Modern Libra

SELECTED

POETRY AND PROSE

OF

John Dryden

The Publisher will be pleased to send, upon
request, a brochure listing each volume
in the *Modern Library College Editions*.

SELECTED
POETRY AND PROSE
OF
John Dryden

EDITED,

WITH AN INTRODUCTION

AND NOTES, BY

EARL MINER

University of California, Los Angeles

Modern Library College Editions

The Modern Library
is published by
Random House, Inc.

Manufactured in the United States of America

CONTENTS

INTRODUCTION

When T. S. Eliot proclaimed himself a classicist in literature, a Catholic in religion, and a royalist in politics, he
took a stand modeled on John Dryden's. Similarly, Eliot's
Dialogue of Dramatic Poetry is an obvious imitation of
Dryden's *Essay of Dramatic Poesy* (1665–1667). Eliot
clearly felt a kinship with Dryden's ideas and principles
and, in addition, admired his combination of roles as a
poet, dramatist, translator, and critic. There are numerous
ironies in such an indebtedness, and one of the best is that
after stealing Dryden's intellectual clothes, Eliot regretted
that Dryden's writing was not sufficiently garbed with
ideas. Moreover, Eliot sometimes had a way of making
what he termed Dryden's virtues seem deadlier than the
faults of other writers: Dryden's poetry merely stated, he
said, but it stated immensely. Yet it was also Eliot who said
that Dryden was, with Milton, one of the two most powerful poets of the seventeenth century, and he praised the
vigor and naturalness of Dryden's language; it was, he
said, "conversational" and "healthy." Now that we can
stand back from Eliot, as well as from the more distant
seventeenth century, we may translate Eliot's rather confused responses—as if to a healthy, relevant poetic classic
who was somehow prosaic—to say that Dryden was a
Christian humanist, a conservative in politics, a poet of
great force, and a master of a wide range of natural lan-

guage. Closer examination of Dryden—however hampered it may be by the lack of biographical information—will show that on such an interpretation Eliot was quite right.

Dryden's Career

Although more information about Dryden's life has survived than about Shakespeare's, Dryden remains the last great English poet of whom so little is known. What is known is largely connected with the circumstances of the publication of his works, so that the facts require us to speak of his career rather than of his personal life. Of course, interpretation is possible, even inevitable, just as interpretation inevitably leads to speculation.

Dryden's birth provides us with the first question involving fact and inviting interpretation. The poet we think of as a conservative in politics and religion and as a man immersed in society was born (by our calendar) on August 19, 1631, at Aldwinckle in Northamptonshire to an apparently radical Puritan family of country gentry. (Two ancestors had been imprisoned for resisting fiscal measures of Charles I.) The next known fact is that in approximately 1646 he left his birthplace to attend Westminster School as King's Scholar. At Westminster he studied under the famous, flogging headmaster, the Rev. Dr. Richard Busby, whose portrait in the National Portrait Gallery in London is enough to frighten anyone who has ever been a student. Dryden's first extant poem, a tortuously Metaphysical elegy on the young Lord Hastings, was included in *Lachrymae Musarum* in 1649. The following year he was admitted pensioner to Trinity College, Cambridge, from which he was graduated Bachelor of Arts in 1654. Little is known of these Cambridge years and even less of the next six, except that his father, Erasmus Dryden, died in 1654, leaving Dryden as eldest son an estate of about £70 a year, a good income then, if he had not needed to support a mother and younger brothers and sisters. The changes in style discernible in the *Heroic Stanzas* on Oliver Cromwell (1658) and in the poems published after the Restoration of Charles II to the English throne suggest that Dryden had been writing more or less steadily since his days at Westminster. If so, nothing more is known to have survived, and in fact only one slight poem, which was included in a letter, survives in manuscript. From 1660 to 1662 his poems on contemporary events brought him to public attention, or perhaps it was rather that new acquaintances and experience brought him to write a new form of "public" poetry. At all events, he was elected one of the Original Fellows of the Royal Society in 1662, revealing that he had arrived as a poet (at the late age of thirty-one) and as a man known to those who were important in the arts, sciences, and government of his time.

The meager poetic evidence prior to 1660 shows Dryden beginning as a late Metaphysical poet as is shown by the poem on Lord Hastings or by the *Heroic Stanzas*. Indeed, he never did wholly discard the conceits, dialectic, and wit of that earlier style—but it was through perfecting a public poetry that he found his stride. Metaphysical poets had explored private experience—what is intimate or unique to each person—and had tried to make the poem's implications universal. Dryden wrote of what was public, what was shared, what brought men and women together rather than what separated them, what put man in time and history, and what defined human personality in relation to God, history, and other men.

Dryden's first great poem, *Annus Mirabilis* (1667), contains both the tragic and the optimistic versions of his view of man. Typically, he shows the tragic in war, and the optimistic in an epic vision of what is possible in peace. The human tragedy is set forth in the picture of Dutch sailors killed or captured by the English during the Second Dutch War (1666).

The son, who thrice three months on th' ocean toss'd,
    Prepar'd to tell what he had pass'd before,
Now sees in English ships the Holland coast
    And parents' arms in vain stretch'd from the shore.

This careful husband had been long away,
    Whom his chaste wife and little children mourn,

Who on their fingers learn'd to tell the day
    On which their father promis'd to return.

Such are the proud designs of humankind,
    And so we suffer shipwreck everywhere!
Alas, what port can such a pilot find,
    Who in the night of fate must blindly steer!

                                        (129–140)

Here he has shown the historical situation, the real times
and places, the little society of the family, and yet, at the
same time, the grander reaches of "humankind" and "fate."
The particularly Drydenian feature is the constant effort to
connect—the immediate with the remote, the real with the
ideal, and the familial with the universally human. Life, in
the poem, becomes a tragic sea journey, the metaphor rising naturally from imaginatively re-created history.

Dryden's optimism often expresses itself in praise of
those great deeds and words that Homer attributed to
Achilles, but Dryden's setting is peace rather than war.
Frequently, as another example from *Annus Mirabilis*
shows, the optimism takes form in a vision of the future.

Instructed ships shall sail to quick commerce,
    By which remotest regions are alli'd,
Which makes one city of the universe,
    Where some may gain and all may be suppli'd.

Then we upon our globe's last verge shall go
    And view the ocean leaning on the sky;
From thence our rolling neighbours we shall know
    And on the lunar world securely pry.

                                        (649–656)

Such hopes are not the intimate or private aspirations distinguishing each of us from all others; they are the hopes of
our race that join and excite people everywhere with visions of exploration, hopes of freedom from want, and
vistas of discoveries in space.

From about 1663 to 1680, however, the main lines of his
career ran in a different direction. Beginning with a farci-
cal play in an old style and some collaborations, he gradu-
ally established himself as the foremost playwright of the

time by introducing witty young "gay couples" into comedy and epic elements into serious drama. He defined the contemporary forms of comedy, tragicomedy, the heroic play, and tragedy and yet found time to write a major nondramatic poem, *Annus Mirabilis*, and criticism, *An Essay of Dramatic Poesy* (1668), and numerous prefaces. By 1667 he had touched nearly every form he was to employ except satire, the verse epistle, and the loose "Pindaric" ode. He was best known during these years as a playwright, but he could also be sure of an audience for historical poetry, songs, and those incomparably various prologues and epilogues in which men, women, and even a child speak a language more colloquial than prose. The opening lines of some of his prologues and epilogues suggest something of the varied naturalness of language and tone that was at Dryden's command on such relaxed occasions.

> I'm thinking (and it almost makes me mad) . . .
>
> . . .
>
> I think, or hope at least, the coast is clear . . .
>
> . . .
>
> Ladies! (I hope there's none behind to hear) . . .
>
> . . .
>
> Is it not strange to hear a poet say . . .
>
> . . .
>
> Lord, how reform'd and quiet we are grown . . .

Dryden's experience as a dramatist no doubt assisted his powers of characterization in nondramatic poetry, and it is clear from these examples that in his language there is a natural vigor that brings to life again these voices from the Restoration playhouse.

In 1668 his literary achievement and staunch royalism won him the Poet Laureateship and an honorary Master of Arts degree. By the 1670s he was well established—he had married Lady Elizabeth Howard in 1663, and the third of his three sons was born in 1669. Various financial arrangements, including part ownership in a theater, gave him hopes (largely unrealized) of a good income. London was still small enough for him to have become acquainted

with almost everyone of consequence in the kingdom. "Mr.
Dryden" was soon well known for his abilities and for his
unusual insight into the significance of the political up-
heavals culminating in the Restoration of Charles II, the
advances in science, and the elements that were most creative in all the arts.

The kingdom had been in a nervous political state
throughout the century—by the time Dryden was twenty-
nine, one king had been beheaded and another restored—
and one of its periodic fits occurred at the end of the 1670s
when yet another revolution appeared to be inevitable.
Partly through spontaneity, partly through foment, a wave
of hysteria grew over what for a time was believed to be a
Popish Plot, an intrigue of Catholics to kill Charles II and
establish on his throne his now Catholic brother, James.
The hand of the Jesuits was suspected everywhere; new
laws were enacted disallowing Catholics from office (the
laws were not always enforced, however); a bill was introduced to exclude James; and agitation was promoted to
have Charles (who had no legitimate issue) declare legitimate his bastard son James, Duke of Monmouth. Dryden
was of course a committed Royalist and must have watched
these events with fear and fascination.

The charges and countercharges, the oaths and denials,
confused anyone at the time who had not already made up
his mind. To Dryden, a conservative, the commotion was
"that plot, the nation's curse,/Bad in itself but represented
worse." The body politic was in a fever and only its head,
the king, seemed capable of cooler counsel. For practical as
well as for theoretical reasons Dryden supported Charles
II, and he gathered all his poetic powers to write *Absalom
and Achitophel* (1681), which is probably the only great
English poem written during, and responding to, a revolutionary situation. Dryden knew his countrymen, and, for
that matter, as the famous opening lines show, he also
knew Charles II very well. He could appreciate that some
people thought that the king had too much power. But,
above all, Dryden yearned for harmony and peace. He
sought to help men understand themselves better by comparing their situation with that of those under the reign of

the biblical King David. The comparison alone had an element of conservativism in it, a reminder that human creatures and human institutions of many eras resemble each other. But whatever political theories might be held, Dryden suggests that any sane man would hesitate to tamper with a system that has been developed over the centuries and that has worked well, if not perfectly. His image is that of an architectural fabric, probably a cathedral or palace—or its Jewish equivalent, the Temple with the Ark of the Covenant.

> What prudent men a settled throne would shake?
> For whatsoe'er their sufferings were before,
> That change they covet makes them suffer more.
> All other errors but disturb a state,
> But innovation is the blow of fate.
> If ancient fabrics nod and threat to fall,
> To patch the flaws and buttress up the wall,
> Thus far 'tis duty; but here fix the mark:
> For all beyond it is to touch our Ark.
>
> (796–804)

The following year (1682) he assisted Nahum Tate in writing a second part to *Absalom and Achitophel*. Dryden's role was that of reviser and creator of a few "characters" or portraits that are the deadlier for their composed amusement.

> He never was a poet of God's making:
> The midwife laid her hand on his thick skull
> With this prophetic blessing, "Be thou dull."
>
> (475–477)

Earlier in 1682 his one bitter poem, *The Medal*, had been published. Its opening lines bespeak his exasperation with the Whigs and the London mob then seething in a revolutionary tumult: "Of all our antic sights and pageantry/ Which English idiots run in crowds to see . . ." As he had the king say in *Absalom and Achitophel*, "Beware the fury of a patient man." *MacFlecknoe* also appeared in 1682, although written earlier. In this poem Dryden's usual composure allowed him to demolish duncery with high spirits.

Beware the amusement of a patient man. It is remarkable that his satires and *Absalom and Achitophel* (if this poem is not a satire) appeared in under two years' time during a career spanning more than four decades.

Charles II died in 1685 and Dryden responded with an ode, *Threnodia Augustalis*. Charles II was widely mourned for himself and for suspicions about his brother, now James II, who succeeded him. James ruled only until 1688, when he fled to France. Like numerous Tories and Anglican clergymen, Dryden could not support William and Mary while James and his son remained alive. As such political problems developed, Dryden found himself examining his religious assumptions as well (the two were closely related throughout the century). Should a man who feared recurrence of revolution in church and state give the assent of his faith to the established Church of England? Or should a belief in the need for central authority lead him to the centuries-old Roman Catholic Church, which claimed infallibility? Like most thinking men in the century, Dryden hesitated and, in the 1680s, wrote poems giving different answers. In 1682 he had produced his confession of Anglicanism, *Religio Laici*, at a time when his wife and perhaps his sons were Catholic. His powers of argument had always concealed his doubts and hesitations, but these doubts led him, in 1685 or 1686, to Catholicism, which then seemed to be the one faith with true authority. However, *The Hind and the Panther* (1687), his longest original poem, again reveals to the careful reader Dryden's doubts about James and rash Catholicism. For better or worse, come what might, Dryden emerged from testing to a final position as a Catholic and a Jacobite. In the Killigrew Ode (1686) he had stated his faith in art and the artist, in *The Hind and the Panther*, his faith in an authoritative Church, and in *A Song for St. Cecilia's Day* (1687), his faith in the human pageant and divine disposition of history. The pageant is that of men in personal relationships and men sharing concern with important events, both of which are constantly revealed in his political, historical, and satiric poems. A less familiar selection from *Threnodia Augustalis* gives a striking vignette of men throughout the

City of London who were elated by news of the (tempo-rary) recovery of Charles II.

> The drooping town in smiles again was dress'd,
>   Gladness in every face express'd,
>   Their eyes before their tongues confess'd.
> Men met each other with erected look;
>   The steps were higher that they took;
> Friends to congratulate their friends made haste,
> And long invet'rate foes saluted as they pass'd.
>
>   (121–127)

These men of London in 1685 were, Dryden saw, a true part of history and of poetry. Such men might at that time be part of the seething London mob, but they might also achieve things that would always be remembered. We have seen that Dryden had such hopes for human achievement in time, but it should be added that he often punctuated the providential scheme of history with passages on the creation or the end of the world. In *The Hind and the Panther*, for example, he starts off an account of the history of toleration and persecution by distinguishing the creation of beasts from that of man.

> One portion of informing fire was giv'n
> To brutes, th' inferior family of Heav'n;
> The Smith Divine, as with a careless beat,
> Struck out the mute creation at a heat;
> But when arriv'd at last to human race,
> The Godhead took a deep consid'ring space,
> And to distinguish man from all the rest
> Unlock'd the sacred treasures of his breast
> And mercy mix'd with reason did impart,
> One to his head, the other to his heart;
> Reason to rule, but mercy to forgive;
> The first is law, the last prerogative.
>
>   (I, 251–262)

Dryden saw in man's very creation that which sets him apart: man shares in the highest attributes of God, and from eternity he has a dignity given him by the God he resembles. Like Pope (although not as brilliantly), Dryden took account of man in his time. Like Milton (although not as grandly), he set his own time in the light of eternity. Like no one but himself among English poets, and unsurpassed in this respect, he ceaselessly sought to extend the area of intersection of the mundane and supernal realms. In addition, next to saving his soul, he sought to affirm the dignity of art, which comes closer to achieving immortality than other human endeavor. The artist—the creator and the man of peace—therefore has a special provision at the day of judgment, which Dryden reveals, at the close of the Killigrew Ode, with the sounding of the last trumpet.

> The sacred poets first shall hear the sound
>   And foremost from the tomb shall bound,
> For they are cover'd with the lightest ground,
> And straight with inborn vigour, on the wing,
> Like mounting larks to the new morning sing.
>   (188–192)

It is no cause for wonder that most readers find the period from about 1678 to 1688 the great decade of his poetry because in these years he showed repeatedly how art might make contemporary events forever relevant; but he was to live twelve years longer, both famous and isolated, denied immediate poetic engagement with his society and yet the author of many thousands of lines of poetry and some of his finest prose. Having lost his Poet Laureateship (to Thomas Shadwell!), he returned to the theater and produced *Don Sebastian* (1690), his greatest tragedy after *All for Love,* and *Amphytrion* (1690), which is, along with *Marriage A-La-Mode,* one of his two finest comedies. But theatrical taste was changing from the full-blooded and high-spirited drama of the Restoration, and Dryden found reason to turn to two kinds of writing that he had practiced intermittently before—translations and verse epistles to his contemporaries. In 1692 he published his *Satires,* translations of Persius and, with others, of Juvenal, that still disturb by their power to make man seem foolish, immoral, and corrupt. In 1697 he published his splendid *Virgil* and, shortly before he died in 1700, his *Fables,* which were chiefly poetic versions of stories in Ovid, Chaucer, and

Boccaccio. It is apparent to anyone who reads these translations that they succeed because they are poems in their
own right and language. But, by the same token, Dryden
felt that these works were representative of abiding civilized values and that he could compare events in his own
day to episodes in the Bible, in Virgil, or in Chaucer and
thereby learn something about the present. To recall Virgil
was to clarify, to appreciate, and to judge. Dryden was
constantly comparing, drawing parallels and analogies, and
alluding to the classics. There is nothing unique in such
classicism; it was central to the belief of generations of humanists. But what is extraordinary is Dryden's sure sense of
what was classical in his own day. His recognition that
Paradise Lost was a classic of Homeric or Virgilian propor-
tions permitted him to allude to it within a few years of its
publication. This work, Dryden suggested, is something all
civilized men will know, something that will abide to tell
men about themselves. No doubt to Dryden, as to Matthew
Arnold two centuries later, the classics contained the best
that had been thought and said. But Dryden believed that,
in addition to classics in the sense that Arnold meant, there
were also modern classics (the fuller title of his own work
is *Fables Ancient and Modern*). He would have added that
all classics were also based on the best that man has done
and believed.

Emerging rather late in life as a major poet, Dryden's poetic skills continued to develop over a career of forty years,
and even the poems of his last decade (1690–1700) show
no loss of power or command of style. There are some who
think his *Fables* contain his finest writing; in any event
they show a lifetime love of narrative poetry that relates
him to Spenser and Milton rather than to the Metaphysi-
cals of the early seventeenth century or to the poets of the
eighteenth century. Every reader has been moved by the
mingling of sad wisdom and bracing lyricism in his last
work, *The Secular Masque*, in which, for example, Mars
(representing the wars of the mid-century) is told:

> Thy sword within the scabbard keep
> And let mankind agree;

> Better the world were fast asleep
>   Than kept awake by thee.
> The fools are only thinner
>   With all our cost and care;
> But neither side a winner,
>   For things are as they were.
>   (63–70)

The same command of voice marks verse epistles like that
To Sir Godfrey Kneller, sometimes complaining of ill treatment by (in this case) Charles II: "Thou hadst thy
Charles a while, and so had I,/ But pass we that unpleasing image by" (100–101). At other times, as in the epistle
To My Dear Friend Mr. Congreve, his usual amiability
leads to that perfection of tone which so many eighteenth-
century poets sought to recapture in their epistles. Dryden
recognizes that he himself has grown old; "But you," he
tells Congreve,

> But you, whom ev'ry Muse and Grace adorn,
> Whom I foresee to better fortune born,
> Be kind to my remains; and, oh, defend
> Against your judgment your departed friend!
> Let not the insulting foe my fame pursue,
> But shade those laurels which descend to you;
> And take for tribute what these lines express:
> You merit more, nor cou'd my love do less.
>   (70–77)

It is small wonder that Congreve later wrote so warmly of
his "departed friend," or that Pope should have thought
that the verse epistle had been given new currency in English. The eighteenth-century admiration for these epistles—
and along with them others to the Duchess of Ormond and
Dryden's cousin John Driden—has in recent years become
better understood, and some of Dryden's admirers think
them among his finest poems.

In a famous phrase in the Preface to *Fables*, Dryden
speaks of "the other harmony of prose." There are very few
examples of major English writers who wrote so harmoni-
ously and well in both prose and verse, and fewer yet

whose work increased in resonance to the end. Yet his very powers of social observation and literary insight revealed to him that the world he had known was altering in the 1690s. As he contemplated approaching death in 1700, he had reason to say,

> 'Tis well an old age is out,
> And time to begin a new.

A century with three revolutions was yielding to a new order. As dramatist and lyric poet, he was to have no heir. But he had given "an auspice to the new" with his verse epistles, satires, translations, and prose. His eminence was recognized by burial in the Poets' Corner of Westminster Abbey and by what would have pleased him more, the continuous publication of his works ever since.

Literary Characteristics

As he sat in Will's Coffee House in the later years of his life, chatting with young writers and taking snuff, Dryden knew, and knew that Europe knew, that he was the foremost English writer of his time. But he also knew that his place in literature was one connected with, and yet different from, an earlier age and the approaching new century. Somewhat ruefully he said that he was "betwixt two ages cast,/ The first of this and hindmost of the last." Today he is most often thought of as the first great Augustan writer in the new age of "Dryden and Pope and Dr. Johnson." By "Augustan," most people mean satire, the heroic couplet, and neoclassicism. Pope may have thought in similar terms, but he praised Dryden for his style:

> Dryden taught to join
> The varying verse, the full resounding line,
> The long majestic march, and energy divine.

Assessing his historical place in *The Lives of the English Poets*, Dr. Johnson spoke of Dryden as one who perfected the old and established the new.

Perhaps no nation ever produced a writer that enriched his language with such variety of models. To him we owe the improvement, perhaps the completion of our metre, the refinement of our language, and much of the correctness of our sentiments. By him we were taught "sapere et fari," to think naturally and express forcibly. . . . He shewed us the true bounds of a translator's liberty. What was said of Rome, adorned by Augustus, may be applied by an easy metaphor to English poetry embellished by Dryden, "lateritiam invenit, marmoream reliquit," he found it brick, and he left it marble.

In addition, Dr. Johnson thought him the father of English criticism and the most natural prose stylist of England. But he also emphasized Dryden's unevenness, wishing he had been more given to revising his first thoughts, and regretted that, given his great powers, Dryden should have sometimes tried to please his audience easily rather than himself at greater effort.

The view of eighteenth-century Dryden—Dryden the translator, critic, neoclassicist, and satirist—is valuable because it reveals important aspects of his literary career and accounts for his century of influence. Those features can easily be demonstrated. His works include nearly 38,500 lines of poetic translation and almost 2,000 pages of prose. Both of the modern selections of his criticism (see the Bibliography, pp. xxxvii–ix) require two volumes. Because many of his translations are of classical writers, he obviously felt the contemporary relevance of Homer, Sophocles, Virgil, Juvenal, Horace, and Ovid. Moreover, the satiric tone pervades much of his writing—for, as he said, "satire will have room whate'er I write."

Among these elements in his legacy to the eighteenth century, satire is the most convenient for illustration. Satire has very ancient origins, but Dryden's new kind drew on the Roman verse satire of Juvenal and Horace, on the practice of French contemporaries like Boileau, and on accessions from such other genres as the epic. The result is new in its creation of full characters, its development of ideas toward a single complex theme, its serious uses of laughter, and its new metaphorical procedures. Dryden's experience of the theater led to unforgettable satiric portraits, and it must be understood that each is as much a literary creation as a character in a play. In *MacFlecknoe* he borrowed actual details of the behavior and writing of the gross though gifted dramatist Thomas Shadwell, but the result is MacFlecknoe, not Shadwell. The character MacFlecknoe is an archetype of the bumbling, dull writer rather than of the historical hearty, skillful, and bumptious playwright. The removal, the degree of art, can be judged by the fact that the poem was in all likelihood designed originally for a different satiric hero modeled on Elkanah Settle, an almost pathetic dramatist and time-server. Better yet, MacFlecknoe, who owes something to both Shadwell and Settle, may be compared with Og and Doeg in *Absalom and Achitophel*, Part II, who are also versions of Shadwell and Settle and are also very different from MacFlecknoe. Again, Achitophel and the unnamed "chief" of *The Medal* are in some sense versions of Anthony Ashley Cooper, Earl of Shaftesbury. Yet the two characters are very different. Achitophel is a heroic figure who has perverted unusual gifts but despite this has still retained his dignity, and the "chief" is a dangerous species of "vermin." Such examples show that Dryden's satiric characters—the same is true of those in poems of praise—are transformed by art to independent life. Various as they are, the satiric passages and satires—as with the panegyrics and passages of praise—were driving toward a central theme.

These and other kinds of poetry practiced by Dryden present a positive association of peace, reason, dynamic order, and creativity; negatively they show an association of strife, willfulness, disruptive disorder, and death-in-life. Deep-seated conservative fears are joined with faith in man's great capacity for achievement. Dryden's satiric tone varies greatly, but even in his one angry poem, *The Medal*, he was judging by positive standards as, for example, the allusions to the Bible show. He himself approached this unique magnification underlying ridicule in two rather different ways. In his *Discourse Concerning Satire*, he suggested in one passage that the very fineness of humorous tone, or consummate art itself, transformed satire.

> To spare the grossness of the names, and to do the thing yet more severely, is to draw a full face, and to make the nose and cheeks stand out, and yet not to employ any depth of shadowing. . . . Neither is it true that this fineness of raillery is offensive. A witty man is tickled while he is hurt in this manner, and a fool feels it not. The occasion of an offence may possibly be given, but he cannot take it. If it be granted that in effect this way does more mischief; that a man is secretly wounded, and though he be not sensible himself; yet there is still a vast difference between the slovenly butchering of a man, and the fineness of a stroke that separates the head from the body, and leaves it standing in its place.

He went on in the *Discourse* to specify three central features of satire. Its very name (from the Latin *satura*, "a dish plentifully stored with all variety of fruits and grains") revealed the variety of its materials. But a proper satire also required "unity of design": for, like a play, "though it consists of many parts, [it] must yet be one in the action, and must drive on the accomplishment of one design." Such formal unity implied a second, thematic feature involving positive as well as negative standards. The satiric poet

> is bound . . . to give his reader some one precept of moral virtue, and to caution him against some one particular vice or folly. Other virtues, subordinate to the first, may be recommended under that chief head; and other vices or follies may be scourged besides that which he principally intends. But he is chiefly to inculcate one virtue, and insist on that.

Finally, Dryden argued that satire required "the majesty of the heroic," or epic, "finely mixed with the venom" of ridicule. Satire was, he said, "undoubtedly a species" of epic poetry. One cannot believe that these characteristics are necessary to all kinds of satire, and they sometimes do not dominate even his own work. But they are principles that give his satiric writing a largeness and nobility of spirit unrivaled in English satire.

Dryden bequeathed characterization, serious themes, and complex tone to Pope, Swift, Dr. Johnson, Byron, and others. Yet differences remain, and not only of emphasis. He would have admired Pope's superior brilliance and extraordinary shimmer of detail, as also Dr. Johnson's *gravitas*, his "grandeur of generality." His peculiar emphasis was, however, upon creating whole new worlds through unusual metaphorical schemes and analogies. *Absalom and Achitophel* is a biblical poem, a retelling of 2 Samuel akin to *Paradise Lost*. But of course the biblical story is also a continuous, closed metaphor, or (in Dryden's word) a parallel for contemporary history. Such creation of a wholly new fictional world—"In pious times, ere priestcraft did begin," for example—was emulated only by Swift. But Swift did not do so in poetry, and his magnification (as in the brilliant second voyage of *Gulliver's Travels*) possesses an irony verging upon misanthropic tragedy. It is peculiar to Dryden alone among English poets since Chaucer that satire should retain dignity, normality, and even affection. One of the strongest passions of his own life as we know it was love for his sons—the same emotion that he allowed Flecknoe to feel for his own silent, dull heir. He not only lent the father his own paternal feelings but also, in one passage, satirized himself along with the "son." (See line 78 and note, p. 188, below.)

Differences in satiric effect, like those in dramatic effect, are in some measure due to differing inclinations in the personality of the writer. Dryden loved and admired people, although he was uncommonly aware of human limitations. He liked to praise, even to the point of outrageous flattery. He flattered the nobility—but also such others as Dr. Charleton, Anne Killigrew, and William Congreve, as poems included in this edition show. Again, we must be aware that he re-creates these people into characters in new worlds. The reader of *MacFlecknoe* who has read Shadwell's best plays will not recognize Shadwell as being the dull writer created from him. Similarly, the reader of *To the Memory of Mr. Oldham* will be hard put to understand, after reading Oldham's own poetry, how he could possibly be thought a successor to Dryden. Praise, or satire, is based on fact and truth; but the real is elevated to an ideal order in which it is transformed into the different fact and truth of art.

In brief, Dryden was a poet, although in some crucial respects different from his successors. To his first really ambitious long poem, *Annus Mirabilis,* he prefixed an Account declaring it to be a historical poem. The significant point here is his definition of historical poetry in terms of a poetic constellation that reveals the coherence of the whole of his nondramatic poetry. With "epic poesy" he associates "the historic and panegyric, which are branches of it." Because satire is but inverted panegyric employing similar topics for similar moral ends, Dryden implied (in 1667) an association of epic, history, and panegyric/satire. The epic afforded grand vision of achievement and large-scale tragedy. History furnished the record of man in biblical, classical, and modern times; panegyric and satire provided the means of passing judgment, of exercising moral control. This passage from the Account (pp. 109–13, below), which probably tells us more about his poetry than any other, underscores the fact that he is not primarily or essentially a satirist. There is more of praise and epic elevation in his poetry than satire, and yet he is not primarily a panegyric or an epic poet either. Of all these terms, historical is the best for his nondramatic poetry, if by "history" we may convey matters both human and divine.

Dryden was a historical progressivist with great faith in what man might achieve in time. In *Annus Mirabilis,* after following the progress of navigation from its rude beginnings to his own day, Dryden looks ahead (line 652) in a vision of hopeful peace, "Where some may gain and all may be suppli'd." In this stanza his hopes lie in trade and exploration and two stanzas later in science. In addressing the Duchess of Ormond, it is beauty that revives Ireland.

> The waste of civil wars, their towns destroy'd,
> Pales unhonour'd, Ceres unemploy'd,

> Were all forgot, and one triumphant day
> Wip'd all the tears of three campaigns away.
>
> (64-67)

Again and again poetry and art triumph even over death, as in the Killigrew Ode. His funeral elegies are almost unique in persistently treating not a sense of loss but of triumph— as the very different poems on Henry Purcell, Anne Killigrew, Charles II, and John Oldham show. Such optimism comes from the fact that Dryden believed that beyond history lay two further orders of time, the immortal and the eternal. The immortal rose from time, but above it, to endure through the rest of human history: "Earth keeps the body, verse preserves the fame." The eternal was God's providential plan of creation, life in time, judgment, and redemption. The interplay between mortal human history, immortal human achievement, and divine disposition in eternity accounts for much of what is most sublime in Dryden's poetry. Passages on creation, on progress, and on the end of the world are scattered throughout his work, substituting for the intense intimacy of Donne a new glory of even imperfect man. Much of the elevation derives from his very unusual belief both in a Providence (allying him with men of the early English Renaissance) and in the modern belief in man's scientific capacities.

Dryden's particular kind of conservative thought is usually termed Christian humanism, which he remade into a living belief in spite of the fact that its assumptions were not held by most of his important contemporaries or by numerous predecessors. He believed that God's essence— and man's highest faculty—was reason, or wisdom. For man, however, faith was superior to reason as a faculty to worship a transcendent God. The will, divine or human, emphasized by Calvinists or the reason claiming the province of faith emphasized by Deists and others seemed to him impious and dangerous. Were it not for his faith in Providence, however, his strong conservative bent might have led to suspicion and querulousness. As for his humanism, he shared with the earlier humanists an admiration for the Graeco-Roman classics, although less for the ancient moralists and rhetoricians than for the poets and historians. The combination of Christianity with humanism gave him faith in man in the present, always excepting the fact that perfection could come only when the trumpet should sound and the dead be raised. Such views did not die with Dryden, but after him they came to be separated and sometimes sentimentalized, sometimes simplified, and sometimes muddled. For all his optimism and good nature, his poetry lacks the sentimentality that was growing up toward the close of the century; by the same token, his poetry is seldom tender, and he therefore seems the least feminine of our poets. Debates on the relative merits of ancient and modern writers did not engage him—like his practice in poetry his criticism reveals his enthusiasm for both and his fitting of both into a single scheme. Humanism indeed continues through the next century and may even be found in the ideals of a Victorian like Arnold. But Christian humanism, after Dryden, died as a necessary basis for literature, and it is no accident therefore that some features of his poetry—for example, the beast fable of *The Hind and the Panther*—are closer to Spenser and to the Middle Ages than to his predecessors in the seventeenth century. All in all, "Dryden and Pope" is a revealing phrase, but what it fails to reveal ("Dryden and Spenser" or "Dryden and Milton") is that he is a major late Renaissance writer. And it is that fact that seems more significant.

As with all writers, the limitations of Dryden's poetry and prose are related to his literary virtues. Writing so much in both modes, he was often careless and was either too busy or too self-indulgent to revise, as Pope so compulsively did. On the old principle that Homer nods, such unevenness may be deplored but need not lead to condemnation. There is a more serious feature of his work, however, that catches some readers unaware. Dryden's lack of intimacy is sometimes a lack of immediacy, or an overprevalence of intellectuality. That is the one serious limitation of his poetry, just as the serious concern with ideas is one of its major merits. It is also sometimes said that his work is coarse, and so it sometimes is—like Spenser's, Shakespeare's, Donne's, and Milton's. But their coarseness is allied, like his, to a fullness of experience that refinement could only jeopardize. Dryden responded so handsomely to the literary virtues of past and contemporary writers and made criticism and what is now called comparative literature so confident, dignified, and pleasurable an enterprise that it is only fair to grant him the same merits. If there is one word for his poetry and prose alike, it is generous. And it is generous in all senses, including the older ones of nobility, graciousness, and magnanimity.

Approaching Dryden

Even accepting that the proper approach to any writer is faithful attention and judgment by normal human values, there is some problem for some readers in their approach to Dryden. His serious concern with ideas, the separation by three centuries, and his extraordinary versatility may leave one wondering where to begin. Students usually find that they come to like and understand Dryden most quickly by starting with poems closest to the post-Romantic assumptions of our day—the songs, odes like *Alexander's Feast,* and elegies like *To the Memory of Mr. Oldham.* The appeal such poems hold today is one reason why so many lyric pieces are included in this volume. From such poems one can move smoothly either to prologues and epilogues or to verse epistles, such as the one to Congreve, which replace singing with speaking. Some readers might prefer to move directly to the rollicking fun of *MacFlecknoe* and then to the sonorities of *Absalom and Achitophel.* At this point, most readers will wish to discover what Dryden has to say about literature in prose, and they will find him at his studied best in *An Essay of Dramatic Poesy* and more relaxed in the Preface to *Fables.* The prose style, or rather styles, are more dated than most of Dryden's admirers care to admit, but they have perhaps never been excelled for naturalness and capaciousness. The final, and in some ways most significant, step possible with this volume is to the poems in which Dryden most clearly, and at greatest

length, expresses his hopes for man in time and eternity—
the bounding "Year of Wonders" (*Annus Mirabilis*) and
the two religious confessions, *Religio Laici* and *The Hind
and the Panther*. Any reader who has read this much of
Dryden will wish to go on to his plays and more of his
prose and translations. For guides to them and texts of a
larger expanse of the works than is included here, the Bibliography may be consulted. No matter what else strikes
such an attentive reader, he will find that some old generali-
zations about Dryden are badly in need of repair and that
the poetry and prose alike constantly yield surprises, fresh
expressions of experience, and unflagging vigor.

Dryden's individual works differ in approach from those
of other early modern writers. Donne's poems rely upon
process, an impetuous, twisting, exciting flow. Milton
writes in grand sentences, and Pope in shimmering couplets. Dryden's basic unit—and it was a discovery made
(though not always practiced) in his prose as well as in his
verse—is the paragraph, the stanza, or such sections as the
portrait of an individual or of an extended comment on life.
His couplets or quatrains are symptoms of the development
and movement of paragraphs, but they are not radical units
within themselves. Of many examples that might be given,
the opening lines of *Absalom and Achitophel* (p. 205,
below) provide the most famous. They show that the paragraph is made up of striking detail. This detail is apparent
in all Dryden's poems when that sweeping forward pressure of his style, which Pope called the "energy divine," can
be resisted for a time. Those opening lines also show that
full understanding requires attention to the tone of voice
and attitude of mind. Finally, such a passage reveals that it
is indeed only a unit, that the paragraph is as subordinate
to a carefully articulated whole as are the lines and couplets to the paragraph, and that, like the lines, the paragraphs move one forcibly over the larger distance.

Three centuries have brought many changes in the English language, but none of any insurmountable difficulty in
reading Dryden. The most important convention to remember for his poetry, as also for Shakespeare's, Donne's,

and that of other earlier poets, is that when verbs end in -*ed* an extra syllable is given; otherwise the fact is indicated by *'d*. For example, *perfum'd* is a two-syllable word and *perfumed* (perfumèd) a three. But in practice Dryden's pronunciation is usually the same as ours, and his *lifted* or *conquer'd* merely employs a more accurately phonetic spelling than contemporary English. However, certain words did have different accents from ours: *commérce, apóstolic, triúmph*. But, as Bridges stated, Dryden's rhythms are so forceful and his style so close to the natural thew and sinew of the language that one need only read and the natural rhythm will disclose where his accents were. The general rule for all poets holds: When in doubt, read aloud.

The meanings of words are another matter. A poet of three centuries ago must be read carefully in order to allay the deception that words that look the same must necessarily mean the same as they do now. A look at the following words in the Glossary will demonstrate the problem: *bent, gust, hovels, jolly,* and *manur'd*. In order that the page will not be cluttered with repeated glossings of such words as *prevent* (anticipate) or *doubt* (expect)—though both words are also used in their modern senses—troublesome words are put into the Glossary, which should be consulted when a line or words seems to make odd sense. Although the matter of pronunciation is very complicated, it does not actually present a difficulty, simply because pronunciation does not affect rhythm or meaning. However, it does affect the larger music and sometimes the specific sense. There are numerous rhymes like *rise/joys, prove/love, come/ Rome*. Not only is seventeenth-century pronunciation often different from ours, but it is often inconsistent and unfixed, which was also lamented by many even in that century. It is sometimes difficult to say whether a rhyme is based on a dominant or an alternative seventeenth-century pronunciation: *nature/creature; here/there; prince/sense; prepar'd/ guard; receive/prerogative; fears/pensioners*. In *The Hind and the Panther,* Dryden rhymes *apostolic* with a word like *like* twice and with *seek*, once. Philologists have shown that Dryden and his contemporaries were not really abusing pronunciation but were instead employing variants or lost pronunciations. Important as they are, such linguistic differences can scarcely be set forth in a text of this kind, except that an occasional note is given. For example, it is significant that *loins* in *MacFlecknoe* (l. 125) is pronounced like *lines*. Such matters, however, are either those common to poets before the nineteenth century or those that attentive reading and a few notes can overcome.

This Edition

Every editor faces certain decisions, and his choices can be better explained than justified. The method of this edition is to present each poetic or prose work with a headnote explaining its circumstances and with footnotes explaining words or passages. The works may be further explicated by reference to the Glossary of obsolete or unusual usages. The works are given in chronological order of composition insofar as that is possible, so that *MacFlecknoe* is assigned to 1678, the year that Oldham set down parts in his copybook, rather than to 1682, when it was first published. The earlier date may not be right, but it is closer to being right than the later and will save readers from the possibility of the old mistake that *MacFlecknoe* was written in response to Thomas Shadwell's poem, *The Medal of John Bays* (if indeed that was by Shadwell). The chronological arrangement also means that *An Essay of Dramatic Poesy* appears where it belongs, early in any edition of Dryden, rather than being tucked in at the end as if it were totally detached from time and poetry.

The selections are entirely whole works, or wholes detached from larger wholes (for example, songs from plays). Nothing is abridged, and therefore many works have been left out. It is painful to exclude plays, most of the translations, many prose pieces, and certain poems. The works that are included show Dryden's range outside drama, and nothing has been included that does not possess true literary merit. Readers new to Dryden may think that a good deal has been brought between two covers; others who, following Sir Walter Scott, think of "glorious John" as an old acquaintance will regret omissions.

The text of this edition is a modernization of an authoritative text based on collations of editions published in Dryden's lifetime. Dryden seldom revised very thoroughly, but the additions—for example, a passage on Achitophel in *Absalom and Achitophel*—are often very significant. These additions are normally followed, although in the same poem (l. 179), *"Assum'd* a patriot's all-atoning name" has been kept rather than the later *"Usurp'd . . ."* because the former is more consistent with Dryden's usual ironic connotations for *patriot* in the poem and, indeed, in the rest of the line. In the one major instance of careful revision included in this edition, *An Essay of Dramatic Poesy,* the second edition (corrected from the first) has been used as the copytext.

The modernization is necessary for a student edition today, but the three particular changes should be made as clear as possible. First, capitalization and italicizing have been altered. Modern practice has been followed, chiefly by reducing the use of both, but also by such procedure as, for example, capitalizing "Nature" when personified and by substituting quotation marks for italics when used for a quotation. Second, and this is a major change, punctuation has been modernized and normalized. The major addition is that of quotation marks for speeches or dialogue, the major reduction, that of heavy internal use of commas by some of Dryden's printers. The old use of question marks for exclamations has been altered to exclamation points. Older vagaries of colons, semicolons, and commas have been altered. The colon has been reduced to a symbol "used before an extended quotation, explanation, example, series, etc." (*Webster's New World Dictionary*). The semicolon has been used as a coordinating sign when conjunctions are not used and to set off highly pointed or complex series. The comma has been used as a coordinating sign with conjunctions and as a subordinating sign. Third, another considerable alteration, Dryden's longer paragraphs have sometimes been broken into smaller units. The spellings used by Dryden (or his printer) are retained when they accord with either modern American or English practice.

Such alterations are appropriate to an edition such as this and are more conservative than changes commonly made in similar editions of Shakespeare. No modernization can claim to represent what the author actually wrote, much less what he intended. But the intention cannot be known. Even Dryden's own practice, like that of most of his contemporaries, was so loose (see the letter to the Duchess of Ormond quoted in the headnote of Dryden's poem to her) that such features were largely determined by his printers. (After rather tortuously searching out the principles of capitalization, one late seventeenth-century grammar desperately concludes that it never begins after the first letter of a word.) It is to be hoped that those who are being introduced to Dryden by this edition will be encouraged to read further in more scholarly "old-spelling" editions and, if they can gain access to them, the old quartos, pamphlets, and folios in which Dryden's works appear as his contemporaries read them. They give a pleasure that no modern edition can offer. The chief aim of modernization is more modest: to bring Dryden as close as possible to readers today while making changes consistently and intelligibly.

It is easier to set oneself this aim than to realize it. Consistency and accuracy are elusive, especially to one attempting a fresh modernized edition. At best, to paraphrase Dryden, to edit the works of another is no great commendation, and I am not so vain as to think I have deserved a greater. But I am sensible of the value of the assistance given me. Mrs. Anne Olin and Miss Carol Green have intelligently and patiently edited a most complicated manuscript. The printers, Messrs. H. Wolff, have done wonders with much marked xeroxes of old-spelling texts. And I am grateful for the help of UCLA students in the Herculean and necessarily rushed task of helping read proof: my thanks to Mr. Ronald S. Baar, Mrs. Melanie Rangno, Mr. Nick Hawranek, Miss Sharon Jaffe, and Miss Patricia Scarpitti. Mrs. Jeanette Wallin has also assisted in this task. Inevitably mistakes will remain, and perhaps the reader can spare them some indulgence. For if Virgil is, as Dryden says, the torture of the grammarian and the plague of the translator, he has himself been the headache of at least one editor.

BIBLIOGRAPHY

These books will serve for further study, as they have served also to provide material for headnotes and notes in this edition. Unpublished material for The California Edition has also been drawn upon.

Editions

Edmund Malone (ed.). *The Critical and Miscellaneous Prose Works of John Dryden.* 3 vols. London, 1800. Ill-organized, but the first serious study of Dryden's biography and prose.

Sir Walter Scott and George Saintsbury (eds.). *The Works of John Dryden.* 18 vols. London, 1882–1892. Apart from Scott's 1808 edition, the only (nearly) complete edition of Dryden at present. There is a biography in Volume I. Scott was Dryden's best editor-critic and the edition is still highly useful.

W. P. Ker (ed.). *Essays of John Dryden.* 2 vols. Oxford, 1900. Handsome and meticulous, but now largely superseded by Watson's edition, below.

George R. Noyes (ed.). *The Poetical Works of Dryden.* Rev. ed. Cambridge, Mass., 1950. The most useful complete one-volume edition of all Dryden's poems, including translations.

Edward N. Hooker, H. T. Swedenberg, Jr., *et al.* (eds.). *The Works of John Dryden* (The California Edition). Berkeley and Los Angeles. Published to date: Vol. I (1956), Vol. VIII (1962), Vol. IX (1967). The most authoritative edition of the works so far published in this edition.

James Kinsley (ed.). *The Poems of John Dryden.* 4 vols. Oxford, 1958. Excellent text, handsomely printed.

George Watson (ed.). *John Dryden: Of Dramatic Poesy and Other Critical Essays.* 2 vols. London and New York: Everyman, 1962. The most useful edition of selected criticism, with valuable notes and index.

Scholarship and Criticism

Samuel Johnson. "Dryden" and "Pope," in G. B. Hill (ed.), *Lives of the English Poets*. 3 vols. Oxford, 1905. Although almost two hundred years old, this criticism is the place for students to begin.

James Russell Lowell. "Dryden," in *The Writings of James Russell Lowell*. 11 vols. Boston, 1890. Vol. III. After Scott, the best nineteenth-century criticism.

A. W. Verall. *Lectures on Dryden*. Cambridge, 1914. Polished remarks.

Mark Van Doren. *John Dryden: A Study of His Poetry*. New York, 1946. The first complete study in this century (first published in 1920; now in paperback also, Indiana University Press).

Thomas Stearns Eliot. *John Dryden: The Poet, the Dramatist, the Critic*. New York, 1932. Brief essays by Dryden's best-known advocate in this century.

Hugh Macdonald. *John Dryden: A Bibliography of Early Editions and of Drydeniana*. Oxford, 1939. The authoritative bibliography of editions in Dryden's lifetime and of comments about him.

Samuel Holt Monk. *John Dryden: A List of Critical Studies Published from 1895 to 1948*. Minneapolis, Minn., 1948. The authoritative bibliography of books and articles about Dryden.

F. L. Huntley. *On Dryden's Essay of Dramatic Poesy*. Ann Arbor, 1951. The most comprehensive study of the work.

Charles E. Ward. *The Life of John Dryden*. Chapel Hill, N. C., 1961. The standard modern biography.

Arthur W. Hoffman. *John Dryden's Imagery*. Gainesville, Fla., 1962. The first study to approach Dryden with current critical methods; selective but very stimulating.

Bernard N. Schilling (ed.). *Dryden: A Collection of Critical Essays*. Englewood Cliffs, N. J., 1963. Selected criticism of this century.

————. *Dryden and the Conservative Myth*. New Haven, Conn., 1961. A study of Dryden's political conservatism in relation to *Absalom and Achitophel*.

James M. Osborn. *John Dryden: Some Biographical Facts and Problems*. Rev. ed. Gainesville, Fla., 1965. A meticulous review (first published in 1940) of the history of Dryden studies, chiefly biographical, with fresh contributions.

Alan Roper. *Dryden's Poetic Kingdoms*. London, 1965. A careful study of Dryden's analogical methods.

Earl Miner. *Dryden's Poetry*. Bloomington, Ind., and London, 1967. Includes a selective bibliography up to January 1965.

Phillip Harth. *Contexts of Dryden's Thought*. Chicago and London, 1968. An excellent study of Dryden's intellectual temper and religious views, primarily as expressed in *Religio Laici*.

SELECTED
POETRY AND PROSE
OF
John Dryden

HEROIC STANZAS

*Consecrated to the Glorious Memory of His Most
Serene and Renowned Highness, Oliver,
Late Lord Protector of This Commonwealth, etc.*

WRITTEN AFTER THE CELEBRATION OF HIS FUNERAL

1659. Oliver Cromwell died on September 3, 1658. He had
been Lord Protector of England since December 1653 and
before that the dominant "Puritan" figure during much of
the Civil Wars. Dryden's elegy appeared with others, including those by two men, earlier or later identified with
the Stuart cause. They were Edmund Waller, the poet, and
Thomas Sprat, later historian of the Royal Society and a
bishop. Contemporary gossip had connected Dryden with
some minor post in the Commonwealth government, but
there is no firm evidence. This poem stresses the character
and achievements of the dead person, the usual technique
that Dryden used in his memorial poems. Cromwell's character (ll. 1–64), foreign success (ll. 65–124), and bringing of peace from strife (ll. 125–148) are all accurately
described. All are matters important to Dryden throughout
his known career and conflict but little with his royalism.
However, the fact of praising Cromwell hardly sorts with
his later views. The verse form is that of the heroic quatrain, which was inspired in large part by William Davenant's epic poem *Gondibert* (1651) and which dominated
even Dryden's early couplet verse.

1

And now 'tis time; for their officious haste,
Who would before have borne him to the sky,
Like eager Romans ere all rites were past
Did let too soon the sacred eagle fly.

2

Though our best notes are treason to his fame
Join'd with the loud applause of public voice;
Since Heav'n, what praise we offer to his name,
Hath render'd too authentic by its choice;

3

Though in his praise no arts can liberal be,
Since they whose Muses have the highest flown   10
Add not to his immortal memory,
But do an act of friendship to their own;

4

Yet 'tis our duty and our interest too
Such monuments as we can build to raise,
Lest all the world prevent what we should do
And claim a title in him by their praise.

5

How shall I then begin, or where conclude
To draw a fame so truly circular?
For in a round what order can be shew'd,
Where all the parts so equal perfect are?   20

6

His grandeur he deriv'd from Heav'n alone,
For he was great ere fortune made him so,
And wars like mists that rise against the sun
Made him but greater seem, not greater grow.

---

4 *eagle*. Was let fly at Roman funerals to carry an emperor's soul among
the gods.
18 *circular*. Circles were emblems of perfection.
22 Adapting Machiavelli's idea of character (*virtù*) and fortune or destiny as factors in greatness.

7

No borrow'd bays his temples did adorn,
But to our crown he did fresh jewels bring,
Nor was his virtue poison'd soon as born
With the too early thoughts of being king.

8

Fortune (that easy mistress of the young
But to her ancient servants coy and hard)   30
Him at that age her favorites rank'd among
When she her best-lov'd Pompey did discard.

9

He, private, mark'd the faults of others' sway,
And set as sea-marks for himself to shun,
Not like rash monarchs who their youth betray
By acts their age too late would wish undone.

10

And yet dominion was not his design;
We owe that blessing not to him but Heaven,
Which to fair acts unsought rewards did join,
Rewards that less to him than us were given.   40

11

Our former chiefs like sticklers of the war
First sought t'inflame the parties, then to poise,
The quarrel lov'd, but did the cause abhor,
And did not strike to hurt but make a noise.

12

War, our consumption, was their gainfull trade;
We inward bled whilst they prolong'd our pain;
He fought to end our fighting and assay'd
To stanch the blood by breathing of the vein.

27 *virtue*. Also *virtú*.
29-30 See Machiavelli, *The Prince* XXV.
31 *that age*. Forty-five, when Cromwell's triumphs began and Pompey's
ended.
41 *former chiefs*. Earlier, ineffective Parliamentary generals.

13

Swift and resistless through the land he pass'd
Like that bold Greek who did the east subdue,   50
And made to battles such heroic haste
As if on wings of victory he flew.

14

He fought secure of fortune as of fame,
Till by new maps the island might be shown,
Of conquests which he strew'd where'er he came
Thick as the galaxy with stars is sown.

15

His palms, though under weights they did not
        stand,
Still thriv'd; no winter could his laurels fade;
Heav'n in his portrait shew'd a workman's hand
And drew it perfect yet without a shade.   60

16

Peace was the prize of all his toils and care,
Which war had banish'd and did now restore;
Bologna's walls thus mounted in the air
To seat themselves more surely than before.

17

Her safety rescu'd Ireland to him owes,
And treacherous Scotland, to no int'rest true,
Yet bless'd that fate which did his arms dispose
Her land to civilize as to subdue.

18

Nor was he like those stars which only shine
When to pale mariners they storms portend;   70

---

⁵⁰ *that bold Greek.* Alexander the Great.
⁶³ *Bologna's walls.* In 1512 beseiging Spaniards undermined a Bolognese
chapel that was said to have risen high in the air with the explosion
and miraculously to have settled unharmed.
⁶⁹ *those stars.* The Hyades; stars had astrological *influence* (71).

He had his calmer influence, and his mine
Did love and majesty together blend.

19

'Tis true, his count'nance did imprint an awe,
And naturally all souls to his did bow,
As wands of divination downward draw
And point to beds where sov'reign gold doth grow.

20

When past all offerings to Feretrian Jove,
He Mars depos'd and arms to gowns made yield;
Successful councils did him soon approve
As fit for close intrigues as open field.   80

21

To suppliant Holland he vouchsaf'd a peace,
Our once bold rival in the British main,
Now tamely glad her unjust claim to cease
And buy our friendship with her idol, gain.

22

Fame of th' asserted sea through Europe blown
Made France and Spain ambitious of his love;
Each knew that side must conquer he would own
And for him fiercely as for empire strove.

23

No sooner was the Frenchman's cause embrac'd
Than the light *monsieur* the grave *don* outweigh'd;   90
His fortune turn'd the scale where it was cast,
Though Indian mines were in the other laid.

24

When absent, yet we conquer'd in his right,
For though some meaner artist's skill were shown

---

⁷¹ *mine.* Old variant for "mien."
⁷⁷ *Feretrian Jove.* To whom spoils of war were dedicated, especially those
taken personally by a Roman from an enemy commander.

In mingling colours, or in placing light,
Yet still the fair designment was his own.

25

For from all tempers he could service draw;
The worth of each with its alloy he knew,
And as the confidant of Nature saw
How she complexions did divide and brew.   100

26

Or he their single virtues did survey
By intuition in his own large breast,
Where all the rich ideas of them lay,
That were the rule and measure to the rest.

27

When such heroic virtue Heav'n sets out,
The stars like Commons sullenly obey,
Because it drains them when it comes about,
And therefore is a tax they seldom pay.

28

From this high spring our foreign conquests flow,
Which yet more glorious triumphs do portend,   110
Since their commencement to his arms they owe,
If springs as high as fountains may ascend.

29

He made us freemen of the continent
Whom Nature did like captives treat before,
To nobler preys the English lion sent,
And taught him first in Belgian walks to roar.

30

That old unquestion'd pirate of the land,
Proud Rome, with dread the fate of Dunkirk heard,

97-100 The imagery is alchemical.
113 *freemen of the continent.* By the cession of Dunkirk in 1658.

And trembling wish'd behind more Alps to stand,
Although an Alexander were her guard.   120

31

By his command we boldly cross'd the line
And bravely fought where southern stars arise,
We trac'd the far-fetch'd gold unto the mine
And that which brib'd our fathers made our prize.

32

Such was our prince; yet own'd a soul above
The highest acts it could produce to show:
Thus poor mechanic arts in public move
Whilst the deep secrets beyond practice go.

33

Nor di'd he when his ebbing fame went less,
But when fresh laurels courted him to live;   130
He seem'd but to prevent some new success,
As if above what triumphs earth could give.

34

His latest victories still thickest came,
As near the center motion does increase,
Till he, press'd down by his own weighty name,
Did, like the vestal, under spoils decease.

35

But first the ocean as a tribute sent
That giant prince of all her watery herd,
And th' isle when her protecting genius went
Upon his obsequies loud sighs conferr'd.   140

---

120 *Alexander.* The Seventh; he was pope from 1655 to 1667.
136 *the vestal.* Tarpeia, a Roman woman who betrayed her city by
letting the Sabines into Rome, asking for reward what the soldiers wore
on their left arms (she meant their gold bracelets). But they crushed
her under the piled bucklers also worn on their left arms.
138 *giant prince.* A large whale came up the Thames on June 3, 1658.
140 *loud sighs.* Stormy winds on August 30, as Cromwell lay dying.

36

No civil broils have since his death arose,
But faction now by habit does obey,
And wars have that respect for his repose,
As winds for halcyons when they breed at sea.

37

His ashes in a peaceful urn shall rest;
His name a great example stands to show
How strangely high endeavours may be blest,
Where piety and valour jointly go.

ASTRAEA REDUX

*A Poem on the Happy Restoration
and Return of His Sacred Majesty
Charles the Second*

> *Iam redit et Virgo, redeunt Sa-
> turnia regna.*
>
> VIRGIL.

1660. Charles II returned to England and to the throne from what he called his travels on May 29, 1660, to the relief and joy of most of the nation. Confusion had followed the death of Cromwell, and even during the Protector's lifetime many had thought it anomalous not to have a hereditary king. The return of Charles brought back to poets the biblical and classical symbolism that had been devised for Tudor and Stuart monarchs. Dryden's title (Justice Returned) and his epigraph from Virgil's *Eclogues* IV, 6 ("Now too the Virgin returns, and the reign of Saturn returns") refer to the virgin goddess Astraea, or justice, who had earlier been associated with Elizabeth I and strong execution of government. Saturn suggests a return to a golden age and to rule interrupted by force. Although in couplets, the poem shows signs, especially near its beginning, of the quatrain movement of *Heroic Stanzas*. It is less unified than that poem, largely because it is more ambitious, more allusive, and more historical in detail. These features look toward Dryden's mature poetry, just as the numerous conceits recall those Metaphysical poets he never quite forgot.

Now with a general peace the world was blest,
While ours, a world divided from the rest,
A dreadful quiet felt, and worser far
Than arms, a sullen interval of war:
Thus when black clouds draw down the lab'ring
    skies,
Ere yet abroad the winged thunder flies,
An horrid stillness first invades the ear,
And in that silence we the tempest fear.
Th' ambitious Swede like restless billows toss'd,
On this hand gaining what on that he lost,   10
Though in his life he blood and ruin breath'd,
To his now guideless kingdom peace bequeath'd.
And Heaven that seem'd regardless of our fate,
For France and Spain did miracles create,
Such mortal quarrels to compose in peace
As nature bred and int'rest did increase.
We sigh'd to hear the fair Iberian bride
Must grow a lily to the lilies' side,
While our cross stars deni'd us Charles his bed
Whom our first flames and virgin love did wed.   20
    For his long absence church and state did groan;
Madness the pulpit, faction seiz'd the throne;
Experienc'd age in deep despair was lost
To see the rebel thrive, the loyal cross'd;
Youth that with joys had unacquainted been
Envi'd gray hairs that once good days had seen;
We thought our sires, not with their own content,
Had ere we came to age our portion spent.
Nor could our nobles hope their bold attempt
Who ruin'd crowns would coronets exempt;   30
For when by their designing leaders taught
To strike at pow'r which for themselves they sought,
The vulgar gull'd into rebellion, arm'd,
Their blood to action by the prize was warm'd.
The sacred purple then and scarlet gown

² *a world,* etc. Virgil, *Eclogues* I, 66 (penitus toto divosos orbe Britannos).
⁷ Often parodied in Dryden's day.
⁹ *ambitious Swede.* Charles X (d. 1660).
¹⁷ *Iberian bride.* Maria Theresa, Infanta of Spain, betrothed to Louis XIV in 1659.
⁸⁵ *purple.* For bishops' gowns. *scarlet.* For peers' gowns.

Like sanguine dye to elephants was shown.
    Thus when the bold Typhoeus scal'd the sky
And forc'd great Jove from his own heaven to fly
(What king, what crown from treasons reach is free,
If Jove and Heaven can violated be?)   40
The lesser gods that shar'd his prosp'rous state
All suffer'd in the exil'd Thund'rer's fate.
The rabble now such freedom did enjoy,
As winds at sea that use it to destroy:
Blind as the Cyclops, and as wild as he,
They own'd a lawless savage liberty,
Like that our painted ancestors so priz'd
Ere empire's arts their breasts had civiliz'd.
    How great were then our Charles his woes, who
   thus
Was forc'd to suffer for himself and us!   50
He, toss'd by fate, and hurried up and down,
Heir to his father's sorrows, with his crown,
Could taste no sweets of youth's desired age,
But found his life too true a pilgrimage.
Unconquer'd yet in that forlorn estate,
His manly courage overcame his fate.
His wounds he took like Romans on his breast,
Which by his virtue were with laurels dress'd.
As souls reach heav'n while yet in bodies pent,
So did he live above his banishment.   60
    That sun which we beheld with cousen'd eyes
Within the water, mov'd along the skies.
How easy 'tis when destiny proves kind
With full spread sails to run before the wind,
But those that 'gainst stiff gales laveering go
Must be at once resolv'd and skilful too.
He would not like soft Otho hope prevent
But stay'd and suffer'd fortune to repent.

---

37 *Typhoeus.* Or Typhon, the monster giant who assaulted heaven in the war against the gods.
45 *Cyclops.* One-eyed Polyphemus; a common comparison for Commonwealth rule.
46 *savage liberty.* Some classical writers and Thomas Hobbes, in *Leviathan* I, xiii, so described primitive society.
51 *toss'd by fate.* Like Virgil's Aeneas (fato profugus).
57 *on his breast.* Not like a coward, on his back.

These virtues Galba in a stranger sought,
And Piso to adopted empire brought.   70
  How shall I then my doubtful thoughts express
That must his suff'rings both regret and bless!
For when his early valour heav'n had cross'd,
And all at Worc'ster but the honour lost,
Forc'd into exile from his rightful throne,
He made all countries where he came his own,
And viewing monarchs' secret arts of sway,
A royal factor for their kingdoms lay.
Thus banish'd David spent abroad his time,
When to be God's anointed was his crime;   80
And when restor'd made his proud neighbours rue
Those choice remarks he from his travels drew.
  Nor is he only by afflictions shown
To conquer others' realms but rule his own;
Recov'ring hardly what he lost before,
His right endears it much, his purchase more.
Inur'd to suffer ere he came to reign,
No rash procedure will his actions stain.
To bus'ness ripen'd by digestive thought,
His future rule is into method brought: 90
As they who first proportion understand
With easy practice reach a master's hand.
  Well might the ancient poets then confer
On night the honour'd name of councilor,
Since struck with rays of prosp'rous fortune blind,
We light alone in dark afflictions find.
In such adversities to scepters train'd,
The name of great his famous grandsire gain'd,
Who yet a king alone in name and right,
With hunger, cold and angry Jove did fight,   100
Shock'd by a covenanting League's vast pow'rs
As holy and as Catholic as ours,

67–70 *soft Otho*. The effeminate Roman (A.D. 32–69), who committed
suicide when courage would have brought him empire, had aided
Galba to become emperor but was passed over as successor in favor of
the *stranger*, Piso.
74 *Worc'ster*. Charles was defeated at Worcester in 1651 and escaped ad-
venturously to France.
79 *David*. 2 Samuel 15–21.
98 *grandsire*. Henri IV of France, who struggled with the Catholic League
that Dryden is comparing to the Commonwealth.

Till fortune's fruitless spite had made it known
Her blows not shook but riveted his throne.
　Some lazy ages lost in sleep and ease
No action leave to busy chronicles,
Such whose supine felicity but makes
In story chasms, in epochës mistakes,
O'er whom time gently shakes his wings of down
Till with his silent sickle they are mown;　　　　　　　　　　110
Such is not Charles his too too active age
Which, govern'd by the wild distemper'd rage
Of some black star infecting all the skies,
Made him at his own cost like Adam wise.
　Tremble, ye nations, who secure before
Laugh'd at those arms that 'gainst ourselves we
　　bore;
Rous'd by the lash of his own stubborn tail
Our lion now will foreign foes assail.
With alga who the sacred altar strows?
To all the sea-gods Charles an off'ring owes:　　　　　　　　120
A bull to thee, Portunus, shall be slain,
A lamb to you, the tempests of the main;
For those loud storms that did against him roar
Have cast his shipwreck'd vessel on the shore.
　Yet as wise artists mix their colours so
That by degrees they from each other go,
Black steals unheeded from the neighb'ring white
Without offending the well cousen'd sight:
So on us stole our blessed change, while we
Th' effect did feel but scarce the manner see.　　　　　　　　130
Frosts that constrain the ground, and birth deny
To flow'rs, that in its womb expecting lie,
Do seldom their usurping pow'r withdraw,
But raging floods pursue their hasty thaw;
Our thaw was mild, the cold not chas'd away
But lost in kindly heat of lengthen'd day.
　Heav'n would no bargain for its blessings drive
But what we could not pay for, freely give.
The Prince of Peace would like himself confer

---

[119] *alga.* Seaweed, an insignificant offering.
[121] *Portunus.* A Roman god of shores and harbors.

A gift unhop'd without the price of war.   140
Yet as he knew his blessings' worth, took care
That we should know it by repeated pray'r,
Which storm'd the skies and ravish'd Charles from
          thence
As heav'n itself is took by violence.
   Booth's forward valour only serv'd to show
He durst that duty pay we all did owe;
Th' attempt was fair, but heav'n's prefixed hour
Not come; so like the watchful traveler
That by the moon's mistaken light did rise,
Lay down again, and clos'd his weary eyes.   150
'Twas Monck whom Providence design'd to loose
Those real bonds false freedom did impose.
The blessed saints that watch'd this turning scene
Did from their stars with joyful wonder lean,
To see small clues draw vastest weights along,
Not in their bulk but in their order strong.
Thus pencils can by one slight touch restore
Smiles to that changed face that wept before.
With ease such fond chimeras we pursue
As fancy frames for fancy to subdue,   160
But when ourselves to action we betake
It shuns the mint like gold that chemists make.
   How hard was then his task, at once to be
What in the body natural we see
Man's architect distinctly did ordain,
The charge of muscles, nerves, and of the brain;
Through viewless conduits spirits to dispense,
The springs of motion from the seat of sense.
'Twas not the hasty product of a day,
But the well ripen'd fruit of wise delay.   170
He like a patient angler, e're he strook
Would let them play a while upon the hook.
Our healthful food the stomach labours thus,
At first embracing what it straight doth crush.

---

145 *Booth*. Sir George Booth led an abortive Royalist uprising against the
   Commonwealth in 1659.
151 *Monck*. General George Monk, or Monck, later Duke of Albermarle,
   commander of forces in Scotland, helped effect the Restoration.
153 *saints*. Imagined as "intelligences" of stars.

Wise leeches will not vain receipts obtrude,
While growing pains pronounce the humours crude;
Deaf to complaints they wait upon the ill
Till some safe crisis authorise their skill.
Nor could his acts too close a vizard wear
To scape their eyes whom guilt had taught to fear   180
And guard with caution that polluted nest
Whence legion twice before was dispossess'd,
Once sacred house which when they enter'd in
They thought the place could sanctify a sin,
Like those that vainly hop'd kind Heav'n would
    wink
While to excess on martyrs' tombs they drink.
And as devouter Turks first warn their souls
To part before they taste forbidden bowls,
So these when their black crimes they went about
First timely charm'd their useless conscience out.   190
Religion's name against itself was made;
The shadow serv'd the substance to invade:
Like zealous missions they did care pretend
Of souls in shew, but made the gold their end.
    Th' incensed pow'rs beheld with scorn from high
An Heaven so far distant from the sky,
Which durst with horses' hoofs that beat the ground
And martial brass belie the thunder's sound.
'Twas hence at length just vengeance thought it fit
To speed their ruin by their impious wit.   200
Thus Sforza, curs'd with a too fertile brain,
Lost by his wiles the pow'r his wit did gain.
    Henceforth their fogue must spend at lesser rate
Than in its flames to wrap a nation's fate.
Suffer'd to live, they are like Helots set
A virtuous shame within us to beget.
For by example most we sinn'd before,
And glass-like, clearness mix'd with frailty bore,
But since reform'd by what we did amiss,

181 *polluted nest.* Parliament, twice dissolved, 1653 and 1659.
185ff. Puritans were often accused of hypocrisy.
201 *Sforza.* Lodovico Sforza (d. 1508) murdered his nephew to become Duke of Milan and later died in French captivity.
205 *Helots.* Slaves whom the Spartans sometimes made drunk in front of children to show the results of intemperance.

We by our suff'rings learn to prize our bliss: 210
Like early lovers whose unpractis'd hearts
Were long the May-game of malicious arts,
When once they find their jealousies were vain
With double heat renew their fires again.
　'Twas this produc'd the joy that hurried o'er
Such swarms of English to the neighb'ring shore,
To fetch that prize by which Batavia made
So rich amends for our impoverish'd trade.
Oh, had you seen from Scheveline's barren shore
(Crowded with troops and barren now no more)   220
Afflicted Holland to his farewell bring
True sorrow, Holland to regret a king;
While waiting him his royal fleet did ride
And willing winds to their low'r'd sails deni'd.
The wavering streamers, flags, and standard out,
The merry seamen's rude but cheerful shout,
And last the cannon's voice that shook the skies ⎫
And, as it fares in sudden ecstasies,　　　　　　　⎬
At once bereft us both of ears and eyes.　　　　　　⎭
The *Naseby*, now no longer England's shame   230
But better to be lost in Charles his name
(Like some unequal bride in nobler sheets),
Receives her lord; the joyful *London* meets
The princely York, himself alone a freight;
The *Swift-sure* groans beneath great Glouc'ster's
　　　　　weight.
Secure as when the halcyon breeds, with these
He that was born to drown might cross the seas.
Heav'n could not own a providence and take
The wealth three nations ventur'd at a stake.
The same indulgence Charles his voyage bless'd   240
Which in his right had miracles confess'd.
The winds that never moderation knew
Afraid to blow too much, too faintly blew;
Or out of breath with joy could not enlarge

[219] *Scheveline*. A village, Scheveningen, near The Hague.
[230] *The Naseby*. A ship named after the Parliamentary victory at Naseby
　in 1645; hence, Charles renamed the ship after himself.
[234] *princely York*. James, Duke of York, later James II.
[235] *Glouc'ster*. Henry, Duke of Gloucester (d. 1660), Charles' fourth son.

Their straiten'd lungs, or conscious of their charge.
The British Amphitrite, smooth and clear,
In richer azure never did appear,
Proud her returning prince to entertain
With the submitted fasces of the main.

   And welcome now (great monarch) to your own;   250
Behold th' approaching cliffs of Albion;
It is no longer motion cheats your view:
As you meet it, the land approacheth you.
The land returns, and in the white it wears
The marks of penitence and sorrow bears.
   But you, whose goodness your descent doth show,
Your heav'nly parentage, and earthly too,
By that same mildness which your father's crown
Before did ravish, shall secure your own.
Not ti'd to rules of policy, you find   260
Revenge less sweet than a forgiving mind.
Thus when th' Almighty would to Moses give
A sight of all he could behold and live,
A voice before his entry did proclaim
Long-suff'ring, goodness, mercy in his name.
Your pow'r to justice doth submit your cause,
Your goodness only is above the laws,
Whose rigid letter while pronounc'd by you
Is softer made. So winds that tempests brew
When through Arabian groves they take their flight,   270
Made wanton with rich odours, lose their spite.
And as those lees that trouble it refine
The agitated soul of generous wine,
So tears of joy for your returning spilt,
Work out and expiate our former guilt.
   Methinks I see those crowds on Dover's strand
Who in their haste to welcome you to land
Chok'd up the beach with their still growing store,
And made a wilder torrent on the shore;

---

246 *Amphitrite*. A goddess, here signifying the sea.
249 *submitted fasces*. Humbly presented emblem of authority; cf. *Annus Mirabilis* 199.
260ff. Charles proposed an Act of Indemnity forgiving British enemies; Dryden usually stressed such mildness in Charles' temper.
262 *Moses*, etc. Exodus 33:20–23 and 34:5–7.

While spurr'd with eager thoughts of past delight   280
Those who had seen you court a second sight,
Preventing still your steps, and making haste
To meet you often wheresoe'er you pass'd.
  How shall I speak of that triumphant day
When you renew'd the expiring pomp of May!
(A month that owns an int'rest in your name:
You and the flow'rs are its peculiar claim.)
That star, that at your birth shone out so bright
It stain'd the duller sun's meridian light,
Did once again its potent fires renew   290
Guiding our eyes to find and worship you.
  And now time's whiter series is begun
Which in soft centuries shall smoothly run;
Those clouds that overcast your morn shall fly,
Dispell'd to farthest corners of the sky.
Our nation with united int'rest blest,
Not now content to poise, shall sway the rest.
  Abroad your empire shall no limits know,
But like the sea in boundless circles flow.
Your much lov'd fleet shall with a wide command   300
Besiege the petty monarchs of the land,
And as old Time his offspring swallow'd down,
Our ocean in its depths all seas shall drown.
Their wealthy trade from pirates' rapine free
Our merchants shall no more advent'rers be;
Nor in the farthest east those dangers fear
Which humble Holland must dissemble here.
Spain to your gift alone her Indies owes,
For what the pow'rful takes not he bestows,
And France that did an exile's presence fear   310
May justly apprehend you still too near.
  At home the hateful names of parties cease,
And factious souls are weari'd into peace.

285 *May*, etc. In 1660 Charles entered London in triumph on his birthday, May 29.
288 *that star*. Had appeared brightly in daylight on May 29, 1630, the day
Charles was born; also alluding to the Star of Bethlehem.
305 *advent'rers*. Punning: one company of traders was the Merchant Ad-
venturers.
310 *an exile's presence*. A treaty with Cromwell made Charles unwelcome
in France.

The discontented now are only they
Whose crimes before did your just cause betray;
Of those your edicts some reclaim from sins,
But most your life and blest example wins.
   Oh, happy prince, whom Heav'n hath taught the
      way,
By paying vows to have more vows to pay!
Oh, happy age! Oh, times like those alone   320
By fate reserv'd for great Augustus' throne!
When the joint growth of arms and arts foreshew
The world a monarch, and that monarch *You.*

---

316 *edicts.* Royal proclamations against rioters and vicious persons (May
  30, 1660).
320-22 Recalling Virgil's prophecy of return of the Golden Age under
  Augustus (*Aeneid* VI, 791 ff.).

TO MY HONOUR'D FRIEND, DR. CHARLETON,

On His Learned and Useful Works;
and More Particularly This of Stonehenge,
by Him Restored to the True Founders.

1662. Dr. Walter Charleton (1620–1707) was a distinguished physician, scientist, and philosopher who appears to have been a major stimulus to Dryden's interest in science. Charleton's *Chorea Gigantum* (1663), which was published with these complimentary verses by Dryden, was one of several attempts to explain the still not wholly certain purpose of the ring of stones at Stonehenge near Salisbury. Charleton's misguided theory that the ring was a Danish coronation site was accepted by very few even at the time. Dryden used the theory as a symbol for lawful freedom in modern science (as opposed to Scholastic Aristotelianism) and in English monarchy (as opposed to extremes of anarchy or tyranny). The poem is the first of Dryden's verse epistles to intellectual or artistic friends, and in it his enthusiasm for contemporary ideas and human achievement (especially English) emerges forcefully. The result is a greater intellectual energy than that found in earlier poems. However, there is little personal relevance other than excitement with ideas.

The longest tyranny that ever sway'd
Was that wherein our ancestors betray'd
Their free-born reason to the Stagirite

---

[3] *the Stagirite.* Aristotle, who was followed by the learned in the Middle Ages.

And made his torch their universal light.
So truth, while only one suppli'd the state,
Grew scarce and dear, and yet sophisticate,
Until 'twas bought, like empiric wares, or charms,
Hard words seal'd up with Aristotle's arms.

   Columbus was the first that shook his throne
And found a temp'rate in a torrid zone;   10
The feverish air fann'd by a cooling breeze,
The fruitful vales set round with shady trees,
And guiltless men who danc'd away their time,
Fresh as their groves and happy as their clime.
Had we still paid that homage to a name,
Which only God and Nature justly claim,
The western seas had been our utmost bound,
Where poets still might dream the sun was drown'd,
And all the stars that shine in southern skies
Had been admir'd by none but savage eyes.   20

   Among th' assertors of free reason's claim
Th' English are not the least in worth or fame.
The world to Bacon does not only owe
Its present knowledge, but its future too.
Gilbert shall live till lodestones cease to draw
Or British fleets the boundless ocean awe.
And noble Boyle, not less in nature seen,
Than his great brother read in states and men.
The circling streams, once thought but pools, of
        blood
(Whether life's fuel, or the body's food)   30
From dark oblivion Harvey's name shall save,
While Ent keeps all the honour that he gave.
   Nor are you, learned friend, the least renown'd,
Whose fame, not circumscrib'd with English ground,

---

[23] *Bacon.* The Royal Society, chartered in 1662, deliberately adopted Sir
   Francis Bacon's *New Atlantis* as a program for action.
[25] *Gilbert.* William Gilbert (d. 1603), royal physician, was the author of
   the first modern study of magnetism.
[27] *noble Boyle.* The Rt. Hon. Robert Boyle (d. 1691), chemist, physicist,
   linguist, and theologian.
[28] *brother.* Roger Boyle (d. 1679), Earl of Orrery, author and political
   figure.
[31] *Harvey.* William Harvey (d. 1657), famous for his study of the circulation of the blood; his last treatise was published at the request of
   George Ent (32), a learned physician.

Flies like the nimble journeys of the light,
And is, like that, unspent too in its flight.
Whatever truths have been by art or chance
Redeem'd from error or from ignorance,
Thin in their authors (like rich veins of ore),
Your works unite and still discover more.   40
Such is the healing virtue of your pen,
To perfect cures on books as well as men.
Nor is this work the least: you well may give
To men new vigour, who make stones to live.
Through you the Danes (their short dominion lost)
A longer conquest than the Saxons boast.
STONEHENGE, once thought a temple, you have
      found
A throne, where kings, our earthly gods, were
      crown'd,
Where by their wond'ring subjects they were seen,
Joy'd with their stature and their princely mien.   50
Our sovereign here above the rest might stand,
And here be chose again to rule the land.

      These ruins shelter'd once his sacred head,
Then when from Worc'ster's fatal field he fled,
Watch'd by the genius of this royal place,
And mighty visions of the Danish race.
His refuge then was for a temple shown,
But, he restor'd, 'tis now become a throne.

---

48 *kings, our earthly gods.* A Royalist conception, with God as King of
kings.
53ff. In the Dedication of his work to Charles II, Charleton recalls that
the king had himself told of visiting Stonehenge after defeat at Worcester.

A *Song*

FROM

THE INDIAN EMPEROR

1665. This, the second song of the play, opens the third
scene of Act IV and comments on the varying fortunes in
love and war of the "Indians" under Montezuma and their
besiegers, the Spaniards. The song belongs to the earlier
tradition of comment on the sad human estate, the *sic vita*
motif that compares man to inferior creatures. Although its
meaning is clear, the fifth line was justly criticized in Dryden's day for illogicality; and his later songs gave up the
agreeable plangency of this one for a livelier note. It received a number of musical settings.

*A pleasant grotto discover'd: in it a fountain spouting;
round about it* Vasquez, Pizarro, *and other Spaniards lying
carelessly unarm'd, and by them many Indian Women, one
of which sings the following Song.*

Song

Ah, fading joy, how quickly art thou past!
      Yet we thy ruin haste;
As if the cares of human life were few
      We seek out new,
And follow fate which would too fast pursue.

See how on every bough the birds express
      In their sweet notes their happiness.

They all enjoy and nothing spare,
   But on their Mother Nature lay their care;
Why then should man, the lord of all below,   10
      Such troubles choose to know
As none of all his subjects undergo?

Hark, hark, the waters fall, fall, fall,
And with a murmuring sound
Dash, dash, upon the ground,
    To gentle slumbers call.

AN ESSAY OF
DRAMATIC POESY

> ———*Fungar vice cotis, acutum*
> *Reddere quae ferrum valet, ex-*
> *sors ipsa secandi.*
> HORAT. *De Arte Poet.*

1665–1667. The "memorable day" on which the dialogue is said to occur was June 3, 1665, a climax in "the late war," that is, the sporadic Second Dutch War (1665–1667). Although it was not published until later, the *Essay* was probably substantially finished by Dryden during a stay with his father-in-law, the Earl of Berkshire, at Charlton, Wiltshire, where Dryden went perhaps in late June 1665 to escape the Great Plague. But the reference to "the late war" in the first sentence of the *Essay* implies a last revision after the Treaty of Breda in July 1667; and Neander later speaks of plays made "since his Majesty's return," "within these seven years." Entered into the *Stationers' Register* for August 6, 1667, it was probably published soon thereafter, although the title page bears the date 1668.

An Essay of Dramatic Poesy is the inner and running title; it is also the more familiar, although the title page version is the more Latinate form, *Of Dramatic Poesy. An Essay.* Because "essay" then meant "an attempt," both versions of the title imply a degree of modesty or hesitation as Dryden set about to write the first major piece of English criticism on drama, and one of the first extended English pieces of criticism as we know it today. In a later "Defence" of the work, he made a bolder claim that his dialogue form was conceived in the tradition of Plato, Cicero, and other

("The Critic," "The Discerner") had borrowed some of his arguments about drama. It has been plausibly suggested that "Lisideius" is derived from an anagram of the Latinized surname of Sir Charles Sedley, and also that it may be a similar Latinizing of *Le Cid,* a famous and controversial play by Corneille, who is much praised by Lisideius. Eugenius ("The Well Born") has been identified with Charles Sackville, who was then Lord Buckhurst and later became Earl of Dorset. Although plausible enough, the identification lacks full proof. At all events, there is no need to assume that Dryden sought simple identification, that there ever was such a conversation and boatride, or that the speakers' opinions need tally at all points with those of their models. The belief that such things may be so is a tribute rather to Dryden's skill in developing the Platonic dramatic setting than to any overwhelming evidence. The arguments advanced by these semi-fictional, or semi-real, speakers are those Dryden thought worthy of serious consideration. It does not follow that he accepted all viewpoints, or that Neander's position is exactly Dryden's own, but the emphasis throughout is essentially patriotic, modern, and liberal.

Three major issues are raised. First, Crites speaks for the superiority of the ancient dramatists and Eugenius for the modern. Second, Lisideius speaks for the superiority of French playwrights and Neander for the English. And third, Crites speaks for the use of blank verse (as nearest prose and actual speech) in serious plays, and Neander for the use of rhyme. Numerous other issues arise, and the actual formulation of points of view is more subtle than bald statement suggests. Behind the specific issues or arguments lie a method and literary perception making Dryden, in Dr. Johnson's phrase, the father of English criticism. The dominant methods are description, comparison, and evaluation (by something more purely literary than moral standards). The Examen of a play by Ben Jonson is the first notable, though rudimentary, example of analytical English criticism.

The three explicit issues provide variations upon two central dramatic—or rather, literary—concerns. The first

concern is quite simply, what is to be the guiding principle
of successful writing? As early as the jests over the two bad
poets (pp. 36–39), Dryden suggests a duality of extremes.
One extreme poet is so tortured in his writing, so committed to emotion, that he is absurd; the other poet is so
unambitious and bound by convention that he fails to
move. In the *Essay* as a whole, the first danger is represented by modern innovations, by English and especially
Spanish variety or violence, and by heightening through
rhyme. The second danger is exemplified by the example
and "rules" of the ancients, by the "correct" practice of the
French, and by a narrow idea of verisimilitude that will
exclude rhymed verse from the stage. It is quite clear that
on balance Dryden is more willing to run the first risk (for
example, to try rhyme or to prefer Shakespeare). But it is
only on balance. The fact that Shakespeare is our Homer
shows how we take our standards from the ancients; and
the fact that Spanish plays are too loose sets a boundary for
English creative variety.

The second concern is less exactly formulated, but it is
the positive version of the first: great achievement in literature is the result of the united faculties of reason, will and
passion, and imagination. The role of reason to judge and
discriminate is shown by the dialogue form itself. The role
of will and passion is to be found, whether agreeably or
not, in the patriotism that is implied by the fictional setting
and comes out in many comments, and, most attractively,
in the love of literature and writers shown throughout the
Essay. Dryden's ambitions, those of the New Man, convey
something of the passion and the desire to succeed in creating a new dramatic poetry which gives the work much of
its fervor. The role of the imagination is implied by the
creation of a semi-fictional form for a critical discussion
and, microcosmically, by two sentences (see fn. 76, below)
of Neander's on the psychology of artistic illusion. Here in
essence is one of Dryden's major aesthetic contributions. It
is amplified (with whatever special pleading) by the insistence in the last main section of the *Essay* that a technique like rhyme is not to be judged by measures of simple

probability in life but by standards of credible artistic re-creation of life.

Few critical essays can have searched so deeply in so natural a prose style and with so special a fictional device. The creation of fictional characters from historical individu-als is familiar in Dryden's greatest poetry, and although that fiction is only partial, it allows *An Essay of Dramatic Poesy* to be considered with John Bunyan's *Pilgrim's Progress* as a second exception to the rule that the seventeenth century created no great prose fiction.

The first edition was dated 1668, probably in mistake for 1667, and the second was dated 1684. Because Dryden uncharacteristically revised this work with great care, the second edition must be the copytext, although with neces-sary corrections from the first.

The epigraph is from Horace, *Ars Poetica*, ll. 304–305: "I shall play the role of a whetstone which, though itself incapable of cutting, yet sharpens steel."

To the Right Honourable Charles Lord Buckhurst.

My Lord,

As I was lately reviewing my loose papers, amongst the rest I found this essay, the writing of which in this rude and undigested manner wherein your Lordship[1] now sees it serv'd as an amusement to me in the country, when the violence of the last plague[2] had driven me from the town. Seeing then our theaters shut up, I was engag'd in these kind of thoughts with the same delight with which men think upon their absent mistresses. I confess I find many things in this discourse which I do not now approve, my judgment being not a little alter'd since the writing of it, but whether for the better or the worse I know not. Neither indeed is it much material in an essay, where all I have said is problematical. For the way of writing plays in verse,

[1] *Lordship.* Charles Sackville (d. 1706), Lord Buckhurst, later Earl of Dorset, who took part in the naval battle referred to at the beginning of the *Essay,* was also known as a poet and man of taste.
[2] *the last plague.* Of 1665.

which I have seem'd to favour, I have since that time laid
the practice of it aside till I have more leisure, because I
find it troublesome and slow. But I am no way alter'd from
my opinion of it, at least with any reasons which have
oppos'd it. For your Lordship may easily observe that none
are very violent against it but those who either have not
attempted it or who have succeeded ill in their attempt.
'Tis enough for me to have your Lordship's example for my
excuse in that little which I have done in it; and I am sure
my adversaries can bring no such arguments against verse
as those with which the fourth act of *Pompey*³ will furnish
me in its defence. Yet, my Lord, you must suffer me a little
to complain of you, that you too soon withdraw from us a
contentment of which we expected the continuance, because you gave it us so early. 'Tis a revolt without occasion
from your party, where your merits had already rais'd you
to the highest commands, and where you have not the excuse of other men, that you have been ill us'd and therefore
laid down arms. I know no other quarrel you can have to
verse than that which Spurina⁴ had to his beauty, when he
tore and mangled the features of his face only because they
pleas'd too well the sight. It was an honour which seem'd
to wait for you, to lead out a new colony of writers from
the mother nation; and upon the first spreading of your
ensigns there had been many in readiness to have follow'd
so fortunate a leader—if not all, yet the better part of
poets.

> *Pars, indocili melior grege; mollis et exspes*
> *Inominata perprimat cubilia.*⁵

I am almost of opinion that we should force you to accept of the command, as sometimes the Praetorian bands
have compell'd their captains to receive the empire. The
court, which is the best and surest judge of writing, has
generally allow'd of verse, and in the town it has found

---

³ *the fourth act of Pompey.* With three others, Buckhurst had translated
Pierre Corneille's play, *La mort de Pompée,* as *Pompey the Great*
(1664).
⁴ *Spurina.* According to Valerius Maximus IV, v.
⁵ *Pars,* etc. Horace, *Epodes* XVI, 37–38. (Let those superior to the herd
go forth; let the soft and hopeless remain inactive on their ill-fated
couches.)

favourers of wit and quality. As for your own particular, my Lord, you have yet youth and time enough to give part of them to the divertisement of the public before you enter into the serious and more unpleasant business of the world. That which the French poet said of the temple of love may be as well apply'd to the temple of the Muses. The words, as near as I can remember them, were these:

> *Le jeune homme, à mauvaise grâce,*
> *N'ayant pas adoré dans le Temple d'Amour;*
> *Il faut qu'il entre, et pour le sage,*
> *Si ce n'est pas son vray séjour,*
> *C'est un giste sur son passage.*[6]

I leave the words to work their effect upon your Lordship in their own language, because no other can so well express the nobleness of the thought, and wish you may be soon call'd to bear a part in the affairs of the nation, where I know the world expects you and wonders why you have been so long forgotten, there being no person amongst our young nobility on whom the eyes of all men are so much bent. But in the meantime your Lordship may imitate the course of Nature, who gives us the flower before the fruit: that, I may speak to you in the language of the Muses, which I have taken from an excellent poem to the King.

> As Nature, when she fruit designs, thinks fit
> By beauteous blossoms to proceed to it,
> And while she does accomplish all the spring,
> Birds to her secret operations sing.[7]

I confess I have no greater reason in addressing this essay to your Lordship than that it might awaken in you the desire of writing something, in whatever kind it be, which might be an honour to our age and country. And methinks it might have the same effect on you which Homer tells us the fight of the Greeks and Trojans before the fleet had on the spirit of Achilles, who though he had

---

[6] *Le jeune homme,* etc. Passage unidentified. (The young man is in bad humor, not having worshiped at the Temple of Love; he *must* go in; and the wise man finds it, if not his true home, at least a refuge on the journey.)

[7] *As Nature,* etc. From Sir William Davenant, *Poem to the King's Most Sacred Majesty.*

resolv'd not to engage, yet found a martial warmth to steal
upon him at the sight of blows, the sound of trumpets, and
the cries of fighting men. For my own part, if in treating of
this subject I sometimes dissent from the opinion of better
wits, I declare it is not so much to combat their opinions as
to defend my own, which were first made public. Sometimes, like a scholar in a fencing-school, I put forth myself
and shew my own ill play on purpose to be better taught.
Sometimes I stand desperately to my arms, like the foot
when deserted by their horse, not in hope to overcome, but
only to yield on more honourable terms. And yet, my Lord,
this war of opinions, you well know, has fallen out among
the writers of all ages and sometimes betwixt friends. Only
it has been prosecuted by some like pedants, with violence
of words, and manag'd by others like gentlemen, with candour and civility. Even Tully had a controversy with his
dear Atticus, and in one of his dialogues[8] makes him sustain the part of an enemy in philosophy, who in his letters
is his confidant of state and made privy to the most
weighty affairs of the Roman Senate. And the same respect
which was paid by Tully to Atticus[9] we find return'd to
him afterwards by Caesar[10] on a like occasion who, answering his book in praise of Cato, made it not so much his
business to condemn Cato as to praise Cicero.

But that I may decline some part of the encounter with
my adversaries, whom I am neither willing to combat nor
well able to resist, I will give your Lordship the relation of
a dispute betwixt some of our wits on the same subject, in
which they did not only speak of plays in verse, but mingled, in the freedom of discourse, some things of the ancient, many of the modern ways of writing, comparing
those with these, and the wits of our nation with those of
others. 'Tis true, they differ'd in their opinions, as 'tis probable they would; neither do I take upon me to reconcile,
but to relate them, and that as Tacitus professes of himself,
"Sine studio partium aut irâ," [11] without passion or interest,

---

[8] *one of his dialogues.* Cicero ("Tully"), *De Legibus.*
[9] *to Atticus.* Cicero, *Ad Atticum* XII, 40.
[10] *by Caesar.* According to Plutarch's Life of Caesar.
[11] *Sine,* etc. Adapting Tacitus, *Annals* I, i (sine ira et studio). (Without
    anger or partiality.)

leaving your Lordship to decide it in favour of which part you shall judge most reasonable, and withal, to pardon the many errors of

> *Your Lordship's*
> *Most obedient humble Servant,*
> John Dreyden[12]

To the Reader.

The drift of the ensuing discourse was chiefly to vindicate the honour[1] of our English writers from the censure of those who unjustly prefer the French before them. This I intimate, lest any should think me so exceeding vain as to teach others an art which they understand much better than myself. But if this incorrect essay, written in the country without the help of books or advice of friends, shall find any acceptance in the world, I promise to myself a better success of the second part,[2] wherein I shall more fully treat of the virtues and faults of the English poets who have written either in this, the epic, or the lyric way.

AN ESSAY OF
DRAMATIC POESY

It was that memorable day in the first summer of the late war when our navy engaged the Dutch, a day wherein the two most mighty and best appointed fleets which any age had ever seen disputed the command of the greater half of the globe, the commerce of nations, and the riches of the universe. While these vast floating bodies on either side mov'd against each other in parallel lines and our countrymen under the happy conduct of his Royal Highness[1] went

---

[12] *Dreyden.* A common variant: also Draydon, Driden.
[1] *vindicate the honour.* Samuel Sorbière's *Relation d'un Voyage en Angleterre* (1664) had criticized the formlessness of English plays.
[2] *the second part.* Never published.
[1] *his Royal Highness.* James, Duke of York, later James II.

breaking, by little and little, into the line of the enemies, the noise of the cannon from both navies reach'd our ears about the city, so that all men being alarm'd with it and in a dreadful suspense of the event, which they knew was then deciding, everyone went following the sound as his fancy led him; and leaving the town almost empty, some took towards the park, some cross the river, others down it, all seeking the noise in the depth of silence.

Amongst the rest, it was the fortune of Eugenius, Crites, Lisideius and Neander to be in company together, three of them persons whom their wit and quality have made known to all the town and whom I have chose to hide under these borrowed names, that they may not suffer by so ill a relation as I am going to make of their discourse.

Taking then a barge which a servant of Lisideius had provided for them, they made haste to shoot the bridge and left behind them that great fall of waters which hind'red them from hearing what they desired; after which, having disengag'd themselves from many vessels which rode at anchor in the Thames and almost block'd up the passage towards Greenwich, they order'd the watermen to let fall their oars more gently; and then, everyone favouring his own curiosity with a strict silence, it was not long ere they perceiv'd the air to break about them like the noise of distant thunder, or of swallows in a chimney: those little undulations of sound, though almost vanishing before they reach'd them, yet still seeming to retain somewhat of their first horror which they had betwixt the fleets. After they had attentively listened till such time as the sound by little and little went from them, Eugenius, lifting up his head and taking notice of it, was the first who congratulated to the rest that happy omen of our nation's victory, adding that we had but this to desire in confirmation of it, that we might hear no more of that noise which was now leaving the English coast. When the rest had concurr'd in the same opinion, Crites, a person of a sharp judgment and somewhat too delicate a taste in wit, which the world have mistaken in him for ill nature, said, smiling to us, that if the concernment of this battle had not been so exceeding great, he could scarce have wish'd the victory at the price he knew he must pay for it, in being subject to the reading and hearing of so many ill verses as he was sure would be made on that subject. Adding, that no argument could scape some of those eternal rhymers who watch a battle with more diligence than the ravens and birds of prey, and the worst of them surest to be first in upon the quarry, while the better able, either out of modesty writ not at all or set that due value upon their poems as to let them be often desired and long expected.

"There are some of those impertinent people of whom you speak," answer'd Lisideius, "who to my knowledge are already so provided, either way, that they can produce not only a panegyric upon the victory but, if need be, a funeral elegy on the Duke—wherein, after they have crown'd his valour with many laurels, they will at last deplore the odds under which he fell, concluding that his courage deserv'd a better destiny." All the company smil'd at the conceit of Lisideius; but Crites, more eager than before, began to make particular exceptions against some writers and said the public magistrate ought to send betimes to forbid them, and that it concern'd the peace and quiet of all honest people that ill poets should be as well silenc'd as seditious preachers.

"In my opinion," replied Eugenius, "you pursue your point too far; for as to my own particular, I am so great a lover of poesy that I could wish them all rewarded who attempt but to do well; at least I would not have them worse us'd than one of their brethren was by Sylla the Dictator: '*Quem in concione vidimus,*' says Tully, '*cum ei libellum malus poeta de populo subjecisset, quod epigramma in eum fecisset tantummodo alternis versibus longiusculis, statim ex iis rebus quas tunc vendebat jubere ei praemium tribui, sub ea conditione ne quid postea scriberet.*'" [2]

"I could wish with all my heart," replied Crites, "that many whom we know were as bountifully thank'd upon the same condition, that they would never trouble us again.

---

[2] *Quem in concione,* etc. Cicero, *Pro Archia Poeta* X. (Sylla, whom we have seen in public meeting—when from the crowd a bad poet handed him an epigram on him written in halting verse—at once ordered the versifier to be paid from the proceeds of things being sold, on the condition that he write no more.)

For amongst others, I have a mortal apprehension of two poets[3] whom this victory with the help of both her wings will never be able to escape."

" 'Tis easy to guess whom you intend," said Lisideius, "and without naming them, I ask you if one of them does not perpetually pay us with clenches upon words and a certain clownish kind of raillery? If now and then he does not offer at a catachresis or Clevelandism,[4] wresting and torturing a word into another meaning? In fine, if he be not one of those whom the French would call *un mauvais buffon*,[5] one who is so much a well-wisher to the satire that he intends, at least, to spare no man, and though he cannot strike a blow to hurt any, yet he ought to be punish'd for the malice of the action, as our witches are justly hang'd because they think themselves to be such and suffer deservedly for believing they did mischief, because they meant it?"

"You have described him," said Crites, "so exactly that I am afraid to come after you with my other extremity of poetry. He is one of those who, having had some advantage of education and converse, knows better than the other what a poet should be but puts it into practice more unluckily than any man. His style and matter are everywhere alike; he is the most calm, peaceable writer you ever read; he never disquiets your passions with the least concernment, but still leaves you in as even a temper as he found you. He is a very leveller in poetry; he creeps along with ten little words in every line and helps out his numbers with *For to* and *Unto* and all the pretty expletives he can find till he drags them to the end of another line, while the sense is left tir'd half way behind it. He doubly starves all his verses, first for want of thought, and then of expression; his poetry neither has wit in it nor seems to have it, like him in Martial.

---

[3] *two poets.* Probably Robert Wild (d. 1679) and Richard Flecknoe (d. 1678—see *MacFlecknoe*), who had, as Dryden wrote, published worthless verses on the battle.

[4] *a catachresis or Clevelandism.* A catachresis bends a word to an unusual purpose, a violence of language like that associated with the Metaphysical conceits of John Cleveland (d. 1658).

[5] *un mauvais buffon.* A wretched jester.

Pauper videri Cinna vult, et est pauper.[6]

He affects plainness to cover his want of imagination; when he writes the serious way, the highest flight of his fancy is some miserable antithesis or seeming contradiction; and in the comic he is still reaching at some thin conceit, the ghost of a jest; and that too flies before him, never to be caught. These swallows which we see before us on the Thames are the just resemblance of his wit: you may observe how near the water they stoop, how many proffers they make to dip, and yet how seldom they touch it; and when they do, 'tis but the surface; they skim over it but to catch a gnat, and then mount into the air and leave it."

"Well, gentlemen," said Eugenius, "you may speak your pleasure of these authors, but though I and some few more about the town may give you a peaceable hearing, yet assure yourselves, there are multitudes who would think you malicious and them injur'd, especially him whom you first described. He is the very Withers[7] of the city; they have bought more editions of his works than would serve to lay under all their pies at the Lord Mayor's Christmas. When his famous poem first came out in the year 1660, I have seen them reading it in the midst of Change time; nay, so vehement they were at it, that they lost their bargain by the candles' ends. But what will you say if he has been received amongst great persons? I can assure you he is this day the envy of one who is lord in the art of quibbling and who does not take it well that any man should intrude so far into his province."

"All I would wish," replied Crites, "is that they who love his writings may still admire him and his fellow poet; *qui Bavium non odit, etc.*[8] is curse sufficient."

"And farther," added Lisideius, "I believe there is no

---

[6] *Pauper*, etc. Martial, *Epigrams* VIII, 19. (Cinna wants to seem poor and poor he is.)

[7] *Withers*. George Withers, a poet (d. 1667) bad enough for Sir John Denham to have saved his life during the Civil Wars by saying that while Withers lived Denham "should not be the worst poet in England."

[8] *qui Bavium*, etc. Ending *"amet tua carmina, Maevi."* Virgil, *Eclogues* III, 90. (Let him who does not detest Bavius love your poems, Maevius.)

man who writes well but would think he had hard measure if their admirers should praise anything of his: *Nam quos contemnimus eorum quoque laudes contemnimus.*" [9]

"There are so few who write well in this age," said Crites, "that methinks any praises should be welcome; they neither rise to the dignity of the last age nor to any of the ancients; and we may cry out of the writers of this time with more reason than Petronius of his, '*Pace vestra liceat dixisse, primi omnium eloquentiam perdidistis*':[10] you have debauched the true old poetry so far, that nature, which is the soul of it, is not in any of your writings."

"If your quarrel," said Eugenius, "to those who now write be grounded only on your reverence to antiquity, there is no man more ready to adore those great Greeks and Romans than I am; but on the other side, I cannot think so contemptibly of the age in which I live or so dishonourably of my own country as not to judge we equal the ancients in most kinds of poesy and in some surpass them; neither know I any reason why I may not be as zealous for the reputation of our age as we find the ancients themselves were in reference to those who lived before them. For you hear your Horace saying,

> *Indignor quidquam reprehendi, non quia crasse*
> *Compositum, illepideve putetur, sed quia nuper.*

And after,

> *Si meliora dies, ut vina, poemata reddit,*
> *Scire velim pretium chartis quotus arroget annus?* [11]

But I see I am engaging in a wide dispute where the arguments are not like to reach close on either side; for poesy is of so large an extent, and so many both of the ancients and moderns have done well in all kinds of it, that in citing one against the other we shall take up more time this evening

---

[9] *Nam quos,* etc. Source unknown. (We despise those who praise what we despise.)

[10] *Pace vestra,* etc. Petronius, *Satyricon* 2. (Permit me to say that you rhetoricians have ruined eloquence.)

[11] *Horace saying,* etc. *Epistles* II, i, 76–77. (I am angry to hear something criticized not for bad writing or lack of appeal but for being new.) And 34–35. (If poems improve like wine with the passing of days, I should like to know what is the best poetic vintage?).

than each man's occasions will allow him. Therefore I would ask Crites to what part of poesy he would confine his arguments, and whether he would defend the general cause of the ancients against the moderns, or oppose any age of the moderns against this of ours."

Crites,[12] a little while considering upon this demand, told Eugenius that, if he pleased, he would limit their dispute to dramatic poesy, in which he thought it not difficult to prove either that the ancients were superior to the moderns or the last age to this of ours.

Eugenius was somewhat surpris'd when he heard Crites make choice of that subject. "For aught I see," said he, "I have undertaken a harder province than I imagin'd, for though I never judg'd the plays of the Greek or Roman poets comparable to ours, yet on the other side those we now see acted come short of many which were written in the last age. But my comfort is, if we are o'ercome, it will be only by our own countrymen; and if we yield to them in this one part of poesy, we more surpass them in all the other; for in the epic or lyric way it will be hard for them to shew us one such amongst them as we have many now living, or who lately were. They can produce nothing so courtly writ, or which expresses so much the conversation of a gentleman, as Sir John Suckling; nothing so even, sweet, and flowing as Mr. Waller; nothing so majestic, so correct as Sir John Denham; nothing so elevated, so copious, and full of spirit, as Mr. Cowley. As for the Italian, French, and Spanish plays, I can make it evident that those who now write surpass them, and that the drama is wholly ours."

All of them were thus far of Eugenius his opinion, that the sweetness of English verse was never understood or practis'd by our fathers. Even Crites himself did not much oppose it; and everyone was willing to acknowledge how much our poesy is improv'd by the happiness of some writers yet living,[13] who first taught us to mould our thoughts into easy and significant words, to retrench the

[12] *Crites.* Because Sir Robert Howard had argued for modern writers, Crites is obviously no simple version of him but a fictionalized character based on him.
[13] *yet living.* Of the four poets named, only Suckling had died by 1665.

superfluities of expression, and to make our rhyme so properly a part of the verse that it should never mislead the sense, but itself be led and govern'd by it.

Eugenius was going to continue this discourse when Lisideius told him that it was necessary before they proceeded further to take a standing measure of their controversy; for how was it possible to be decided who writ the best plays before we know what a play should be?—but, this once agreed on by both parties, each might have recourse to it either to prove his own advantages or to discover the failings of his adversary.

He had no sooner said this but all desir'd the favour of him to give the definition of a play; and they were the more importunate because neither Aristotle, nor Horace, nor any other who had writ of that subject had ever done it.

Lisideius, after some modest denials, at last confess'd he had a rude notion of it, indeed rather a description than a definition, but which serv'd to guide him in his private thoughts when he was to make a judgment of what others writ: that he conceiv'd a play ought to be, "A just and lively image of human nature, representing its passions and humours and the changes of fortune to which it is subject, for the delight and instruction of mankind."

This definition, though Crites rais'd a logical objection against it, that it was only *a genere et fine*,[14] and so not altogether perfect, was yet well received by the rest; and after they had given order to the watermen to turn their barge and row softly that they might take the cool of the evening in their return, Crites, being desired by the company to begin, spoke on behalf of the ancients in this manner: "If confidence presage a victory, Eugenius in his own opinion has already triumphed over the ancients; nothing seems more easy to him than to overcome those whom it is our greatest praise to have imitated well; for we do not only build upon their foundations, but by their models. Dramatic poesy had time enough, reckoning from Thespis (who first invented it) to Aristophanes, to be born, to grow

[14] *a genere et fine.* By the larger class and the purpose of literature—not by the single species of drama.

up, and to flourish in maturity. It has been observed of arts
and sciences that in one and the same century they have
arriv'd to great perfection, and no wonder, since every age
has a kind of universal genius which inclines those that live
in it to some particular studies. The work then being
push'd on by many hands must of necessity go forward.

"Is it not evident in these last hundred years (when the
study of philosophy has been the business of all the *virtuosi*
in Christendom) that almost a new nature has been reveal'd to us? That more errors of the School have been de-
tected, more useful experiments in philosophy have been
made, more noble secrets in optics, medicine, anatomy, astronomy discover'd than in all those credulous and doting
ages from Aristotle to us? So true it is that nothing spreads
more fast than science, when rightly and generally cultivated.

"Add to this the more than common emulation that was
in those times of writing well, which though it be found in
all ages and all persons that pretend to the same reputation, yet poesy being then in more esteem than now it is
had greater honours decreed to the professors of it; and
consequently the rivalship was more high between them.
They had judges ordain'd to decide their merit and prizes
to reward it. And historians have been diligent to record of
Aeschylus, Euripides, Sophocles, Lycophron, and the rest
of them, both who they were that vanquish'd in these wars
of the theater, and how often they were crown'd. While the
Asian kings and Grecian commonwealths scarce afforded
them a nobler subject than the unmanly luxuries of a debauch'd court or giddy intrigues of a factious city. '*Alit
aemulatio ingenia,*' says Paterculus, '*et nunc invidia, nunc
admiratio incitationem accendit*':[15] Emulation is the spur of
wit, and sometimes envy, sometimes admiration quickens
our endeavours.

"But now, since the rewards of honour are taken away,
that virtuous emulation is turn'd into direct malice, yet so
slothful that it contents itself to condemn and cry down
others without attempting to do better. 'Tis a reputation
too unprofitable to take the necessary pains for it; yet,

[15] *Alit aemulatio,* etc. Paterculus, *Historia Romana* I, 17.

wishing they had it, that desire is incitement enough to hinder others from it. And this, in short, Eugenius, is the reason why you have now so few good poets and so many severe judges. Certainly, to imitate the ancients well much labour and long study is required, which pains, I have already shewn, our poets would want encouragement to take, if yet they had ability to go through the work. Those ancients have been faithful imitators and wise observers of that nature which is so torn and ill represented in our plays; they have handed down to us a perfect resemblance of her, which we, like ill copiers, neglecting to look on, have render'd monstrous and disfigur'd. But that you may know how much you are indebted to those your masters and be ashamed to have so ill requited them, I must remember you that all the rules[16] by which we practise the drama at this day (either such as relate to the justness and symmetry of the plot or the episodical ornaments, such as descriptions, narrations, and other beauties which are not essential to the play) were delivered to us from the observations which Aristotle made of those poets who either liv'd before him or were his contemporaries. We have added nothing of our own, except we have the confidence to say our wit is better, of which none boast in this our age, but such as understand not theirs. Of that book[17] which Aristotle has left us περὶ τῆς ποιητικῆς, Horace his *Art of Poetry* is an excellent comment and, I believe, restores to us that second book of his concerning comedy which is wanting in him.

"Out of these two have been extracted the famous rules which the French call *des trois unités*,[18] or the three unities which ought to be observ'd in every regular play, namely, of time, place, and action.

"The unity of time they comprehend in twenty-four hours, the compass of a natural day, or as near it as can be

---

[16] *the rules.* From Horace and their own interpretations, continental critics deduced literary rules attributed to Aristotle and designed to facilitate writing. Most notable were the three unities (time, place, action), of which action alone is Aristotelian.

[17] *that book.* Aristotle's *Poetics* proposed to treat all poetry, but only his comments on tragedy survive.

[18] *des trois unités.* Corneille's third discourse, *Discours des trois Unités* (1660), and other works are heavily drawn upon by Dryden in his *Essay,* parts of which are called in passing *discourse.*

contriv'd, and the reason of it is obvious to everyone, that the time of the feigned action or fable of the play should be proportion'd as near as can be to the duration of that time in which it is represented. Since therefore all plays are acted on the theater in a space of time much within the compass of twenty-four hours, that play is to be thought the nearest imitation of Nature whose plot or action is confin'd within that time. And by the same rule which concludes this general proportion of time, it follows that all the parts of it are (as near as may be) to be equally subdivided, namely, that one act take not up the suppos'd time of half a day, which is out of proportion to the rest, since the other four are then to be straiten'd within the compass of the remaining half; for it is unnatural that one act, which being spoke or written is not longer than the rest, should be suppos'd longer by the audience. 'Tis therefore the poet's duty to take care that no act should be imagin'd to exceed the time in which it is represented on the stage and that the intervals and inequalities of time be suppos'd to fall out between the acts.

"This rule of time, how well it has been observed by the ancients, most of their plays will witness. You see them in their tragedies (wherein to follow this rule is certainly most difficult), from the very beginning of their plays, falling close into that part of the story which they intend for the action or principal object of it, leaving the former part to be delivered by narration; so that they set the audience, as it were, at the post where the race is to be concluded, and saving them the tedious expectation of seeing the poet set out and ride the beginning of the course, they suffer you not to behold him till he is in sight of the goal and just upon you.

"For the second unity, which is that of place, the ancients meant by it that the scene ought to be continu'd through the play in the same place where it was laid in the beginning. For the stage on which it is represented, being but one and the same place, it is unnatural to conceive it many, and those far distant from one another. I will not deny but by the variation of painted scenes, the fancy (which in these cases will contribute to its own deceit)

may sometimes imagine it several places with some appearance of probability; yet it still carries the greater likelihood of truth if those places be suppos'd so near each
other, as in the same town or city, which may all be com-
prehended under the larger denomination of one place. For
a greater distance will bear no proportion to the shortness
of time which is allotted in the acting to pass from one of
them to another; for the observation of this, next to the
ancients, the French are to be most commended. They tie
themselves so strictly to the unity of place that you never
see in any of their plays a scene chang'd in the middle of
an act; if the act begins in a garden, a street, or chamber,
'tis ended in the same place. And that you may know it to
be the same, the stage is so supplied with persons that it is
never empty all the time; he who enters second has business with him who was on before; and before the second
quits the stage, a third appears who has business with him.

"This Corneille calls *la liaison des scènes*, the continuity
or joining of the scenes; and 'tis a good mark of a well
contriv'd play when all the persons are known to each
other, and every one of them has some affairs with all the
rest.

"As for the third unity, which is that of action, the ancients meant no other by it than what the logicians do by
their *finis*, the end or scope of any action: that which is the
first in intention and last in execution. Now the poet is to
aim at one great and complete action, to the carrying on of
which all things in his play, even the very obstacles, are to
be subservient; and the reason of this is as evident as any
of the former.

"For two actions equally labour'd and driven on by the
writer would destroy the unity of the poem; it would be no
longer one play, but two. Not but that there be many actions in a play, as Ben Jonson has observed in his *Discoveries;* but they must be all subservient to the great one, which
our language happily expresses in the name of 'under-
plots': such as in Terence's *Eunuch* is the difference and
reconcilement of Thais and Phaedria, which is not the chief
business of the play but promotes the marriage of Chaerea
and Chremes's sister, principally intended by the poet.

There ought to be but one action, says Corneille, that is, one complete action which leaves the mind of the audience in a full repose. But this cannot be brought to pass but by many other imperfect actions which conduce to it and hold the audience in a delightful suspense of what will be.

"If by these rules (to omit many other drawn from the precepts and practice of the ancients) we should judge our modern plays, 'tis probable that few of them would endure the trial; that which should be the business of a day takes up in some of them an age; instead of one action they are the epitomes of a man's life; and for one spot of ground (which the stage should represent) we are sometimes in more countries than the map can shew us.

"But if we will allow the ancients to have contriv'd well, we must acknowledge them to have written better; questionless we are depriv'd of a great flock of wit in the loss of Menander among the Greek poets, and of Caecilius, Afranius, and Varius among the Romans. We may guess at Menander's excellency by the plays of Terence, who translated some of them and yet wanted so much of him that he was call'd by C. Caesar,[19] the half-Menander; and may judge of Varius by the testimonies of Horace, Martial, and Velleius Paterculus. 'Tis probable that these, could they be recover'd, would decide the controversy; but so long as Aristophanes and Plautus are extant, while the tragedies of Euripides, Sophocles, and Seneca are in our hands, I can never see one of those plays which are now written but it increases my admiration of the ancients. And yet I must acknowledge further that, to admire them as we ought, we should understand them better than we do. Doubtless many things appear flat to us, the wit of which depended on some custom or story which never came to our knowledge, or perhaps on some criticism in their language, which being so long dead and only remaining in their books, 'tis not possible they should make us understand perfectly. To read Macrobius explaining the propriety and elegancy of many words in Virgil, which I had before pass'd over without consideration as common things, is enough to assure me that I ought to think the same of Terence; and that in

[19] *by C. Caesar.* See Suetonius, *Vita Terentii.*

the purity of his style (which Tully so much valued that he ever carried his works about him) there is yet left in him great room for admiration, if I knew but where to place it. In the meantime I must desire you to take notice that the greatest man of the last age[20] (Ben Jonson) was willing to give place to them in all things. He was not only a professed imitator of Horace but a learned plagiary of all the others; you track him everywhere in their snow. If Horace, Lucan, Petronius Arbiter, Seneca, and Juvenal had their own from him, there are few serious thoughts which are new in him; you will pardon me therefore if I presume he lov'd their fashion when he wore their clothes. But since I have otherwise a great veneration for him, and you, Eugenius, prefer him above all other poets, I will use no farther argument to you than his example: I will produce before you Father Ben, dress'd in all the ornaments and colours of the ancients; you will need no other guide to our party if you follow him; and whether you consider the bad plays of our age or regard the good plays of the last, both the best and worst of the modern poets will equally instruct you to admire the ancients."

Crites had no sooner left speaking, but Eugenius, who had waited with some impatience for it, thus began: "I have observ'd in your speech that the former part of it is convincing as to what the moderns have profited by the rules of the ancients, but in the latter you are careful to conceal how much they have excell'd them. We own all the helps we have from them and want neither veneration nor gratitude while we acknowledge that to overcome them we must make use of the advantages we have receiv'd from them. But to these assistances we have joined our own industry, for (had we sat down with a dull imitation of them) we might then have lost somewhat of the old perfection but never acquir'd any that was new. We draw not therefore after their lines but those of nature, and having the life before us, besides the experience of all they knew, it is no wonder if we hit some airs and features which they

[20] *the greatest man of the last age.* Later Neander prefers Shakespeare, but Crites' favor for Jonson was an orthodox preference in the 1660s.

have miss'd. I deny not what you urge of arts and sciences, that they have flourish'd in some ages more than others, but your instance in philosophy makes for me. For if natural causes be more known now than in the time of Aristotle, because more studied, it follows that poesy and other arts may with the same pains arrive still nearer to perfection; and that granted, it will rest for you to prove that they wrought more perfect images of human life than we, which, seeing in your discourse you have avoided to make good, it shall now be my task to shew you some part of their defects and some few excellencies of the moderns. And I think there is none among us can imagine I do it enviously or with purpose to detract from them; for what interest of fame or profit can the living lose by the reputation of the dead? On the other side it is a great truth which Velleius Paterculus affirms, '*Audita visis libentius laudamus; et praesentia invidia, praeterita admiratione prosequimur; et his nos obrui, illis instrui credimus.*' [21] That praise or censure is certainly the most sincere which unbrib'd posterity shall give us.

"Be pleased then in the first place to take notice that the Greek poesy, which Crites has affirm'd to have arriv'd to perfection in the reign of the old comedy, was so far from it that the distinction of it into acts was not known to them, or if it were, it is yet so darkly deliver'd to us that we cannot make it out.

"All we know of it is from the singing of their chorus, and that too is so uncertain that in some of their plays we have reason to conjecture they sung more than five times. Aristotle indeed divides the integral parts of a play into four: [22] first, the *protasis*, or entrance, which gives light only to the characters of the persons and proceeds very little into any part of the action; secondly, the *epitasis*, or working up of the plot where the play grows warmer (the de-

---

[21] *Audita,* etc. *Historia Romana* II, 92. (We are apt to praise what we hear rather than what we see; we regard the present with envy and the past with admiration, believing ourselves overcome by the one while we learn from the other.)

[22] *Aristotle indeed divides,* etc. Dryden follows Renaissance interpretations of Aristotle, *Poetics* XII, rather than Aristotle himself. Added in the second edition, the term *status* used below comes from J. C. Scaliger, *Poetices* I, ix, which may well be Dryden's source in this passage.

sign or action of it is drawing on, and you see something
promising that it will come to pass); thirdly, the *catastasis*,
call'd by the Romans, *status*, the heighth and full growth of
the play (we may call it properly the counterturn, which
destroys that expectation, embroils the action in new difficulties, and leaves you far distant from that hope in which
it found you, as you may have observ'd in a violent stream
resisted by a narrow passage: it runs round to an eddy, and
carries back the waters with more swiftness than it brought
them on); lastly, the *catastrophe*, which the Grecians call'd
λύσις, the French *le dénouement*, and we the discovery
or unravelling of the plot; there you see all things settling
again upon their first foundations, and the obstacles which
hindered the design or action of the play once remov'd, it
ends with that resemblance of truth and nature that the
audience are satisfied with the conduct of it. Thus this
great man deliver'd to us the image of a play, and I must
confess it is so lively that from thence much light has been
deriv'd to the forming it more perfectly into acts and
scenes. But what poet first united to five the number of the
acts I know not; only we see it so firmly establish'd in the
time of Horace that he gives it for a rule in comedy, 'Neu
brevior quinto, neu sit productior actu.' [23] So that you see
the Grecians cannot be said to have consummated this art,
writing rather by entrances than by acts and having rather
a general undigested notion of a play than knowing how
and where to bestow the particular graces of it.

"But since the Spaniards at this day allow but three acts,
which they call *jornadas*,[24] to a play, and the Italians in
many of theirs follow them—when I condemn the ancients,
I declare it is not altogether because they have not five
acts to every play, but because they have not confin'd
themselves to one certain number. 'Tis building an house
without a model; and when they succeeded in such undertakings, they ought to have sacrific'd to fortune, not to the
Muses.

---

[23] *Neu brevior*, etc. Dryden misremembered Horace, *Ars Poetica* 189, but
the idea—that plays should be no longer or shorter than five acts—is
the same.
[24] *jornadas*. The term regularly used by Calderón. The practice was begun earlier by Lope de Vega, who called such a division *acto*.

"Next, for the Plot, which Aristotle call'd [ὁ] μῦθος and often τῶν πραγμάτων σύνθεσις,[25] and from him the Romans *fabula*, it has already been judiciously observ'd by a late writer[26] that in their tragedies it was only some tale deriv'd from Thebes or Troy, or at least something that happen'd in those two ages, which was worn so threadbare by the pens of all the epic poets, and even by tradition itself of the talkative Greeklings (as Ben Jonson calls them), that before it came upon the stage it was already known to all the audience. And the people so soon as ever they heard the name of Oedipus knew as well as the poet that he had kill'd his father by a mistake and committed incest with his mother, before the play; that they were now to hear of a great plague, an oracle, and the ghost of Laius. So that they sat with a yawning kind of expectation till he was to come with his eyes pull'd out and speak a hundred or more verses in a tragic tone in complaint of his misfortunes. But one *Oedipus, Hercules,* or *Medea* had been tolerable; poor people they 'scap'd not so good cheap. They had still the *chapon bouillé* set before them till their appetites were cloy'd with the same dish; and the novelty being gone, the pleasure vanish'd; so that one main end of dramatic poesy in its definition, which was to cause delight, was of consequence destroy'd.

"In their comedies, the Romans generally borrow'd their plots from the Greek poets; and theirs was commonly a little girl stolen or wander'd from her parents, brought back unknown to the city, there got with child by some lewd young fellow, who, by the help of his servant, cheats his father, and when her time comes, to cry '*Juno Lucina, fer opem,*' [27] one or other sees a little box or cabinet which was carried away with her, and so discovers her to her friends, if some god do not prevent it by coming down in a machine and taking the thanks of it to himself.

"By the plot you may guess much of the characters of the persons. An old father who would willingly, before he

25 *Aristotle call'd,* etc. The terms may be rendered "myth" and "the arrangement of events."
26 *a late writer.* A recent writer: Sir Robert Howard, Preface, *Four New Plays* (1665).
27 *Juno,* etc. Terence, *Andria* III, i, 15. (Lucina Juno, perform your task.) Lucina, goddess of childbirth, was sometimes identified with Juno.

dies, see his son well married; his debauch'd son, kind in
his nature to his mistress but miserably in want of money; a
servant or slave, who has so much wit to strike in with him
and help to dupe his father; a braggadochio captain; a parasite; and a lady of pleasure.

"As for the poor honest maid on whom the story is built
and who ought to be one of the principal actors in the play,
she is commonly a mute in it. She has the breeding of the
old Elizabeth way, which was for maids to be seen and not
to be heard; and it is enough you know she is willing to be
married when the fifth act requires it.

"These are plots built after the Italian mode of houses;
you see through them all at once. The characters are indeed the imitations of nature, but so narrow as if they had
imitated only an eye or an hand and did not dare to venture on the lines of a face or the proportion of a body.

"But in how strait a compass soever they have bounded
their plots and characters, we will pass it by if they have
regularly pursued them and perfectly observ'd those three
unities of time, place, and action, the knowledge of which
you say is deriv'd to us from them. But in the first place,
give me leave to tell you, that the unity of place, however
it might be practised by them, was never any of their rules.
We neither find it in Aristotle, Horace, or any who have
written of it, till in our age the French poets[28] first made it
a precept of the stage. The unity of time, even Terence
himself (who was the best and most regular of them) has
neglected. His *Heautontimorumenos,* or *Self-Punisher,*
takes up visibly two days, says Scaliger,[29] the two first acts
concluding the first day, the three last the day ensuing.
And Euripides, in tying himself to one day, has committed
an absurdity never to be forgiven him. For in one of his
tragedies he has made Theseus go from Athens to Thebes,
which was about forty English miles, under the walls of it
to give battle, and appear victorious in the next act; and
yet from the time of his departure to the return of the *nun-
tius,* who gives the relation of his victory, Aethra and the

---

[28] *the French poets.* Who took the "rule" from the Italian humanist Castel-
    vetro.
[29] *says Scaliger.* In *Poetices* VI, iii.

Chorus have but thirty-six verses, which is not for every mile a verse.

"The like error is as evident in Terence his *Eunuch*, when Laches, the old man, enters by mistake into the house of Thais, where betwixt his exit and the entrance of Pythias, who comes to give ample relation of the disorders he has rais'd within, Parmeno, who was left upon the stage, has not above five lines to speak. '*C'est bien employer un temps si court*,' [30] says the French poet who furnish'd me with one of the observations. And almost all their tragedies will afford us examples of the like nature.

" 'Tis true, they have kept the continuity, or as you call'd it, *liaison des scènes*, somewhat better. Two do not perpetually come in together, talk, and go out together, and other two succeed them, and do the same throughout the act, which the English call by the name of single scenes. But the reason is, because they have seldom above two or three scenes, properly so call'd in every act; for it is to be accounted a new scene, not only every time the stage is empty; but every person who enters, though to others, makes it so, because he introduces a new business. Now the plots of their plays being narrow and the persons few, one of their acts was written in a less compass than one of our well-wrought scenes, and yet they are often deficient even in this. To go no further than Terence, you find in the *Eunuch* Antipho ent'ring single in the midst of the third act after Chremes and Pythias were gone off. In the same play you have likewise Dorias beginning the fourth act alone; and after she has made a relation of what was done at the soldiers' entertainment (which by the way was very inartificial, because she was presum'd to speak directly to the audience and to acquaint them with what was necessary to be known, but yet should have been so contriv'd by the poet as to have been told by persons of the drama to one another, and so by them to have come to the knowledge of the people), she quits the stage, and Phaedria enters next, alone likewise. He also gives you an account of himself and of his returning from the country in mono-

---

[30] *C'est bien*, etc. (This is not bad use of time.) Taken like much else from Corneille's *Third Discourse*.

logue, to which unnatural way of narration Terence is subject in all his plays. In his *Adelphi,* or *Brothers,* Syrus and
Demea enter after the scene was broken by the departure
of Sostrata, Geta, and Canthara; and indeed you can
scarce look into any of his comedies where you will not
presently discover the same in interruption.

"But as they have fail'd both in laying of their plots and
in managing of them, swerving from the rules of their own
art by mis-representing nature to us, in which they have ill
satisfied one intention of a play, which was delight, so in
the instructive part they have err'd worse. Instead of punishing vice and rewarding virtue, they have often shewn a
prosperous wickedness and an unhappy piety. They have
set before us a bloody image of revenge in *Medea*[31] and
given her dragons to convey her safe from punishment. A
Priam and Astyanax murder'd, and Cassandra ravish'd,
and the lust and murder ending in the victory of him who
acted them. In short, there is no indecorum in any of our
modern plays, which if I would excuse I could not shadow
with some authority from the ancients.

"And one farther note of them let me leave you. Tragedies and comedies were not writ then as they are now,
promiscuously, by the same person, but he who found his
genius bending to the one never attempted the other way.
This is so plain, that I need not instance to you that Aristophanes, Plautus, Terence, never any of them writ a tragedy; Aeschylus, Euripides, Sophocles, and Seneca never
meddled with comedy:[32] the sock and buskin[33] were not
worn by the same poet. Having then so much care to excel
in one kind, very little is to be pardon'd them if they mis-
carried in it; and this would lead me to the consideration of
their wit, had not Crites given me sufficient warning not to
be too bold in my judgment of it, because the languages
being dead and many of the customs and little accidents on
which it depended lost to us, we are not competent judges
of it. But though I grant that here and there we may miss

---

[31] *Medea.* That of Euripides.
[32] *never meddled,* etc. Euripides is now known to have written at least
one comedy, and Sophocles a satirical play.
[33] *sock and buskin.* Comic *soccus* and tragic *cothurnus* worn on the
Roman stage.

the application of a proverb or a custom, yet a thing well said will be wit in all languages; and though it may lose something in the translation, yet to him who reads it in the original, 'tis still the same; he has an idea of its excellency, though it cannot pass from his mind into any other expression or words than those in which he finds it. When Phaedria in the *Eunuch* had a command from his mistress to be absent two days, and encouraging himself to go through with it, said, '*Tandem ego non illa caream, si opus sit, vel totum triduum?*' [34] Parmeno, to mock the softness of his master, lifting up his hands and eyes, cries out as it were in admiration, '*Hui! universum triduum!*'—the elegancy of which *universum*, though it cannot be render'd in our language, yet leaves an impression on our souls. But this happens seldom in him, in Plautus oft'ner, who is infinitely too bold in his metaphors and coining words, out of which many times his wit is nothing, which questionless was one reason why Horace falls upon him so severely in those verses:

> *Sed proavi nostri Plautinos et numeros, et*
> *Laudavere sales, nimium patienter utrumque*
> *Ne dicam stolide.*[35]

For Horace himself was cautious to obtrude a new word on his readers and makes custom and common use the best measure of receiving it into our writings.

> *Multa renascentur quae nunc cecidere, cadentque*
> *Quae nunc sunt in honore vocabula, si volet usus,*
> *Quem penes, arbitrium est, et jus, et norma loquendi.*[36]

"The not observing this rule is that which the world has blam'd in our satirist Cleveland; to express a thing hard and unnaturally is his new way of elocution. 'Tis true, no poet but may sometimes use a catachresis; Virgil does it:

---

[34] *Tandem,* etc. Terence, *Eunuch* II, i. Phaedria asks, "Am I then to do without her, if it comes to that, for three whole days?" And Parmeno replies, "A three days' forever!"

[35] *Sed proavi nostri,* etc. *Ars Poetica* 270–72. (Our ancestors even praised the versification and bite of Plautus, being too patient with them, not to say stupid.)

[36] *Multa renascentur,* etc. *Ars Poetica* 70–72. (Many terms will be reborn that died and others now respectable will go, if usage so decides, it being the arbitrement, law, and rule of speech.)

Mixtaque ridenti colocasia fundet acantho—[37]

in his Eclogue of Pollio. And in his seventh *Aeneid:*

> . . . *mirantur et undae,*
> *Miratur nemus, insuetum fulgentia longe,*
> *Scuta virum fluvio, pictasque innare carinas.*[38]

And Ovid once so modestly that he asks leave to do it:

> . . . *si verbo audacia detur*
> *Haud metuam summi dixisse Palatia caeli*—[39]

calling the court of Jupiter by the name of Augustus his palace; though in another place he is more bold, where he says, '*Et longas visent Capitolia pompas.*' [40] But to do this always and never be able to write a line without it, though it may be admir'd by some few pedants, will not pass upon those who know that wit is best convey'd to us in the most easy language, and is most to be admir'd when a great thought comes dress'd in words so commonly receiv'd that it is understood by the meanest apprehensions, as the best meat is the most easily digested. But we cannot read a verse of Cleveland's without making a face at it, as if every word were a pill to swallow; he gives us many times a hard nut to break our teeth, without a kernel for our pains. So that there is this difference betwixt his satires and Doctor Donne's, that the one gives us deep thoughts in common language, though rough cadence; the other gives us common thoughts in abstruse words. 'Tis true, in some places his wit is independent of his words, as in that of *The Rebel Scot:*

> Had Cain been Scot, God wou'd have chang'd his doom;
> Not forc'd him wander, but confin'd him home.[41]

---

[37] *Mistaque,* etc. *Eclogues* IV, 20. (Pour out the beans mingled with the smiling acanthus.)

[38] *mirantur,* etc. *Aeneid* VIII (not VII), 91–93.
> The woods and waters wonder at the gleam
> Of shields and painted ships that stem the stream.
>   (Trans. Dryden.)

[39] *si verbo,* etc. *Metamorphoses* I, 175–76. "If I may be so bold," Ovid begins; Dryden later rendered the expression, "the Louvre of the sky."

[40] *Et longas,* etc. *Metamorphoses* I, 561. (And capitals view long processions.)

[41] *Had Cain,* etc. *The Rebel Scot* 63–64.

" '*Si sic omnia dixisset!*' " [42] This is wit in all languages:
'tis like mercury, never to be lost or kill'd; and so that
other:

> For beauty like white-powder makes no noise,
> And yet the silent hypocrite destroys.[43]

You see the last line is highly metaphorical, but it is so soft
and gentle that it does not shock us as we read it.

"But to return from whence I have digress'd to the consideration of the ancients' writing and their wit (of which
by this time you will grant us in some measure to be fit
judges), though I see many excellent thoughts in Seneca,
yet he of them who had a genius most proper for the stage
was Ovid; he had a way of writing so fit to stir up a pleasing admiration and concernment, which are the objects of a
tragedy, and to shew the various movements of a soul combating betwixt two different passions that, had he liv'd in
our age or in his own could have writ with our advantages,
no man but must have yielded to him. And therefore I am
confident the *Medea* is none of his; for though I esteem it
for the gravity and sententiousness of it, which he himself
concludes to be suitable to a tragedy, '*Omne genus scripti
gravitate tragaedia vincit,*' [44] yet it moves not my soul
enough to judge that he, who in the epic way wrote things
so near the drama as the story of Myrrha, of Caunus and
Biblis, and the rest, should stir up no more concernment
where he most endeavor'd it. The masterpiece of Seneca I
hold to be that scene in the *Troades*, where Ulysses is seeking for Astyanax to kill him. There you see the tenderness
of a mother so represented in Andromache that it raises
compassion to a high degree in the reader and bears the
nearest resemblance of anything in the tragedies of the ancients to the excellent scenes of passion in Shakespeare or
in Fletcher. For love-scenes you will find few among them;
their tragic poets dealt not with that soft passion, but with
lust, cruelty, revenge, ambition, and those bloody actions

---

[42] *Si sic,* etc. Juvenal, *Satires* X, 123–24. (If only he had always spoken
thus.)

[43] *For beauty,* etc. *Rupertismus,* 39–40. *White-powder* is arsenic. The poem
is not thought to be Cleveland's by recent editors.

[44] *Omne genus,* etc. *Tristia* II, 381. (Tragedy excels in gravity all other
kinds of writing.)

they produc'd, which were more capable of raising horror than compassion in an audience, leaving love untouch'd, whose gentleness would have temper'd them, which is the most frequent of all the passions, and which, being the private concernment of every person, is sooth'd by viewing its own image in a public entertainment.

"Among their comedies, we find a scene or two of tenderness, and that where you would least expect it, in Plautus; but to speak generally, their lovers say little when they see each other, but *'Anima mea, vita mea'*; 'ζωὴ καὶ ψυχή,' [45] as the women in Juvenal's time us'd to cry out in the fury of their kindness: then indeed to speak sense were an offense. Any sudden gust of passion (as an ecstasy of love in an unexpected meeting) cannot better be express'd than in a word and a sigh breaking one another. Nature is dumb on such occasions, and to make her speak would be to represent her unlike herself. But there are a thousand other concernments of lovers, as jealousies, complaints, contrivances, and the like, where not to open their minds at large to each other were to be wanting to their own love and to the expectation of the audience, who watch the movements of their minds as much as the changes of their fortunes. For the imaging of the first is properly the work of a poet; the latter he borrows from the historian."

Eugenius was proceeding in that part of his discourse when Crites interrupted him. "I see," said he, "Eugenius and I are never like to have this question decided betwixt us, for he maintains the moderns have acquir'd a new perfection in writing; I can only grant they have alter'd the mode of it. Homer describ'd his heroes men of great appetites, lovers of beef broil'd upon the coals, and good fellows, contrary to the practice of the French romances, whose heroes neither eat, nor drink, nor sleep, for love. Virgil makes Aeneas a bold avower of his own virtues,

Sum pius Aeneas fama super aethera notus,[46]

---

[45] *Anima mea,* etc. My soul, my life; life and soul.
[46] *Sum pius Aeneas,* etc. Contracting *Aeneid* I, 378–79. (I am Aeneas the just, known to fame throughout the world.)

which in the civility of our poets is the character of a Fan-
faron or Hector; for with us the knight takes occasion to
walk out, or sleep, to avoid the vanity of telling his own
story, which the trusty squire is ever to perform for him. So
in their love scenes, of which Eugenius spoke last, the ancients were more hearty, we more talkative: they writ love
as it was then the mode to make it, and I will grant thus
much to Eugenius, that perhaps one of their poets, had he
liv'd in our age,

> Si foret hoc nostrum fato delapsus in aevum[47]

(as Horace says of Lucilius), he had alter'd many things;
not that they were not natural before, but that he might
accommodate himself to the age in which he liv'd. Yet in
the meantime we are not to conclude anything rashly
against those great men, but preserve to them the dignity
of masters and give that honour to their memories (Quos
Libitina sacravit[48]) part of which we expect may be paid to
us in future times."

This moderation of Crites, as it was pleasing to all the
company, so it put an end to that dispute, which Eugenius,
who seem'd to have the better of the argument, would urge
no farther. But Lisideius, after he had acknowledg'd himself of Eugenius his opinion concerning the ancients, yet
told him he had forborne, till his discourse were ended, to
ask him why he preferr'd the English plays above those of
other nations? and whether we ought not to submit our
stage to the exactness of our next neighbours?

"Though," said Eugenius, "I am at all times ready to
defend the honour of my country against the French and to
maintain we are as well able to vanquish them with our
pens as our ancestors have been with their swords, yet if
you please," added he, looking upon Neander, "I will commit this cause to my friend's management; his opinion of
our plays is the same with mine, and besides, there is no

---

[47] Si foret, etc. Horace, Satires I, x, 68. (If he had been deferred by fate
to this our age.)
[48] Quos Libitina sacravit. Horace, Epistles II, i, 49. (Those whom the Funeral Goddess has consecrated.)

reason, that Crites and I, who have now left the stage
should re-enter so suddenly upon it, which is against the
laws of comedy."

"If the question had been stated," replied Lisideius,
"who had writ best, the French or English forty years ago,
I should have been of your opinion and adjudg'd the
honour to our own nation, but since that time," said he,
turning towards Neander, "we have been so long together
bad Englishmen[49] that we had not leisure to be good poets.
Beaumont, Fletcher, and Jonson (who were only capable
of bringing us to that degree of perfection which we have)
were just then leaving the world; as if, in an age of so
much horror, wit and those milder studies of humanity had
no farther business among us. But the Muses, who ever
follow peace, went to plant in another country; it was then
that the great Cardinal of Richelieu began to take them
into his protection and that, by his encouragement, Corneille and some other Frenchmen reform'd their theatre
(which before was as much below ours as it now surpasses
it and the rest of Europe). But because Crites in his discourse for the ancients has prevented me by observing
many rules of the stage which the moderns have borrow'd
from them, I shall only, in short, demand of you, whether
you are not convinc'd that of all nations the French have
best observ'd them? In the unity of time you find them so
scrupulous that it yet remains a dispute among their poets
whether the artificial day of twelve hours more or less be
not meant by Aristotle, rather than the natural one of
twenty-four, and consequently whether all plays ought not
to be reduc'd into that compass? This I can testify, that in
all their dramas writ within these last twenty years and
upwards, I have not observ'd any that have extended the
time to thirty hours. In the unity of place they are full as
scrupulous, for many of their critics limit it to that very
spot of ground where the play is suppos'd to begin; none of
them exceed the compass of the same town or city.

"The unity of action in all their plays is yet more conspicuous, for they do not burden them with under-plots, as

---

[49] *bad Englishmen.* Bad for rebelling and executing a king. Beaumont,
Fletcher, and Jonson had died before war started in 1642.

the English do, which is the reason why many scenes of
our tragicomedies[50] carry on a design that is nothing of kin
to the main plot and that we see two distinct webs in a
play, like those in ill wrought stuffs, and two actions, that
is, two plays carried on together to the confounding of the
audience, who, before they are warm in their concernments
for one part, are diverted to another, and by that means
espouse the interest of neither. From hence likewise it
arises that the one half of our actors are not known to the
other. They keep their distances as if they were Montagues
and Capulets and seldom begin an acquaintance till the
last scene of the fifth act, when they are all to meet upon
the stage. There is no theatre in the world has anything so
absurd as the English tragicomedy. 'Tis a drama of our
own invention, and the fashion of it is enough to proclaim
it so: here a course of mirth, there another of sadness and
passion, and a third of honour and a duel. Thus in two
hours and a half we run through all the fits of Bedlam. The
French affords you as much variety on the same day, but
they do it not so unseasonably, or mal à propos[51] as we. Our
poets present you the play and the farce together, and our
stages still retain somewhat of the original civility of the
Red Bull:[52]

Atque ursum et pugiles media inter carmina poscunt.[53]

"The end of tragedies or serious plays, says Aristotle,[54] is
to beget admiration, compassion, or concernment; but are
not mirth and compassion things incompatible? And is it
not evident that the poet must of necessity destroy the
former by intermingling of that latter? That is, he must
ruin the sole end and object of his tragedy to introduce
somewhat that is forced into it and is not of the body of it.

---

[50] *tragicomedies.* Of the kind mingling the serious and comic.

[51] *mal à propos.* Lisideius, proponent of French drama, uses five of the
six French expressions Dryden introduces into the *Essay.* These expressions, like a number of others, appear to have been introduced into
English by Dryden.

[52] *Red Bull.* A rowdy theater that closed early in the Restoration.

[53] *Atque ursum,* etc. Altering Horace, *Epistles* II, i, 185–86. (They will
call for a bearfight or boxers in the middle of a play.)

[54] *Aristotle. Poetics* VI gives pity (*compassion*) and fear (*concernment*) as
tragic responses; the Renaissance added admiration (awe, wonder),
sometimes replacing fear with it.

Would you not think that physician mad who, having pre-scribed a purge, should immediately order you to take re-stringents?

"But to leave our plays and return to theirs, I have noted one great advantage they have had in the plotting of their tragedies, that is, they are always grounded upon some known history, according to that of Horace, 'Ex noto fictum carmen sequar,' [55] and in that they have so imitated the ancients that they have surpass'd them. For the an-cients, as was observ'd before, took for the foundation of their plays some poetical fiction such as under that consid-eration could move but little concernment in the audience, because they already knew the event of it. But the French goes farther:

> Atque ita mentitur, sic veris falsa remiscet,
> Primo ne medium, medio ne discrepet imum.[56]

"He so interweaves truth with probable fiction that he puts a pleasing fallacy upon us, mends the intrigues of fate, and dispenses with the severity of history to reward that virtue which has been render'd to us there unfortunate. Sometimes the story has left the success so doubtful that the writer is free, by the privilege of a poet, to take that which of two or more relations will best suit with his de-sign: as for example in the death of Cyrus,[57] whom Justin and some others report to have perish'd in the Scythian war but Xenophon affirms to have died in his bed of extreme old age. Nay more, when the event is past dispute, even then we are willing to be deceiv'd and the poet, if he con-trives it with appearance of truth, has all the audience of his party, at least during the time his play is acting. So naturally we are kind to virtue when our own interest is not in question, that we take it up as the general concernment of mankind. On the other side, if you consider the historical plays of Shakespeare, they are rather so many chronicles of

---

[55] *Ex noto*, etc. *Ars Poetica* 240. (I shall create my poems from familiar matter.)

[56] *Atque ita mentitur*, etc. *Ars Poetica* 151–52. (Homer creates, so combin-ing false with true that there is no discrepancy between beginning and middle or middle and end.)

[57] *the death of Cyrus*. See Justinus I, 8, ii, 3 and xxxviii, 3; also Xenophon, *Cyropaedia* VIII, 7.

kings, or the business many times of thirty or forty years, cramp'd into a representation of two hours and an half, which is not to imitate or paint Nature, but rather to draw her in miniature, to take her in little, to look upon her through the wrong end of a perspective, and receive her images not only much less, but infinitely more imperfect than the life. This, instead of making a play delightful, renders it ridiculous:

> *Quodcumque ostendis mihi sic, incredulus odi.*[58]

For the spirit of man cannot be satisfied but with truth, or at least verisimility; and a poem is to contain, if not τὰ ἔτυμα, yet ἐτύμοισιν ὁμοῖα,[59] as one of the Greek poets has express'd it.

"Another thing in which the French differ from us and from the Spaniards is that they do not embarrass or cumber themselves with too much plot; they only represent so much of a story as will constitute one whole and great action sufficient for a play; we, who undertake more, do but multiply adventures which, not being produc'd from one another, as effects from causes, but barely following, constitute many actions in the drama and consequently make it many plays.

"But by pursuing closely one argument which is not cloy'd with many turns, the French have gain'd more liberty for verse, in which they write. They have leisure to dwell on a subject which deserves it and to represent the passions (which we have acknowledg'd to be the poet's work) without being hurried from one thing to another, as we are in the plays of Calderón, which we have seen lately upon our theaters under the name of Spanish plots. I have taken notice but of one tragedy of ours whose plot has that uniformity and unity of design in it which I have commended in the French, and that is *Rollo*,[60] or rather, under the name of *Rollo*, the story of Bassianus and Geta in Herodian; there indeed the plot is neither large nor intricate

---

[58] *Quodcumque*, etc. *Ars Poetica* 188. (It is so incredible that I hate whatever of this kind you show me.)

[59] τὰ ἔτυμα, etc. Hesiod, *Theogony* 27. (The truth, the likeness of truth.)

[60] *Rollo*. A sensational play (1639) thought jointly written by Chapman, Fletcher, Jonson, and Massinger and based on Herodian III–IV.

but just enough to fill the minds of the audience, not to
cloy them. Besides, you see it founded upon the truth of
history; only the time of the action is not reduceable to the
strictness of the rules; and you see in some places a little
farce mingled, which is below the dignity of the other
parts. And in this all our poets are extremely peccant. Even
Ben Jonson himself in *Sèjanus* and *Catiline* has given us
this oleo of a play, this unnatural mixture of comedy and
tragedy, which to me sounds just as ridiculously as the history of David with the merry humours of Golias.[61] In *Sejanus* you may take notice of the scene betwixt Livia and
the physician, which is a pleasant satire upon the artificial
helps of beauty. In *Catiline* you may see the parliament of
women, the little envies of them to one another, and all that
passes betwixt Curio and Fulvia: scenes admirable in their
kind but of an ill mingle with the rest.

"But I return again to the French writers who, as I have
said, do not burden themselves too much with plot, which
has been reproach'd to them by an ingenious person of our
nation[62] as a fault, for he says they commonly make but one
person considerable in a play; they dwell on him and his
concernments, while the rest of the persons are only subservient to set him off. If he intends this by it, that there is
one person in the play who is of greater dignity than the
rest, he must tax not only theirs, but those of the ancients
and, which he would be loth to do, the best of ours; for 'tis
impossible but that one person must be more conspicuous
in it than any other, and consequently the greatest share in
the action must devolve on him. We see it so in the management of all affairs; even in the most equal aristocracy,
the balance cannot be so justly pois'd but some one will be
superior to the rest, either in parts, fortune, interest, or the
consideration of some glorious exploit, which will reduce
the greatest part of business into his hands.

"But if he would have us to imagine that in exalting one
character the rest of them are neglected, and that all of
them have not some share or other in the action of the play,

[61] *Golias.* Probably the droll of medieval popular literature, but probably
also a pun on "Golia's" (Goliath's).

[62] *an ingenious person*, etc. Thomas Sprat, replying to Sorbière, in his
Observations on M. de Sorbier's Voyage into England (1665).

I desire him to produce any of Corneille's tragedies wherein every person (like so many servants in a well govern'd family) has not some employment, and who is not necessary to the carrying on of the plot, or at least to your understanding it.

"There are indeed some protatic persons in the ancients whom they make use of in their plays, either to hear or give the relation; but the French avoid this with great address, making their narrations only to, or by such, who are some way interested in the main design. And now I am speaking of relations, I cannot take a fitter opportunity to add this in favor of the French, that they often use them with better judgment and more à propos than the English do. Not that I commend narrations in general, but there are two sorts of them, one of those things which are antecedent to the play and are related to make the conduct of it more clear to us. But 'tis a fault to choose such subjects for the stage as will force us on that rock, because we see they are seldom listen'd to by the audience, and that is many times the ruin of the play. For being once let pass without attention, the audience can never recover themselves to understand the plot; and indeed it is somewhat unreasonable that they should be put to so much trouble as, that to comprehend what passes in their sight, they must have recourse to what was done, perhaps, ten or twenty years ago.

"But there is another sort of relations, that is, of things hap'ning in the action of the play and suppos'd to be done behind the scenes, and this is many times both convenient and beautiful. For by it the French avoid the tumult to which we are subject in England by representing duels, battles, and the like, which render our stage too like the theaters where they fight prizes. For what is more ridiculous than to represent an army with a drum and five men behind it, all which the hero of the other side is to drive in before him; or to see a duel fought, and one slain with two or three thrusts of the foils, which we know are so blunted that we might give a man an hour to kill another in good earnest with them.

"I have observ'd that in all our tragedies the audience cannot forbear laughing when the actors are to die; 'tis the

most comic part of the whole play. All *passions* may be
lively represented on the stage, if to the well-writing of
them the actor supplies a good commanded voice and
limbs that move easily and without stiffness; but there are
many *actions* which can never be imitated to a just height.
Dying especially is a thing which none but a Roman gladi-
ator could naturally perform on the stage, when he did not
imitate or represent, but do it; and therefore it is better to
omit the representation of it.

"The words of a good writer which describe it lively will
make a deeper impression of belief in us than all the actor
can insinuate into us when he seems to fall dead before us,
as a poet in the description of a beautiful garden or a
meadow will please our imagination more than the place
itself can please our sight. When we see death represented
we are convinc'd it is but fiction, but when we hear it related, our eyes (the strongest witnesses) are wanting,
which might have undeceiv'd us; and we are all willing to
favour the sleight when the poet does not too grossly impose on us. They therefore who imagine these relations
would make no concernment in the audience are deceiv'd,
by confounding them with the other, which are of things
antecedent to the play; those are made often in cold blood
(as I may say) to the audience, but these are warm'd with
our concernments, which were before awaken'd in the
play. What the philosophers say of motion, that when it is
once begun it continues of itself and will do so to eternity
without some stop put to it,[63] is clearly true on this occasion; the soul, being already mov'd with the characters and
fortunes of those imaginary persons, continues going of its
own accord, and we are no more weary to hear what becomes of them when they are not on the stage than we are
to listen to the news of an absent mistress. But it is objected that, if one part of the play may be related, then
why not all? I answer: some parts of the action are more fit
to be represented, some to be related. Corneille says judiciously that the poet is not oblig'd to expose to view all
particular actions which conduce to the principal; he ought

---

[63] *when it is once*, etc. The principle of inertia had been formulated in
Cartesian physics.

to select such of them to be seen which will appear with the greatest beauty, either by the magnificence of the show, or the vehemence of passions which they produce, or some other charm which they have in them, and let the rest arrive to the audience by narration. 'Tis a great mistake in us to believe the French present no part of the action on the stage; every alteration or crossing of a design, every new-sprung passion and turn of it is a part of the action, and much the noblest, except we conceive nothing to be action till the players come to blows, as if the painting of the hero's mind were not more properly the poet's work than the strength of his body. Nor does this anything contradict the opinion of Horace, where he tells us,

> *Segnius irritant animos demissa per aurem,*
> *Quam quae sunt oculis subjecta fidelibus.*

For he says immediately after,

> *. . . non tamen intus*
> *Digna geri promes in scaenam; multaque tolles*
> *Ex oculis, quae mox narret facundia praesens.*

Among which many he recounts some:

> *Nec pueros coram populo Medea trucidet,*
> *Aut in avem Procne mutetur, Cadmus in anguem, etc.*[64]

"That is, those actions which by reason of their cruelty will cause aversion in us or, by reason of their impossibility, unbelief, ought either wholly to be avoided by a poet, or only [to be] deliver'd by narration. To which we may have leave to add such as to avoid tumult (as was before hinted), or to reduce the plot into a more reasonable compass of time, or for defect of beauty in them, are rather to be related than presented to the eye. Examples of all these

---

[64] *Segnius,* etc., . . . *Non tamen,* etc., . . . and *Nec pueros,* etc. Dryden takes from Horace, *Ars Poetica* 180–87. (What finds entrance through the ears stirs the mind less deeply than what is presented to the reliability of the eyes . . . Still, what is to take place behind the scenes should not be brought on the stage, and what the facile tongue of the actor may relate should be denied the eyes. Medea should not carve up her boys before the audience, . . . Procne turn into a bird, or Cadmus into a snake.)

kinds are frequent, not only among all the ancients but in
the best receiv'd of our English poets. We find Ben Jonson
using them in his *Magnetic Lady*, where one comes out
from dinner and relates the quarrels and disorders of it to
save the undecent appearance of them on the stage and to
abbreviate the story, and this in express imitation of Terence, who had done the same before him in his *Eunuch*,
where Pythias makes the like relation of what had happen'd within at the soldiers' entertainment. The relations
likewise of Sejanus' death and the prodigies before it are
remarkable, the one of which was hid from sight to avoid
the horror and tumult of the representation, the other to
shun the introducing of things impossible to be believ'd. In
that excellent play the *King and no King*, Fletcher goes yet
farther, for the whole unravelling of the plot is done by
narration in the fifth act, after the manner of the ancients;
and it moves great concernment in the audience, though it
be only a relation of what was done many years before the
play. I could multiply other instances, but these are sufficient to prove that there is no error in choosing a subject
which requires this sort of narrations; in the ill management of them, there may.

"But I find I have been too long in this discourse, since
the French have many other excellencies not common to
us, as that you never see any of their plays end with a
conversion, or simple change of will, which is the ordinary
way which our poets use to end theirs. It shews little art in
the conclusion of a dramatic poem, when they who have
hinder'd the felicity during the four acts, desist from it in
the fifth without some powerful cause to take them off their
design; and though I deny not but such reasons may be
found, yet it is a path that is cautiously to be trod, and the
poet is to be sure he convinces the audience that the motive is strong enough. As for example, the conversion of the
usurer in *The Scornful Lady*[65] seems to me a little forc'd,
for being an usurer, which implies a lover of money to the
highest degree of covetousness (and such the poet has rep-

---

[65] *The Scornful Lady*. Like *A King and no King* (above), a joint work of
Beaumont and Fletcher.

resented him), the account he gives for the sudden change is that he has been dup'd by the wild young fellow, which in reason might render him more wary another time, and make him punish himself with harder fare and coarser clothes to get up again what he had lost. But that he should look on it as a judgment and so repent, we may expect to hear in a sermon, but I should never endure it in a play.

"I pass by this; neither will I insist on the care they take that no person after his first entrance shall ever appear but the business which brings him upon the stage shall be evident, which rule, if observ'd, must needs render all the events in the play more natural; for there you see the probability of every accident in the cause that produc'd it, and that which appears chance in the play will seem so reasonable to you that you will there find it almost necessary, so that in the exit of the actor you have a clear account of his purpose and design in the next entrance (though, if the scene be well wrought, the event will commonly deceive you), for there is nothing so absurd, says Corneille, as for an actor to leave the stage only because he has no more to say.

"I should now speak of the beauty of their rhyme and the just reason I have to prefer that way of writing in tragedies before ours in blank verse; but because it is partly receiv'd by us and therefore not altogether peculiar to them, I will say no more of it in relation to their plays. For our own, I doubt not but it will exceedingly beautify them, and I can see but one reason why it should not generally obtain, that is, because our poets write so ill in it. This indeed may prove a more prevailing argument than all others which are us'd to destroy it, and therefore I am only troubled when great and judicious poets, and those who are acknowledg'd such, have writ or spoke against it; as for others they are to be answer'd by that one sentence of an ancient author: 'Sed ut primo ad consequendos eos quos priores ducimus accendimur, ita ubi aut praeteriri, aut aequari eos posse desperavimus, studium cum spe senescit: quod, scilicet, assequi non potest, sequi desinit; . . .

*praeteritoque eo in quo eminere non possumus, aliquid in
quo nitamur conquirimus.' "* [66]

Lisideius concluded in this manner, and Neander after a
little pause thus answer'd him. "I shall grant Lisideius,
without much dispute, a great part of what he has urg'd
against us, for I acknowledge that the French contrive
their plots more regularly and observe the laws of comedy
and decorum of the stage (to speak generally) with more
exactness than the English. Farther, I deny not but he has
tax'd us justly in some irregularities of ours which he has
mention'd; yet, after all, I am of opinion that neither our
faults nor their virtues are considerable enough to place
them above us.

"For the lively imitation of nature[67] being in the definition of a play, those which best fulfil that law ought to be
esteem'd superior to the others. 'Tis true, those beauties of
the French poesy are such as will raise perfection higher
where it is, but are not sufficient to give it where it is not;
they are indeed the beauties of a statue but not of a man,
because not animated with the soul of poesy, which is imitation of humour and passions: and this Lisideius himself,
or any other, however biased to their party, cannot but
acknowledge, if he will either compare the humours of our
comedies or the characters of our serious plays with theirs.
He who will look upon theirs which have been written till
these last ten years or thereabouts will find it an hard matter to pick out two or three passable humours amongst
them. Corneille himself, their arch-poet, what has he produc'd except *The Liar*,[68] and you know how it was cri'd up
in France; but when it came upon the English stage,
though well translated and that part of Dorant acted to so
much advantage as I am confident it never receiv'd in its
own country, the most favourable to it would not put it in

---

[66] *Sed ut primo*, etc. Paterculus, *Historia Romana* I, 17. (But as we aspire at first to surpass those we consider the greatest so, when we have
come to despair of surpassing or equaling them, our efforts weaken
with our hope—which is to say that what one cannot bring off successfully one no longer seeks; . . . and setting aside that in which we
cannot be eminent, we seek something else in which we can do better.)
[67] *the lively imitation*. What follows shows Dryden's stress on *lively*.
[68] *The Liar*. Le Menteur (1642).

competition with many of Fletcher's or Ben Jonson's. In the rest of Corneille's comedies, you have little humour; he tells you himself his way is first to shew two lovers in good intelligence with each other, in the working up of the play to embroil them by some mistake, and in the latter end to clear it and reconcile them.

"But of late years Molière, the younger Corneille, Quinault,[69] and some others have been imitating afar off the quick turns and graces of the English stage. They have mix'd their serious plays with mirth, like our tragicomedies, since the death of Cardinal Richelieu, which Lisideius and many others not observing, have commended that in them for a virtue which they themselves no longer practise. Most of their new plays are, like some of ours, deriv'd from the Spanish novels. There is scarce one of them without a veil[70] and a trusty Diego who drolls much after the rate of the *Adventures*.[71] But their humours, if I may grace them with that name, are so thin sown that never above one of them comes up in any play. I dare take upon me to find more variety of them in some one play of Ben Jonson's than in all theirs together, as he who has seen *The Alchemist, The Silent Woman,* or *Bartholomew Fair* cannot but acknowledge with me.

"I grant the French have performed what was possible on the groundwork of the Spanish plays; what was pleasant before they have made regular. But there is not above one good play to be writ on all those plots; they are too much alike to please often, which we need not the experience of our own stage to justify. As for their new way of mingling mirth with serious plot, I do not with Lisideius condemn the thing, though I cannot approve their manner of doing it. He tells us we cannot so speedily recollect ourselves after a scene of great passion and concernment as to pass to another of mirth and humour and to enjoy it with any relish. But why should he imagine the soul of man more heavy than his senses? Does not the eye pass from an

---

[60] *the younger Corneille.* Thomas (d. 1709), brother of Pierre. *Quinault.* Phillipe (d. 1688) then highly popular, later eclipsed by Racine.

[70] *a veil.* Indicated a Spanish or Moorish woman on the Restoration stage.

[71] *Adventures. The Adventures of Five Hours,* Sir Samuel Tuke's adaption of *Los Empeños de seis horas* by Coello, a play with a comic servant, Diego.

unpleasant object to a pleasant in a much shorter time than is requir'd to this? And does not the unpleasantness of the first commend the beauty of the latter? The old rule of logic might have convinc'd him that contraries, when plac'd near, set off each other. A continued gravity keeps the spirit too much bent; we must refresh it sometimes, as we bait in a journey that we may go on with greater ease. A scene of mirth mix'd with tragedy has the same effect upon us which our music has betwixt the acts, which we find a relief to us from the best plots and language of the stage if the discourses have been long. I must therefore have stronger arguments ere I am convinc'd that compassion and mirth in the same subject destroy each other, and in the meantime cannot but conclude to the honour of our nation, that we have invented, increas'd, and perfected a more pleasant way of writing for the stage than was ever known to the ancients or moderns of any nation, which is tragicomedy.

"And this leads me to wonder why Lisideius and many others should cry up the barrenness of the French plots above the variety and copiousness of the English. Their plots are single; they carry on one design which is push'd forward by all the actors, every scene in the play contributing and moving towards it. Our plays, besides the main design, have under-plots or by-concernments of less considerable persons, and intrigues, which are carried on with the motion of the main plot—just as they say the orb of the fix'd stars and those of the planets, though they have motions of their own, are whirl'd about by the motion of the *primum mobile* in which they are contain'd.[72] That similitude expresses much of the English stage: for if contrary motions may be found in nature to agree, if a planet can go east and west at the same time, one way by virtue of his own motion, the other by the force of the first mover, it will not be difficult to imagine how the under-plot, which is only different, not contrary to the great design, may naturally be conducted along with it.

[72] *just as they say,* etc. As often in his poetry, Dryden argued his point with astronomical and political analogies.

"Crites[73] has already shewn us from the confession of the French poets that the unity of action is sufficiently preserv'd if all the imperfect actions of the play are conducing to the main design; but when those petty intrigues of a play are so ill order'd that they have no coherence with the other, I must grant that Lisideius has reason to tax that want of due connexion; for coordination[74] in a play is as dangerous and unnatural as in a state. In the meantime he must acknowledge our variety, if well order'd, will afford a greater pleasure to the audience.

"As for his other argument, that by pursuing one single theme they gain an advantage to express and work up the passions, I wish any example he could bring from them would make it good, for I confess their verses are to me the coldest I have ever read. Neither indeed is it possible for them, in the way they take, so to express passion as that the effects of it should appear in the concernment of an audience, their speeches being so many declamations which tire us with the length; so that instead of persuading us to grieve for their imaginary heroes, we are concern'd for our own trouble, as we are in tedious visits of bad company, we are in pain till they are gone. When the French stage came to be reform'd by Cardinal Richelieu, those long harangues were introduc'd to comply with the gravity of a churchman. Look upon the *Cinna* and the *Pompey;* they are not so properly to be called plays as long discourses of reason of state; and *Polyeucte* in matters of religion is as solemn as the long stops upon our organs. Since that time it is grown into a custom, and their actors speak by the hour-glass, like our parsons; nay, they account it the grace of their parts and think themselves disparag'd by the poet if they may not twice or thrice in a play entertain the audience with a speech of an hundred lines. I deny not but this may suit well enough with the French; for as we, who are a more sullen people, come to be diverted at our plays, so they who are of an airy and gay temper come thither to

---

[73] *Crites.* Dryden mistakenly gives "Eugenius."
[74] *coordination.* Equality, opposed to the hierarchical subordination (Shakespeare's "degree") that Dryden thought necessary to society.

make themselves more serious. And this I conceive to be one reason why comedies are more pleasing to us and tragedies to them. But to speak generally, it cannot be deni'd that short speeches and replies are more apt to move the passions and beget concernment in us than the other, for it is unnatural for anyone in a gust of passion to speak long together, or for another in the same condition to suffer him without interruption. Grief and passion are like floods rais'd in little brooks by a sudden rain; they are quickly up, and if the concernment be pour'd unexpectedly in upon us, it overflows us. But a long sober shower gives them leisure to run out as they came in without troubling the ordinary current. As for comedy, repartee is one of the chiefest graces; the greatest pleasure of the audience is a chase of wit kept up on both sides and swiftly manag'd. And this our forefathers, if not we, have had in Fletcher's plays to a much higher degree of perfection than the French poets can reasonably hope to reach.

"There is another part of Lisideius his discourse in which he has rather excus'd our neighbours than commended them, that is, for aiming only to make one person considerable in their plays. 'Tis very true what he has urged, that one character in all plays, even without the poet's care, will have advantage of all the others, and that the design of the whole drama will chiefly depend on it. But this hinders not that there may be more shining characters in the play, many persons of a second magnitude, nay, some so very near, so almost equal to the first, that greatness may be oppos'd to greatness, and all the persons be more considerable, not only by their quality, but their action. 'Tis evident that the more the persons are, the greater will be the variety of the plot. If then the parts are manag'd so regularly that the beauty of the whole be kept entire, and that the variety become not a perplex'd and confus'd mass of accidents, you will find it infinitely pleasing to be led in a labyrinth of design, where you see some of your way before you yet discern not the end till you arrive at it. And that all this is practicable, I can produce for examples many of our English plays: as *The Maid's Tragedy,*[75] *The Alchemist,*

[75] *The Maid's Tragedy.* By Beaumont and Fletcher.

The Silent Woman. I was going to have named *The Fox,*
but that the unity of design seems not exactly observ'd in
it, for there appear two actions in the play, the first naturally ending with the fourth act, the second forc'd from it
in the fifth, which yet is the less to be condemn'd in him,
because the disguise of Volpone, though it suited not with
his character as a crafty or covetous person, agreed well
enough with that of a voluptuary, and by it the poet gain'd
the end at which he aim'd, the punishment of vice and the
reward of virtue, both which that disguise produc'd. So
that to judge equally of it, it was an excellent fifth act, but
not so naturally proceeding from the former.

"But to leave this and pass to the latter part of Lisideius
his discourse which concerns relations, I must acknowledge
with him that the French have reason when they hide that
part of the action which would occasion too much tumult
on the stage and to choose rather to have it made known
by narration to the audience. Farther, I think it very convenient, for the reasons he has given, that all incredible
actions were remov'd; but whether custom has so insinuated itself into our countrymen, or nature has so form'd
them to fierceness, I know not; but they will scarcely suffer
combats and other objects of horror to be taken from them.
And indeed, the indecency of tumults is all which can be
objected against fighting. For why may not our imagination
as well suffer itself to be deluded with the probability of it
as with any other thing in the play? For my part, I can
with as great ease persuade myself that the blows which
are struck are given in good earnest, as I can that they who
strike them are kings or princes, or those persons which
they represent.[76] For objects of incredibility I would be satisfied from Lisideius, whether we have any so remov'd from
all appearance of truth as are those of Corneille's
Andromède—a play which has been frequented the most
of any he has writ? If the Perseus, or the son of an heathen
god, the Pegasus, and the monster were not capable to
choke a strong belief, let him blame any representation of

[76] *For why may not,* etc. This and the preceding sentence on literary illusion and the working of the imagination offer one of Dryden's major
contributions to English aesthetic thought and relate to the concern
with what is "natural" in rhyme in Neander's discourse, below.

ours hereafter. Those indeed were objects of delight; yet
the reason is the same as the probability: for he makes it
not a ballette[77] or masque but a play, which is to resemble
truth. But for death, that it ought not to be represented, I
have besides the arguments alleg'd by Lisideius, the authority of Ben Jonson, who has forborne it in his tragedies;
for both the death of Sejanus and Catiline are related,
though in the latter I cannot but observe one irregularity of
that great poet: he has remov'd the scene in the same act
from Rome to Catiline's army, and from thence again to
Rome, and besides has allow'd a very inconsiderable time
after Catiline's speech for the striking of the battle and the
return of Petreius, who is to relate the event of it to the
Senate; which I should not animadvert on him, who was
otherwise a painful observer of τὸ πρέπον, or the decorum
of the stage, if he had not us'd extreme severity in his judgment on the incomparable Shakespeare for the same fault.
To conclude on this subject of relations, if we are to be
blam'd for shewing too much of the action, the French are
as faulty for discovering too little of it; a mean betwixt both
should be observed by every judicious writer, so as the audience may neither be left unsatisfied by not seeing what is
beautiful, or shock'd by beholding what is either incredible
or indecent.

"I hope I have already prov'd in this discourse that,
though we are not altogether so punctual as the French in
observing the laws of comedy, yet our errors are so few,
and little, and those things wherein we excel them so considerable, that we ought of right to be preferr'd before
them. But what will Lisideius say if they themselves acknowledge they are too strictly bounded by those laws, for
breaking which he has blam'd the English? I will allege
Corneille's words, as I find them in the end of his *Discourse
of the Three Unities*, 'Il est facile aux spéculatifs d'estre
sévères, etc.' 'Tis easy for speculative persons to judge severely, but if they would produce to public view ten or
twelve pieces of this nature, they would perhaps give more
latitude to the rules than I have done, when by experience
they had known how much we are limited and constrain'd

---

[77] *ballette.* Ballet; the first recorded English usage.

by them, and how many beauties of the stage they banish'd
from it.' To illustrate a little what he has said, by their
servile observations of the unities of time and place and
integrity of scenes they have brought on themselves that
dearth of plot and narrowness of imagination which may
be observ'd in all their plays. How many beautiful accidents might naturally happen in two or three days which
cannot arrive with any probability in the compass of
twenty-four hours? There is time to be allowed also for maturity of design, which amongst great and prudent persons,
such as are often represented in tragedy, cannot with any
likelihood of truth be brought to pass at so short a warning.
Farther, by tying themselves strictly to the unity of place
and unbroken scenes, they are forc'd many times to omit
some beauties which cannot be shewn where the act began
but might, if the scene were interrupted, and the stage
clear'd for the persons to enter in another place. And therefore the French poets are often forc'd upon absurdities, for
if the act begins in a chamber, all the persons in the play
must have some business or other to come thither, or else
they are not to be shewn that act, and sometimes their
characters are very unfitting to appear there. As, suppose it
were the King's bed-chamber, yet the meanest man in the
tragedy must come and dispatch his business there, rather
than in the lobby or courtyard (which is fitter for him) for
fear the stage should be clear'd and the scenes broken.
Many times they fall by it into a greater inconvenience, for
they keep their scenes unbroken and yet change the place,
as in one of their newest plays,[78] where the act begins in
the street. There a gentleman is to meet his friend; he sees
him with his man coming out from his father's house; they
talk together, and the first goes out; the second, who is a
lover, has made an appointment with his mistress; she appears at the window, and then we are to imagine the scene
lies under it. This gentleman is call'd away and leaves his
servant with his mistress; presently her father is heard from
within; the young lady is afraid the servingman should be
discover'd, and thrusts him into a place of safety, which is

[78] newest plays. Apparently referring to Thomas Corneille, L'Amour à
la Mode (1651), Act III.

suppos'd to be her closet. After this, the father enters to the
daughter, and now the scene is in a house, for he is seeking
from one room to another for this poor Philipin, or French
Diego, who is heard from within, drolling and breaking
many a miserable conceit on the subject of his sad condition. In this ridiculous manner the play goes forward, the
stage being never empty all the while; so that the street,
the window, the two houses, and the closet are made to
walk about and the persons to stand still. Now what, I
beseech you, is more easy than to write a regular French
play or more difficult than to write an irregular English
one, like those of Fletcher or of Shakespeare?

"If they content themselves as Corneille did with some
flat design which, like an ill riddle, is found out ere it be
half propos'd, such plots we can make every way regular
as easily as they; but whene'er they endeavour to rise to
any quick turns and counterturns of plot, as some of them
have attempted since Corneille's plays have been less in
vogue, you see they write as irregularly as we, though they
cover it more speciously. Hence the reason is perspicuous
why no French plays, when translated, have, or ever can,
succeed on the English stage. For if you consider the plots,
our own are fuller of variety; if the writing, ours are more
quick and fuller of spirit. And therefore 'tis strange mistake
in those who decry the way of writing plays in verse, as if
the English therein imitated the French. We have borrowed nothing from them; our plots are weav'd in English
looms. We endeavour therein to follow the variety and
greatness of characters which are deriv'd to us from Shakespeare and Fletcher; the copiousness and well-knitting of
the intrigues we have from Jonson, and for the verse itself
we have English precedents of elder date than any of Corneille's plays. Not to name our old comedies before
Shakespeare, which were all writ in verse of six feet,[79] or
alexandrines, such as the French now use, I can shew in
Shakespeare many scenes of rhyme together, and the like

---

[79] *in verse of six feet.* Dryden is too categorical about the verse of "all"
pre-Shakespearean comedy. His phrase, *six feet,* is, however, one of
many seventeenth-century remarks showing that poets conceived of lines
in meter rather than, as some modern critics have argued, syllable count
alone.

in Ben Jonson's tragedies, in *Catiline* and *Sejanus* sometimes thirty or forty lines—I mean besides the chorus, or
the monologues, which by the way, shew'd Ben no enemy
to this way of writing, especially if you read his *Sad Shepherd*, which goes sometimes on rhyme, sometimes on blank
verse, like an horse who eases himself on trot and amble.
You find him likewise commending Fletcher's pastoral of
The Faithful Shepherdess, which is for the most part
rhyme, though not refin'd to that purity to which it
hath since been brought. And these examples are enough
to clear us from a servile imitation of the French.

"But to return whence I have digress'd, I dare boldly
affirm these two things of the English drama: first, that we
have many plays of ours as regular as any of theirs and
which, besides, have more variety of plot and characters;
and secondly, that in most of the irregular plays of Shakespeare or Fletcher (for Ben Jonson's are for the most part
regular), there is a more masculine fancy and greater spirit
in the writing than there is in any of the French. I could
produce, even in Shakespeare's and Fletcher's works, some
plays which are almost exactly form'd, as *The Merry Wives
of Windsor* and *The Scornful Lady*.[80] But because (generally speaking) Shakespeare, who writ first, did not perfectly
observe the laws of comedy, and Fletcher, who came
nearer to perfection, yet through carelessness made many
faults, I will take the pattern of a perfect play from Ben
Jonson, who was a careful and learned observer of the dramatic laws, and from all his comedies I shall select *The
Silent Woman*, of which I will make a short examen[81] according to those rules which the French observe."

As Neander was beginning to examine *The Silent
Woman*, Eugenius earnestly regarding him, "I beseech you,
Neander," said he, "gratify the company and me in particular so far, as before you speak of the play, to give us a
character of the author; and tell us frankly your opinion,

---

[80] *The Merry Wives of Windsor.* Shakespeare's comedy, like Beaumont and
Fletcher's, *The Scornful Lady,* covers about two days. Dryden must
have forgot *The Tempest,* which represents about three hours and also
has unity of place.

[81] *examen.* Examination, analysis. The word is recorded early in the century, but Dryden no doubt took it from Corneille's *Théâtre* (1660).

whether you do not think all writers, both French and English, ought to give place to him?"

"I fear," replied Neander, "that in obeying your commands I shall draw some envy on myself. Besides, in performing them, it will be first necessary to speak somewhat
of Shakespeare and Fletcher, his rivals in poesy, and one of
them, in my opinion, at least his equal, perhaps his superior.

"To begin then with Shakespeare,[82] he was the man who
of all modern, and perhaps ancient, poets had the largest
and most comprehensive soul. All the images of nature
were still present to him, and he drew them not laboriously
but luckily.[83] When he describes anything, you more than
see it, you feel it too. Those who accuse him to have
wanted learning give him the greater commendation; he
was naturally learn'd; he needed not the spectacles of
books to read Nature; he look'd inwards and found her
there. I cannot say he is everywhere alike; were he so, I
should do him injury to compare him with the greatest of
mankind.[84] He is many times flat, insipid, his comic wit
degenerating into clenches, his serious swelling into bom-
bast. But he is always great when some great occasion is
presented to him: no man can say he ever had a fit subject
for his wit and did not then raise himself as high above the
rest of poets, '*Quantum lenta solent, inter viburna cu-
pressi.*' [85] The consideration of this made Mr. Hales[86] of
Eton say that there was no subject of which any poet ever
writ but he would produce it much better done in Shake-

---

[82] *Shakespeare.* Dryden's heterodoxy in preferring Shakespeare above Jonson has of course since become orthodoxy. The description is "a perpetual model of encomiastic criticism: exact without minuteness, and
lofty without exaggeration." (Dr. Johnson, Life of Dryden.)

[83] *he drew them,* etc. Much of the language implies a comparison between
poetry and painting of a kind Dryden often used. The implication, by
long tradition from Mannerist art criticism, is a distinction between
the *luck* of genius and the labor of a craftsman. The appeal to painting
in literary criticism is a common symptom of impatience with the
"rules." The stress on figurative language and looking inward are
similar symptoms of Dryden's aesthetic stand.

[84] *the greatest of mankind.* Editors have avoided glossing the phrase. Perhaps Homer or Socrates is meant.

[85] *Quantum lenta solent,* etc. Virgil, *Eclogues* I, 25. (As cypresses are
given to rising above the bending willows.)

[86] *Mr. Hales.* John (d. 1656), Fellow of Eton College.

speare; and however others are now generally preferr'd before him yet the age wherein he liv'd, which had contemporaries with him Fletcher and Jonson, never equall'd them to him in their esteem. And in the last king's court,[87] when Ben's reputation was at highest, Sir John Suckling, and with him the greater part of the courtiers, set our Shakespeare far above him.

"Beaumont and Fletcher, of whom I am next to speak, had, with the advantage of Shakespeare's wit, which was their precedent, great natural gifts improv'd by study, Beaumont especially being so accurate a judge of plays that Ben Jonson, while he liv'd, submitted all his writings to his censure and 'tis thought us'd his judgment in correcting, if not contriving, all his plots. What value he had for him appears by the verses he writ to him, and therefore I need speak no farther of it. The first play that brought Fletcher and him in esteem was their *Philaster*, for before that they had written two or three very unsuccessfully, as the like is reported of Ben Jonson before he writ *Every Man in his Humour*. Their plots were generally more regular than Shakespeare's, especially those which were made before Beaumont's death, and they understood and imitated the conversation of gentlemen much better, whose wild debaucheries and quickness of wit in repartees no poet before them could paint as they have done. Humour, which Ben Jonson deriv'd from particular persons, they made it not their business to describe; they represented all the passions very lively, but above all, love. I am apt to believe the English language in them arriv'd to its highest perfection; what words have since been taken in are rather superfluous than ornamental. Their plays are now the most pleasant and frequent entertainments of the stage, two of theirs being acted through the year for one of Shakespeare's or Jonson's. The reason is, because there is a certain gayety in their comedies and pathos in their more serious plays which suits generally with all men's humours. Shakespeare's language is likewise a little obsolete, and Ben Jonson's wit comes short of theirs.

[87] *the last king's court.* That of Charles I.

"As for Jonson, to whose character I am now arriv'd, if we look upon him while he was himself (for his last plays were but his dotages), I think him the most learned and judicious writer which any theater ever had. He was a most severe judge of himself as well as others. One cannot say he wanted wit, but rather that he was frugal of it. In his works you find little to retrench or alter. Wit and language, and humour also in some measure, we had before him, but something of art was wanting to the drama till he came. He manag'd his strength to more advantage than any who preceded him. You seldom find him making love in any of his scenes or endeavouring to move the passions; his genius was too sullen and saturnine to do it gracefully, especially when he knew he came after those who had performed both to such an height. Humour was his proper sphere, and in that he delighted most to represent mechanic people. He was deeply conversant in the ancients, both Greek and Latin, and he borrow'd boldly from them: there is scarce a poet or historian among the Roman authors of those times whom he has not translated in *Sejanus* and *Catiline*. But he has done his robberies so openly that one may see he fears not to be taxed by any law. He invades authors like a monarch, and what would be theft in other poets is only victory in him. With the spoils of these writers he so represents old Rome to us, in its rites, ceremonies, and customs, that if one of their poets had written either of his tragedies, we had seen less of it than in him. If there was any fault in his language 'twas that he weav'd it too closely and laboriously, in his comedies especially. Perhaps, too, he did a little too much romanize our tongue, leaving the words which he translated almost as much Latin as he found them, wherein though he learnedly followed their language, he did not enough comply with the idiom of ours. If I would compare him with Shakespeare, I must acknowledge him the more correct poet, but Shakespeare the greater wit. Shakespeare was the Homer or father of our dramatic poets, Jonson was the Virgil, the pattern of elaborate writing. I admire him, but I love Shakespeare. To conclude of him, as he has given us the most correct plays, so in the precepts which he has laid down in his *Discoveries*[88] we have as many and profitable rules for perfecting the stage as any wherewith the French can furnish us.

"Having thus spoken of the author, I proceed to the examination[89] of his comedy, *The Silent Woman*."

EXAMEN OF *The Silent Woman*

"To begin first with the length of the action, it is so far from exceeding the compass of a natural day that it takes not up an artificial one. 'Tis all included in the limits of three hours and an half, which is no more than is requir'd for the presentment on the stage: a beauty perhaps not much observ'd; if it had, we should not have look'd on the Spanish translation of *Five Hours*[90] with so much wonder. The scene of it is laid in London; the latitude of place is almost as little as you can imagine, for it lies all within the compass of two houses and, after the first act, in one. The continuity of scenes is observ'd more than in any of our plays, except his own *Fox* and *Alchemist*.[91] They are not broken above twice or thrice at most in the whole comedy, and in the two best of Corneille's plays, the *Cid* and *Cinna*, they are interrupted once. The action of the play is entirely one, the end or aim of which is the settling Morose's estate on Dauphine. The intrigue of it is the greatest and most noble of any pure unmix'd comedy in any language: you see in it many persons of various characters and humours, and all delightful—as first, Morose, or an old man, to whom all noise but his own talking is offensive. Some who would be thought critics say this humour of his is forc'd, but to remove that objection we may consider him first to be naturally of a delicate hearing, as many are to whom all

---

[88] *Discoveries. Timber: Or Discoveries* (1640) concludes with rather disconnected comments on dramaturgy that only Dryden's patriotism could prefer to the critical writings of Corneille.

[89] *the examination.* This "examen" is the first English example of sustained analysis of a single work; its example was followed later by Thomas Rymer rather than by Dryden himself.

[90] *Five Hours.* See note 71, above.

[91] *the continuity,* etc. This and the preceding sentence much exaggerate *Epicoene's* "continuity," which is better observed by Jonson in *The Alchemist* and *Volpone*.

sharp sounds are unpleasant; and secondly, we may attribute much of it to the peevishness of his age or the wayward authority of an old man in his own house, where he may make himself obeyed; and to this the poet seems to allude in his name Morose. Beside this, I am assur'd from divers persons that Ben Jonson was actually acquainted with such a man, one altogether as ridiculous as he is here represented. Others say it is not enough to find one man of such an humour; it must be common to more, and the more common the more natural. To prove this, they instance in the best of comical characters, Falstaff: there are many men resembling him, old, fat, merry, cowardly, drunken, amorous, vain, and lying. But to convince these people I need but tell them that humour is the ridiculous extravagance of conversation, wherein one man differs from all others. If then it be common, or communicated to many, how differs it from other men's? Or what indeed causes it to be ridiculous so much as the singularity of it? As for Falstaff, he is not properly one humour, but a miscellany of humours or images drawn from so many several men. That wherein he is singular is his wit, or those things he says, *praeter expectatum*, unexpected by the audience; his quick evasions when you imagine him surprised which, as they are extremely diverting of themselves, so receive a great addition from his person, for the very sight of such an unwieldy old debauch'd fellow is a comedy alone.

"And here, having a place so proper for it, I cannot but enlarge somewhat upon this subject of humour into which I am fallen. The ancients had little of it in their comedies, for the τὸ γελοῖον[92] of the old comedy, of which Aristophanes was chief, was not so much to imitate a man as to make the people laugh at some odd conceit which had commonly somewhat of unnatural or obscene in it. Thus when you see Socrates brought upon the stage, you are not to imagine him made ridiculous by the imitation of his actions, but rather by making him perform something very unlike himself, something so childish and absurd, as by comparing it with the gravity of the true Socrates makes a ridiculous object for the spectators. In their new comedy, which suc-

[92] τὸ γελοῖον. Aristotle, *Poetics* V. (The ridiculous.)

ceeded, the poets sought indeed to express the ἦθος, as in
their tragedies the πάθος,[93] of mankind. But this ἦθος
contain'd only the general characters of men and manners
—as old men, lovers, servingmen, courtesans, parasites,
and such other persons as we see in their comedies, all
which they made alike, that is, one old man or father, one
lover, one courtesan so like another as if the first of them
had begot the rest of every sort: 'ex homine hunc natum
dicas.' [94] The same custom they observ'd likewise in their
tragedies. As for the French, though they have the word
humeur among them, yet they have small use of it in their
comedies or farces, they being but ill imitations of the
ridiculum, or that which stirr'd up laughter in the old comedy. But among the English 'tis otherwise, where by humour is meant some extravagant habit, passion, or affection, particular (as I said before) to some one person, by
the oddness of which he is immediately distinguish'd from
the rest of men, which being lively and naturally represented most frequently begets that malicious pleasure in
the audience which is testified by laughter, as all things
which are deviations from customs are ever the aptest to
produce it. Though by the way, this laughter is only accidental, as the person represented is fantastic or bizarre; but
pleasure is essential to it, as the imitation of what is natural. The description of these humours drawn from the
knowledge and observation of particular persons was the
peculiar genius and talent of Ben Jonson, to whose play I
now return.

"Besides Morose, there are at least nine or ten different
characters and humours in *The Silent Woman,* all which
persons have several concernments of their own, yet are all
us'd by the poet to the conducting of the main design to
perfection. I shall not waste time in commending the writing of this play, but I will give you my opinion that there is
more wit and acuteness of fancy in it than in any of Ben
Jonson's. Besides that, he has here describ'd the conversation of gentlemen in the persons of True-Wit and his
friends with more gayety, air, and freedom than in the rest

---

[93] ἦθος, etc. *Ethos* suggests settled character, *pathos* the aroused emotions.
[94] *ex homine,* etc. Terence, *Eunuch* 460.

of his comedies. For the contrivance of the plot, 'tis extreme elaborate and yet withal easy; for the λύσις, or untying of it, 'tis so admirable that when it is done no one of the audience would think the poet could have miss'd it; and yet it was conceal'd so much before the last scene that any other way would sooner have enter'd into your thoughts. But I dare not take upon me to commend the fabric of it, because it is altogether so full of art that I must unravel every scene in it to commend it as I ought. And this excellent contrivance is still the more to be admir'd, because 'tis comedy where the persons are only of common rank and their business private, not elevated by passions or high concernments as in serious plays. Here everyone is a proper judge of all he sees; nothing is represented but that with which he daily converses, so that by consequence all faults lie open to discovery and few are pardonable. 'Tis this which Horace has judiciously observ'd:

> Creditur ex medio quia res arcessit habere
> Sudoris minimum, sed habet Comedia tanto
> Plus oneris, quanto veniae minus.[95]

"But our poet, who was not ignorant of these difficulties, has made use of all advantages, as he who designs a large leap takes his rise from the highest ground. One of these advantages is that which Corneille has laid down as the greatest which can arrive to any poem and which he himself could never compass above thrice in all his plays, viz., the making choice of some signal and long-expected day whereon the action of the play is to depend. This day was that design'd by Dauphine for the settling of his uncle's estate upon him, which to compass he contrives to marry him. That the marriage had been plotted by him long beforehand is made evident by what he tells True-Wit in the second act, that in one moment he had destroy'd what he had been raising many months.

"There is another artifice of the poet which I cannot here omit, because by the frequent practise of it in his comedies

---

[95] Creditur, etc. Epistles II, i, 168–70. (Many think that because comedy takes its material from daily life it requires little effort; actually, its burden is heavier, because so much less is allowed for deviation.)

he has left it to us almost as a rule, that is, when he has any character or humour wherein he would shew a *coup de maistre* or his highest skill, he recommends it to your observation by a pleasant description of it before the person first appears. Thus, in *Bartholomew Fair* he gives you the pictures of Numps and Cokes, and in this those of Daw, Lafoole, Morose, and the Collegiate Ladies, all which you hear describ'd before you see them. So that before they come upon the stage you have a longing expectation of them which prepares you to receive them favourably, and when they are there, even from their first appearance you are so far acquainted with them that nothing of their humour is lost to you.

"I will observe yet one thing further of this admirable plot; the business of it rises in every act. The second is greater than the first, the third than the second, and so forward to the fifth. There too you see, till the very last scene, new difficulties arising to obstruct the action of the play; and when the audience is brought into despair that the business can naturally be effected then, and not before, the discovery is made. But that the poet might entertain you with more variety all this while, he reserves some new characters to show you, which he opens not till the second and third act. In the second Morose, Daw, the Barber, and Otter, in the third the Collegiate Ladies; all which he moves afterwards in by-walks or under-plots as diversions to the main design lest it should grow tedious, though they are still naturally join'd with it and somewhere or other subservient to it. Thus, like a skilful chess player, by little and little he draws out his men and makes his pawns of use to his greater persons.

"If this comedy and some others of his were translated into French prose (which would now be no wonder to them, since Molière has lately given them plays out of verse which have not displeas'd them), I believe the controversy would soon be decided betwixt the two nations, even making them the judges.[96] But we need not call our

---

[96] *If this comedy,* etc. The paragraph gives more of Dryden's patriotic exaggeration. He was speaking of hopes, not fact, as he might have if this had been written twenty-five years later.

heroes to our aid. Be it spoken to the honour of the English, our nation can never want in any age such who are able to dispute the empire of wit with any people in the universe. And though the fury of a civil war and power for twenty years together abandon'd to a barbarous race of men, enemies of all good learning, had buried the Muses under the ruins of monarchy, yet with the restoration of our happiness, we see reviv'd poesy lifting up its head and already shaking off the rubbish which lay so heavy on it. We have seen since his Majesty's return many dramatic poems which yield not to those of any foreign nation and which deserve all laurels but the English. I will set aside flattery and envy: it cannot be deni'd but we have had some little blemish either in the plot or writing of all those plays which have been made within these seven years (and perhaps there is no nation in the world so quick to discern them or so difficult to pardon them as ours). Yet if we can persuade ourselves to use the candour of that poet who (though the most severe of critics) has left us this caution by which to moderate our censures—

> . . . *ubi plura nitent in carmine, non ego paucis*
> *Offendar maculis*—[97]

if, in consideration of their many and great beauties, we can wink at some slight and little imperfections; if we, I say, can be thus equal to ourselves, I ask no favour from the French. And if I do not venture upon any particular judgment of our late plays, 'tis out of the consideration which an ancient writer gives me: '*Vivorum, ut magna admiratio, ita censura difficilis*' [98]—betwixt the extremes of admiration and malice 'tis hard to judge upright of the living. Only I think it may be permitted me to say that as it is no less'ning to us to yield to some plays, and those not many of our own nation in the last age, so can it be no addition to pronounce of our present poets that they have far surpass'd all the ancients and the modern writers of other countries."

---

[97] . . . *ubi plura*, etc. Horace, *Ars Poetica* 351–52. (When many beauties shine in a poem, I shall not take offense with a few blemishes.)
[98] *Vivorum*, etc. Paterculus, *Historia Romana* II, 36.

This was the substance of what was then spoke on that occasion, and Lisideius, I think, was going to reply, when he was prevented thus by Crites. "I am confident," said he, "that the most material things that can be said have been already urg'd on either side; if they have not, I must beg of Lisideius that he will defer his answer till another time; for I confess I have a joint quarrel to you both, because you have concluded, without any reason given for it, that rhyme is proper for the stage. I will not dispute how ancient it hath been among us to write this way; perhaps our ancestors knew no better till Shakespeare's time. I will grant it was not altogether left by him and that Fletcher and Ben Jonson us'd it frequently in their pastorals and sometimes in other plays. Farther, I will not argue whether we receiv'd it originally from our own countrymen or from the French, for that is an inquiry of as little benefit as theirs who in the midst of the late plague were not so solicitous to provide against it as to know whether we had it from the malignity of our own air or by transportation from Holland. I have therefore only to affirm that it is not allowable in serious plays; for comedies, I find you already concluding with me. To prove this I might satisfy myself to tell you how much in vain it is for you to strive against the stream of the people's inclination, the greatest part of which are prepossess'd so much with those excellent plays of Shakespeare, Fletcher, and Ben Jonson (which have been written out of rhyme) that except you could bring them such as were written better in it, and those too by persons of equal reputation with them, it will be impossible for you to gain your cause with them who will still be judges. This it is to which in fine all your reasons must submit. The unanimous consent of an audience is so powerful that even Julius Caesar (as Macrobius[99] reports of him) when he was perpetual dictator was not able to ballance it on the other side. But when Laberius, a Roman knight, at his request contended in the mime with another poet, he was forc'd to cry out, *'Etiam favente me victus es, Laberi!'*

[99] *Macrobius.* In *Saturnalia* II, 7. Caesar's remark from Macrobius, *Etiam,* etc., follows. (You are defeated, Laberius, in spite of my favor.)

"But I will not on this occasion take the advantage of the greater number, but only urge such reasons against rhyme as I find in the writings of those who have argu'd for the other way. First, then, I am of opinion that rhyme is unnatural in a play, because dialogue there is presented as the effect of sudden thought. For a play is the imitation of nature, and since no man without premeditation speaks in rhyme, neither ought he to do it on the stage; this hinders not but the fancy may be there elevated to an higher pitch of thought than it is in ordinary discourse, for there is a probability that men of excellent and quick parts may speak noble things *ex tempore*. But those thoughts are never fetter'd with the numbers or sound of verse without study, and therefore it cannot be but unnatural to present the most free way of speaking in that which is the most constrain'd. For this reason, says Aristotle,[100] 'tis best to write tragedy in that kind of verse which is the least such, or which is nearest prose, and this amongst the ancients was the iambic, and with us is blank verse, or the measure of verse kept exactly without rhyme. These numbers therefore are fittest for a play; the others for a paper of verses or a poem, blank verse being as much below them, as rhyme is improper for the drama. And if it be objected that neither are blank verses made *ex tempore*, yet as nearest nature, they are still to be preferr'd.

"But there are two particular exceptions which many besides myself have had to verse, by which it will appear yet more plainly how improper it is in plays. And the first of them is grounded on that very reason for which some have commended rhyme: they say the quickness of repartees in argumentative scenes receives an ornament from verse. Now what is more unreasonable than to imagine that a man should not only imagine the wit but the rhyme too upon the sudden? This nicking of him who spoke before both in sound and measure is so great an happiness that you must at least suppose that the persons of your play to be born poets,

---

[100] *says Aristotle.* In *Poetics* V, he says rather that the iambic meter is closest to speech.

> . . . . *Arcades omnes,*
> *Et cantare pares, et respondere parati;*[101]

they must have arriv'd to the degree of '*quicquid conabar dicere,*' [102] to make verses almost whether they will or no. If they are anything below this, it will look rather like the design of two than the answer of one; it will appear that your actors hold intelligence together, that they perform their tricks like fortune-tellers, by confederacy. The hand of art will be too visible in it against that maxim of all professions, '*Ars est celare artem,*' that it is the greatest perfection of art to keep itself undiscover'd. Nor will it serve you to object that, however you manage it, 'tis still known to be a play, and consequently the dialogue of two persons understood to be the labour of one poet. For a play is still an imitation of nature; we know we are to be deceiv'd, and we desire to be so; but no man ever was deceiv'd but with a probability of truth, for who will suffer a gross lie to be fasten'd on him? Thus we sufficiently understand that the scenes which represent cities and countries to us are not really such, but only painted on boards and canvas. But shall that excuse the ill painture or designment of them? Nay rather ought they not to be labour'd with so much the more diligence and exactness to help the imagination—since the mind of man does naturally tend to truth, and therefore the nearer anything comes to the imitation of it, the more it pleases.

"Thus, you see, your rhyme is incapable of expressing the greatest thoughts naturally; and the lowest it cannot with any grace, for what is more unbefitting the majesty of verse than to call a servant, or bid a door be shut in rhyme? And yet you are often forc'd on this miserable necessity. But verse, you say, circumscribes a quick and luxuriant fancy, which would extend itself too far on every subject did not the labour which is requir'd to well turn'd and pol-

---

[101] *Arcades omnes,* etc. Virgil, *Eclogues* VII, 4–5.
  Both young Arcadians, both alike inspir'd
  To sing and answer as the song requir'd.
             (Trans. Dryden.)
[102] *quicquid, etc.* Dryden immediately renders the phrase, which is unidentified.

ish'd rhyme set bounds to it. Yet this argument, if granted, would only prove that we may write better in verse, but not more naturally. Neither is it able to evince that, for he who wants judgment to confine his fancy in blank verse may want it as much in rhyme; and he who has it will avoid errors in both kinds. Latin verse was as great a confinement to the imagination of those poets as rhyme to ours, and yet you find Ovid saying too much on every subject. 'Nescivit,' says Seneca, 'quod bene cessit relinquere';[103] of which he gives you one famous instance in his description of the Deluge.

> Omnia pontus erat, deerant quoque litora ponto.
> Now all was sea, nor had that sea a shore.

Thus Ovid's fancy was not limited by verse, and Virgil needed not verse to have bounded his.

"In our own language we see Ben Jonson confining himself to what ought to be said, even in the liberty of blank verse, and yet Corneille, the most judicious of the French poets, is still varying the same sense an hundred ways and dwelling eternally on the same subject, though confin'd by rhyme. Some other exceptions I have to verse, but since these I have nam'd are for the most part already public, I conceive it reasonable they should first be answer'd."

"It concerns me less than any," said Neander (seeing he had ended), "to reply to this discourse, because when I should have prov'd that verse may be natural in plays, yet I should always be ready to confess that those which I have written in this kind come short of that perfection which is requir'd.[104] Yet since you are pleas'd I should undertake this province, I will do it, though with all imaginable respect and deference, both to that person[105] from whom you

---

[103] Nescivit, etc. Marcus Seneca the rhetorician said this of Ovid in Controversiae IX, 5. (He does not know when to leave well enough alone.) It was Lucius Seneca (Quaestiones Naturales III, 27) who praised the verse quoted.

[104] It concerns me less than any, etc. The remark actually reveals the sensitivity usually hidden by Dryden's Olympian detachment.

[105] that person. Although both here may refer (if differing punctuation be allowed) to respect and deference, it probably means "both to you and

have borrow'd your strongest arguments, and to whose judgment when I have said all, I finally submit. But before I proceed to answer your objections, I must first remember you that I exclude all comedy from my defence; and next that I deny not but blank verse may be also us'd, and content myself only to assert that in serious plays where the subject and characters are great and the plot unmix'd with mirth, which might allay or divert these concernments which are produc'd, rhyme is there as natural, and more effectual, than blank verse.

"And now having laid down this as a foundation, to begin with Crites, I must crave leave to tell him that some of his arguments against rhyme reach no farther than from the faults or defects of ill rhyme to conclude against the use of it in general. May not I conclude against blank verse by the same reason? If the words of some poets who write in it are either ill chosen or ill placed (which makes not only rhyme but all kind of verse in any language unnatural), shall I, for their vicious affectation, condemn those excellent lines of Fletcher which are written in that kind? Is there anything in rhyme more constrain'd than this line in blank verse?—'I Heav'n invoke, and strong resistance make' [106]—where you see both the clauses are plac'd unnaturally, that is, contrary to the common way of speaking, and that without the excuse of a rhyme to cause it. Yet you would think me very ridiculous if I should accuse the stubbornness of blank verse for this and not rather the stiffness of the poet. Therefore, Crites, you must either prove that words, though well chosen and duly plac'd, yet render not rhyme natural in itself, or that however natural and easy the rhyme may be, yet it is not proper for a play. If you insist on the former part, I would ask you what other conditions are requir'd to make rhyme natural in itself, besides an election of apt words and a right disposition of them? For the due choice of your words expresses your sense naturally, and the due placing them adapts the rhyme to it. If

---

to *that person*." That person may be Aristotle or, perhaps more likely, Sir Robert Howard; see footnote 122, below.

[106] *I Heav'n invoke*, etc. Unidentified; perhaps manufactured for the occasion.

you object that one verse may be made for the sake of
another, though both the words and rhyme be apt, I answer it cannot possibly so fall out; for either there is a dependance of sense betwixt the first line and the second, or
there is none. If there be that connection, then in the natural position of the words the latter line must of necessity
flow from the former; if there be no dependance, yet still
the due ordering of words makes the last line as natural in
itself as the other. So that the necessity of a rhyme never
forces any but bad or lazy writers to say what they would
not otherwise. 'Tis true, there is both care and art requir'd
to write in verse. A good poet never establishes the first line
till he has sought out such a rhyme as may fit the sense,
already prepar'd to heighten the second. Many times the
close of the sense falls into the middle of the next verse or
farther off, and he may often prevail himself of the same
advantages in English which Virgil had in Latin; he may
break off in the hemistich and begin another line. Indeed,
the not observing these two last things makes plays which
are writ in verse so tedious, for though, most commonly,
the sense is to be confin'd to the couplet, yet nothing that
does 'perpetuo tenore fluere,' [107] run in the same channel,
can please always. 'Tis like the murmuring of a stream,
which not varying in the fall, causes at first attention, at
last drowsiness. Variety of cadences is the best rule, the
greatest help to the actors, and refreshment to the audience.

"If then verse may be made natural in itself, how becomes it unnatural in a play? You say the stage is the representation of nature and no man in ordinary conversation
speaks in rhyme. But you foresaw when you said this that
it might be answer'd, neither does any man speak in blank
verse, or in measure without rhyme. Therefore you concluded that which is nearest nature is still to be preferr'd.
But you took no notice that rhyme might be made as natural as blank verse, by the well placing of the words, etc. All
the difference between them, when they are both correct is
the sound in one, which the other wants; and if so, the
sweetness of it and all the advantage resulting from it,

---

[107] *perpetuo tenore fluere.* Cicero, *De Oratore* VI, 21.

which are handled in the Preface to *The Rival Ladies*,[108] will yet stand good.

"As for that place of Aristotle where he says plays should be writ in that kind of verse which is nearest prose, it makes little for you, blank verse being properly but measur'd prose. Now measure alone in any modern language does not constitute verse; those of the ancients in Greek and Latin consisted in quantity of words and a determinate number of feet. But when, by the inundation of the Goths and Vandals into Italy new languages were introduced and barbarously mingled with the Latin, of which the Italian, Spanish, French, and ours (made out of them and the Teutonic) are dialects, a new way of poesy was practis'd; new, I say, in those countries, for in all probability it was that of the conquerors in their own nations. At least we are able to prove, that the eastern people have us'd it from all antiquity (*Vide* Daniel, his *Defence of Rhyme*). This new way consisted in measure or number of feet and rhyme. The sweetness of rhyme and observation of accent supplying the place of quantity in words, which could neither exactly be observ'd by those barbarians who knew not the rules of it, neither was it suitable to their tongues as it had been to the Greek and Latin. No man is tied in modern poesy to observe any farther rule in the feet of his verse, but that they be dissyllables, whether spondee, trochee, or iambic it matters not; only he is obliged to rhyme. Neither do the Spanish, French, Italian or Germans acknowledge at all, or very rarely, any such kind of poesy as blank verse amongst them. Therefore at most 'tis but a poetic prose, a '*sermo pedestris*,' and as such most fit for comedies, where I acknowledge rhyme to be improper.

"Farther, as to that quotation of Aristotle, our couplet verses may be render'd as near prose as blank verse itself by using those advantages I lately nam'd, as breaks in an hemistich, or running the sense into another line, thereby making art and order appear as loose and free as nature; or not tying ourselves to couplets strictly, we may use the benefit of the Pindaric way practis'd in *The Siege of*

---

[108] *The Rival Ladies.* Dryden's Epistle Dedicatory to that play (1664), his first extant criticism, argues the merits of rhymed verse.

Rhodes,[109] where the numbers vary and the rhyme is dispos'd carelessly and far from often chiming. Neither is that other advantage of the ancients to be despis'd, of changing the kind of verse when they please with the change of the scene or some new entrance, for they confine not themselves always to iambics, but extend their liberty to all lyric numbers and sometimes even to hexameter. But I need not go so far to prove that rhyme, as it succeeds to all other offices of Greek and Latin verse, so especially to this of plays, since the custom of nations at this day confirms it; the French, Italian, and Spanish tragedies are generally writ in it, and sure the universal consent of the most civiliz'd parts of the world ought in this, as it doth in other customs, to include the rest.

"But perhaps you may tell me I have propos'd such a way to make rhyme natural, and consequently proper to plays, as is unpracticable, and that I shall scarce find six or eight lines together in any play where the words are so plac'd and chosen as is requir'd to make it natural. I answer, no poet need constrain himself at all times to it. It is enough he makes it his general rule, for I deny not but sometimes there may be a greatness in placing the words otherwise; and sometimes they may sound better, sometimes also the variety itself is excuse enough. But if, for the most part, the words be plac'd as they are in the negligence of prose, it is sufficient to denominate the way practicable; for we esteem that to be such which in the trial oft'ner succeeds than misses. And thus far you may find the practice made good in many plays; where you do not, remember still that if you cannot find six natural rhymes together, it will be as hard for you to produce as many lines in blank verse, even among the greatest of our poets, against which I cannot make some reasonable exception.

"And this, Sir, calls to my remembrance the beginning of your discourse, where you told us we should never find the audience favourable to this kind of writing till we could produce as good plays in rhyme as Ben Jonson, Fletcher,

---

[109] *The Seige of Rhodes.* Sir William Davenant's opera, or heroic play (1656). In the same year Cowley's influential loose "Pindarics" were published in his *Poems.*

and Shakespeare had writ out of it. But it is to raise envy to
the living to compare them with the dead. They are honour'd and almost ador'd by us, as they deserve; neither do I
know any so presumptuous of themselves as to contend
with them. Yet give me leave to say thus much without
injury to their ashes, that not only we shall never equal
them, but they could never equal themselves, were they to
rise and write again. We acknowledge them our fathers in
wit, but they have ruin'd their estates themselves before
they came to their children's hands. There is scarce an humour, a character, or any kind of plot which they have not
us'd. All comes sullied or wasted to us, and were they to
entertain this age, they could not now make so plenteous
treatments out of such decay'd fortunes. This therefore will
be a good argument to us either not to write at all or to
attempt some other way. There is no bays to be expected
in their walks:

> . . . *Tentanda via est qua me quoque possum*
> *Tollere humo.*[110]

"This way of writing in verse, they have only left free to
us; our age is arriv'd to a perfection in it which they never
knew and which (if we may guess by what of theirs we
have seen in verse as *The Faithful Shepherdess* and *Sad
Shepherd*)[111] 'tis probable they never could have reach'd.
For the genius of every age is different, and though ours
excel in this, I deny not but that to imitate nature in that
perfection which they did in prose is a greater commendation than to write in verse exactly. As for what you have
added, that the people are not generally inclin'd to like this
way, if it were true, it would be no wonder that betwixt the
shaking off an old habit and the introducing of a new there
should be difficulty. Do we not see them stick to Hopkins
and Sternhold's Psalms[112] and forsake those of David, I

---

[110] *Tentanda via,* etc. Virgil, *Georgics* III, 8–9.
> New ways I must attempt, my groveling name
> To raise aloft and wing my flight to fame.
> (Trans. Dryden.)

[111] *The Faithful Shepherdess.* Jonson's unfinished play, like Fletcher's
Sad Shepherd, was written partly in rhyme.

[112] *Hopkins and Sternhold's Psalms,* etc. The limping verse rendering of
the Psalms by Thomas Sternhold (d. 1549) and John Hopkins (d. 1570)

mean Sandys his translation of them? If by the people you
understand the multitude, the οἱ πολλοί, 'tis no matter
what they think. They are sometimes in the right, sometimes in the wrong; their judgment is a mere lottery. 'Est
ubi plebs recte putat, est ubi peccat' [113]—Horace says it of
the vulgar judging poesy. But if you mean the mix'd audience of the populace and the noblesse, I dare confidently
affirm that a great part of the latter sort are already favourable to verse and that no serious plays written since the
King's return have been more kindly receiv'd by them than
The Siege of Rhodes, the *Mustapha*,[114] *The Indian Queen*,
and *Indian Emperor*.

"But I come now to the inference of your first argument.
You said that the dialogue of plays is presented as the
effect of sudden thought, but no man speaks suddenly or *ex
tempore* in rhyme. And you inferr'd from thence that
rhyme, which you acknowledge to be proper to epic poesy,
cannot equally be proper to dramatic unless we could suppose all men born so much more than poets that verses
should be made in them, not by them.

"It has been formerly urg'd by you and confess'd by me
that, since no man spoke any kind of verse *ex tempore*, that
which was nearest nature was to be preferr'd. I answer
you, therefore, by distinguishing betwixt what is nearest to
the nature of comedy, which is the imitation of common
persons and ordinary speaking, and what is nearest the nature of a serious play. This last is indeed the representation of nature, but 'tis nature wrought up to an higher
pitch. The plot, the characters, the wit, the passions, the
descriptions are all exalted above the level of common converse as high as the imagination of the poet can carry them
with proportion to verisimility. Tragedy we know is wont
to image to us the minds and fortunes of noble persons and
to portray these exactly; heroic rhyme is nearest nature, as
being the noblest kind of modern verse.

---

was often criticized by Dryden and others, but it held popular favor over
the far superior *Paraphrase upon the Psalms* (1636) of George Sandys
(d. 1644).

[113] *Est ubi plebs*, etc. Adopting Horace, *Epistles* II, i, 63. (It is when the
multitude think they are right that they are wrong.)

[114] *Mustapha*. A heroic play (1665) by Robert Boyle, Earl of Orrery.

Indignatur enim privatis et prope socco
Dignis carminibus narrari cena Thyestae,[115]

says Horace; and in another place,

Effutire levis indigna Tragoedia versus.[116]

Blank verse is acknowledg'd to be too low for a poem, nay more, for a paper of verses; but if too low for an ordinary sonnet, how much more for tragedy, which is by Aristotle in the dispute betwixt the epic poesy and the dramatic, for many reasons he there alleges, rank'd above it?

"But setting this defence aside, your argument is almost as strong against the use of rhyme in poems as in plays; for the epic way is everywhere interlac'd with dialogue or discursive scenes; and therefore you must either grant rhyme to be improper there, which is contrary to your assertion, or admit it into plays by the same title which you have given it to poems. For though tragedy be justly preferr'd above the other, yet there is a great affinity between them, as may easily be discover'd in that definition of a play which Lisideius gave us. The genus of them is the same, a just and lively image of human nature in its actions, passions, and traverses of fortune; so is the end namely for the delight and benefit of mankind. The characters and persons are still the same, *viz.*, the greatest of both sorts; only the manner of acquainting us with those actions, passions, and fortunes is different. Tragedy performs it *viva voce* or by action, in dialogue, wherein it excels the epic poem which does it chiefly by narration and therefore is not so lively an image of human nature. However, the agreement betwixt them is such that if rhyme be proper for one, it must be for the other. Verse, 'tis true, is not the effect of sudden thought; but this hinders not that sudden thought may be represented in verse, since those thoughts are such as must be higher than nature can raise them without premeditation, especially to a continuance of them even out of verse; and consequently you cannot imagine them to have been

---

[115] *Indignatur,* etc. Horace, *Ars Poetica* 90–91. (The banquet of Thyestes scorns to be told in language of daily life suitable to comedy.)
[116] *Effutire,* etc. *Ars Poetica* 231. (Tragedy scorns to chatter in trifling verses.)

sudden either in the poet or the actors. A play, as I have said, to be like nature, is to be set above it; as statues which are plac'd on high are made greater than the life, that they may descend to the sight in their just proportion.

"Perhaps I have insisted too long on this objection; but the clearing of it will make my stay shorter on the rest. You tell us, Crites, that rhyme appears most unnatural in repartees, or short replies, when he who answers, it being presum'd he knew not what the others would say, yet makes up that part of the verse which was left incomplete, and supplies both the sound and measure of it. This you say looks rather like the confederacy of two than the answer of one.

"This, I confess, is an objection which is in every man's mouth who loves not rhyme. But suppose, I beseech you, the repartee were made only in blank verse, might not part of the same argument be turn'd against you? For the measure is as often suppli'd there as it is in rhyme. The latter half of the hemistich as commonly made up or a second line subjoin'd as a reply to the former, which any one leaf in Jonson's plays will sufficiently clear to you. You will often find in the Greek tragedians and in Seneca that when a scene grows up into the warmth of repartees (which is the close fighting of it) the latter part of the trimeter is suppli'd by him who answers, and yet it was never observ'd as a fault in them by any of the ancient or modern critics. The case is the same in our verse as it was in theirs, rhyme to us being in lieu of quantity to them. But if no latitude is to be allow'd a poet, you take from him not only his license of *quidlibet audendi*,[117] but you tie him up in a straiter compass than you would a philosopher. This is indeed *Musas colere severiores:*[118] you would have him follow Nature, but he must follow her on foot; you have dismounted him from his Pegasus.

"But you tell us this supplying the last half of a verse or adjoining a whole second to the former looks more like the design of two than the answer of one. Suppose we ac-

---

[117] *quidlibet audendi. Ars Poetica* 10. (Daring anything.)
[118] *Musas colere severiores*. Martial, *Epigrams* IX, xi, 17. (To cultivate the severer Muses.)

knowledge it? How comes this confederacy to be more dis-pleasing to you than in a dance which is well contriv'd? You see there the united design of many persons to make up one figure; after they have separated themselves in many petty divisions, they rejoin one by one into a gross. The confederacy is plain amongst them, for chance could never produce anything so beautiful; and yet there is noth-ing in it that shocks your sight. I acknowledge the hand of art appears in repartee, as of necessity it must in all kinds of verse. But there is also the quick and poignant brevity of it (which is an high imitation of nature in those sudden gusts of passion) to mingle with it, and this join'd with the cadency and sweetness of the rhyme leaves nothing in the soul of the hearer to desire. 'Tis an art which appears, but it appears only like the shadowings of painture, which be-ing to cause the rounding of it cannot be absent, but while that is consider'd they are lost. So while we attend to the other beauties of the matter, the care and labour of the rhyme is carri'd from us or at least drown'd in its own sweetness, as bees are sometimes buri'd in their honey. When a poet has found the repartee, the last perfection he can add to it is to put it into verse. However good the thought may be, however apt the words in which 'tis couch'd, yet he finds himself at a little unrest while rhyme is wanting; he cannot leave it till that comes naturally and then is at ease and sits down contented.

"From replies, which are the most elevated thoughts of verse, you pass to those which are most mean and which are common with the lowest of household conversation. In these, you say, the majesty of verse suffers. You instance in the calling of a servant or commanding a door to be shut in rhyme. This, Crites, is a good observation of yours but no argument, for it proves no more but that such thoughts should be waiv'd, as often as may be, by the address of the poet. But suppose they are necessary in the places where he uses them, yet there is no need to put them into rhyme. He may place them in the beginning of a verse and break it off, as unfit, when so debas'd for any other use. Or granting the worst, that they require more room than the hemistich will allow, yet still there is a choice to be made of the best words and least vulgar (provided they be apt) to express such thoughts. Many have blam'd rhyme in general for this fault, when the poet with a little care might have redress'd it. But they do it with no more justice than if English poesy should be made ridiculous for the sake of the Water Poet's rhymes.[119] Our language is noble, full, and significant; and I know not why he who is master of it may not clothe ordinary things in it as decently as the Latin, if he use the same diligence in his choice of words:

> *Delectus verborum origo est eloquentiae.*[120]

It was the saying of Julius Caesar, one so curious in his, that none of them can be chang'd but for a worse. One would think 'unlock the door' was a thing as vulgar as could be spoken, and yet Seneca could make it sound high and lofty in his Latin:

> *Reserate clusos regii postes laris.*[121]
> Set wide the palace gates.

"But I turn from this exception, both because it happens not above twice or thrice in any play that those vulgar thoughts are us'd, and then too were there no other apology to be made, yet the necessity of them (which is alike in all kind of writing) may excuse them. For if they are little and mean in rhyme, they are of consequence such in blank verse. Besides that the great eagerness and precipitation with which they are spoken makes us rather mind the substance than the dress, that for which they are spoken rather than what is spoke. For they are always the effect of some hasty concernment, and something of consequence depends on them.

"Thus, Crites, I have endeavour'd to answer your objections; it remains only that I should vindicate an argument for verse which you have gone about to overthrow. It had formerly been said that the easiness of blank verse renders the poet too luxuriant, but that the labour of rhyme bounds

[119] *the Water Poet's rhymes.* The doggerel of John Taylor (d. 1653), a Thames waterman, had been popular earlier in the century.
[120] *Delectus verborum,* etc. Cicero, *Brutus* 72. (The choice of words is the fount of eloquence.)
[121] *Reserate clusos,* etc. *Hippolytus* 860.

and circumscribes an over-fruitful fancy. The scene there being commonly confin'd to the couplet and the words so order'd that the rhyme naturally follows them, not they the rhyme. To this you answer'd that it was no argument to the question in hand, for the dispute was not which way a man may write best but which is most proper for the subject on which he writes.

"First give me leave, Sir, to remember you that the argument against which you rais'd this objection was only secondary; it was built on this hypothesis, that to write in verse was proper for serious plays. Which supposition being granted (as it was briefly made out in that discourse by shewing how verse might be made natural), it asserted that this way of writing was an help to the poet's judgment, by putting bounds to a wild, overflowing fancy. I think therefore it will not be hard for me to make good what it was to prove on that supposition. But you add that were this let pass, yet he who wants judgment in the liberty of his fancy may as well shew the defect of it when he is confin'd to verse; for he who has judgment will avoid errors, and he who has it not will commit them in all kinds of writing.

"This argument, as you have taken it from a most acute person,[122] so I confess it carries much weight in it. But by using the word 'judgment' here indefinitely, you seem to have put a fallacy upon us. I grant he who has judgment, that is, so profound, so strong, or rather so infallible a judgment that he needs no helps to keep it always pois'd and upright, will commit no faults either in rhyme or out of it. And on the other extreme, he who has a judgment so weak and craz'd that no helps can correct or amend it shall write scurvily out of rhyme and worse in it. But the first of these judgments is no where to be found, and the latter is not fit to write at all. To speak therefore of judgment as it is in the best poets, they who have the greatest proportion of it want other helps than from it within. As for example you would be loth to say that he who is indued with a sound judgment has no need of history, geography, or moral philosophy to write correctly. Judgment is indeed the master-

[122] *a most acute person.* Sir Robert Howard.

workman in a play, but he requires many subordinate
hands, many tools to his assistance. And verse I affirm to be
one of these. 'Tis a rule and line by which he keeps his
building compact and even, which otherwise lawless imagination would raise either irregularly or loosely. At least if
the poet commits errors with this help, he would make
greater and more without it. 'Tis (in short) a slow and
painful, but the surest kind, of working. Ovid, whom you
accuse for luxuriancy in verse, had perhaps been farther
guilty of it had he writ in prose. And for your instance of
Ben Jonson who, you say, writ exactly without the help of
rhyme, you are to remember 'tis only an aid to a luxuriant
fancy, which his was not. As he did not want imagination,
so none ever said he had much to spare. Neither was verse
then refin'd so much to an help to that age as it is to ours.
Thus, then, the second thoughts being usually the best, as
receiving the maturest digestion from judgment, and the
last and most mature product of those thoughts being artful and labour'd verse, it may well be inferr'd that verse is a
great help to a luxuriant fancy; and this is what that argument which you oppos'd was to evince."

Neander was pursuing this discourse so eagerly that Eugenius had call'd to him twice or thrice ere he took notice
that the barge stood still and that they were at the foot of
Somerset Stairs, where they had appointed it to land. The
company were all sorry to separate so soon, though a great
part of the evening was already spent, and stood awhile
looking back on the water, upon which the moonbeams
play'd and made it appear like floating quick-silver. At
last they went up through a crowd of French people who
were merrily dancing in the open air and nothing concern'd
for the noise of guns which had alarm'd the town that
afternoon. Walking thence together to the Piazza they
parted there, Eugenius and Lisideius to some pleasant appointment they had made, and Crites and Neander to their
several lodgings.

ANNUS MIRABILIS

The Year of Wonders, 1666

AN HISTORICAL POEM: CONTAINING
THE PROGRESS AND VARIOUS SUCCESSES OF OUR NAVAL
WAR WITH HOLLAND, UNDER THE CONDUCT OF HIS
HIGHNESS PRINCE RUPERT, AND HIS GRACE THE DUKE
OF ALBEMARLE. AND DESCRIBING THE FIRE OF LONDON

> *Multum interest res poscat, an homines latius imperare velint.*
> TRAJAN. Imperator. ad Plin.

> *Urbs antiqua ruit, multos dominata per annos.*
> VIRG.

1666. Dryden's first major nondramatic poem was published in 1667. Although "An Historical Poem," it has numerous elements in common with the epic of *Paradise Lost* and the panegyric of Abraham Cowley's *Ode to the Royal Society,* both of which were also published in the same year. The poem, his last major use of the heroic quatrain, deals primarily with the Second Dutch War and the Great Fire of London, the "wonders" of 1666. There is some allusion as well to the plague of 1665. In his Account of the poem, Dryden makes clear how conscious he was of writing historical poetry, but history was then thought to involve the hand of God and various portents as well as natural events. The fact was important because there were those who were unreconciled to, or disaffected from, the Restoration settlement and who had been claiming that misrule was about to bring disaster or that divine retribution would fall upon the king and his government. Dryden had a broader conception of history than that, but he argued in similar terms that the faults bringing trouble lay in the nation's past, in its enemies, and indeed in human nature itself. The two main actions—naval war and fire—are therefore brought together on the one hand by a shared tragic view of man's condition and frustrated effort and on the other by a vision of the triumphs possible to constructive effort secured through peace and justice. The first line introduces "arts" ambiguously, but they come to be those of war and peace, with the digression on navigation and the praise of the Royal Society stressing knowledge and with the conclusion of the poem emphasizing trade. Although the tragic version of these values is very strong in the poem, the optimistic version predominates thematically and in the bounding energy of the style.

The Account is especially significant for its definition of historical poetry—which is so percipient for Dryden's career—and for its discussion of imagination, wit, diction, and imagery. The verses to Anne Hyde, Duchess of York, embedded in the Account were evidently known to the town by circulation in manuscript. They show the poet emerging with mixed success from the attempt to write naturally and yet with moving imagery in a poem of address. He still found it easier to write narrative poetry in quatrains than to write verse epistles in couplets, and it was the former rather than the latter that showed him in full stride as a poet.

The first epigraph is adapted from Pliny, *Epistolae* X, 33: "It matters greatly whether the occasion demands, or whether men wish to extend their power." The second is from Virgil, *Aeneid* II, 363: "An ancient and imperial city falls." (Trans. Dryden.)

To the Metropolis of Great Britain,
the Most Renowned and Late Flourishing
City of London, in Its Representatives

the Lord Mayor and Court of Aldermen,
the Sheriffs and Common Council of It.

As perhaps I am the first who ever presented a work of this
nature to the metropolis of any nation, so is it likewise con-
sonant to justice that he who was to give the first example
of such a dedication should begin it with that city which
has set a pattern to all others of true loyalty, invincible
courage, and unshaken constancy. Other cities have been
prais'd for the same virtues, but I am much deceiv'd if any
have so dearly purchas'd their reputation; their fame has
been won them by cheaper trials than an expensive though
necessary war, a consuming pestilence, and a more consuming fire. To submit yourselves with that humility to the
judgments of Heaven, and at the same time to raise yourselves with that vigour above all human enemies; to be
combatted at once from above and from below, to be struck
down and to triumph: I know not whether such trials have
been ever parallel'd in any nation; the resolution and successes of them never can be. Never had prince or people
more mutual reason to love each other, if suffering for each
other can endear affection. You have come together a pair
of matchless lovers, through many difficulties; he, through
a long exile, various traverses of fortune, and the interposi-
tion of many rivals, who violently ravish'd and withheld
you from him; and certainly you have had your share in
sufferings. But Providence has cast upon you want of trade
that you might appear bountiful to your country's necessi-
ties; and the rest of your afflictions are not more the effects
of God's displeasure (frequent examples of them having
been in the reign of the most excellent princes), than occasions for the manifesting of your Christian and civil virtues.
To you therefore this *Year of Wonders* is justly dedicated,
because you have made it so: you who are to stand a
wonder to all years and ages and who have built yourselves
an immortal monument on your own ruins. You are now a
phœnix in her ashes and, as far as humanity can approach,
a great emblem of the suffering deity. But Heaven never
made so much piety and virtue to leave it miserable. I have
heard indeed of some virtuous persons who have ended

unfortunately, but never of any virtuous nation: Providence is engag'd too deeply when the cause becomes so general. And I cannot imagine it has resolv'd the ruin of that people at home which it has blessed abroad with such successes. I am therefore to conclude that your sufferings are at an end and that one part of my poem has not been more an history of your destruction than the other a prophecy of your restoration. The accomplishment of which happiness, as it is the wish of all true Englishmen, so is by none more passionately desired than by

> *The greatest of your admirers, and*
> *most humble of your servants,*
> John Dryden.

An Account of the Ensuing Poem,
in a Letter to the Honorable
Sir Robert Howard.

Sir,

I am so many ways oblig'd to you, and so little able to return your favours that, like those who owe too much, I can only live by getting farther into your debt. You have not only been careful of my fortune, which was the effect of your nobleness, but you have been solicitous of my reputation, which is that of your kindness. It is not long since I gave you the trouble of perusing a play[1] for me and now, instead of an acknowledgment, I have given you a greater, in the correction of a poem. But since you are to bear this persecution, I will at least give you the encouragement of a martyr: you could never suffer in a nobler cause. For I have chosen the most heroic subject which any poet could desire: I have taken upon me to describe the motives, the beginning, progress, and successes of a most just and necessary war; in it, the care, management, and prudence of

---

[1] *a play. Secret Love, or the Maiden Queen* (early 1667). Sir Robert Howard was Dryden's brother-in-law, a politician, and a critic with whom Dryden sometimes disagreed. Crites of *An Essay of Dramatic Poesy* is a fictionalizing of Howard.

our King; the conduct and valour of a royal admiral [2] and of two incomparable generals; the invincible courage of our captains and seamen; and three glorious victories, the result of all. After this I have, in the fire, the most deplorable but withal the greatest argument that can be imagin'd: the destruction being so swift, so sudden, so vast and miserable, as nothing can parallel in story. The former part of this poem, relating to the war, is but a due expiation for my not serving my king and country in it. All gentlemen are almost oblig'd to it; and I know no reason we should give that advantage to the commonalty of England to be foremost in brave actions, which the noblesse of France would never suffer in their peasants. I should not have written this but to a person who has been ever forward to appear in all employments whither his honour and generosity have call'd him. The latter part of my poem, which describes the fire, I owe first to the piety and fatherly affection of our monarch to his suffering subjects and in the second place to the courage, loyalty, and magnamity of the city, both which were so conspicuous that I have wanted words to celebrate them as they deserve.

I have call'd my poem *historical*, not *epic*, though both the actions and actors are as much heroic as any poem can contain. But since the action is not properly one, nor that accomplish'd in the last successes, I have judg'd it too bold a title for a few stanzas which are little more in number than a single *Iliad* or the longest of the *Aeneids*. For this reason (I mean not of length, but broken action, ti'd too severely to the laws of history), I am apt to agree with those who rank Lucan rather among historians in verse, than epic poets,[3] in whose room, if I am not deceiv'd, Silius Italicus,[4] though a worse writer, may more justly be admitted. I have chosen to write my poem in quatrains, or

---

[2] *royal admiral*, etc. James, Duke of York, later James II. The *generals* are Prince Rupert, cousin of Charles II and the greatest Royalist general in the Civil Wars, and George Monck (or Monk), now Duke of Albemarle; see *Astraea Redux* 151 and stanza 191, below.

[3] *those who rank Lucan*, etc. Petronius, *Satyricon* 118; Quintilian, *Institutes* X, i, 90; Sir William Davenant, Preface to *Gondibert*. Dryden has Davenant particularly in mind.

[4] *Silicus Italicus*. His epic, *Punica*, lacks the ornate dignity of Lucan's *Pharsalia*.

stanzas of four in alternate rhyme, because I have ever
judg'd them more noble and of greater dignity, both for the
sound and number, than any other verse in use amongst us;
in which I am sure I have your approbation. The learned
languages have, certainly, a great advantage of us in not
being tied to the slavery of any rhyme, and were less constrain'd in the quantity of every syllable—which they
might vary with spondees or dactyls, besides so many other
helps of grammatical figures,[5] for the lengthening or ab-
breviation of them—than the modern are in the close of
that one syllable, which often confines, and more often cor-
rupts the sense of all the rest. But in this necessity of our
rhymes, I have always found the couplet verse most easy
(though not so proper for this occasion), for there the work
is sooner at an end, every two lines concluding the labour
of the poet; but in quatrains he is to carry it farther on, and
not only so, but to bear along in his head the troublesome
sense of four lines together. For those who write correctly
in this kind must needs acknowledge that the last line of
the stanza is to be consider'd in the composition of the first.
Neither can we give ourselves the liberty of making any
part of a verse for the sake of a rhyme, or concluding with
a word which is not current English, or using the variety of
female rhymes, all which our fathers practis'd; and for the
female rhymes, they are still in use amongst other nations:
with the Italian in every line, with the Spaniard promiscuously, with the French alternately, as those who have read
the *Alarique,* the *Pucelle,*[6] or any of their later poems will
agree with me. And besides this, they write in alexandrines, or verses of six feet, such as amongst us is the old
translation of Homer, by Chapman;[7] all which, by lengthening of their chain, makes the sphere of their activity the
larger.

I have dwelt too long upon the choice of my stanza,
which you may remember is much better defended in the

---

[5] *grammatical figures.* Arbitrary ways for determining scansion of Latin
verse.
[6] *the Alarique,* etc. Two then recent French epics: Georges de Scudéry's
Alaric ou Rome Sauvée (1654) and Jean Chapelain's *Pucelle* (1656).
[7] *Chapman.* George Chapman in fact used fourteeners for his rendering of
the *Iliad* and pentameter for his *Odyssey.*

Preface to *Gondibert*,[8] and therefore I will hasten to acquaint you with my endeavours in the writing. In general I
will only say, I have never yet seen the description of any
naval fight in the proper terms which are us'd at sea; and if
there be any such in another language, as that of Lucan in
the third of his *Pharsalia*, yet I could not prevail myself of
it in the English, the terms of arts in every tongue bearing
more of the idiom of it than any other words. We hear, indeed, among our poets, of the thund'ring of guns, the
smoke, the disorder, and the slaughter; but all these are
common notions. And certainly as those who, in a logical
dispute, keep in general terms would hide a fallacy, so those
who do it in any poetical description would veil their ignorance.

> *Descriptas servare vices operumque colores*
> *Cur ego, si nequeo ignoroque, poeta salutor?* [9]

For my own part, if I had little knowledge of the sea, yet I
have thought it no shame to learn; and if I have made some
few mistakes, 'tis only, as you can bear me witness, because
I have wanted opportunity to correct them, the whole
poem being first written, and now sent you from a place,
where I have not so much as the converse of any seaman.[10]
Yet, though the trouble I had in writing it was great, it was
more than recompens'd by the pleasure; I found myself so
warm in celebrating the praises of military men, two such
especially as the Prince and General, that it is no wonder if
they inspir'd me with thoughts above my ordinary level.
And I am well satisfi'd that as they are incomparably the
best subject I have ever had, excepting only the royal family, so also, that this I have written of them is much better
than what I have perform'd on any other. I have been
forc'd to help out other arguments, but this has been boun-

---

[8] *better defended*, etc. Davenant argued that the heroic quatrain was
more pleasurable and various than couplets.

[9] *Descriptas*, etc. Horace, *Ars Poetica* 86–87. (If I cannot keep the accepted rules and tone of poetry—if I do not know such things—why
am I called a poet?)

[10] *For my own part*, etc. Because only three stanzas (146–48) are remarkable for nautical terms, the use of terms from "arts" hardly justified
either Dryden's enthusiasm or Dr. Johnson's censure (Life of Dryden).
But the issue of "correctness" is one dividing critics and poets of the
seventeenth century from the eighteenth century.

tiful to me; they have been low and barren of praise, and I
have exalted them, and made them fruitful; but here—
Omnia sponte sua reddit justissima tellus.[11] I have had a
large, a fair, and a pleasant field, so fertile, that without my
cultivating it has given me two harvests in a summer and
in both oppress'd the reaper. All other greatness in subjects
is only counterfeit, it will not endure the test of danger; the
greatness of arms is only real; other greatness burdens a
nation with its weight, this supports it with its strength.
And as it is the happiness of the age, so is it the peculiar
goodness of the best of kings, that we may praise his subjects without offending him; doubtless it proceeds from a
just confidence of his own virtue, which the lustre of no
other can be so great as to darken in him: for the good or
the valiant are never safely prais'd under a bad or a degenerate prince.

But to return from this digression to a farther account of
my poem, I must crave leave to tell you, that as I have
endeavour'd to adorn it with noble thoughts, so much more
to express those thoughts with elocution. The composition
of all poems is or ought to be of wit, and wit in the poet, or
wit writing (if you will give me leave to use a school distinction), is no other than the faculty of imagination in the
writer which, like a nimble spaniel,[12] beats over and ranges
through the field of memory till it springs the quarry it
hunted after; or, without metaphor, which searches over all
the memory for the species or ideas of those things which it
designs to represent. Wit written is that which is well de-
fin'd, the happy result of thought or product of that imagination. But to proceed from wit in the general notion of it
to the proper wit of an heroic or historical poem, I judge it
chiefly to consist in the delightful imaging of persons, actions, passions, or things. 'Tis not the jerk or sting of an
epigram, nor the seeming contradiction of a poor antithesis
(the delight of an ill judging audience in a play of rhyme),

---

[11] *Omnia sponte,* etc. An aphorism resembling numerous Latin sayings.
(Perfectly just, the earth returns everything of its own free will.)
[12] *a nimble spaniel.* The traditional emblem for "fancy" or imagination.
Although unusually abstract for Dryden, the passage is one of his most
significant for its distinctions and relations between imagination, wit,
and fancy.

nor the jingle of a more paranomasia; neither is it so much the morality of a grave sentence, affected by Lucan, but more sparingly used by Virgil; but it is some lively and apt description, dress'd in such colours of speech that it sets before your eyes the absent object as perfectly and more delightfully than nature. So then the first happiness of the poet's imagination is properly invention, or finding of the thought; the second is fancy, or the variation, driving,[13] or moulding of that thought, as the judgment represents it proper to the subject; the third is elocution, or the art of clothing and adorning that thought so found and varied, in apt, significant, and sounding words; the quickness of the imagination is seen in the invention, the fertility in the fancy, and the accuracy in the expression. For the two first of these Ovid is famous amongst the poets, for the latter Virgil. Ovid images more often the movements and affections of the mind, either combating between two contrary passions, or extremely discompos'd by one; his words therefore are the least part of his care, for he pictures nature in disorder, with which the study and choice of words is inconsistent. This is the proper wit of dialogue or discourse and, consequently, of the drama, where all that is said is to be suppos'd the effect of sudden thought; which, though it excludes not the quickness of wit in repartees, yet admits not a too curious election of words, too frequent allusions, or use of tropes, or, in fine, anything that shows remoteness of thought or labour in the writer. On the other side, Virgil speaks not so often to us in the person of another, like Ovid, but in his own; he relates almost all things as from himself and thereby gains more liberty than the other to express his thoughts with all the graces of elocution, to write more figuratively, and to confess as well the labour as the force of his imagination. Though he describes his Dido well and naturally in the violence of her passions, yet he must yield in that to the Myrrha, the Biblis, the Althaea of Ovid; for, as great an admirer of him as I am, I must acknowledge that, if I see not more of their souls than I see of Dido's, at least I have a greater concernment for them; and

[13] *driving.* An edition of 1688, whose changes are possibly Dryden's, reads "deriving."

that convinces me that Ovid has touch'd those tender
strokes more delicately than Virgil could.

But when action or persons are to be describ'd, when
any such image is to be set before us, how bold, how mas-
terly are the strokes of Virgil! We see the objects he represents us within their native figures, in their proper motions;
but we so see them as our own eyes could never have beheld them so beautiful in themselves. We see the soul of
the poet, like that universal one of which he speaks, in-
forming and moving through all his pictures,

> . . . totamque infusa per artus
> Mens agitat molem, et magno se corpore miscet;[14]

we behold him embellishing his images, as he makes Venus
breathing beauty upon her son Aeneas.

> . . . lumenque juventae
> Purpureum, et laetos oculis afflarat honores:
> Quale manus addunt ebori decus, aut ubi flavo
> Argentum, Pariusve lapis circundatur auro.[15]

See his tempest, his funeral sports, his combat of Turnus
and Aeneas, and his *Georgics*, which I esteem the divinest
part of all his writings, the plague, the country, the battle
of bulls, the labour of the bees, and those many other excellent images of nature, most of which are neither great in
themselves, nor have any natural ornament to bear them
up; but the words wherewith he describes them are so excellent that it might be well appli'd to him which was said
by Ovid, *Materiam superabat opus;*[16] the very sound of his
words has often somewhat that is connatural to the subject,
and while we read him, we sit, as in a play, beholding the

---

[14] *totamque infusa,* etc. Virgil, *Aeneid* VI, 726-27. (And mind, suffused
throughout, moves the entire mass and mingles with the mighty body.)
[15] *Aeneid* I, 590-93.

> His mother goddess, with her hands divine,
> Had form'd his curling locks and made his temples shine,
> And giv'n his rolling eyes a sparkling grace,
> And breath'd a youthful vigour on his face:
> Like polish'd iv'ry, beauteous to behold,
> Or Parian marble when enchas'd in gold.

(Trans. Dryden.)

[16] *Materiam,* etc. Ovid, *Metamorphoses* II, 5. (The workmanship surpassed
the material.)

scenes of what he represents. To perform this, he made frequent use of tropes, which you know change the nature of a known word, by applying it to some other signification; and this is it which Horace means in his epistle to the Pisos.

> *Dixeris egregie notum si callida verbum*
> *Reddiderit junctura novum.*[17]

But I am sensible I have presum'd too far, to entertain you with a rude discourse of that art which you both know so well and put into practise with so much happiness. Yet before I leave Virgil, I must own the vanity to tell you, and by you the world, that he has been my master in this poem: I have followed him every where, I know not with what success, but I am sure with diligence enough; my images are many of them copied from him and the rest are imitations of him. My expressions also are as near as the idioms of the two languages would admit of in translation. And this, Sir, I have done with that boldness, for which I will stand accomptable to any of our little critics who, perhaps, are not better acquainted with him than I am. Upon your first perusal of this poem, you have taken notice of some words which I have innovated (if it be too bold for me to say refin'd) upon his Latin which, as I offer not to introduce into English prose, so I hope they are neither improper, nor altogether unelegant in verse; and in this Horace will again defend me.

> *Et nova, fictaque nuper habebunt verba fidem, si*
> *Graeco fonte cadant, parce detorta.*[18]

The inference is exceeding plain; for if a Roman poet might have liberty to coin a word, supposing only that it was derived from the Greek, was put into a Latin termination, and that he us'd this liberty but seldom, and with modesty: how much more justly may I challenge that privilege to do it with the same prerequisites, from the best and

---

[17] *Dixeris,* etc. *Ars Poetica* 47-48. (You will write well if the skill of your context makes a familiar word fresh.)

[18] *Et nova,* etc. *Ars Poetica* 52-53. (New words and coinages will gain acceptance if they come from a Greek source with but slight change.)

most judicious of Latin writers? In some places, where
either the fancy or the words were his, or any others', I
have noted it in the margin that I might not seem a plagiary; in others I have neglected it, to avoid as well the tedi-
ousness as the affectation of doing it too often.

Such descriptions or images, well wrought, which I
promise not for mine, are, as I have said, the adequate
delight of heroic poesy, for they beget admiration, which is
its proper object; as the images of the burlesque, which is
contrary to this, by the same reason beget laughter; for the
one shows Nature beautified, as in the picture of a fair
woman, which we all admire; the other shows her deformed, as in that of a lazar, or of a fool with distorted face
and antic gestures, at which we cannot forbear to laugh,
because it is a deviation from Nature.[19] But though the
same images serve equally for the epic poesy, and for the
historic and panegyric, which are branches of it, yet a several sort of sculpture is to be used in them: if some of them
are to be like those of Juvenal, *stantes in curribus Aemil-
iani*,[20] heroes drawn in their triumphal chariots and in their
full proportion; others are to be like that of Virgil, *spirantia
mollius aera*:[21] there is somewhat more of softness and tenderness to be shown in them.

You will soon find I write not this without concern. Some
who have seen a paper of verses which I wrote last year to
her Highness the Duchess have accus'd them of that only
thing I could defend in them; they have said I did *humi
serpere*,[22] that I wanted not only height of fancy but dignity of words to set it off; I might well answer with that of
Horace, *Nunc non erat his locus*,[23] I knew I address'd them
to a lady and accordingly I affected the softness of expres-

---

[19] *Such descriptions,* etc. Although continuing his discussion of imagery
and poetic effect, Dryden turns to distinctions and connections between
epic, history, and panegyric. The ideas are traditional, but their relationship to each other and to actual poetic practice at once depart from
earlier criticism and forecast the central directions of Dryden's work
hereafter.

[20] *stantes in curribus,* etc. *Satires* VIII, 3. (The Aemilians standing in
their chariots.)

[21] *spirantia,* etc. *Aeneid* VI, 847. (More softly shaped statues of breathing
bronze.)

[22] *humi serpere. Ars Poetica* 28. (Crawl on the ground.)

[23] *Nunc non erat,* etc. *Ars Poetica* 19. (This was not the place for them.)

sion and the smoothness of measure rather than the height of thought, and in what I did endeavour it is no vanity to say I have succeeded. I detest arrogance, but there is some difference betwixt that and a just defence. But I will not farther bribe your candour, or the readers'. I leave them[24] to speak for me and, if they can, to make out that character, not pretending to a greater, which I have given them.

Verses to Her Highness the Duchess, on the Memorable Victory Gain'd by the Duke Against the Hollanders, June the 3rd, 1665, and on Her Journey Afterwards into the North.

MADAM,

When, for our sakes, your hero you resign'd
To swelling seas and every faithless wind,
When you releas'd his courage and set free
A valour fatal to the enemy,
You lodg'd your country's cares within your breast
(The mansion where soft love should only rest),
And ere our foes abroad were overcome,
The noblest conquest you had gain'd at home.
Ah, what concerns did both your souls divide!
Your honour gave us what your love deni'd,   10
And 'twas for him much easier to subdue
Those foes he fought with than to part from you.
That glorious day, which two such navies saw,
As each, unmatch'd, might to the world give law,
Neptune, yet doubtful whom he should obey,
Held to them both the trident of the sea;
The winds were hush'd, the waves in ranks were
    cast,
As awfully as when God's people pass'd:
Those, yet uncertain on whose sails to blow,
These, where the wealth of nations ought to flow.   20

---

[24] *I leave them.* Referring to *verses* several lines before.
[17-18] Exodus 14:21-22.

Then with the Duke your Highness rul'd the
    day;
While all the brave did his command obey,
The fair and pious under you did pray.
How pow'rful are chaste vows! the wind and tide
You brib'd to combat on the English side.
Thus to your much lov'd lord you did convey
An unknown succour, sent the nearest way.
New vigour to his wearied arms you brought
(So Moses was upheld while Israel fought).
While, from afar, we heard the cannon play   30
Like distant thunder on a shiny day,
For absent friends we were asham'd to fear,
When we consider'd what you ventur'd there.
Ships, men, and arms our country might restore,
But such a leader could supply no more.
With generous thoughts of conquest he did burn,
Yet fought not more to vanquish than return.
Fortune and victory he did pursue,
To bring them, as his slaves, to wait on you.
Thus beauty ravish'd the rewards of fame,   40
And the fair triumph'd when the brave o'rcame.
Then, as you meant to spread another way
By land your conquests far as his by sea,
Leaving our southern clime, you march'd along
The stubborn north, ten thousand cupids strong.
Like commons the nobility resort
In crowding heaps to fill your moving court;
To welcome your approach the vulgar run,
Like some new envoy from the distant sun.
And country beauties by their lovers go,   50
Blessing themselves and wond'ring at the show:
So when the new-born phoenix first is seen,
Her feather'd subjects all adore their queen;
And, while she makes her progress through the east,
From every grove her numerous trains increase:
Each poet of the air her glory sings,

28–29 Exodus 17:11–12.
52 ff. Cf. *Threnodia Augustalis* 364 ff.

And round him the pleas'd audience clap their
     wings.

And now, Sir, 'tis time I should relieve you from the
tedious length of this account. You have better and more
profitable employment for your hours, and I wrong the
public to detain you longer. In conclusion, I must leave my
poem to you with all its faults, which I hope to find fewer
in the printing by your emendations. I know you are not of
the number of those, of whom the younger Pliny speaks,
*Nec sunt parum multi qui carpere amicos suos judicium
vocant;*[1] I am rather too secure of you on that side. Your
candour in pardoning my errors may make you more remiss
in correcting them, if you will not withal consider that they
come into the world with your approbation and through
your hands. I beg from you the greatest favor you can confer upon an absent person, since I repose upon your management what is dearest to me, my fame and reputation;
and therefore I hope it will stir you up to make my poem
fairer by many of your blots; if not, you know the story of
the gamester who married the rich man's daughter, and
when her father denied the portion, christened all the children by his surname, that if, in conclusion, they must beg,
they should do so by one name, as well as by the other. But
since the reproach of my faults will light on you, 'tis but
reason I should do you that justice to the readers to let
them know that if there be any thing tolerable in this
poem, they owe the argument to your choice, the writing to
your encouragement, the correction to your judgment, and
the care of it to your friendship, to which he must ever
acknowledge himself to owe all things, who is,

                                   Sir,

                          *The most obedient and most
                             faithful of your servants,*
                                   John Dryden.

*From Charleton in Wiltshire,
Novem. 10, 1666.*

---

[1] *Nec sunt,* etc. Pliny, *Epistles* VII, 28. (There are many who call it dis-
cernment to criticize their friends.)

ANNUS MIRABILIS

The Year of Wonders, 1666

1

In thriving arts long time had Holland grown,
  Crouching at home, and cruel when abroad:
Scarce leaving us the means to claim our own.
  Our King they courted and our merchants aw'd.

2

Trade, which like blood should circularly flow,
  Stopp'd in their channels, found its freedom lost;
Thither the wealth of all the world did go
  And seem'd but shipwreck'd on so base a coast.

3

For them alone the heav'ns had kindly heat,
  In eastern quarries ripening precious dew;[a]   10
For them the Idumæan balm did sweat,
  And in hot Ceylon spicy forests grew.

4

The sun but seem'd the lab'rer of their year;
  Each waxing moon suppli'd her wat'ry store[b]
To swell those tides, which from the line did bear
  Their brim-full vessels to the Belg'an shore.

5

Thus mighty in her ships stood Carthage long
  And swept the riches of the world from far,

---

[a] *In eastern quarries, etc. Precious stones at first are dew, condens'd
and harden'd by the warmth of the sun or subterranean fires.* [The lettered footnotes are Dryden's; material added to them in this edition is
set off in brackets.]

[b] *Each waxing, etc. According to their opinion, who think that great heap
of waters under the line is depressed into tides by the moon, towards
the poles.*

---

8 *so base.* Cf. the French, Les Pais-bas, for the Netherlands.
17ff. Echoing the Virgilian view of Carthage (Holland): "Stout for the
war and studious of their trade" (*Aeneid* I, 13–14, trans. Dryden).
England's first "Punic War" with Holland was that of 1652–1654; Dry-

Yet stoop'd to Rome, less wealthy, but more strong:
    And this may prove our second Punic War.   20

6

What peace can be where both to one pretend?
    (But they more diligent, and we more strong)
Or if a peace, it soon must have an end,
    For they would grow too pow'rful were it long.

7

Behold two nations, then, engag'd so far
    That each sev'n years the fit must shake each
        land,
Where France will side to weaken us by war,
    Who only can his vast designs withstand.

8

See how he feeds th' Iberian[c] with delays,
    To render us his timely friendship vain,   30
And, while his secret soul on Flanders preys,
    He rocks the cradle of the babe of Spain.

9

Such deep designs of empire does he lay
    O'er them whose cause he seems to take in hand,
And, prudently, would make them lords at sea
    To whom with ease he can give laws by land.

10

This saw our King, and long within his breast
    His pensive counsels balanc'd to and fro;
He griev'd the land he freed should be oppress'd,
    And he less for it than usurpers do.   40

11

His gen'rous mind the fair ideas drew
    Of fame and honour which in dangers lay,

---

[c] *th' Iberian. The Spaniard.*

---

den predicts that the second will end like that in which Rome destroyed
Carthage.
[40]*usurpers.* Cromwell, who came to replace Charles I as the central figure
of government, had brilliantly executed the First Dutch War.

Where wealth, like fruit on precipices, grew,
    Not to be gather'd but by birds of prey.

12

The loss and gain each fatally were great,
    And still his subjects call'd aloud for war;
But peaceful kings o'er martial people set
    Each others poise and counter-balance are.

13

He first survey'd the charge with careful eyes,
    Which none but mighty monarchs could
        maintain;   50
Yet judg'd, like vapours that from limbecs rise,
    It would in richer showers descend again.

14

At length resolv'd t' assert the wat'ry ball,
    He in himself did whole armadoes bring;
Him, aged seamen might their master call,
    And choose for general were he not their King.

15

It seems as every ship their sovereign knows,
    His awful summons they so soon obey:
So hear the scaly herd when Proteus blows,[d]
    And so to pasture follow through the sea.   60

16

To see this fleet upon the ocean move
    Angels drew wide the curtains of the skies,
And Heav'n, as if there wanted lights above,
    For tapers made two glaring comets rise;

[d] *when Proteus blows. Or Caeruleus Proteus immania ponti armenta, et
magnas pascit sub gurgite Phocas.* Virg. [As often, Dryden's note (referring to Virgil, *Georgics* IV, 387–89 and 394–95) gives the idea rather
than the exact wording of the original.]

<hr>

[51] *limbecs.* The first clear indication of the strain of alchemical language
and thought in the poem.
[54] Echoing Virgil: "And in himself alone an army brought" (*Aeneid* VII,
706–7, trans. Dryden).
[64] *comets.* Seen in November and December 1664.

17

Whether they unctuous exhalations are,
    Fir'd by the sun, or seeming so alone,
Or each some more remote and slippery star,
    Which looses footing when to mortals shown;

18

Or one that bright companion of the sun
    Whose glorious aspect seal'd our newborn King,   70
And now a round of greater years begun,
    New influence from his walks of light did bring.

19

Victorious York did, first, with fam'd success,
    To his known valour make the Dutch give place;
Thus Heav'n our Monarch's fortune did confess,
    Beginning conquest from his royal race.

20

But since it was decreed, auspicious King,
    In Britain's right that thou should'st wed the main,
Heav'n, as a gage, would cast some precious thing
    And therefore doom'd that Lawson should be slain.   80

21

Lawson amongst the foremost met his fate,
    Whom sea-green Sirens from the rocks lament:
Thus as an off'ring for the Grecian State,
    He first was kill'd who first to battle went.

22

Their chief* blown up, in air, not waves expir'd,
    To which his pride presum'd to give the law;
The Dutch confess'd Heav'n present and retir'd,
    And all was Britain the wide ocean saw.

* *The Admiral of Holland.* [The starred notes are Dryden's.]

80 Sir John Lawson, long distinguished for naval service, is compared to
    Protesilaus, the first Greek ashore at Troy and killed by Hector; see
    Metamorphoses XII, 67–69, and *Iliad* II, 695–702.
85 *chief.* Admiral Opdam.

23

To nearest ports their shatter'd ships repair,
   Where by our dreadful cannon they lay aw'd: 90
So reverently men quit the open air
   When thunder speaks the angry gods abroad.

The Attempt at Berghen

24

And now approach'd their fleet from India, fraught
   With all the riches of the rising sun,
And precious sand from southern climates[e] brought,
   (The fatal regions where the war begun).

25

Like hunted castors, conscious of their store,
   Their waylaid wealth to Norway's coasts they
      bring;
There first the north's cold bosom spices bore,
   And winter brooded on the eastern spring.   100

26

By the rich scent we found our perfum'd prey,
   Which flank'd with rocks did close in covert lie;
And round about their murdering cannon lay,
   At once to threaten and invite the eye.

27

Fiercer than cannon and than rocks more hard,
   The English undertake th' unequal war;
Seven ships alone, by which the port is barr'd,
   Besiege the Indies and all Denmark dare.

28

These fight like husbands, but like lovers those:
   These fain would keep, and those more fain enjoy;   110

[e] *southern climates, Guinea.*

[93] *their fleet from India.* In July 1665 English ships pursued a Dutch
treasure fleet that stopped at Bergen on its return from the New World.
India: the West Indies.

And to such height their frantic passion grows,
   That what both love, both hazard to destroy.

29

Amidst whole heaps of spices lights a ball,
   And now their odours arm'd against them fly:
Some preciously by shatter'd porc'lain fall,
   And some by aromatic splinters die.

30

And though by tempests of the prize bereft,
   In heaven's inclemency some ease we find;
Our foes we vanquish'd by our valour left
   And only yielded to the seas and wind.   120

31

Nor wholly lost we so deserv'd a prey;
   For storms, repenting, part of it restor'd,
Which, as a tribute from the Baltic Sea,
   The British ocean sent her mighty lord.

32

Go, mortals, now, and vex yourselves in vain
   For wealth, which so uncertainly must come,
When what was brought so far, and with such pain,
   Was only kept to lose it nearer home.

33

The son, who twice three months on th' ocean toss'd,
   Prepar'd to tell what he had pass'd before,   130
Now sees in English ships the Holland coast
   And parents' arms in vain stretch'd from the shore.

34

This careful husband had been long away,
   Whom his chaste wife and little children mourn,
Who on their fingers learn'd to tell the day
   On which their father promis'd to return.

[119] That is: We left our foes, etc.

35

Such are the proud designs of humankind,[f]
  And so we suffer shipwreck everywhere!
Alas, what port can such a pilot find,
  Who in the night of fate must blindly steer!   140

36

The undistinguish'd seeds of good and ill
  Heav'n, in his bosom, from our knowledge hides,
And draws them in contempt of human skill,
  Which oft, for friends, mistaken foes provides.

37

Let Münster's prelate ever be accurst,
  In whom we seek the German faith[g] in vain;
Alas, that he should teach the English first
  That fraud and avarice in the Church could
    reign!

38

Happy who never trust a stranger's will,
  Whose friendship's in his interest understood!   150
Since money giv'n but tempts him to be ill
  When pow'r is too remote to make him good.

War Declar'd by France

39

Till now, alone the mighty nations strove;
  The rest, at gaze, without the lists did stand,
And threat'ning France, plac'd like a painted Jove,
  Kept idle thunder in his lifted hand.

---

[f] *Such are, etc.* from Petronius. *Si, bene calculum ponas ubique fit
naufragium.* [*Satyricon* 115.]
[g] *the German faith.* Tacitus saith of them, *Nullos mortalium fide aut
armis ante Germanos esse.* [*Annals* XIII, liv. (No one surpasses the
Germans for arms or loyalty.)]

---

145 *Münster's prelate.* Bernhard von Galen, Bishop of Münster, an unreli-
able ally of England against Holland, had accepted English subsidies.
155 *threat'ning France.* After numerous threats, France formally declared
war on January 6, 1666.

40

That eunuch guardian of rich Holland's trade,
   Who envies us what he wants pow'r t' enjoy!
Whose noiseful valour does no foe invade
   And weak assistance will his friends destroy.   160

41

Offended that we fought without his leave,
   He takes this time his secret hate to show,
Which Charles does with a mind so calm receive
   As one that neither seeks nor shuns his foe.

42

With France, to aid the Dutch, the Danes unite:
   France as their tyrant, Denmark as their slave.
But when with one three nations join to fight,
   They silently confess that one more brave.

43

Louis had chas'd the English from his shore,
   But Charles the French as subjects does invite.   170
Would Heav'n for each some Solomon restore,
   Who, by their mercy, may decide their right.

44

Were subjects so but only by their choice
   And not from birth did forc'd dominion take,
Our prince alone would have the public voice
   And all his neighbours' realms would deserts
     make.

45

He without fear a dangerous war pursues,
   Which without rashness he began before.
As honour made him first the danger choose,
   So still he makes it good on virtue's score.   180

[157] *That eunuch guardian.* Louis XIV (as in 169, below).
[165] *the Danes unite.* In February 1666.

46

The doubled charge his subjects' love supplies,
   Who, in that bounty, to themselves are kind:
So glad Egyptians see their Nilus rise
   And in his plenty their abundance find.

Prince Rupert and Duke Albemarle Sent to Sea

47

With equal pow'r he does two chiefs create,
   Two such as each seem'd worthiest when alone,
Each able to sustain a nation's fate,
   Since both had found a greater in their own.

48

Both great in courage, conduct and in fame,
   Yet neither envious of the other's praise;   190
Their duty, faith, and int'rest too the same,
   Like mighty partners equally they raise.

49

The Prince long time had courted fortune's love,
   But once possess'd did absolutely reign:
Thus with their Amazons the heroes strove,
   And conquer'd first those beauties they would
      gain.

50

The Duke beheld, like Scipio, with disdain
   That Carthage, which he ruin'd, rise once more,
And shook aloft the fasces of the main
   To fright those slaves with what they felt before.   200

51

Together to the wat'ry camp they haste,
   Whom matrons passing to their children show:

---

[188] See 762, below.
[199] the fasces. Symbols of authority. Cf. Astraea Redux 249; Threnodia
   Augustalis 517.

Infants' first vows for them to Heav'n are cast,
   And future people[h] bless them as they go.

52

With them no riotous pomp nor Asian train
   T' infect a navy with their gaudy fears,
To make slow fights and victories but vain;
   But war, severely, like itself, appears.

53

Diffusive of themselves where'er they pass,
   They make that warmth in others they expect;   210
Their valour works like bodies on a glass
   And does its image on their men project.

Duke of Albemarle's Battle, First Day

54

Our fleet divides, and straight the Dutch appear,
   In number and a fam'd commander bold;
The narrow seas can scarce their navy bear,
   Or crowded vessels can their soldiers hold.

55

The Duke, less numerous but in courage more,
   On wings of all the winds to combat flies;
His murdering guns a loud defiance roar,
   And bloody crosses on his flagstaffs rise.   220

56

Both furl their sails and strip them for the fight;
   Their folded sheets dismiss the useless air:
Th' Elean Plains[i] could boast no nobler sight
   When struggling champions did their bodies bare.

---

[h] *future people, Examina infantium futurusque populus. Plin. Jun. in pan. ad Traj.* [Younger Pliny, *Panegyricus* XXVI.]
[i] *Th' Elean, etc. Where the Olympic games were celebrated.*

---

213 *Our fleet divides.* Poor English naval intelligence led to a nearly disastrous division of the fleet in May and June. Albemarle was as much foolhardy as brave.

57

Borne each by other in a distant line,
    The sea-built forts in dreadful order move:
So vast the noise, as if not fleets did join,
    But lands unfix'd[k] and floating nations strove.

58

Now pass'd, on either side they nimbly tack,
    Both strive to intercept and guide the wind;   230
And, in its eye, more closely they come back
    To finish all the deaths they left behind.

59

On high-rais'd decks the haughty Belgians ride,
    Beneath whose shade our humble frigates go:
Such port the elephant bears, and so defi'd
    By the rhinoceros, her unequal foe.

60

And as the build, so different is the fight;
    Their mounting shot is on our sails design'd;
Deep in their hulls our deadly bullets light
    And through the yielding planks a passage find.   240

61

Our dreaded admiral from far they threat,
    Whose batter'd rigging their whole war receives;
All bare, like some old oak which tempests beat,
    He stands and sees below his scatter'd leaves.

62

Heroes of old, when wounded, shelter sought,
    But he, who meets all danger with disdain,
Ev'n in their face his ship to anchor brought
    And steeple-high stood propp'd upon the main.

---

[k] *lands unfix'd. From Virgil: Credas innare revulsas Cycladas, etc.*
    [Aeneid VIII, 691 ff.]

---

[233] *Belgians.* Common usage for the Dutch.

63

At this excess of courage all amaz'd,
   The foremost of his foes awhile withdraw: 250
With such respect in enter'd Rome they gaz'd,
   Who on high chairs the god-like fathers saw.

64

And now, as where Patroclus' body lay,
   Here Trojan chiefs advanc'd, and there the Greek,
Ours o'er the Duke their pious wings display,
   And theirs the noblest spoils of Britain seek.

65

Meantime, his busy mariners he hastes,
   His shatter'd sails with rigging to restore;
And willing pines ascend his broken masts,
   Whose lofty heads rise higher than before.   260

66

Straight to the Dutch he turns his dreadful prow,
   More fierce th' important quarrel to decide.
Like swans, in long array his vessels show,
   Whose crests, advancing, do the waves divide.

67

They charge, re-charge, and all along the sea
   They drive and squander the huge Belgian fleet.
Berkeley alone, who nearest danger lay,
   Did a like fate with lost Creüsa meet.

68

The night comes on, we eager to pursue
   The combat still, and they asham'd to leave,   270

253-54 See *Iliad* XVII.
267 Dryden's first version ran, "Berkeley alone, not making equal way." His
change probably indicates a fear of reflecting on Berkeley's undoubted
heroism, but the first version was more accurate and more analogous to
the fate of Creusa, Aeneas's wife, who could not escape Troy (*Aeneid* II,
736-40).
269 *The night comes on,* etc. One of many night pieces in Dryden, many
of which are, like this, introduced by a version of the Virgilian formula,
Nox erat.

Till the last streaks of dying day withdrew,
   And doubtful moonlight did our rage deceive.

69

In th' English fleet each ship resounds with joy
   And loud applause of their great leader's fame.
In fiery dreams the Dutch they still destroy,
   And, slumb'ring, smile at the imagin'd flame.

70

Not so the Holland fleet, who, tir'd and done,
   Stretch'd on their decks like weary oxen lie;
Faint sweats all down their mighty members run
   (Vast bulks which little souls but ill supply).   280

71

In dreams they fearful precipices tread,
   Or, shipwreck'd, labour to some distant shore,
Or in dark churches walk among the dead;
   They wake with horror and dare sleep no more.

Second Day's Battle

72

The morn they look on with unwilling eyes,
   Till, from their main-top, joyful news they hear
Of ships, which by their mould bring new supplies,
   And in their colours Belgian lions bear.

73

Our watchful general had discern'd from far
   This mighty succour which made glad the foe;   290
He sigh'd but, like a father of the war,
   His face spake hope, while deep his sorrows flow.[1]

74

His wounded men he first sends off to shore
   (Never, till now, unwilling to obey).

[1] *His face, etc. Spem vultu simulat premit alto corde dolorem.* Virg. [*Aeneid* I, 209.]

209-84 Greatly admired by Dr. Johnson (Life of Dryden).

They, not their wounds, but want of strength
   deplore,
  And think them happy who with him can stay.

75

Then, to the rest, "Rejoyce," said he, "today
  In you the fortune of Great Britain lies;
Among so brave a people you are they
  Whom Heav'n has chose to fight for such a prize.   300

76

If number English courages could quell,
  We should at first have shunn'd, not met our foes,
Whose numerous sails the fearful only tell:
  Courage from hearts and not from numbers
    grows."

77

He said, nor needed more to say; with haste
  To their known stations cheerfully they go;
And all at once, disdaining to be last,
  Solicit every gale to meet the foe.

78

Nor did th' encourag'd Belgians long delay,
  But, bold in others, not themselves, they stood: 310
So thick, our navy scarce could shear their way,
  But seem'd to wander in a moving wood.

79

Our little fleet was now engag'd so far,
  That, like the swordfish in the whale, they fought.
The combat only seem'd a civil war,
  Till through their bowels we our passage wrought.

80

Never had valour, no not ours before,
  Done aught like this upon the land or main,
Where not to be o'ercome was to do more
  Than all the conquests former kings did gain.   320

81

The mighty ghosts of our great Harries rose,
    And armed Edwards look'd with anxious eyes
To see this fleet among unequal foes,
    By which fate promis'd them their Charles should
      rise.

82

Meantime the Belgians tack upon our rear,
    And raking chase-guns through our sterns they
      send;
Close by, their fire-ships like jackals appear,
    Who on their lions for the prey attend.

83

Silent in smoke of cannons they come on
    (Such vapours once did fiery Cacus hide);   330
In these the height of pleas'd revenge is shown,
    Who burn contented by another's side.

84

Sometimes, from fighting squadrons of each fleet
    (Deceiv'd themselves, or to preserve some friend),
Two grapling Aetna's on the ocean meet,
    And English fires with Belgian flames contend.

85

Now, at each tack, our little fleet grows less;
    And, like maim'd fowl, swim lagging on the main.
Their greater loss their numbers scarce confess
    While they lose cheaper than the English gain.   340

86

Have you not seen when, whistled from the fist,
    Some falcon stoops at what her eye design'd,

---

[326] *chase-guns.* Mounted fore or aft, not on the sides.
[330] *Cacus.* Virgil, in *Aeneid* VIII, 251–55, describes the monster, "fiery Cacus," tracked and slain by Hercules.

And, with her eagerness, the quarry miss'd,
    Straight flies at check and clips it down the wind,

87

The dastard crow that to the wood made wing
    And sees the groves no shelter can afford,
With her loud caws her craven kind does bring,
    Who safe in numbers cuff the noble bird?

88

Among the Dutch thus Albemarle did fare;
    He could not conquer, and disdain'd to fly.   350
Past hope of safety, 'twas his latest care,
    Like falling Caesar, decently to die.

89

Yet pity did his manly spirit move
    To see those perish who so well had fought;
And generously with his despair he strove,
    Resolv'd to live till he their safety wrought.

90

Let other Muses write his prosp'rous fate,
    Of conquer'd nations tell and kings restor'd,
But mine shall sing of his eclips'd estate,
    Which, like the sun's, more wonders does afford.   360

91

He drew his mighty frigates all before,
    On which the foe his fruitless force employs;
His weak ones deep into his rear he bore,
    Remote from guns as sick men are from noise.

92

His fiery cannon did their passage guide,
    And foll'wing smoke obscur'd them from the foe.

---

344 *flies at check*, etc. Turns from proper quarry to baser prey, then flies
rapidly down the wind.
349 *thus Albemarle*, etc. His foolhardiness was criticized at the time; Dryden quickly turned from such matters to Albemarle's consideration for
his men.

Thus Israel safe from the Egyptians' pride
   By flaming pillars and by clouds did go.

93

Elsewhere the Belgian force we did defeat,
   But here our courages did theirs subdue: 370
So Xenophon once led that fam'd retreat
   Which first the Asian empire overthrew.

94

The foe approach'd; and one, for his bold sin,
   Was sunk (as he that touch'd the Ark was slain);
The wild waves master'd him and suck'd him in,
   And smiling eddies dimpled on the main.

95

This seen, the rest at awful distance stood,
   As if they had been there as servants set,
To stay, or to go on, as he thought good,
   And not pursue, but wait on his retreat.   380

96

So Lybian huntsmen, on some sandy plain,
   From shady coverts rous'd, the lion chase:
The kingly beast roars out with loud disdain,
   And slowly moves, unknowing to give place.[m]

97

But if some one approach to dare his force,
   He swings his tail and swiftly turns him round,
With one paw seizes on his trembling horse
   And with the other tears him to the ground.

98

Amidst these toils succeeds the balmy night,
   Now hissing waters the quench'd guns restore;   390

[m] *The simile is Virgil's, Vestigia retro improperata refert, etc. [Aeneid IX, 792 ff.]*

367–68 *Thus Israel*, etc. Exodus 13:21–22.
371 *So Xenophon.* Who led the Greeks on a brilliant long retreat through the enemy in the fourth century B.C.
374 *as he that touch'd*, etc. 1 Chronicles 13:9–10.

And weary waves,[n] withdrawing from the fight,
　　Lie lull'd and panting on the silent shore.

99

The moon shone clear on the becalmed flood,
　　Where, while her beams like glittering silver play,
Upon the deck our careful general stood
　　And deeply mus'd on the succeeding day.[o]

100

"That happy sun," said he, "will rise again,
　　Who twice victorious did our navy see,
And I alone must view him rise in vain,
　　Without one ray of all his star for me.　　　　　　400

101

Yet, like an English gen'ral will I die,
　　And all the ocean make my spacious grave.
Women and cowards on the land may lie,
　　The sea's a tomb that's proper for the brave."

102

Restless he pass'd the remnants of the night
　　Till the fresh air proclaim'd the morning nigh,
And burning ships, the martyrs of the fight,
　　With paler fires beheld the eastern sky.

Third Day

103

But now, his stores of ammunition spent,
　　His naked valour is his only guard;　　　　　　410
Rare thunders are from his dumb cannon sent,
　　And solitary guns are scarcely heard.

---

[n] *weary waves. From Statius Sylv. Nec trucibus fluviis idem sonus: occidit horror æquoris, ac terris maria acclinata quiescunt.* [Silvae V, iv, 5–6.]

[o] *The third of June, famous for two former victories.*

---

395 *our careful general.* Albemarle.

104

Thus far had fortune pow'r, here forc'd to stay,
　　Nor longer durst with virtue be at strife:
This as a ransom Albemarle did pay
　　For all the glories of so great a life.

105

For now brave Rupert from afar appears,
　　Whose waving streamers the glad gen'ral knows;
With full spread sails his eager navy steers,
　　And every ship in swift proportion grows.   420

106

The anxious Prince had heard the cannon long,
　　And from that length of time dire omens drew
Of English over-match'd and Dutch too strong,
　　Who never fought three days but to pursue.

107

Then, as an eagle (who, with pious care,
　　Was beating widely on the wing for prey),
To her now silent eyrie does repair
　　And finds her callow infants forc'd away;

108

Stung with her love she stoops upon the plain,
　　The broken air loud whistling as she flies;   430
She stops, and listens, and shoots forth again,
　　And guides her pinions by her young ones' cries:

109

With such kind passion hastes the Prince to fight,
　　And spreads his flying canvas to the sound;

417-20 The earlier version (below) may have been changed for its blasphemy, but Dryden frequently compared human with divine (e.g., 454,
below).

　　　　For now brave Rupert's navy did appear,
　　　　　Whose waving streamers from afar he knows:
　　　　As in his fate something divine there were,
　　　　　Who dead and buried the third day arose.

Him, whom no danger, were he there, could fright,
    Now, absent, every little noise can wound.

110

As in a drought the thirsty creatures cry
    And gape upon the gather'd clouds for rain,
And first the martlet meets it in the sky,
    And with wet wings joys all the feather'd train: 440

111

With such glad hearts did our despairing men
    Salute th' appearance of the Prince's fleet,
And each ambitiously would claim the ken
    That with first eyes did distant safety meet.

112

The Dutch, who came like greedy hinds before
    To reap the harvest their ripe ears did yield,
Now look like those when rolling thunders roar,
    And sheets of lightning blast the standing field.

113

Full in the Prince's passage hills of sand
    And dang'rous flats in secret ambush lay,   450
Where the false tides skim o'er the cover'd land
    And seamen with dissembled depths betray:

114

The wily Dutch who, like fall'n angels, fear'd
    This new Messiah's coming, there did wait,
And round the verge their braving vessels steer'd,
    To tempt his courage with so fair a bait.

115

But he, unmov'd, contemns their idle threat,
    Secure of fame when ere he please to fight;

---

439 *the martlet.* A kind of swallow; swallows were thought to foretell
weather and were associated with water; see *The Hind and the Panther*
III, 427 ff., especially 441–44, 508–10, 570–71.
449 ff. Rupert showed his usual skill, but the ensuing battle with the ships
of the gifted Dutch admiral De Ruyter ended inconclusively.

His cold experience tempers all his heat
   And inbred worth does boasting valour slight.   460

116

Heroic virtue did his actions guide,
   And he the substance, not th' appearance, chose;
To rescue one such friend he took more pride
   Than to destroy whole thousands of such foes.

117

But, when approach'd, in strict embraces bound,
   Rupert and Albemarle together grow;
He joys to have his friend in safety found,
   Which he to none but to that friend would owe.

118

The cheerful soldiers with new stores suppli'd
   Now long to execute their spleenful will;   470
And in revenge for those three days they tri'd,
   Wish one, like Joshua's, when the sun stood still.

Fourth Day's Battle

119

Thus re-enforc'd, against the adverse fleet
   Still doubling ours, brave Rupert leads the way.
With the first blushes of the morn they meet
   And bring night back upon the newborn day.

120

His presence soon blows up the kindling fight,
   And his loud guns speak thick like angry men;
It seem'd as slaughter had been breath'd all night
   And death new pointed his dull dart again.   480

121

The Dutch too well his mighty conduct knew
   And matchless courage since the former fight,

---

469 *soldiers.* That is, fighting men, the sailors.
472 Joshua 10:12–14.

Whose navy like a stiff stretch'd cord did show
   Till he bore in and bent them into flight.

122

The wind he shares while half their fleet offends
   His open side, and high above him shows,
Upon the rest at pleasure he descends,
   And, doubly harm'd, he double harms bestows.

123

Behind, the gen'ral mends his weary pace,
   And sullenly to his revenge he sails: 490
So glides some trodden serpent on the grass
   And long behind his wounded volume trails.ᵖ

124

Th' increasing sound is borne to either shore,
   And for their stakes the throwing nations fear.
Their passions double with the cannons' roar,
   And with warm wishes each man combats there.

125

Pli'd thick and close as when the fight begun,
   Their huge unwieldy navy wastes away:
So sicken waning moons too near the sun
   And blunt their crescents on the edge of day.   500

126

And now reduc'd on equal terms to fight,
   Their ships like wasted patrimonies show:
Where the thin scatt'ring trees admit the light
   And shun each others' shadows as they grow.

127

The warlike Prince had sever'd from the rest
   Two giant ships, the pride of all the main,

ᵖ *So glides, etc.* From Virgil, *Quum medii nexus, extremaeque agmina caudae solvuntur; tardosque trahit sinus ultimus orbes, etc.* [*Georgics* III, 423–24.]

500 *crescents.* (a) moons; (b) naval formations.
502 *wasted patrimonies.* Inherited woods, their trees cut and sold by a spendthrift heir.

Which, with his one, so vigorously he press'd
   And flew so home they could not rise again.

128

Already batter'd, by his lee they lay,
   In vain upon the passing winds they call;   510
The passing winds through their torn canvas play,
   And flagging sails on heartless sailors fall.

129

Their open'd sides receive a gloomy light,
   Dreadful as day let in to shades below;
Without, grim death rides bare-fac'd in their sight
   And urges ent'ring billows as they flow.

130

When one dire shot, the last they could supply,
   Close by the board the prince's mainmast bore;
All three now helpless by each other lie,
   And this offends not, and those fear no more.   520

131

So have I seen some fearful hare maintain
   A course till tir'd before the dog she lay,
Who, stretch'd behind her, pants upon the plain,
   Past pow'r to kill as she to get away.

132

With his loll'd tongue he faintly licks his prey;
   His warm breath blows her flix up as she lies;
She, trembling, creeps upon the ground away
   And looks back to him with beseeching eyes.

133

The prince unjustly does his stars accuse,
   Which hinder'd him to push his fortune on,   530
For what they to his courage did refuse
   By mortal valour never must be done.

521-28 Recalling Ovid, *Metamorphoses* I, 533-39.

134

This lucky hour the wise Batavian takes
    And warns his tatter'd fleet to follow home,
Proud to have so got off with equal stakes,
    Where 'twas a triumph not to be o'ercome.q

135

The gen'ral's force, as kept alive by fight,
    Now, not oppos'd, no longer can pursue,
Lasting till Heav'n had done his courage right,
    When he had conquer'd he his weakness knew.   540

136

He casts a frown on the departing foe
    And sighs to see him quit the wat'ry field;
His stern fix'd eyes no satisfaction show
    For all the glories which the fight did yield.

137

Though, as when fiends did miracles avow,
    He stands confess'd ev'n by the boastful Dutch,
He only does his conquest disavow
    And thinks too little what they found too much.

138

Return'd, he with the fleet resolv'd to stay;
    No tender thoughts of home his heart divide;   550
Domestic joys and cares he puts away,
    For realms are households which the great must
      guide.

139

As those who unripe veins in mines explore,
    On the rich bed again the warm turf lay

---

q *From Horace: Quos opimus fallere et effugere est triumphus.* [*Odes* IV,
  iv, 51–52.]

---

533 *the wise Batavian.* De Ruyter, *Batavian* being yet another word for the
  Dutch. Dryden's mixed admiration and dislike for the Dutch reflects
  widespread ambiguous English attitudes in the century.
543 Mark 3:11.

Till time digests the yet imperfect ore,
    And know it will be gold another day:

140

So looks our Monarch on this early fight,
    Th' essay, and rudiments of great success,
Which all-maturing time must bring to light,
    While he, like Heav'n, does each day's labour
      bless.   560

141

Heav'n ended not the first or second day,
    Yet each was perfect to the work design'd;
God and kings work, when they their work survey,
    And passive aptness in all subjects find.

His Majesty Repairs the Fleet

142

In burden'd vessels first, with speedy care,
    His plenteous stores do season'd timber send;
Thither the brawny carpenters repair
    And as the surgeons of maim'd ships attend.

143

With cord and canvas from rich Hamburg sent,
    His navy's molted wings he imps once more;   570
Tall Norway fir, their masts in battle spent,
    And English oak sprung leaks and planks restore.

144

All hands employ'd, the royal work grows warm,[r]
    Like labouring bees on a long summer's day,
Some sound the trumpet for the rest to swarm,
    And some on bells of tasted lilies play;

---

[r] *Fervet opus: the same similitude in Virgil.* [Echoing *Aeneid* I, 430–36
and VI, 707–9.]

565ff. These nautical matters: (a) excited Charles' interest, as in this passage; (b) lead to the poem's digression (617 ff.); and (c) were a concern of the Royal Society (657 ff.).

145

With gluey wax some new foundation lay
　Of virgin combs, which from the roof are hung;
Some arm'd within doors, upon duty stay,
　Or tend the sick or educate the young.　　　　　580

146

So here, some pick out bullets from the sides,
　Some drive old oakum through each seam and
　　rift;
Their left-hand does the calking-iron guide,
　The rattling mallet with the right they lift.

147

With boiling pitch another near at hand
　(From friendly Sweden brought) the seams instops,
Which well paid o'er the salt-sea waves withstand
　And shakes them from the rising beak in drops.

148

Some the gall'd ropes with dauby marling bind,
　Or sere-cloth masts with strong tarpaulin coats;　　590
To try new shrouds one mounts into the wind,
　And one, below, their ease or stiffness notes.

149

Our careful Monarch stands in person by,
　His new-cast cannons' firmness to explore,
The strength of big-corn'd powder loves to try
　And ball and cartridge sorts for every bore.

150

Each day brings fresh supplies of arms and men
　And ships which all last winter were abroad,
And such as fitted since the fight had been,
　Or new from stocks were fall'n into the road.　　　600

[586] *instops.* The only usage recorded.

Loyal London Describ'd

151

The goodly *London* in her gallant trim
  (The phoenix daughter of the vanish'd old),
Like a rich bride does to the ocean swim
  And on her shadow rides in floating gold.

152

Her flag aloft spread ruffling to the wind
  And sanguine streamers seem the flood to fire;
The weaver, charm'd with what his loom design'd,
  Goes on to sea and knows not to retire.

153

With roomy decks, her guns of mighty strength
  (Whose low-laid mouths each mounting billow
    laves),   610
Deep in her draught, and warlike in her length,
  She seems a sea-wasp flying on the waves.

154

This martial present, piously design'd,
  The loyal city give their best-lov'd King,
And with a bounty ample as the wind,
  Built, fitted, and maintain'd to aid him bring.

Digression Concerning Shipping and Navigation

155

By viewing Nature, Nature's handmaid, Art,
  Makes mighty things from small beginnings grow:
Thus fishes first to shipping did impart
  Their tail the rudder and their head the prow.   620

156

Some log, perhaps, upon the waters swam
  An useless drift, which, rudely cut within

---

[601] *London*. Several ships bore the name, all ending disastrously. The one
Dryden speaks of replaced one that exploded March 7, 1665.

And hollow'd, first a floating trough became,
   And cross some riv'let passage did begin.

157

In shipping such as this the Irish kern
   And untaught Indian on the stream did glide,
Ere sharp-keel'd boats to stem the flood did learn,
   Or fin-like oars did spread from either side.

158

Add but a sail, and Saturn so appear'd
   When, from lost empire, he to exile went   630
And with the golden age to Tiber steer'd,
   Where coin and first commerce he did invent.

159

Rude as their ships was navigation then;
   No useful compass or meridian known,
Coasting, they kept the land within their ken,
   And knew no north but when the pole-star shone.

160

Of all who since have us'd the open sea,
   Than the bold English none more fame have won;
Beyond the year and out of Heav'n's high-way,[s]
   They make discoveries where they see no sun.   640

161

But what so long in vain and yet unknown
   By poor mankind's benighted wit is sought
Shall in this age to Britain first be shown,
   And hence be to admiring nations taught.

162

The ebbs of tides and their mysterious flow
   We as art's elements shall understand,

-----

[s] *Extra annui solique vias.* Virg. [*Aeneid* VI, 796. See also *Threnodia Augustalis* 353; *Britannia Rediviva* 306.]

-----

629 *Saturn.* Who, deposed by Jove, took laws, arts, peace—the Golden Age —to Italy.
641ff. Matters under study by members of the Royal Society.

And as by line upon the ocean go,
    Whose paths shall be familiar as the land.

163

Instructed ships shall sail to quick commerce,[t]
    By which remotest regions are alli'd,   650
Which makes one city of the universe,
    Where some may gain and all may be suppli'd.

164

Then we upon our globe's last verge shall go
    And view the ocean leaning on the sky;
From thence our rolling neighbours we shall know
    And on the lunar world securely pry.

Apostrophe to the Royal Society

165

This I foretell from your auspicious care,
    Who great in search of God and nature grow,
Who best your wise Creator's praise declare,
    Since best to praise His works is best to know.   660

166

O truly royal! who behold the law
    And rule of beings in your Maker's mind
And thence, like limbecs, rich ideas draw
    To fit the levell'd use of humankind.

167

But first the toils of war we must endure
    And from th' injurious Dutch redeem the seas.
War makes the valiant of his right secure
    And gives up fraud to be chastis'd with ease.

[t] *By a more exact measure of longitude.*

---

[654] *leaning.* The visual effect from looking on the ocean from a height at
the shore, Dryden's usual image of shore and seascapes.
[659] *God and nature.* So defending the Royal Society against charges of
atheism.

168

Already were the Belgians on our coast,
    Whose fleet more mighty every day became   670
By late success, which they did falsely boast
    And now by first appearing seem'd to claim.

169

Designing, subtle, diligent, and close,
    They knew to manage war with wise delay;
Yet all those arts their vanity did cross
    And, by their pride, their prudence did betray.

170

Nor stay'd the English long but, well suppli'd,
    Appear as numerous as th' insulting foe.
The combat now by courage must be tri'd,
    And the success the braver nation show.   680

171

There was the Plymouth squadron new come in,
    Which in the straits last winter was abroad,
Which twice on Biscay's working bay had been
    And on the Midland Sea the French had aw'd.

172

Old expert Allen, loyal all along,
    Fam'd for his action on the Smyrna fleet,
And Holmes, whose name shall live in epic song,
    While music numbers, or while verse has feet.

173

Holmes, the Achates of the gen'ral's fight,
    Who first bewitch'd our eyes with Guinea Gold: 690

681-84 The "Plymouth Squadron" under Sir Jeremy Smyth had been in the
    Midland (Mediterranean) Sea preventing the union of the French fleet;
    Smyth now led the Blue Squadron of the refitted fleet.
685 *Allen.* Sir Thomas Allin, a loyal Royalist, had attacked a Dutch Smyrna
    convoy in 1665 and now led the White Squadron.
687 *Holmes.* Sir Robert Holmes, rear admiral of the Red Squadron under
    Rupert and Albemarle. He had conquered the Gold Coast for England,
    returning with enticing gold, as Cato the Censor had entered Rome
    with a fig picked three days before in Carthage.

As once old Cato in the Roman's sight
  The tempting fruits of Afric did unfold.

174

With him went Spragg, as bountiful as brave,
  Whom his high courage to command had brought;
Harman, who did the twice fir'd *Harry* save,
  And in his burning ship undaunted fought.

175

Young Hollis, on a Muse by Mars begot,
  Born, Caesar-like, to write and act great deeds,
Impatient to revenge his fatal shot,
  His right hand doubly to his left succeeds.   700

176

Thousands were there in darker fame that dwell,
  Whose deeds some nobler poem shall adorn,
And though to me unknown they, sure, fought well,
  Whom Rupert led and who were British born.

177

Of every size an hundred fighting sail,
  So vast the navy now at anchor rides
That underneath it the press'd waters fail,
  And with its weight it shoulders off the tides.

178

Now anchors weigh'd, the seamen shout so shrill
  That heav'n and earth and the wide ocean rings;   710
A breeze from westward waits their sails to fill
  And rests, in those high beds, his downy wings.

---

603 *Spragg.* Edward Spragge, vice-admiral of the Blue Squadron, knighted
  for bravery in June 1665.
605 *Harman.* Sir John Harman, rear admiral of the Blue, in June had
  snatched victory from grave danger. It is not certain that he was on
  this sailing.
607 *Hollis.* Sir Fretcheville Hollis or Holles, wild but gallant, lost an
  arm on June 7, 1665.

179

The wary Dutch this gathering storm foresaw
 And durst not bide it on the English coast;
Behind their treach'rous shallows they withdraw
 And there lay snares to catch the British host.

180

So the false spider, when her nets are spread,
 Deep ambush'd in her silent den does lie,
And feels, far off, the trembling of her thread,
 Whose filmy cord should bind the struggling fly; 720

181

Then, if at last, she find him fast beset,
 She issues forth and runs along her loom;
She joys to touch the captive in her net,
 And drags the little wretch in triumph home.

182

The Belgians hop'd that with disorder'd haste
 Our deep-cut keels upon the sands might run,
Or, if with caution leisurely were pass'd,
 Their numerous gross might charge us one by one.

183

But with a fore-wind pushing them above
 And swelling tide that heav'd them from below, 730
O'er the blind flats our warlike squadrons move,
 And with spread sails to welcome battle go.

184

It seem'd as there the British Neptune stood
 With all his host of waters at command,
Beneath them to submit th' officious flood,
 And with his trident shov'd them off the sand.[u]

[u] *Levat ipse Tridenti, et vastas aperit Syrtes, etc.* Virg. [*Aeneid* I, 145–46.]

---

[713]ff. Battle commenced July 25, 1665.

185

To the pale foes they suddenly draw near
   And summon them to unexpected fight;
They start like murderers when ghosts appear
   And draw their curtains in the dead of night.   740

Second Battle

186

Now van to van the foremost squadrons meet,
   The midmost battles hasting up behind,
Who view, far off, the storm of falling sleet
   And hear their thunder rattling in the wind.

187

At length the adverse admirals appear
   (The two bold champions of each country's
      right);
Their eyes describe the lists as they come near
   And draw the lines of death before they fight.

188

The distance judg'd for shot of every size,
   The linstocks touch, the pond'rous ball expires;   750
The vig'rous seaman every port-hole plies
   And adds his heart to every gun he fires.

189

Fierce was the fight on the proud Belgians' side
   For honour, which they seldom sought before,
But now they by their own vain boasts were ti'd
   And forc'd, at least in show, to prize it more.

190

But sharp remembrance on the English part
   And shame of being match'd by such a foe

---

740 *curtains.* Such as completely enclosed beds; echoing Shakespeare, 2
Henry IV I, i, 70–73.
747 *describe.* A Ciceronian expression meaning to arrange the whole plan of
battle.

Rouse conscious virtue up in every heart,
   And seeming to be stronger makes them so.[w]   760

191

Nor long the Belgians could that fleet sustain,
   Which did two gen'rals' fates and Caesar's bear.
Each several ship a victory did gain,
   As Rupert or as Albemarle were there.

192

Their batter'd admiral too soon withdrew,
   Unthank'd by ours for his unfinish'd fight,
But he the minds of his Dutch masters knew,
   Who call'd that Providence which we call'd flight.

193

Never did men more joyfully obey
   Or sooner understood the sign to fly;   770
With such alacrity they bore away
   As if to praise them all the states stood by.

194

O famous leader of the Belgian fleet,
   Thy monument inscrib'd such praise shall wear
As Varro, timely flying, once did meet,
   Because he did not of his Rome despair.

195

Behold that navy, which a while before
   Provok'd the tardy English to the fight,
Now draw their beaten vessels close to shore,
   As larks lie dar'd to shun the hobbies' flight.   780

---

[w] *Possunt quia posse videntur*. Virg. [*Aeneid* V, 231.]

---

762 *Caesar's*. Charles II's. In his Life of Caesar, Plutarch tells how Caesar's
encouragement—and declaration that they carried him and his fortune
—led the mariners to brave action and safety in a storm.

765 *Their batter'd admiral*. The skillful De Ruyter was not at fault, but
rather some cowardly Dutch officers and crews. Dryden handsomely
compares him to C. Terrentius Varro, who valiantly reorganized the
shattered Roman fleet after the battle of Cannae.

196

Whoe'er would English monuments survey
   In other records may our courage know,
But let them hide the story of this day,
   Whose fame was blemish'd by too base a foe.

197

Or if too busily they will inquire
   Into a victory which we disdain,
Then let them know the Belgians did retire
   Before the patron saint[x] of injur'd Spain.

198

Repenting England this revengeful day
   To Philip's manes[y] did an off'ring bring: 790
England, which first by leading them astray
   Hatch'd up rebellion to destroy her king.

199

Our fathers bent their baneful industry
   To check a monarchy that slowly grew,
But did not France or Holland's fate foresee,
   Whose rising pow'r to swift dominion flew.

200

In fortune's empire blindly thus we go
   And wander after pathless destiny,
Whose dark resorts since prudence cannot know
   In vain it would provide for what shall be.   800

201

But whate'er English to the bless'd shall go
   And the fourth Harry or first Orange meet,

---

[x] *patron saint: St. James, on whose day this victory was gain'd.*
[y] *Philip's manes. Philip the second, of Spain, against whom the Hol-
landers rebelling, were aided by Queen Elizabeth.*

---

802 *the fourth Harry,* etc. Paraphrase: Whatever Englishman has gone to
heaven and met Henri IV or William the Silent would find Henri disowning the French under Louis XIV as a foe to England and William
detesting Dutch naval power directed against his benefactor, England.

Find him disowning of a Bourbon foe,
 And him detesting a Batavian fleet.

202

Now on their coasts our conquering navy rides,
 Waylays their merchants and their land besets;
Each day new wealth without their care provides;
 They lie asleep with prizes in their nets.

203

So, close behind some promontory lie
 The huge leviathans t' attend their prey,   810
And give no chase, but swallow in the fry,
 Which through their gaping jaws mistake the way.

Burning of the Fleet in the Vlie
by Sir Robert Holmes

204

Nor was this all: in ports and roads remote
 Destructive fires among whole fleets we send;
Triumphant flames upon the water float,
 And out-bound ships at home their voyage end.

205

Those various squadrons, variously design'd,
 Each vessel freighted with a several load,
Each squadron waiting for a several wind,
 All find but one, to burn them in the road.   820

206

Some bound for Guinea, golden sand to find,
 Bore all the gauds the simple natives wear;
Some for the pride of Turkish courts design'd,
 For folded turbans finest Holland bear.

813ff. After the battle of July 25, 1665, the English preyed on the Dutch coast and destroyed a Dutch squadron off Vlie Island. The Dutch later returned the compliment by sailing up the Thames.

207

Some English wool, vex'd in a Belgian loom
   And into cloth of spongy softness made,
Did into France or colder Denmark doom,
   To ruin with worse ware our staple trade.

208

Our greedy seamen rummage every hold,
   Smile on the booty of each wealthier chest   830
And, as the priests who with their gods make bold,
   Take what they like and sacrifice the rest.

Transitum to the Fire of London

209

But ah! how unsincere are all our joys!
   Which, sent from Heav'n, like lightning make no
      stay;
Their palling taste the journey's length destroys,
   Or grief, sent post, o'ertakes them on the way.

210

Swell'd with our late successes on the foe,
   Which France and Holland wanted power to
      cross,
We urge an unseen fate to lay us low
   And feed their envious eyes with English loss.   840

211

Each element his dread command obeys,
   Who makes or ruins with a smile or frown,
Who as by one he did our nation raise,
   So now he with another pulls us down.

212

Yet, London, empress of the northern clime,
   By an high fate thou greatly didst expire,

---

825 *English wool.* Esteemed the finest, it was eagerly sought and often
   smuggled out of England.
841 *his.* Antecedent, *fate,* 839.

Great as the world's, which at the death of time
    Must fall and rise a nobler frame by fire.[z]

213

As when some dire usurper Heav'n provides
    To scourge his country with a lawless sway,   850
His birth, perhaps, some petty village hides
    And sets his cradle out of fortune's way;

214

Till fully ripe his swelling fate breaks out
    And hurries him to mighty mischiefs on;
His prince, surpris'd at first, no ill could doubt,
    And wants the pow'r to meet it when 'tis known:

215

Such was the rise of this prodigious fire,
    Which in mean buildings first obscurely bred,
From thence did soon to open streets aspire
    And straight to palaces and temples spread.   860

216

The diligence of trades and noiseful gain,
    And luxury, more late, asleep were laid;
All was the Night's, and in her silent reign
    No sound the rest of nature did invade.

217

In this deep quiet, from what source unknown,
    Those seeds of fire their fatal birth disclose;
And first, few scatt'ring sparks about were blown,
    Big with the flames that to our ruin rose.

---

[z] *Quum mare quum tellus correptaque regia Coeli, ardeat, etc.* Ovid.
[*Metamorphoses* I, 256 ff.]

849-53 Glancing at Cromwell, born as it were in a petty village.
857 *this prodigious fire.* The Great Fire of London began about 2 A.M.,
Sunday, September 2, 1666, in the shop of the king's baker. It burned
for four days destroying, especially on its terrible third day, over half
of the City of London.
863 *All was the Night's.* Echoing Seneca, *Controversiae* VII, 1 (16), 27.
866 *seeds.* From Latin, *semina,* favored especially by Lucretius in account-
ing for generation of many kinds of life and things.

218

Then in some close-pent room it crept along
 And, smould'ring as it went, in silence fed,   870
Till th' infant monster, with devouring strong,
 Walk'd boldly upright with exalted head.

219

Now like some rich or mighty murderer,
 Too great for prison, which he breaks with gold,
Who fresher for new mischiefs does appear
 And dares the world to tax him with the old:

220

So scapes th' insulting fire his narrow jail
 And makes small outlets into open air;
There the fierce winds his tender force assail·
 And beat him downward to his first repair.   880

221

The winds, like crafty courtesans, withheld
 His flames from burning but to blow them more,[a]
And every fresh attempt he is repell'd
 With faint denials, weaker than before.

222

And now, no longer letted of his prey,
 He leaps up at it with enrag'd desire,
O'er-looks the neighbours with a wide survey,
 And nods at every house his threat'ning fire.

223

The ghosts of traitors from the Bridge descend
 With bold fanatic spectres to rejoice;   890

[a] *like crafty, etc. Haec arte tractabat cupidum virum, ut illius animum inopia accenderet.* [Terence, *Heautontimorumenos* 366–67.]

---

889 The stanza was extravagantly admired by Dr. Johnson and Sir Walter Scott. Dryden alludes to Fifth Monarchy men executed in 1661 and other rebels executed in 1662, whose heads had been impaled above Southwark gate tower on London Bridge. The specters rejoiced that the bridge was partially burned.

About the fire into a dance they bend
   And sing their Sabbath notes with feeble voice.

224

Our Guardian Angel saw them where he sat
   Above the palace of our slumb'ring King,
He sigh'd, abandoning his charge to fate,
   And, drooping, oft look'd back upon the wing.

225

At length the crackling noise and dreadful blaze
   Call'd up some waking lover to the sight,
And long it was ere he the rest could raise,
   Whose heavy eyelids yet were full of night.   900

226

The next to danger, hot pursu'd by fate,
   Half cloth'd, half naked, hastily retire;
And frighted mothers strike their breasts, too late,
   For helpless infants left amidst the fire.

227

Their cries soon waken all the dwellers near;
   Now murmuring noises rise in every street;
The more remote run stumbling with their fear
   And in the dark men justle as they meet.

228

So weary bees in little cells repose;
   But if night-robbers lift the well-stor'd hive,
     910
An humming through their waxen city grows,
   And out upon each other's wings they drive.

229

Now streets grow throng'd and busy as by day;
   Some run for buckets to the hallow'd choir,
Some cut the pipes, and some the engines play,
   And some more bold mount ladders to the fire.

[914] Fire buckets were kept in churches.

230

In vain: for from the east a Belgian wind
    His hostile breath through the dry rafters sent;
The flames impell'd soon left their foes behind
    And forward with a wanton fury went.   920

231

A quay of fire ran all along the shore
    And lighten'd all the river with the blaze;[b]
The waken'd tides began again to roar,
    And wond'ring fish in shining waters gaze.

232

Old Father Thames rais'd up his reverend head
    But fear'd the fate of Simois would return;
Deep in his ooze he sought his sedgy bed
    And shrunk his waters back into his urn.

233

The fire meantime walks in a broader gross;
    To either hand his wings he opens wide;   930
He wades the streets, and straight he reaches cross
    And plays his longing flames on th' other side.

234

At first they warm, then scorch, and then they take;
    Now with long necks from side to side they feed;
At length, grown strong, their mother fire forsake
    And a new colony of flames succeed.

235

To every nobler portion of the town
    The curling billows roll their restless tide;
In parties now they straggle up and down,
    As armies, unoppos'd, for prey divide.   940

[b] *Sigaea igni freta lata relucent.* Virg. [*Aeneid* II, 312.]

---

917 *a Belgian wind.* A strong northeast wind drove the fire.
925 The Xanthus was aided by its tributary, Simois, to drown Achilles,
    and for this they were attacked by Hephaestus in flames (*Iliad* XXI,
    305 ff.).

236

One mighty squadron, with a side-wind sped,
   Through narrow lanes his cumber'd fire does
      haste,
By pow'rful charms of gold and silver led,
   The Lombard Bankers and the Change to waste.

237

Another backward to the Tow'r would go
   And slowly eats his way against the wind,
But the main body of the marching foe
   Against th' imperial palace is design'd.

238

Now day appears, and with the day the King,
   Whose early care had robb'd him of his rest;   950
Far off the cracks of falling houses ring,
   And shrieks of subjects pierce his tender breast.

239

Near as he draws, thick harbingers of smoke
   With gloomy pillars cover all the place,
Whose little intervals of night are broke
   By sparks that drive against his sacred face.

240

More than his guards his sorrows made him known,
   And pious tears which down his cheeks did
      show'r;
The wretched in his grief forgot their own
   (So much the pity of a king has pow'r).   960

241

He wept the flames of what he lov'd so well
   And what so well had merited his love.

---

944 That is, the property of the bankers of Lombard Street and the nearby
Royal Exchange.
949 ff. The king and his brother James never showed to better advantage
together than during the crisis of the fire.
953 *smoke.* One account said the smoke trailed for fifty miles.

For never prince in grace did more excel,
   Or royal city more in duty strove.

242

Nor with an idle care did he behold
   (Subjects may grieve, but monarchs must
     redress):
He chears the fearful, and commends the bold,
   And makes despairers hope for good success.

243

Himself directs what first is to be done
   And orders all the succours which they bring.   970
The helpful and the good about him run
   And form an army worthy such a king.

244

He sees the dire contagion spread so fast
   That where it seizes all relief is vain,
And therefore must unwillingly lay waste
   That country which would else the foe maintain.

245

The powder blows up all before the fire;
   Th' amazed flames stand gather'd on a heap,
And from the precipice's brink retire,
   Afraid to venture on so large a leap.   980

246

Thus fighting fires awhile themselves consume,
   But straight, like Turks, forc'd on to win or die,
They first lay tender bridges of their fume
   And o'er the breach in unctuous vapours fly.

247

Part stays for passage till a gust of wind
   Ships o'er their forces in a shining sheet;
Part, creeping under ground, their journey blind
   And, climbing from below, their fellows meet.

[982] *Turks.* Who slaughtered any retreating infantrymen with rear cavalry.

248

Thus, to some desert plain or old wood-side,
    Dire night-hags come from far to dance their
        round,   990
And o'er broad rivers on their fiends they ride
    Or sweep in clouds above the blasted ground.

249

No help avails: for, Hydra-like, the fire
    Lifts up his hundred heads to aim his way.
And scarce the wealthy can one half retire
    Before he rushes in to share the prey.

250

The rich grow suppliant, and the poor grow proud;
    Those offer mighty gain, and these ask more.
So void of pity is th' ignoble crowd,
    When others' ruin may increase their store.   1000

251

As those who live by shores with joy behold
    Some wealthy vessel split or stranded nigh,
And from the rocks leap down for shipwreck'd gold
    And seek the tempest which the others fly:

252

So these but wait the owners' last despair,
    And what's permitted to the flames invade;
Ev'n from their jaws they hungry morsels tear
    And on their backs the spoils of Vulcan lade.

253

The days were all in this lost labour spent,
    And when the weary King gave place to night,   1010
His beams he to his royal brother lent
    And so shone still in his reflective light.

1008 *Vulcan.* Roman god of the forge (Greek, Hephaestus); hence, fire.

254

Night came, but without darkness or repose,
   A dismal picture of the gen'ral doom,
Where souls distracted when the trumpet blows
   And half unready with their bodies come.

255

Those who have homes, when home they do repair
   To a last lodging call their wand'ring friends.
Their short uneasy sleeps are broke with care
   To look how near their own destruction tends.   1020

256

Those who have none sit round where once it was
   And with full eyes each wonted room require,
Haunting the yet warm ashes of the place,
   As murder'd men walk where they did expire.

257

Some stir up coals and watch the Vestal fire;
   Others in vain from sight of ruin run,
And, while through burning lab'rinths they retire,
   With loathing eyes repeat what they would shun.

258

The most in fields like herded beasts lie down,
   To dews obnoxious on the grassy floor,   1030
And while their babes in sleep their sorrows drown,
   Sad parents watch the remnants of their store.

259

While by the motion of the flames they guess
   What streets are burning now, and what are near,
An infant, waking, to the paps would press,
   And meets, instead of milk, a falling tear.

1013ff. Recalling the Ovidian *Dies irae* (stanza 212) in a passage on the
Judgment Day, a favorite kind of subject for Dryden.

260

No thought can ease them but their Sovereign's care,
  Whose praise th' afflicted as their comfort sing;
Ev'n those whom want might drive to just despair
  Think life a blessing under such a king.   1040

261

Meantime he sadly suffers in their grief,
  Out-weeps an hermit, and out-prays a saint;
All the long night he studies their relief,
  How they may be suppli'd, and he may want.

King's Prayer

262

"O God," said he, "Thou patron of my days,
  Guide of my youth in exile and distress!
Who me, unfriended, brought'st by wondrous ways
  The kingdom of my fathers to possess;

263

Be Thou my judge, with what unwearied care
  I since have labour'd for my people's good,   1050
To bind the bruises of a civil war
  And stop the issues of their wasting blood.

264

Thou, who hast taught me to forgive the ill
  And recompense, as friends, the good misled,
If mercy be a precept of Thy will,
  Return that mercy on Thy servant's head.

265

Or if my heedless youth has stept astray,
  Too soon forgetful of Thy gracious hand,
On me alone Thy just displeasure lay,
  But take Thy judgments from this mourning land.   1060

1053ff. See *Astraea Redux* 258 ff.

266

We all have sinn'd, and Thou hast laid us low
    As humble earth from whence at first we came:
Like flying shades before the clouds we show
    And shrink like parchment in consuming flame.

267

O let it be enough what Thou hast done
    When spotted deaths ran arm'd through every
       street
With poison'd darts, which not the good could shun,
    The speedy could out-fly, or valiant meet.

268

The living few, and frequent funerals then,
    Proclaim'd Thy wrath on this forsaken place,   1070
And now those few who are return'd again
    Thy searching judgments to their dwellings trace.

269

O pass not, Lord, an absolute decree
    Or bind Thy sentence unconditional,
But in Thy sentence our remorse foresee,
    And, in that foresight, this Thy doom recall.

270

Thy threatenings, Lord, as Thine, Thou may'st
    revoke;
    But, if immutable and fix'd they stand,
Continue still Thyself to give the stroke
    And let not foreign foes oppress thy land."   1080

271

Th' Eternal heard and from the heav'nly choir
    Chose out the cherub with the flaming sword,

1066 *spotted deaths.* From the plague of 1665.
1045-80 Dryden recalls the famous "King's Prayer" of *Eikon Basilike*, the
Royalist propaganda triumph for Charles I. The passage also parallels
in the fire section the repairing of the fleet (565 ff.) in the naval
section.

And bade him swiftly drive th' approaching fire
   From where our naval magazines were stor'd.

272

The blessed minister his wings display'd,
   And like a shooting star he cleft the night;
He charg'd the flames, and those that disobey'd
   He lash'd to duty with his sword of light.

273

The fugitive flames, chastis'd, went forth to prey
   On pious structures by our fathers rear'd,   1090
By which to heav'n they did effect the way,
   Ere faith in Churchmen without works was heard.

274

The wanting orphans saw with wat'ry eyes
   Their founders' charity in dust laid low
And sent to God their ever-answer'd cries
   (For He protects the poor who made them so).

275

Nor could thy fabric, Paul's, defend thee long,
   Though thou wert sacred to thy Maker's praise,
Though made immortal by a poet's song,
   And poets' songs the Theban walls could raise.   1100

276

The daring flames peep'd in and saw from far
   The awful beauties of the sacred choir,
But since it was prophan'd by civil war,
   Heav'n thought it fit to have it purg'd by fire.

[1084] *our naval magazines.* It was thought a miracle that the fire had stopped
short at the Tower and its crucial naval stores.
[1097] *Paul's.* St. Paul's Cathedral, burned the terrible third day.
[1099] *a poet's song.* Edmund Waller, *Upon His Majesty's Repairing of
Paul's* (ca. 1635).
[1100] *Theban walls.* Magically raised by Amphion's lyre.
[1103] *prophan'd by civil war.* Much of the cathedral was rented for secular
uses during the Commonwealth.

277

Now down the narrow streets it swiftly came
    And, widely opening, did on both sides prey.
This benefit we sadly owe the flame,
    If only ruin must enlarge our way.

278

And now four days the sun had seen our woes,
    Four nights the moon beheld th' incessant fire;   1110
It seem'd as if the stars more sickly rose
    And farther from the fev'rish north retire.

279

In th' empyrean Heaven (the bless'd abode),
    The thrones and the dominions prostrate lie,
Not daring to behold their angry God;
    And an hush'd silence damps the tuneful sky.

280

At length th' Almighty cast a pitying eye,
    And mercy softly touch'd His melting breast;
He saw the town's one half in rubbish lie
    And eager flames give on to storm the rest.   1120

281

An hollow chrystal pyramid he takes,
    In firmamental waters dipp'd above;
Of it a broad extinguisher he makes
    And hoods the flames that to their quarry strove.

282

The vanquish'd fires withdraw from every place
    Or, full with feeding, sink into a sleep;
Each household genius shows again his face
    And, from the hearths, the little lares creep.

283

Our King this more than natural change beholds;
    With sober joy his heart and eyes abound;   1130

To the All-good his lifted hands he folds
   And thanks Him low on his redeemed ground.

284

As when sharp frosts had long constrain'd the earth,
   A kindly thaw unlocks it with mild rain,
And first the tender blade peeps up to birth,
   And straight the green fields laugh with promis'd
      grain:

285

By such degrees the spreading gladness grew
   In every heart, which fear had froze before;
The standing streets with so much joy they view
   That with less grief the perish'd they deplore.   1140

286

The father of the people open'd wide
   His stores and all the poor with plenty fed:
Thus God's annointed God's own place suppli'd
   And fill'd the empty with his daily bread.

287

This royal bounty brought its own reward
   And in their minds so deep did print the sense,
That if their ruins sadly they regard,
   'Tis but with fear the sight might drive him
      thence.

City's Request to the King Not to Leave Them

288

But so may he live long, that town to sway
   Which by his auspice they will nobler make,   1150
As he will hatch their ashes by his stay
   And not their humble ruins now forsake.

289

They have not lost their loyalty by fire,
   Nor is their courage or their wealth so low

That from his wars they poorly would retire
    Or beg the pity of a vanquish'd foe.

                        290
Not with more constancy the Jews of old,
    By Cyrus from rewarded exile sent,
Their royal city did in dust behold,
    Or with more vigour to rebuild it went.   1160

                        291
The utmost malice of their stars is past,
    And two dire comets which have scourg'd the
        town
In their own plague and fire have breath'd their last,
    Or dimly in their sinking sockets frown.

                        292
Now frequent trines the happier lights among,
    And high-rais'd Jove from his dark prison freed
(Those weights took off that on his planet hung),
    Will gloriously the new-laid work succeed.

                        293
Methinks already, from this chemic flame,
    I see a city of more precious mold: 1170
Rich as the town which gives the Indies^c name,
    With silver pav'd and all divine with gold.

                        294
Already, labouring with a mighty fate,
    She shakes the rubbish from her mounting brow,
And seems to have renew'd her charter's date,
    Which Heav'n will to the death of time allow.

---

^c *Mexico.*

1157–58 Ezra I–III.
1165 *trines.* See the Glossary; the Killigrew Ode 41–43; *Britannia Rediviva*
33.
1166 *Jove.* The planet Jupiter.
1160–72 The alchemical fire process renders a baser London into a more
    golden London.

295

More great than human now, and more August,[d]
   New deifi'd she from her fires does rise,
Her widening streets on new foundations trust,
   And opening into larger parts she flies.   1180

296

Before, she like some shepherdess did show,
   Who sat to bathe her by a river's side,
Not answering to her fame, but rude and low,
   Nor taught the beauteous arts of modern pride.

297

Now, like a maiden queen, she will behold
   From her high turrets, hourly suitors come;
The East with incense and the West with gold
   Will stand like suppliants to receive her doom.

298

The silver Thames, her own domestic flood,
   Shall bear her vessels like a sweeping train,   1190
And often wind (as of his mistress proud)
   With longing eyes to meet her face again.

299

The wealthy Tagus and the wealthier Rhine
   The glory of their towns no more shall boast;
And Seine, that would with Belgian rivers join,
   Shall find her lustre stain'd and traffic lost.

300

The vent'rous merchant, who design'd more far
   And touches on our hospitable shore,
Charm'd with the splendour of this Northern Star,
   Shall here unlade him and depart no more.   1200

[d] *Augusta, the old name of London.* [The name meant "city of Augustus" and is certainly as old as the fourth century A.D. and perhaps older.]

1191 *often wind.* The passage well describes the unexpected twists of the Thames in the London area.
1193 *Tagus.* A Spanish river said to have golden sands.
1195 *Seine.* That is, Louis XIV.

301

Our pow'rful navy shall no longer meet,
    The wealth of France or Holland to invade;
The beauty of this town, without a fleet,
    From all the world shall vindicate her trade.

302

And while this fam'd emporium we prepare,
    The British ocean shall such triumphs boast
That those who now disdain our trade to share
    Shall rob like pirates on our wealthy coast.

303

Already we have conquer'd half the war,
    And the less dang'rous part is left behind;   1210
Our trouble now is but to make them dare
    And not so great to vanquish as to find.

304

Thus to the eastern wealth through storms we go,
    But now, the Cape once doubled, fear no more;
A constant trade-wind will securely blow
    And gently lay us on the spicy shore.

1201-4 Dryden's pacifism is made clear.
1209 Echoing Virgil, *Eclogues* IX, 59.

A Song

FROM

TYRRANIC LOVE

1669. *Tyrannic Love* is a heroic tragedy about the mad passion of the Roman tyrant Maximin for the resolute St. Catharine and about his attempts upon her chastity and religion. At the beginning of Act IV, the tribune and conjurer, Nigrinius, invokes two spirits, "mild Nakar" and his beloved, "soft Damilcar," who are of a middle kind, "Not in their natures simply good or ill." The situation and the song (twice set to music) give an example of what Dryden later called "that fairy kind of writing" that he passed on from the Elizabethans to Pope for *The Rape of the Lock*.

Song

  Nakar *and* Damilcar *descend in clouds, and sing.*

Nakar	Hark, my Damilcar, we are call'd below!
Dam.	Let us go, let us go!
	Go to relieve the care
	Of longing lovers in despair!
Nakar	Merry, merry, merry, we sail from the east
	Half tippled at a rainbow feast.
Dam.	In the bright moonshine while winds whistle loud,
	Tivy, tivy, tivy, we mount and we fly,
	All racking along in a downy white cloud;
	And lest our leap from the sky should prove too far,
	We slide on the back of a new-falling star.

10

Nakar   And drop from above,
        In a jelly of love!
Dam.   But now the sun's down, and the element's
            red,
        The spirits of fire against us make head!
Nakar   They muster, they muster, like gnats in the
            air;
        Alas! I must leave thee, my fair,
        And to my light horsemen repair.
Dam.   O stay, for you need not to fear 'em tonight;
        The wind is for us and blows full in their
            sight;   20
        And o'er the wide ocean we fight!
        Like leaves in the autumn our foes will fall
            down,
        And hiss in the water—
Both   And hiss in the water and drown!
Nakar   But their men lie securely entrench'd in a
            cloud,
        And a trumpeter-hornet to battle sounds loud.
Dam.   Now mortals that spy
        How we tilt in the sky
        With wonder will gaze
        And fear such events as will ne'er come to
            pass!   30
Nakar   Stay you to perform what the man will have
            done.
Dam.   Then call me again when the battle is won.
Both   So ready and quick is a spirit of air
        To pity the lover and succour the fair,
        That, silent and swift, the little soft god
        Is here with a wish and is gone with a nod.

        The clouds part, Nakar *flies up, and* Damilcar
            down.

---

¹³ *jelly.* The alga, nostoc, appears as a jellylike mass on dry soil after a
rain and was long thought to be the remains of a fallen star.
²²⁻³⁰ Probably Dryden's first echo of Milton—*Paradise Lost* I, 301–15.

Epilogue

FROM

TYRANNIC LOVE

1669. *Tyrannic Love* ends in a welter of deaths, including that of Maximin's daughter, Valeria, who, distraught with love, dies by her own hand. As Dryden shows in *Mac-Flecknoe* (l. 78) and in this best known of his epilogues, he found a certain amusement in the heroic posturing of some of his huffing heroes. He here had Eleanor (Ellen, Nell, Nelly) Gwynn (1650–1687), the irrepressible "Protestant" mistress of Charles II since 1668, rise up to deliver comment, on this strange resurrection at Eastertime, on her seductive powers, and on the "dull poet" who could show *her* dying for love. Her magnetism is clearly evident in the Epilogue, just as it also is in Charles' withdrawing her from the stage for a time after this play and in his deathbed request to James, "Let not poor Nelly starve." She was paid a good pension.

Spoken by Mrs. Ellen, *when she was to be carried off dead by the bearers.*[1]

To the Bearer	Hold; are you mad? you damn'd confounded dog!
	I am to rise and speak the Epilogue.
To the Audience	I come, kind gentlemen, strange news to tell ye:
	I am the ghost of poor departed Nelly.

[1] *bearers.* Dead bodies had to be borne off the apron stage in full view of the audience.

Sweet ladies, be not frighted; I'll be
        civil;
I'm what I was, a little harmless
        devil.
For after death, we sprites have
        just such natures
We had for all the world when
        human creatures;
And therefore I that was an actress
        here
Play all my tricks in Hell, a goblin
        there.   10
Gallants, look to't, you say there are
        no sprites,
But I'll come dance about your beds
        at nights.
And, faith, you'll be in a sweet kind
        of taking,
When I surprise you between sleep
        and waking.
To tell you true, I walk because I
        die
Out of my calling in a tragedy.
O poet, damn'd dull poet, who
        could prove
So senseless! to make Nelly die for
        love;
Nay, what's yet worse, to kill me
        in the prime
Of Easter-Term, in tart and cheese-
        cake time!   20
I'll fit the fop, for I'll not one word
        say
T'excuse his godly out-of-fashion
        play,
A play which if you dare but twice
        sit out,
You'll all be slander'd and be
        thought devout.

But farewell, gentlemen, make
    haste to me;
I'm sure ere long to have your
    company.
As for my Epitaph when I am gone,
I'll trust no poet but will write my
    own.

Here Nelly *lies, who, though she
    liv'd a slattern,*   30
*Yet di'd a princess acting in St.
    Cathar'ne.*

Songs

FROM

AN EVENING'S LOVE

1668. Published in 1671, the play is one with a "Spanish plot" from Calderón. It features two of the so-called "gay couples" common in Restoration comedy—a pair of young Englishmen who woo a pair of Spanish sisters, each of the four fearing commitment almost as much as estrangement. The First Song is one that Wildblood hopes, in reference to Jacintha and himself, will "encourage one another to a breach by the dangers of possession." The Second Song (Act II) is, according to Wildblood, "a song *al' Angloise*" to serenade the two sisters. The Third Song (Act IV) is sung by Beatrix, the "woman" of the sisters, at the request of Jacintha, "to draw [Wildblood] nearer." The Fourth Song (Act IV) is sung by Wildblood, who "never sung in all my life," and Jacintha, "Upon condition the best singer shall wear the breeches" after marriage. It is much the best of the four and captures the devil-may-care gayety of Dryden's early comedy.

I
Song

You charm'd me not with that fair face,
   Though it was all divine;
To be another's is the grace
   That makes me wish you mine.

2

The gods and Fortune take their part
   Who like young monarchs fight,
And boldly dare invade that heart
   Which is another's right.

3

First mad with hope we undertake
   To pull up every bar,   10
But once possess'd, we faintly make
   A dull defensive war.

4

Now every friend is turn'd a foe
   In hope to get our store,
And passion makes us cowards grow,
   Which made us brave before.

II
Song

After the pangs of a desperate lover,
When day and night I have sigh'd all in vain,
Ah, what a pleasure it is to discover
In her eyes pity, who causes my pain!

2

When with unkindness our love at a stand is,
And both have punish'd ourselves with the pain,
Ah, what a pleasure the touch of her hand is,
Ah, what a pleasure to press it again!

3

When the denial comes fainter and fainter,
And her eyes give what her tongue does deny,   10
Ah, what a trembling I feel when I venture,
Ah, what a trembling does usher my joy!

4

When, with a sigh, she accords me the blessing,
And her eyes twinkle 'twixt pleasure and pain;
Ah, what a joy 'tis beyond all expressing,
Ah, what a joy to hear, "Shall we again?"

III
Song

Calm was the even, and clear was the sky,
   And the new budding flowers did spring,
When all alone went Amyntas and I
   To hear the sweet nightingale sing;
I sat, and he laid him down by me,
   But scarcely his breath he could draw,
For when with a fear he began to draw near,
   He was dash'd with, "A ha ha ha ha!"

2

He blush'd to himself and lay still for a while,
   And his modesty curb'd his desire,   10
But straight I convinc'd all his fear with a smile,
   Which added new flames to his fire.
"O Sylvia," said he, "you are cruel
   To keep your poor lover in awe";
Then once more he press'd with his hand to my
     breast,
   But was dash'd with "A ha ha ha ha!"

3

I knew 'twas his passion that caus'd all his fear,
   And therefore I piti'd his case;
I whisper'd him softly, "There's nobody near,"
   And laid my cheek close to his face;   20
But as he grew bolder and bolder,
   A shepherd came by us and saw,

And just as our bliss we began with a kiss,
　　He laugh'd out with, "A ha ha ha ha!"

IV
Song

Damon　　Celimena of my heart,
　　　　　　None shall ere bereave you;
　　　　　　If, with your good leave, I may
　　　　　　Quarrel with you once a day,
　　　　　　I will never leave you.

2

Celimena　Passion's but an empty name
　　　　　　Where respect is wanting;
　　　　　　Damon, you mistake your aim:
　　　　　　Hang your heart and burn your flame,
　　　　　　If you must be ranting.　　　　　　　10

3

Damon　　Love as dull and muddy is
　　　　　　As decaying liquor;
　　　　　　Anger sets it on the lees
　　　　　　And refines it by degrees,
　　　　　　Till it works it quicker.

4

Celimena　Love by quarrels to beget
　　　　　　Wisely you endeavour,
　　　　　　With a grave physician's wit
　　　　　　Who to cure an ague fit
　　　　　　Put me in a fever.　　　　　　　　20

5

Damon　　Anger rouses love to fight
　　　　　　And his only bait is;
　　　　　　'Tis the spur to dull delight

And is but an eager bite,
When desire at height is.

6

Celimena   If such drops of heat can fall
In our wooing weather,
If such drops of heat can fall,
We shall have the devil and all
When we come together.   30

Prologue

AURENG-ZEBE

1675. After a decade or more of writing serious plays mostly in rhyme, after justifying rhymed verse for serious plays in *An Essay of Dramatic Poesy*, and after writing *Aureng-Zebe*, his finest rhymed play, Dryden turned away from rhyme with "another taste of wit." The taste of the time was also changing, but he reveals here an indifference bordering on contempt for his audience and their tastes in the light of both his own sense of art and the great achievements of Shakespeare.

Our author by experience finds it true
'Tis much more hard to please himself than you,
And out of no feign'd modesty this day
Damns his laborious trifle of a play:
Not that it's worse than what before he writ,
But he has now another taste of wit,
And, to confess a truth (though out of time),
Grows weary of his long-lov'd mistress, rhyme.
Passion's too fierce to be in fetters bound,
And Nature flies him like enchanted ground.   10
What verse can do he has perform'd in this,
Which he presumes the most correct of his,
But spite of all his pride a secret shame
Invades his breast at Shakespeare's sacred name:
Aw'd when he hears his godlike Romans rage,
He, in a just despair, would quit the stage
And to an age less polish'd, more unskill'd,

Does with disdain the foremost honours yield.
As with the greater dead he dares not strive,
He wou'd not match his verse with those who live: 20
Let him retire, betwixt two ages cast,
The first of this and hindmost of the last.
A losing gamester, let him sneak away;
He bears no ready money from the play.
The fate which governs poets thought it fit
He shou'd not raise his fortunes by his wit.
The clergy thrive, and the litigious bar;
Dull heroes fatten with the spoils of war;
All southern vices, Heav'n be prais'd, are here,
But wit's a luxury you think too dear.   30
When you to cultivate the plant are loath,
'Tis a shrewd sign 'twas never of your growth,
And wit in northern climates will not blow
Except, like orange trees, 'tis hous'd from snow.
There needs no care to put a playhouse down:
'Tis the most desert place of all the town.
We and our neighbours, to speak proudly, are
Like monarchs, ruin'd with expensive war.
While, like wise English, unconcern'd you sit
And see us play the tragedy of wit.   40

24 *play*. Gaming; also perhaps this play, drama.
37 *neighbours*. The other theater, at Dorset Garden.
38 *expensive war*. Such as that then underway between Louis XIV and the
   Prince of Orange. Dryden praises the peace policy of Charles II (39).

MACFLECKNOE

1678? This satire of dull writers, especially of playwrights, was published unauthorized in 1682 and authorized, although without its author's name, in 1684. Parts of it had, however, been set down by John Oldham in 1678, and since approximately 1680 there were echoes of it in contemporary writings. The exact date of completion of the poem in its present form is not certainly known, but 1678 is the most likely year. Recently it has been shown that in all probability Elkanah Settle (1648–1724) rather than Thomas Shadwell (?1642–1692) was first designed to be Prince of Dullness. However, it is true that in March of that year Dryden had written a prologue for Shadwell's play, *A True Widow*, and relations between the two men had included certain differences of opinion, particularly on the best forms of contemporary drama.

But it is not known for certain what particular cause led Dryden to the devastating but enormously humorous characterization of a dramatist of considerable ability—there were many worse about than Shadwell and even Settle. However, it is evident that the satire is directed at a character at once mindless, artless, uncreative, and boring. The poem tightly weaves allusions to plays, playwrights, and numerous works both classical and modern (see, e.g., ll. 134–38n). Some of these are identified in the notes, but the main tenor of argument is that MacFlecknoe is associated with a dull line of playwrights from Dekker to Flecknoe and Shadwell, who wrote for the city; and that he is dissociated from a line of great dramatists running from Jonson to Etherege. The coronation situation parodies that of Charles II and introduces a largely metaphorical strain of politics. Another strain of religious detail serves primar-

ily to control judgment. The laughter, for all its deadliness,
is curiously affectionate.

MACFLECKNOE

All human things are subject to decay,
And when Fate summons, monarchs must obey:
This Flecknoe found who, like Augustus, young
Was call'd to Empire and had govern'd long
In prose and verse, was own'd without dispute
Through all the realms of Nonsense, absolute.
    This aged Prince now flourishing in peace
And blest with issue of a large increase,
Worn out with business, did at length debate
To settle the succession of the state,   10
And pond'ring which of all his sons was fit
To reign and wage immortal war with wit,
Cri'd, " 'Tis resolv'd; for Nature pleads that he
Should only rule who most resembles me;
Sh—— alone my perfect image bears,
Mature in dullness from his tender years.
Sh—— alone of all my sons is he
Who stands confirm'd in full stupidity.
The rest to some faint meaning make pretence,
But Sh—— never deviates into sense.   20
Some beams of wit on other souls may fall,
Strike through, and make a lucid interval,
But Sh——'s genuine night admits no ray;
His rising fogs prevail upon the day;
Besides his goodly fabric fills the eye
And seems design'd for thoughtless majesty,
Thoughtless as monarch oaks that shade the plain
And, spread in solemn state, supinely reign.
    "Heywood and Shirley were but types of thee,

[3] *Flecknoe.* The contemporary *type* (see 29) of a dull poet. On Richard
  Flecknoe, see *An Essay of Dramatic Poesy* note 3.
[27] *monarch oaks.* The oak, king of plants as the lion is king of beasts;
  the oak was also royal because one had sheltered Charles II after
  defeat at Worcester.
[29] *Heywood and Shirley.* Thomas Heywood (d. 1641) and James Shirley
  (d. 1666), dramatists. *Types* are either characteristic specimens, as

Thou last great prophet of tautology;   30
Even I, a dunce of more renown than they,
Was sent before but to prepare thy way
And, coarsely clad in Norwich drugget, came
To teach the nations in thy greater name.
My warbling lute, the lute I whilom strung
When to King John of Portugal I sung,
Was but the prelude to that glorious day
When thou on silver Thames did'st cut thy way
With well tim'd oars before the royal barge,
Swell'd with the pride of thy celestial charge,   40
And big with hymn, commander of an host,
The like was ne'er in Epsom blankets toss'd.

"Methinks I see the new Arion sail,
The lute still trembling underneath thy nail.
At thy well sharpen'd thumb, from shore to shore
The treble squeaks for fear, the basses roar;
Echoes from Pissing Alley, 'Sh——' call,
And 'Sh——' they resound from Aston Hall.
About thy boat the little fishes throng,
As at the morning toast that floats along.   50
Sometimes as prince of thy harmonious band
Thou wield'st thy papers in thy threshing hand.
St. Andre's feet ne'er kept more equal time,

Flecknoe and Shadwell of dull poets, or prophetic similitudes, as Heywood and Shirley of Flecknoe. Christ had several prophetic types before Him, as the following lines develop.

[30-32] His way prepared by John the Baptist (Matthew 3:3-4), Christ was
the last prophet. "Prophet, Priest, and King," Christ's three traditional roles are repeatedly parodied in Flecknoe and Shadwell, showing
them to be in a sense anti-Christs.

[33] *Norwich drugget*. A coarse cloth (see 214). Shadwell was from Norwich,
north of London (see also 170).

[36] Flecknoe boasted of the patronage of the king of Portugal.

[42] *in Epsom blankets toss'd*. Like Shadwell's Sir Samuel Hearty, the coarse
figure who sold the *bargains* (181) of *The Virtuoso;* also alluding to
Shadwell's *Epsom Wells.*

[43] *Arion*. A Greek musician, saved when song-loving dolphins carried him
ashore as he played his lyre.

[47] *Pissing Alley*. One with the name existed in the old City of London,
the scene of most of the poem, another near the Thames and this particular scene.

[48] *Aston Hall*. Unidentified.

[37-50] A tissue of echoes from Edmund Waller, *Of the Danger His Majesty*
(being Prince) Escaped in the Road at Saint Anderes. Both Flecknoe
and Shadwell took pride in their musical gifts.

[53] *St. Andre*. A French dancing master, choreographer of Shadwell's
Psyche.

Not ev'n the feet of thy own *Psyche's* rhyme,
Though they in number as in sense excel;
So just, so like tautology they fell
That, pale with envy, Singleton forswore ⎤
The lute and sword which he in triumph bore ⎬
And vow'd he ne'er would act Villerius more." ⎦
    Here stopp'd the good old sire and wept for joy   60
In silent raptures of the hopeful boy.
All arguments, but most his plays, persuade
That for anointed dullness he was made.

    Close to the walls which fair Augusta bind
(The fair Augusta much to fears inclin'd),
An ancient fabric rais'd t' inform the sight,
There stood of yore, and Barbican it hight:
A watchtower once, but now, so Fate ordains,
Of all the pile an empty name remains.
From its old ruins brothel-houses rise,   70
Scenes of lewd loves and of polluted joys,
Where their vast courts the mother-strumpets keep,
And, undisturb'd by watch, in silence sleep.
Near these a Nursery erects its head,
Where queens are form'd and future heroes bred,
Where unfledg'd actors learn to laugh and cry, ⎤
Where infant punks their tender voices try, ⎬
And little Maximins the gods defy. ⎦
    Great Fletcher never treads in buskins here,
Nor greater Jonson dares in socks appear.   80
But gentle Simkin just reception finds

57-59 *Singleton*, etc. John Singleton (d. 1686), a musician to the king and in the theater. *Villerius.* A character in Sir William Davenant's opera, *The Seige of Rhodes* (1656).
64-65 *Augusta*, etc. London; see *Annus Mirabilis* 1177. Her fears are those of extreme anti-Catholics.
67 *Barbican.* A tower, in a disreputable area of the same name, outside the wall on the northwest of the City of London.
72 ff. *Where their vast courts.* One of many parodies in the poem of Abraham Cowley's unfinished epic, *Davideis* (1657)—showing how everything good becomes debased when touched by Shadwell.
74 *Nursery.* Erected by Lady Davenant in 1671, it was one of several schools for training actors and actresses when the theaters opened after the Commonwealth.
78 *little Maximins. Maximus* means "greatest"; Dryden gibes at his own ranting tyrant in *Tyrannic Love.*
80 *socks.* The emblem of comedy (Latin, *soccus*).
81 *Simkin.* A traditional droll, admired by the character Timothy in Shadwell's play, *The Miser* (1672).

Amidst this monument of vanish'd minds;
Pure clenches the suburbian Muse affords,
And Panton waging harmless war with words.
Here Flecknoe, as a place to fame well known,
Ambitiously design'd his Sh——'s throne.
For ancient Dekker prophesi'd long since ⎫
That in this pile should reign a mighty prince, ⎬
Born for a scourge of wit and flail of sense, ⎭
To whom true dulness should some *Psyches* owe,   90
But worlds of *Misers* from his pen should flow;
Humorists and *Hypocrites* it should produce,
Whole Raymond families and tribes of Bruce.

   Now Empress Fame had publish'd the renown
Of Sh——'s coronation through the town.
Rous'd by report of Fame, the nations meet
From near Bun Hill and distant Watling Street.
No Persian carpets spread th' imperial way,
But scatter'd limbs of mangled poets lay;
From dusty shops neglected authors come,   100
Martyrs of pies and relics of the bum.
Much Heywood, Shirley, Ogilby there lay,
But loads of Sh—— almost chok'd the way.
Bilk'd stationers for yeomen stood prepar'd,
And Herringman was captain of the guard.

   The hoary Prince in majesty appear'd,
High on a throne of his own labours rear'd.
At his right hand our young Ascanius sat,
Rome's other hope and pillar of the state.
His brows thick fogs, instead of glories, grace,   110

---

[83] *suburbian*. London suburbs were thought disreputable.
[84] *Panton*. A punster? See *clinches* in the Glossary.
[87] *Dekker*. Thomas (d. 1632), dramatist and enemy of Ben Jonson.
[90-93] Mention of four of Shadwell's plays and also of characters from two of them, *The Humourists* (1671) and *The Virtuoso*.
[94] *Empress Fame*. In Virgil, *Aeneid* IV, 173 ff., Fame spreads word of Dido's fall.
[97] *Bun Hill*. Another "suburbian" area, northeast of the Barbican coronation scene. *Watling Street*, near St. Paul's, was actually closer but was more *distant* in true values.
[101] Odd papers were used for wrapping meat pies and for toilet paper.
[102] *Ogilby*. John Ogilby (d. 1676), enterprising printer, poet, and factotum, who, like Flecknoe, became a type of the bad poet.
[105] *Herringman*. Publisher of Shadwell—and of Dryden until a break in 1678.

And lambent dullness play'd around his face.
As Hannibal did to the altars come,
Sworn by his sire a mortal foe to Rome,
So Sh—— swore, nor should his vow be vain,
That he till death true dullness would maintain,
And in his father's right and realm's defence
Ne'er to have peace with wit nor truce with sense.

   The King himself the sacred unction made,
As king by office and as priest by trade;
In his sinister hand, instead of ball,   120
He plac'd a mighty mug of potent ale;
Love's Kingdom to his right he did convey,
At once his sceptre and his rule of sway,
Whose righteous lore the Prince had practis'd young,
And from whose loins recorded *Psyche* sprung.
His temples last with poppies were o'erspread,
That nodding seem'd to consecrate his head.
Just at that point of time, if Fame not lie,
On his left hand twelve reverend owls did fly:
So Romulus, 'tis sung, by Tiber's brook,   130
Presage of sway from twice six vultures took.
Th' admiring throng loud acclamations make
And omens of his future empire take.
The sire then shook the honours of his head
And from his brows damps of oblivion shed
Full on the filial dullness; long he stood,
Repelling from his breast the raging god;
At length burst out in this prophetic mood.
   "Heavens bless my son; from Ireland let him reign

[106-11] Mingling parodies of Milton's grand Satan and Virgil's young hero, Ascanius: *Paradise Lost* II, 1 ff.; *Aeneid* XII, 168 and II, 682–84. *his own labours*. Flecknoe's books, published at his own expense.

[112-13] For Hannibal's oath, see Livy, *History* XXI, i.

[118-19] See 30–32*n*.

[120] *sinister*. (a) Left; (b) of evil omen.

[122] *Love's Kingdom*. Flecknoe's play (1664); both words of the title are played on in the passage.

[125] *loins*. Appropriately pronounced "lines." *Psyche*. Shadwell's opera; the "soul" engendered by the *loins* of *Love's Kingdom*.

[126] *poppies*. (a) A soporific (Virgil, *Aeneid* IV, 486); (b) a sterilizing agent (Virgil, *Georgics* I, 78); (c) an aphrodisiac that does not fertilize (Sir Thomas Browne, *Vulgar Errors* VII, 7).

[130] *So Romulus*. According to Plutarch, Life of Romulus.

[134-38] Alluding to: Jupiter in *Aeneid* X, 113–15; the frenzied Sibyl, *Aeneid* VI, 46–51 and 77–82; Helenus' prophecy when possessed by the

To far Barbadoes on the western main;   140
Of his dominion may no end be known,
And greater than his father's be his throne.
Beyond *Love's Kingdom* let him stretch his pen";
He paus'd, and all the people cri'd, "Amen."
   "Then thus," continu'd he, "my son, advance
Still in new impudence, new ignorance.
Success let others teach, learn thou from me
Pangs without birth and fruitless industry.
Let *Virtuosos* in five years be writ,
Yet not one thought accuse thy toil of wit.   150
Let gentle George in triumph tread the stage,
Make Dorimant betray and Loveit rage;
Let Cully, Cockwood, Fopling, charm the pit
And in their folly shew the writer's wit.
Yet still thy fools shall stand in thy defence
And justify their author's want of sense.
Let 'em be all by thy own model made
Of dullness, and desire no foreign aid,
That they to future ages may be known
Not copies drawn, but issue of thy own.   160
Nay let thy men of wit too be the same,
All full of thee and differing but in name,
But let no alien Sedley interpose
To lard with wit thy hungry *Epsom* prose.
And when false flowers of rhetoric thou would'st cull,
Trust nature, do not labour to be dull,
But write thy best, and top, and in each line
Sir Formal's oratory will be thine.
Sir Formal, though unsought, attends thy quill

---

god, *Aeneid* III, 369 ff.; and God's beaming on the Son, *Paradise Lost*
VI. 719–22. Other allusions have been suggested.
139–40 *Ireland.* Regarded as savage and illiterate; between it and *Barbadoes*
lies empty sea.
144 *all the people cri'd, "Amen."* Nehemiah 8:6.
147–48 *Aeneid* XII, 435–46; Aeneas urging Ascanius to valor.
149 Some said Shadwell wrote hastily, others said slowly.
151 *gentle George.* George Etherege. Some of his highly successful characters
in his three plays are named.
158, 163–64 Sir Charles Sedley had, Shadwell said, revised his play, *A True
Widow* (1678).
168–69 Sir Formal speaks "flowers of rhetoric" in *The Virtuoso.*

And does thy northern dedications fill.   170
   "Nor let false friends seduce thy mind to fame
By arrogating Jonson's hostile name.
Let Father Flecknoe fire thy mind with praise
And Uncle Ogilby thy envy raise.
Thou art my blood, where Jonson has no part:
What share have we in nature or in art?
Where did his wit on learning fix a brand
And rail at arts he did not understand?
Where made he love in Prince Nicander's vein
Or swept the dust in *Psyche*'s humble strain?   180
Where sold he bargains, 'whip-stitch, kiss my arse,'
Promis'd a play and dwindled to a farce?
When did his Muse from Fletcher scenes purloin,
As thou whole Eth'rege dost transfuse to thine?
But so transfus'd as oil on waters flow;
His always floats above, thine sinks below.
   "This is thy province, this thy wondrous way
New humours to invent for each new play;
This is that boasted bias of thy mind,
By which one way, to dullness, 'tis inclin'd,   190
Which makes thy writings lean on one side still
And in all changes that way bends thy will.
   "Nor let thy mountain belly make pretence
Of likeness; thine's a tympany of sense.
A tun of man in thy large bulk is writ,
But sure thou 'rt but a kilderkin of wit.
Like mine thy gentle numbers feebly creep,
Thy tragic Muse gives smiles, thy comic sleep.
With whate'er gall thou set'st thyself to write,
Thy inoffensive satires never bite.   200
In thy felonious heart though venom lies,

---

[170] *northern dedications.* By 1678 Shadwell had dedicated five plays to the Duke or Duchess of Newcastle.
[172] *Jonson's hostile name.* Shadwell's not unworthy claim to be the continuer of Jonsonian comedy annoyed Dryden.
[173-74] In *Aeneid* III, 342–43, it is father Aeneas and uncle Hector.
[179] *Prince Nicander's vein,* etc. In *Psyche,* the prince shows "industrious love"; the Prologue says the "subject's humble."
[181] *bargains.* Obscene rejoinders to provoked remarks.
[189] *that boasted bias.* In the Epilogue to *The Humourists,* Shadwell defined a Jonsonian humor as a "bias of the mind."
[195-96] A tun holds four kilderkins.

It does but touch thy Irish pen and dies.
Thy genius calls thee not to purchase fame
In keen iambics, but mild anagram:
Leave writing plays, and choose for thy command
Some peaceful province in Acrostic Land.
There thou may'st wings display and altars raise,
And torture one poor word ten thousand ways.
Or if thou would'st thy diff'rent talents suit,
Set thy own songs and sing them to thy lute."   210
  He said, but his last words were scarcely
    heard,
For Bruce and Longvil had a trap prepar'd
And down they sent the yet declaiming bard.
Sinking he left his drugget robe behind,
Borne upwards by a subterranean wind.
The mantle fell to the young prophet's part
With double portion of his father's art.

---

204 *keen iambics.* Satire, written by the Romans in iambic verse.
207 Dryden rejects "shaped" poems as silly, but it is unclear whether
   Herbert's "Easter Wings" and "The Altar" are specifically meant.
212-13 *Bruce and Longvil.* Send the talking Sir Formal through a trapdoor
   in *The Virtuoso* III.
215-17 In 2 Kings 2:9–13 Elisha takes up the prophetic mantle of Elijah
   with half his *art.* Also echoing Cowley's elegy on Crashaw, asking half
   the art of his friend.

A Song

FROM

THE SPANISH FRIAR

1680. *The Spanish Friar* mixed mirth and gravity, dignity and indecency, and other elements skillfully enough to become Dryden's most continuous theatrical success. For political and religious reasons it managed to please—or upset —Charles II, James II, Mary Queen of William III, and generations of theater audiences. In Act V the Queen says to Teresa: "To soothe my sadness/ Sing me the song which poor Olympia made/ When false Bireno left her." It is the standard Restoration example of the unimagistic lyric style and of songs of feminine regret. The composer Captain Pack originally set it to music.

I

Farewell, ungrateful traitor,
   Farewell, my perjur'd swain,
Let never injur'd creature
   Believe a man again.
The pleasure of possessing
Surpasses all expressing,
But 'tis too short a blessing,
   And love too long a pain.

II

'Tis easy to deceive us
   In pity of your pain,
But when we love you leave us
   To rail at you in vain.

10

Before we have descri'd it
There is no bliss beside it,
But she that once has tri'd it
    Will never love again.

III

The passion you pretended
    Was only to obtain,
But when the charm is ended
    The charmer you disdain.   20
Your love by ours we measure
Till we have lost our treasure,
But dying is a pleasure
    When living is a pain.

THE EPILOGUE
SPOKEN TO THE KING

At the Opening the Play-House
at Oxford on Saturday last,
Being March the Nineteenth, 1681

1681. The first play performed during Charles II's stay in
Oxford for the crucial 1681 sitting of Parliament was *Tam-
erlane the Great* by Charles Saunders (dates unknown).
Dryden had advised Saunders on the play and had furnished him with an earlier Epilogue. The present poem
was written for a special Oxford performance of the play,
and it conveys an unusual degree of relaxed calm for that
contentious time. The image of the world as a camera ob-
scura projection in Oxford is an unusual one; other images
—the world as stage, of *discordia concors*, and the like—
are very much older, and all drive toward a hope for calm
wisdom.

As from a darken'd room some optic glass
Transmits the distant species as they pass,
The world's large landscape is from far descri'd,
And men contracted on the paper glide:
Thus crowded Oxford represents mankind,
And in these walls Great Britain seems confin'd.
Oxford is now the public theater,
And you both audience are and actors here.
The gazing world on the new scene attend,
Admire the turns, and wish a prosp'rous end.   10

This place, the seat of peace, the quiet cell,
Where arts remov'd from noisy business dwell,
Shou'd calm your wills, unite the jarring parts,
And with a kind contagion seize your hearts.
Oh! may its genius like soft music move
And tune you all to concord and to love.
Our ark that has in tempests long been toss'd
Cou'd never land on so secure a coast.
From hence you may look back on civil rage
And view the ruins of the former age.   20
Here a New World its glories may unfold,
And here be sav'd the remnants of the Old.
But while your days on public thoughts are bent
Past ills to heal and future to prevent,
Some vacant hours allow to your delight: ⎫
Mirth is the pleasing business of the night, ⎬
The king's prerogative, the people's right. ⎭
Were all your hours to sullen cares confin'd,
The body wou'd be jaded by the mind.
'Tis wisdom's part betwixt extremes to steer: 30
Be gods in senates, but be mortals here.

---

[11] *the quiet cell.* Dryden often wrote of collegiate *cells* or retreats.
[17] *ark.* The "ship of state"; Noah's ark.

THE PROLOGUE

To the University of Oxford

1681? It is not known what play this Prologue introduced, and the date of delivery is also unclear. But it is generally assumed that it was recited at a time close to the preceding *Epilogue Spoken to the King*. In all, Dryden wrote nine prologues and epilogues for plays performed at Oxford University, the majority touching either upon political matters or flattering the good taste of the dons. The famous preference for Oxford (Athens) over Cambridge (Thebes) concluding this Prologue probably tells us more about his attitude toward his old university, Cambridge, than toward his audience at Oxford, and more about the actors' preference for the quiet of the theater in the Tennis Courts, as opposed to the rowdiness of London, than about their love of learning.

Tho' actors cannot much of learning boast,
Of all who want it, we admire it most.
We love the praises of a learned pit,
As we remotely are alli'd to wit.
We speak our poets' wit and trade in ore,
Like those who touch upon the golden shore,
Betwixt our judges can distinction make,
Discern how much, and why, our poems take;
Mark if the fools, or men of sense, rejoice,
Whether th' applause be only sound or voice.   10
When our fop gallants or our City folly
Clap over-loud, it makes us melancholy;

---

⁶ *the golden shore.* Of the New World, whence gold was appropriated.

We doubt that scene which does their wonder raise,
And for their ignorance contemn their praise.
Judge then, if we who act and they who write
Shou'd not be proud of giving you delight.
London likes grossly, but this nicer pit
Examines, fathoms all the depths of wit;
The ready finger lays on every blot,
Knows what shou'd justly please and what shou'd
                    not.   20
Nature herself lies open to your view,
You judge by her what draught of her is true,
Where outlines false, and colours seem too faint,
Where bunglers dawb, and where true poets paint.
But by the sacred genius of this place,
By every Muse, by each domestic grace,
Be kind to wit which but endeavours well
And where you judge presumes not to excel.
Our poets hither for adoption come,
As nations su'd to be made free of Rome,   30
Not in the suffragating tribes to stand,
But in your utmost, last provincial band.
If his ambition may those hopes pursue,
Who with religion loves your arts and you,
Oxford to him a dearer name shall be
Than his own mother university.
Thebes did his green, unknowing youth engage;
He chooses Athens in his riper age.

---

[31] *suffragating tribes.* Referring to the *jus suffragi:* that is, poets cannot
  claim to be members of Oxford but may hope for the benefits of association.

ABSALOM AND ACHITOPHEL

A Poem

*—Si propius stes
Te capiet magis—*

1681. The Introduction to this volume touches on the rise in England of a state of near revolution connected with the Popish Plot and the crisis over bills to exclude from the succession James, Duke of York, the Catholic brother of the king, and on agitation to have Charles' illegitimate son, James, Duke of Monmouth, declared heir. The struggle began to turn in favor of the Royalists on March 28, 1681, when Charles dissolved the Parliament sitting at Oxford with a speech that served as the model for David's at the end of this poem. Dryden's contemporaries recognized at once that the poem concerned their own time, although everything in it is consistently said of Israel under David, and the pretense, or the allegory, is maintained throughout. And yet there was considerable confusion over who precisely was being alluded to especially in the lesser portraits (or "characters," as they were called). The confusion resulted partly from the fact that Dryden made real, that is, artistically independent, characters out of the differing reality of historical persons, and partly because he maintained his biblical parallel so rigorously (although close reading will show passages true of David's or of Charles' reign alone).

Earlier writings of many kinds offered Dryden a choice

of parallels for events in his own day. The Bible, French
history of the Ligue of the Duke of Guise, Elizabethan history with its Protestant Association to protect the queen,
the history of Venice, and classical history of various periods
were used repeatedly by Dryden and his contemporaries.
He and they believed that, whatever accidental differences
might exist, mankind was the same always and everywhere
and that therefore, as he said in his Life of Plutarch, "having the causes before our eyes, we cannot easily be de-
ceived in the effects, if we have judgment enough but to
draw the parallel." The parallel he chose was one adopting
2 Samuel (a close knowledge of which greatly heightens
appreciation of the poem's details and skill). The choice
was much the most appropriate for a Royalist, because although almost all men at that time believed that the Bible
could be glossed to reveal the truth about civil affairs, the
story of David was closely involved in Stuart and Tudor
theories of kingship. If no writer used the parallel as brilliantly as Dryden, that is because no one had ever taken
the artistic possibilities of the biblical story so seriously, or
his own time seriously enough, as history. The parallel was
also useful in giving a greater sense of action than the
poem in fact possesses. The only episodes are those of
Achitophel's temptations of Absalom, of Absalom's temptation of the people, and of David's speech. The former two
are considerably heightened by allusions to *Paradise Lost*
and *Paradise Regained.* The poem's lack of action (in
which it resembles *MacFlecknoe*) is probably due to Dryden's writing a poetry more seriously concerned with metaphors and ideas, but it was probably also true that he did
not wish to suggest the possibility of undertakings that
might lead to civil war. The resolution is, at all events, in
terms of personalities and principle (ll. 759 ff.). The
principle is that of the conservative case for maintaining a
system that has been hard won and well tested and that is
superior to any likely actual (as opposed to merely theoretical) alternative.

The poem was at once a source of Royalist joy and a
goad to anti-Royalist replies. There were four issues of the
first edition and, in all, seven publications of the poem in

English in 1681. (It was also translated into Latin and
French, and a sequel, *The Second Part of Absalom and
Achitophel*, by Nahum Tate with Dryden's help, appeared
in 1682.) The first version to call itself the second edition
has twelve lines on Achitophel (ll. 180–91) and four on
Absalom (ll. 957–60) not in earlier printings. It is not
clear whether these were omitted by the printer from the
earlier issues or added by Dryden after later composition.
Because the passages are favorable to both characters,
there has been discussion whether Dryden sought to be
fair, to be yet more skillfully satiric, or to modify in some
other way two of the central characters of the poem. There
has also been much discussion over the genre of the poem,
with some of the designations being mock heroic, satire,
epyllion (little epic), political poem, and historical poem.
It is agreed that all these elements are to be found in the
poem and that it is unified, but there is little agreement on
the center of that unity. The tone of the poem is especially
important, as is shown by comparison with *The Medal* and
with the lines written by Dryden for *Absalom and Achitophel*, Part II.

The epigraph is from Horace, *Ars Poetica* 361–62:
"If you stand closer, you will be more taken."

To the Reader

'Tis not my intention to make an apology for my poem:
some will think it needs no excuse, and others will receive
none. The design, I am sure, is honest, but he who draws
his pen for one party must expect to make enemies of the
other. For Wit and Fool are consequents of Whig and
Tory, and every man is a knave or an ass to the contrary
side. There's a treasury of merits[1] in the fanatic church as
well as in the papist, and a pennyworth to be had of saint-
ship, honesty, and poetry for the lewd, the factious, and
the blockheads. But the longest chapter in Deuteronomy

---

[1] *treasury of merits.* Formed by the supererogatory goodness of Catholic
saints.

has not curses enough for an anti-Bromingham.[2] My comfort is their manifest prejudice to my cause will render their judgment of less authority against me. Yet if a poem have a genius, it will force its own reception in the world. For there's a sweetness in good verse which tickles even while it hurts, and no man can be heartily angry with him who pleases him against his will. The commendation of adversaries is the greatest triumph of a writer, because it never comes unless extorted. But I can be satisfied on more easy terms: if I happen to please the more moderate sort, I shall be sure of an honest party and, in all probability, of the best judges, for the least concern'd are commonly the least corrupt. And, I confess, I have laid in for those, by rebating the satire (where justice would allow it), from carrying too sharp an edge. They who can criticize so weakly as to imagine I have done my worst may be convinc'd, at their own cost, that I can write severely with more ease than I can gently. I have but laugh'd at some men's follies, when I could have declaim'd against their vices, and other men's virtues I have commended as freely as I have tax'd their crimes.

And now, if you are a malicious reader, I expect you should return upon me that I affect to be thought more impartial than I am. But if men are not to be judg'd by their professions, God forgive you Commonwealthsmen[3] for professing so plausibly for the government. You cannot be so unconscionable as to charge me for not subscribing of my name, for that would reflect too grossly upon your own party, who never dare, though they have the advantage of a jury to secure them. If you like not my poem, the fault may possibly be in my writing (though 'tis hard for an author to judge against himself); but more probably 'tis in your morals, which cannot bear the truth of it. The violent, on both sides, will condemn the character of Absalom[4] as either too favourably or too hardly drawn. But they are not the violent whom I desire to please. The fault, on the right hand, is to extenuate, palliate, and indulge, and, to confess

[2] *anti-Bromingham.* A Tory; a supporter of the king.
[3] *Commonwealthsmen.* Supporters of the "Good Old Cause," anti-Royalists.
[4] *Absalom.* See poem 17–18n.

freely, I have endeavour'd to commit it. Besides the respect which I owe his birth, I have a greater for his heroic virtues, and David himself could not be more tender of the young man's life than I would be of his reputation. But since the most excellent natures are always the most easy and, as being such, are the soonest perverted by ill counsels, especially when baited with fame and glory, 'tis no more a wonder that he withstood not the temptations of Achitophel [5] than it was for Adam not to have resisted the two devils, the serpent and the woman. The conclusion of the story I purposely forbore to prosecute, because I could not obtain from myself to shew Absalom unfortunate. The frame of it was cut out but for a picture to the waist, and if the draught be so far true, 'tis as much as I design'd.

Were I the inventor, who am only the historian, I should certainly conclude the piece with the reconcilement of Absalom to David. And who knows but this may come to pass? Things were not brought to an extremity where I left the story. There seems yet to be room left for a composure; hereafter, there may only be for pity. I have not so much as an uncharitable wish against Achitophel but am content to be accus'd of a good natur'd error, and to hope with Origen[6] that the Devil himself may, at last, be sav'd. For which reason, in this poem, he is neither brought to set his house in order nor to dispose of his person afterwards as he in wisdom shall think fit.[7] God is infinitely merciful, and his vicegerent[8] is only not so, because he is not infinite.

The true end of satire is the amendment of vices by correction. And he who writes honestly is no more an enemy to the offender than the physician to the patient when he prescribes harsh remedies to an inveterate disease, for those are only in order to prevent the chirurgeon's work of an *ense rescindendum*,[9] which I wish not to my very ene-

---

[5] *Achitophel*. See poem 150n. It will be observed that no Restoration names have been given in this epistle or the poem.
[6] *Origen*, etc. The first hint of Achitophel's diabolical character; this was traditional.
[7] *to set his house in order*, etc. And, as in 2 Samuel, thereafter to hang himself.
[8] *his vicegerent*. The king; God is King of kings.
[9] *an ense rescindendum*. Something that must be cut off with the sword (Ovid, *Metamorphoses* I, 191; Virgil, *Aeneid* XII, 389).

mies. To conclude all, if the body politic[10] have any analogy to the natural, in my weak judgment, an Act of Oblivion were as necessary in a hot, distemper'd state, as an opiate would be in a raging fever.

ABSALOM AND ACHITOPHEL

A Poem

In pious times, ere priestcraft did begin,
Before polygamy was made a sin;
When man on many multipli'd his kind,
Ere one to one was cursedly confin'd;
When nature prompted, and no law deni'd
Promiscuous use of concubine and bride;
Then Israel's monarch, after Heaven's own heart,
His vigorous warmth did variously impart
To wives and slaves, and wide as his command
Scatter'd his Maker's image through the land.   10
  Michal, of royal blood, the crown did wear,
A soil ungrateful to the tiller's care;
Not so the rest, for several mothers bore
To godlike David several sons before.
But since like slaves his bed they did ascend,
No true succession could their seed attend.
  Of all this numerous progeny was none
So beautiful, so brave as Absalom.

---

[10] *the body politic*, etc. Referring to the old belief of correspondence between the *corpus* of human society and the human body; similarly, the king had a natural body and a body politic (his subjects) between which there was a mystic "privity"; see *Threnodia Augustalis* 61–62*n*.

1–10 The idea of Christian liberty to do things forbidden by the Law (Old Testament) is wittily inverted. If the patriarchs had many wives, and David his inclinations, Christian liberty should allow Charles II his mistresses. His queen, Catherine of Braganza (d. 1705)—see the *Michal* of 11—was sterile at this time, and a secret court debate discussed the allowability of polygamy or divorce.

16 *No true succession.* So disposing of Monmouth's claims.

17–18 *Absalom.* 2 Samuel, especially 14:25. A type of pride in personal appearance. Based on James, Duke of Monmouth, an illegitimate son of Charles II, executed in 1685 for treason. Dryden obviously felt some sympathy, as did the biblical David, but the parallel and the details condemn Monmouth.

Whether, inspir'd by some diviner lust,
His father got him with a greater gust,   20
Or that his conscious destiny made way
By manly beauty to imperial sway,
Early in foreign fields he won renown
With kings and states alli'd to Israel's crown;
In peace the thoughts of war he could remove
And seem'd as he were only born for love.
Whate'er he did was done with so much ease,
In him alone 'twas natural to please.
His motions all accompanied with grace,
And paradise was open'd in his face.   30
With secret joy indulgent David view'd
His youthful image in his son renew'd;
To all his wishes nothing he deny'd
And made the charming Annabel his bride.
What faults he had (for who from faults is free?)
His father could not, or he would not, see.
Some warm excesses which the law forbore
Were constru'd youth that purg'd by boiling o'er,
And Amnon's murder, by a specious name,
Was call'd a just revenge for injur'd fame.   40
Thus prais'd and lov'd the noble youth remain'd
While David undisturb'd in Sion reign'd.
But life can never be sincerely blest;
Heaven punishes the bad and proves the best.
    The Jews, a headstrong, moody, murmuring race
As ever tri'd th' extent and stretch of grace,
God's pamper'd people whom, debauch'd with ease,
No king could govern nor no god could please
(Gods they had tri'd of every shape and size
That god-smiths could produce, or priests devise),   50
These Adam-wits, too fortunately free,
Began to dream they wanted liberty;

³⁰ Echoing Dante, *Paradiso* XVIII, 21.
³⁴ *Annabel.* Anne, Countess of Buccleuch (d. 1732), greatly admired by Dryden and his contemporaries.
³⁹ *Amnon's murder.* 2 Samuel 13; the Restoration parallel, if any, is uncertain.
⁴⁵ *The Jews.* Representing the English.
⁵¹ *Adam-wits.* Fools, like Adam, who sinned while free in a desire for power.

And when no rule, no precedent was found
Of men by laws less circumscrib'd and bound,
They led their wild desires to woods and caves
And thought that all but savages were slaves.
They who, when Saul was dead, without a blow
Made foolish Ishbosheth the crown forgo,
Who banish'd David did from Hebron bring
And, with a general shout, proclaim'd him king: 60
Those very Jews, who at their very best
Their humour more than loyalty express'd,
Now wonder'd why so long they had obey'd
An idol monarch which their hands had made,
Thought they might ruin him they could create,
Or melt him to that golden calf, a state.
   But these were random bolts; no form'd design
Nor interest made the factious crowd to join.
The sober part of Israel, free from stain,
Well knew the value of a peaceful reign,   70
And looking backward with a wise affright,
Saw seams of wounds dishonest to the sight;
In contemplation of whose ugly scars,
They curst the memory of civil wars.
The moderate sort of men, thus qualifi'd,
Inclin'd the balance to the better side,
And David's mildness manag'd it so well
The bad found no occasion to rebel.
But when to sin our bias'd nature leans,
The careful Devil is still at hand with means   80
And providently pimps for ill desires:
The Good Old Cause reviv'd, a plot requires.
Plots, true or false, are necessary things
To raise up commonwealths and ruin kings.
   Th' inhabitants of old Jerusalem

---

56 Hobbes and some classical writers believed that primitive society was
  absolutely but anarchically and miserably free.
57 *Saul.* Ruler of Israel before David; representing Oliver Cromwell.
58 *Ishbosheth.* 2 Samuel 3–4; representing the ineffectual Richard Cromwell.
59 *Hebron.* 2 Samuel 5:1–5; representing Scotland, where Charles II was
  crowned on January 1, 1651.
64 *idol.* Also idle.
66 *a state.* A nation not ruled by a king; not a kingdom.
82 See To the Reader note 3.

Were Jebusites—the town so call'd from them,
And theirs the native right—
But when the chosen people grew more strong,
The rightful cause at length became the wrong,
And every loss the men of Jebus bore,   90
They still were thought God's enemies the more.

Thus, worn and weaken'd, well or ill content,
Submit they must to David's government;
Impoverish'd, and depriv'd of all command,
Their taxes doubled as they lost their land
And, what was harder yet to flesh and blood,
Their gods disgrac'd and burnt like common wood.
This set the heathen priesthood in a flame,
For priests of all religions are the same;
Of whatsoe'er descent their godhead be,   100
Stock, stone, or other homely pedigree,
In his defence his servants are as bold
As if he had been born of beaten gold.
The Jewish Rabbins, tho' their enemies,
In this conclude them honest men and wise,
For 'twas their duty, all the learned think,
T' espouse his cause by whom they eat and drink.

   From hence began that Plot, the nation's curse,
Bad in itself but represented worse;
Rais'd in extremes and in extremes decri'd,   110
With oaths affirm'd, with dying vows deni'd;
Not weigh'd or winnow'd by the multitude,
But swallow'd in the mass, unchew'd and crude.
Some truth there was, but dash'd and brew'd with
      lies
To please the fools and puzzle all the wise.
Succeeding times did equal folly call
Believing nothing or believing all.

---

⁸⁶ *Jebusites.* Representing Roman Catholics.
⁹⁴⁻⁹⁵ Referring to the Test Acts requiring officeholders to take the Anglican sacrament and to penal laws against Catholics.
¹⁰⁸⁻⁹ The Popish Plot began from the anti-Catholic feeling and the political agitation described. In 1678 there were rumors of Jesuit plots
against Charles II in favor of his Catholic brother James. Witnesses like
Titus Oates (on whom Corah is based, 632 ff., below) sprang up, in-
flamed the nation, and led to the condemnation or execution of over
thirty persons by mid-1681. Dryden no doubt is correct in implying
that Shaftesbury exploited rather than originated the Plot.

Th' Egyptian rites the Jebusites embrac'd,
Where gods were recommended by their taste.
Such savory deities must needs be good,   120
As serv'd at once for worship and for food.
By force they could not introduce these gods,
For ten to one in former days was odds.
So fraud was us'd (the sacrificer's trade):
Fools are more hard to conquer than persuade.
Their busy teachers mingled with the Jews,
And rak'd, for converts, ev'n the court and stews,
Which Hebrew priests the more unkindly took,
Because the fleece accompanies the flock.
Some thought they God's anointed meant to slay   130
By guns, invented since full many a day;
Our author swears it not, but who can know
How far the Devil and Jebusites may go?

   This Plot, which fail'd for want of common sense,
Had yet a deep and dangerous consequence,
For, as when raging fevers boil the blood,
The standing lake soon floats into a flood,
And every hostile humour, which before
Slept quiet in its channels, bubbles o'er:
So several factions from this first ferment   140
Work up to foam and threat the government.
Some by their friends, more by themselves, thought
      wise
Oppos'd the power to which they could not rise.
Some had in courts been great, and thrown from
      thence,
Like fiends, were harden'd in impenitence.
Some by their Monarch's fatal mercy grown
From pardon'd rebels kinsmen to the throne,
Were rais'd in power and public office high:
Strong bands, if bands ungrateful men could tie.
   Of these the false Achitophel was first: 150

118-21 A disgusting passage on transubstantiation. *Egyptian rites* are
   French, hence Catholic: transubstantiation.
130-34 Dryden breaks his historical parallel for a laugh at his credulous
   contemporaries.
136-41 To the Reader note 10.
144-45 Like Milton's fallen angels, *Paradise Lost.*
150 *Achitophel.* In 2 Samuel the evil counselor of David. A type of pride.

A name to all succeeding ages curst.
For close designs and crooked counsels fit,
Sagacious, bold, and turbulent of wit;
Restless, unfix'd in principle and place,
In power unpleas'd, impatient of disgrace.
A fiery soul which, working out its way, ⎫
Fretted the pigmy body to decay   ⎬
And o'er-inform'd the tenement of clay. ⎭

   A daring pilot in extremity;
Pleas'd with the danger when the waves went
    high,   160
He sought the storms, but for a calm unfit,
Would steer too nigh the sands to boast his wit.
Great wits are sure to madness near alli'd,
And thin partitions do their bounds divide;
Else why should he, with wealth and honour blest,
Refuse his age the needful hours of rest?
Punish a body which he could not please,
Bankrupt of life, yet prodigal of ease?
And all to leave what with his toil he won
To that unfeather'd, two-legg'd thing, a son,   170
Got while his soul did huddled notions try,
And born a shapeless lump, like anarchy.
In friendship false, implacable in hate;
Resolv'd to ruin or to rule the state.
To compass this the triple bond he broke, ⎫
The pillars of the public safety shook,   ⎬
And fitted Israel for a foreign yoke.   ⎭
Then, seiz'd with fear, yet still affecting fame,
Assum'd a patriot's all-atoning name.

---

in intellect (162, etc.). Often called Satanic and from Commonwealth times the figure of an evil, scheming politician. Based on Anthony Ashley Cooper (d. 1683), Earl of Shaftesbury, leader of the Whigs. Dryden's epic epithet *false* refers to his shifting under Cromwell and Charles II as well as his perversion of great gifts. Like Milton's Satan, he is truly dangerous and great, unlike the "chief" of *The Medal*.

156-58 Shaftesbury's smallness of size with largeness of ambition.

170 Shaftesbury's son, also named Anthony, lacked his father's gifts; he is defined as Plato was said to have defined man, *implumis bipes*.

175 *the triple bond*. Alliance with Holland and Sweden in 1668, agitated against by Shaftesbury, but no more disreputably than by all parties from 1668 to 1683.

179 *Assum'd*. From early editions; fits Dryden's contempt (179–85) better than the later "Usurp'd."

So easy still it proves in factious times   180
With public zeal to cancel private crimes;
How safe is treason, and how sacred ill,
Where none can sin against the people's will,
Where crowds can wink, and no offence be known,
Since in another's guilt they find their own!
    Yet fame deserv'd no enemy can grudge;
The statesman we abhor but praise the judge.
In Israel's courts ne'er sat an Abbethdin
With more discerning eyes or hands more clean:
Unbrib'd, unsought the wretched to redress,   190
Swift of dispatch and easy of access.
Oh, had he been content to serve the crown
With virtues only proper to the gown,
Or had the rankness of the soil been freed
From cockle that oppress'd the noble seed,
David for him his tuneful harp had strung,
And Heaven had wanted one immortal song.
But wild ambition loves to slide, not stand,
And fortune's ice prefers to virtue's land.
    Achitophel, grown weary to possess   200
A lawful fame and lazy happiness,
Disdain'd the golden fruit to gather free
And lent the crowd his arm to shake the tree.
Now manifest of crimes contriv'd long since,
He stood at bold defiance with his prince,
Held up the buckler of the people's cause
Against the crown and skulk'd behind the laws.
The wish'd occasion of the Plot he takes,
Some circumstances finds, but more he makes.
By buzzing emissaries fills the ears   210
Of list'ning crowds with jealosies and fears
Of arbitrary counsels brought to light,
And proves the king himself a Jebusite.

188 *Abbethdin*. One of two high Jewish judges.
180–91 Added in the second edition. In fact, Shaftesbury's service as judge
    is obscure.
195 *cockle*. Emblem of error, sedition, etc. *Threnodia Augustalis* 354–55.
196–97 David would have written praise of him rather than writing one of
    his Psalms.
204 *manifest of*. A Latinism: revealed in, evident with.
213 *the king himself a Jebusite*. Dryden probably did not know that
    Charles was a crypto-Catholic.

Weak arguments! which yet he knew full well
Were strong with people easy to rebel.
For govern'd by the moon, the giddy Jews
Tread the same track when she the prime renews;
And once in twenty years, their scribes record,
By natural instinct they change their lord.

Achitophel still wants a chief, and none   220
Was found so fit as warlike Absalom:
Not that he wish'd his greatness to create
(For politicians neither love nor hate),
But for he knew, his title not allow'd,
Would keep him still depending on the crowd,
That kingly power, thus ebbing out, might be
Drawn to the dregs of a democracy.
Him he attempts with studi'd arts to please
And sheds his venom in such words as these.

"Auspicious Prince! at whose nativity   230
Some royal planet rul'd the southern sky;
Thy longing country's darling and desire,
Their cloudy pillar and their guardian fire;
Their second Moses, whose extended wand
Divides the seas and shews the promis'd land;
Whose dawning day in every distant age
Has exercis'd the sacred prophets' rage;
The people's prayer, the glad diviners' theme,
The young men's vision and the old men's dream!
Thee, Saviour, thee, the nation's vows confess   240
And, never satisfi'd with seeing, bless.
Swift, unbespoken pomps thy steps proclaim,
And stammering babes are taught to lisp thy name.

218-19 At twenty-year intervals: the Long Parliament, the Restoration, and the Popish Plot.

227 Democracy was then a scare word.

230-31 Shaftesbury and Monmouth were devotees of astrology; so was Dryden, but for private affairs.

233 *cloudy pillar*, etc. Exodus 13:21.

234 *their second Moses*. Their Savior, their Christ (240). Dryden was alluding to Christ's temptation of the kingdoms (in *Paradise Regained* II, 300 through IV, 393), by Satan, revealing Achitophel as a true Satan, Absalom as a false Christ.

239 Joel 2:28.

240 After Lucretius I, 6: "Thee, goddess, thee the clouds and tempests fear" (trans. Dryden).

How long wilt thou the general joy detain,
Starve and defraud the people of thy reign?
Content ingloriously to pass thy days
Like one of virtue's fools that feeds on praise,
Till thy fresh glories, which now shine so bright,
Grow stale and tarnish with our daily sight?
   "Believe me, royal youth, thy fruit must be   250
Or gather'd ripe, or rot upon the tree.
Heav'n has to all allotted, soon or late,
Some lucky revolution of their fate,
Whose motions, if we watch and guide with skill,
(For human good depends on human will),
Our Fortune rolls as from a smooth descent
And from the first impression takes the bent;
But if unseiz'd, she glides away like wind,
And leaves repenting folly far behind.
Now, now she meets you with a glorious prize   260
And spreads her locks before her as she flies.
   "Had thus old David, from whose loins you spring,
Not dar'd, when fortune call'd him, to be king,
At Gath an exile he might still remain,
And heaven's anointing oil had been in vain.
Let his successful youth your hopes engage,
But shun th' example of declining age:
Behold him setting in his western skies,
The shadows length'ning as the vapours rise.
He is not now, as when on Jordan's sand   270
The joyful people throng'd to see him land,
Cov'ring the beach and black'ning all the strand,
But like the Prince of Angels from his height,
Comes tumbling downward with diminish'd light,
Betray'd by one poor Plot to public scorn
(Our only blessing since his curst return),

258-61 In the emblem books, Fortune or Occasion on a wheel, or as here
on a ball, sped by with hair streaming in front to be seized; the figure
was bald behind to frustrate those who had delayed.
264 *Gath.* 1 Samuel 27:1–4; representing Brussels.
270 *Jordan's sand.* 2 Samuel 19:9–15; here representing Dover beach; but see
820.
273-74 Achitophel attributes to David his own role as Lucifer; Isaiah 14:
12–13.

Those heaps of people which one sheaf did bind,
Blown off and scatter'd by a puff of wind.
        "What strength can he to your designs oppose,
Naked of friends and round beset with foes?   280
If Pharaoh's doubtful succour he should use,
A foreign aid would more incense the Jews;
Proud Egypt would dissembled friendship bring,
Foment the war, but not support the king;
Nor would the royal party e'r unite
With Pharaoh's arms t' assist the Jebusite;
Or if they should, their interest soon would break,
And with such odious aid make David weak.
        "All sorts of men by my successful arts,
Abhorring kings, estrange their alter'd hearts   290
From David's rule; and 'tis the general cry,
'Religion, Commonwealth, and Liberty!'
If you as champion of the public good
Add to their arms a chief of royal blood,
What may not Israel hope, and what applause
Might such a general gain by such a cause?
Not barren praise alone, that gaudy flower
Fair only to the sight, but solid power;
And nobler is a limited command
Giv'n by the love of all your native land   300
Than a successive title, long, and dark,
Drawn from the mouldy rolls of Noah's Ark."
        What cannot praise effect in mighty minds,
When flattery soothes, and when ambition blinds!
Desire of power, on earth a vicious weed,
Yet, sprung from high, is of celestial seed;
In God 'tis glory, and when men aspire,
'Tis but a spark too much of heavenly fire.
        Th' ambitious youth, too covetous of fame,
Too full of angel's metal in his frame,   310
Unwarily was led from virtue's ways,
Made drunk with honour and debauch'd with praise.

---

[281] *Pharaoh*. Represents Louis XIV.
[285-86] The biblical parallel is convenient, but many Englishmen feared an
  alliance of the king with France for Catholicism.
[310] *angel's metal*. Also "mettle" and the coin, angel-noble, an old double
  pun.

Half loath, and half consenting to the ill
(For loyal blood within him struggled still),
He thus repli'd—"And what pretence have I
To take up arms for public liberty?
My father governs with unquestion'd right,
The faith's defender and mankind's delight;
Good, gracious, just, observant of the laws,
And Heav'n by wonders has espous'd his cause.   320
Whom has he wrong'd in all his peaceful reign?
Who sues for justice to his throne in vain?
What millions has he pardon'd of his foes,
Whom just revenge did to his wrath expose?
Mild, easy, humble, studious of our good,
Inclin'd to mercy and averse from blood.
If mildness ill with stubborn Israel suit
His crime is God's beloved attribute.
What could he gain, his people to betray,
Or change his right for arbitrary sway?   330
Let haughty Pharaoh curse with such a reign
His fruitful Nile and yoke a servile train.

   "If David's rule Jerusalem displease,
The dog star heats their brains to this disease.
Why then should I, encouraging the bad,
Turn rebel and run popularly mad?
Were he a tyrant who, by lawless might,
Oppress'd the Jews and rais'd the Jebusite,
Well might I mourn, but nature's holy bands
Would curb my spirits and restrain my hands;   340
The people might assert their liberty,
But what was right in them were crime in me.
His favour leaves me nothing to require,

---

318 *mankind's delight.* Emperor Titus was *deliciae generis humanae* to Suetonius VIII (1).
326-28 Charles signed execution warrants against his will, showing the mercy
(*God's beloved attribute*) that Dryden usually emphasizes in him. Dryden holds the old view that God's essence is reason (wisdom) and that
the essential will of the Calvinists is an attribute properly placed, with
others, beneath mercy; cf. *The Medal* 91–92.
329-30 Insisting that the king had his rights and the subjects their rights to
liberty and property; see 759 ff.
334 *the dog star.* Sirius; its heats brought diseases or madness.
337-42 Royalist doctrine: passive resistance is all that is permissible, even
under a tyrant, whom God alone punishes.

Prevents my wishes, and outruns desire.
    "What more can I expect while David lives?
All but his kingly diadem he gives;
And that—" But there he paus'd; then sighing, said,
"Is justly destin'd for a worthier head.
For when my father from his toils shall rest
And late augment the number of the blest,   350
His lawful issue shall the throne ascend,
Or the collateral line where that shall end.
His brother, though oppress'd with vulgar spite,
Yet dauntless and secure of native right,
Of every royal virtue stands possess'd,
Still dear to all the bravest and the best.
His courage foes, his friends his truth, proclaim,
His loyalty the king, the world his fame.
His mercy even th' offending crowd will find,
For sure he comes of a forgiving kind.   360
Why should I then repine at heaven's decree,
Which gives me no pretence to royalty?
    "Yet, oh, that Fate, propitiously inclin'd,
Had rais'd my birth or had debas'd my mind,
To my large soul not all her treasure lent,
And then betray'd it to a mean descent.
I find, I find my mounting spirits bold,
And David's part disdains my mother's mold.
Why am I scanted by a niggard birth?
My soul disclaims the kindred of her earth,   370
And made for empire, whispers me within:
'Desire of greatness is a godlike sin.'"
    Him staggering so when Hell's dire agent found,
While fainting virtue scarce maintain'd her ground,
He pours fresh forces in and thus replies.
    "Th' eternal God, supremely good and wise,
Imparts not these prodigious gifts in vain;
What wonders are reserv'd to bless your reign?
Against your will your arguments have shown
Such virtue's only given to guide a throne.   380

---

348 *a worthier head*. That of James, Duke of York; no such *brother* (353)
    enters the biblical episode.
373 *Him staggering*, etc. Miltonic syntax, recalling also Satan's pressure on
    Eve in *Paradise Lost*.

Not that your father's mildness I contemn,
But manly force becomes the diadem.
'Tis true, he grants the people all they crave,
And more perhaps than subjects ought to have,
For lavish grants suppose a monarch tame,
And more his goodness than his wit proclaim.
   "But when should people strive their bonds to
      break,
If not when kings are negligent or weak?
Let him give on till he can give no more;
The thrifty Sanhedrin shall keep him poor,   390
And every sheckle which he can receive
Shall cost a limb of his prerogative.
To ply him with new plots shall be my care
Or plunge him deep in some expensive war,
Which when his treasure can no more supply,
He must with the remains of kingship buy.
His faithful friends, our jealousies and fears
Call Jebusites and Pharaoh's pensioners:
Whom, when our fury from his aid has torn,
He shall be naked left to public scorn.   400
   "The next successor, whom I fear and hate,
My arts have made obnoxious to the state,
Turn'd all his virtues to his overthrow,
And gain'd our elders to pronounce a foe.
His right, for sums of necessary gold,
Shall first be pawn'd and afterwards be sold,
Till time shall ever-wanting David draw
To pass your doubtful title into law;
If not, the people have a right supreme
To make their kings, for kings are made for them.   410
   "All empire is no more than pow'r in trust,
Which when resum'd, can be no longer just.
Succession, for the general good design'd,
In its own wrong a nation cannot bind;
If altering that the people can relieve,
Better one suffer than a nation grieve.

---

³⁹⁹ *Sanhedrin.* The Jewish high council, representing the House of
Commons.
⁴⁰¹ *next successor.* James.
⁴⁰⁹⁻¹⁶ Republican theory: cf. Dryden's Royalist (759 ff.).

The Jews well know their power; ere Saul they
    chose,
God was their king, and God they durst depose.
    "Urge now your piety, your filial name,
A father's right, and fear of future fame: 420
The public good, that universal call
To which even Heav'n submitted, answers all.
Nor let his love enchant your generous mind;
'Tis Nature's trick to propagate her kind—
Our fond begetters, who would never die,
Love but themselves in their posterity.
Or let his kindness by th' effects be tri'd,
Or let him lay his vain pretence aside.
God said he lov'd your father; could he bring
A better proof than to anoint him king?   430
It surely shew'd he lov'd the shepherd well,
Who gave so fair a flock as Israel.
    "Would David have you thought his darling son?
What means he then to alienate the crown?
The name of godly he may blush to bear:
'Tis after God's own heart to cheat his heir.
He to his brother gives supreme command,
To you a legacy of barren land,
Perhaps th' old harp on which he thrums his lays,
Or some dull Hebrew ballad in your praise.   440
    "Then the next heir, a prince severe and wise,
Already looks on you with jealous eyes,
Sees through the thin disguises of your arts,
And marks your progress in the people's hearts.
Though now his mighty soul its grief contains,
He meditates revenge who least complains;
And like a lion, slumb'ring in the way,
Or sleep-dissembling while he waits his prey,
His fearless foes within his distance draws,
Constrains his roaring and contracts his paws;   450
Till at the last, his time for fury found,

417-18 That is, the Commonwealth declared God its king but deposed Him
    for Cromwell.
436 Genesis 27:6–29.
439-40 Though he loved music, Charles did not write great poetry like the
    Psalms attributed to David.

He shoots with sudden vengeance from the ground;
The prostrate vulgar passes o'er and spares,
But with a lordly rage his hunters tears.
    "Your case no tame expedients will afford;
Resolve on death or conquest by the sword,
Which for no less a state than life you draw;
And self-defence is nature's eldest law.
Leave the warm people no considering time,
For then rebellion may be thought a crime.   460
Prevail yourself of what occasion gives,
But try your title while your father lives;
And that your arms may have a fair pretence,
Proclaim you take them in the king's defence,
Whose sacred life each minute would expose
To plots from seeming friends and secret foes.
    "And who can sound the depth of David's soul?
Perhaps his fear his kindness may control.
He fears his brother, though he loves his son,
For plighted vows too late to be undone.   470
If so, by force he wishes to be gain'd,
Like women's lechery to seem constrain'd;
Doubt not, but when he most affects the frown,
Commit a pleasing rape upon the crown.
Secure his person to secure your cause:
They who possess the prince possess the laws."
    He said, and this advice above the rest
With Absalom's mild nature suited best;
Unblam'd of life (ambition set aside),
Not stain'd with cruelty nor puff'd with pride,   480
How happy had he been if destiny
Had higher plac'd his birth, or not so high!
His kingly virtues might have claim'd a throne
And blest all other countries but his own;
But charming greatness, since so few refuse,
'Tis juster to lament him than accuse.
Strong were his hopes a rival to remove,
With blandishments to gain the public love,

446-54 A common zoographical detail about lions from ancient times.
458 *self-defence*, etc. So Hobbes, *Leviathan* I, xiv.
468-69 *kindness* is subject, *fear* object.
484 Clearly showing Dryden's settled opposition to Monmouth.

To head the faction while their zeal was hot,
And popularly prosecute the Plot.   490
To farther this, Achitophel unites
The malcontents of all the Israelites,
Whose differing parties he could wisely join
For several ends to serve the same design.

 The best, and of the princes some were such,
Who thought the power of monarchy too much—
Mistaken men, and patriots in their hearts,
Not wicked, but seduc'd by impious arts:
By these the springs of property were bent
And wound so high they crack'd the government.   500
The next for interest sought t' embroil the state,
To sell their duty at a dearer rate,
And make their Jewish markets of the throne,
Pretending public good to serve their own.
Others thought kings an useless heavy load
Who cost too much and did too little good.
These were for laying honest David by
On principles of pure good husbandry.
With them join'd all th' harranguers of the throng
That thought to get preferment by the tongue.   510

 Who follow next a double danger bring,
Not only hating David, but the king.
The Solymaean rout, well vers'd of old
In godly faction and in treason bold,
Cow'ring and quaking at a conqueror's sword,
But lofty to a lawful prince restor'd,
Saw with disdain an ethnic plot begun
And scorn'd by Jebusites to be outdone.
Hot Levites headed these, who pull'd before
From th' Ark, which in the Judges' day they bore,   520
Resum'd their cant, and with a zealous cry
Pursu'd their old belov'd theocracy,

495-98 These *best* were the men of property who decided events in 1642,
1660, and 1688, the century's three revolutions in England.
499-500 That is, a subject's right to property was a theme so played on that,
like an overwound spring, it snapped the whole of which it was a part.
512 *the king.* That is, royal rule as well as the particular king.
513 *Solymaean rout.* The London rabble; Solyma was another name for
Jerusalem.
517 *ethnic.* Of the gentiles; here, Jebusites, Catholics.

Where Sanhedrin and priest enslav'd the nation
And justifi'd their spoils by inspiration;
For who so fit for reign as Aaron's race,
If once dominion they could found in grace?
These led the pack, tho' not of surest scent,
Yet deepest mouth'd against the government.

A numerous host of dreaming saints succeed,
Of the true old enthusiastic breed;   530
'Gainst form and order they their power employ,
Nothing to build and all things to destroy.

But far more numerous was the herd of such
Who think too little and who talk too much.
These, out of mere instinct, they knew not why,
Ador'd their fathers' God, and property
And, by the same blind benefit of fate,
The Devil and the Jebusite did hate:
Born to be sav'd, even in their own despite,
Because they could not help believing right.   540
Such were the tools, but a whole Hydra more
Remains, of sprouting heads too long to score.

Some of their chiefs were princes of the land;
In the first rank of these did Zimri stand,
A man so various that he seem'd to be
Not one, but all mankind's epitome.
Stiff in opinions, always in the wrong,
Was everything by starts and nothing long,
But in the course of one revolving moon,
Was chemist, fiddler, statesman, and buffoon;   550
Then all for women, painting, rhiming, drinking,
Besides ten thousand freaks that di'd in thinking.
Blest madman, who could every hour employ
With something new to wish or to enjoy!

---

525 *Aaron's race.* The clergy.
526 *dominion.* That is, power, which was for Dryden founded on natural
law, not grace, and law was the ethical expression of divine reason; see
The Hind and the Panther I, 160–96.
544 *Zimri.* Based on George Villiers (d. 1687), second Duke of Buckingham, gifted but debauched, restless, and spendthrift. The political sides
recall Zimri, servant of Elah (1 Kings 16:8–20; 2 Kings 9:31), and the
personal Zimri lover of Cozbi (Numbers 25; Buckingham was lover of
the Countess of Shrewsbury and slayer of her husband in 1668). Dryden
also models on Bacon's fiddler in "Of the True Greatness of Kingdoms
and Estates."

Railing and praising were his usual themes,
And both (to shew his judgment) in extremes;
So over-violent or over-civil
That every man with him was God or Devil.
In squand'ring wealth was his peculiar art:
Nothing went unrewarded but desert.   560
Begger'd by fools, whom still he found too late,
He had his jest, and they had his estate.
He laugh'd himself from court, then sought relief
By forming parties but could ne'er be chief
For, spite of him, the weight of business fell
On Absalom and wise Achitophel;
Thus, wicked but in will, of means bereft,
He left not faction but of that was left.

   Titles and names 'twere tedious to rehearse
Of lords below the dignity of verse.
Wits, warriors, Commonwealthsmen were the best—   570
Kind husbands and mere nobles all the rest.
And therefore in the name of dulness be
The well-hung Balaam and cold Caleb free.
And canting Nadab let oblivion damn,
Who made new porridge for the Paschal Lamb.
Let friendship's holy band some names assure;
Some their own worth, and some let scorn secure.
Nor shall the rascal rabble here have place,
Whom kings no titles gave and God no grace;
Not bull-fac'd Jonas, who could statutes draw   580
To mean rebellion and make treason law.

   But he, tho' bad, is follow'd by a worse,
The wretch who Heaven's anointed dar'd to curse:

---

574 *well-hung*, etc. Fluent (Numbers 22:5-6) and licentious (Revelation
2:14); so *cold* also means impotent. Balaam probably suggests Theophi-
lus Hastings (d. 1701), seventh Earl of Huntingdon, who soon left the
Whigs, and Caleb, Arthur Capel (d. 1683), Earl of Essex, though also
identified by some as the notorious Ford, Lord Grey of Wark; cf. *mere
nobles*, 572.
575 *Nadab*. Son of Aaron the Levite (Exodus 6:23; Leviticus 10:1), based
on William, Lord Howard of Escrick (d. 1694), a Dissenter.
576 Explanation: Although Dissenters dismissed the Anglican liturgy as
porridge (a fact), when in the Tower the dissenting Howard took the
sacrament according to the Prayer Book, substituting "lamb's wool"
(ale with apple pulp) for wine.
581 *Jonas*. Based on Sir William Jones (d. 1682), one of the most skillful
Whig hands.

Shimei, whose youth did early promise bring
Of zeal to God and hatred to his king,
Did wisely from expensive sins refrain
And never broke the sabbath but for gain;
Nor ever was he known an oath to vent
Or curse, unless against the government.   590
    Thus, heaping wealth by the most ready way
Among the Jews, which was to cheat and pray;
The city, to reward his pious hate
Against his master, chose him magistrate;
His hand a vare of justice did uphold;
His neck was loaded with a chain of gold.
During his office treason was no crime.
The sons of Belial had a glorious time;
For Shimei, though not prodigal of pelf,
Yet lov'd his wicked neighbour as himself;   600
When two or three were gather'd to declaim
Against the monarch of Jerusalem,
Shimei was always in the midst of them,
And if they curst the king when he was by,
Would rather curse than break good company.
If any durst his factious friends accuse,
He pack'd a jury of dissenting Jews,
Whose fellow-feeling in the godly cause
Would free the suff'ring saint from human laws.
For laws are only made to punish those   610
Who serve the King and to protect his foes.
If any leisure time he had from power
(Because 'tis sin to misemploy an hour),
His business was, by writing, to persuade
That kings were useless and a clog to trade,
And that his noble style he might refine,
No Rechabite more shunn'd the fumes of wine.
Chaste were his cellars, and his shrieval board
The grossness of a city feast abhorr'd;

585 *Shimei.* A man of Saul's house (Cromwell's cause) who cursed David (2
   Samuel 16:5; 1 Kings 2:36–46); based on Slingsby Bethel (d. 1697), determined opponent of the throne and a London sheriff in 1680.
598 *the sons of Belial.* Rioters (Judges 19:22–25; *Paradise Lost* I, 500–5)
   and rebels (Deuteronomy 13:13; 2 Samuel 20:1–2); perhaps punning on
   Balliol College, where Whigs met during the Oxford Parliament.
617 *Rechabite.* Jeremiah 35:14.

His cooks, with long disuse, their trade forgot: 620
Cool was his kitchen, tho' his brains were hot.
Such frugal virtue malice may accuse,
But sure 'twas necessary to the Jews;
For towns once burnt, such magistrates require
As dare not tempt God's providence by fire.
With spiritual food he fed his servants well,
But free from flesh that made the Jews rebel,
And Moses' laws he held in more account,
For forty days of fasting in the mount.

  To speak the rest, who better are forgot,   630
Would tire a well-breath'd witness of the plot.
Yet, Corah, thou shalt from oblivion pass:
Erect thyself, thou monumental brass,
High as the serpent of thy metal made,
While nations stand secure beneath thy shade.
What tho' his birth were base, yet comets rise
From earthy vapours ere they shine in skies.
Prodigious actions may as well be done
By weaver's issue as by prince's son.
This arch-attestor for the public good   640
By that one deed ennobles all his blood.
Who ever ask'd the witnesses' high race,
Whose oath with martyrdom did Stephen grace?

  Ours was a Levite, and as times went then,
His tribe were Godalmighty's gentlemen.
Sunk were his eyes, his voice was harsh and loud,
Sure signs he neither choleric was nor proud;
His long chin prov'd his wit; his saintlike grace
A church vermilion, and a Moses' face;
His memory, miraculously great,   650

624 *towns once burnt.* London, as related in *Annus Mirabilis.*
632 *Corah.* The rebel of Numbers 16, based on Titus Oates (d. 1705), the
fertile central witness of the Popish Plot. First Anabaptist, then Anglican chaplain, next Roman priest abroad, then separated, then again
trained as priest, then a repatriate to London in June 1678, by August
he had launched the Plot.
633 *brass.* Numbers 21:6–9; Jeremiah 6:28.
642–43 On Stephen Martyr, Acts 6:9–15.
649 *A church vermilion,* etc. Recalling the vermilion house of Jehoiakim,
who "shed innocent blood" (Jeremiah 22:13–19). On the stage a red
face indicated a luxurious priest, as Dryden's Father Dominic in *The
Spanish Friar.* The rosiness is that of a man with false revelation, a
false Moses (Exodus 34:29).

Could plots exceeding man's belief repeat,
Which therefore cannot be accounted lies,
For human wit could never such devise.
Some future truths are mingled in his book,
But where the witness fail'd the prophet spoke;
Some things like visionary flights appear;
The spirit caught him up the Lord knows where,
And gave him his rabbinical degree
Unknown to foreign university.
His judgment yet his memory did excel,   660
Which piec'd his wondrous evidence so well
And suited to the temper of the times,
Then groaning under Jebusitic crimes.
Let Israel's foes suspect his heav'nly call,
And rashly judge his writ apocryphal;
Our laws for such affronts have forfeits made:
He takes his life, who takes away his trade.
    Were I myself in witness Corah's place,
The wretch who did me such a dire disgrace
Should whet my memory, though once forgot,   670
To make him an appendix of my Plot.
His zeal to heav'n made him his prince despise
And load his person with indignities,
But zeal peculiar privilege affords,
Indulging latitude to deeds and words.
And Corah might for Agag's murder call,
In terms as coarse as Samuel us'd to Saul.
What others in his evidence did join
(The best that could be had for love or coin),
In Corah's own predicament will fall: 680
For *witness* is a common name to all.
    Surrounded thus with friends of every sort,
Deluded Absalom forsakes the court;
Impatient of high hopes, urg'd with renown,
And fir'd with near possession of a crown.
Th' admiring crowd are dazzled with surprize

---

659 *university.* Salamanca, from which Oates, contradicted by authorities, claimed to be doctor of divinity.
676 *Agag's murder.* The biblical (1 Samuel 15) and Restoration significances are unclear. Agag is perhaps Lord Stafford, executed in December 1680; see *On the Marriage of . . . Mrs. Anastasia Stafford.*

And on his goodly person feed their eyes;
His joy conceal'd, he sets himself to show,
On each side bowing popularly low;
His looks, his gestures, and his words he frames,　　　690
And with familiar ease repeats their names.
Thus, form'd by nature, furnish'd out with arts,
He glides unfelt into their secret hearts;
Then with a kind compassionating look
And sighs bespeaking pity ere he spoke,
Few words he said, but easy those and fit,
More slow than Hybla drops and far more sweet.
　　"I mourn, my countrymen, your lost estate,
Tho' far unable to prevent your fate;
Behold a banish'd man, for your dear cause　　　700
Expos'd a prey to arbitrary laws!
Yet, oh! that I alone cou'd be undone,
Cut off from empire and no more a son!
Now all your liberties a spoil are made; ⎤
Egypt and Tyrus intercept your trade, ⎬
And Jebusites your sacred rites invade. ⎦
My father, whom with reverence yet I name,
Charm'd into ease, is careless of his fame,
And brib'd with petty sums of foreign gold,
Is grown in Bathsheba's embraces old,　　　710
Exalts his enemies, his friends destroys,
And all his pow'r against himself employs.
He gives, and let him give my right away,
But why should he his own and yours betray?
He only, he can make the nation bleed,
And he alone from my revenge is freed.
Take then my tears" (with that he wip'd his eyes)
" 'Tis all the aid my present power supplies;
No court informer can these arms accuse,
These arms may sons against their fathers use,　　　720
And 'tis my wish the next successor's reign
May make no other Israelite complain."

---

[607] *Hybla drops.* Sicilian honey; a classical allusion.
[705] *Tyrus.* Holland, the Carthage of *Annus Mirabilis* 17 ff.
[709-10] Acknowledging Charles' dependence on Louis XIV for money and his fondness for women, perhaps particularly Louise de Kéroualle (d. 1734), Duchess of Portsmouth.

Youth, beauty, graceful action seldom fail;
But common interest always will prevail,
And pity never ceases to be shown
To him who makes the people's wrongs his own.
The crowd (that still believes their kings oppress)
With lifted hands their young Messiah bless,
Who now begins his progress to ordain,
With chariots, horsemen, and a numerous train;   730
From east to west his glories he displays,
And like the sun the promis'd land surveys.
Fame runs before him, as the morning star,
And shouts of joy salute him from afar;
Each house receives him as a guardian god
And consecrates the place of his abode;
But hospitable treats did most commend
Wise Issachar, his wealthy western friend.

This moving court that caught the people's eyes
And seem'd but pomp did other ends disguise;   740
Achitophel had form'd it, with intent
To sound the depths and fathom where it went,
The people's hearts; distinguish friends from foes,
And try their strength before they came to blows;
Yet all was colour'd with a smooth pretence
Of specious love and duty to their prince.
Religion and redress of grievances,
Two names that always cheat and always please,
Are often urg'd; and good King David's life
Endanger'd by a brother and a wife.   750
Thus, in a pageant show a Plot is made,
And peace itself is war in masquerade.

Oh, foolish Israel! never warn'd by ill,
Still the same bait, and circumvented still!
Did ever men forsake their present ease,
In midst of health imagine a disease,

729ff. 2 Samuel 15:1–6; Monmouth set west on July 26, 1680, to rally popular favor.
738 *Wise Issachar.* Representing Thomas Thynne (d. 1682) of Wiltshire, the "Protestant Squire," wise after the fashion of Issachar in Genesis 44:14, "a strong ass."
750 *a brother and a wife.* The queen and James were Catholic. Oates had absolved James of any plot but was urged by Shaftesbury to accuse him; his doing so strained the credulity of all but the most fanatic.

Take pains contingent mischiefs to foresee,
Make heirs for monarchs, and for God decree?
    What shall we think! can people give away
Both for themselves and sons their native sway?   760
Then they are left defenseless to the sword
Of each unbounded arbitrary lord;
And laws are vain, by which we right enjoy,
If kings unquestion'd can those laws destroy.
    Yet, if the crowd be judge of fit and just,
And kings are only officers in trust,
Then this resuming cov'nant was declar'd
When kings were made, or is for ever barr'd;
If those who gave the scepter could not tie
By their own deed their own posterity,   770
How then could Adam bind his future race?
How could his forfeit on mankind take place?
Or how could heavenly justice damn us all,
Who ne'er consented to our father's fall?
Then kings are slaves to those whom they command
And tenants to their people's pleasure stand.
Add, that the pow'r for property allow'd
Is mischievously seated in the crowd;
For who can be secure of private right,
If sovereign sway may be dissolv'd by might?   780
Nor is the people's judgment always true:
The most may err as grossly as the few
And faultless kings run down by common cry
For vice, oppression, and for tyranny.
What standard is there in a fickle rout
Which, flowing to the mark, runs faster out?
Nor only crowds, but Sanhedrins may be
Infected with this public lunacy
And share the madness of rebellious times,
To murder monarchs for imagin'd crimes.   790
If they may give and take whene'er they please,
Not kings alone (the godhead's images),
But government itself at length must fall
To nature's state, where all have right to all.
    Yet, grant our lords the people kings can make,
What prudent men a settled throne would shake?

For whatsoe'er their sufferings were before,
That change they covet makes them suffer more.
All other errors but disturb a state,
But innovation is the blow of fate.   800
If ancient fabrics nod and threat to fall,
To patch the flaws and buttress up the wall,
Thus far 'tis duty; but here fix the mark:
For all beyond it is to touch our Ark.
To change foundations, cast the frame anew,
Is work for rebels who base ends pursue:
At once divine and human laws control,
And mend the parts by ruin of the whole.
The tampering world is subject to this curse,
To physic their disease into a worse.   810
   Now what relief can righteous David bring?
How fatal 'tis to be too good a king!
Friends he has few, so high the madness grows,
Who dare be such must be the people's foes;
Yet some there were, ev'n in the worst of days;
Some let me name, and naming is to praise.
   In this short file Barzillai first appears,
Barzillai crown'd with honour and with years;
Long since, the rising rebels he withstood
In regions waste beyond the Jordan's flood,   820
Unfortunately brave to buoy the state,
But sinking underneath his master's fate,
In exile with his godlike prince he mourn'd,
For him he suffer'd and with him return'd.
The court he practis'd, not the courtier's art;
Large was his wealth, but larger was his heart,
Which well the noblest objects knew to choose,

759-810 Dryden's "passage on government"; cf. also *To My Honour'd Kinsman*, 171 ff. Dryden emphasizes: (a) inherited liberties of English subjects, guaranteed by laws (759–64); (b) the hereditary nature of the throne and obedience to it (765–80); (c) the danger in following the judgment of the many (780–94); and (d) the prudence of retaining a functioning system and of repairing only its minor flaws (795–810).

817 *Barzillai*. Most appropriately the "very aged, very great man" who "had provided the king of sustenance" in 2 Samuel 19:32, based on James Butler (d. 1688) the now aged, great first Duke of Ormond (or Ormonde), a devoted Royalist independent in his integrity and generous with his wealth to the Royalist cause and to numerous beneficiaries.

820 *beyond the Jordan's flood*. In Ireland as Lord Lieutenant for Charles I.

The fighting warrior and recording Muse.
  His bed could once a fruitful issue boast;
Now more than half a father's name is lost.   830
His eldest hope, with every grace adorn'd,
By me (so Heav'n will have it) always mourn'd
And always honour'd, snatch'd in manhood's prime
By' unequal fates and providence's crime,
Yet not before the goal of honour won,
All parts fulfill'd of subject and of son;
Swift was the race but short the time to run.
O narrow circle but of pow'r divine,
Scanted in space but perfect in thy line!
By sea, by land, thy matchless worth was known,   840
Arms thy delight, and war was all thy own;
Thy force, infus'd, the fainting Tyrians propp'd,
And haughty Pharaoh found his fortune stopp'd.

  Oh, ancient honour, Oh, unconquer'd hand,
Whom foes unpunish'd never could withstand!
But Israel was unworthy of thy name:
Short is the date of all immoderate fame.
It looks as Heaven our ruin had design'd
And durst not trust thy fortune and thy mind.
Now free from earth, thy disemcumb'red soul   850
Mounts up and leaves behind the clouds and starry
    pole;
From thence thy kindred legions may'st thou bring
To aid the guardian angel of thy King.

  Here stop, my Muse, here cease thy painful flight;
No pinions can pursue immortal height;
Tell good Barzillai thou canst sing no more,

---

831 *His eldest hope.* Dryden's ideal young courtier, Thomas, Earl of Ossory, who had died in 1680, had been distinguished for bravery, loyalty, and honesty.

832-34 See Virgil, *Aeneid* V, 49-50. The *unequal fates* recall Virgil's *fata iniquia* (*Aeneid* II, 257 and X, 380).

839-40 The circle emblem for perfection is combined with the formula of the brevity of that which is extraordinary; see 847.

844-45 Cf. *Aeneid* VI, 878-80. (Oh, for the goodness, for the old perfect honor, and for the stout right hand unvanquished in war. None would have advanced on him without injury, whether when he tore against the foe afoot or when he dug his spurs into the flanks of his foaming horse.)

847 Rendering Martial IV, xxix, 7, an idea in 844-45 and in the Killigrew Ode 147-48.

And tell thy soul she should have fled before;
Or fled she with his life and left this verse
To hang on her departed patron's hearse?
Now take thy steepy flight from Heaven and see   860
If thou canst find on earth another *he;*
Another he would be too hard to find;
See then whom thou canst see not far behind.

    Zadoc the priest whom, shunning power and
      place,
His lowly mind advanc'd to David's grace;
With him the Sagan of Jerusalem,
Of hospitable soul and noble stem;
Him of the western dome, whose weighty sense
Flows in fit words and heavenly eloquence.
The prophets' sons, by such example led,   870
To learning and to loyalty were bred,
For colleges on bounteous kings depend,
And never rebel was to arts a friend.
To these succeed the pillars of the laws,
Who best cou'd plead and best can judge a cause.

    Next them a train of loyal peers ascend:
Sharp judging Adriel the Muses' friend,
Himself a Muse—in Sanhedrin's debate
True to his prince, but not a slave of state,
Whom David's love with honours did adorn,   880
That from his disobedient son were torn.

    Jotham of piercing wit and pregnant thought,
Indu'd by nature and by learning taught
To move assemblies, who but only try'd

---

⁸⁶⁴ *Zadoc the priest.* Mentioned in 2 Samuel 8; the phrase is the title of a contemporary piece of religious music; based on William Sancroft (d. 1693), the reserved Archbishop of Canterbury.

⁸⁶⁶ *Sagan of Jerusalem.* Based on Henry Compton (d. 1713), Bishop of London, youngest son of the Earl of Northampton and a strong anti-Catholic. *Sagan* was the rank next high priest (archbishop).

⁸⁶⁸ *Him of the western dome.* John Dolben (d. 1686), Archbishop of York, patron of *prophets' sons*, boys at Dryden's school, Westminster.

⁸⁷⁷ *Sharp judging Adriel.* Based on John Sheffield (d. 1721), then Earl of Mulgrave, in 1703 Duke of Buckingham and Normanby; a patron of Dryden and *sharp* for his Essay on Satire.

⁸⁸⁰⁻⁸¹ In 1679 Charles II gave Mulgrave two offices taken from Monmouth.

⁸⁸² *Jotham.* Based on George Savile (d. 1695), first Baron Savile, later Marquis of Halifax, distinguished for his prose style, for his policy of "trimming" between political extremes, and for persuasive eloquence against the Exclusion Bill. He had supported Shaftesbury's (*worse*) side until 1680.

The worse awhile, then chose the better side.
Nor chose alone, but turn'd the balance too,
So much the weight of one brave man can do.

Hushai, the friend of David in distress,
In public storms of manly steadfastness;
By foreign treaties he inform'd his youth   890
And join'd experience to his native truth.
His frugal care suppli'd the wanting throne,
Frugal for that but bounteous of his own;
'Tis easy conduct when exchequers flow,
But hard the task to manage well the low;
For sovereign power is too depress'd or high
When kings are forc'd to sell or crowds to buy.

Indulge one labour more, my weary Muse,
For Amiel—who can Amiel's praise refuse?
Of ancient race by birth, but nobler yet   900
In his own worth, and without title great;
The Sanhedrin long time as chief he rul'd,
Their reason guided and their passion cool'd;
So dextrous was he in the crown's defence,
So form'd to speak a loyal nation's sense,
That as their band was Israel's tribes in small,
So fit was he to represent them all.
Now rasher charioteers the seat ascend,
Whose loose carriers his steady skill commend;
They like th' unequal ruler of the day   910
Misguide the seasons and mistake the way,
While he withdrawn at their mad labour smiles
And safe enjoys the sabbath of his toils.

These were the chief, a small but faithful band ⎫
Of worthies, in the breach who dar'd to stand   ⎬
And tempt th' united fury of the land.   ⎭

---

888 *Hushai.* Friend of David (2 Samuel 25–27) influential in Achitophel's
defeat; based on Laurence Hyde (d. 1711), Earl of Rochester from
1682, one of Dryden's persistent benefactors, a diplomat (890), and
first lord of the Treasury (892 ff.).

899 *Amiel.* One of the "able men for strength of service" (1 Chronicles
26:4–8), based on Edward Seymour (d. 1708), Speaker of the Commons where he was master of procedure; his was one of the old and
noble families of England.

908–11 Subsequent speakers of the House are mere Phaetons to Seymour's
Apollo; Phaeton stole his father's chariot of the sun and drove disastrously. The comparison was traditional for those whose ambitions led
them past loyalty.

With grief they view'd such powerful engines bent
To batter down the lawful government:
A numerous faction with pretended frights,
In Sanhedrins to plume the regal rights;   920
The true successor from the court remov'd;
The plot by hireling witnesses improv'd.
These ills they saw, and as their duty bound,
They shew'd the King the danger of the wound:
That no concessions from the throne would please,
But lenitives fomented the disease;
That Absalom, ambitious of the crown,
Was made the lure to draw the people down;
That false Achitophel's pernicious hate
Had turn'd the Plot to ruin church and state;   930
The council violent, the rabble worse,
That Shimei taught Jerusalem to curse.

   With all these loads of injuries oppress'd,
And long revolving in his careful breast
Th' event of things, at last, his patience tir'd,
Thus from his royal throne by Heav'n inspir'd,
The godlike David spoke; with awfull fear
His train their Maker in their master hear.

   "Thus long have I, by native mercy sway'd,
My wrongs dissembl'd, my revenge delay'd: 940
So willing to forgive th' offending age,
So much the father did the king assuage.
But now so far my clemency they slight,
Th' offenders question my forgiving right.
That one was made for many, they contend,
But 'tis to rule, for that's a monarch's end.
They call my tenderness of blood, my fear,
Though manly tempers can the longest bear.
Yet since they will divert my native course,
'Tis time to shew I am not good by force.   950
Those heap'd affronts that haughty subjects bring
Are burthens for a camel, not a king:
Kings are the public pillars of the state,
Born to sustain and prop the nation's weight;

---

[944] Charles had tried to prevent the trial of his minister, Danby, and angered many in the Commons by pardoning him in March 1679.

If my young Samson will pretend a call
To shake the column, let him share the fall.

    "But, oh, that yet he would repent and live!
How easy 'tis for parents to forgive!
With how few tears a pardon might be won
From nature pleading for a darling son!   960
Poor pitied youth, by my paternal care
Rais'd up to all the height his frame could bear;
Had God ordain'd his fate for empire born,
He would have given his soul another turn;
Gull'd with a patriot's name, whose modern sense
Is one that would by law supplant his prince:
The people's brave, the politician's tool,
Never was patriot yet but was a fool.

    "Whence comes it that religion and the laws
Should more be Absalom's than David's cause?   970
His old instructor, e're he lost his place,
Was never thought endu'd with so much grace.
Good heav'ns, how faction can a patriot paint!
My rebel ever proves my people's saint;
Would *they* impose an heir upon the throne?
Let Sanhedrins be taught to give their own.

    "A king's at least a part of government,
And mine as requisite as their consent;
Without my leave a future king to choose,
Infers a right the present to depose;   980
True, they petition me t' approve their choice,
But Esau's hands suit ill with Jacob's voice.
My pious subjects for my safety pray,
Which to secure they take my power away.
From plots and treasons Heaven preserve my years,
But save me most from my petitioners,
Unsatiate as the barren womb or grave;
God cannot grant so much as they can crave.

    "What then is left but with a jealous eye
To guard the small remains of royalty?   990

---

966 *supplant.* The change from *destroy* in the first edition suggests some
    softening of criticism.
982 Genesis 27:26–36.
987 According to Proverbs 30:16, "The grave; and the barren womb" are
    among the four insatiable things.

The law shall still direct my peaceful sway,
And the same law teach rebels to obey;
Votes shall no more establish'd pow'r control,
Such votes as make a part exceed the whole;
No groundless clamours shall my friends remove,
Nor crowds have power to punish e're they prove;
For gods and godlike kings their care express
Still to defend their servants in distress.

"Oh, that my power to saving were confin'd;
Why am I forc'd, like Heaven, against my mind   1000
To make examples of another kind?
Must I at length the sword of justice draw?
Oh, curst effects of necessary law!
How ill my fear they by my mercy scan:
Beware the fury of a patient man.
They could not be content to look on grace
Her hinder parts, but with a daring eye
To tempt the terror of her front and die.

"By their own arts 'tis righteously decreed,
Those dire artificers of death shall bleed.   1010
Against themselves their witnesses will swear,
Till viper-like their mother plot they tear
And suck for nutriment that bloody gore
Which was their principle of life before.
Their Belial with their Belzebub will fight;
Thus on my foes my foes shall do me right;
Nor doubt th' event: for factious crowds engage
In their first onset all their brutal rage;
Then, let 'em take an unresisted course,
Retire and traverse, and delude their force,   1020
But when they stand all breathless, urge the fight,
And rise upon 'em with redoubled might;

1000-5 Dryden's orthodox theology gives *mind* as most significant, the
  divine essence, or wisdom, and *justice* or *law*, the ethical expression of
  wisdom and an attribute along with *grace* or mercy. The king here ac-
  tively assumes his part as God's vicegerent. See 326–28*n* and 526*n*.
1006-10 The man who looks on God's face dies, though Moses (Exodus
  33:20–23) saw his "back parts"—or grace; the Whigs asked for the
  front, law, which will be mortal.
1012-14 *Till viper-like,* etc. Aptly recalling the offspring of Errour in Spenser, *The Faerie Queene* I, i, 25–26.
1015 *Belial . . . Belzebub.* Devils, recalling two of Milton's principal fallen
  angels in *Paradise Lost.*

For lawful pow'r is still superior found;
When long driven back, at length it stands the
    ground."
    He said. Th' Almighty, nodding, gave consent,
And peals of thunder shook the firmament.
Henceforth a series of new time began;
The mighty years in long procession ran:
Once more the godlike David was restor'd,
And willing nations knew their lawful lord.   1030

---

⁹³⁹⁻¹⁰²⁵ The speech resolves the poem more dramatically than the casual
    ending in 2 Samuel by using an address or proclamation from the
    throne, recalling Charles' speech to the Oxford Parliament and using
    arguments from *His Majesty's Declaration,* for which Dryden wrote a
    defense.
¹⁰²⁵⁻³⁰ The prophetic past tense; for divine confirmation (cf. *Aeneid* IX,
    104-6) and institution of a new age (see *Astraea Redux* 320-22n).

THE MEDAL

A Satire Against Sedition

*Per Graium populos, mediaeque
per Elidis urbem
Ibat ovans; divumque sibi posce-
bat honores.*

1681–1682. The Royalists (or Tories) had seized the initiative by the time of *Absalom and Achitophel* and so were able to have Shaftesbury committed to the Tower on July 2, 1681, charged with high treason. But the anti-Royalists (or Whigs) were still very active and packed the jury, so getting the charges against Shaftesbury returned with an "Ignoramus" on November 24. His followers had a triumphant medal struck, showing on its one side the bust of their leader, and on its other a view of London with the Bridge, the Tower, a rising sun dispelling clouds, and the motto *Laetamur* (see ll. 10–15). Just as the king had been the meaningful center of *Absalom and Achitophel* though he was, as it were, usually offstage, so now does the personality of the unnamed "chief," Shaftesbury, dominate this poem. The difference between him and the character Achitophel shows how fully both are artistic creations. Achitophel had possessed heroic though perverted qualities; the "chief" is "base," "venal," and distasteful. Another change is the more prominent function of the seething London populace, whose greater and more ominous reality seems to lessen the validity of the prediction of divine order at the end of the poem.

The poem is remarkable for its air of fury that, from the evidence in the prefatory "Epistle to the Whigs," seems partly feigned, a satiric device common enough in Roman

and earlier English satire. On the other hand, *The Medal* is
Dryden's single angry poem, working by techniques of
diminution and debasement rather than amplification;
moreover, the poem's most moving lines (91–134) question whether man as a social, historical, or individual creature is capable of anything but rashness and folly. Such
doubt is at once disturbing and productive of the dark,
fearsome power of the poem. Comparison with *Absalom
and Achitophel* Parts I and II reveals how important the
biblical parallel might be and how overpowering the contemporary scene undistanced by that parallel might seem.
The structural patterning of the poem on the scenes depicted on the two sides of the medal heightens the particu-
larity of Dryden's satire.

Because the poem responds to the release of Shaftesbury
on November 24, 1681, and was circulating by March 16,
1682, it must have been written near the turn of the year.
The epigraph is from Virgil, *Aeneid* VI, 588–89:

> Thro' Elis and the Grecian towns he flew;
> Th' audacious wretch four fiery coursers drew;
> He wav'd a torch aloft and, madly vain,
> Sought godlike worship from a servile train.
>
> (Trans. Dryden.)

Epistle to the Whigs

For to whom can I dedicate this poem with so much justice
as to you? 'Tis the representation of your own hero; 'tis the
picture drawn at length which you admire and prize so
much in little. None of your ornaments are wanting—neither the landscape of the Tower, nor the rising sun, nor the
Anno Domini of your new sovereign's coronation. This
must needs be a grateful undertaking to your whole party,
especially to those who have not been so happy as to purchase the original. I hear the 'graver has made a good
market of it: all his kings are bought up already, or the
value of the remainder so enhanc'd that many a poor Po-

lander[1] who would be glad to worship the image is not able
to go to the cost of him but must be content to see him
here. I must confess I am no great artist, but sign-post
painting will serve the turn to remember a friend by, especially when better is not to be had. Yet for your comfort the
lineaments are true; and though he sat not five times to me
as he did to B.,[2] yet I have consulted history, as the Italian
painters do when they wou'd draw a Nero or a Caligula:
though they have not seen the man, they can help their
imagination by a statue of him and find out the colouring
from Suetonius and Tacitus.[3] Truth is, you might have
spar'd one side of your medal: the head wou'd be seen to
more advantage if it were plac'd on a spike of the Tower, a
little nearer to the sun. Which wou'd then break out to a
better purpose. You tell us in your Preface to the *No-
Protestant Plot*[4] that you shall be forc'd hereafter to leave
off your modesty; I suppose you mean that little which is
left you, for it was worn to rags when you put out this
medal. Never was there practis'd such a piece of notorious
impudence in the face of an establish'd government. I believe when he is dead you will wear him in thumb-rings, as
the Turks did Scanderbeg,[5] as if there were virtue in his
bones to preserve you against monarchy.

Yet all this while you pretend not only zeal for the public
good, but a due veneration for the person of the King. But
all men who can see an inch before them may easily detect
those gross fallacies. That it is necessary for men in your
circumstances to pretend both is granted you, for without
them there could be no ground to raise a faction. But I
would ask you one civil question, what right has any man
among you, or any Association[6] of men (to come nearer to
you), who out of Parliament cannot be consider'd in public

---

[1] *Polander.* A Whig; Shaftesbury made a joke of himself by seeking the
elective Polish kingship in 1675.

[2] *B.* George Bower, artist of the medal.

[3] *Suetonius and Tacitus.* Roman historians.

[4] *No-Protestant Plot.* A Whig tract in three parts (1681–1682), probably
by Robert Ferguson, "the Plotter."

[5] *Scanderbeg.* George Castriota, "Iskander Beg" (d. 1467), an Albanian
prince in the Turkish wars; after capturing Alessio, the Turks made
amulets of his disinterred bones.

[6] *Association.* Shaftesbury was accused of a design to form a hyper-Prot-
estant, anti-Royalist group with such a name on the model of an Association to protect Elizabeth I; see pp. 241–42, below.

capacity, to meet, as you daily do in factious clubs, to vilify the government in your discourses and to libel it in all your writings? Who made you judges in Israel? Or how is it consistent with your zeal of the public welfare to promote sedition? Does your definition of "loyal," which is to serve the King according to the laws, allow you the licence of traducing the executive power, with which you own he is invested? You complain that his Majesty has lost the love and confidence of his people; and by your very urging it, you endeavour what in you lies to make him lose them. All good subjects abhor the thought of arbitrary power, whether it be in one or many; if you were the patriots you would seem, you would not at this rate incense the multitude to assume it; for no sober man can fear it, either from the King's disposition or his practice or even, where you would odiously lay it, from his ministers. Give us leave to enjoy the government and the benefit of laws under which we were born and which we desire to transmit to our posterity. You are not the trustees of the public liberty; and if you have not right to petition[7] in a crowd, much less have you to intermeddle in the management of affairs or to arraign what you do not like, which in effect is everything that is done by the King and Council.

Can you imagine that any reasonable man will believe you respect the person of his Majesty, when 'tis apparent that your seditious pamphlets are stuff'd with particular reflexions on him? If you have the confidence to deny this, 'tis easy to be evinc'd from a thousand passages, which I only forbear to quote because I desire they should die and be forgotten. I have perus'd many of your papers; and to show you that I have, the third part of your *No-Protestant Plot* is much of it stolen from your dead author's pamphlet call'd *The Growth of Popery*,[8] as manifestly as Milton's *Defence of the English People* is from Buchanan,[9] *De jure regni apud Scotos,* or your first Covenant and new Associ-

---

[7] *you have not right to petition.* Royalist "addresses" were distinguished from critical "petitions" to the throne, which were forbidden in groups larger than ten or twenty (by law: 13 Car. II. c. 5).

[8] *The Growth of Popery. An Account of* (1677), by Andrew Marvell (d. 1678).

[9] *Buchanan.* George (d. 1582), Scottish humanist famous for his Latin style and his republicanism.

ation, from the holy League[10] of the French Guisards. Any-one who reads Davila[11] may trace your practices all along. There were the same pretences for reformation and loyalty, the same aspersions of the king, and the same grounds of a rebellion. I know not whether you will take the historian's word, who says it was reported that Poltrot, a Huguenot, murder'd Francis Duke of Guise by the instigations of Theodore Beza;[12] or that it was a Huguenot minister, otherwise call'd a Presbyterian (for our Church abhors so devilish a tenet), who first writ a treatise of the lawfulness of deposing and murdering kings of a different persuasion in religion. But I am able to prove from the doctrine of Calvin and principles of Buchanan that they set the people above the magistrate, which if I mistake not is your own fundamental and which carries your loyalty no farther than your liking.

When a vote of the House of Commons goes on your side, you are as ready to observe it as if it were pass'd into a law; but when you are pinch'd with any former and yet unrepealed Act of Parliament, you declare that in some cases you will not be oblig'd by it. The passage is in the same third part of the No-Protestant Plot and is too plain to be denied. The late copy of your intended Association you neither wholly justify nor condemn. But as the Papists, when they are unoppos'd, fly out into all the pageantries of worship but in times of war when they are hard press'd by arguments, lie close entrench'd behind the Council of Trent: so, now, when your affairs are in a low condition you dare not pretend that to be a legal combination; but whensoever you are afloat, I doubt not but it will be maintain'd and justify'd to purpose. For indeed there is nothing to defend it but the sword: 'tis the proper time to say anything when men have all things in their power.

In the meantime you wou'd fain be nibbling at a parallel betwixt this Association and that in the time of Queen

[10] *the holy League*, etc. The Ligue of the Guisards was a Catholic anti-Royalist movement led by the Duke of Guise against the then Protestant king, Henri IV (d. 1610).
[11] *Davila*. Italian historian (d. 1631), author of the very popular *Storia delle Guerre Civilia di Francia*.
[12] *Beza*. Théodore de Béze (d. 1605), successor to Calvin.

Elizabeth. But there is this small difference betwixt them,
that the ends of the one are directly opposite to the other:
one with the Queen's approbation and conjunction, as head
of it, the other without either the consent or knowledge of
the King, against whose authority it is manifestly design'd.
Therefore you do well to have recourse to your last evasion,
that it was contriv'd by your enemies and shuffled into the
papers that were seiz'd, which yet you see the nation is not
so easy to believe as your own jury. But the matter is not
difficult to find twelve men in Newgate[13] who wou'd acquit
a malefactor.

I have one only favour to desire of you at parting, that
when you think of answering this poem, you wou'd employ
the same pens against it who have combatted with so much
success against *Absalom and Achitophel;* for then you may
assure yourselves of a clear victory without the least reply.
Rail at me abundantly, and, not to break a custom, do it
without wit; by this method you will gain a considerable
point, which is wholly to waive the answer of my arguments. Never own the bottom of your principles, for fear
they shou'd be treason. Fall severely on the miscarriages of
government, for if scandal be not allow'd, you are no free-
born subjects. If God has not bless'd you with the talent of
rhyming, make use of my poor stock and welcome; let your
verses run upon my feet; and for the utmost refuge of notorious blockheads reduc'd to the last extremity of sense, turn
my own lines upon me, and, in utter despair of your own
satire, make me satirize myself. Some of you have been
driven to this bay already.[14] But above all the rest commend me to the Nonconformist parson who writ *The Whip
and Key.* I am afraid it is not read so much as the piece
deserves, because the bookseller is every week crying help
at the end of his *Gazette* to get it off. You see I am charitable enough to do him a kindness, that it may be publish'd
as well as printed, and that so much skill in Hebrew deri-

---

[13] *Newgate.* The prison.
[14] *Some of you,* etc. *Absalom and Achitophel* evoked desperate counter-
blasts, some of which paraphrased or parodied Dryden; among the
many was one attributed to the Calvinist parson Christopher Nesse,
A Whip for the Fool's Back (1681); another, *A Key* to Dryden's earlier
poem (1682).

vations may not lie for wastepaper in the shop. Yet I half
suspect he went no farther for his learning than the index
of Hebrew names and etymologies which is printed at the
end of some English Bibles. If "Achitophel" signify the
"Brother of a Fool," the authour of that poem will pass with
his readers for the next of kin. And perhaps 'tis the relation
that makes the kindness. Whatever the verses are, buy 'em
up, I beseech you, out of pity; for I hear the conventicle is
shut up and the brother of Achitophel out of service.

Now footmen, you know, have the generosity to make a
purse for a member of their society who has had his livery
pull'd over his ears, and even Protestant socks are bought
up among you out of veneration to the name. A dissenter in
poetry from sense and English will make as good a Protestant rhymer as a Dissenter from the Church of England a
Protestant parson. Besides, if you encourage a young be-
ginner, who knows but he may elevate his style a little
above the vulgar epithets of "prophane," and "saucy Jack,"
and "atheistic scribbler," with which he treats me when the
fit of enthusiasm is strong upon him; by which well-
manner'd and charitable expressions I was certain of his
sect before I knew his name. What wou'd you have more of
a man? He has damn'd me in your cause from Genesis to
the Revelations and has half the texts of both the Testaments against me, if you will be so civil to yourselves as to
take him for your interpreter, and not to take them for Irish
witnesses.[15] After all, perhaps you will tell me that you retain'd him only for the opening of your cause and that your
main lawyer is yet behind. Now if it so happen he meet
with no more reply than his predecessors, you may either
conclude that I trust to the goodness of my cause, or fear
my adversary, or disdain him, or what you please, for the
short on 't is, 'tis indifferent to your humble servant, whatever your party says or thinks of him.

---

[15] *Irish witnesses.* Who first testified for, then against, Shaftesbury's cause
in the Popish Plot.

THE MEDAL

A Satire Against Sedition

Of all our antic sights and pageantry
Which English idiots run in crowds to see,
The Polish Medal bears the prize alone:
A monster more the favourite of the town
Than either fairs or theatres have shown.
Never did Art so well with Nature strive,
Nor ever idol seem'd so much alive;
So like the man: so golden to the sight,
So base within, so counterfeit and light.
One side is fill'd with title and with face;   10
And, lest the King shou'd want a regal place,
On the reverse, a tow'r the town surveys,
O'er which our mounting sun his beams displays.
The word, pronounc'd aloud by shrieval voice,
Laetamur, which in Polish is "rejoice."
The day, month, year, to the great act are join'd,
And a new canting holiday design'd.
Five days he sat for every cast and look,
Four more than God to finish Adam took.
But who can tell what essence angels are,   20
Or how long Heav'n was making Lucifer?
Oh, cou'd the style that copi'd every grace
And plough'd such furrows for an eunuch face,
Cou'd it have form'd his ever-changing will,
The various piece had tir'd the 'graver's skill!
    A martial hero first, with early care
Blown, like a pigmy by the winds, to war.
A beardless chief, a rebel e'r a man
(So young his hatred to his prince began).
Next this (how wildly will ambition steer!)   30
A vermin wriggling in th' usurper's ear.

---

³ *Polish.* See Epistle footnote 1.
¹⁴ *shrieval voice.* Voice of London's Whig sheriffs.
³¹ *vermin.* That is, the earwig, common metaphor for whisperer or parasite, recalling Satan, who whispered temptations in Eve's ear (Milton, *Paradise Lost* IV).

Bart'ring his venal wit for sums of gold,
He cast himself into the saint-like mould,
Groan'd, sigh'd, and pray'd, while godliness was
    gain,
The loudest bagpipe of the squeaking train.
But, as 'tis hard to cheat a juggler's eyes,
His open lewdness he cou'd ne'er disguise.
There split the Saint, for hypocritic zeal
Allows no sins but those it can conceal.
Whoring to scandal gives too large a scope: 40
Saints must not trade, but they may interlope.
Th' ungodly principle was all the same,
But a gross cheat betrays his partner's game.
Besides, their pace was formal, grave, and slack;
His nimble wit outran the heavy pack.
Yet still he found his fortune at a stay,
Whole droves of blockheads choking up his way;
They took, but not rewarded, his advice;
Villain and wit exact a double price.
Pow'r was his aim, but thrown from that pretence,   50
The wretch turn'd loyal in his own defence,
And malice reconcil'd him to his prince.
Him in the anguish of his soul he serv'd,
Rewarded faster still than he deserv'd.
Behold him now exalted into trust;
His counsel's oft convenient, seldom just.
Ev'n in the most sincere advice he gave
He had a grudging still to be a knave.
The frauds he learnt in his fanatic years
Made him uneasy in his lawful gears.   60
At best as little honest as he cou'd
And, like white witches, mischievously good.
To his first bias longingly he leans
And *rather* wou'd be great by wicked means.
Thus, fram'd for ill, he loos'd our triple hold
(Advice unsafe, precipitous, and bold).

---

[37] *open lewdness.* Shaftesbury was called "the greatest whoremaster in England."
[50-53] Referring to Shaftesbury's period of support of Charles II.
[62] *white witches.* Who use their powers for good.
[65] *triple hold.* See *Absalom and Achitophel* 175n.

From hence those tears! that Ilium of our woe!
Who helps a pow'rful friend forearms a foe.
What wonder if the waves prevail so far
When he cut down the banks that made the bar?   70
Seas follow but their nature to invade,
But he by art our native strength betray'd.
So Sampson to his foe his force confess'd
And to be shorn lay slumb'ring on her breast.
But when this fatal counsel, found too late,
Expos'd its author to the public hate,
When his just sovereign, by no impious way,
Cou'd be seduc'd to arbitrary sway,
Forsaken of that hope he shifts the sail,
Drives down the current with a pop'lar gale,   80
And shews the fiend confess'd without a veil.

He preaches to the crowd that pow'r is lent
But not convey'd to kingly government,
That claims successive bear no binding force,
That coronation oaths are things of course;
Maintains the multitude can never err,
And sets the people in the papal chair.
The reason's obvious: "Int'rest never lies";
The most have still their int'rest in their eyes;
The pow'r is always theirs, and pow'r is ever
      wise.   90

Almighty crowd, thou shorten'st all dispute;
Pow'r is thy essence, wit thy attribute!
Nor faith nor reason make thee at a stay;
Thou leapst o'er all eternal truths in thy Pindaric
      way!
Athens, no doubt, did righteously decide
When Phocion and when Socrates were tri'd:
As righteously they did those dooms repent;
Still they were wise, whatever way they went.

---

[73] *Sampson to his foe.* Delilah, who cut Samson's hair, which Sampson had *confess'd* to be his source of strength.

[82-87] See *Absalom and Achitophel* 200-7.

[92] *Pow'r,* etc. Inverting Dryden's view that reason (wit) was God's essence, will and power but attributes. See *Absalom and Achitophel* 326-28n and 1000-5n.

[96] *Phocion,* etc. Athenians executed Phocion on a charge of treason in 317 B.C., and Socrates on a charge of impiety in 399 B.C. They later regretted both executions and raised statues in honor of the victims.

Crowds err not though to both extremes they run,
To kill the father and recall the son.   100
Some think the fools were most, as times went then,
But now the world's o'erstock'd with prudent men.
The common cry is ev'n religion's test;
The Turk's is at Constantinople best;
Idols in India, Popery at Rome;
And our own worship only true at home,
And true but for the time; 'tis hard to know
How long we please it shall continue so.
This side today, and that tomorrow burns;
So all are God-a'mighties in their turns.   110
A tempting doctrine, plausible and new:
What fools our fathers were, if this be true!
Who, to destroy the seeds of civil war,
Inherent right in monarchs did declare;
And, that a lawful pow'r might never cease,
Secur'd succession to secure our peace.
Thus, property and sovereign sway at last
In equal balances were justly cast;
But this new Jehu spurs the hot-mouth'd horse,
Instructs the beast to know his native force,   120
To take the bit between his teeth and fly
To the next headlong steep of anarchy.
Too happy England, if our good we knew;
Wou'd we possess the freedom we pursue!
The lavish government can give no more;
Yet we repine, and plenty makes us poor.
God tri'd us once; our rebel-fathers fought;
He glutted 'em with all the pow'r they sought,
Till master'd by their own usurping brave,
The freeborn subject sunk into a slave.   130
We loath our manna, and we long for quails:
Ah, what is man, when his own wish prevails!
How rash, how swift to plunge himself in ill;
Proud of his pow'r and boundless in his will!

100 To *kill* Charles I, *recall* Charles II.
119 *Jehu.* The wild horseman of 2 Kings 9:20.
127-30 Freedom sought by the Commonwealthsmen ended in the oligarchy
  of Cromwell and his major generals.
131 *manna.* A favorite allusion of Dryden's to Numbers 11, manna being an
  emblem of divine Providence, the episode a type of human ingratitude.

That kings can do no wrong we must believe:
None can they do, and must they all receive?
Help, Heaven! or sadly we shall see an hour
When neither wrong nor right are in their pow'r!
Already they have lost their best defence,
The benefit of laws, which they dispense.   140
No justice to their righteous cause allow'd,
But baffled by an arbitrary crowd.
And medals 'grav'd, their conquest to record,
The stamp and coin of their adopted lord.

The man who laugh'd but once to see an ass
Mumbling to make the cross-grain'd thistles pass,
Might laugh again to see a jury chaw
The prickles of unpalatable law.
The witnesses that, leech-like, liv'd on blood,
Sucking for them were med'cinally good;   150
But when they fasten'd on *their* fester'd sore, ⎫
Then justice and religion they forswore,   ⎬
Their maiden oaths debauch'd into a whore.   ⎭
Thus men are rais'd by factions and decri'd,
And rogue and saint distinguish'd by their side.
They rack ev'n Scripture to confess their cause,
And plead a call to preach in spite of laws.
But that's no news to the poor injur'd page;
It has been us'd as ill in every age,
And is constrain'd, with patience, all to take;   160
For what defence can Greek and Hebrew make?
Happy who can this talking trumpet seize;
They make it speak whatever sense they please!
'Twas fram'd at first our oracle t' enquire;   ⎫
But since our sects in prophecy grow higher,   ⎬
The text inspires not them, but they the text   ⎭
    inspire.

London, thou great emporium of our isle,
O thou too bounteous, thou too fruitful Nile,

---

140 *laws.* Dryden included law with king and Parliament as the three bases of the English Constitution.

145 *The man,* etc. Crassus, according to a story by Lucilius, *Reliquae.*

156-57 Referring to those Sects that took politics from individual interpretation of Scriptures or the *call* of the Holy Spirit.

How shall I praise or curse to thy desert!
Or separate thy sound from thy corrupted part!   170
I call'd thee Nile; the parallel will stand;
Thy tides of wealth o'erflow the fatten'd land;
Yet monsters from thy large increase we find
Engender'd on the slime thou leav'st behind.
Sedition has not wholly seiz'd on thee;
Thy nobler parts are from infection free.
Of Israel's tribes thou hast a numerous band,
But still the Canaanite is in the land.
Thy military chiefs are brave and true,
Nor are thy disenchanted burghers few.   180
The head is loyal which thy heart commands,
But what's a head with two such gouty hands?
The wise and wealthy love the surest way,
And are content to thrive and to obey.
But wisdom is to sloth too great a slave;
None are so busy as the fool and knave.
    Those let me curse: what vengeance will they
      urge,
Whose ordures neither plague nor fire can purge,
Nor sharp experience can to duty bring,
Nor angry Heav'n, nor a forgiving king!   190
In Gospel phrase their chapmen they betray:
Their shops are dens; the buyer is their prey.
The knack of trades is living on the spoil;
They boast ev'n when each other they beguile.
Customs to steal is such a trivial thing
That 'tis their charter to defraud their King.
All hands unite of every jarring sect;
They cheat the country first and then infect.
They, for God's cause, their monarchs dare
    dethrone,
And they'll be sure to make his cause their own.   200
Whether the plotting Jesuit laid the plan

181 The *head* is the Royalist Sir John Moore, elected Lord Mayor of London in 1681; the two *hands* are the Whig sheriffs elected about the same time.
188 *neither plague nor fire.* See *Annus Mirabilis*, headnote.
191 The traditional charge, hypocrisy, against Puritans.

Of murd'ring kings, or the French Puritan,
Our sacrilegious sects their guides outgo,
And kings and kingly pow'r wou'd murder too.

   What means their trait'rous combination less,
Too plain t' evade, too shameful to confess.
But treason is not own'd when 'tis descri'd;
Successful crimes alone are justifi'd.
The men who no conspiracy wou'd find—
Who doubts, but had it taken, they had join'd?   210
Join'd in a mutual cov'nant of defence,
At first without, at last against, their prince.
If sovereign right by sovereign pow'r they scan,
The same bold maxim holds in God and man:
God were not safe, His thunder cou'd they shun,
He shou'd be forc'd to crown another Son.
Thus when the heir was from the vineyard thrown,
The rich possession was the murd'rer's own.
In vain to sophistry they have recourse;
By proving theirs no plot, they prove 'tis worse: 220
Unmask'd rebellion and audacious force.
Which though not actual, yet all eyes may see
'Tis working in th' immediate pow'r to be;
For from pretended grievances they rise,
First to dislike and after to despise.
Then, Cyclop-like in human flesh to deal,
Chop up a minister at every meal;
Perhaps not wholly to melt down the King,
But clip his regal rights within the ring,
From thence t' assume the pow'r of peace and war   230
And ease him by degrees of public care.
Yet to consult his dignity and fame,
He shou'd have leave to exercise the name
And hold the cards while Commons play'd the game.

201-2 Both the French Guisards, supported by Jesuits, and French Calvinists contributed to anti-Royalist theory.
205 *combination*. The Whig Association.
217 *when the heir*, etc. Matthew 21:33–39.
228-29 Coins could be melted for their valuable metal and bore, within a
   ring, the sovereign's head. Early unmilled coins still circulated, so making clipping of edges profitable, although, when clipped within the
   ring, coins ceased to be legal tender.

For what can pow'r give more than food and
    drink,
To live at ease, and not be bound to think?
These are the cooler methods of their crime,
But their hot zealots think 'tis loss of time;
On utmost bounds of loyalty they stand,
And grin and whet like a Croatian band   240
That waits impatient for the last command.
Thus outlaws open villainy maintain:
They steal not but in squadrons scour the plain;
And if their pow'r the passengers subdue,
The most have right, the wrong is in the few.
Such impious axioms foolishly they show,
For in some soils republics will not grow;
Our temp'rate isle will no extremes sustain
Of pop'lar sway or arbitrary reign,
But slides between them both into the best,   250
Secure in freedom, in a monarch blest.
And though the climate, vex'd with various winds,
Works through our yielding bodies on our minds,
The wholesome tempest purges what it breeds,
To recommend the calmness that succeeds.
    But thou, the pander of the people's hearts
(O crooked soul and serpentine in arts),
Whose blandishments a loyal land have whor'd
And broke the bonds she plighted to her Lord;
What curses on thy blasted name will fall!   260
Which age to age their legacy shall call,
For all must curse the woes that must descend on all.
Religion thou hast none; thy mercury
Has pass'd through every sect or theirs through thee.
But what thou giv'st, that venom still remains,
And the pox'd nation feels thee in their brains.
What else inspires the tongues and swells the breasts
Of all thy bellowing renegado priests

---

257 *serpentine.* One of many suggestions of Shaftesbury's Satanic role in the
    poem.
258-59 The biblical metaphor for Israel's betrayal of Jehovah.
263 *Religion thou hast none.* Shaftesbury was thought a freethinker. *Mer-*
    cury was used as a dangerous cure for syphilis: *the pox'd* of 266.

That preach up thee for God, dispense thy laws,
And with thy stum ferment their fainting cause?   270
Fresh fumes of madness raise, and toil, and sweat,
To make the formidable cripple great.
Yet shou'd thy crimes succeed, shou'd lawless pow'r
Compass those ends thy greedy hopes devour,
Thy canting friends thy mortal foes wou'd be;
Thy god and theirs will never long agree.
For thine (if thou hast any) must be one
That lets the world and humankind alone,
A jolly god that passes hours too well
To promise Heav'n or threaten us with Hell;   280
That unconcern'd can at rebellion sit,
And wink at crimes he did himself commit.
A tyrant theirs; the Heav'n their priesthood paints
A conventicle of gloomy sullen saints;
A Heav'n, like Bedlam, slovenly and sad,
Foredoom'd for souls with false religion mad.
      Without a vision poets can foreshow
What all but fools by common sense may know:
If true succession from our isle shou'd fail,
And crowds profane with impious arms prevail,   290
Not thou nor those thy factious arts engage ⎫
Shall reap that harvest of rebellious rage,   ⎬
With which thou flatter'st thy decrepit age. ⎭
The swelling poison of the sev'ral sects,
Which wanting vent, the nation's health infects
Shall burst its bag, and fighting out their way
The various venoms on each other prey.
The Presbyter, puff'd up with spiritual pride,
Shall on the necks of the lewd nobles ride,
His brethren damn, the civil pow'r defy,   300
And parcel out republic prelacy.
But short shall be his reign; his rigid yoke
And tyrant pow'r will puny sects provoke;
And frogs and toads and all the tadpole train

---

270 Stale wines were refermented with new, or *stum*.
272 *cripple*. Shaftesbury had a running sore that drained by a silver tube
inserted by his physician, John Locke.
294-97 Cf. *Absalom and Achitophel* 1012–14; *The Hind and the Panther*
III, 1277–88.

Will croak to Heav'n for help from this devouring
    crane.
The cut-throat sword and clamorous gown shall jar
In sharing their ill-gotten spoils of war;
Chiefs shall be grudg'd the part which they pretend,
Lords envy lords, and friends with every friend
About their impious merit shall contend.   310
The surly Commons shall respect deny
And justle peerage out with property.
Their gen'ral either shall his trust betray
And force the crowd to arbitrary sway,
Or they suspecting his ambitious aim,
In hate of kings shall cast anew the frame
And thrust out Collatine that bore their name.

    Thus inborn broils the factions wou'd engage,
Or wars of exil'd heirs, or foreign rage,
Till halting vengeance overtook our age: 320
And our wild labours, wearied into rest,
Reclin'd us on a rightful monarch's breast.

—Pudet haec opprobria, vobis
Et dici potuisse, et non potuisse refelli.

₃₀₄₋₅ In the Aesopian fable, ungrateful frogs asked Jove to replace their
quiet King Log; he sent a crane that devoured them.
₂₉₈₋₃₁₇ The rebellion, rivalry, autocracy, and final royal restoration of the
years between 1642 and 1660 will come again.
₃₁₇ *Collatine.* Predicting that if made king, Monmouth would be later
forced to abdicate because related to Charles II, as Lucius Tarquinus
Collatinus was for being related to the last Tarquin king, whom he had
helped dethrone.
₃₂₃₋₂₄ *Pudet haec opprobria,* etc. Altered from Ovid, *Metamorphoses* I,
757-58. (It is shameful that this opprobrium can be spoken of you and
that it cannot be refuted.)

PROLOGUE TO THE DUCHESS ON HER RETURN FROM SCOTLAND

1682. Mary of Este and Modena (1658–1718), the second wife of James, Duke of York, was one of those foremost beauties of the time that Dryden liked to praise. Other passages on her are in the Killigrew Ode (ll. 134 ff.) and in *Britannia Rediviva* (ll. 304 ff.). James had returned in March 1682 from the Scottish exile prudently imposed upon him by Charles II during the Popish Plot, and after a trip back to the north brought his duchess to Whitehall on May 27. Dryden and Thomas Otway had celebrated the Duke's earlier return with a Prologue and an Epilogue for a special performance of Otway's *Venice Preserv'd,* and the Prologue to the Duchess was written for a similar occasion on May 31. The beautiful Duchess became a symbol of the peace Dryden hoped would follow upon the victories of Charles II over his domestic enemies.

When factious rage to cruel exile drove
The queen of beauty and the court of love,
The Muses droop'd with their forsaken arts,
And the sad Cupids broke their useless darts.
Our fruitful plains to wilds and deserts turn'd,
Like Eden's face when banish'd man it mourn'd;
Love was no more when loyalty was gone,
The great supporter of his awful throne.
Love cou'd no longer after beauty stay
But wander'd northward to the verge of day,   10
As if the sun and he had lost their way.
But now th' illustrious nymph, return'd again,

Brings every grace triumphant in her train;
The wond'ring Nereids, though they rais'd no storm,
Foreslow'd her passage to behold her form;
Some cri'd "A Venus," some, "A Thetis pass'd,"
But this was not so fair, nor that so chaste.
Far from her sight flew faction, strife, and pride,
And envy did but look on her and di'd.
Whate'er we suffer'd from our sullen fate,   10
Her sight is purchas'd at an easy rate;
Three gloomy years against this day were set,
But this one mighty sum has clear'd the debt.
Like Joseph's dream, but with a better doom,
The famine past, the plenty still to come.
For her the weeping heav'ns become serene,
For her the ground is clad in cheerful green,
For her the nightingales are taught to sing,
And Nature has for her delay'd the spring.
The Muse resumes her long-forgotten lays,   30
And love, restor'd, his ancient realm surveys,
Recalls our beauties, and revives our plays;
His waste dominions peoples once again,
And from her presence dates his second reign.
But awful charms on her fair forehead sit,
Dispensing what she never will admit.
Pleasing, yet cold, like Cynthia's silver beam,
The people's wonder, and the poet's theme.
Distemper'd zeal, sedition, canker'd hate,
No more shall vex the Church and tear the State;   40
No more shall faction civil discords move,
Or only discords of too tender love:
Discord like that of music's various parts,
Discord that makes the harmony of hearts,
Discord that only this dispute shall bring,
Who best shall love the Duke and serve the King.

24-25 *Joseph's dream.* Pharaoh's dream, interpreted by Joseph: seven years
    of plenty followed by seven years of dearth; Genesis 41.
37 *Cynthia.* Diana, goddess of the moon and of chastity.

The Second Part of

ABSALOM AND ACHITOPHEL

A POEM

1682. Both the events following the King's speech at the end of the first part of *Absalom and Achitophel* and the great popularity of the poem led to a call for a sequel. According to a note published in an edition of *The Second Part of Absalom and Achitophel* in 1716, the earlier poem "was applauded by everyone; and several persons pressing [Dryden] to write a second part, he, upon declining it himself, spoke to Mr. [Nahum] Tate to write one, and gave him his advice in the direction of it." The passage here is accepted as Dryden's because, although most who have read Tate's usual competent but untranscendent work think that much else in the poem is by Dryden, everyone agrees that the portraits of Doeg (based on Elkanah Settle) and of Og (based on Thomas Shadwell) could only be by him. Tate's continuation has some virtues and interest, but its account of events from September 1682 lacks the force and coherence of the original poem while also not possessing the directed anger of *The Medal*. Dryden's rollicking portraits are once again wholly new in kind, as comparison with *MacFlecknoe*, the first part of *Absalom and Achitophel*, and *The Medal* would show.

Levi, thou art a load; I'll lay thee down   400
And show rebellion bare without a gown,

400 *Levi*. The clergy.

Poor slaves in metre, dull and addlepated,
Who rhime below ev'n David's Psalms translated:
Some in my speedy pace I must outrun,
As lame Mephibosheth the wizard's son;
To make quick way I'll leap o'er heavy blocks,
Shun rotten Uzza as I wou'd the pox,
And hasten Og and Doeg to rehearse,
Two fools that crutch their feeble sense on verse,
Who by my Muse to all succeeding times   410
Shall live in spite of their own doggerel rhimes.
    Doeg, though without knowing how or why,
Made still a blund'ring kind of melody,
Spurr'd boldly on and dash'd through thick and
        thin,
Through sense and nonsense, never out nor in,
Free from all meaning, whether good or bad,
And in one word, heroically mad;
He was too warm on picking-work to dwell ⎤
But faggotted his notions as they fell,   ⎬
And if they rhym'd and rattl'd all was well. ⎦   420
Spiteful he is not, though he wrote a satire,
For still there goes some *thinking* to ill-nature;
He needs no more than birds and beasts to think;
All his occasions are to eat and drink.
If he call rogue and rascal from a garret,
He means you no more mischief than a parrot;
The words for friend and foe alike were made;
To fetter 'em in verse is all his trade.
For almonds he'll cry whore to his own mother

---

[403] *David's Psalms translated.* See *Essay of Dramatic Poesy,* note 112.

[405] *Mephibosheth.* Samuel Pordage (d ?1691), whose father had been arraigned for dealings with evil spirits.

[407] *Uzza.* Identified in 1716 as "J. H.," but unknown. The name implies impudent extremism (I Chronicles 13:7–11) and the line, syphilis.

[412] *Doeg.* The "fearful, uneasy" Edomite traitor of 1 Samuel 22; based on Elkanah Settle (d. 1724), who grew vain after the great success of his play, *The Empress of Morocco* (1673). First a court poet, then a Shaftesbury man, then not, then again a Whig, his career was indeed "uneasy" and ultimately pathetic in its degradation.

[415] *sense and nonsense.* Settle claimed to write rapt with inspiration.

[429] Combining (a) allusion to Shakespeare, *Troilus and Cressida* V, ii, 193–95, which provides imagery for 425–29; and (b) the story that, upon Thomas Otway's challenge to a duel, Settle wrote an apology, saying he was "the son of a whore" for having written against Otway.

And call young Absalom King David's brother.   430
Let him be gallows-free by my consent
And nothing suffer since he nothing meant;
Hanging supposes human soul and reason:
This animal's below committing treason.
Shall he be hang'd who never cou'd rebel?
That's a preferment for Achitophel.
The woman that committed buggery
Was rightly sentenc'd by the law to die,
But 'twas hard fate that to the gallows led
The dog that never heard the statute read.   440
Railing in other men may be a crime,
But ought to pass for mere instinct in him;
Instinct he follows and no farther knows,
For to write verse with him is to *transprose*.
'Twere pity treason at his door to lay,
"Who makes Heaven's gate a lock to its own key":
Let him rail on, let his invective Muse
Have four-and-twenty letters to abuse,
Which if he jumbles to one line of sense,
Indict him of a capital offence.   450
In fireworks give him leave to vent his spite:
Those are the only serpents he can write;
The height of his ambition is, we know,
But to be master of a puppet-show;
On that one stage his works may yet appear,
And a month's harvest keeps him all the year.

   Now stop your noses, readers, all and some,
For here's a tun of midnight-work to come,
Og from a treason tavern rolling home.

---

430 In Settle's *Absalom Senior*, Absalom is the Duke of York, uncle of
Dryden's Absalom-Monmouth.
444 To transverse was to put prose into verse; for all writers but Doeg,
to *transprose* is the opposite.
446 Adapting the second line of *Absalom Senior*.
448 In the alphabet, *i* and *j*, like *u* and *v*, were counted as one letter.
451 *fireworks*. Including squibs and *serpents* (452) in the Whig cele-
brations in which Settle had a hand.
454 *puppet-show*. The humblest entertainments were not too humble for
Settle and, in fact, in his last years he descended so far.
459 *Og*. "Gigantic," an enemy of Israel (Deuteronomy 3:1); based on
Thomas Shadwell (see *MacFlecknoe*, headnote). Shadwell had become a
Whig propagandist and probably author of the scurrilous, ill-written
attack on Dryden, *The Medal of John Bayes*.

Round as a globe, and liquor'd ev'ry chink,   460
Goodly and great he sails behind his link;
With all this bulk there's nothing lost in Og,
For ev'ry inch that is not fool is rogue,
A monstrous mass of foul corrupted matter,
As all the devils had spew'd to make the batter.
When wine has given him courage to blaspheme,
He curses God, but God before curst him;
And if man cou'd have reason none has more
That made his paunch so rich and him so poor.
With wealth he was not trusted, for Heav'n knew   470
What 'twas of old to pamper up a Jew;
To what wou'd he on quail and pheasant swell
That ev'n on tripe and carrion cou'd rebel?
    But though Heav'n made him poor (with rev'rence
        speaking),
    never was a poet of God's making:
The midwife laid her hand on his thick skull
With this prophetic blessing, "Be thou dull";
Drink, swear, and roar; forbear no lewd delight
Fit for thy bulk; do anything but write;
Thou art of lasting make like thoughtless men,   480
A strong nativity—but for the pen,
Eat opium, mingle arsenic in thy drink,
Still thou may'st live avoiding pen and ink.
I see, I see, 'tis counsel given in vain,
For treason botch'd in rhyme will be thy bane;
Rhyme is the rock on which thou art to wreck;
'Tis fatal to thy fame and to thy neck;
Why should thy metre good King David blast?
A psalm of his will surely be thy last.
Dar'st thou presume in verse to meet thy foes,   490
Thou whom the penny pamphlet foil'd in prose?
Doeg, whom God for mankind's mirth has made,
O'ertops thy talent in thy very trade;

---

477 *"Be thou dull."* The original italicizes only this, implying that the
  midwife says no more. However, it might be argued that much of what
  follows continues her remarks.
490-91 Apparently: Do you presume to attack in the verse of *The Medal
  of John Bayes*—you, who have been disposed of in a cheap prose
  pamphlet?

Doeg to thee, thy paintings are so coarse,
A poet is, though he's the poet's horse.
A double noose thou on thy neck dost pull,
For writing treason and for writing dull;
To die for faction is a common evil,
But to be hang'd for nonsense is the devil;
Had'st thou the glories of thy King express'd,   500
Thy praises had been satire at the best;
But thou in clumsy verse, unlick'd, unpointed,
Hast shamefully defi'd the Lord's anointed.
    I will not rake the dunghill of thy crimes,
For who wou'd read thy life that reads thy rhymes?
But of King David's foes be this the doom,
May all be like the young man Absalom;
And for my foes may this their blessing be,
To talk like Doeg and to write like thee.

506-7 That is, dead (2 Samuel 18:32).

RELIGIO LAICI;

Or A Layman's Faith

A POEM

> *Ornari res ipsa negat; contenta doceri.*

1682. The explicit occasion of the first of Dryden's two religious confessions was the translation in 1682 of Father Simon's *Histoire Critique du Vieux Testament* by a young friend, Henry Dickinson. Simon had examined the textual confusion of the Old Testament in order to put into doubt the Protestant case for reliance on the Bible alone, rather than with church tradition, as a guide or Rule of Faith. Dryden obviously shared to some extent Simon's concern with what he thought the misuse of Scripture (see *The Medal*, ll. 156 ff., and below, ll. 398 ff.), but he shared with Rome, as well as with Canterbury, the belief that Simon's position was suspiciously radical (see ll. 252 ff.). Because he did not agree with the thesis of the book, he must have written the poem out of friendship. But it is also evident that he seized the occasion as one on which to assess and to express his own religious beliefs. Moreover, the issue of where final religious authority lay was the crucial one for him and most of his thinking contemporaries. The problem was to pick one's way through such errors as the excessive rationalism in matters of faith of the Deists (see especially, ll. 184 ff.), the corruptions in Catholic tradition (ll. 356 ff.), and the anarchy of private judgment (ll. 398 ff.). Obviously Dryden was searching for reli-

gious certainty (see especially ll. 276 ff.). The salvation
of one's soul depended upon choice of the true Rule of
Faith outside the individual, and yet the choice of external
authority had to be made within (ll. 303–304).

Dryden's solution is almost ostentatiously Anglican. His
lengthy Preface (which covers in prose the same ground
covered in verse by the poem and is therefore omitted
here) reports that he showed his poem for criticism "to a
judicious and learned friend, . . . zealous in the service of
Church and State"; and in prose and verse alike he goes
out of his way to submit to his "Mother Church." Such
gestures testify to a period of religious uncertainty, a crisis
of conscience that his skill in debating ideas largely conceals. Yet the doctrine is wholly Anglican, as is shown by
the repeated editions of the poem and by the absence of
any contemporary suspicion of Catholicism. The issues are
those that concerned intellectual Protestants and Catholics;
his answer in 1682 suited his Anglican contemporaries, if
not his Catholic wife and possibly Catholic sons. In another
five years he would give, however, a Catholic solution in
The Hind and the Panther to the same problem of the Rule
of Faith. The imagery of the much admired opening of this
poem is largely traditional, and Dryden himself explains at
the end of the poem the reason for the increasingly unimagistic nature of the poem. The point is touched upon in
the epigraph from Manilius, *Astronomica,* III, 139: "The
topic refuses to be adorned, for it is content with being
explained."

RELIGIO LAICI [1]

Dim as the borrow'd beams of moon and stars
To lonely, weary, wand'ring travellers
Is reason to the soul; and as on high,
Those rolling fires discover but the sky,
Not light us here, so reason's glimmering ray
Was lent not to assure our doubtful way
But guide us upward to a better day.

[1] *Religio Laici*. The Religion of a Layman.

And as those nightly tapers disappear
When day's bright lord ascends our hemisphere,
So pale grows reason at religion's sight,   10
So dies, and so dissolves in supernatural light.
   Some few, whose lamp shone brighter, have been
     led
From cause to cause to nature's secret head
And found that one first principle must be;
But what, or who, that UNIVERSAL HE,
Whether some soul encompassing this ball,
Unmade, unmov'd, yet making, moving all;
Or various atoms' interfering dance
Leap'd into form (the noble work of chance);
Or this great all was from eternity: 20
Not ev'n the Stagirite himself could see,
And Epicurus guess'd as well as he:
As blindly grop'd they for a future state,
As rashly judg'd of providence and fate.
   But least of all could their endeavours find   *Opinions of the*
What most concern'd the good of humankind;   *several sects of*
                                              philosophers
For happiness was never to be found,   *concerning the*
But vanish'd from 'em like enchanted ground.   *Summum Bonum.*
One thought content the good to be enjoy'd;
This every little accident destroy'd;   30
The wiser madmen did for virtue toil,
A thorny or at best a barren soil;
In pleasure some their glutton souls would steep,
But found their line too short, the well too deep,
And leaky vessels which no bliss cou'd keep.
Thus, anxious thoughts in endless circles roll,
Without a centre where to fix the soul;
In this wild maze their vain endeavours end.
How can the less the greater comprehend?
Or finite reason reach infinity?   40
For what cou'd fathom GOD were more than He.
   The Deist thinks he stands on firmer ground,   *System of*
                                             Deism.

[12] *Some few.* Like Aristotle the Stagirite (21) and the atomist Epicurus
(22).
[25-38] Lacking faith in revelation, the best minds, like Milton's fallen angels
debating philosophy, end in "Vain wisdom all, and false philosophy"
(*Paradise Lost* II, 565).

Cries, "εὑρεκα: the mighty secret's found;
God is that spring of good, supreme and best;
We, made to serve, and in that service blest;
If so, some rules of worship must be given,
Distributed alike to all by Heaven,
Else God were partial and to some deni'd
The means His justice shou'd for all provide.
This general worship is to PRAISE and PRAY,   50
One part to borrow blessings, one to pay;
And when frail nature slides into offence,
The sacrifice for crimes is penitence.
Yet since th' effects of Providence, we find,
Are variously dispens'd to humankind—
That vice triumphs and virtue suffers here
(A brand that sovereign justice cannot bear)—
Our reason prompts us to a future state,
The last appeal from fortune and from fate,
Where God's all-righteous ways will be declar'd,   60
The bad meet punishment, the good reward."

Thus man by his own strength to Heaven wou'd   *Of reveal'd*
    soar   *religion.*
And wou'd not be oblig'd to God for more.
Vain, wretched creature, how art thou misled
To think thy wit these God-like notions bred!
These truths are not the product of thy mind
But dropp'd from Heaven and of a nobler kind.
Reveal'd religion first inform'd thy sight,
And reason saw not till faith sprung the light.
Hence all thy natural worship takes the source: 70
'Tis Revelation what thou think'st discourse.
Else, how com'st thou to see these truths so clear,
Which so obscure to heathens did appear?
Not Plato these, nor Aristotle found,
Nor he whose wisdom oracles renown'd.   *Socrates.*

---

⁴⁸ εὑρεκα. Dryden's spelling (instead of εὑρηκα) and meter show that his
pronunciation of Greek was based on concepts of accent rather than on
concepts of quantity derived from Latin.
⁴²ff. Those believing not only (43–61) in a religion reduced to principles
inherent to all religions, but also (62–65) in the powers of man's un-
aided reason to arrive at ultimate religious truth; see 25–38n. Dryden
commonly associates Deism, Socinianism, and natural religion; see *The
Hind and the Panther* I, 52–61.

Hast thou a wit so deep or so sublime,
Or canst thou lower dive or higher climb?
Canst thou, by reason, more of Godhead know
Than Plutarch, Seneca, or Cicero?
Those giant wits, in happier ages born   80
(When arms and arts did Greece and Rome adorn),
Knew no such system, no such piles cou'd raise
Of natural worship, built on pray'r and praise,
To one sole GOD.
Nor did remorse to expiate sin prescribe,
But slew their fellow creatures for a bribe;
The guiltless victim groan'd for their offence,
And cruelty and blood was penitence.
If sheep and oxen cou'd atone for men,
Ah! at how cheap a rate the rich might sin!   90
And great oppressors might Heav'n's wrath beguile
By offering his own creatures for a spoil!
   Dar'st thou, poor worm, offend Infinity?
And must the terms of peace be given by thee?
Then thou art justice in the last appeal;
Thy easy God instructs thee to rebel
And, like a king remote and weak, must take
What satisfaction thou art pleas'd to make.
   But if there be a pow'r too just and strong
To wink at crimes and bear unpunish'd wrong,   100
Look humbly upward, see his will disclose
The forfeit first and then the fine impose:
A mulct thy poverty cou'd never pay
Had not eternal wisdom found the way
And with celestial wealth suppli'd thy store:
His justice makes the fine, his mercy quits the score.
See God descending in thy human frame,
Th' offended suff'ring in th' offender's name;
All thy misdeeds to Him imputed see,
And all His righteousness devolv'd on thee.   110
   For granting we have sinn'd and that th' offence
Of man is made against omnipotence,

---

80 Echoing Virgil, *Aeneid* VI, 649: "Teucer's old heroic race,/Born better times and happier years to grace" (trans. Dryden).
107 The Incarnation, a mystery understood by faith rather than natural
reason.

Some price that bears proportion must be paid,
And infinite with infinite be weigh'd.
See then the Deist lost: remorse for vice
Not paid, or paid, inadequate in price;
What farther means can reason now direct,
Or what relief from human wit expect?
That shews us sick, and sadly are we sure
Still to be sick till Heav'n reveal the cure;   120
If then Heav'n's will must needs be understood
(Which must, if we want cure, and Heaven be
        good),
Let all records of will reveal'd be shown, ⎫
With Scripture, all in equal balance thrown, ⎬
And our one Sacred Book will be that one. ⎭

   Proof needs not here, for whether we compare
That impious, idle, superstitious ware
Of rites, lustrations, offerings (which before
In various ages various countries bore)
With Christian faith and virtues, we shall find   130
None answ'ring the great ends of humankind
But this one rule of life: that shews us best
How God may be appeas'd and mortals blest.
Whether from length of time its worth we draw,
The world is scarce more ancient than the Law;
Heav'n's early care prescrib'd for every age,
First in the soul, and after in the page.
Or whether more abstractedly we look,
Or on the writers, or the written book,
Whence, but from Heav'n, cou'd men unskill'd in
        arts,   140
In several ages born, in several parts,
Weave such agreeing truths? or how, or why
Shou'd all conspire to cheat us with a lie?
Unask'd their pains, ungrateful their advice,
Starving their gain, and martyrdom their price.
   If on the Book itself we cast our view,

---

135 *the Law.* Of Moses, the Ten Commandments.
140 ff. Preparing for the argument for the reliability of Scripture, and
turning to the New Testament.

Concurrent heathens prove the story true;
The doctrine, miracles, which must convince,
For Heav'n in them appeals to human sense;
And though they prove not, they confirm the cause,   150
When what is taught agrees with nature's laws.

    Then for the style: majestic and divine,
It speaks no less than God in every line:
Commanding words, whose force is still the same
As the first "Fiat" that produc'd our frame. Let their be Light
All faiths beside, or did by arms ascend,
Or sense indulg'd has made mankind their friend;
This only doctrine does our lusts oppose,
Unfed by nature's soil in which it grows;
Cross to our interests, curbing sense and sin,   160
Oppress'd without and undermin'd within,
It thrives through pain, its own tormentors tires,
And with a stubborn patience still aspires.
To what can reason such effects assign,
Transcending nature, but to laws divine?
Which in that sacred volume are contain'd,
Sufficient, clear, and for that use ordain'd.

    But stay; the Deist here will urge anew,   *Objection of*
No supernatural worship can be true,   *the Deist.*
Because a general law is that alone   170
Which must to all and everywhere be known,
A style so large as not *this* Book can claim
Nor aught that bears reveal'd religion's name.
'Tis said the sound of a Messiah's birth
Is gone through all the habitable earth,
But still that text must be confin'd alone
To what was then inhabited and known;
And what provision cou'd from thence accrue
To Indian souls and worlds discover'd new?
In other parts it helps that ages past   180
The Scriptures there were known and were imbrac'd,
Till sin spread once again the shades of night:

152-55 Christian praise of biblical *style* often followed the opinion attributed
    to Longinus that God's *Fiat*, "Let there be light," was the most sub-
    lime phrase in all writing.

What's that to these who never saw the light?
  Of all objections this indeed is chief   *The objection*
To startle reason, stagger frail belief.   *answer'd.*
We grant, 'tis true, that Heav'n from human sense
Has hid the secret paths of Providence;
But boundless wisdom, boundless mercy may
Find ev'n for those bewilder'd souls a way;
If from His nature foes may pity claim,   190
Much more may strangers who ne'er heard His
    name.
And though no name be for salvation known,
But that of His eternal Son's alone,
Who knows how far transcending goodness can
Extend the merits of that Son to man?
Who knows what reasons may His mercy lead,
Or ignorance invincible may plead?
  Not only charity bids hope the best,
But more the great Apostle has express'd:
"That, if the Gentiles (whom no Law inspir'd)   200
By nature did what was by Law requir'd,
They, who the written rule had never known,
Were to themselves both rule and law alone;
To nature's plain indictment they shall plead,
And by their conscience be condemn'd or freed."
Most righteous doom! because a rule reveal'd
Is none to those from whom it was conceal'd.
Then those who follow'd reason's dictates right,
Liv'd up, and lifted high their natural light,
With Socrates may see their Maker's face,   210
While thousand rubric-martyrs want a place.
  Nor does it balk my charity to find
Th' Egyptian bishop of another mind;

184-85 Dryden's admission accounts for his radical belief that the virtuous
heathen may be saved and suggests that otherwise Deism might appear
to be irrefutable.
200-5 St. Paul, Romans 2:14–15.
211 *rubric-martyrs.* Those in the calendar of saints.
213 *Th' Egyptian bishop.* St. Athanasius (d. 373) opponent at the Council
of Nicaea of Arius, who had heretically denied Christ's divinity. The
Creed formerly attributed to the saint begins with two sentences
sometimes referred to as the Preface: "Whosoever will be saved: before
all things it is necessary that he hold the Catholic faith. Which faith
[see 219] except everyone do keep whole and unfettered: without
doubt he shall perish everlastingly" (*Book of Common Prayer*).

For though his Creed eternal truth contains,
'Tis hard for man to doom to endless pains
All who believ'd not all his zeal requir'd
Unless he first cou'd prove he was inspir'd.
Then let us either think he meant to say,
This faith, *where publish'd,* was the only way;
Or else conclude that, Arius to confute,   220
The good old man, too eager in dispute,
Flew high, and as his Christian fury rose
Damn'd all for heretics who durst oppose.

Thus far my charity this path has tri'd
(A much unskillful, but well meaning guide);
Yet what they are, ev'n these crude thoughts were
    bred
By reading that which better thou hast read,
Thy matchless author's work, which thou, my friend,
By well translating better dost commend.

*Digression
to the
translator
of Father
Simon's
Critical
History
of the
Old Testa-
ment.*

Those youthful hours which, of thy equals most   230
In toys have squander'd or in vice have lost,
Those hours hast thou to nobler use employ'd,
And the severe delights of truth enjoy'd.
Witness this weighty book in which appears
The crabbed toil of many thoughtful years
Spent by thy author in the sifting care
Of Rabbins' old sophisticated ware
From gold divine, which he who well can sort
May afterwards make algebra a sport.
A treasure, which if country curates buy,   240
They Junius and Tremellius may defy,
Save pains in various readings and translations,
And without Hebrew make most learn'd quotations;
A work so full with various learning fraught,
So nicely ponder'd, yet so strongly wrought,
As nature's height and art's last hand requir'd,
As much as man cou'd compass, uninspir'd.
Where we may see what errors have been made
Both in the copier's and translator's trade,

228 *my friend.* Henry Dickinson.
241 *Junius and Tremellius.* Learned sixteenth-century Calvinist divines,
    whose joint Latin translation of the Bible was criticized by Father
    Simon.

How Jewish, Popish interests have prevail'd,   250
And where infallibility has fail'd.
    For some, who have his secret meaning guess'd,
Have found our author not too much a priest;
For fashion-sake he seems to have recourse
To Pope, and Councils, and tradition's force;
But he that old traditions cou'd subdue
Cou'd not but find the weakness of the new;
If Scripture, though deriv'd from heav'nly birth,
Has been but carelessly preserv'd on earth,
If God's own people, who of God before   260
Knew what we know and had been promis'd more
In fuller terms of Heaven's assisting care,
And who did neither time nor study spare
To keep this Book untainted, unperplex'd,
Let in gross errors to corrupt the text,
Omitted paragraphs, embroil'd the sense,
With vain traditions stopp'd the gaping fence
Which every common hand pull'd up with ease:
What safety from such brushwood-helps as these?
If *written words* from time are not secur'd,   270
How can we think have *oral sounds* endur'd?
Which thus transmitted, if *one* mouth has fail'd,
Immortal lies on ages are entail'd;
And that some such have been is prov'd too plain,
If we consider interest, church, and gain.
    "Oh," but says one, "tradition set aside,   *Of the*
Where can we hope for an unerring guide?   *infalli-*
                                                         bility of
For since th' original scripture has been lost,   *tra-*
All copies disagreeing, maim'd the most,   *dition,*
                                                      in general.
Or Christian faith can have no certain ground,   280
Or truth in church tradition must be found."
    Such an omniscient Church we wish indeed:
'Twere worth both Testaments and cast in the
        Creed;

252-53 Simon antagonized, for differing reasons, Catholics and Protestants
alike.
282-83 Too much should not be made of this: it is an example of the
meaningless concession in contemporary theological controversy, and
there are a number of parallels in Anglican writing.

But if this Mother be a guide so sure,
As can all doubts resolve, all truth secure,
Then her infallibility as well
Where copies are corrupt, or lame, can tell,
Restore lost canon with as little pains,
As truly explicate what still remains,
Which yet no council dare pretend to do,   290
Unless, like Esdras, they cou'd write it new:
Strange confidence, still to interpret true,
Yet not be sure that all they have explain'd
Is in the blest original contain'd.
More safe, and much more modest 'tis to say,
"God wou'd not leave mankind without a way,"
And that the Scriptures, though not everywhere
Free from corruption, or entire, or clear,
Are uncorrupt, sufficient, clear, entire
In all things which our needful faith require.   300
If others in the same glass better see
'Tis for *themselves* they look, but not for *me*:
For *MY* salvation must its doom receive
Not from what *OTHERS*, but what *I* believe.

    Must *all tradition* then be set aside?

*Objection
on behalf of
Tradition
urg'd by
Father
Simon.*

This to affirm were ignorance or pride.
Are there not many points, some needful sure,
To saving faith that Scripture leaves obscure?
Which every sect will wrest a several way
(For what one sect interprets, all sects may):   310
We hold, and say we prove from Scripture plain,
That Christ is GOD; the bold Socinian
From the same Scripture urges he's but MAN.
Now what appeal can end th' important suit?
Both parts talk loudly, but the rule is mute.

    Shall I speak plain and, in a nation free,
Assume an honest layman's liberty?
I think (according to my little skill,
To my own Mother-Church submitting still)

---

291 *Esdras.* 2 Esdras 14.
316-19 The submissiveness to his Church is unnecessary; he is merely working up to the point, accepted by Canterbury, that early tradition agreeing with Scripture should be accepted (334-45).

That many have been sav'd, and many may,   320
Who never heard this question brought in play.
Th' unletter'd Christian, who believes in gross,
Plods on to Heaven, and ne'er is at a loss:
For the strait gate wou'd be made straiter yet,
Were none admitted there but men of wit.
The few, by nature form'd, with learning fraught,
Born to instruct, as others to be taught,
Must study well the sacred page and see
Which doctrine, this, or that, does best agree
With the whole tenor of the work divine,   330
And plainliest points to Heav'n's reveal'd design;
Which exposition flows from genuine sense,
And which is forc'd by wit and eloquence.

   Not that tradition's parts are useless here,
When general, old, disinteress'd, and clear;
That ancient Fathers thus expound the page
Gives truth the reverend majesty of age,
Confirms its force, by biding every test,
For best authority's next rules are best.
And still the nearer to the spring we go   340
More limpid, more unsoil'd the waters flow.
Thus, first traditions were a proof alone,
Cou'd we be certain such they were, so known;
But since some flaws in long descent may be,
They make not truth but probability.
Even Arius and Pelagius durst provoke
To what the centuries preceding spoke.
Such difference is there in an oft-told tale,
But truth by its own sinews will prevail.
Tradition written therefore more commends   350
Authority, than what from voice descends;
And this, as perfect as its kind can be,
Rolls down to us the sacred history,
Which, from the universal Church receiv'd,

---

³³⁹ Some editors emend to: *best authorities, next rules, are best;* but
Dryden is saying that the rules of the best authority (the fathers, tradition) are nearest (*next*) in time to revealed Scripture.
³⁴⁰ The heretics Arius and Pelagius dared to *provoke/To,* or appeal to,
tradition; the phrase may also suggest appeal to a higher ecclesiastical
tribunal. Perhaps Dryden was thinking of their arguments before early
councils.

Is tri'd, and after, for itself believ'd.

    The partial Papists wou'd infer from hence
Their Church, in last resort, shou'd judge the
    sense.

*The second
objection.
Answer to
the
objection.*

But first they wou'd assume, with wondrous art,
Themselves to be the whole who are but part
Of that vast frame, the Church; yet grant they were   360
The handers down, can they from thence infer
A right t' interpret? or wou'd they alone,
Who brought the present, claim it for their own?
The Book's a common largess to mankind,
Not more for them than every man design'd;
The welcome news is in the letter found,
The carrier's not commission'd to expound.
It speaks itself, and what it does contain
In all things needful to be known is plain.

    In times o'ergrown with rust and ignorance,   370
A gainful trade their clergy did advance;
When want of learning kept the laymen low,
And none but priests were authoriz'd to know;
When what small knowledge was in them did dwell,
And he a god who cou'd but read or spell;
Then Mother Church did mightily prevail:
She parcel'd out the Bible by retail,
But still expounded what she sold or gave
To keep it in her power to damn and save;
Scripture was scarce, and as the market went,   380
Poor laymen took salvation on content,
As needy men take money, good or bad;
God's word they had not, but the priests' they had;
Yet, whate'er false conveyances they made,
The lawyer still was certain to be paid.
In those dark times they learn'd their knack so well
That by long use they grew infallible;
At last, a knowing age began t' enquire
If they the Book, or that did them inspire;
And, making narrower search they found, tho' late,   390

---

[356] *Papists.* Roman Catholics; the Catholic claim to Church authority, like
    certain arguments of Deism, seemed so dangerously strong to Dryden
    as to need rebuttal.
[366] *The welcome news.* "Gospel" means "good news."

That what they thought the priests', was their estate:
Taught by the will produc'd (the written Word)
How long they had been cheated on record.
Then every man who saw the title fair
Claim'd a child's part and put in for a share,
Consulted soberly his private good,
And sav'd himself as cheap as e'er he cou'd.
'Tis true, my friend (and far be flattery hence),
This good had full as bad a consequence:
The Book thus put in every vulgar hand,   400
Which each presum'd he best cou'd understand,
The common rule was made the common prey
And at the mercy of the rabble lay.
The tender page with horny fists was gall'd,
And he was gifted most that loudest bawl'd;
The Spirit gave the doctoral degree, ⎫
And every member of a company   ⎬
Was of his trade and of the Bible free. ⎭
Plain truths enough for needful use they found,
But men wou'd still be itching to expound;   410
Each was ambitious of th' obscurest place,
No measure ta'n from knowledge, all from grace.
Study and pains were now no more their care;
Texts were explain'd by fasting and by prayer;
This was the fruit the private spirit brought,
Occasion'd by great zeal and little thought.
While crowds unlearn'd, with rude devotion warm,
About the sacred viands buzz and swarm,
The fly-blown text creates a crawling brood
And turns to maggots what was meant for food.   420
"A thousand daily sects rise up and die;
A thousand more the perish'd race supply."
So all we make of Heaven's discover'd will
Is not to have it or to use it ill.
The danger's much the same: on several shelves

---

412 It was a main effort of Thomas Aquinas and Richard Hooker to recon-
    cile *knowledge* (reason) with faith (in *grace*), a dilemma throughout
    Christianity.
417–20 Developing the imagery in Samuel Butler, *Hudibras* III, ii, 7–12.
421–22 Quotation unidentified.

If others wreck us, or we wreck ourselves.
    What then remains, but waiving each extreme,
The tides of ignorance and pride to stem?
Neither so rich a treasure to forgo,
Nor proudly seek beyond our pow'r to know.   430
Faith is not built on disquisitions vain;
The things we *must* believe are few and plain;
But since men *will* believe more than they need,
And every man will make himself a creed,
In doubtful questions 'tis the safest way
To learn what unsuspected ancients say;
For 'tis not likely we shou'd higher soar
In search of Heav'n than all the Church before;
Nor can we be deceiv'd, unless we see
The Scripture and the Fathers disagree.   440
If after all, they stand suspected still
(For no man's faith depends upon his will),
'Tis some relief that points not clearly known
Without much hazard may be let alone;
And after hearing what our Church can say,
If still our reason runs another way,
That private reason 'tis more just to curb
Than by disputes the public peace disturb,
For points obscure are of small use to learn:
But common quiet is mankind's concern.   450
    Thus have I made my own opinions clear:
Yet neither praise expect nor censure fear;
And this unpolish'd, rugged verse I chose,
As fittest for discourse and nearest prose;
For while from sacred truth I do not swerve,
Tom Sternhold's or Tom Shadwell's rhymes will
        serve.

370-426 Characteristic spicing of argument with satire or irony.
428 Sectarian *ignorance;* Catholic *pride.*
433-40 Like many Anglicans, Dryden leans toward Catholicism on this issue.
454 *nearest prose.* Probably in its emphasis upon clarity with a minimum
  of imagery and metaphor. Dr. Johnson (Life of Dryden) said that
  though the poem is "prosaic in some parts," it "rises to high poetry in
  others."
456 Thomas Sternhold and Thomas Shadwell are associated in *The Second
  Part of Absalom and Achitophel,* 403; see *An Essay of Dramatic Poesy*
  note 112.

TO THE EARL
OF ROSCOMMON

*On His Excellent Essay of
Translated Verse*

1684. Earlier plans of the Royal Society to emulate the
French Academy with a committee on the English language had not borne fruit. According to Fenton's edition of
The Works of Edmund Waller (1744), about 1684, "in
imitation of the learned and polite assemblies, with which
he had been acquainted abroad," Wentworth Dillon,
fourth Earl of Roscommon (?1632–1685), "began to form
a Society for the refining, and fixing the standard of language; in which design his great friend Mr. Dryden was a
principal assistant," as indeed, he had been a member of
the committee of the Royal Society. From 1683 to 1685
there are numerous signs of a desire to clarify what seemed
linguistic and literary confusion. Original poems on the art
of poetry and translations of classical poems (especially
Horace, *Ars Poetica*) renewed interest in criteria for
translation, and concern over the lack of certainty of pronunciation and other elements of language all show symptoms of concern. Dryden himself returned to *An Essay of
Dramatic Poesy* in 1684, revising it along stricter grammatical lines. His concern with words, as well as his desire not
to be tyrannized by rigid classifications of meaning, can be
glimpsed in this poem in the recurrent play upon *translation:* meaning "transferral" (ll. 3, 7), "rendering into another language" (title, ll. 35, 54, 63), and "transported"
or "transformed" (l. 48). The poem is a history of poetry
in the guise of translation, in all these senses, from nation

to nation and so is based upon a progress piece of verse,
yielding at the end to a royal progress of Homer and Virgil
into the stately palace of English poetry. The poem marks
a step forward in Dryden's development of the verse epistle
from the early poem to Dr. Charleton and toward later
poems to William Congreve, Sir Godfrey Kneller, John
Driden, and others.

Whether the fruitful Nile or Tyrian shore
The seeds of arts and infant science bore,
'Tis sure the noble plant, translated first,
Advanc'd its head in Grecian gardens nurs'd.
The Grecians added verse; their tuneful tongue
Made nature first and nature's God their song.
Nor stopp'd translation here: for conquering Rome
With Grecian spoils brought Grecian numbers home,
Enrich'd by those Athenian Muses more
Than all the vanquish'd world cou'd yield before.   10
'Till barb'rous nations and more barb'rous times
Debas'd the majesty of verse to rhymes,
Those rude at first, a kind of hobbling prose
That limp'd along and tinkl'd in the close;
But Italy, reviving from the trance
Of Vandal, Goth, and monkish ignorance,
With pauses, cadence, and well-vowell'd words,
And all the graces a good ear affords,
Made rhyme an art, and Dante's polish'd page
Restor'd a silver, not a golden age;   20
Then Petrarch follow'd, and in him we see ⎫
What rhyme improv'd in all its height can be: ⎬
At best a pleasing sound and fair barbarity; ⎭
The French pursu'd their steps; and Britain last
In manly sweetness all the rest surpass'd.
    The wit of Greece, the gravity of Rome
Appear exalted in the British loom:

¹ It was debated whether civilization began in Egypt or Phoenicia. For the
    cultivation image, see *Threnodia Augustalis* 346–63; *To Mr. Congreve*
    1–12.
⁵⁻⁶ Referring to *The Works and the Days* and the *Theogony* of Hesiod,
    one of the earliest of Greek poets.
¹¹⁻²⁵ Witty rhyming attacks on rhyme were traditional.

The Muses' empire is restor'd again,
In Charles his reign and by Roscommon's pen.
Yet modestly he does his work survey,   30
And calls a finish'd poem an *Essay;*
For all the needful rules are scatter'd here, ⎱
Truth smoothly told and pleasantly severe   ⎬
(So well is art disguis'd, for nature to appear). ⎰
Nor need those rules to give translation light,
His own example is a flame so bright
That he, who but arrives to copy well,
Unguided will advance, unknowing will excel.
Scarce his own Horace cou'd such rules ordain,
Or his own Virgil sing a nobler strain.   40
   How much in him may rising Ireland boast,
How much in gaining him has Britain lost!
Their island in revenge has ours reclaim'd;
The more instructed we, the more we still are
      sham'd.
'Tis well for us his generous blood did flow
Deriv'd from British channels long ago,
That here his conquering ancestors were nurs'd,
And Ireland but translated England first;
By this reprisal we regain our right,
Else must the two contending nations fight,   50
A nobler quarrel for his native earth
Than what divided Greece for Homer's birth.
   To what perfection will our tongue arrive,
How will invention and translation thrive,
When authors nobly born will bear their part
And not disdain th' inglorious praise of art!
Great gen'rals thus, descending from command,
With their own toil provoke the soldier's hand.
How will sweet Ovid's ghost be pleas'd to hear
His fame augmented by an English peer,   60   *The Earl
                                                  of Mulgrave.*

36-40 Roscommon had translated Horace, *Odes* I, xxii and III, vi; *Ars
   Poetica;* and Virgil, *Eclogue* VI.
41-52 Roscommon's estates were Irish, his ancestry English.
54 *invention.* Original writing, opposed to *translation.*
57-58 In view of Roscommon's honorary military position, Dryden uses the
   old formula, *Dux exemplo praeit,* for his example as a writer.
59-60 On Mulgrave, see *Absalom and Achitophel* 877n.* Roscommon's *Essay*
   had praised him, and Dryden had assisted his "Helen to Paris" in *Ovid's
   Epistles, Translated* (1680).

How he embellishes his Helen's loves,
Outdoes his softness and his sense improves!
When these translate and teach translators too,
Nor firstling kid, nor any vulgar vow
Shou'd at Apollo's grateful altar stand;
Roscommon writes; to that auspicious hand,
Muse, feed the bull that spurns the yellow sand;
Roscommon, whom both court and camps commend,
True to his prince and faithful to his friend;
Roscommon, first in fields of honour known,   70
First in the peaceful triumphs of the gown,
He both Minervas justly makes his own.
Now let the few belov'd by Jove, and they
Whom infus'd Titan form'd of better clay,
On equal terms with ancient wit engage,
Nor mighty Homer fear, nor sacred Virgil's page:
Our English palace opens wide in state,
And without stooping they may pass the gate.

70-72 The two *Minervas* are her aspects of learning and warfare.

74 *infus'd Titan*. The reference is to Prometheus, who created man before
   the classical flood, as in Ovid, *Metamorphoses* I, 78–86; but the phrasing
   is closer to Juvenal, *Satires* XIV, 33–35.

77-78 Virgil's Aeneas had to stoop to enter the palace of Evander (*Aeneid*
   VIII, 359–69), but Virgil himself and Homer will enter with unbent
   majesty into English poetry.

TO THE MEMORY OF
MR. OLDHAM

1684. Little is known of the life of John Oldham (1653–1683) and less of Dryden's relation with him, although the young man had clearly aroused Dryden's hopes and affection. Dryden emphasized two facts: Oldham's preceding him in satire (ll. 5–10) and the cacaphonous style usual in Oldham's poetry (ll. 13–21). Much of the poem is concerned with defining the nature of their relationship by a series of Roman allusions: to the assistance (ll. 8–10) by the older Nisus to his younger friend Euryalus to win the race (Virgil, *Aeneid* V, 328); to the mourning (l. 22) for a brother (Catullus, *Elegy* LXV) or of a promising young comrade-in-arms, as was Pallas to Aeneas (*Aeneid* XI, 97–98); and at last to Augustus mourning the death of a most promising successor (*Aeneid* VI, 854–86, verses echoed or paraphrased by Dryden in ll. 24–25).

Farewell, too little and too lately known,
Whom I began to think and call my own,
For sure our souls were near alli'd, and thine
Cast in the same poetic mould with mine.
One common note on either lyre did strike,
And knaves and fools we both abhorr'd alike;
To the same goal did both our studies drive;
The last set out the soonest did arrive.
Thus Nisus fell upon the slippery place,
While his young friend perform'd and won the race.   10
O early ripe! to thy abundant store
What could advancing age have added more?
It might (what nature never gives the young)

Have taught the numbers of thy native tongue.
But satire needs not those, and wit will shine
Through the harsh cadence of a rugged line.
A noble error, and but seldom made,
When poets are by too much force betray'd.
Thy generous fruits, though gather'd ere their
    prime,
Still show'd a quickness, and maturing time   20
But mellows what we write to the dull sweets of
    rhyme.
Once more, hail and farewell; farewell, thou young,
But, ah, too short Marcellus of our tongue;
Thy brows with ivy and with laurels bound,
But fate and gloomy night encompass thee around.

FOUR TRANSLATIONS

In addition to his poetry and critical prose, Dryden wrote some twenty-eight plays and translated nearly 38,500 lines of verse and about two thousand pages of prose. In this volume his plays are represented, though most inadequately, by some of his prologues and epilogues. The following four translations of three classical poets give some, if again an inadequate, idea of his powers as a translator. It is, after all, impossible to do more than mention his classic version of Virgil's *Eclogues, Georgics,* and *Aeneid;* his powerful rendering of the satirists, Persius and Juvenal; his selections from Homer and Theocritus; or the magnificent, rather more romantic group he called *Fables,* including portions of Ovid's *Metamorphoses;* some *novelle* of Boccaccio; and Chaucerian tales. In Dryden, the humanist respect for classics found full tribute in practice.

As might be expected, he not only translated but also expounded the critical principles of translation. He distinguished three kinds: "metaphrase," so-called literal translation; "paraphrase," or looser rendering yet adhering to the sense and spirit of the original; and "imitation," developing the original along new lines. He chose the middle way, giving tribute to metaphrase by his close attention to the best scholarship on his originals and to imitation by allowing himself considerable margins for selection, omission, addition, and adaptation. His catholic taste permitted him to imagine that his "soul" was peculiarly like that of the authors he chose. And his desire not merely to render but rather to create original English poems led him to the ideal of writing a poem such as that which the translated author would have written had he lived in the seventeenth century. Such principles may seem obvious, inevitable, or merely characteristic of Dryden, but they represent the first, and to this day the most articulate, theory of poetic translation. Similarly, his translations remain the translations of a poet. Those who study them closely usually come away convinced that they are not only the finest English version of their authors but also the truest.

In the unabashed seventeenth-century manner, Dryden often borrowed from earlier translators or pillaged the notes of learned commentators. At the same time, he used his translations as a proving ground for his own styles, often experimenting with long and short lines, unusual rhythmic effects, risky subjects, and, to him, new poetic forms. Many signs of such experimentation will be found in the passage from Lucretius and in the poems from Ovid. With the Horatian ode, Dryden undertook his first essay in the loose "Pindaric" ode, which was to be the form he used for all his greatest lyrics. Perhaps in the end it is no injustice to the classical poets to say that the English poems are as much Dryden's as theirs, simply because they actually are English poems.

In the second of his miscellanies, *Sylvae* (1685), Dryden included a large number of translations by himself and others. His own include five selections from the *De Rerum Natura* of Lucretius as well as three odes and an epode by Horace. For centuries the scientific and philosophical Epicureanism of Lucretius had made him suspect to Christian readers. To the seventeenth century, with its rising interest in science, the reasoned eloquence of this Latin treatment "Of the Nature of Things" was well-nigh irresistible. Yet Dryden did not, as he might well have done, choose the most scientific or historical selections for translation. Instead he chose those dealing with the human condition, and among them is that soberest of the consolations of philosophy, "Against the Fear of Death." Dryden did not always exhibit such an interest in sustained care with his poetry, but among his translations of Horace, the twenty-third ode of the third book is similarly remarkable—for its combination of polish and sustained lyric strength. The lighter Epicureanism tinged with Stoicism that marks the Horatian ethos at its best is fully embodied in natural English. Although other classical poets were always held in

higher regard, Ovid was to Dryden, as he also was to
medieval and Renaissance poets, the classical poet to
whom he was most likely to turn for translation. Dryden
alluded to nearly all Ovid's works at one time or another
and similarly rendered, early or late, some of Ovid's
epistles, his *Art of Love*, and his *Metamorphoses*. It is a
matter of regret that the selections from the *Metamorphoses* are too long for inclusion here. Dryden did, however, render two of Ovid's love elegies (*Amores*) that well
convey the gayer and, it must be added, the naughtier
sides of Ovid and Dryden alike. The first selection wittily
reveals that the Roman elegy was really any poem written
in the elegiac distich (couplets of a full hexameter line followed by a curtailed shorter line), and that the subject was
more often love than death. In a sense, seventeenth-
century love poetry began in the sixteenth century with the
naturalization of the Roman love elegy by Donne. The wit,
realism, cynicism, and open physicality certainly do not say
everything about love, but they are a relief from more solemn swellings. In the first elegy of the first book, Ovid is
humorously shown by Dryden to be driven to write love
poetry when he would rather write epics. In the fourth
elegy of the first book, the stock figure of the desperate
lover is shown to be adulterous and unromantic, more concerned with the tricks of sex than elevations of soul. These
elegies were translated at an unknown date and are included at this point purely for convenience.

Translation

OF THE LATTER PART OF THE THIRD BOOK OF

LUCRETIUS

Against the Fear of Death

What has this bugbear death to frighten man,
If souls can die as well as bodies can?
For, as before our birth we felt no pain

When Punic arms infested land and main,
When heav'n and earth were in confusion hurl'd
For the debated empire of the world,
Which aw'd with dreadful expectation lay,
Sure to be slaves, uncertain who shou'd sway:
So, when our mortal frame shall be disjoin'd,
The lifeless lump, uncoupled from the mind,   10
From sense of grief and pain we shall be free;
We shall not feel, because we shall not *be*.
Though earth in seas, and seas in heav'n were lost,
We shou'd not move, we only shou'd be toss'd.

Nay, ev'n suppose when we have suffer'd fate
The soul cou'd feel in her divided state,
What's that to us? For we are only we
While souls and bodies in one frame agree.
Nay, tho' our atoms shou'd revolve by chance,
And matter leap into the former dance,   20
Tho' time our life and motion cou'd restore
And make our bodies what they were before—
What gain to us wou'd all this bustle bring?
The new-made man wou'd be another thing;
When once an interrupting pause is made,
That individual being is decay'd.
We who are dead and gone shall bear no part
In all the pleasures nor shall feel the smart
Which to that other mortal shall accrue,
Whom of our matter time shall mould anew.   30

For backward if you look, on that long space
Of ages past, and view the changing face
Of matter, toss'd and variously combin'd
In sundry shapes, 'tis easy for the mind
From thence t' infer that seeds of things have been
In the same order as they now are seen,
Which yet our dark remembrance cannot trace,
Because a pause of life, a gaping space,
Has come betwixt, where memory lies dead,
And all the wand'ring motions from the sense are
    fled.   40

⁴ *Punic. Carthaginian,* referring to wars between Rome and Carthage
(*Punic*) earlier; see 249*n.*

For whosoe'er shall in misfortunes live
Must *be*, when those misfortunes shall arrive;
And since the man who *is* not, feels not woe
(For death exempts him, and wards off the blow
Which we, the living, only feel and bear),
What is there left for us in death to fear?
When once that pause of life has come between,
'Tis just the same as we had never been.

 And therefore if a man bemoan his lot,
That after death his mould'ring limbs shall rot,   50
Or flames, or jaws of beasts devour his mass,
Know he's an unsincere, unthinking ass.
A secret sting remains within his mind—
The fool is to his own cast offals kind;
He boasts no sense can after death remain, ⎫
Yet makes himself a part of life again— ⎬
As if some other he could feel the pain. ⎭
If, while he live, this thought molest his head,
"What wolf or vulture shall devour me dead?"
He wastes his days in idle grief nor can   60
Distinguish 'twixt the body and the man,
But thinks himself can still himself survive,
And what when dead he feels not, feels alive.
Then he repines that he was born to die,
Nor knows in death there is no other he,
No living he remains his grief to vent,
And o'er his senseless carcass to lament.
If after death 'tis painful to be torn
By birds and beasts, then why not so to burn,
Or drench'd in floods of honey to be soak'd,   70
Imbalm'd to be at once preserv'd and chok'd,
Or on an ayery mountain's top to lie
Expos'd to cold and heav'n's inclemency,
Or crowded in a tomb to be oppress'd
With monumental marble on thy breast?
 But to be snatch'd from all thy household joys,

---

⁵⁴ *offals*. Both the parts of slain or dead animals unfit for food and the
 bodies of slain men; senses played on in 50–75.
⁶⁰⁻⁷¹ Roman methods of treating corpses for burial.
⁷² *ayery*. The original spelling, an apparent play on *airy* and *aerie* or
 eyrie.

From thy chaste wife and thy dear prattling boys,
Whose little arms about thy legs are cast
And climbing for a kiss prevent their mother's haste,
Inspiring secret pleasure thro' thy breast—   80
All these shall be no more; thy friends oppress'd,
Thy care and courage now no more shall free.
"Ah, wretch," thou cri'st, "ah! miserable me,
One woeful day sweeps children, friends, and wife,
And all the brittle blessings of my life!"
Add one thing more, and all thou say'st is true:
Thy want and wish of them is vanish'd too,
Which well consider'd were a quick relief
To all thy vain imaginary grief.
For thou shalt sleep and never wake again   90
And, quitting life, shall quit thy living pain.
But we thy friends shall all those sorrows find
Which in forgetful death thou leav'st behind;
No time shall dry our tears nor drive thee from
     our mind.
The worst that can befall thee, measur'd right,
Is a sound slumber and a long good night.
     Yet thus the fools that would be thought the wits
Disturb their mirth with melancholy fits,
When healths go round, and kindly brimmers flow
Till the fresh garlands on their foreheads glow,   100
They whine and cry, "Let us make haste to live;
Short are the joys that human life can give."
Eternal preachers that corrupt the draught
And pall the god that never thinks with thought;
Idiots with all that thought, to whom the worst
Of death is want of drink and endless thirst,
Or any fond desire as vain as these.
     For ev'n in sleep the body, wrapp'd in ease,
Supinely lies as in the peaceful grave,
And wanting nothing, nothing can it crave.   110
Were that sound sleep eternal, it were death,
Yet the first atoms then, the seeds of breath,
Are moving near to sense; we do but shake
And rouse that sense, and straight we are awake.

95ff. Cf. 251 ff.

Then death to us and death's anxiety
Is less than nothing, if a less cou'd be.
For then our atoms, which in order lay,
Are scatter'd from their heap and puff'd away,
And never can return into their place,
When once the pause of life has left an empty space.   120
   And last, suppose great Nature's voice shou'd call
To thee, or me, or any of us all,
"What dost thou mean, ungrateful wretch, thou vain,
Thou mortal thing, thus idly to complain
And sigh and sob, that thou shalt be no more?
For if thy life were pleasant heretofore,
If all the bounteous blessings I cou'd give
Thou hast enjoy'd, if thou hast known to live,
And pleasure not leak'd thro' thee like a sieve,
Why dost thou not give thanks, as at a plenteous
    feast
Cramm'd to the throat with life, and rise and take   130
    thy rest?
But if my blessings thou hast thrown away,
If undigested joys pass'd thro' and wou'd not stay,
Why dost thou wish for more to squander still?
If life be grown a load, a real ill,
And I wou'd all thy cares and labours end,
Lay down thy burden, fool, and know thy friend.
To please thee I have empti'd all my store;
I can invent and can supply no more,
But run the round again, the round I ran before.   140
Suppose thou art not broken yet with years,
Yet still the self-same scene of things appears,
And wou'd be ever, cou'd'st thou ever live;
For life is still but life—there's nothing new to give."
What can we plead against so just a bill?
We stand convicted, and our cause goes ill.
   But if a wretch, a man oppress'd by fate,
Shou'd beg of Nature to prolong his date,
She speaks aloud to him with more disdain:
"Be still, thou martyr fool, thou covetous of pain."   150
But if an old decrepit sot lament,
"What thou," she cries, "who hast outliv'd content!

Dost thou complain, who hast enjoy'd my store?
But this is still th' effect of wishing more!
Unsatisfi'd with all that Nature brings,
Loathing the present, liking absent things,
From hence it comes thy vain desires at strife
Within themselves have tantaliz'd thy life,
And ghastly death appear'd before thy sight
E'er thou hadst gorg'd thy soul and senses with
    delight.   160
Now leave those joys unsuiting to thy age
To a fresh comer and resign the stage."
    Is Nature to be blam'd if thus she chide?
No, sure; for 'tis her business to provide
Against this ever-changing frame's decay
New things to come and old to pass away.
One being worn, another being makes;
Chang'd but not lost, for Nature gives and takes:
New matter must be found for things to come,
And these must waste like those and follow Nature's
    doom.   170
All things, like thee, have time to rise and rot
And from each other's ruin are begot,
For life is not confin'd to him or thee;
'Tis giv'n to all for use, to none for property.
    Consider former ages past and gone,
Whose circles ended long e'er thine begun,
Then tell me, fool, what part in them thou hast?
Thus may'st thou judge the future by the past.
What horror seest thou in that quiet state,
What bugbear dreams to fright thee after fate?   180
No ghost, no goblins, that still passage keep,
But all is there serene in that eternal sleep.
For all the dismal tales that poets tell,
Are verifi'd on earth and not in hell.
No Tantalus looks up with fearful eye
Or dreads th' impending rock to crush him from on
    high:
But fear of chance on earth disturbs our easy hours,

---

[185] *Tantalus.* According to the lesser known version of his punishment with
the ever-impending stone; his sin is variously given.

Or vain imagin'd wrath of vain imagin'd pow'rs.
No Tityus torn by vultures lies in hell,
Nor cou'd the lobes of his rank liver swell   190
To that prodigious mass for their eternal meal,
Not tho' his monstrous bulk had cover'd o'er
Nine spreading acres or nine thousand more,
Not tho' the globe of earth had been the giants'
       floor;
Nor in eternal torments cou'd he lie,
Nor cou'd his corps sufficient food supply:
But he's the Tityus who by love oppress'd,
Or tyrant passion preying on his breast,
And ever anxious thoughts, is robb'd of rest.
The Sisyphus is he whom noise and strife   200
Seduce from all the soft retreats of life,
To vex the government, disturb the laws;
Drunk with the fumes of popular applause,
He courts the giddy crowd to make him great
And sweats and toils in vain to mount the sovereign
       seat.
For still to aim at pow'r and still to fail,
Ever to strive and never to prevail,
What is it, but in reason's true account
To heave the stone against the rising mount;
Which urg'd, and labour'd, and forc'd up with pain,   210
Recoils and rolls impetuous down and smokes along
       the plain.
Then still to treat thy ever-craving mind
With ev'ry blessing and of ev'ry kind,
Yet never fill thy rav'ning appetite,
Though years and seasons vary thy delight—
Yet nothing to be seen of all the store,
But still the wolf within thee barks for more:
This is the fable's moral which they tell
Of fifty foolish virgins damn'd in hell

---

[189] *Tityus*. The giant. For attempting to ravish Latona, he was placed
    in Hades where his liver was perpetually devoured; he was said to cover
    nine acres when stretched out.
[211] A happy example of a heptameter line; for one of the hexameters see
    205.
[219] *fifty foolish virgins*. The Danaides, who murdered the men betrothed
    to them, and thus, as Lucretius says, were punished.

To leaky vessels which the liquor spill,   220
To vessels of their sex, which none cou'd ever fill.
As for the dog, the Furies and their snakes,
The gloomy caverns and the burning lakes,
And all the vain infernal trumpery,
They neither are, nor were, nor e'er can be.
But here on earth the guilty have in view
The mighty pains to mighty mischiefs due:
Racks, prisons, poisons, the Tarpeian rock,
Stripes, hangmen, pitch, and suffocating smoke,
And last, and most, if these were cast behind,   230
Th' avenging horror of a conscious mind
Whose deadly fear anticipates the blow
And sees no end of punishment and woe,
But looks for more at the last gasp of breath:
This makes an hell on earth and life a death.
   Meantime, when thoughts of death disturb thy
     head,
Consider Ancus great and good is dead;
Ancus, thy better far, was born to die,
And thou, dost thou bewail mortality?
So many monarchs with their mighty state   240
Who rul'd the world were overrul'd by Fate.
That haughty king who lorded o'er the main
And whose stupendous bridge did the wild waves
     restrain
(In vain they foam'd, in vain they threaten'd wreck,
While his proud legions march'd upon their back),
Him Death, a greater monarch, overcame,
Nor spared his guards the more for their immortal
     name.
The Roman chief, the Carthaginian dread,
Scipio the thunderbolt of war is dead,
And like a common slave by Fate in triumph led.   250

---

²²¹ Introducing an idea from Proverbs 30:16, that the womb (with the grave, earth, and fire) is one of the four insatiable things.

²²²⁻²³ Features of the classical underworld.

²²⁸ *the Tarpeian rock.* From which felons were hurled to death.

²³⁷ *Ancus.* Fourth king of Rome, valorous as Romulus and wise as Numa; see *Threnodia Augustalis* 465 ff.

²⁴² *that haughty king.* Xerxes, who bridged the Hellespont.

²⁴⁹ *Scipio.* Publius Cornelius, "Scipio Africanus," a conqueror of Carthage,

   The founders of invented arts are lost,
And wits who made eternity their boast:
Where now is Homer, who possess'd the throne?
Th' immortal work remains, the mortal author's gone.
Democritus, perceiving age invade,
His body weaken'd, and his mind decay'd,
Obey'd the summons with a cheerful face,
Made haste to welcome death and met him half the
    race.
That stroke, ev'n Epicurus cou'd not bar,
Though he in wit surpass'd mankind as far }   260
As does the midday sun the midnight star.
And thou, dost thou disdain to yield thy breath,
Whose very life is little more than death?
More than one half by lazy sleep possess'd,
And when awake thy soul but nods at best,
Daydreams and sickly thoughts revolving in thy
    breast.
Eternal troubles haunt thy anxious mind
Whose cause and cure thou never hop'st to find,
But still uncertain, with thyself at strife,
Thou wander'st in the labyrinth of life.   270
   O if the foolish race of man who find
A weight of cares still pressing on their mind
Cou'd find as well the cause of this unrest
And all this burden lodg'd within the breast,
Sure they wou'd change their course, nor live as now,
Uncertain what to wish or what to vow.
Uneasy both in country and in town,
They search a place to lay their burden down.
One, restless in his palace, walks abroad
And vainly thinks to leave behind the load   280
But straight returns, for he's as restless there
And finds there's no relief in open air.
Another to his villa wou'd retire
And spurs as hard as if it were on fire;

one of the greatest of Roman generals and renowned for highest Roman
integrity.
252 A striking addition by Dryden.
255 *Democritus.* The classical atomist and early philosopher of the school
later called Epicurean.

No sooner enter'd at his country door,
But he begins to stretch, and yawn, and snore,
Or seeks the city which he left before.
Thus every man o'erworks his weary will
To shun himself and to shake off his ill;
The shaking fit returns and hangs upon him still.   290
No prospect of repose nor hope of ease,
The wretch is ignorant of his disease,
Which known wou'd all his fruitless trouble spare,
For he wou'd know the world not worth his care:
Then wou'd he search more deeply for the cause
And study Nature well and Nature's laws;
For in this moment lies not the debate,
But on our future, fix'd, eternal state,
That never-changing state which all must keep
Whom death has doom'd to everlasting sleep.   300

Why are we then so fond of mortal life,
Beset with dangers and maintain'd with strife?
A life which all our care can never save;
One fate attends us and one common grave.
Besides we tread but a perpetual round;
We ne'er strike out but beat the former ground,
And the same mawkish joys in the same track are
    found.
For still we think an absent blessing best,
Which cloys and is no blessing when possess'd—
A new arising wish expells it from the breast.   310
The fev'rish thirst of life increases still;
We call for more and more and never have our fill,
Yet know not what tomorrow we shall try,
What dregs of life in the last draught may lie.
Nor, by the longest life we can attain,
One moment from the length of death we gain,
For all behind belongs to his eternal reign.
When once the Fates have cut the mortal thread,
The man as much to all intents is dead
Who dies today, and will as long be so,   320
As he who di'd a thousand years ago.

HORACE

Ode XXIX, Book III

PARAPHRASED IN PINDARIC VERSE, AND INSCRIB'D TO THE
RIGHT HONOURABLE LAWRENCE, EARL OF ROCHESTER

I

Descended of an ancient line
   That long the Tuscan scepter sway'd,
Make haste to meet the generous wine,
   Whose piercing is for thee delay'd;
The rosy wreath is ready made,
   And artful hands prepare
The fragrant Syrian oil that shall perfume thy hair.

II

When the wine sparkles from afar,
   And the well-natur'd friend cries, "Come away,"
Make haste and leave thy business and thy care—   10
   No mortal int'rest can be worth thy stay.

III

Leave for a while thy costly country seat
   And, to be great indeed, forget
The nauseous pleasures of the great;
    Make haste and come,
Come and forsake thy cloying store,
   Thy turret that surveys from high
The smoke and wealth and noise of Rome,
   And all the busy pageantry
That wise men scorn and fools adore: 20
Come, give thy soul a loose and taste the pleasures of
      the poor.

²¹ *give thy soul a loose.* Often quoted and praised by James Russell Lowell
  as an example of Dryden's manly and free dignity.

IV

Sometimes 'tis grateful to the rich to try
A short vicissitude and fit of poverty:
   A savoury dish, a homely treat,
   Where all is plain, where all is neat,
   Without the stately spacious room,
The Persian carpet or the Tyrian loom,
Clear up the cloudy foreheads of the great.

V

The sun is in the Lion mounted high;
   The Syrian star   30
   Barks from afar
And with his sultry breath infects the sky;
The ground below is parch'd, the heav'ns above us
      fry.
   The shepherd drives his fainting flock
   Beneath the covert of a rock
   And seeks refreshing rivulets nigh;
   The Sylvans to their shades retire—
Those very shades and streams new shades and
      streams require
And want a cooling breeze of wind to fan the raging
      fire.

VI

Thou, what befits the new Lord May'r,   40
   And what the City faction dare,
   And what the Gallic arms will do,
   And what the quiver-bearing foe,
   Art anxiously inquisitive to know:
But God has, wisely, hid from human sight

---

27 *the Tyrian loom.* Cloth, especially the famous purple esteemed by Greeks and Romans.
30 *the Syrian star.* Sirius, the dog star, thought to bring sickening or maddening heat.
37 *Sylvans.* Woodland spirits.
40-42 The contemporary allusions are those of "imitation" rather than "paraphrase" translation: *Lord May'r* of London; the *City faction* of Whiggish commercial interests; the *Gallic arms* of Louis XIV bent on conquest.

The dark decrees of future fate
And sown their seeds in depth of night;
He laughs at all the giddy turns of state,
When mortals search too soon and fear too late.

VII

Enjoy the present smiling hour   50
And put it out of Fortune's pow'r.
The tide of bus'ness, like the running stream,
Is sometimes high and sometimes low,
A quiet ebb or a tempestuous flow,
And always in extreme.
Now with a noiseless, gentle course
It keeps within the middle bed,
Anon it lifts aloft the head
And bears down all before it with impetuous force,
And trunks of trees come rolling down,   60
Sheep and their folds together drown,
Both house and homestead into seas are borne,
And rocks are from their old foundations torn,
And woods made thin with winds their scatter'd
honours mourn.

VIII

Happy the man, and happy he alone,
He who can call today his own,
He who secure within can say,
"Tomorrow do thy worst, for I have liv'd today.
Be fair or foul, or rain or shine,
The joys I have possess'd in spite of fate are mine.   70
Not Heav'n itself upon the past has pow'r,
But what has been, has been, and I have had my
hour."

IX

Fortune that with malicious joy
Does man her slave oppress,

---

[65] *Happy the man.* The "happy man," an ideal referred to in the Horatian phrase, *ille beatus*, led the independent, retired, moderate life described here and much influenced ideals in Dryden's century and the next.

Proud of her office to destroy,
Is seldom pleas'd to bless.
Still various and unconstant still,
But with an inclination to be ill,
Promotes, degrades, delights in strife,
And makes a lottery of life.   80
I can enjoy her while she's kind,
But when she dances in the wind
And shakes her wings and will not stay,
I puff the prostitute away;
The little or the much she gave is quietly resign'd;
Content with poverty, my soul I arm,
And virtue, tho' in rags, will keep me warm.

                    x
            What is 't to me
Who never sail in her unfaithful sea,
If storms arise, and clouds grow black,   90
If the mast split and threaten wreck?
Then let the greedy merchant fear
            For his ill-gotten gain
And pray to gods that will not hear,
While the debating winds and billows bear
            His wealth into the main.
For me, secure from Fortune's blows
(Secure of what I cannot lose),
In my small pinnace I can sail,
            Contemning all the blust'ring roar,   100
                And running with a merry gale,
With friendly stars my safety seek
Within some little winding creek,
            And see the storm ashore.

82-84 The bug image, which is not in Horace, is traditional for the glittering and annoying.

OVID'S AMOURS

Book I.   Elegy I

For mighty wars I thought to tune my lute
And make my measures to my subject suit.
Six feet for ev'ry verse the Muse design'd,
But Cupid, laughing when he saw my mind,
From ev'ry second verse a foot purloin'd.

   "Who gave thee, boy, this arbitrary sway,
On subjects not thy own commands to lay,
Who Phoebus only and his laws obey?
'Tis more absurd than if the Queen of Love
Shou'd in Minerva's arms to battle move,   10
Or manly Pallas from that Queen shou'd take
Her torch and o'er the dying lover shake.
In fields as well may Cynthia sow the corn,
Or Ceres wind in woods the bugle horn.
As well may Phoebus quit the trembling string
For sword and shield, and Mars may learn to sing.
Already thy dominions are too large;
Be not ambitious of a foreign charge.
If thou wilt reign o'er all and ev'rywhere,
The god of music for his harp may fear.   20
Thus when with soaring wings I seek renown,
Thou pluck'st my pinions, and I flutter down.
Cou'd I on such mean thoughts my Muse employ,
I want a mistress or a blooming boy."

   Thus I complain'd; his bow the stripling bent
And chose an arrow fit for his intent.
The shaft his purpose fatally pursues—
"Now, poet, there's a subject for thy Muse,"

3-5 Cupid curtails every second hexameter to change an epic measure to
    elegiac distichs for love elegies.
8 *Phoebus.* Inventer and god of poetry, music, and other high arts.
9-16 Impossible exchanges of roles between Venus (9), goddess of love, and
    Minerva (10) or Pallas Athene (11, the Greek equivalent), goddess of
    war; of Cynthia (13) or Diana, goddess of the hunt, and Ceres (14),
    goddess of agriculture; and of Phoebus (15) and Mars (16), god of war.
20 *the god of music.* See 8n.

He said. Too well, alas, he knows his trade,
For in my breast a mortal wound he made.   30
Far hence, ye proud hexameters, remove;
My verse is pac'd and travell'd into love.
With myrtle wreaths my thoughtful brows enclose,
While in unequal verse I sing my woes.

OVID'S AMOURS

Book I.   Elegy IV

*To his mistress, whose husband
is invited to a feast with them.
The poet instructs her how to
behave herself in his company.*

Your husband will be with us at the treat—
May that be the last supper he shall eat.
And am poor I, a guest invited there,
Only to see, while he may touch, the fair?
To see you kiss and hug your nauseous lord,
While his lewd hand descends below the board?
Now wonder not that Hippodamia's charms,
At such a sight, the Centaurs urg'd to arms,
That in a rage they threw their cups aside,
Assail'd the bridegroom and wou'd force the bride.   10
I am not half a horse (I wish I were),
Yet hardly can from you my hands forbear.
  Take then my counsel which, observ'd, may be
Of some importance both to you and me.
Be sure to come before your man be there;
There's nothing can be done, but come howe'er.
Sit next him (that belongs to decency),
But tread upon my foot in passing by.
Read in my looks what silently they speak

---

[34] *unequal verse.* The *pac'd* distichs; see 3–5n.
[7] *Hippodamia.* At her marriage to Perithous, the intoxicated Centaurs
  (half man, half horse) threatened to ravish the women present.

And slyly, with your eyes, your answer make.   20
My lifted eyebrow shall declare my pain;
My right hand to his fellow shall complain,
And on the back a letter shall design,
Besides a note that shall be writ in wine.
Whene'er you think upon our last embrace,
With your forefinger gently touch your face.
If any word of mine offend my dear,
Pull with your hand the velvet of your ear.
If you are pleas'd with what I do or say,
Handle your rings or with your fingers play.   30
As suppliants use at altars, hold the board
Whene'er you wish the devil may take your lord.
When he fills for you, never touch the cup
But bid th' officious cuckold drink it up.
The waiter on those services employ;
Drink you, and I will snatch it from the boy,
Watching the part where your sweet mouth has
       been,
And thence, with eager lips, will suck it in.
If he with clownish manners thinks it fit
To taste and offers you the nasty bit,   40
Reject his greasy kindness and restore
Th' unsav'ry morsel he had chew'd before.
Nor let his arms embrace your neck, nor rest
Your tender cheek upon his hairy breast.
Let not his hand within your bosom stray
And rudely with your pretty bubbies play.
But above all let him no kiss receive;
That's an offence I never can forgive.
Do not, O do not that sweet mouth resign,
Lest I rise up in arms and cry, " 'Tis mine!"   50
I shall thrust in betwixt and, void of fear,
The manifest adult'rer will appear.
      These things are plain to sight, but more I doubt
What you conceal beneath your petticoat.
Take not his leg between your tender thighs,
Nor with your hand provoke my foe to rise.

18-32 Ovid's passage on love's sign language was often imitated in the
sixteenth and seventeenth centuries.

How many love-inventions I deplore
Which I myself have practis'd all before!
How oft have I been forc'd the robe to lift
In company, to make a homely shift   60
For a bare bout ill huddled o'er in haste,
While o'er my side the fair her mantle cast.
You to your husband shall not be so kind,
But lest you shou'd, your mantle leave behind.
Encourage him to tope but kiss him not,
Nor mix one drop of water in his pot.
If he be fuddled well and snores apace,
Then we may take advice from time and place.
When all depart, while compliments are loud,
Be sure to mix among the thickest crowd: 70
There I will be, and there we cannot miss
Perhaps to grubble or at least to kiss.

    Alas, what length of labour I employ
Just to secure a short and transient joy!
For night must part us, and when night is come,
Tuck'd underneath his arms he leads you home.
He locks you in, I follow to the door,
His fortune envy and my own deplore.
He kisses you, he more than kisses too;
Th' outrageous cuckold thinks it all his due.   80
But add not to his joy by your consent,
And let it not be giv'n, but only lent;
Return no kiss nor move in any sort;
Make it a dull and a malignant sport.
Had I my wish, he shou'd no pleasure take,
But slubber o'er your business for my sake.
And whate'er fortune shall this night befall,
Coax me tomorrow by forswearing all.

THRENODIA AUGUSTALIS

*A Funeral-Pindaric Poem
Sacred to the Happy Memory of
King Charles II*

> *Fortunati ambo, si quid mea
> carmina possunt,
> Nulla dies unquam memori vos
> eximet aevo!*

1685. Charles II died of uremic poisoning on Friday, February 6, 1685. Dryden's poem, which was later than most in appearing (ll. 1 ff.), probably awaited the confirmation of his Poet Laureateship. But he also took pains to establish details for a poem that was both accurate and lyrical. The attack of illness came suddenly (stanza I) on Monday, February 2, after prolonged good health and just as the King was enjoying assurance of rule. On hearing the news, his brother James rushed to the sickroom, not fully dressed (stanza II). After the most fearsome medical treatment, or mistreatment, which the King bore patiently (stanzas V–VI), he seemed to recover on Thursday (stanza III). But the inevitable outcome was clear, and Charles approached death with great dignity (stanza VI); in full consciousness, he blessed his miscellaneous family and subjects, asking pardon of those whom he might have mistreated (stanzas VII–VIII). In the second half of the poem Dryden essayed the difficult feat, rendered yet more difficult in a lyric, of true and yet appropriate judgment on Charles (stanzas IX–XIV) and the still more difficult task of assessing with enthusiasm the phlegmatic personality of James. The portrait of Charles (which bears comparison with the King of *Absalom and Achitophel*) stresses his mildness, his interest in art and learning, and his peaceable nature. The portrait of the new King emphasizes "warlike" heroism and his reputation as a man of his word. The poem concludes with a prediction of the kind Dryden liked to make: an almost Utopian picture of "English loyalty" at home and the success of a "conquering navy" abroad. The poem shows the differing virtues of the brothers, implicitly judging them both, rather to the favor of Charles.

Apart from his outstanding translation of Horace's Ode xxix, Book III, *Threnodia Augustalis* is Dryden's first poem in the form of the loose "Pindaric" ode in which most of his greatest lyrics were written. For some reason his printer did not follow the usual practice of indenting lines according to decreasing length of metrical feet, and this edition is probably the first in which the usual practice has been adopted for this ode. The title is not completely clear; it appears to mean a threnode by a priest of Augustus, that is, a funeral poem interspersed with prayers by the Poet Laureate of the two kings. The imagery and allusions employ the traditional store of royalist symbolism developed from Roman through Stuart times and, as is usual with Dryden, mingle Christian and pagan, classical and biblical, medieval and modern elements.

The epigraph is from Virgil, *Aeneid* IX, 446–47:

> O happy friends! for; if my verse can give
> Immortal life, your fame shall ever live.
> (Trans. Dryden.)

I

Thus long my grief has kept me dumb;
Sure there's a lethargy in mighty woe;
   Tears stand congeal'd and cannot flow,
And the sad soul retires into her inmost room;
Tears, for a stroke foreseen, afford relief,
But unprovided for a sudden blow,
    Like Niobe we marble grow
      And petrify with grief.

---

7 *Niobe*. Stricken with grief for her children that were slain by Apollo and Diana for her own impiety, she was turned to stone.

    Our British Heav'n was all serene;
        No threat'ning cloud was nigh,   10
Not the least wrinkle to deform the sky;
We liv'd as unconcern'd and happily
As the first age in nature's golden scene;
    Supine amidst our flowing store,
We slept securely, and we dreamt of more;
When suddenly the thunder-clap was heard;
It took us unprepar'd and out of guard,
    Already lost before we fear'd.
Th' amazing news of Charles at once were spread,
    At once the general voice declar'd,   20
        "Our gracious Prince was dead."
No sickness known before, no slow disease
    To soften grief by just degrees,
But like an hurricane on Indian seas
        The tempest rose,
    An unexpected burst of woes,
    With scarce a breathing space betwixt,
This Now becalm'd and perishing the next.
    As if great Atlas from his height
    Shou'd sink beneath his heav'nly weight   30
And, with a mighty flaw, the flaming wall
      (As once it shall)
Shou'd gape immense and rushing down o'erwhelm
    this nether ball:
So swift and so surprizing was our fear;
Our Atlas fell indeed, but Hercules was near.

          II

    His pious brother, sure the best
        Who ever bore that name,
    Was newly risen from his rest
      And, with a fervent flame,
His usual morning vows had just addres'd   40
        For his dear sovereign's health,

---

[31] *the flaming wall.* Echoing Lucretius, *De Rerum Natura* I, 73: "flammantia moenia mundi."

[29-35] Hercules (James II) once relieved Atlas (Charles II) of the burden of the world. Both were types of kings, Hercules of the warlike or heroic; see 466 ff.

And hop'd to have 'em heard
In long increase of years,
In honour, fame, and wealth;
Guiltless of greatness thus he always pray'd,
Nor knew nor wish'd those vows he made
On his own head shou'd be repay'd.
Soon as th' ill omen'd rumor reach'd his ear
(Ill news is wing'd with fate and flies apace),
Who can describe th' amazement in his face! 50
Horror in all his pomp was there,
Mute and magnificent without a tear;
And then the hero first was seen to fear.
Half unarray'd he ran to his relief,
So hasty and so artless was his grief;
Approaching Greatness met him with her charms
Of pow'r and future state,
But look'd so ghastly in a brother's fate,
He shook her from his arms.
Arriv'd within the mournful room, he saw 60
A wild Distraction void of awe
And arbitrary Grief unbounded by a law.
God's image, God's anointed lay
Without motion, pulse, or breath,
A senseless lump of sacred clay,
An image, now, of death.
Amidst his sad attendants' groans and cries,
The lines of that ador'd, forgiving face
Distorted from their native grace;
An iron slumber sat on his majestic eyes. 70
The pious Duke—forbear, audacious Muse,
No terms thy feeble art can use
Are able to adorn so vast a woe—
The grief of all the rest like subject-grief did show,
His like a sovereign did transcend;

61-62 A complicated point. In traditional symbolism, a king had his body natural (Charles' body is now dying) and his body politic made up of his subjects, and a mystic privity existed between them. What James discovers is an ironic arbitrariness among the attendant subjects (body politic), ironic because Charles II (Dryden implies) was never himself arbitrary. Only at this moment does one of Charles' bodies show lawlessness. The same kind of point is made in 136-37; see also *Absalom and Achitophel*, To the Reader note 10.
70 *iron slumber.* A Virgilianism: *Aeneid* X, 745-46.

No wife, no brother, such a grief cou'd know,
    Nor any name but friend.

III

O wondrous changes of a fatal scene,
    Still varying to the last!
  Heav'n, though its hard decree was pass'd,   80
Seem'd pointing to a gracious turn again,
And Death's up-lifted arm arrested in its haste.
    Heav'n half repented of the doom
    And almost griev'd it had foreseen
What by foresight it will'd eternally to come.
    Mercy above did hourly plead
    For her resemblance here below,
    And mild Forgiveness intercede
      To stop the coming blow.
New Miracles approach'd th' ethereal throne,   90
Such as his wondrous life had oft and lately known,
    And urg'd that still they might be shown.
On earth his pious brother pray'd and vow'd,
Renouncing greatness at so dear a rate,
    Himself defending what he cou'd
From all the glories of his future fate.
      With him th' innumerable crowd
        Of armed prayers
Knock'd at the gates of Heav'n, and knock'd aloud,
The first well-meaning, rude petitioners.   100
    All for his life assail'd the throne,
All wou'd have brib'd the skies by off'ring up their
    own.
So great a throng not Heav'n itself cou'd bar;
'Twas almost borne by force as in the Giants' war.
The pray'rs, at least, for his reprieve were heard;
His death, like Hezekiah's, was deferr'd:
    Against the sun the shadow went;
    Five days, those five degrees, were lent
To form our patience and prepare th' event.

103-4 The gigantomachy against Zeus, related by many classical writers.
105-9 The King's illness extended through *five degrees*, or days, rather like
good King Hezekiah, who was given a respite when "sick unto death"
(2 Kings 20:1-11).

The second causes took the swift command, 110
   The med'cinal head, the ready hand,
   All eager to perform their part,
All but eternal doom was conquer'd by their art;
   Once more the fleeting soul came back
     T' inspire the mortal frame,
And in the body took a doubtful stand,
Doubtful and hov'ring like expiring flame
That mounts and falls by turns and trembles o'er the
     brand.

IV

The joyful short-liv'd news soon spread around,
Took the same train, the same impetuous bound; 120
The drooping town in smiles again was dress'd,
   Gladness in every face express'd,
   Their eyes before their tongues confess'd.
Men met each other with erected look;
   The steps were higher that they took;
Friends to congratulate their friends made haste,
And long invet'rate foes saluted as they pass'd.
Above the rest heroic James appear'd
Exalted more, because he more had fear'd;
   His manly heart, whose noble pride 130
     Was still above
   Dissembled hate or varnish'd love,
Its more than common transport cou'd not hide
But like an eagre* rode in triumph o'er the tide.
    Thus, in alternate course
   The tyrant passions, hope and fear,
    Did in extremes appear
And flash'd upon the soul with equal force.
    Thus, at half ebb, a rolling sea
   Returns and wins upon the shore; 140
The wat'ry herd, affrighted at the roar,
   Rest on their fins awhile, and stay,
   Then backward take their wond'ring way;
   The prophet wonders more than they

---

* *An eagre is a tide swelling above another tide, which I have myself
observ'd on the River Trent.* [Dryden's note.]

At prodigies but rarely seen before,
And cries, "A king must fall, or kingdoms change their
    sway!"
Such were our counter-tides at land, and so
   Presaging of the fatal blow
   In their prodigious ebb and flow.
The royal soul, that like the lab'ring moon   150
   By charms of art was hurried down,
Forc'd with regret to leave her native sphere,
   Came but awhile on liking here;
   Soon weary of the painful strife,
   And made but faint essays of life:
       An evening light
       Soon shut in night,
A strong distemper and a weak relief,
Short intervals of joy and long returns of grief.

       v
   The sons of art all med'cines tri'd   160
And every noble remedy appli'd;
   With emulation each essay'd
   His utmost skill, nay more, they pray'd;
Never was losing game with better conduct play'd.
Death never won a stake with greater toil,
   Nor e're was fate so near a foil;
   But, like a fortress on a rock,
Th' impregnable disease their vain attempts did
    mock;
They min'd it near, they batter'd from afar
With all the cannon of the med'cinal war;   170
   No gentle means cou'd be essay'd,
'Twas beyond parley when the siege was laid.
   Th' extremest ways they first ordain,
Prescribing such intolerable pain
   As none but Caesar cou'd sustain;
   Undaunted Caesar underwent
   The malice of their art, nor bent

150-57 Ancient belief held that the moon labored in agony during an
eclipse and might then be brought down by enchanters; *her* (152)
refers to *soul* and *moon* (150), both feminine in Latin.

Beneath whate'er their pious rigour cou'd invent;
  In five such days he suffer'd more
Than any suffer'd in his reign before;   180
  More, infinitely more, than he
Against the worst of rebels cou'd decree,
A traitor or twice-pardon'd enemy.
  Now art was tir'd without success,
No racks cou'd make the stubborn malady confess.
  The vain insurancers of life
And he who most perform'd and promis'd less,
Even Short himself, forsook th' unequal strife.
  Death and despair was in their looks;
No longer they consult their memories or books;   190
  Like helpless friends, who view from shore
The lab'ring ship and hear the tempest roar,
  So stood they with their arms across,
  Not to assist, but to deplore
        Th' inevitable loss.

                    VI
  Death was denounc'd; that frightful sound
  Which even the best can hardly bear;
  He took the summons void of fear
And, unconcern'dly, cast his eyes around,
As if to find and dare the grisly challenger.   200
  What death cou'd do he lately tri'd,
  When in four days he more than di'd.
The same assurance all his words did grace;
The same majestic mildness held its place,
Nor lost the monarch in his dying face.
Intrepid, pious, merciful, and brave,
He look'd as when he conquer'd and forgave.

                    VII
  As if some angel had been sent
  To lengthen out his government
And to foretell as many years again   210
As he had number'd in his happy reign,

---

[188] *Short.* Thomas (d. 1685), a Tory and Catholic physician, one among
many who had ministered to Charles II.

So cheerfully he took the doom
    Of his departing breath,
Nor shrunk nor stepp'd aside for death,
But with unalter'd pace kept on,
Providing for events to come
    When he resign'd the throne.
Still he maintain'd his kingly state
And grew familiar with his fate.
Kind, good, and gracious to the last,   220
On all he lov'd before his dying beams he cast:
  O truly good, and truly great,
For glorious as he rose, benignly so he set!
    All that on earth he held most dear
    He recommended to his care,
        To whom both Heav'n
        The right had giv'n
And his own love bequeath'd supreme command;
He took and press'd that ever-loyal hand,
    Which cou'd in peace secure his reign,   230
    Which cou'd in wars his pow'r maintain,
That hand on which no plighted vows were ever
    vain.
    Well for so great a trust he chose
    A prince who never disobey'd,
Not when the most severe commands were laid,
Nor want, nor exile with his duty weigh'd;
A prince on whom (if Heav'n its eyes cou'd close)
The welfare of the world it safely might repose.

        VIII
    That king who liv'd to God's own heart
    Yet less serenely died than he;   240
    Charles left behind no harsh decree
    For schoolmen with laborious art
      To save from cruelty;

235-36 In some crises, Charles II had to send his brother into exile while
a storm was weathered. James, who had an absolute concept of loyalty
to a king, always obeyed at once.
237-38 See 29-35.
239-45 David on his deathbed charged Solomon with vengeance on his
enemies; Charles was more merciful. In 244 *those* may include Monmouth, then in Holland.

Those for whom love cou'd no excuses frame
   He graciously forgot to name.
Thus far my Muse, though rudely, has design'd
Some faint resemblance of his godlike mind,
But neither pen nor pencil can express
   The parting brothers' *tenderness*,
   Though that's a term too mean and low   250
(The blest above a kinder word may know);
   But what they did and what they said,
   The monarch who triumphant went,
     The militant who stay'd,
Like painters, when their height'ning arts are spent,
   I cast into a shade.
   That all forgiving king,
   The type of Him above,
   That inexhausted spring
   Of clemency and love,   260
   Himself to his next self accus'd,
And ask'd that pardon which he ne'er refus'd
   For faults not his, for guilt and crimes
Of godless men and of rebellious times;
   For an hard exile, kindly meant,
   When his ungrateful country sent
Their best Camillus into banishment,
And forc'd their sov'reign's act—they cou'd not his
     consent.
Oh, how much rather had that injur'd chief
   Repeated all his suff'rings past   270
   Than hear a pardon begg'd at last,
Which giv'n cou'd give the dying no relief;
   He bent, he sunk beneath his grief;
   His dauntless heart wou'd fain have held
   From weeping, but his eyes rebell'd.
Perhaps the godlike hero in his breast
   Disdain'd or was asham'd to show
   So weak, so womanish a woe,

253-54 Adapting concepts of the Church militant and the Church triumphant.
267 *their best Camillus*. M. Furius Camillus, a very devout Roman general, similar at several points to James.

Which yet the brother and the friend so plenteously
    confess'd.

       IX

Amidst that silent show'r the royal mind   280
    An easy passage found
  And left its sacred earth behind,
Nor murm'ring groan express'd, nor labouring
    sound,
  Nor any least tumultuous breath;
Calm was his life, and quiet was his death.
  Soft as those gentle whispers were
  In which th' Almighty did appear;
By the still voice the prophet knew him there.
That peace which made thy prosperous reign to
    shine,
That peace thou leav'st to thy imperial line,   290
That peace, O happy shade, be ever thine!

       X

For all those joys thy Restoration brought,
  For all the miracles it wrought,
For all the healing balm thy mercy pour'd
  Into the nation's bleeding wound,
  And care that after kept it sound;
  For numerous blessings yearly shower'd
  And property with plenty crown'd;
  For freedom, still maintain'd alive,
Freedom, which in no other land will thrive,   300
Freedom, an English subject's sole prerogative,
  Without whose charms ev'n peace wou'd be
  But a dull, quiet slavery:
For these and more, accept our pious praise;
    'Tis all the subsidy
    The present age can raise;
The rest is charg'd on late posterity.
  Posterity is charg'd the more,
  Because the large abounding store
To them and to their heirs is still entail'd by thee.   310

288 *the still voice.* 1 Kings 19:12.

Succession, of a long descent,
Which chastely in the channels ran
And from our demigods began,
Equal almost to time in its extent,
Through hazards numberless and great,
Thou hast deriv'd this mighty blessing down,
And fix'd the fairest gem that decks th' imperial
crown.
Not faction, when it shook thy regal seat,
Not senates, insolently loud
(Those echoes of a thoughtless crowd),   320
Not foreign or domestic treachery,
Could warp thy soul to their unjust decree.
So much thy foes thy manly mind mistook,
Who judg'd it by the mildness of thy look;
Like a well temper'd sword, it bent at will
But kept the native toughness of the steel.

                    XI

Be true, O Clio, to thy hero's name!
But draw him strictly so
That all who view the piece may know;
He needs no trappings of fictitious fame;   330
The load's too weighty; thou may'st choose
Some parts of praise and some refuse;
Write, that his annals may be thought more lavish than
the Muse.
In scanty truth thou hast confin'd
The virtues of a royal mind,
Forgiving, bounteous, humble, just, and kind:
His conversation, wit, and parts,
His knowledge in the noblest, useful arts
Were such dead authors cou'd not give,
But habitudes of those who live,   340
Who, lighting him, did greater lights receive;
He drain'd from all and all they knew,

311-26 *Succession*, etc. Charles II insisted upon legitimacy for succession,
realizing that anything else would hazard the throne; he therefore un-
shakably disallowed Monmouth.
327 *Clio*. Muse of history.
333 *annals*. The barest, least adorned form of history, according to Dryden
in his Life of Plutarch.

His apprehension quick, his judgment true,
    That the most learn'd with shame confess
His knowledge more, his reading only less.

XII

Amidst the peaceful triumphs of his reign,
What wonder if the kindly beams he shed
    Reviv'd the drooping arts again,
        If Science rais'd her head,
And soft Humanity that from rebellion fled?   350
Our isle, indeed, too fruitful was before,
    But all uncultivated lay
Out of the solar walk and Heav'n's high way,
    With rank Geneva weeds run o'er,
And cockle, at the best, amidst the corn it bore;
    The royal husbandman appear'd,
        And plough'd, and sow'd, and till'd,
The thorns he rooted out, the rubbish clear'd,
        And bless'd th' obedient field,
When straight a double harvest rose,   360
    Such as the swarthy Indian mows,
    Or happier climates near the line,
Or paradise manur'd and dress'd by hands divine.

XIII

As when the newborn phoenix takes his way
His rich paternal regions to survey,
Of airy choristers a numerous train
Attend his wond'rous progress o'er the plain:
    So rising from his father's urn,
    So glorious did our Charles return;
    Th' officious Muses came along,   370

---

³⁵³ Cf. *Annus Mirabilis* 639; *Britannia Rediviva* 306.
³⁵⁵ *cockle*. See *Absalom and Achitophel* 195n.
³⁵⁰⁻⁶³ For the dual cultivation metaphor: *To the Earl of Roscommon*
    1 ff.; *To Mr. Congreve* 1 ff.
³⁶⁴ᶠᶠ. The *phoenix* comparison had appeared in *Verses to the Duchess;*
    it yields to the *birds of paradise* (poets) (380), who were said always
    to stay on the wing, lacking legs, and to feed on dew. Some think
    this a criticism of Charles for not paying the monies due Dryden for
    his offices; but for a less indulgent attitude, see *To Sir Godfrey Kneller*
    97–101.

A gay harmonious choir like angels ever young
(The Muse that mourns him now his happy triumph
    sung);
Even *they* cou'd thrive in his auspicious reign,
   And such a plenteous crop they bore
   Of purest and well-winnow'd grain
   As Britain never knew before.
Tho' little was their hire and light their gain,
   Yet somewhat to their share he threw;
   Fed from his hand, they sung and flew
Like birds of paradise that liv'd on morning dew.   380
O never let their lays his name forget!
The pension of a prince's praise is great.
Live then, thou great encourager of arts,
   Live ever in our thankful hearts;
Live blest above, almost invok'd below,
   Live and receive this pious vow,
Our patron once, our guardian angel now.
   Thou Fabius of a sinking state,
Who didst by wise delays divert our fate
   When faction like a tempest rose   390
     In death's most hideous form,
   Then art to rage thou didst oppose
     To weather out the storm;
   Not quitting thy supreme command,
Thou heldst the rudder with a steady hand
Till safely on the shore the bark did land,
   The bark that all our blessings brought,
Charg'd with thyself and James, a doubly royal
    fraught.

XIV

   O frail estate of human things,
    And slippery hopes below!   400
Now to our cost your emptiness we know
   (For 'tis a lesson dearly bought),

---

³⁸⁸ *Fabius.* Q. Fabius Maximus, the Roman general who thwarted Hannibal by patient delays, a just comparison for the policy of Charles II
in bad times.

Assurance here is never to be sought.
  The best, and best belov'd of kings,
  And best deserving to be so,
When scarce he had escap'd the fatal blow
  Of faction and conspiracy,
  Death did his promis'd hopes destroy;
He toil'd, he gain'd, but liv'd not to enjoy.
  What mists of Providence are these   410
    Through which we cannot see!
So saints, by supernatural pow'r set free,
Are left at last in martyrdom to die;
Such is the end of oft-repeated miracles.
  Forgive me, Heav'n, that impious thought;
  'Twas grief for Charles to madness wrought
  That question'd thy supreme decree!
  Thou didst his gracious reign prolong,
  Even in thy saints' and angels' wrong,
His fellow citizens of immortality.   420
  For twelve long years of exile borne,
Twice twelve we number'd since his blest return;
  So strictly wer't thou just to pay,
  Ev'n to the driblet of a day.
  Yet still we murmur and complain
The quails and manna shou'd no longer rain;
Those miracles 'twas needless to renew;
The Chosen Flock has now the Promis'd Land in
    view.

                          xv
A warlike prince ascends the regal state,
  A prince long exercis'd by fate;   430
Long may he keep, tho' he obtains it late.
Heroes in Heaven's peculiar mold are cast;
They and their poets are not form'd in haste;
Man was the first in God's design, and man was made
    the last.

421-24 Charles was proclaimed king on February 5, 1648-9; his *blest return*
  was in 1660; he died on February 6, 1684-5, the *driblet of a day* off
  from the Scottish proclamation.
426-28 Cf. *The Medal* 131n.
430 *long exercis'd by fate*. So Virgil's Aeneas, *Aeneid* III, 182.

False heroes made by flattery so,
Heav'n can strike out, like sparkles, at a blow;
But e'er a prince is to perfection brought,
He costs omnipotence a second thought.
     With toil and sweat,
  With hard'ning cold and forming heat,   440
   The Cyclops did their strokes repeat
Before th' impenetrable shield was wrought.
It looks as if the Maker wou'd not own
    The noble work for his
Before 'twas tri'd and found a masterpiece.

XVI

View then a monarch ripen'd for a throne.
  Alcides thus his race began;
   O'er infancy he swiftly ran;
The future god at first was more than man;
   Dangers and toils and Juno's hate   450
   Even o'er his cradle lay in wait,
   And there he grappled first with Fate;
In his young hands the hissing snakes he press'd,
So early was the deity confess'd;
Thus by degrees he rose to Jove's imperial seat;
Thus difficulties prove a soul *legitimately* great.
Like his, our hero's infancy was tri'd;
Betimes the Furies did their snakes provide
  And to his infant arms oppose
His father's rebels and his brother's foes;   460
The more oppress'd, the higher still he rose;
  Those were the preludes of his fate
  That form'd his manhood, to subdue
The Hydra of the many-headed, hissing crew.

XVII

As after Numa's peaceful reign,
The martial Ancus did the scepter wield,

---

441 *Cyclops*. Workmen of Vulcan, they made Aeneas' shield (Virgil, *Aeneid*, VIII).
447-55 *Alcides*, or Hercules (see 36), in two actions that were types of a king's quelling rebellion: strangling snakes in his cradle and over-coming the Lernean hydra as one of his labors.

Furbish'd the rusty sword again,
    Resum'd the long forgotten shield,
And led the Latins to the dusty field:
    So James the drowsy genius wakes   470
    Of Britain long entranc'd in charms,
    Restive and slumb'ring on its arms;
'Tis rous'd and with a new strung nerve the spear
        already shakes.
    No neighing of the warrior steeds,
    No drum, or louder trumpet, needs
T' inspire the coward, warm the cold—
His voice, his sole appearance makes 'em bold.
Gaul and Batavia dread th' impending blow;
Too well the vigour of that arm they know;
They lick the dust and crouch beneath their fatal
        foe.   480
    Long may they fear this awful prince
    And not provoke his ling'ring sword;
    Peace is their only sure defence,
    Their best security his word;
In all the changes of his doubtful state,
His truth, like Heav'n's, was kept inviolate;
For him to promise is to make it fate.
His valour can triumph o'er land and main;
With broken oaths his fame he will not stain,
With conquest basely bought and with inglorious
        gain.   490

XVIII

For once, O Heav'n, unfold thy adamantine book
    And let his wond'ring Senate see,
If not thy firm immutable decree,
At least the second page of strong contingency,
Such as consists with wills originally free;
    Let them with glad amazement look
    On what their happiness may be;
Let them not still be obstinately blind

465-69 *Ancus Martius*, the warlike grandson of peaceable good King Numa,
    led the Romans against the Latins—Dryden's comparison is less accurate
    for details than personalities.
492 *Senate.* Parliament, especially the Commons.

Still to divert the good thou hast design'd,
  Or with malignant penury 500
To starve the royal virtues of his mind.
Faith is a Christian's and a subject's test;
O give them to believe and they are surely blest!
They do; and with a distant view I see
Th' amended vows of English loyalty.
And all beyond that object, there appears
The long retinue of a prosperous reign,
  A series of successful years,
In orderly array, a martial, manly train.
  Behold ev'n to remoter shores 510
  A conquering navy proudly spread;
The British cannon formidably roars,
  While starting from his oozy bed
Th' asserted Ocean rears his reverend head
To view and recognize his ancient lord again,
  And with a willing hand restores
    The fasces of the main.

514-17 A formula of the river or ocean god raising his head above the
waters, as in *Astraea Redux* 246–49 and numerous classical writings.

TO THE PIOUS MEMORY
OF THE ACCOMPLISH'D
YOUNG LADY
MRS. ANNE KILLIGREW,

Excellent in the Two Sister-Arts of
Poesy and Painting

AN ODE

1685. The beautiful Anne Killigrew (1660–1685) died in June 1685. By autumn of that year her *Poems* appeared with Dryden's ode as a tribute to her, the daughter of one friend, the Rev. Dr. Henry Killigrew, and the niece of another, the droll Thomas Killigrew. The young woman was one of a number of Restoration bluestockings, of whom the best known was "the Matchless Orinda," Mrs. Katherine Philips, who also was a poet, a virtuous woman, and a victim of smallpox (stanza VIII). Anne Killigrew was a painter of real gifts, one or two of her paintings having been sometimes thought the work of the best hands of the day. She practiced both the "French" (in fact mostly Flemish and Italian) landscape style (stanza VI) and the "English" portrait style, which Dryden himself preferred (stanza VII). Her poetic ability was correspondingly low, although the ethical quality of her verse (stanzas IV–V) is beyond dispute. Dryden's praise must be understood in such terms of friendship, of mingled talents, and of virtue. Above all, he describes and praises poetic genius. This ode, which Dr. Johnson thought undoubtedly the finest in English, shows that Dryden's mastery of the Pindaric stanza afforded him opportunity to express his faith in artistic genius and his own art.

I

Thou youngest virgin-daughter of the skies,
Made in the last promotion of the blest,
Whose palms new pluck'd from Paradise
In spreading branches more sublimely rise
Rich with immortal green above the rest,
Whether adopted to some neighb'ring star,
Thou roll'st above us in thy wand'ring race,
 Or in procession fix'd and regular
 Mov'd with the heavens' majestic pace,
 Or call'd to more superior bliss,   10
Thou tread'st with seraphims the vast abyss,
Whatever happy region is thy place,
Cease thy celestial song a little space
(Thou wilt have time enough for hymns divine,
 Since Heav'n's eternal year is thine);
Hear then a mortal Muse thy praise rehearse
  In no ignoble verse,
But such as thy own voice did practice here
When thy first fruits of poesy were giv'n
To make thyself a welcome inmate there,   20
 While yet a young probationer
 And candidate of Heav'n.

II

If by traduction came thy mind,
 Our wonder is the less to find
A soul so charming from a stock so good;
Thy father was transfus'd into thy blood;
So wert thou born into the tuneful strain
(An early, rich, and inexhausted vein).
 But if thy preëxisting soul
 Was form'd at first with myriads more,   30

6-11 Envisioning the older geocentric universe: whether the "intelligence" or angel of a star near earth, whether in the outer sphere of the fixed stars, or whether with seraphim in God's immediate presence.

It did through all the mighty poets roll
  Who Greek or Latin laurels wore
And was that Sappho last which once it was before.
  If so, then cease thy flight, O heav'n-born mind!
  Thou hast no dross to purge from thy rich ore,
  Nor can thy soul a fairer mansion find
  Than was the beauteous frame she left behind:
Return, to fill or mend the choir of thy celestial kind.

III

  May we presume to say that at thy birth
New joy was sprung in Heav'n as well as here on
      earth?   40
For sure the milder planets did combine
On thy auspicious horoscope to shine,
And ev'n the most malicious were in trine.
    Thy brother-angels at thy birth
    Strung each his lyre and tun'd it high,
    That all the people of the sky
  Might know a poetess was born on earth;
      And then, if ever, mortal ears
      Had heard the music of the spheres!
      And if no clust'ring swarm of bees   50
On thy sweet mouth distill'd their golden dew.
  'Twas that such vulgar miracles
  Heav'n had not leisure to renew;
For all the blest fraternity of love
Solemniz'd there thy birth and kept thy holiday
    above.

IV

O gracious God! How far have we
Prophan'd thy heav'nly gift of poesy!
Made prostitute and profligate the Muse,
Debas'd to each obscene and impious use,

23-33 Two theories of the origin of the soul: *traduction* or transfusion by
  the father at conception; and the Platonic or Pythagorean transmigra-
  tion of a *preëxisting soul*.
33 *Sappho*. The Greek poetess.
48-49 After sinning in Eden and becoming mortal, man could no longer
  hear the music of the spheres, except, some said, at the Nativity.
50-51 Bees on the infant Plato's mouth foretold his eloquence.

Whose harmony was first ordain'd above   60
For tongues of angels and for hymns of love!
O wretched we! Why were we hurri'd down
   This lubric and adult'rate age
   (Nay added fat pollutions of our own)
   T' increase the steaming ordures of the stage?
What can we say t' excuse our second Fall?
Let this thy Vestal, Heav'n, atone for all!
   Her Arethusian stream remains unsoil'd,
   Unmix'd with foreign filth and undefil'd;
Her wit was more than man, her innocence a child!   70

V

   Art she had none, yet wanted none,
   For nature did that want supply;
   So rich in treasures of her own,
   She might our boasted stores defy;
Such noble vigour did her verse adorn
That it seem'd borrow'd where 'twas only born.
   Her morals, too, were in her bosom bred,
     By great examples daily fed,
What in the best of books, her father's life, she read.
   And to be read herself she need not fear;   80
   Each test and ev'ry light her Muse will bear,
   Though Epictetus with his lamp were there.
   Ev'n love (for love sometimes her Muse express'd)
Was but a lambent flame which play'd about her
         breast,
   Light as the vapours of a morning dream,
   So cold herself, whilst she such warmth express'd,
   'Twas Cupid bathing in Diana's stream.

VI

   Born to the spacious empire of the Nine,
   One would have thought she should have been
      content

[66] See 48–49n.
[68] Arethusa was nymph of a pure Ortygian spring.
[82] The Stoic philosopher Epictetus, as described by Lucian in *The Ignorant Book-Collector*.

To manage well that mighty government;   90
But what can young ambitious souls confine?
    To the next realm she stretch'd her sway,
    For Painture near adjoining lay,
A plenteous province and alluring prey.
A Chamber of Dependences was fram'd
(As conquerors will never want pretence,
    When arm'd, to justify the offence),
And the whole fief in right of poetry she claim'd.
    The country open lay without defence,
    For poets frequent inroads there had made,   100
        And perfectly could represent
    The shape, the face, with ev'ry lineament;
And all the large domains which the dumb sister
            sway'd,
        All bow'd beneath her government,
        Receiv'd in triumph wheresoe'er she went.
Her pencil drew whate'er her soul design'd,
And oft the happy draught surpass'd the image in
            her mind.
The sylvan scenes of herds and flocks
And fruitful plains and barren rocks
Of shallow brooks that flow'd so clear   110
The bottom did the top appear;
Of deeper, too, and ampler floods,
Which as in mirrors shew'd the woods;
Of lofty trees with sacred shades
And perspectives of pleasant glades
Where nymphs of brightest form appear
And shaggy satyrs standing near,
Which them at once admire and fear;
The ruins, too, of some majestic piece,
Boasting the pow'r of ancient Rome or Greece,   120
Whose statues, friezes, columns broken lie,
And though defac'd, the wonder of the eye:
What nature, art, bold fiction e'er durst frame,
Her forming hand gave feature to the name.

93 *the next realm.* Painting; France; and schools of "French" painting.
95 *Chamber of Dependences.* A diplomatic device of Louis XIV to subvert
   a *province.*
103 *the dumb sister.* Painting.

So strange a concourse ne'er was seen before,
But when the peopl'd ark the whole creation bore.

VII

The scene then chang'd; with bold, erected look
Our martial King the sight with reverence strook;
For not content t' express his outward part,
Her hand call'd out the image of his heart;   130
His warlike mind, his soul devoid of fear,
His high-designing thoughts were figur'd there,
As when, by magic, ghosts are made appear.
    Our phoenix Queen was portray'd, too, so
        bright—
Beauty alone could beauty take so right;
Her dress, her shape, her matchless grace
Were all observ'd, as well as heav'nly face.
With such a peerless majesty she stands
As in that day she took the crown from sacred
        hands,
Before a train of heroines was seen,   140
In beauty foremost, as in rank the Queen!
    Thus nothing to her genius was deni'd,
But like a ball of fire the further thrown,
    Still with a greater blaze she shone,
And her bright soul broke out on ev'ry side.
What next she had design'd, Heav'n only knows,
To such immod'rate growth her conquest rose
That fate alone its progress could oppose.

VIII

    Now all those charms, that blooming grace,
The well-proportion'd shape, and beauteous face   150

---

126 *the peopl'd ark.* In his *Ode. of Wit*, Cowley had established the ark as
a metaphor of poetic wit.
127 *The scene then chang'd.* The landscape of France is changed to England and the implied English tradition of portrait painting.
128 *Our martial King*, James II, excellently painted by Anne Killigrew.
134 *Our phoenix Queen.* Queen Mary; see *The Prologue to the Duchess*,
headnote.
147-48 Echoing the epigraph for Anne Killigrew's *Poems*, Martial, *Epigrams* VI, xxix, 7: "Immodicis brevis et aetas, et rara senectus"; the
first portion of which is rendered more closely in *Absalom and Achitophel* 847.

Shall never more be seen by mortal eyes.
In earth the much lamented virgin lies!
   Not wit nor piety could fate prevent,
   Nor was the cruel Destiny content
   To finish all the murder at a blow,
To sweep at once her life, and beauty too,
But like a harden'd felon took a pride
    To work more mischievously slow,
    And plunder'd first and then destroy'd.
O double sacrilege on things divine,   160
To rob the relic and deface the shrine!
    But thus Orinda di'd:
   Heav'n by the same disease did both translate;
As equal were their souls, so equal was their fate.

       IX
   Meantime her warlike brother on the seas
   His waving streamers to the winds displays
And vows for his return with vain devotion pays.
    Ah, generous youth, that wish forbear;
    The winds too soon will waft thee here!
    Slack all thy sails and fear to come;   170
Alas, thou know'st not, thou art wreck'd at home!
No more shalt thou behold thy sister's face;
Thou hast already had her last embrace.
But look aloft, and if thou ken'st from far
Among the Pleiads a new-kindl'd star,
If any sparkles, than the rest, more bright,
'Tis she that shines in that propitious light.

       X
When in mid-air the golden trump shall sound
   To raise the nations underground;

---

[162] *Orinda.* Mrs. Katherine Philips (d. 1664), "the Matchless Orinda," a
far better poet than Anne Killigrew, also died of smallpox. She was
celebrated in an elegy by Cowley, *On the Death of Mrs. Katherine
Philips,* whose imagery Dryden borrows in 160–61. Dryden echoes other
prefatory material in the *Poems by the Matchless Orinda* and poems
by Anne Killigrew as well.
[165] *her warlike brother.* Henry Killigrew (d. 1712), naval captain, later
admiral, was then sailing against pirates in the Mediterranean.
[175] *the Pleiads.* The seven stars of the Pleiades, a name derived from the
Greek word for "to sail."

When in the valley of Jehosaphat,   180
The judging God shall close the book of fate
   And there the last assizes keep
  For those who wake and those who sleep;
    When rattling bones together fly
From the four corners of the sky;
When sinews o'er the skeletons are spread,
Those cloth'd with flesh, and life inspires the dead:
The sacred poets first shall hear the sound
  And foremost from the tomb shall bound,
For they are cover'd with the lightest ground,   190
And straight with inborn vigour, on the wing,
Like mounting larks to the new morning sing.
There thou, sweet saint, before the choir shalt go
As harbinger of Heav'n the way to show,
The way which thou so well hast learn'd below.

180-81 *Jehosaphat* or Jehoshaphat means "God judges"; cf. Joel 3:2.

TO SIR GEORGE ETHEREGE

Mr. Dryden's *Answer*

1686. In 1685, Sir George Etherege (?1635–1691) went as English minister to Ratisbon (now Regensburg, Bavaria), from where he sent official and personal reports to the Earl of Middleton, the Secretary of State. Among the personal reports (most of which talk of gambling, chasing resistant women, unwelcome drinking, and loneliness for England) were two poems (sent in January and April, 1686) in the kind of dog-trot octosyllabic couplets that Dryden imitates in his poem. No poet, Middleton evidently showed Etherege's two poems to Dryden, whose anonymous reply was transparent even to Etherege's secretary. Once Dryden had entered as verse correspondent, Etherege turned back to prose. Dryden elsewhere criticizes the lack of dignity in the comic octosyllabic couplet associated with Samuel Butler's *Hudibras,* but in this informal bantering he gains an effect similar to some of his prologues and epilogues.

The opening lines have been interpreted as a play on Etherege's age, which Dryden is not likely to have known, and also as a play on talk of latitude in Etherege's second verse letter. Perhaps the best explanation holds that Dryden was saying that Etherege took the warmth of London (at "fifty-one" degrees) to the "chill degree" of Ratisbon, that he either thought or pretended to think was "fifty-three." It is true, however, that ll. 9 ff. treat age. More clearly, Dryden maintains throughout the air of aristocratic negligence that was cultivated by Etherege and other Restoration courtiers. There is also something of the "wild debaucheries, and quickness of wit in repartees" that in *An*

Essay of Dramatic Poesy Dryden associated with the gentlemen in Beaumont and Fletcher's plays. The poem is
Dryden's only surviving *jeu d'esprit*, and Etherege must
have appreciated its suavity and even the lightly acidulous
wit of the conclusion.

To you who live in chill degree
(As map informs) of fifty-three,
And do not much for cold atone
By bringing thither fifty-one,
(Methinks) all climes shou'd be alike
From tropic e'en to pole arctic.
Since you have such a constitution
As cannot suffer diminution,
You can be old in grave debate
And young in love's affairs of state,   10
And both to wives and husbands show
The vigour of a plenipo—
Like mighty missioner you come
Ad partes infidelium,
A work of wondrous merit sure,
So far to go, so much endure,
And all to preach to German dame,
Where sound of Cupid never came.
Less had you done, had you been sent
As far as Drake or Pinto went,   20
For cloves and nutmegs to the line-a,
Or even for oranges to China;
That had indeed been charity   ⎫
Where love-sick ladies helpless lie ⎬
Chopp'd and for want of liquor dry. ⎭
   But you have made your zeal appear
Within the circle of the Bear;
What region of the world so dull,

11-12 Etherege is *plenipo*, plenipotentiary, to the husbands as ambassador
   with full powers, and to the wives in the Latinate sense of full-potent.
14 "To regions of the infidels"; perhaps also "To regions of the unfaithful
   ones."
20 Sir Francis Drake went to the New World, Fernám Mendes Pinto to
   Asia.
27 *the Bear.* An eating house in Drury Lane; also Ursa Major.

That is not of your labours full?
Triptolemus (so sing the nine)   30
Strew'd plenty from his cart divine,
But (spite of all those fable-makers)
He never sow'd on Almaine acres;
No, that was left by fate's decree
To be perform'd and sung by thee.
    Thou break'st thro' forms with as much ease
As the French king thro' articles;
In grand affairs thy days are spent ⎫
In waging weighty compliment,   ⎬
With such as monarchs represent;   ⎭   40
They whom such vast fatigues attend
Want some soft minutes to unbend,
To show the world that now and then
Great ministers are mortal men.
Then Rhenish rummers walk the round,
In bumpers every king is crown'd,
Besides three holy miter'd Hectors
And the whole College of Electors;
No health of potentate is sunk
That pays to make his envoy drunk.   50
    These Dutch delights I mention'd last
Suit not, I know, your English taste—
For wine to leave a whore or play,
Was ne'er your excellency's way;
Nor need the title give offence,
For here you were his excellence:
For gaming, writing, speaking, keeping,
His excellence for all but sleeping.
Now if you tope in form, and treat, ⎫
'Tis the sour sauce to the sweet meat, ⎬   60
The fine you pay for being great.   ⎭
    Nay, there's a harder imposition,
Which is (indeed) the court petition,
That setting worldly pomp aside

30-31 *Triptolemus.* See Ovid, *Metamorphoses* V, 642–61 and such other
fable-makers as Pausanias.
36-37 Louis XIV often broke treaties.
47-48 The German *College of Electors* comprised five secular rulers and
three miter'd Hectors, the archbishops of Mainz, Cologne, and Trier.
51-52 Etherege disliked drinking.

(Which poet has at font defi'd),
You wou'd be pleas'd in humble way
To write a trifle call'd a play;
This truly is a degradation
But wou'd oblige the crown and nation,
Next to your wise negotiation;   70
If you pretend, as well you may,
Your high degree, your friends will say
The Duke St. Aignan made a play;
If Gallic peer affect you scarce,
His Grace of Bucks. has made a farce,
And you whose comic wit is terse-all,
Can hardly fall below *Rehearsal*.
Then finish what you once began,
But scribble faster if you can,
For yet no George, to our discerning,   80
E'er writ without a ten year's warning.

66-67 James II had requested another comedy from Etherege.
73 *play.* A tragicomedy, *Bradamante* (1637).
74-81 References to George Villiers, Duke of Buckingham ("Zimri"), part
    author of *The Rehearsal* (a parody of heroic plays by Dryden and
    others), begun in 1663 but not performed until 1671.

THE HIND
AND THE PANTHER

A Poem, in Three Parts

—*Antiquam exquirite matrem.*
Et vera, incessu, patuit dea.—
VIRG.

1686–1687. Dryden's longest original poem appeared amid
a storm of religious controversy, to which it was itself inevitably a contribution. The date of Dryden's conversion to
Catholicism is still uncertain. He had perhaps decided as
early as the Battle of Sedgemoor on July 6, 1685 (see Part
II, ll. 654 ff. in context), and by January 19, 1686, he was
publicly known to have attended Mass. It is clear, however, that his conversion hinged upon the central issue of
Religio Laici—the Rule of Faith, the proper authority for
belief and salvation. His answer is shown in Part II (most
briefly, ll. 479–85). Like many before him, he could say
"my doubts are done" only when he had trusted the guid-
ance of his faith to a Church whose claim to authority was
complete and whose government (like monarchy?) was
continuous in legitimate succession (Part II, ll. 578 ff.). He
knew that to become a Catholic was to gain little present
advantage and certain trouble in the future (Part III, ll.
225 ff.), and in one of the most moving passages of the poem
(Part III, ll. 281 ff.), he pictured himself as the prodigal
son who has, at great cost and after struggle, given up his
ambitious dreams. The three personal passages (Part I, ll.
64 ff.; Part II, ll. 654 ff.; Part III, ll. 235 ff.) testify best to
Dryden's commitment in the poem.

Most readers are likely to wonder about this strange

beast fable for churches, kings, or even ordinary individuals. As Dryden himself says (Part III, ll. 1–9), Spenser's *Mother Hubbard's Tale* and, more especially, Aesop were major sources. John Ogilby's *Fables of Aesop Paraphras'd in Verse* furnished him with numerous details and the basic plots of the fables of the Swallows and of the Pigeons in Part III. Spenser had helped to suggest how a beast fable could be used to convey historical as well as ethical significance. As Dryden had glossed Restoration history by biblical history in *Absalom and Achitophel* after the manner of one kind of parabolic reading of Scripture, so now he glossed Scripture and beast lore by following another traditional gloss of the Bible: the *moraliter* gloss referring to the Church. It was easy in seventeenth-century or earlier thought to consider either the Book of God's Word (the Bible) or the Book of His Works (the creation) as a source of truth, and both were read symbolically with types (David as a type of Christ) and correspondences (the lion corresponding as king among beasts to human kings).

Dryden was assisted in relating beast lore to religion by the tradition of sacred zoography, or religious study of beasts, and in particular perhaps by the *Historia Animalium Sacra* of Wolfgang Franzius that discussed at length the moral, ecclesiastical, and typological significances of quadrupeds and birds. Such thought had drawn upon traditions from the earlier Renaissance, the Middle Ages, and antiquity. Dryden knew that most of his contemporaries would find "this mysterious writ" rather obscure and partly for that reason found it useful to introduce humor or absurdity into a work intermittently satiric. It will be observed, for example, that the occasional absurdities are directed chiefly at the Anglican Panther and not at all at the "sober" Catholic Hind. Moreover, the poet found a real pleasure (e.g., Part II, ll. 714–20; Part III, ll. 22–29) in moving with his beast fable, or in dropping it, sometimes in adjusting it so subtly that we cannot say where it begins or ends, and sometimes (e.g., Part III, ll. 14–15) in making his points by contradicting or opposing the two elements of the fable. By the time a reader attentive to Dryden's techniques reaches the fables of the Swallows and the Pigeons in Part III, he will find it altogether suitable to artistic logic that a Catholic Hind should tell an Anglican Panther about sexually misbehaving Catholic Poultry that is nonetheless better than Anglican Pigeons. The fabulous element is to-day one of the most interesting aspects of the poem.

In view of the complexity and unusual character of the poem, a brief résumé may be of use. The poem opens with a description of the Catholic Hind, "immortal and un-chang'd" (Part I, ll. 1–34). There follow "characters" of other beasts who are representatives of Reformed Churches (Part I, ll. 35–510). Movement through this gallery is twice interrupted, the first time for Dryden to counter the Fox's Socinianism (denial of Christ's divinity) and natural religion with his own belief in a supernatural and tran-scendent religion approached by faith rather than the un-aided reason. This passage (Part I, ll. 62–149) is the best known in the poem. The other interruption (Part I, ll. 239–307) includes a creation passage and a plea for religious toleration; it is also aimed at countering a tendency repre-sented by the more-or-less Presbyterian Wolf. Dryden now pleads for reason in the face of the "deform'd" supernatu-ralism which would displace divine and human wisdom with willfulness. In other words, he has emphasized faith, reason, and their perversions. At the close of Part I, the Panther and Hind meet.

Their talk throughout Part II centers on contemporary issues of religious controversy in a way "chiefly concerning Church authority": Anglican hedging over relations with James II and with Catholics (Part II, ll. 1–59); infallibil-ity, tradition, and the Rule of Faith (Part II, ll. 60–388); the Catholic as the true Church (Part II, ll. 389–638); and the welcome given by the Catholic Church to those who come to it (Part II, ll. 639–48). At its end, Part II alludes to James II (Part II, ll. 654–62) along with Dryden's per-sonal attestation and closes with talk of the Hind and her guest, the Panther. Part II is the most theological section of the poem and therefore probably the least close to modern issues and interests, but it is set forth with great clarity and occasional splendor (e.g., Part II, ll. 499 ff.).

Part III opens with the *apologia* for the fable (Part III.

ll. 1–15) and goes on (Part III, ll. 16–426) to debate the
social and political implications of the religious stands
taken by the Hind and the Panther. Then the Panther relates her fable of the Swallows (Part III, ll. 427–638),
where Dryden manages the difficult feat of at once having
the Panther foretell the destruction of English Catholics, of
having her acknowledge unaware through the Swallow
type that the Catholic is the true Church, and of warning
James II of the dangers attendant upon the measures he
was taking on the counsel of his rasher advisers. More discussion (Part III, ll. 639–905) of the motivations of the
opposing sides (including the personal passage on Dryden's conversion) yields to the Hind's fable of the Pigeons
(Part III, ll. 906–1288), which foretells a religious toleration in England in which the relative merits of the Catholic
Poultry and the Anglican Pigeon will lead the Pigeon to
decline away. The poem ends with a brief apostrophe to
the Hind (Part III, ll. 1289–98). Simply, Part I deals with
the past of the Catholic and other churches, Part II with
contemporary issues, and Part III with the religious future
of England. Mingled with this temporal sequence is, however, the timelessness of divine Providence in the typologies of the beasts.

As the epistle—To the Reader—and the poem itself
show, Dryden entered the controversy of the time in prose.
James II had published, in 1686, *Two Papers Written by
the Late King Charles II. Together with a Copy of a Paper
Written by the Late Duchess of York,* the first two briefly
arguing the Catholic case, the last justifying conversion.
Edward Stillingfleet, then Dean of St. Paul's, countered all
three papers with an *Answer.* A Catholic *Defence* then appeared, with Dryden writing in favor of the duchess'
paper. Stillingfleet returned with *A Vindication of the Answer,* to which Dryden refers in the epistle and the poem,
chiefly on the issue of whether or not there was a Protestant treatise of humility, Dryden saying that the only one
he knew of was a treatise by one Duncomb, referring to a
work by an E. D. (probably Eleazor Duncon or Dun-
combe) translated, as he says, from Alonzo Rodriguez. For
his part Stillingfleet probably had in mind William Allen's

Practical Discourse of Humility. This exchange now has
little significance, but it was regarded at the time as the
opening round of a controversy that had, by the time the
poem was in press, come to a climax with James' Declaration for Liberty of Conscience (or Declaration of Indulgence) on April 4, 1687. Dryden had anticipated but not
"so soon expected" this general toleration and, as he hints,
was led by it to revise part of the Hind's fable in Part III
and perhaps a very few other passages. As might be expected, the poem was read with great interest, whether in
anger or enthusiasm, and was quickly reprinted. Today the
old controversies are less interesting than Dryden's evident
commitment and his creation of a poem extraordinary in its
almost medieval fable. Almost bursting at the seams with
miscellaneous bustle, ideas, and figures, the poem contains
almost all the various types of poetry that Dryden had
touched upon outside the theater. *The Hind and the
Panther* is crucial to an understanding of Dryden's Christian humanism and especially of his religion. Its importance in his writings is, among his less known poems, that
of *Absalom and Achitophel* among his more familiar.

The double epigraph is taken from Virgil, *Aeneid* III,
96: "Seek out your ancient mother"; and *Aeneid* I, 405:
"The true goddess is known by her stately movement"
(both referring to the Catholic Hind).

To the Reader

The nation is in too high a ferment for me to expect
either fair war or even so much as fair quarter from a
reader of the opposite party. All men are engag'd either on
this side or that, and tho' conscience is the common word
which is given by both, yet if a writer fall among enemies
and cannot give the marks of *their* conscience, he is
knock'd down before the reasons of his own are heard. A
Preface, therefore, which is but a bespeaking of favour,
is altogether useless. What I desire the reader should know
concerning me he will find in the body of the poem, if he
have but the patience to peruse it. Only this advertisement

let him take beforehand, which relates to the merits of
the cause. No general characters of parties (call 'em
either Sects or Churches) can be so fully and exactly
drawn as to comprehend all the several members of 'em, at
least all such as are receiv'd under that denomination. For
example, there are some of the Church by Law Establish'd
who envy not liberty of conscience to Dissenters, as being
well satisfied that, according to their own principles, they
ought not to persecute them. Yet these, by reason of their
fewness, I could not distinguish from the numbers of the
rest with whom they are embodied in one common name.
On the other side there are many of our Sects, and more
indeed than I could reasonably have hop'd, who have withdrawn themselves from the communion of the Panther[1]
and embrac'd this gracious Indulgence[2] of His Majesty
in point of toleration. But neither to the one nor the other
of these is this satire any way intended; 'tis aim'd only at
the refractory and disobedient on either side. For those
who are come over to the royal party are consequently
suppos'd to be out of gunshot. Our physicians have observ'd that in process of time some diseases have abated of
their virulence and have in a manner worn out their malignity so as to be no longer mortal; and why may not I suppose the same concerning some of those who have formerly been enemies to kingly government as well as Catholic religion? I hope they have now another notion of both,
as having found, by comfortable experience, that the doctrine of persecution is far from being an article of our
faith.

'Tis not for any private man to censure the proceedings
of a foreign prince, but without suspicion of flattery I
may praise our own, who has taken contrary measures,
and those more suitable to the spirit of Christianity. Some
of the Dissenters in their addresses to His Majesty have
said "That he has restor'd God to his Empire over Conscience." I confess I dare not stretch the figure to so great
a boldness, but I may safely say that conscience is the
royalty and prerogative of every private man. He is ab-

---

[1] *the Panther*. The Anglican *Church by Law Establish'd,* as above.
[2] *Indulgence*. See headnote.

solute in his own breast and accountable to no earthly
power for that which passes only betwixt God and him.
Those who are driven into the fold are, generally speaking,
rather made hypocrites than converts.[3]

This Indulgence being granted to all the Sects, it ought
in reason to be expected that they should both receive it
and receive it thankfully. For at this time of day to refuse
the benefit and adhere to those whom they have esteem'd
their persecutors, what is it else but publicly to own that
they suffer'd not before for conscience sake, but only out
of pride and obstinacy to separate from a Church for those
impositions which they now judge may be lawfully obey'd?
After they have so long contended for their classical
ordination (not to speak of rites and ceremonies), will
they at length submit to an episcopal? If they can go so
far out of complaisance to their old enemies, methinks a
little reason should persuade 'em to take another step and
see whither that wou'd lead 'em.

Of the receiving this toleration thankfully, I shall say no
more than that they ought, and I doubt not they will, consider from what hands they receiv'd it. 'Tis not from a
Cyrus, a heathen prince and a foreigner,[4] but from a
Christian king, their native sovereign, who expects a return in specie from them, that the kindness which he has
graciously shown them may be retaliated on those of his
own persuasion.

As for the poem in general, I will only thus far satisfy
the reader: that it was neither impos'd on me, nor so
much as the subject given me by any man. It was written
during the last winter and the beginning of this spring,
though with long interruptions of ill health and other hin-
drances. About a fortnight before I had finish'd it, His
Majesty's Declaration[5] for Liberty of Conscience came
abroad, which, if I had so soon expected, I might have
spar'd myself the labour of writing many things which are
contain'd in the third part of it. But I was always in some

[3] Dryden as usual condemns Louis XIV, here alluding to the Revocation
of the Edict of Nantes in 1685 and subsequent persecution of French
Protestants.
[4] Cyrus, etc. See Ezra 1:1-4.
[5] Declaration. See headnote.

hope that the Church of England might have been persuaded to have taken off the penal laws and the Test, which was one design of the poem when I propos'd to myself the writing of it.

'Tis evident that some part of it was only occasional and not first intended. I mean that defence of myself to which every honest man is bound when he is injuriously attack'd in print; and I refer myself to the judgment of those who have read the *Answer* to *The Defence of the Late King's Papers*, and that of the Duchess (in which last I was concerned [6]), how charitably I have been represented there. I am now inform'd both of the author and supervisors of his pamphlet and will reply when I think he can affront me; for I am of Socrates' opinion that all creatures cannot. In the meantime let him consider whether he deserv'd not a more severe reprehension than I gave him formerly for using so little respect to the memory of those whom he pretended to answer and, at his leisure, look out for some original treatise of humility written by any Protestant in English (I believe I may say in any other tongue), for the magnified piece of Duncomb on that subject, which either he must mean or none, and with which another of his fellows has upbraided me, was translated from the Spanish of Rodriguez, tho' with the omission of the 17th, the 24th, the 25th, and the last chapter, which will be found in comparing of the books.

He would have insinuated to the world that Her late Highness died not a Roman Catholic; he declares himself to be now satisfied to the contrary, in which he has giv'n up the cause, for matter of fact was the principal debate betwixt us. In the meantime he would dispute the motives of her change: how prepost'rously let all men judge, when he seem'd to deny the subject of the controversy, the change itself. And because I would not take up this ridiculous challenge, he tells the world I cannot argue; but he may as well infer that a Catholic cannot fast, because he will not take up the cudgels against Mrs. James[7] to confute the Protestant religion.

---

[6] See headnote.
[7] Mrs. Elinor James was an eccentric Anglican religious controversialist.

I have but one word more to say concerning the poem
as such and abstracting from the matters either religious
or civil which are handled in it. The first part, consisting
most in general characters and narration, I have endeavour'd to raise and give it the majestic turn of heroic
poesy. The second, being matter of dispute and chiefly
concerning Church authority, I was oblig'd to make as
plain and perspicuous as possibly I cou'd, yet not wholly
neglecting the numbers, though I had not frequent occasions for the magnificence of verse. The third, which has
more of the nature of domestic conversation is, or ought
to be, more free and familiar than the two former.

There are in it two episodes,[8] or fables, which are in-
terwoven with the main design, so that they are properly
parts of it, though they are also distinct stories of themselves. In both of these I have made use of the common
places of satire, whether true or false, which are urg'd by
the members of the one Church against the other. At
which I hope no reader of either party will be scandaliz'd,
because they are not of my invention, but as old, to my
knowledge, as the times of Boccace[9] and Chaucer on the
one side, and as those of the Reformation on the other.

THE HIND
AND THE PANTHER

The First Part

A milk white Hind,[1] immortal and unchang'd,
Fed on the lawns and in the forest rang'd;
Without unspotted, innocent within,
She fear'd no danger, for she knew no sin.

---

[8] *two episodes*. Of the Swallows and of the Pigeons in the Third Part.
[9] *Boccace*. Boccaccio.
[1] *Hind*. The Catholic Church. In these notes, references to parts of the
poem are given as I, II, and III: I, 1 is the first line of the poem. But
a note in one particular part referring to lines in the same part has
no roman numeral.

Yet had she oft been chas'd with horns and hounds
And Scythian shafts, and many winged wounds
Aim'd at her heart; was often forc'd to fly,
And doom'd to death though fated not to die.
   Not so her young, for their unequal line
Was hero's make, half human, half divine.   10
Their earthly mold obnoxious was to fate;
Th' immortal part assum'd immortal state.
Of these a slaughtered army lay in blood,
Extended o'er the Caledonian wood,
Their native walk; whose vocal blood arose
And cri'd for pardon on their perjur'd foes;
Their fate was fruitful, and the sanguine seed
Endu'd with souls, increas'd the sacred breed.
So captive Israel multipli'd in chains
A numerous exile and enjoy'd her pains.   20
With grief and gladness mix'd, their mother view'd
Her martyr'd offspring and their race renew'd;
Their corps to perish, but their kind to last,
So much the deathless plant the dying fruit
     surpass'd.
   Panting and pensive now she rang'd alone
And wander'd in the kingdoms once her own.
The common hunt, though from their rage restrain'd
By sov'reign pow'r, her company disdain'd:
Grinn'd as they pass'd and with a glaring eye
Gave gloomy signs of secret enmity.   30
'Tis true, she bounded by and tripp'd so light
They had not time to take a steady sight.
For truth has such a face and such a mien
As to be lov'd needs only to be seen.
   The bloody *Bear*, an *Independent* beast,
Unlick'd to form, in groans her hate express'd.

---

[6] *Scythian shafts.* Recalls the *Scythia sagitta* of Ovid, *Metamorphoses* X, 588; and *winged wounds* is a metonomy for spears or darts as in Virgil, *Aeneid* II, 529 and elsewhere.

[9] *her young.* Mortal Catholics making up the immortal Church.

[14] *Caledonian wood.* Britain, the *Caledonia silva* of classical writers; see III, 3.

[15] *vocal blood.* Genesis 4:10.

[19-20] *Israel.* Exodus 1:7.

[35] *Bear.* Independents (Congregationalists), who lacked the ecclesiastical *form* of Rome and Canterbury.

Among the timorous kind the *Quaking Hare*
Profess'd neutrality but would not swear.
Next her the *Buffoon Ape,* as atheists use,
Mimic'd all sects and had his own to choose;   40
Still when the Lion look'd, his knees he bent
And pay'd at Church a courtier's compliment.

    The bristl'd *Baptist Boar,* impure as he
(But whiten'd with the foam of sanctity),
With fat pollutions fill'd the sacred place
And mountains levell'd in his furious race;
So first rebellion founded was in grace!
But since the mighty ravage which he made
In German forests had his guilt betray'd,
With broken tusks and with a borrow'd name   50
He shunn'd the vengeance and conceal'd the shame,
So lurk'd in sects unseen. With greater guile
False *Reynard* fed on consecrated spoil;
The graceless beast by Athanasius first
Was chas'd from Nice; then by Socinus nurs'd
His impious race their blasphemy renew'd
And nature's King through nature's optics view'd.
Revers'd, they view'd him lessen'd to their eye,
Nor in an infant could a God descry:
New swarming sects to this obliquely tend;   60
Hence they began, and here they all will end.

    What weight of ancient witness can prevail
If private reason hold the public scale?
But gracious God, how well dost Thou provide
For erring judgments an unerring guide!
Thy throne is darkness in th' abyss of light,
A blaze of glory that forbids the sight;
O teach me to believe Thee thus conceal'd

---

[37] *Hare.* The Friends, or Quakers, who refused to take oaths and were
much persecuted.
[39] *Ape.* Atheists or freethinkers pretending to religion for profit.
[41] *Lion.* The king; here James II.
[43] *Baptist Boar.* The wretched Anabaptists, so violent at Münster in 1532,
and English counterparts.
[53] *False Reynard.* Those denying the Incarnation: Arians (54–55), Socinians
(55–56), and adherents of natural religion (56–59), including no doubt the
Deists attacked in *Religio Laici* 42 ff. The *consecrated spoil* seems to be
Christ's divinity and the transubstantiated Host of the Eucharist, a
second Christian mystery that Dryden treats next.

And search no farther than Thyself reveal'd,
But her alone for my director take   70
Whom Thou hast promis'd never to forsake!
My thoughtless youth was wing'd with vain desires,
My manhood, long misled by wand'ring fires,
Follow'd false lights; and when their glimps was
    gone,
My pride struck out new sparkles of her own.
Such was I, such by nature still I am,
Be Thine the glory and be mine the shame.
   Good life be now my task: my doubts are done
(What more could fright my faith than Three in
    One?);
Can I believe eternal God could lie   80
Disguis'd in mortal mold and infancy?
That the great maker of the world could die?
And after that trust my imperfect sense
Which calls in question His omnipotence?
Can I my reason to my faith compel,
And shall my sight, and touch, and taste rebel?
Superior faculties are set aside—
Shall their subservient organs be my guide?
Then let the moon usurp the rule of day
And winking tapers show the sun his way;   90
For what my senses can themselves perceive
I need no revelation to believe.
Can they who say the Host should be descri'd
By sense define a body glorifi'd?
Impassible and penetrating parts?
Let them declare by what mysterious arts
He shot that body through th' opposing might
Of bolts and bars impervious to the light
And stood before his train confess'd in open sight.
   For since thus wond'rously he pass'd, 'tis plain   100
One single place two bodies did contain,

---

71 *promis'd.* In Matthew 28:20.
80-92 The hierarchy of faith, reason, and sense is traditional Catholic
    and Anglican thought; Dryden argues also that transubstantiation is
    similar to the mysteries of the Trinity and Incarnation, accepted by
    Anglicans.
96-99 John 20:19, 26.

And sure the same omnipotence as well
Can make one body in more places dwell.
Let reason then at her own quarry fly—
But how can finite grasp infinity?
  'Tis urg'd again that faith did first commence
By miracles, which are appeals to sense,
And thence concluded that our sense must be
The motive still of credibility.
For latter ages must on former wait,   110
And what began belief must propagate.
  But winnow well this thought, and you shall find
'Tis light as chaff that flies before the wind.
Were all those wonders wrought by pow'r divine
As means or ends of some more deep design?
Most sure as means, whose end was this alone,
To prove the godhead of th' eternal Son.
God thus asserted, man is to believe
Beyond what sense and reason can conceive,
And for mysterious things of faith rely   120
On the proponent, Heav'n's authority.
If then our faith we for our guide admit,
Vain is the farther search of human wit,
As when the building gains a surer stay,
We take th' unuseful scaffolding away:
Reason by sense no more can understand;
The game is play'd into another hand.
  Why choose we then like bilanders to creep ⎫
Along the coast and land in view to keep,   ⎬
When safely we may launch into the deep? ⎭   130
In the same vessel which our Saviour bore, ⎫
Himself the pilot, let us leave the shore   ⎬
And with a better guide a better world explore. ⎭
Could He his godhead veil with flesh and blood
And not veil these again to be our food?
His grace in both is equal in extent;
The first affords us life, the second nourishment.

[106] *'Tis urg'd.* In contemporary Anglican controversy.
[127] *another hand.* Faith.
[135] *our food.* The Host in the Eucharist.

And if He can, why all this frantic pain
To construe what His clearest words contain
And make a riddle what He made so plain?   140
To take up half on trust, and half to try—
Name it not faith but bungling bigotry.
Both knave and fool the merchant we may call
To pay great sums and to compound the small.
For who wou'd break with heav'n and wou'd not break
        for all?
Rest then, my soul, from endless anguish freed,
Nor sciences thy guide, nor sense thy creed.
Faith is the best ensurer of thy bliss;
The bank above must fail before the venture miss.
    But heav'n and heav'n-born faith are far from
        thee,   150
Thou first apostate to divinity.
Unkennel'd range in thy Polonian plains;
A fiercer foe th' insatiate *Wolf* remains.
    Too boastful Britain, please thyself no more
That beasts of prey are banish'd from thy shore:
The Bear, the Boar, and every savage name,
Wild in effect, though in appearance tame,
Lay waste thy woods, destroy thy blissful bow'r,
And muzzl'd though they seem, the mutes devour.
More haughty than the rest, the wolfish race   160
Appear with belly gaunt and famish'd face:
Never was so deform'd a beast of Grace.
His ragged tail betwixt his legs he wears
Close clapp'd for shame, but his rough crest he
        rears
And pricks up his predestinating ears.
His wild disorder'd walk, his haggard eyes

---

139 *His clearest words.* "This is my body" (Matthew 26:26), a favorite
Catholic text.
148 *Faith is the best ensurer.* Faith here corrects the perverted rationalism
of the Fox; reason later corrects the perverted grace of the Wolf.
150 *thee.* The Fox.
153 *Wolf.* Presbyterians and others who deformed grace (162) with violence,
passion, and willfulness.
159 *muzzl'd.* By the Test Acts and penal laws.
163-64 Alluding to the Geneva cloak and black skull cap favored by Presbyterians.

Did all the bestial citizens surprise.
Though fear'd and hated, yet he ruled awhile
As captain or companion of the spoil.
Full many a year his hateful head had been   170
For tribute paid, nor since in Cambria seen;
The last of all the litter 'scap'd by chance
And from Geneva first infested France.
Some authors thus his pedigree will trace,
But others write him of an upstart race,
Because of Wycliffe's brood no mark he brings
But his innate antipathy to kings.
These last deduce him from th' Helvetian kind,
Who near the Leman Lake his consort lin'd.
That fi'ry Zwinglius first th' affection bred,   180
And meagre Calvin bless'd the nuptial bed.
In Israel some believe him whelp'd long since,   *Vid. Pref.*
When the proud Sanhedrin oppress'd the prince.   *to Heyl.*
Or, since he will be Jew, derive him high'r   *Hist. of*
When Corah with his brethren did conspire   *Presb.*
From Moses' hand the sov'reign sway to wrest
And Aaron of his ephod to divest,
Till opening earth made way for all to pass
And cou'd not bear the burden of a *class*.
The Fox and he came shuffl'd in the dark,   190
If ever they were stow'd in Noah's ark;
Perhaps not made, for all their barking train
The *Dog* (a common species) will contain;
And some wild curs, who from their masters ran, ⎫
Abhorring the supremacy of man,   ⎬
In woods and caves the rebel race began.   ⎭

   O happy pair, how well have you increas'd;
What ills in Church and state have you redress'd!

---

169 *captain* during the Civil Wars, *companion* in the Commonwealth.
171 Wolves were said to have been exterminated in Wales in the tenth century.
173 *Geneva*. From where Calvinism went to French Huguenots.
176Calvin's ideas resembled Wycliffe's more than those of other medieval reformers.
179–81 Sexual imagery (see the Glossary), with a play on *Leman*.
182 Dryden's note refers to Peter Heylyn, *Aërius Redivivus* (1670), ridiculing the Presbyterian claim to descent from the Jewish Sanhedrin.
185 *Corah*. Numbers 16; cf. *Absalom and Achitophel* 632 ff.
193 *The Dog*. Pagans: the ultimate in the tendencies of the Fox and Wolf who were formerly believed to be canine.

With teeth untri'd and rudiments of claws,
Your first essay was on your native laws;   200
Those having torn with ease and trampl'd down,
Your fangs you fasten'd on the miter'd crown
And freed from God and monarchy your town.
What though your native kennel still be small,
Bounded betwixt a puddle and a wall,
Yet your victorious colonies are sent
Where the north ocean girds the continent.
Quicken'd with fire below, your monsters breed
In fenny Holland and in fruitful Tweed,
And like the first the last affects to be   210
Drawn to the dregs of a democracy.
As where in fields the fairy rounds are seen
A rank, sour herbage rises on the green:
So, springing where these midnight elves advance,
Rebellion prints the footsteps of the dance.
Such are their doctrines, such contempt they show
To heav'n above and to their prince below
As none but traitors and blasphemers know.
God like the tyrant of the skies is plac'd,
And kings like slaves beneath the crowd debas'd.   220
So fulsome is their food that flocks refuse
To bite, and only dogs for physic use.
As where the lightning runs along the ground,
No husbandry can heal the blasting wound,
Nor bladed grass, nor bearded corn succeeds,
But scales of scurf and putrefaction breeds:
Such wars, such waste, such fiery tracks of dearth
Their zeal has left, and such a teemless earth.
But as the poisons of the deadliest kind
Are to their own unhappy coasts confin'd;   230
As only Indian shades of sight deprive,
And magic plants will but in Colchos thrive:

---

205 *a puddle and a wall.* Lake Geneva and the Alps.
207-9 The North Sea lies between *fenny Holland* and the *Tweed,* the river
  boundary with Scotland, where Presbyterianism flourished.
212 *fairy rounds.* Patches blighted by fairies' dancing or by lightning.
219 That is, the Calvinists' predestinating God is a perversion like *tyrant*
  Zeus.
231 *Indian shades.* The fabled poisonous shade of the upas tree.
232 *Colchos.* Home of the sorceress Medea.

So Presbyt'ry and pestilential zeal
Can only flourish in a commonweal.
    From Celtic woods is chas'd the wolfish crew;
But, ah! some pity e'en to brutes is due—
Their native walks, methinks, they might enjoy
Curb'd of their native malice to destroy.
Of all the tyrannies on human kind
The worst is that which persecutes the mind.   240
Let us but weigh at what offence we strike;
'Tis but because we cannot think alike.
In punishing of this, we overthrow
The laws of nations and of nature too.
Beasts are the subjects of tyrannic sway,
Where still the stronger on the weaker prey.
Man only of a softer mold is made,
Not for his fellows' ruin, but their aid.
Created kind, beneficent, and free,
The noble image of the Deity.   250
    One portion of informing fire was giv'n
To brutes, th' inferior family of Heav'n;
The Smith Divine, as with a careless beat,
Struck out the mute creation at a heat;
But when arriv'd at last to human race,
The Godhead took a deep consid'ring space,
And to distinguish man from all the rest
Unlock'd the sacred treasures of his breast
And mercy mix'd with reason did impart,
One to his head, the other to his heart;   260
Reason to rule, but mercy to forgive;
The first is law, the last prerogative.
And like his mind his outward form appear'd, ⎫
When issuing naked to the wond'ring herd, ⎪
He charm'd their eyes, and for they lov'd, they ⎬
      fear'd; ⎭
Not arm'd with horns of arbitrary might, ⎫
Or claws to seize their furry spoils in fight, ⎬
Or with increase of feet t' o'ertake 'em in their flight; ⎭

---

235 *From Celtic woods.* From France; see To the Reader note 3.
251–62 The *brutes* are created by a casual will (253) and man by reason
(256); see 148n.

Of easy shape and pliant ev'ry way,
Confessing still the softness of his clay,
And kind as kings upon their coronation day; } 270
With open hands and with extended space
Of arms to satisfy a large embrace.
Thus kneaded up with milk, the new made man
His kingdom o'er his kindred world began,
Till knowledge misappli'd, misunderstood,
And pride of empire sour'd his balmy blood.
Then, first rebelling, his own stamp he coins;
The murd'rer Cain was latent in his loins,
And blood began its first and loudest cry 280
For diff'ring worship of the Deity.
Thus persecution rose, and farther space
Produc'd the mighty hunter of his race.
Not so the blessed Pan his flock increas'd,
Content to fold 'em from the famish'd beast;
Mild were his laws; the Sheep and harmless Hind
Were never of the persecuting kind.
Such pity now the pious pastor shows,
Such mercy from the British Lion flows,
That both provide protection for their foes. } 290
    O happy regions, Italy and Spain,
Which never did those monsters entertain!
The Wolf, the Bear, the Boar can there advance
No native claim of just inheritance.
And self-preserving laws, severe in show,
May guard their fences from th' invading foe.
Where birth has plac'd 'em, let 'em safely share
The common benefit of vital air.

---

274 *milk*. Associated in emblems with Nature's flowing breasts and the
suckling breasts of Charity; also the milk of human kindness.
280 Genesis 4:10.
283 *the mighty hunter*. Nimrod, type of the persecutor of one's fellow
creatures, Genesis 10:9; *Paradise Lost* XII, 24 ff.
284 *Pan*. Christ, a humanist equivalent.
286 *the Sheep*. A type of the true Church and of Christ.
288-89 *the pious pastor*. Pope Innocent XI, who assisted Protestants in wars
against the Turks. *British Lion*. James II, as opposed to the French
king; see the headnote for James' Declaration.
263-90 The progress piece of toleration and persecution runs from the
creation of man through 1687.
291-96 The lack of such animals in Italy and Spain provided Dryden with
a lame defense of the Inquisition.

Themselves unharmful, let them live unharm'd,
Their jaws disabl'd and their claws disarm'd;   300
Here only in nocturnal howlings bold,
They dare not seize the Hind nor leap the fold.
More pow'erful and as vigilant as they,
The Lion awfully forbids the prey.
Their rage repress'd though pinch'd with famine
        sore,
They stand aloof and tremble at his roar;
Much is their hunger, but their fear is more.
    These are the chief; to number o'er the rest
And stand like Adam, naming ev'ry beast,
Were weary work; nor will the Muse describe   310
A slimy-born and sun-begotten tribe
Who, far from steeples and their sacred sound,
In fields their sullen conventicles found;
These gross, half-animated lumps I leave,
Nor can I think what thoughts they can conceive.
But if they think at all, 'tis sure no high'r
Than matter put in motion may aspire.
Souls that can scarce ferment their mass of clay,
So drossy, so divisible are they,
As wou'd but serve pure bodies for allay;   320
Such souls as shards produce, such beetle things
As only buzz to heav'n with ev'ning wings,
Strike in the dark, offending but by chance,
Such are the blindfold blows of ignorance.
They know not beings and but hate a name,
To them the Hind and *Panther* are the same.
    The Panther sure the noblest, next the Hind,
And fairest creature of the spotted kind;
Oh, could her inborn stains be wash'd away,
She were too good to be a beast of prey!   330
How can I praise or blame and not offend,
Or how divide the frailty from the friend!

308-26 The wretched and fanatic sects, distinguished by irrationality and
persecution. They met in *conventicles,* even in *fields* (313).
327 *Panther.* The Church of England; a type of beauty (except for a deformed face) and cruelty; also called "pardalis" for the female and
"leopard" from her bastard ancestry from the lion (from Latin, *leo*)
and the pard. Dryden emphasizes these matters and the sexuality zoo-
graphers attributed to the panther.

Her faults and virtues lie so mix'd that she
Nor wholly stands condemn'd nor wholly free.
Then, like her injur'd Lion let me speak;
He cannot bend her and he would not break.
Unkind already and estrang'd in part,
The Wolf begins to share her wand'ring heart.
Though unpolluted yet with actual ill,
She half commits who sins but in her will.   340
If, as our dreaming Platonists report,
There could be spirits of a middle sort,
Too black for Heav'n and yet too white for Hell,
Who just dropp'd half way down, nor lower fell;
So pois'd, so gently she descends from high,
It seems a soft dismission from the sky.

Her house not ancient, whatso'er pretence
Her clergy heralds make in her defence.
A second century not halfway run
Since the new honours of her blood begun.   350
A Lion old, obscene, and furious made
By lust, compress'd her mother in a shade.
Then, by a left-hand marr'age weds the dame,
Cov'ring adult'ry with a specious name;
So schism begot, and sacrilege and she,
A well-match'd pair, got graceless heresy.
God's and kings' rebels have the same good cause
To trample down divine and human laws;
Both would be call'd reformers, and their hate
Alike destructive both to Church and state;   360
The fruit proclaims the plant; a lawless prince ⎤
By luxury reform'd incontinence;   ⎥
By ruins, charity; by riots, abstinence;   ⎦
Confessions, fasts, and penance set aside;   ⎤
O with what ease we follow such a guide,   ⎥
Where souls are starv'd and senses gratify'd! ⎦

342 *spirits of a middle sort. Paradise Lost* III, 462: "Betwixt th' angelical
and human kind."
350 Since Henry VIII's Act of Supremacy (1534).
351 *A Lion.* Henry VIII.
355-56 The complex sexuality recalls Milton's Satan, Sin, and Death,
Paradise Lost II, 727 ff.
361-64 Admitting late medieval corruption, Dryden argues that Henry VIII
made bad worse and good bad.

Where marr'age pleasures midnight pray'r supply,
And matin bells (a melancholy cry)
Are tun'd to merrier notes, "increase" and "multiply."
Religion shows a rosy colour'd face,   370
Not hatter'd out with drudging works of grace;
A down hill Reformation rolls apace.
What flesh and blood wou'd crowd the narrow gate
Or, till they waste their pamper'd paunches, wait?
All wou'd be happy at the cheapest rate.

   Though our lean faith these rigid laws has giv'n,
The full fed Mussulman goes fat to Heav'n,
For his Arabian prophet with delights
Of sense allur'd his eastern proselytes.
The jolly Luther, reading him, began   380
T' interpret Scriptures by his Alcoran,
To grub the thorns beneath our tender feet
And make the paths of Paradise more sweet;
Bethought him of a wife e'er halfway gone
(For 'twas uneasy travailing alone),
And in this masquerade of mirth and love,
Mistook the bliss of heav'n for Bacchanals above.
Sure he presum'd of praise who came to stock
Th' ethereal pastures with so fair a flock,
Burnish'd and batt'ning on their food to show   390
The diligence of careful herds below.
   Our Panther, though like these she chang'd her
      head,
Yet as the mistress of a monarch's bed
Her front erect with majesty she bore,
The crozier wielded and the miter wore.
Her upper part, of decent discipline,
Show'd affectation of an ancient line,
And fathers, councils, Church and Church's head,
Were on her reverend phylacteries read.
But what disgrac'd and disavow'd the rest   400

---

384 When he married in 1525 at age forty-two, Luther (d. 1546) was more
   than *halfway gone,* but the phrase is a *double entendre.*
376-91 Christians thought the Muslim paradise a scandal; Catholics had
   long since compared Luther with Mahomet. On *jolly* see the Glossary.
392 *these.* The nonconformist *herds* of 391.
395 *crozier* and *miter* are emblems of episcopacy.
397 That is, affected to possess.

Was Calvin's brand that stigmatiz'd the beast.
Thus, like a creature of a double kind
In her own labyrinth she lives confin'd.
To foreign lands no sound of her is come,
Humbly content to be despis'd at home.

  Such is her faith; where good cannot be had,
At least she leaves the refuse of the bad.
Nice in her choice of ill, though not of best,
And least deform'd, because reform'd the least.
In doubtful points betwixt her diff'ring friends,   410
Where one for substance, one for sign contends,
Their contradicting terms she strives to join;
Sign shall be substance, substance shall be sign.
A real presence all her sons allow,
And yet 'tis flat idolatry to bow,
Because the godhead's there they know not how.
Her novices are taught that bread and wine
Are but the visible and outward sign
Receiv'd by those who in communion join.
But th' inward grace, or the thing signifi'd,   420
His blood and body, who to save us di'd—
The faithful this thing signify'd receive.
What is't those faithful then partake or leave?
For what is signifi'd and understood
Is, by her own confession, flesh and blood.
Then by the same acknowledgement we know
They take the sign and take the substance too.
The lit'ral sense is hard to flesh and blood,
But nonsense never can be understood.

  Her wild belief on ev'ry wave is toss'd,   430
But sure no church can better morals boast.
True to her king her principles are found;
O that her practice were but half so sound!

---

402 *creature of a double kind.* Leo-pard (see 327*n*); also like another
  cruel double creature, the Minotaur in the labyrinth (403).
417 *novices.* Catechists.
410-29 Differing Protestant conceptions of the Eucharist including Luth-
  eran consubstantiation (a real presence of Christ with, but not in, the
  elements) and Calvinist belief in a purely symbolic rite. Dryden merci-
  lessly exposes Anglican contradictions and wittily argues for transubstantiation, although *hard to flesh and blood.*
430 *Her wild belief,* etc. James 1:6.

Steadfast in various turns of state she stood
And seal'd her vow'd affection with her blood.
Nor will I meanly tax her constancy,
That int'rest or obligement made the tie—
Bound to the fate of murder'd monarchy
(Before the sounding ax so falls the vine
Whose tender branches round the poplar twine.)   440
She chose her ruin and resign'd her life,
In death undaunted as an Indian wife;
A rare example, but some souls we see
Grow hard and stiffen with adversity;
Yet these by fortune's favours are undone;
Resolv'd into a baser form they run,
And bore the wind but cannot bear the sun.
Let this be nature's frailty or her fate,
Or Isgrim's* counsel, her new chosen mate;
Still she's the fairest of the fallen crew,   450
No mother more indulgent but the true.

   Fierce to her foes, yet fears her force to try,
Because she wants innate authority;
For how can she constrain them to obey
Who has herself cast off the lawful sway?
Rebellion equals all, and those who toil
In common theft will share the common spoil.
Let her produce the title and the right
Against her old superiors first to fight;
If she reform by text, ev'n that's as plain   460
For her own rebels to reform again.
As long as words a diff'rent sense will bear
And each may be his own interpreter,
Our airy faith will no foundation find;
The Word's a weathercock for ev'ry wind;
The Bear, the Fox, the Wolf, by turns prevail;
The most in pow'r supplies the present gale.
The wretched Panther cries aloud for aid

* *The Wolf* [The starred notes are Dryden's.]

438-40 Combining two Aesopian fables, "The Husbandman and the Wood"
   and "The Gourd and the Pine."
443 *an Indian wife.* Who burned herself with her husband's corpse.
443-47 Aesop, "The Sun, the Wind, and the Traveler."
451 *the true.* The Hind.

To Church and councils whom she first betray'd;
No help from Fathers or traditions' train—   470
Those ancient guides she taught us to disdain.
And by that Scripture which she once abus'd
To Reformation stands herself accus'd.
What bills for breach of laws can she prefer,
Expounding which she owns herself may err?
And after all her winding ways are tri'd,   ⎫
If doubts arise she slips herself aside   ⎬
And leaves the private conscience for the guide. ⎭
If then that conscience set th' offender free,
It bars her claim to Church authority.   480
How can she censure or what crime pretend,
But Scripture may be constru'd to defend?
Ev'n those whom for rebellion she transmits
To civil pow'r her doctrine first acquits,
Because no disobedience can ensue
Where no submission to a judge is due,
Each judging for himself by her consent,
Whom thus absolv'd she sends to punishment.
Suppose the magistrate revenge her cause,
'Tis only for transgressing human laws.   490
How answ'ring to its end a church is made,
Whose pow'r is but to counsel and persuade!
O solid rock on which secure she stands!
Eternal house not built with mortal hands!
O sure defence against th' infernal gate,
A patent during pleasure of the state!
   Thus is the Panther neither lov'd nor fear'd,
A mere mock queen of a divided herd,
Whom soon by lawful pow'r she might control,
Herself a part submitted to the whole.   500
Then, as the moon, who first receives the light
By which she makes our nether regions bright,
So might she shine, reflecting from afar
The rays she borrow'd from a better star,
Big with the beams which from her mother flow

---

470 The syntax is unclear: perhaps *Fathers' or traditions'*.
493-90 Matthew 16:18, a prime Catholic text for authority.
504 *a better star*. The sun; the Catholic Church.

And reigning o'er the rising tides below.
Now, mixing with a savage crowd, she goes
And meanly flatters her invet'rate foes.
Rul'd while she rules, and losing ev'ry hour
Her wretched remnants of precarious pow'r.   510
    One evening while the cooler shade she sought,
Revolving many a melancholy thought,
Alone she walk'd, and look'd around in vain
With rueful visage for her vanish'd train;
None of her sylvan subjects made their court;
Levées and couchées pass'd without resort.
So hardly can usurpers manage well
Those whom they first instructed to rebel:
More liberty begets desire of more;
The hunger still increases with the store.   520
Without respect they brush'd along the wood,
Each in his clan and fill'd with loathsome food,
Ask'd no permission to the neighb'ring flood.
The Panther full of inward discontent
Since they wou'd go before 'em wisely went,
Supplying want of pow'r by drinking first,
As if she gave 'em leave to quench their thirst.
    Among the rest, the Hind, with fearful face,
Beheld from far the common wat'ring place,
Nor durst approach, till with an awful roar   530
The sovereign Lion bade her fear no more.
Encourag'd thus she brought her younglings nigh,
Watching the motions of her Patron's eye,
And drank a sober draught; the rest amaz'd
Stood mutely still, and on the stranger gaz'd,
Survey'd her part by part and sought to find
The ten-horn'd monster in the harmless Hind,
Such as the Wolf and Panther had design'd.
They thought at first they dream'd, for 'twas
        offence
With them to question certitude of sense,   540

---

506 *the rising tides.* Of the Sects.
528ff. The opening of I is recalled, but the *fearful face* contradicts l. 4.
537 *The ten-horn'd monster.* Of Revelations 13:1. Catholics complained
  of Protestant misrepresentation.

Their guide in faith; but nearer when they drew
And had the faultless object full in view,
Lord, how they all admir'd her heav'nly hue!
Some, who before her fellowship disdain'd,
Scarce, and but scarce, from inborn rage restrain'd,
Now frisk'd about her and old kindred feign'd.
Whether for love or int'rest, ev'ry sect
Of all the savage nation shew'd respect;
The viceroy Panther could not awe the herd;
The more the company the less they fear'd.   550
The surly Wolf with secret envy burst
Yet cou'd not howl: the Hind had seen him first;
But what he durst not speak, the Panther durst.
    For when the herd suffic'd did late repair
To ferny heaths and to their forest lair,
She made a mannerly excuse to stay,
Proff'ring the Hind to wait her half the way;
That since the sky was clear, an hour of talk
Might help her to beguile the tedious walk.
With much good will the motion was embrac'd,   560
To chat awhile on their adventures pass'd;
Nor had the grateful Hind so soon forgot
Her friend and fellow-suff'rer in the Plot.
Yet wond'ring how of late she grew estrang'd,
Her forehead cloudy and her count'nance chang'd,
She thought this hour th' occasion would present
To learn her secret cause of discontent
Which, well she hop'd, might be with ease redress'd,
Consid'ring her a well-bred civil beast
And more a gentlewoman than the rest.   570
After some common talk what rumours ran,
The lady of the spotted muff began.

539-43 Cf. 25-34.
551-52 An old superstition: when man and wolf met, the first to see the
    other struck him dumb.
558 *hour of talk*. II and III.
563 *the Plot*. The Popish Plot; see *Absalom and Achitophel,* headnote.
569-72 It is always the Panther at whom these humorous sallies are directed.

The Second Part

"Dame," said the Panther, "times are mended well
Since late among the Philistines you fell;
The toils were pitch'd, a spacious tract of ground
With expert huntsmen was encompass'd round;
Th' enclosure narrow'd, the sagacious pow'r
Of hounds and death drew nearer ev'ry hour.
'Tis true, the younger Lion 'scap'd the snare,
But all your priestly calves lay struggling there
As sacrifices on their altars laid,
While you their careful mother wisely fled,   10
Not trusting destiny to save your head.
For whate'er promises you have appli'd
To your unfailing Church, the surer side
Is four fair legs in danger to provide.
And whate'er tales of Peter's chair you tell
Yet, saving reverence of the miracle,
The better luck was yours to 'scape so well."
   "As I remember," said the sober Hind,
"Those toils were for your own dear self design'd
As well as me, and with the selfsame throw   20
To catch the quarry and the vermin too
(Forgive the sland'rous tongues that call'd you
         so).
Howe'er you take it now, the common cry
Then ran you down for your rank loyalty;
Besides, in Popery they thought you nurs'd
(As evil tongues will ever speak the worst),
Because some forms and ceremonies some
You kept, and stood in the main question dumb.
Dumb you were born indeed, but thinking long,
The Test it seems at last has loos'd your tongue.   30
And to explain what your forefathers meant

---

[14] Aesop, "The Fox and the Cat."
[1-17] The Popish Plot, fomented by *Philistines* or Whigs, from which
   James, *the younger Lion* (7) escaped, though priests (*calves*, the young
   of deer) were executed (8–9).
[21] *quarry*. See the Glossary for words of the hunt in this passage.
[28] *dumb*. Anglican evasiveness in Eucharistic doctrine; see also 203.
[30] *Test*. The Test Acts required a declaration against transubstantiation.

By real presence in the Sacrament
(After long fencing push'd, against a wall),
Your salvo comes, that He's not there at all;
There chang'd your faith, and what may change
    may fall.
Who can believe what varies every day,
Nor ever was, nor will be at a stay?"
  "Tortures may force the tongue untruths to tell,
And I ne'er own'd myself infallible,"
Repli'd the Panther; "grant such presence were,   40
Yet in your sense I never own'd it there.
A real *virtue* we by faith receive,
And that we in the Sacrament believe."
  "Then," said the Hind, "as you the matter state,
Not only Jesuits can equivocate;
For 'real,' as you now the word expound,
From solid substance dwindles to a sound.
Methinks an Aesop's fable you repeat:
You know who took the shadow for the meat.
Your Church's substance thus you change at will   50
And yet retain your former figure still.
I freely grant you spoke to save your life,
For then you lay beneath the butcher's knife.
Long time you fought, redoubl'd batt'ry bore
But, after all, against yourself you swore,
Your former self, for ev'ry hour your form
Is chopp'd and chang'd like winds before a storm.
Thus fear and int'rest will prevail with some,
For all have not the gift of martyrdom."
  The Panther grinn'd at this, and thus repli'd: 60
"That men may err was never yet deni'd.
But if that common principle be true,
The cannon, Dame, is level'd full at you.
But shunning long disputes, I fain wou'd see
That wondrous wight, Infallibility.
Is he from Heav'n, this mighty champion, come,

48-49 In Aesop's "The Dog and the Shadow," a dog with meat in his
mouth drops it into the water when he tries to get its reflection. Anglicans drop the real presence of Christ (*meat*) for a *shadow* and so lose
both.

Or lodg'd below in subterranean Rome?
First seat him somewhere and derive his race,
Or else conclude that nothing has no place."
    "Suppose (though I disown it)," said the Hind,   70
"The certain mansion were not yet assign'd,
The doubtful residence no proof can bring
Against the plain existence of the thing.
Because philosophers may disagree
If sight b' emission or reception be,
Shall it be thence inferr'd I do not see?
But you require an answer positive,
Which yet when I demand, you dare not give,
For fallacies in universals live.
I then affirm that this unfailing guide   80
In Pope and gen'ral councils must reside;
Both lawful, both combin'd, what one decrees
By numerous votes the other ratifies;
On this undoubted sense the Church relies.
'Tis true, some doctors in a scantier space,
I mean, in each apart, contract the place.
Some, who to greater length extend the line,
The Church's after acceptation join.
This last circumference appears too wide,
The Church diffus'd is by the council ti'd,   90
As members by their representatives
Oblig'd to laws which prince and senate gives.
    "Thus some contract, and some enlarge the space:
In Pope and council who denies the place,
Assisted from above with God's unfailing grace?
Those canons all the needful points contain,
Their sense so obvious and their words so plain
That no disputes about the doubtful text
Have hitherto the lab'ring world perplex'd;
If any shou'd in after times appear,   100

---

67 Recalling *Roma Sotteranea*, a previously inhabited Roman cavern that
had been recently rediscovered.
75 The physiology of sight, whether by reception from the object or by
emission of eyebeams, was debated for centuries.
70–95 In fact, the *locus* of infallibility had not been *assign'd*, whether: (a)
Pope; (b) general council; (c) Pope and general council; (d) Pope,
general council, and Church. Dryden chooses (c) as *via media* analogous
to English polity, with legality and unity.
90 *canons.* Pronouncements by Church councils.

New councils must be call'd to make the meaning
    clear;
Because in them the pow'r supreme resides,
And all the promises are to the guides.
This may be taught with sound and safe defence.
   "But mark how sandy is your own pretence,
Who setting councils, Pope, and Church aside,
Are ev'ry man his own presuming guide.
The sacred books, you say, are full and plain,
And ev'ry needful point of truth contain;
All who can read interpreters may be.   110
Thus though your sev'ral churches disagree,
Yet ev'ry saint has to himself alone
The secret of this philosophic stone.
These principles your jarring Sects unite,
When diff'ring doctors and disciples fight.
Though Luther, Zwinglius, Calvin, holy chiefs,
Have made a battle royal of beliefs,
Or like wild horses sev'ral ways have whirl'd
The tortur'd text about the Christian world,
Each Jehu lashing on with furious force,   120
That Turk or Jew cou'd not have us'd it worse.
No matter what dissension leaders make
Where ev'ry private man may save a stake,
Rul'd by the Scripture and his own advice
Each has a blind bypath to Paradise,
Where driving in a circle slow or fast,
Opposing Sects are sure to meet at last.
A wondrous charity you have in store
For all reform'd to pass the narrow door,
So much that Mahomet had scarcely more.   130
For he, kind prophet, was for damning none,
But Christ and Moses were to save their own;
Himself was to secure his chosen race,
Though reason good for Turks to take the place,
And he allow'd to be the better man
In virtue of his holier *Alcoran*."

[120] *Jehu.* The furious driver of 2 Kings 9:20.
[126] *in a circle.* In circular logic.
[128-30] The Koran accepts Hebrew figures and Christ as true prophets,
   though Mahomet is most illustrious.

"True," said the Panther, "I shall ne'er deny
My breth'ren may be sav'd as well as I,
Though Huguenots contemn our ordination,
Succession, ministerial vocation,   140
And Luther, more mistaking what he read,
Misjoins the sacred Body with the Bread.
Yet, Lady, still remember I maintain,
The Word in needful points is only plain."

    "Needless or needful I not now contend,
For still you have a loophole for a friend"
(Rejoin'd the matron), "but the rule you lay
Has led whole flocks and leads them still astray
In weighty points and full damnation's way.
For did not Arius first, Socinus now,   150
The Son's eternal godhead disavow,
And did not these by Gospel texts alone
Condemn our doctrine and maintain their own?
Have not all heretics the same pretence
To plead the Scriptures in their own defence?
How did the Nicene council then decide
That strong debate—was it by Scripture tri'd?
No, sure to those the rebel would not yield;
Squadrons of texts he marshall'd in the field;
That was but civil war, an equal set,   160
Where piles with piles, and eagles eagles met.
With texts point blank and plain he fac'd the foe,
And did not Satan tempt our Saviour so?
The good old bishops took a simpler way,
Each ask'd but what he heard his father say,
Or how he was instructed in his youth,
And by tradition's force upheld the truth."

    The Panther smil'd at this; "And when," said
        she,
"Were those first councils disallow'd by me?
Or where did I at sure tradition strike,   170
Provided still it were apostolic?"

---

[144] See *Religio Laici* 297–300; Church of England Article VI.
[161] Echoing Lucan, *Pharsalia* I, 7.
[169-70] To episcopacy, Canterbury added the authority of the *first* [four]
    councils and other *sure tradition* as principles closest to Rome.

    "Friend," said the Hind, "you quit your former
      ground,
Where all your faith you did on Scripture found;
Now 'tis tradition join'd with Holy Writ;
But thus your memory betrays your wit."

    "No," said the Panther, "for in that I view
When your tradition's forg'd and when 'tis true.
I set 'em by the rule, and as they square ⎫
Or deviate from undoubted doctrine there ⎬
This oral fiction, that old faith declare." ⎭   180

    (*Hind.*) "The council steer'd it seems a diff'rent
      course—
They tri'd the Scripture by tradition's force;
But you tradition by the Scripture try; ⎫
Pursu'd by Sects, from this to that you fly, ⎬
Nor dare on one foundation to rely. ⎭
The Word is then depos'd, and in this view
You rule the Scripture, not the Scripture you."

    Thus said the Dame and, smiling, thus pursu'd,
"I see tradition then is disallow'd,
When not evinc'd by Scripture to be true,   190
And Scripture as interpreted by you.
But here you tread upon unfaithful ground,
Unless you cou'd infallibly expound,
Which you reject as odious popery
And throw that doctrine back with scorn on me.
Suppose we on things traditive divide
And both appeal to Scripture to decide;
By various texts we both uphold our claim,
Nay, often ground our titles on the same;
After long labour lost and time's expense,   200
Both grant the words and quarrel for the sense.
Thus all disputes forever must depend,
For no dumb rule can controversies end.
Thus when you said tradition must be tri'd
By Sacred Writ, whose sense yourselves decide,
You said no more but that yourselves must be
The judges of the Scripture sense, not we.

189ff. Church authority, the central argument of II, emerges clearly.

Against our Church tradition you declare
And yet your clerks wou'd sit in Moses' chair;
At least 'tis prov'd against your argument,　　　　　210
The rule is far from plain where all dissent."

　　"If not by Scriptures, how can we be sure"
(Repli'd the Panther) "what tradition's pure?
For you may palm upon us new for old;
All, as they say, that glitters is not gold."

　　"How but by following her," repli'd the Dame,
"To whom deriv'd from sire to son they came;
Where ev'ry age does on another move
And trusts no farther than the next above;
Where all the rounds like Jacob's ladder rise,　　　220
The lowest hid in earth, the topmost in the skies."

　　Sternly the savage did her answer mark,
Her glowing eyeballs glitt'ring in the dark,
And said but this, "Since lucre was your trade,
Succeeding times such dreadful gaps have made
'Tis dangerous climbing: to your sons and you
I leave the ladder and its omen too."

　　(Hind.) "The Panther's breath was ever fam'd for
　　　　　sweet,
But from the Wolf such wishes oft I meet;
You learn'd this language from the blatant beast,　　230
Or rather did not speak but were possess'd.
As for your answer, 'tis but barely urg'd;
You must evince tradition to be forg'd;
Produce plain proofs, unblemish'd authors use
As ancient as those ages they accuse;
Till when 'tis not sufficient to defame:
An old possession stands till elder quits the claim.
Then for our int'rest, which is nam'd alone
To load with envy, we retort your own.
For when traditions in your faces fly,　　　　　240

209 Matthew 23:2-3, implying heresy.
215 Proverbial.
220-27 Jacob's ladder (Genesis 28:12-15) is given as an *omen* of the gallows
　　to the Hind by the Panther, who forgets it is a type of Christ's descent.
228 *sweet*. The aroma by which panthers lured animals to their destruc-
　　tion.
230 *the blatant beast*. The wolf; slander in Spenser, *The Faerie Queene*
　　V, xii and VI.
233 *barely urg'd*. Argued without proof.

Resolving not to yield, you must decry:
As when the cause goes hard, the guilty man
Excepts and thins his jury all he can;
So when you stand of other aid bereft,
You to the twelve Apostles would be left.
   "Your friend the Wolf did with more craft
      provide
To set those toys, traditions, quite aside,
And Fathers too, unless when reason spent
He cites 'em but sometimes for ornament.
But, Madam Panther, you, though more sincere,   250
Are not so wise as your adulterer;
The private spirit is a better blind
Than all the dodging tricks your authors find.
For they who left the Scripture to the crowd ⎫
Each for his own peculiar judge allow'd;   ⎬
The way to please 'em was to make 'em proud. ⎭
Thus, with full sails they ran upon the shelf;
Who cou'd suspect a cousenage from himself?
On his own reason safer 'tis to stand
Than be deceiv'd and damn'd at second hand.   260
But you who Fathers and traditions take,
And garble some, and some you quite forsake,
Pretending Church authority to fix,
And yet some grains of private spirit mix,
Are like a mule made up of diff'ring seed,
And that's the reason why you never breed,
At least not propagate your kind abroad,
For home Dissenters are by statutes aw'd.
And yet they grow upon you ev'ry day,   ⎫
While you (to speak the best) are at a stay,   ⎬ 270
For sects that are extremes abhor a middle way. ⎭
Like tricks of state to stop a raging flood ⎫
Or mollify a mad-brain'd Senate's mood: ⎬
Of all expedients never one was good.   ⎭
Well may they argue (nor can you deny),

---

[237] See *Religio Laici* 425–26.
[265-67] See also I, 402–5.
[268] *statutes*. Penal laws such as: Act of Uniformity (1662), Conventicle Act (1664), Five Mile Act (1665).

If we must fix on Church authority,
Best on the best, the fountain, not the flood,
That must be better still, if this be good.
Shall she command who has herself rebell'd?
Is Antichrist by Antichrist expell'd?   280
Did we a lawful tyranny displace
To set aloft a bastard of the race?
Why all these wars to win the Book, if we ⎫
Must not interpret for ourselves, but she? ⎬
Either be wholly slaves or wholly free. ⎭
For purging fires traditions must not fight,
But they must prove episcopacy's right:
Thus those led horses are from service freed;
You never mount 'em but in time of need.
Like mercenaries hir'd for home defence,   290
They will not serve against their native prince;
Against domestic foes of hierarchy
These are drawn forth to make fanatics fly,
But when they see their countrymen at hand, ⎫
Marching against 'em under Church command, ⎬
Straight they forsake their colours and disband." ⎭

   Thus she, nor cou'd the Panther well enlarge
With weak defence against so strong a charge;
But said, "For what did Christ his Word provide,
If still his Church must want a living guide?   300
And if all saving doctrines are not there,
Or sacred pen-men cou'd not make 'em clear,
From after ages we should hope in vain
For truths which men inspir'd cou'd not explain."

   "Before the Word was written," said the Hind,
"Our Saviour preach'd His faith to human kind;
From His Apostles the first age receiv'd
Eternal truth, and what they taught, believ'd.
Thus by tradition faith was planted first,
Succeeding flocks succeeding pastors nurs'd.   310
This was the way our wise Redeemer chose ⎫
(Who sure could all things for the best dispose) ⎬
To fence His fold from their encroaching foes. ⎭

He cou'd have writ Himself, but well foresaw
Th' event would be like that of Moses' law;
Some difference wou'd arise, some doubts remain,
Like those which yet the jarring Jews maintain.
No written laws can be so plain, so pure,
But wit may gloss and malice may obscure—
Not those indicted by His first command:
A prophet grav'd the text, an angel held his hand.   320
Thus faith was e'er the written Word appear'd,
And men believ'd not what they read but heard.
   "But since th' Apostles cou'd not be confin'd
To these, or those, but severally design'd
Their large commission 'round the world to blow,
To spread their faith they spread their labours too.
Yet still their absent flock their pains did share;
They hearken'd still, for love produces care.
And as mistakes arose, or discords fell,   330
Or bold seducers taught 'em to rebel,
As charity grew cold or faction hot,
Or long neglect their lessons had forgot,
For all their wants they wisely did provide,
And preaching by epistles was suppli'd:
So great physicians cannot all attend,
But some they visit, and to some they send.
Yet all those letters were not writ to all,
Nor first intended, but occasional,
Their absent sermons; nor if they contain   340
All needful doctrines, are those doctrines plain.
Clearness by frequent preaching must be wrought;
They writ but seldom, but they daily taught.
And what one saint has said of holy Paul,
'He darkly writ,' is true appli'd to all.
For this obscurity could Heav'n provide   ⎫
More prudently than by a living guide,   ⎬
As doubts arose, the difference to decide?   ⎭
A guide was therefore needful, therefore made,
And if appointed, sure to be obey'd.   350

320-21 Exodus 32:16 and 34:28.
344-45 See 2 Peter 3:16.

"Thus, with due rev'rence to th' Apostles' Writ,
By which my sons are taught, to which submit,
I think those truths their sacred works contain
The Church alone can certainly explain,
That following ages, leaning on the past,
May rest upon the primitive at last.
Nor wou'd I thence the Word no rule infer,
But none without the Church interpreter.
Because, as I have urg'd before, 'tis mute
And is itself the subject of dispute.   360
But what th' Apostles their successors taught, ⎫
They to the next, from them to us is brought, ⎬
Th' undoubted sense which is in Scripture sought. ⎭
From hence the Church is arm'd, when errors   ⎫
    rise,   ⎪
To stop their entrance and prevent surprise;   ⎬
And safe entrench'd within, her foes without   ⎪
    defies.   ⎭
By these, all fest'ring sores her councils heal, ⎫
Which time or has disclos'd, or shall reveal,   ⎬
For discord cannot end without a last appeal.   ⎭
Nor can a council national decide   ⎫   370
But with subordination to her guide   ⎬
(I wish the cause were on that issue tri'd).   ⎭
Much less the Scripture, for suppose debate
Betwixt pretenders to a fair estate
Bequeath'd by some legator's last intent
(Such is our dying Saviour's Testament):
The will is prov'd, is open'd, and is read;
The doubtful heirs their diff'ring titles plead;
All vouch the words their int'rest to maintain,
And each pretends by those his cause is plain.   380
Shall then the testament award the right?
No, that's the Hungary for which they fight,
The field of battle, subject of debate,
The thing contended for, the fair estate.
The sense is intricate; 'tis only clear

370-1 The Anglican episcopate would have had to submit to Rome.
382 *Hungary*. Then being disputed for by Turkish and German forces.

What vowels and what consonants are there.
Therefore 'tis plain: its meaning must be tri'd
Before some judge appointed to decide."

"Suppose" (the fair Apostate said) "I grant
The faithful flock some living guide should want;   390
Your arguments an endless chase pursue;
Produce this vaunted leader to our view,
This mighty Moses of the chosen crew."

The Dame, who saw her fainting foe retir'd,
With force renew'd to victory aspir'd;
And looking upward to her kindred sky,
As once our Saviour own'd his Deity,
Pronounc'd his words—"She whom ye seek
    am I."

Nor less amaz'd this voice the Panther heard
Than were those Jews to hear a god declar'd.   400

Then thus the matron modestly renew'd:
"Let all your prophets and their Sects be view'd
And see to which of 'em yourselves think fit
The conduct of your conscience to submit;
Each proselyte wou'd vote his doctor best
With absolute exclusion to the rest;
Thus wou'd your Polish Diet disagree,
And end as it began, in anarchy.
Yourself the fairest for election stand,
Because you seem crown-gen'ral of the land,   410
But soon against your superstitious lawn
Some Presbyterian sabre wou'd be drawn;
In your establish'd laws of sov'reignty
The rest some fundamental flaw wou'd see
And call rebellion gospel liberty.

305-88 Dryden argues the priority and superiority of the oral catechesis to
    the written, a traditional English Catholic view, without quite explicitly
    ruling out the role of the written word, which orthodox Catholicism
    allowed with the oral.
394-98 Beginning the poem's climax, which continues in offers of reconcilia-
    tion by the Hind, and part of the Panther's *hour of grace* (III, 893).
407-10 Polish allusions: unanimity being required in the Diet, a single
    vetoer would be destroyed; *crown-gen'ral* was the title of Sobieski as he
    pursued his ambitions to be elected king, which he was (John III) as
    Dryden wrote.
411 *lawn.* Bishop's fine linen vestments, *superstitious* to the Sects.

To Church decrees your articles require
Submission modifi'd, if not entire;
Homage deny'd, to censures you proceed,
But when Curtana will not do the deed,
You lay that pointless clergy-weapon by,   420
And to the laws, your sword of justice, fly.
    "Now this your Sects the more unkindly take
(Those prying varlets hit the blots you make),
Because some ancient friends of yours declare
Your only rule of faith the Scriptures are,
Interpreted by men of judgment sound,
Which ev'ry sect will for themselves expound,
Nor think less rev'rence to their doctors due
For sound interpretation than to you.
    "If then, by able heads are understood   430
Your brother prophets who reform'd abroad,
Those able heads expound a wiser way
That their own sheep their shepherd shou'd obey.
But if you mean yourselves are only sound,   ⎫
That doctrine turns the Reformation 'round,   ⎬
And all the rest are false reformers found,   ⎭
Because in sundry points you stand alone,   ⎫
Not in communion join'd with any one,   ⎬
And therefore must be all the Church or none.   ⎭
Then, till you have agreed whose judge is best,   440
Against this forc'd submission they protest;
While sound and sound a diff'rent sense explains,
Both play at hard-head till they break their brains,
And from their chairs each other's force defy
While unregarded thunders vainly fly.
    "I pass the rest, because your Church alone
Of all usurpers best cou'd fill the throne.
But neither you, nor any Sect beside   ⎫
For this high office can be qualifi'd   ⎬
With necessary gifts requir'd in such a guide. ⎭   450
For that which must direct the whole must be   ⎫
Bound in one bond of faith and unity;   ⎬
But all your sev'ral Churches disagree.   ⎭

---

[419] *Curtana*. The blunt sword of mercy, part of English regalia since Edward the Confessor.
[445] *thunders*. Ecclesiastical deprecations, excommunications, etc.

The consubstantiating Church and priest
Refuse communion to the Calvinist;
The French reform'd from preaching you restrain,
Because you judge their ordination vain;
And so they judge of yours, but donors must
    ordain.
  "In short, in doctrine or in discipline
Not one reform'd can with another join,   460
But all from each as from damnation fly;
No union they pretend but in non-popery.
Nor, shou'd their members in a synod meet,
Cou'd any church presume to mount the seat
Above the rest, their discords to decide;
None wou'd obey, but each wou'd be the guide;
And face to face dissensions wou'd encrease,
For only distance now preserves the peace.
All in their turns accusers and accus'd;
Babel was never half so much confus'd.   470
What one can plead, the rest can plead as well,
For amongst equals lies no last appeal,
And all confess themselves are fallible.
  "Now, since you grant some necessary guide,
All who can err are justly laid aside;
Because a trust so sacred to confer
Shows want of such a sure interpreter,
And how can he be needful who can err?
Then, granting that unerring guide we want,
That such there is you stand oblig'd to grant;   480
Our Saviour else were wanting to supply
Our needs and obviate that necessity.
It then remains that Church can only be
The guide which owns unfailing certainty,
Or else you slip your hold and change your side,
Relapsing from a necessary guide.
But this annex'd condition of the crown,
Immunity from errors, you disown;
Here then you shrink and lay your weak
    pretensions down.

---

454 Lutherans.
487-88 Absolute Royalism held that kings cannot err *de jure*.

For petty royalties you raise debate,   490
But this unfailing universal state
You shun, nor dare succeed to such a glorious
    weight.
And for that cause those promises detest
With which our Saviour did his Church invest,
But strive t' evade and fear to find 'em true,
As conscious they were never meant to you;
All which the mother Church asserts her own,
And with unrivall'd claim ascends the throne.
  "So when of old th' Almighty Father sat
In council to redeem our ruin'd state,   500
Millions of millions at a distance round
Silent the sacred consistory crown'd
To hear what mercy mix'd with justice cou'd
    propound,
All prompt with eager pity to fulfill
The full extent of their Creator's will;
But when the stern conditions were declar'd,
A mournful whisper through the host was heard,
And the whole hierarchy with heads hung down
Submissively declin'd the pondrous proffer'd crown.
Then, not till then, th' eternal Son from high   510
Rose in the strength of all the Deity,
Stood forth t' accept the terms and underwent
A weight which all the frame of Heav'n had bent,
Nor He Himself cou'd bear but as omnipotent.
Now, to remove the least remaining doubt
That ev'n the blear-ey'd Sects may find her out,
Behold what heav'nly rays adorn her brows,
What from His wardrobe her belov'd allows
To deck the wedding-day of His unspotted
    spouse.
Behold what marks of majesty she brings,   520
Richer than ancient heirs of eastern kings;
Her right hand holds the sceptre and the keys
To show whom she commands and who obeys:
With these to bind or set the sinner free,

---

519 *unspotted.* Unlike the Panther; immaculate.

With that t' assert spiritual royalty.

"One in herself not rent by schism, but sound,   *Marks of*
Entire, one solid shining diamond,   *the Catho-*
Not sparkles shatter'd into Sects like you;   *lic Church*
One is the Church and must be to be true: *Nicene*
One central principle of unity.   *Creed.*
As undivided, so from errors free,   530
As one in faith, so one in sanctity.

Thus she, and none but she, th' insulting rage
Of heretics oppos'd from age to age:
Still when the giant-brood invades her throne,
She stoops from Heav'n and meets 'em half way
    down
And with paternal thunder vindicates her crown.
But like Egyptian sorcerers you stand
And vainly lift aloft your magic wand
To sweep away the swarms of vermin from the
    land;   540
You cou'd like them, with like infernal force
Produce the plague but not arrest the course.
But when the boils and botches with disgrace
And public scandal sat upon the face,
Themselves attack'd, the Magi strove no more,
They saw God's finger and their fate deplore;
Themselves they cou'd not cure of the dishonest
    sore.

"Thus one, thus pure, behold her largely spread
Like the fair ocean from her mother bed;
From east to west triumphantly she rides;   550
All shores are water'd by her wealthy tides.

"The Gospel sound diffus'd from pole to pole
Where winds can carry and where waves can roll,
The selfsame doctrine of the sacred page
Convey'd to ev'ry clime in ev'ry age.

"Here let my sorrow give my satire place
To raise new blushes on my British race;

490-525 Cf. *Paradise Lost* III, 203–65 and *ibid.*, II, 417 ff. For 517–19, cf.
    also *The Faerie Queene* I, xii, 22–23 and Revelations 21:2.
535-37 In the gigantomachy, Athene (Rome) struck down the giants (here-
    tics) with the thunder of Zeus (God).
538-42 Exodus 8:7.
543-47 Exodus 9:11.

Our sailing ships like common shores we use,
And through our distant colonies diffuse
The draughts of dungeons and the stench of
    stews,   560
Whom, when their homebred honesty is lost,
We disembogue on some far Indian coast:
Thieves, pandars, palliards, sins of ev'ry sort—
Those are the manufactures we export,
And these the missionaires our zeal has made.
For, with my country's pardon be it said,
Religion is the least of all our trade.

   "Yet some improve their traffic more than we,
For they on gain, their only god, rely,
And set a public price on piety.   570
Industrious of the needle and the chart
They run full sail to their Japonian mart:
Prevention fear, and prodigal of fame
Sell all of Christian to the very name,
Nor leave enough of that to hide their naked
    shame.

   "Thus, of three marks which in the Creed we
    view,
Not one of all can be appli'd to you:
Much less the fourth; in vain alas you seek
Th' ambitious title of apostolic;
Godlike descent! 'tis well your blood can be   580
Prov'd noble in the third or fourth degree;
For all of ancient that you had before
(I mean what is not borrow'd from our store)
Was error fulminated o'er and o'er.
Old heresies condemn'd in ages past,
By care and time recover'd from the blast.

   "'Tis said with ease, but never can be prov'd,
The Church her old foundations has remov'd

568-75 The Dutch were then the only Europeans allowed to trade with
Japan, at the cost (so other countries alleged) of denying their Christianity.
526-86 The marks or notes of the Church, or necessary distinguishing
properties of the true Church (as distinct from heretical groups), are
here based on the Catholic version of the Nicene Creed: "Credo . . . Et
unam sanctam catholicam et apostolicam Ecclesiam." The Anglican
version omits sanctity.

And built new doctrines on unstable sands:
Judge that, ye winds and rains; you prov'd her, yet
    she stands.   590
Those ancient doctrines charg'd on her for new—
Show when, and how, and from what hands they
    grew.
We claim no pow'r when heresies grow bold
To coin new faith but still declare the old.
How else cou'd that obscene disease be purg'd
When controverted texts are vainly urg'd?
To prove tradition new, there's somewhat more
Requir'd than saying, 'twas not us'd before.
Those monumental arms are never stirr'd
Till schism or heresy call down Goliath's sword.   600
   "Thus, what you call corruptions are in truth
The first plantations of the Gospel's youth,
Old standard faith; but cast your eyes again
And view those errors which new Sects maintain
Or which of old disturb'd the Church's peaceful
    reign,
And we can point each period of the time
When they began, and who begot the crime,
Can calculate how long th' eclipse endur'd,
Who interpos'd, what digits were obscur'd;
Of all which are already pass'd away,   610
We know the rise, the progress, and decay.
   "Despair at our foundations then to strike
Till you can prove your faith Apostolic,
A limpid stream drawn from the native source,
Succession lawful in a lineal course.
Prove any church oppos'd to this our head
So one, so pure, so unconfin'dly spread,
Under one chief of the spiritual state,
The members all combin'd and all subordinate.
Show such a seamless coat, from schism so free,   620
In no communion join'd with heresy;

590 Matthew 7:25.
599–600 See 1 Samuel 21:9.
614 *native source.* See 277n.
620 *seamless coat.* Unity; John 19:23.

If such a one you find, let truth prevail,
Till when your weights will in the balance fail:
A church unprincipl'd kicks up the scale.

   "But if you cannot think (nor sure you can
Suppose in God what were unjust in man),
That He, the fountain of eternal grace,
Should suffer falsehood for so long a space
To banish truth and to usurp her place;
That sev'n successive ages should be lost   630
And preach damnation at their proper cost;
That all your erring ancestors should die,
Drown'd in th' abyss of deep idolatry;
If piety forbid such thoughts to rise,
Awake and open your unwilling eyes;
God has left nothing for each age undone
From this to that wherein He sent His Son:
Then think but well of Him, and half your work
   is done.

   "See how His Church adorn'd with ev'ry grace
With open arms, a kind forgiving face,   640
Stands ready to prevent her long-lost sons'
   embrace.
Not more did Joseph o'er his brethren weep,
Nor less himself cou'd from discovery keep,
When in the crowd of suppliants they were seen,
And in their crew his best beloved Benjamin.
That pious Joseph in the Church behold,
To feed your famine and refuse your gold:
The Joseph you exil'd, the Joseph whom you
   sold."

   Thus, while with heav'nly charity she spoke,
A streaming blaze the silent shadows broke,   650
Shot from the skies a cheerful azure light;
The birds obscene to forests wing'd their flight,
And gaping graves receiv'd the wand'ring guilty
   sprite.

*The re-
nunciation
of the Bene-
dictines to
the abbey
lands.*

---

[630] *sev'n successive ages.* Changed from *nine* in the first edition, shortening
the centuries of British faith from the adoption of Christianity to the
Lollards, rather than to Edward II.
[639-41] See Luke 15:11–32, and on the prodigal son, see III, 288–97.
[642-48] Details of the Joseph story are treated allegorically: Reformation

Such were the pleasing triumphs of the sky
For James his late nocturnal victory,
The pledge of his Almighty patron's love,
The fireworks which his angel made above.
I saw myself the lambent easy light

*Poëta
loquitur.*

Gild the brown horror and dispel the night;
The messenger with speed the tidings bore,   660
News which three lab'ring nations did restore,
But heav'n's own *nuncius* was arriv'd before.

By this, the Hind had reach'd her lonely cell,
And vapours rose, and dews unwholesome fell.
When she, by frequent observation wise,
As one who long on Heav'n had fix'd her eyes,
Discern'd a change of weather in the skies.
The western borders were with crimson spread;
The moon descending look'd all flaming red;
She thought good manners bound her to invite   670
The stranger dame to be her guest that night.
'Tis true, coarse diet and a short repast,
(She said) were weak inducements to the taste
Of one so nicely bred and so unus'd to fast.
But what plain fare her cottage cou'd afford,
A hearty welcome at a homely board
Was freely hers; and, to supply the rest,
An honest meaning and an open breast.
Last, with content of mind, the poor man's wealth,
A grace-cup to their common Patron's health.   680
This she desir'd her to accept and stay,
For fear she might be wilder'd in her way,
Because she wanted an unerring guide;
And then the dew-drops on her silken hide

(bondage), Catholic charity (weeping), Catholic affection for England
(Benjamin), monastic charities (feeding brothers), and renunciation of
abbey lands (Dryden's note).
654-62 Dryden testifies to a celestial display on the night of victory over
Monmouth's rebel forces, July 6, 1685, at Sedgemoor. Because this testimony comes in a personal passage and is not confirmed by any known
evidence, it must be symbolic—of divine sanction of James and of some
matter special to Dryden.
668-69 Sedgemoor lies in the west of England.
679 *content of mind*, etc. Lucretius, *De Rerum Natura* V, 1118.

Her tender constitution did declare,
Too ladylike a long fatigue to bear
And rough inclemencies of raw nocturnal air.

But most she fear'd that travelling so late,
Some evil-minded beasts might lie in wait
And without witness wreak their hidden hate.   690

    The Panther, though she lent a list'ning ear,
Had more of Lion in her than to fear;
Yet wisely weighing, since she had to deal
With many foes, their numbers might prevail,
Return'd her all the thanks she cou'd afford,
And took her friendly hostess at her word.

Who ent'ring first her lowly roof (a shed
With hoary moss and winding ivy spread,
Honest enough to hide an humble hermit's
    head),

Thus graciously bespoke her welcome guest: 700
"So might these walls with your fair presence blest
Become your dwelling-place of everlasting rest,
Not for a night or quick revolving year,
Welcome an owner, not a sojourner.
This peaceful seat, my poverty secures;
War seldom enters but where wealth allures;
Nor yet despise it, for this poor abode
Has oft receiv'd and yet receives a god;
A god victorious of the Stygian race
Here laid his sacred limbs and sanctified the place.   710
This mean retreat did mighty Pan contain;
Be emulous of him and pomp disdain,
And dare not to debase your soul to gain."

    The silent stranger stood amaz'd to see
Contempt of wealth and wilful poverty;
And though ill habits are not soon controll'd,
Awhile suspended her desire of gold;
But civily drew in her sharpen'd paws,
Not violating hospitable laws,
And pacif'd her tail and lick'd her frothy jaws.   720

672-90 The Hind turns satirist.
701-4 Another offer of reconciliation.
707-10 In *Aeneid* VIII, 362-65, the *god victorious* is Hercules who, like
   Pan (711 and I, 284), is a humanist type of Christ.

The Hind did first her country cates provide,
Then couch'd herself securely by her side.

The Third Part

Much malice mingl'd with a little wit
Perhaps may censure this mysterious writ,
Because the Muse has peopl'd Caledon
With panthers, bears, and wolves, and beasts
    unknown,
As if we were not stock'd with monsters of our
    own.
Let Aesop answer, who has set to view
Such kinds as Greece and Phrygia never knew;
And Mother Hubbard in her homely dress
Has sharply blam'd a British Lioness,
That Queen, whose feast the factious rabble keep,   10
Expos'd obscenely naked and asleep.
Led by those great examples, may not I
The wanted organs of their words supply?
If men transact like brutes, 'tis equal then
For brutes to claim the privilege of men.
  Others our Hind of folly will indict,
To entertain a dang'rous guest by night.
Let those remember that she cannot die
Till rolling time is lost in round eternity;
Nor need she fear the Panther, though untam'd,   20
Because the Lion's peace was now proclaim'd;
The wary savage would not give offence
To forfeit the protection of her Prince,
But watch'd the time her vengeance to complete,
When all her furry sons in frequent senate met.
Meanwhile she quench'd her fury at the flood

---

[3] *Caledon.* Britain; see I, 14*n*.
[6] *Aesop.* See headnote.
[8] *Mother Hubbard.* Spenser, *Mother Hubbard's Tale.*
[10] *Queen.* Elizabeth I. "Queen Bess' Day" was noisily celebrated by anti-Catholic crowds.
[21] *the Lion's peace.* James' Declaration; see headnote.
[25] *furry sons.* (a) Of the Panther; (b) clergy with the fur hoods of university graduates.

And with a Lenten salad cool'd her blood.
Their commons, though but coarse, were nothing
    scant,
Nor did their minds an equal banquet want.
    For now the Hind, whose noble nature strove   30
T' express her plain simplicity of love,
Did all the honours of her house so well
No sharp debates disturb'd the friendly meal.
She turn'd the talk, avoiding that extreme,
To common dangers past, a sadly pleasing theme,
Rememb'ring ev'ry storm which toss'd the state,
When both were objects of the public hate,
And dropp'd a tear betwixt for her own
    children's fate.
    Nor fail'd she then a full review to make
Of what the Panther suffer'd for her sake: 40
Her lost esteem, her truth, her loyal care,
Her faith unshaken to an exil'd heir,
Her strength t' endure, her courage to defy,
Her choice of honourable infamy.
On these, prolixly thankful, she enlarg'd,
Then with acknowledgments herself she charg'd;
For friendship, of itself an holy tie,
Is made more sacred by adversity.
Now should they part, malicious tongues wou'd say,
They met like chance companions on the way,   50
Whom mutual fear of robbers had possess'd;
While danger lasted, kindness was profess'd,
But that once o'er, the short-liv'd union ends,
The road divides, and there divide the friends.
    The Panther nodded when her speech was done
And thank'd her coldly in a hollow tone,
But said her gratitude had gone too far
For common offices of Christian care.
If to the lawful heir she had been true,
She paid but Caesar what was Caesar's due.   60
"I might," she added, "with like praise describe
Your suff'ring sons and so return your bribe,

30-54 A review of events from the Popish Plot to 1686.

But incense from my hands is poorly priz'd,
For gifts are scorn'd where givers are despis'd.
I serv'd a turn and then was cast away;
You, like the gaudy fly, your wings display,
And sip the sweets, and bask in your great
    Patron's day."
    This heard, the Matron was not slow to find
What sort of malady had seiz'd her mind;
Disdain, with gnawing envy, fell despite,   70
And canker'd malice stood in open sight.
Ambition, int'rest, pride without control,
And jealousy, the jaundice of the soul,
Revenge, the bloody minister of ill,
With all the lean tormenters of the will.
'Twas easy now to guess from whence arose
Her new made union with her ancient foes,
Her forc'd civilities, her faint embrace,
Affected kindness with an alter'd face;
Yet durst she not too deeply probe the wound,   80
As hoping still the nobler parts were sound,
But strove with anodynes t' assuage the smart
And mildly thus her med'cine did impart.
    "Complaints of lovers help to ease their pain;
It shows a rest of kindness to complain,
A friendship loth to quit its former hold
And conscious merit may be justly bold.
But much more just your jealousy would show,
If others' good were injury to you;
Witness, ye heav'ns, how I rejoyce to see   90
Rewarded worth and rising loyalty.
Your warrior offspring that upheld the crown,
The scarlet honours of your peaceful gown,
Are the most pleasing objects I can find,
Charms to my sight and cordials to my mind:
When virtue spoomes before a prosp'rous gale
My heaving wishes help to fill the sail,
And if my pray'rs for all the brave were heard,

66-67 Aesop, "The Fly and the Ant."
93 *scarlet honours*. Academic and ecclesiastical distinctions, from doctors'
    robes, etc.

Caesar should still have such and such should still
    reward.
  "The labour'd earth your pains have sow'd and
    till'd;   100
'Tis just you reap the product of the field.
Yours be the harvest; 'tis the beggars' gain
To glean the fallings of the loaded wain.
Such scatter'd ears as are not worth your care
Your charity for alms may safely spare,
And alms are but the vehicles of pray'r.
My daily bread is lit'rally implor'd;
I have no barns nor granaries to hoard;
If Caesar to his own his hand extends,
Say which of yours his charity offends: 110
You know he largely gives to more than are his
    friends.
Are you defrauded when he feeds the poor?
Our mite decreases nothing of your store;
I am but few, and by your fare you see
My crying sins are not of luxury.
Some juster motive sure your mind withdraws,
And makes you break our friendship's holy laws,
For barefac'd envy is too base a cause.
  "Show more occasion for your discontent;
Your love, the Wolf, wou'd help you to invent   120
Some German quarrel, or as times go now,
Some French, where force is uppermost, will do.
When at the fountain's head, as merit ought
To claim the place, you take a swilling draught,
How easy 'tis an envious eye to throw
And tax the sheep for troubling streams below,
Or call her (when no farther cause you find)
An enemy profess'd of all your kind.
But then, perhaps, the wicked world wou'd think
The Wolf design'd to eat as well as drink."   130

100-8 The biblical Ruth; English Catholics glean like her; in biblical
    glosses she is a type of the true Church.
109-11 James' solicitations for Huguenots fleeing to England from French
    Catholic persecution; see To the Reader note 3.
121-22 *German quarrel*. A *querrelle d'Aleman* was a quarrel on slight or
    pretended provocation, as those of Louis XIV.
123-30 Aesop, "The Wolf and the Lamb."

    This last allusion gall'd the Panther more,
Because indeed it rubb'd upon the sore.
Yet seem'd she not to winch, though shrewdly
      pain'd,
But thus her passive character maintain'd.
    "I never grudg'd, whate'er my foes report,
Your flaunting fortune in the Lion's court.
You have your day, or you are much beli'd,
But I am always on the suff'ring side;
You know my doctrine, and I need not say
I will not, but I cannot disobey.
On this firm principle I ever stood: 140
He of my sons who fails to make it good
By one rebellious act renounces to my blood."
    "Ah," said the Hind, "how many sons have you
Who call you mother whom you never knew!
But most of them who that relation plead
Are such ungracious youths as wish you dead.
They gape at rich revenues which you hold
And fain would nibble at your grandame gold,
Enquire into your years, and laugh to find   150
Your crazy temper shows you much declin'd.
Were you not dim, and doted, you might see
A pack of cheats that claim a pedigree,
No more of kin to you than you to me.
Do you not know that for a little coin
Heralds can foist a name into the line;
They ask you blessing but for what you have,
But once possess'd of what with care you save,
The wanton boys wou'd piss upon your grave.
    "Your sons of latitude that court your grace,   160
Though most resembling you in form and face,
Are far the worst of your pretended race.
And, but I blush your honesty to blot,
Pray God you prove 'em lawfully begot;
For in some Popish libels I have read
The Wolf has been too busy in your bed.

---

[160] *sons of latitude.* The Latitudinarians (*broad-way sons* in 229), or Moderate Divines, favoring Protestant rather than Catholic elements in Anglicanism and accommodation with Dissenters.
[164-66] In his *Defense of the Duchess of York's Paper* (see headnote), Dry-

At least their hinder parts, the belly piece,
The paunch, and all that Scorpio claims are his.
Their malice, too, a sore suspicion brings,
For though they dare not bark, they snarl at kings;   170
Nor blame 'em for intruding in your line;
Fat bishoprics are still of right divine.
    "Think you your new French proselytes are come
To starve abroad, because they starv'd at home?
Your benefices twinkl'd from afar;
They found the new Messiah by the star;
Those Swisses fight on any side for pay,
And 'tis the living that conforms, not they.
Mark with what management their tribes divide, ⎫
Some stick to you and some to t' other side,   ⎬   180
That many churches may for many mouths   ⎭
    provide.
More vacant pulpits wou'd more converts make;
All wou'd have latitude enough to take;
The rest unbenefic'd, your Sects maintain,   ⎫
For ordinations without cures are vain,   ⎬
And chamber practice is a silent gain.   ⎭
Your sons of breadth at home are much like these,
Their soft and yielding metals run with ease,
They melt and take the figure of the mould,
But harden and preserve it best in gold."   190
    "Your Delphic sword," the Panther then repli'd,
"Is double-edg'd and cuts on either side.
Some sons of mine who bear upon their shield
Three steeples argent in a sable field
Have sharply tax'd your converts who, unfed,
Have follow'd you for miracles of bread;
Such who themselves of no religion are,
Allur'd with gain, for any will declare.
Bare lies with bold assertions they can face,
But dint of argument is out of place.   200

---

den compared Latitudinarians and Presbyterians. The controversy over
the Royal Papers is discussed through 217.
[194] Dryden makes up arms borne by no Anglican bishop, but probably to
designate three bishops active in controversy in 1686 and 1687.

The grim logician puts 'em in a fright;
'Tis easier far to flourish than to fight.
  "Thus our eighth Henry's marriage they
      defame;
They say the schism of beds began the game,
Divorcing from the Church to wed the Dame,
Though largely prov'd and by himself profess'd,
That conscience, conscience wou'd not let him rest,
I mean, not till possess'd of her he lov'd
And old, uncharming Catherine was remov'd.
For sundry years before did he complain,   210
And told his ghostly confessor his pain.
With the same impudence, without a ground,
They say that, look the Reformation round,
No treatise of humility is found.
But if none were, the Gospel does not want;
Our Saviour preach'd it, and I hope you grant
The Sermon in the Mount was Protestant."
  "No doubt," repli'd the Hind, "as sure as all
The writings of Saint Peter and Saint Paul.
On that decision let it stand or fall.   220
Now for my converts, who you say unfed
Have follow'd me for miracles of bread,
Judge not by hearsay, but observe at least
If since their change their loaves have been
      increas'd.
The Lion buys no converts; if he did,
Beasts wou'd be sold as fast as he cou'd bid.
Tax those of int'rest who conform for gain,
Or stay the market of another reign.
Your broad-way sons wou'd never be too nice
To close with Calvin, if he paid their price;   230
But rais'd three steeples high'r, wou'd change their
      note,
And quit the cassock for the canting-coat.
Now, if you damn this censure, as too bold,

---

201 *grim logician.* In Dryden's *Defense* this was a phrase for Stillingfleet,
  who then used it back at Dryden.
227-28 Dryden foresees Catholic suffering; see also 427 ff.

Judge by yourselves and think not others sold.

"Meantime my sons, accus'd by fame's report,
Pay small attendance at the Lion's court,
Nor rise with early crowds, nor flatter late
(For silently they beg who daily wait).
Preferment is bestow'd that comes unsought;
Attendance is a bribe, and then 'tis bought.   240
How they shou'd speed, their fortune is untri'd,
For not to ask is not to be deni'd.
For what they have, their God and King they bless,
And hope they shou'd not murmur had they less.
But, if reduc'd subsistence to implore,
In common prudence they wou'd pass your door;
Unpiti'd Hudibras, your champion friend,
Has shown how far your charities extend.
This lasting verse shall on his tomb be read,
'He sham'd you living and upbraids you dead.'   250

"With odious atheist names you load your
          foes;
Your lib'ral clergy why did I expose?
It never fails in charities like those.
In climes where true religion is profess'd
That imputation were no laughing jest.
But *Imprimatur* with a chaplain's name,
Is here sufficient licence to defame.
What wonder is't that black detraction thrives?
The homicide of names is less than lives,
And yet the perjur'd murderer survives."   260

    This said, she paus'd a little and suppress'd
The boiling indignation of her breast;
She knew the virtue of her blade nor wou'd
Pollute her satire with ignoble blood:
Her panting foes she saw before her lie,
And back she drew the shining weapon dry:
So when the gen'rous lion has in sight
His equal match, he rouses for the fight,

---

247 *Hudibras.* Samuel Butler (d. 1680), famous for his Anglican satire in
    Hudibras and for his supposed neglect by king and bishops.
256 *Imprimatur.* The licensing formula, for most books in the power of the
    Archbishop of Canterbury and the Bishop of London, by law: 14
    Charles II. c. 33.

But when his foe lies prostrate on the plain,
He sheaths his paws, uncurls his angry mane   270
And, pleas'd with bloodless honours of the day,
Walks over and disdains th' inglorious prey.
So JAMES, if great with less we may compare,
Arrests his rolling thunderbolts in air,
And grants ungrateful friends a lengthen'd space
T' implore the remnants of long suff'ring grace.

   This breathing time the Matron took, and then
Resum'd the thread of her discourse again.
"Be vengeance wholly left to pow'rs divine,
And let Heav'n judge betwixt your sons and mine.   280
If joys hereafter must be purchas'd here
With loss of all that mortals hold so dear,
Then welcome infamy and public shame
And, last, a long farewell to worldly fame.
'Tis said with ease, but, oh, how hardly tri'd ⎫
By haughty souls to human honour ti'd!   ⎬
O sharp convulsive pangs of agonizing pride! ⎭
Down then, thou rebel, never more to rise,   ⎫
And what thou didst and dost so dearly prize, ⎬
That fame, that darling fame, make that thy ⎭
   sacrifice.   290
'Tis nothing thou hast giv'n; then add thy tears
For a long race of unrepenting years;
'Tis nothing yet, yet all thou hast to give;
Then add those *maybe* years thou hast to live.
Yet nothing still: then poor and naked come; ⎫
Thy father will receive his unthrift home,   ⎬
And thy blest Saviour's blood discharge the ⎭
   mighty sum.

   "Thus" (she pursu'd) "I discipline a son
Whose uncheck'd fury to revenge wou'd run;
He champs the bit, impatient of his loss,   300
And starts aside and flounders at the cross.
Instruct him better, gracious God, to know,

---

[279] Romans 12:19.
[218-97] The personal section of III.
[287-97] Luke 15:23. The prodigal son was glossed as the errant Christian
returning to God. Dryden's reluctant forfeiting of *fame* (290) is moving. Cf. II, 639–41.

As thine is vengeance, so forgiveness, too.
That suff'ring from ill tongues he bears no more
Than what his sovereign bears and what his Saviour
      bore.
   "It now remains for you to school your child,
And ask why God's anointed he revil'd;
A king and princess dead! did Shimei worse?
The curser's punishment should fright the curse.
Your son was warn'd and wisely gave it o'er,   310
But he who counsell'd him has paid the score;
The heavy malice cou'd no higher tend,
But woe to him on whom the weights descend:
So to permitted ills the daemon flies;
His rage is aim'd at him who rules the skies;
Constrain'd to quit his cause, no succour found,
The foe discharges ev'ry tire around,
In clouds of smoke, abandoning the fight,
But his own thund'ring peals proclaim his flight.
   "In Henry's change his charge as ill succeeds;   320
To that long story little answer needs;
Confront but Henry's words with Henry's deeds.
Were space allow'd, with ease it might be prov'd
What springs his blessed Reformation mov'd.
The dire effects appear'd in open sight,
Which from the cause he calls a distant flight,
And yet no larger leap than from the sun to light.
   "Now last your sons a double paean sound:
A *Treatise of Humility* is found.
'Tis found, but better had it ne'er been sought   330
Than thus in Protestant procession brought.
The fam'd original through Spain is known,
Rodriguez' work, my celebrated son,
Which yours by ill-translating made his own,
Conceal'd its author and usurp'd the name,
The basest and ignoblest theft of fame.

---

308 *king and princess.* Charles II and Anne Hyde, deceased Duchess of
   York, whose *Papers* were criticized by Stillingfleet, who is compared to
   Shimei (2 Samuel 16:5–13); cf. *Absalom and Achitophel* 585 ff.
309 See 1 Kings 2:36–46.
311 *he who counsell'd.* Reference uncertain.
313–15 Cf. *Paradise Lost* IV, 996 ff.

My altars kindl'd first that living coal;
Restore, or practice better what you stole;
That virtue could this humble verse inspire;
'Tis all the restitution I require."   340
    Glad was the Panther that the charge was clos'd
And none of all her fav'rite sons expos'd.
For laws of arms permit each injur'd man
To make himself a saver where he can.
Perhaps the plunder'd merchant cannot tell
The names of pirates in whose hands he fell,
But at the den of thieves he justly flies,
And ev'ry Algerine is lawful prize;
No private person in the foe's estate
Can plead exemption from the public fate.   350
Yet Christian laws allow not such redress;
Then let the greater supersede the less.
But let th' abbetors of the Panther's crime
Learn to make fairer wars another time.
Some characters may sure be found to write ⎫
Among her sons, for 'tis no common sight, ⎬
A spotted dam and all her offspring white. ⎭
    The savage, though she saw her plea controll'd,
Yet wou'd not wholly seem to quit her hold
But offer'd fairly to compound the strife   360
And judge conversion by the convert's life.
" 'Tis true," she said, "I think it somewhat strange
So few shou'd follow profitable change,
For present joys are more to flesh and blood
Than a dull prospect of a distant good.
'Twas well alluded by a son of mine
(I hope to quote him is not to purloin):
Two magnets, Heav'n and earth, allure to bliss,
The larger loadstone that, the nearer this;
The weak attraction of the greater fails,   370
We nod awhile, but neighbourhood prevails;
But when the greater proves the nearer too,

³³⁷ Isaiah 6:6.
³⁰⁶⁻⁴⁰ Returning to the controversy over the Royal Papers.
³⁵¹ *Christian laws.* Requiring forgiveness, as Luke 6:31, etc.
³⁵⁸ *her plea.* Made in 191–217.
³⁶⁶ *a son of mine.* Reference uncertain.

I wonder more your converts come so slow.
Methinks in those who firm with me remain
It shows a nobler principle than gain."
  "Your inf'rence wou'd be strong" (the Hind
    repli'd)
"If yours were in effect the suff'ring side.
Your clergy sons their own in peace possess,
Nor are their prospects in reversion less.
My proselytes are struck with awful dread;   380
Your bloody comet-laws hang blazing o'er their
    head.
The respite they enjoy but only lent,
The best they have to hope protracted punishment.
Be judge yourself, if int'rest may prevail,
Which motives, yours or mine, will turn the scale.
While pride and pomp allure, and plenteous ⎫
    ease,   ⎪
That is, till man's predominant passions cease; ⎬
Admire no longer at my slow encrease.   ⎭
  "By education most have been misled;
So they believe, because they so were bred.   390
The priest continues what the nurse began,
And thus the child imposes on the man.
The rest I nam'd before, nor need repeat,
But int'rest is the most prevailing cheat,
The sly seducer both of age and youth;
They study that and think they study truth.
When int'rest fortifies an argument,   ⎫
Weak reason serves to gain the will's assent, ⎬
For souls already warp'd receive an easy bent. ⎭
  "Add long prescription of establish'd laws,   400
And pique of honour to maintain a cause,
And shame of change, and fear of future ill,
And Zeal, the blind conductor of the will,
And chief among the still mistaking crowd, ⎫
The fame of teachers obstinate and proud,   ⎬
And more than all, the private judge allow'd, ⎭

---

381 *bloody comet-laws.* Penal laws against Dissenters and Catholics were
often called "sanguinary laws" by them.

Disdain of Fathers which the dance began,
And last, uncertain who's the narrower span,
The clown unread and half-read gentleman."

   To this the Panther, with a scornful smile: 410
"Yet still you travail with unwearied toil
And range around the realm without control
Among my sons for proselytes to prole,
And here and there you snap some silly soul.
You hinted fears of future change in state;
Pray Heav'n you did not prophesy your fate;
Perhaps you think your time of triumph near
But may mistake the season of the year;
The Swallows' fortune gives you cause to fear."

   "For charity" (repli'd the Matron), "tell   420
What sad mischance those pretty birds befell."

   "Nay, no mischance" (the savage Dame
     repli'd)
"But want of wit in their unerring guide,
And eager haste, and gaudy hopes, and giddy
     pride.
Yet, wishing timely warning may prevail,
Make you the moral, and I'll tell the tale.

   "The Swallow, privileg'd above the rest
Of all the birds as man's familiar guest,
Pursues the sun in summer brisk and bold,
But wisely shuns the persecuting cold,   430
Is well to chancels and to chimneys known,
Though 'tis not thought she feeds on smoke alone.
From hence she has been held of heav'nly line,
Endu'd with particles of soul divine.
This merry chorister had long possess'd
Her summer seat and feather'd well her nest,
Till frowning skies began to change their cheer,
And time turn'd up the wrong side of the year;

---

⁴³⁴ *particles of soul divine.* Horace, *Satires* II, ii, 79.
⁴³⁵⁻³⁷ Catholic prosperity under James will end with his reign.
⁴²⁷⁻⁶³⁸ The fable of the Swallows adapts John Ogilby's, Aesopian fable I, xl, "The Parliament of the Birds," and details from sacred zoography treating the Swallow as a type of the true Church. Dryden's point is complex: James is being led by rash advisers like Father Petres (the Martin) into courses that Dryden and other moderate Catholics feared

The shedding trees began the ground to strow
With yellow leaves, and bitter blasts to blow.   440
Sad auguries of winter thence she drew,
Which by instinct, or prophecy, she knew;
When prudence warn'd her to remove betimes
And seek a better heav'n and warmer climes.

   "Her sons were summon'd on a steeple's height
And, call'd in common council, vote a flight;
The day was nam'd, the next that shou'd be fair;
All to the gen'ral rendezvous repair;
They try their flutt'ring wings and trust
     themselves in air.

But whether upward to the moon they go,   450
Or dream the winter out in caves below,
Or hawk at flies elsewhere, concerns us not to
     know.

   "Southwards, you may be sure, they bent their
     flight,
And harbour'd in a hollow rock at night;
Next morn they rose and set up ev'ry sail;
The wind was fair but blew a mack'rel gale;
The sickly young sat shiv'ring on the shore,
Abhorr'd salt water never seen before,
And pray'd their tender mothers to delay
The passage and expect a fairer day.   460

   "With these the Martin readily concurr'd,
A Church-begot and Church-believing bird,
Of little body but of lofty mind,
Round belli'd, for a dignity design'd,
And much a dunce, as Martins are by kind.
Yet often quoted canon-laws, and code,
And Fathers which he never understood;
But little learning needs in noble blood.

---

would be disastrous; they wished accommodation with the Establishment (as the Swallow with Man in Aesop). Dryden also shows that the
Panther—many Anglicans—is cruel in desiring the destruction of Catholics. Because, however, the Swallow's wintering symbolized endurance
of persecution by the true Church, the Panther unwittingly gives the
title to Rome.

450-52 The wintering of Swallows was not understood until the nineteenth
century.

461 *Martin*. Based especially on Father Petres, but representing as well
other rash advisers of James II.

For, sooth to say, the Swallow brought him in,
Her household chaplain and her next of kin.   470
In superstition silly to excess,
And casting schemes by planetary guess;
In fine, shortwing'd, unfit himself to fly,
His fear foretold foul weather in the sky.

"Besides, a Raven from a wither'd oak,
Left of their lodging, was observ'd to croak.
That omen lik'd him not, so his advice
Was present safety bought at any price
(A seeming pious care that cover'd cowardice).
To strengthen this, he told a boding dream   480
Of rising waters and a troubl'd stream,
Sure signs of anguish, dangers, and distress,
With something more not lawful to express;
By which he slyly seem'd to intimate
Some secret revelation of their fate.
For, he concluded, once upon a time,
He found a leaf inscrib'd with sacred rhyme,
Whose antique characters did well denote
The Sibyl's hand of the Cumaean grot;
The mad divineress had plainly writ,   490
A time shou'd come (but many ages yet)
In which, sinister destinies ordain,
A Dame shou'd drown with all her feather'd train,
And seas from thence be call'd the Chelidonian
    main.
At this, some shook for fear; the more devout
Arose and bless'd themselves from head to foot.
" 'Tis true, some stagers of the wiser sort
Made all these idle wonderments their sport;
They said their only danger was delay,
And he who heard what ev'ry fool cou'd say   500
Wou'd never fix his thoughts but trim his time
    away.

---

470 *household chaplain.* Confessor of James II.
475-76 Virgil, *Eclogues* IX, 15. The Raven is based on Anglican divines in
    the midst of controversy, especially Thomas Tennison.
480-85 Flood is an image of political disorder, what is not *lawful* (483) is
    rebellion; cf. II, 272-73.
494 *Chelidonian.* From the Greek word for "swallow," in analogy with
    the Icarian Sea.

The passage yet was good; the wind, 'tis true,
Was somewhat high, but that was nothing new,
Nor more than usual equinoxes blew.

The sun (already from the scales declin'd)
Gave little hopes of better days behind
But change from bad to worse of weather and of
    wind.

Nor need they fear the dampness of the sky
Should flag their wings and hinder them to fly,
'Twas only water thrown on sails too dry.   510

But least of all philosophy presumes
Of truth in dreams from melancholy fumes;
Perhaps the Martin, hous'd in holy ground,
Might think of ghosts that walk their midnight
    round,
Till grosser atoms, tumbling in the stream
Of fancy, madly met and clubb'd into a dream.
As little weight his vain presages bear
Of ill effect to such alone who fear.
Most prophecies are of a piece with these;
Each Nostradamus can foretell with ease,   520
Not naming persons and confounding times,
One casual truth supports a thousand lying rimes.

   "Th' advice was true, but fear had seiz'd the most,
And all good counsel is on cowards lost.
The question crudely put, to shun delay,
'Twas carri'd by the major part to stay.

   "His point thus gain'd, Sir Martin dated thence
His pow'r, and from a priest became a prince.
He order'd all things with a busy care
And cells and refectories did prepare,   530
And large provisions laid of winter fare.

But now and then let fall a word or two
Of hope that Heav'n some miracle might show,
And for their sakes the sun shou'd backward go,
Against the laws of nature upward climb,

---

505 *scales.* Libra in the zodiac; beginning autumn.
520 *Nostradamus.* Recalling "Nostradamus' Prophecy" (ca. 1672), an anti-
    Royalist poem in the tradition of political predictions during the Com-
    monwealth.

And, mounted on the Ram, renew the prime,
For which two proofs in sacred story lay,
Of Ahaz' dial and of Joshua's day.
In expectation of such times as these
A chapel hous'd 'em, truly call'd of ease;   540
For Martin much devotion did not ask;
They pray'd sometimes, and that was all their task.
    "It happen'd (as beyond the reach of wit
Blind prophecies may have a lucky hit)
That, this accomplish'd, or at least in part,
Gave great repute to their new Merlin's art.
Some Swifts,* the giants of the Swallow kind,
Large limb'd, stout-hearted, but of stupid mind
(For Swisses or for Gibeonites design'd),
These lubbers, peeping through a broken pane   550
To suck fresh air, survey'd the neighbouring plain,
And saw (but scarcely cou'd believe their eyes)
New blossoms flourish and new flow'rs arise,
As God had been abroad, and walking there,
Had left his footsteps and reform'd the year:
The sunny hills from far were seen to glow
With glittering beams, and in the meads below
The burnish'd brooks appear'd with liquid gold
        to flow.
At last they heard the foolish Cuckoo sing,
Whose note proclaim'd the holy day of spring.   560
    "No longer doubting, all prepare to fly
And repossess their patrimonial sky.
The priest before 'em did his wings display,
And, that good omens might attend their way,
As luck wou'd have it, 'twas St. Martin's Day.
    "Who but the Swallow now triumphs alone?
The canopy of heaven is all her own,
Her youthful offspring to their haunts repair,
And glide along in glades and skim in air,

* Other-wise call'd Martlets.

---

539 Ram. Aries in the zodiac; early spring.
538 2 Kings 20:11; Joshua 10:12–14.
547-60 This perplexing passage probably refers to Englishmen like Tyrconnel who claimed a triumph for James II and Catholicism in Ireland.
565 St. Martin's Day. November 11.

And dip for insects in the purling springs,   570
And stoop on rivers to refresh their wings.
Their mothers think a fair provision made,
That ev'ry son can live upon his trade,
And, now the careful charge is off their hands,
Look out for husbands and new nuptial bands;
The youthful widow longs to be suppli'd, ⎫
But first the lover is by lawyers ti'd   ⎬
To settle jointure-chimneys on the bride. ⎭
So thick they couple in so short a space,
That Martin's marr'age-off'rings rise apace;   580
Their ancient houses, running to decay,
Are furbish'd up and cemented with clay;
They teem already; store of eggs are laid,
And brooding mothers call Lucina's aid.
Fame spreads the news, and foreign fowls appear ⎫
In flocks to greet the new returning year,   ⎬
To bless the founder and partake the cheer.   ⎭

    "And now 'twas time (so fast their numbers rise)
To plant abroad and people colonies;
The youth drawn forth, as Martin had desir'd   590
(For so their cruel destiny requir'd),
Were sent far off on an ill-fated day;   ⎫
The rest wou'd need conduct 'em on their way,   ⎬
And Martin went, because he fear'd alone to stay. ⎭

    "So long they flew with inconsiderate haste
That now their afternoon began to waste;
And, what was ominous, that very morn
The sun was enter'd into Capricorn,
Which by their bad astronomers' account,
That week the Virgin balance shou'd remount;   600
An infant moon eclips'd him in his way
And hid the small remainders of his day.
The crowd, amaz'd, pursu'd no certain mark,
But birds met birds and justled in the dark;
Few mind the public in a panic fright,

572-84 Normal family concerns in the seventeenth century.
585 *foreign fowls*. Foreign Catholic priests.
598 *Capricorn*. In the zodiac; beginning of winter.
600 *Virgin balance*. Libra; see 504n. The Swallows confuse the season.

And fear increas'd the horror of the night.
Night came, but unattended with repose,
Alone she came, no sleep their eyes to close,
Alone and black she came, no friendly stars
    arose.
  "What shou'd they do, beset with dangers   610
    round,
No neighb'ring dorp, no lodging to be found,
But bleaky plains and bare unhospitable ground?
The later brood, who just began to fly,
Sick-feather'd and unpractis'd in the sky,
For succour to their helpless mother call;
She spread her wings; some few beneath 'em
    crawl;
She spread 'em wider yet but cou'd not cover all.
T' augment their woes, the winds began to move
Debate in air for empty fields above,
Till Boreas got the skies and pour'd amain   620
His rattling hail-stones mix'd with snow and rain.
  "The joyless morning late arose and found
A dreadful desolation reign around,
Some buried in the snow, some frozen to the
    ground;
The rest were struggling still with death and lay
The Crows' and Ravens' rights, an undefended prey,
Excepting Martin's race, for they and he
Had gain'd the shelter of a hollow tree,
But soon discover'd by a sturdy clown,
He headed all the rabble of a town,   630
And finish'd 'em with bats or poll'd 'em down.
Martin himself was caught alive and tri'd
For treas'nous crimes, because the laws provide
No Martin there in winter shall abide.
High on an oak which never leaf shall bear
He breath'd his last, expos'd to open air,
And there his corps, unbless'd, are hanging still,

607-9 A night piece begun with a version of the Virgilian formula, *nox erat*.
635 *an oak*. The gallows.

To show the change of winds with his prophetic
    bill."

    The patience of the Hind did almost fail,
For well she mark'd the malice of the tale,   640
Which ribald art their Church to Luther owes;
In malice it began, by malice grows;
He sow'd the Serpent's teeth, an iron-harvest
    rose.

But most in Martin's character and fate
She saw her slander'd sons, the Panther's hate,
The people's rage, the persecuting state,
Then said, "I take th' advice in friendly part,
You clear your conscience or at least your heart;
Perhaps you fail'd in your foreseeing skill,
For Swallows are unlucky birds to kill.   650
As for my sons, the family is bless'd
Whose ev'ry child is equal to the rest;
No church reform'd can boast a blameless line;
Such Martins build in yours and more than mine,
Or else an old fanatic author lies
Who summ'd their scandals up by centuries.
But through your parable I plainly see
The bloody laws, the crowd's barbarity,
The sunshine that offends the purblind sight;
Had some their wishes, it wou'd soon be night.   660
Mistake me not, the charge concerns not you,
Your sons are malcontents, but yet are true,
As far as nonresistance makes 'em so,
But that's a word of neutral sense, you know,
A passive term which no relief will bring,
But trims betwixt a rebel and a king."

632-38 An earlier law (27 Eliz. c. 2, re-enacted 1 Jac. I. c. 4), enforced only
    in hysterical times, rendered Catholic priests subject to being hanged,
    drawn, and quartered.
638 *prophetic bill.* Superstition held that when certain birds were hung
    by the feet their bills would point the quarter of the wind.
641-43 Luther is compared to Cadmus (*Metamorphoses* III, 95 ff.) inter-
    preted satanically out of Milton (*Paradise Lost* IX, 503-6).
650 *Swallows,* etc. An old superstition.
655 *fanatic author.* John White (d. 1644), a Dissenter, wrote *The First
    Century of Scandalous Malignant* [Anglican] *Priests* (1643); that is,
    Father Petres is bad but many Anglicans are worse.
658 *bloody laws.* See 632-38n.

"Rest well assur'd," the Pardalis repli'd,
"My sons wou'd all support the regal side,
Though Heav'n forbid the cause by battle shou'd
    be tri'd."

    The Matron answer'd with a loud amen,.   670
And thus pursu'd her argument again.
"If as you say, and as I hope no less,
Your sons will practise what yourself profess,
What angry pow'r prevents our present peace?
The Lion, studious of our common good
Desires (and kings' desires are ill withstood)
To join our nations in a lasting love;
The bars betwixt are easy to remove,
For sanguinary laws were never made above.
If you condemn that prince of tyranny,   680
Whose mandate forc'd your Gallic friends to fly,
Make not a worse example of your own,
Or cease to rail at causeless rigour shown,
And let the guiltless person throw the stone.
His blunted sword your suff'ring brotherhood
Have seldom felt, he stops it short of blood,
But you have ground the persecuting knife
And set it to a razor edge on life.
Curs'd be the wit which cruelty refines,
Or to his father's rod the Scorpion joins;   690
Your finger is more gross than the great
    monarch's loins.
But you perhaps remove that bloody note,
And stick it on the first Reformers' coat.
O let their crime in long oblivion sleep;
'Twas theirs indeed to make, 'tis yours to keep.
Unjust, or just, is all the question now;
'Tis plain that not repealing you allow.
    "To name the Test wou'd put you in a rage;
You charge not that on any former age,
But smile to think how innocent you stand,   700
Arm'd by a weapon put into your hand.

---

[679] *sanguinary laws.* Cf. 381*n*, 632–38*n*, and 658.
[680] *prince.* Louis XIV; the syntax appears to be deliberately ambiguous.
[685] *blunted sword.* See II, 419*n*.
[690-91] 1 Kings 12:10–11.

Yet still remember that you wield a sword
Forg'd by your foes against your sovereign lord,
Design'd to hew th' imperial cedar down,
Defraud succession, and disheir the crown.
T' abhor the makers and their laws approve,
Is to hate traitors and the treason love.
What means it else, which now your children say,
'We made it not, nor will we take away.'

  "Suppose some great oppressor had by slight   710
Of law disseis'd your brother of his right,
Your common sire surrend'ring in a fright;
Would you to that unrighteous title stand,
Left by the villain's will to heir the land?
More just was Judas, who his Saviour sold;
The sacrilegious bribe he cou'd not hold,
Nor hang in peace before he render'd back the
    gold.
What more could you have done than now you do,
Had Oates and Bedlow and their Plot been true?
Some specious reasons for those wrongs were
    found;   720
The dire magicians threw their mists around,
And wise men walk'd as on enchanted ground.
But now when Time has made th' imposture
    plain
(Late though he follow'd Truth and limping held
    her train),
What new delusion charms your cheated eyes
    again?
The painted harlot might awhile bewitch,
But why the hag uncas'd and all obscene with itch?
  "The first Reformers were a modest race;
Our peers possess'd in peace their native place,
And when rebellious arms o'erturn'd the state,   730
They suffer'd only in the common fate;
But now the sov'reign mounts the regal chair,

---

704 *imperial cedar.* 2 Samuel 7:2; 2 Kings 14:9.
715–17 Matthew 27:3–5.
719 *Oates and Bedlow.* Principal witnesses in the Popish Plot.
726–27 Recalling Duessa, *The Faerie Queene* I, viii, 46.

And mitr'd seats are full, yet David's bench is bare.
Your answer is, they were not dispossess'd;
They need but rub their metal on the Test
To prove their ore: 'twere well if gold alone
Were touch'd and tri'd on your discerning stone;
But that unfaithful Test, unfound will pass
The dross of atheists and sectarian brass,
As if th' experiment were made to hold   740
For base productions and reject the gold;
Thus men ungodded may to places rise,
And Sects may be preferr'd without disguise;
No danger to the Church or state from these;
The Papist only has his writ of ease.
No gainful office gives him the pretence
To grind the subject or defraud the prince.
Wrong conscience or no conscience may deserve
To thrive, but ours alone is privileg'd to starve.
   " 'Still thank yourselves,' you cry, 'your noble race   750
We banish not, but they forsake the place.
Our doors are open.' True, but e'er they come,
You toss your censing Test and fume the room;
As if 'twere Toby's rival to expel
And fright the fiend who could not bear the smell."
   To this the Panther sharply had repli'd, ⎫
But having gain'd a verdict on her side, ⎬
She wisely gave the loser leave to chide; ⎭
Well satisfi'd to have the butt and peace; ⎫
And for the plaintiff's cause she car'd the less, ⎬   760
Because she su'd *in forma pauperis;* ⎭
Yet thought it decent something shou'd be said,
For secret guilt by silence is betray'd:
So neither granted all, nor much deni'd,
But answer'd with a yawning kind of pride.
   "Methinks such terms of proferr'd peace you
      bring

728-33 Under the Tudors, Catholic peers were allowed seats in the Lords;
   they had suffered with Anglicans in the Interregnum, but are now
   denied seats although now under a Catholic king.
739 *atheists*, etc. Who lacked Catholic compunction in taking the Anglican
   sacrament prescribed by Test Acts.
745 *writ of ease.* Certificate of discharge from office.
754-55 Tobit 6–8.

As once Aeneas to th' Italian king;
By long possession all the land is mine;
You strangers come with your intruding line
To share my sceptre, which you call to join.   770
You plead like him an ancient pedigree
And claim a peaceful seat by fate's decree.
In ready pomp your sacrificer stands
T' unite the Trojan and the Latin bands,
And that the league more firmly may be ti'd,
Demand the fair Lavinia for your bride.
Thus plausibly you veil th' intended wrong,
But still you bring your exil'd gods along,
And will endeavour in succeeding space
Those household poppits on our hearths to place.   780
Perhaps some barb'rous laws have been preferr'd;
I spake against the Test but was not heard;
These to rescind and peerage to restore
My gracious sov'reign wou'd my vote implore;
I owe him much but owe my conscience more."
    "Conscience is then your plea," repli'd the Dame,
"Which well-inform'd will ever be the same.
But yours is much of the Cameleon hue,
To change the dye with ev'ry diff'rent view.
When first the Lion sat with awful sway,   790
Your conscience taught you duty to obey;
He might have had your statutes and your Test;
No conscience but of subjects was profess'd.
He found your temper and no farther tri'd,
But on that broken reed your Church reli'd.
In vain the Sects assay'd their utmost art
With offer'd treasure to espouse their part,
Their treasures were a bribe too mean to move
        his heart.
But when by long experience you had prov'd
How far he cou'd forgive, how well he lov'd,   800
A goodness that excell'd his godlike race,
And only short of Heav'n's unbounded grace,

A flood of mercy that o'erflowed our isle,
Calm in the rise and fruitful as the Nile,
Forgetting whence your Egypt was suppli'd,
You thought your sov'reign bound to send the tide,
Nor upward look'd on that immortal spring
But vainly deem'd he durst not be a king.

"Then conscience, unrestrain'd by fear, began
To stretch her limits and extend the span,　　　　　810
Did his indulgence as her gift dispose,
And made a wise alliance with her foes.
Can conscience own th' associating name
And raise no blushes to conceal her shame?
For sure she has been thought a bashful dame.
But if the cause by battle shou'd be tri'd,
You grant she must espouse the regal side:
O Proteus conscience, never to be ti'd!
What Phoebus from the tripod shall disclose
Which are in last resort your friends or foes?　　　820
Homer, who learn'd the language of the sky,
The seeming Gordian knot wou'd soon untie;
Immortal pow'rs the term of 'conscience' know,
But 'int'rest' is her name with men below."

"Conscience or int'rest be't, or both in one"
(The Panther answer'd in a surly tone),
"The first commands me to maintain the crown;
The last forbids to throw my barriers down.
Our penal laws no sons of yours admit;
Our Test excludes your tribe from benefit.　　　　830
These are my banks your ocean to withstand,
Which proudly rising overlooks the land,
And once let in, with unresisted sway
Wou'd sweep the pastors and their flocks away.
Think not my judgment leads me to comply
With laws unjust, but hard necessity;
Imperious need which cannot be withstood
Makes ill authentic for a greater good.

790-812 James II and the Anglican hierarchy started off on good terms in 1685 on his pledge in Privy Council to uphold the Establishment; he assumed their support with his good will and they assumed his support; disagreement followed. See 952-54.
813 *associating name*. Referring to the anti-Catholic Whig Association condemned by Dryden in *The Medal*.

Possess your soul with patience and attend;
A more auspicious planet may ascend;   840
Good fortune may present some happier time
With means to cancel my unwilling crime
(Unwilling, witness, all ye pow'rs above),
To mend my errors and redeem your love;
That little space you safely may allow;
Your all-dispensing pow'r protects you now."
    "Hold," said the Hind, " 'tis needless to explain;
You wou'd postpone me to another reign,
Till when you are content to be unjust;
Your part is to possess and mine to trust.   850
A fair exchange propos'd, of future chance
For present profit and inheritance.
Few words will serve to finish our dispute—
Who will not now repeal wou'd persecute;
To ripen green revenge your hopes attend,
Wishing that happier planet wou'd ascend.
For shame let conscience be your plea no more; ⎫
To will hereafter proves she might before;   ⎬
But she's a bawd to gain and holds the door. ⎭
    "Your care about your banks infers a fear   860
Of threat'ning floods and inundations near;
If so, a just reprise would only be
Of what the land usurp'd upon the sea;
And all your jealousies but serve to show
Your ground is, like your neighbour nation, low.
T' entrench in what you grant unrighteous laws
Is to distrust the justice of your cause,
And argues that the true religion lies
In those weak adversaries you despise.
    "Tyrannic force is that which least you fear;   870
The sound is frightful in a Christian's ear;
Avert it, Heav'n, nor let that plague be sent
To us from the dispeopled continent.
    "But piety commands me to refrain;
Those pray'rs are needless in this Monarch's reign.

---

⁸⁴⁰ *more auspicious planet.* As in 856, probably William and Mary.
⁸⁶⁵ *Your ground,* etc. Meaning Holland, where William of Orange was
    closely watching English events.

Behold! how he protects your friends oppress'd,
Receives the banish'd, succours the distress'd;
Behold, for you may read an honest open breast.
He stands in daylight and disdains to hide
An act to which by honour he is ti'd,   880
A generous, laudable, and kingly pride.
Your Test he would repeal, his peers restore,
This when he says he means, he means no more."
    "Well," said the Panther, "I believe him just,
And yet—"
                "And yet, 'tis but because you must;
You would be trusted, but you would not trust."
The Hind thus briefly, and disdain'd t' enlarge
On pow'r of kings and their superior charge
As Heav'n's trustees before the people's choice,
Tho' sure the Panther did not much rejoyce   890
To hear those echoes giv'n of her once loyal voice.
    The Matron woo'd her kindness to the last
But cou'd not win; her hour of grace was past.
Whom thus persisting when she could not bring
To leave the Wolf and to believe her King,
She gave her up and fairly wish'd her joy
Of her late treaty with her new ally,
Which well she hop'd wou'd more successful prove
Than was the Pigeons' and the Buzzard's love.
The Panther ask'd what concord there cou'd be   900
Betwixt two kinds whose natures disagree?
The Dame repli'd, " 'Tis sung in ev'ry street,
The common chat of gossips when they meet;
But since unheard by you, 'tis worth your while
To take a wholesome tale, tho' told in homely style.
    "A plain good man, whose name is understood
(So few deserve the name of plain and good),
Of three fair lineal lordships stood possess'd
And liv'd, as reason was, upon the best;
Inur'd to hardships from his early youth,   910
Much had he done and suffer'd for his truth;

872–77 See To the Reader note 3, III, 109–11n.
908 England, Wales, Scotland.

At land and sea, in many a doubtful fight,
Was never known a more advent'rous knight
Who oft'ner drew his sword and always for the
    right.

   "As fortune wou'd (his fortune came tho' late),
He took possession of his just estate,
Nor rack'd his tenants with increase of rent,
Nor liv'd too sparing, nor too largely spent,
But overlook'd his hinds; their pay was just
And ready, for he scorn'd to go on trust;   920
Slow to resolve, but in performance quick,
So true, that he was awkward at a trick.
For little souls on little shifts rely,
And coward arts of mean expedients try:
The noble mind will dare do anything but lie.
False friends (his deadliest foes) could find no
    way
But shows of honest bluntness to betray.
That unsuspected plainness he believ'd;
He look'd into himself and was deceiv'd.
Some lucky planet sure attends his birth,   930
Or Heav'n wou'd make a miracle on earth,
For prosp'rous honesty is seldom seen,
To bear so dead a weight and yet to win.
It looks as fate with nature's law would strive,
To show plaindealing once an age may thrive,
And when so tough a frame she could not bend,
Exceeded her commission to befriend.

   "This grateful man, as Heav'n increas'd his store,
Gave God again and daily fed his poor;
His house with all convenience was purvey'd;   940
The rest he found but rais'd the fabric where he
    pray'd,
And in that sacred place his beauteous wife
Employ'd her happiest hours of holy life.

   "Nor did their alms extend to those alone
Whom common faith more strictly made their own;

---

⁹¹⁵ *late*. Born in 1633, James II acceded in 1685.
⁹²⁸ *False friends*, etc. Including rash Catholics especially and also un-
reliable turncoats.
⁹⁴¹ *the fabric*. The Catholic chapel in Whitehall.

A sort of Doves were hous'd too near their hall,
Who cross the proverb and abound with gall.
Tho' some, 'tis true, are passively inclin'd,
The greater part degenerate from their kind:
Voracious birds that hotly bill and breed,   950
And largely drink, because on salt they feed.
Small gain from them their bounteous owner
    draws
Yet, bound by promise, he supports their cause,
As corporations privileg'd by laws.
    "That house which harbour to their kind affords
Was built long since, God knows, for better birds,
But flutt'ring there they nestle near the throne,
And lodge in habitations not their own,
By their high crops and corny gizzards known.
Like Harpies they could scent a plenteous board—   960
Then to be sure they never fail'd their lord.
The rest was form and bare attendance paid;
They drunk, and eat, and grudgingly obey'd.
The more they fed, they raven'd still for more,
They drain'd from Dan and left Beersheba poor;
All this they had by law, and none repin'd;
The pref'rence was but due to Levi's kind,
But when some lay-preferment fell by chance,
The gourmands made it their inheritance.
When once possess'd, they never quit their claim,   970
For then 'tis sanctifi'd to Heav'n's high name,
And hallow'd thus they cannot give consent
The gift should be prophan'd by worldly
    management.
    "Their flesh was never to the table serv'd,
Tho' 'tis not thence inferr'd the birds were starv'd,
But that their master did not like the food,
As rank and breeding melancholy blood.
Nor did it with his gracious nature suit,
Ev'n tho' they were not Doves, to persecute;

947 *gall.* Proverbially lacked by Doves and Pigeons.
950–51 Pigeons were thought lecherous; but *salt* also refers to *salarium,*
    state endowments for the Established Church. Cf. *jolly birds* 991.
952 See 790–812n.
965 That is, the whole country; 1 Samuel 3:20.
967 *Levi's kind.* The (Anglican) priesthood.

Yet he refus'd (nor could they take offence)   980
Their glutton kind should teach him abstinence.
Nor consecrated grain their wheat he thought,
Which new from treading in their bills they brought,
But left his hinds each in his private pow'r,
That those who like the bran might leave the flour.
He for himself, and not for others chose,
Nor would he be impos'd on, nor impose;
But in their faces his devotion paid
And sacrifice with solemn rites was made,
And sacred incense on his altars laid.   990

   "Besides these jolly birds, whose crops impure
Repay'd their commons with their salt manure,
Another farm he had behind his house,
Not overstock'd but barely for his use,
Wherein his poor domestic poultry fed,
And from his pious hands receiv'd their bread.
Our pamper'd Pigeons with malignant eyes
Beheld these inmates and their nurseries;
Tho' hard their fare, at ev'ning and at morn
A cruse of water and an ear of corn,   1000
Yet still they grudg'd that modicum and thought
A sheaf in ev'ry single grain was brought;
Fain would they filch that little food away,
While unrestrain'd those happy gluttons prey.
And much they griev'd to see so nigh their hall
The bird that warn'd St. Peter of his fall;
That he should raise his miter'd crest on high
And clap his wings and call his family
To sacred rites; and vex th' ethereal pow'rs
With midnight matins at uncivil hours;   1010
Nay more, his quiet neighbours should molest,
Just in the sweetness of their morning rest.

   "Beast of a bird, supinely when he might
Lie snug and sleep, to rise before the light;
What if his dull forefathers us'd that cry,
Cou'd he not let a bad example die?

982 *their wheat*. The Host in the Anglican sacrament.
995 *domestic poultry*. Catholics, especially priests and nuns.
1013 The idea of a supine Cock is humorous to Dryden if not to Anglicans.

The world was fall'n into an easier way;
This age knew better than to fast and pray.
Good sense in sacred worship would appear
So to begin as they might end the year.   1020
Such feats in former times had wrought the falls
Of crowing Chanticleers in cloister'd walls.
Expell'd for this, and for their lands, they fled,
And Sister Partlet with her hooded head
Was hooted hence, because she would not pray
    abed.
The way to win the restive world to God
Was to lay by the disciplining rod,
Unnatural fasts, and foreign forms of pray'r;
Religion frights us with a mien severe.
'Tis prudence to reform her into ease   1030
And put her in undress to make her pleas;
A lively faith will bear aloft the mind,
And leave the luggage of good works behind.
    "Such doctrines in the Pigeon-house were taught:
You need not ask how wondrously they wrought;
But sure the common cry was all for these
Whose life and precept both encourag'd ease.
Yet fearing those alluring baits might fail,
And holy deeds o'er all their arts prevail
(For vice, tho' frontless, and of harden'd face   1040
Is daunted at the sight of awful Grace),
An hideous figure of their foes they drew,
Nor lines, nor looks, nor shades, nor colours true,
And this grotesque design expos'd to public view.
One would have thought it some Egyptian piece
With garden-gods and barking deities,
More thick than Ptolemy has stuck the skies.
All so perverse a draught, so far unlike,

1006-23 The Cock was a type of the vigilant priest for warning Peter (Matthew 26) and of lechery, as Dryden also intimates.
1022-33 *Chanticleer* and *Partlet*, priests and nuns, also recalling The Nun's Priest's Tale.
1032-33 Protestants stressed faith leading to good works; Catholics stressed good works as a sign of faith.
1045-46 Anubis, an idol with a dog's head and man's body, was called *lutrator*, the barker, by Romans.
1047 *Ptolemy*. Egyptian geographer, astronomer, mathematician in the second century A.D.

It was no libel where it meant to strike;
Yet still the daubing pleas'd, and great and small   1050
To view the monster crowded Pigeon-hall.
There Chanticleer was drawn upon his knees
Adoring shrines and stocks of sainted trees,
And by him a misshapen, ugly race;
The curse of God was seen on ev'ry face;
No Holland emblem could that malice mend,
But still the worse the look, the fitter for a fiend.

   "The master of the farm displeas'd to find
So much of rancour in so mild a kind,
Enquir'd into the cause and came to know   1060
The passive Church had struck the foremost blow,
With groundless fears and jealousies possess'd,   ⎫
As if this troublesome intruding guest   ⎬
Would drive the birds of Venus from their nest,   ⎭
A deed his inborn equity abhorr'd,
But int'rest will not trust, tho' God should plight His
      word.

   "A law, the source of many future harms,
Had banish'd all the Poultry from the farms,
With loss of life if any should be found
To crow or peck on this forbidden ground.   1070
That bloody statute chiefly was design'd
For Chanticleer the white of clergy kind;
But after-malice did not long forget
The lay that wore the robe and coronet;
For them, for their inferiors and allies,
Their foes a deadly shibboleth devise,
By which unrighteously it was decreed,   ⎫
That none to trust or profit should succeed   ⎬
Who would not swallow first a poisonous, wicked   ⎭
      weed,
Or that to which old Socrates was curs'd,   1080
Or henbane-juice to swell 'em till they burst.

1056 *Holland emblem.* Unfavorable representation of Charles II in Dutch
emblems had been a stated *casus belli* in 1671–1672.
1042–57 See I, 537n. on "representing."
1072 *the white.* Referring to priestly surplices.
1076 *a deadly shibboleth.* The Test Acts; Judges 12:6.

The patron (as in reason) thought it hard
To see this inquisition in his yard,
By which the sovereign was of subjects' use
    debarr'd.

  "All gentle means he tri'd which might withdraw
Th' effects of so unnatural a law,
But still the Dove-house obstinately stood
Deaf to their own and to their neighbours' good,
'And which was worse (if any worse could be),'
Repented of their boasted loyalty,   1090
Now made the champions of a cruel cause
And drunk with fumes of popular applause;
For those whom God to ruin has design'd
He fits for fate and first destroys their mind.

  "New doubts indeed they daily strove to raise,
Suggested dangers, interpos'd delays,
And emissary Pigeons had in store,
Such as the Meccan prophet us'd of yore
To whisper counsels in their patron's ear,
And veil'd their false advice with zealous fear.   1100
The master smiled to see 'em work in vain,
To wear him out and make an idle reign;
He saw but suffer'd their protractive arts,
And strove by mildness to reduce their hearts,
But they abus'd that grace to make allies,
And fondly clos'd with former enemies;
For fools are double fools endeav'ring to be wise.

  "After a grave consult what course were best,
One more mature in folly than the rest
Stood up and told 'em, with his head aside,   1110
That desp'rate cures must be to desp'rate ills appli'd;
And therefore since their main impending fear
Was from th' increasing race of Chanticleer,
Some potent bird of prey they ought to find,

1089 An often quoted line from Roger Boyle, Earl of Orrery's *Black Prince* II, i, 273.
1093-94 Proverbial.
1097-98 A common Christian aspersion on Mahomet.
1102 About this time Dryden wrote Etherege, wishing James II would follow the "noble idleness" of Charles II—that is, moderation and patience.

A foe profess'd to him and all his kind:
Some haggard Hawk who had her eyry nigh,
Well pounc'd to fasten, and well wing'd to fly;
One they might trust their common wrongs to wreak;
'The Musquet and the Kastril were too weak,
Too fierce the Falcon, but above the rest   1120
The noble Buzzard ever pleas'd me best;
Of small renown, 'tis true, for not to lie,
We call him but a Hawk by courtesy.
I know he haunts the Pigeon-house and farm,
And more, in time of war, has done us harm,
But all his hate on trivial points depends;
Give up our forms and we shall soon be friends.
For Pigeons' flesh he seems not much to care;
Cramm'd Chickens are a more delicious fare.
On this high potentate, without delay,   1130
I wish you would confer the sovereign sway;
Petition him t' accept the government
And let a splendid embassy be sent.'
    "This pithy speech prevail'd, and all agreed
Old enmity's forgot, the Buzzard should succeed.
    "Their welcome suit was granted soon as
        heard,
His lodgings furnish'd, and a train prepar'd
With *B's* upon their breast appointed for his
        guard.
He came, and crown'd with great solemnity,
'God save King Buzzard,' was the gen'ral cry.   1140
    "A portly Prince and goodly to the sight,
He seem'd a son of Anak for his height,
Like those whom stature did to crowns prefer,
Black-brow'd and bluff like Homer's Jupiter;
Broad-back'd and brawny, built for love's delight,
A prophet form'd to make a female proselyte.
A theologue more by need than genial bent,
By breeding sharp, by nature confident.
Int'rest in all his actions was discern'd;

[1119] *Musquet . . . Kastril.* The small hawk; a common falcon.
[1142] *son of Anak.* A giant; Numbers 13:3.
[1143] 1 Samuel 9:2.

More learn'd than honest, more a wit than learn'd.   1150
Or forc'd by fear, or by his profit led,.
Or both conjoin'd, his native clime he fled,
But brought the virtues of his heav'n along,
A fair behaviour and a fluent tongue.
And yet with all his arts he could not thrive,
The most unlucky parasite alive.
Loud praises to prepare his paths he sent,
And then himself pursu'd his compliment;
But by reverse of fortune chas'd away,
His gifts no longer than their author stay;   1160
He shakes the dust against th' ungrateful race
And leaves the stench of ordures in the place.
    "Oft has he flatter'd and blasphem'd the same,
For in his rage he spares no sov'reign's name:
The hero and the tyrant change their style
By the same measure that they frown or smile.
When well receiv'd by hospitable foes,
The kindness he returns is to expose;
For courtesies, tho' undeserv'd and great,
No gratitude in felon minds beget;   1170
As tribute to his wit the churl receives the treat.
His praise of foes is venomously nice;
So touch'd, it turns a virtue to a vice:
'A Greek, and bountiful, forewarns us twice.'
Sev'n sacraments he wisely does disown,
Because he knows confession stands for one;
Where sins to sacred silence are convey'd
And not for fear or love to be betray'd;
But he, uncall'd, his patron to control,
Divulg'd the secret whispers of his soul,   1180
Stood forth th' accusing Satan of his crimes

1152 *his native clime he fled.* Burnet frequently traveled out of Scotland
and England. After disagreements with the court in 1685, for example,
Burnet went to France and then further south before settling in Holland. His travel accounts exemplified his notorious inaccuracy and vanity as well as an unusual faultfinding.
1154 *a fluent tongue.* Burnet was a brilliant, popular preacher.
1161 Luke 10:10–11; also the befouling harpy.
1163 *the same.* Charles II specifically, others generally.
1175–78 *Sev'n sacraments.* Anglicans retained but two of the Roman and
Greek seven. They omitted confession (part of penance) allegedly because it requires *sacred silence* of a priest.
1181 *accusing.* Rendering "diabolical."

And offer'd to the Moloch of the times.
Prompt to assail, and careless of defence,
Invulnerable in his impudence,
He dares the world, and eager of a name
He thrusts about and justles into fame.
Frontless, and satire-proof he scours the streets,
And runs an Indian muck at all he meets.
So fond of loud report that not to miss
Of being known (his last and utmost bliss),   1190
He rather would be known for what he is.

  "Such was and is the Captain of the Test,
Tho' half his virtues are not here express'd;
The modesty of fame conceals the rest.
The spleenful Pigeons never could create
A prince more proper to revenge their hate;
Indeed, more proper to revenge, than save,
A king, whom in his wrath, th' Almighty gave;
For all the grace the landlord had allow'd
But made the Buzzard and the Pigeons proud,   1200
Gave time to fix their friends and to seduce the
      crowd.
They long their fellow subjects to enthrall,
Their patron's promise into question call,
And vainly think he meant to make 'em lords
      of all.

  "False fears their leaders fail'd not to suggest,
As if the Doves were to be dispossess'd;
Nor sighs, nor groans, nor goggling eyes did want,
For now the Pigeons too had learn'd to cant.
The House of Pray'r is stock'd with large increase;
Nor doors nor windows can contain the press,   1210
For birds of ev'ry feather fill th' abode;

[1182] *Moloch.* Amorite god worshiped with human sacrifice.
[1170-86] In a shameful episode in 1675, Burnet testified in Parliament against
his patron, Lauderdale, and at the same time his fulsome dedication
to Lauderdale came from the press.
[1141-98] The Buzzard was based on William of Orange as soldier (1125)
and possible king (1140), on Gilbert Burnet (d. 1715) for personal details, and on the Hawk for typologies of impiety and Judas. The
brilliant but shifty Burnet was notorious in early life for exploiting and
betraying patrons.
[1198] 1 Samuel 8:16–18; Aesop, "The Frogs Desiring a King."

Ev'n atheists out of envy own a god,
And reeking from the stews, adult'rers come,
Like Goths and Vandals to demolish Rome.
That conscience which to all their crimes was mute
Now calls aloud and cries to persecute.
No rigour of the laws to be releas'd,
And much the less, because it was their Lord's
    request;
They thought it great their Sov'reign to control
And nam'd their pride nobility of soul.   1220
  " 'Tis true, the Pigeons and their prince-elect
Were short of pow'r their purpose to effect,
But with their quills did all the hurt they cou'd
And cuff'd the tender Chickens from their food;
And much the Buzzard in their cause did stir,
Tho' naming not the patron to infer,
With all respect, he was a gross idolater.
  "But when th' imperial owner did espy
That thus they turn'd his grace to villainy,
Not suff'ring wrath to discompose his mind,   1230
He strove a temper for th' extremes to find,
So to be just as he might still be kind.
Then, all maturely weigh'd, pronounc'd a doom
Of sacred strength for ev'ry age to come.
By this the Doves their wealth and state possess,
No rights infring'd but license to oppress;
Such pow'r have they as factious lawyers long
To crowns ascrib'd, that kings can do no wrong.
But since his own domestic birds have tri'd
The dire effects of their destructive pride,   1240
He deems that proof a measure to the rest,
Concluding well within his kingly breast
His fowl of nature, too, unjustly were oppress'd.
He therefore makes all birds of ev'ry sect
Free of his farm, with promise to respect
Their sev'ral kinds alike and equally protect.

[1226-27] Burnet made the charge in a pamphlet defending the Test Acts.
[1243] *fowl of nature.* Wild fowl (not pure-blooded *domestic* Catholics); the Sects, overjoyed by the Declaration.

His gracious edict the same franchise yields
To all the wild increase of woods and fields,
And who in rocks aloof, and who in steeples
    builds.
To Crows the like impartial grace affords,   1250
And Choughs, and Daws, and such republic birds;
Secur'd with ample privilege to feed,
Each has his district and his bounds decreed,
Combin'd in common int'rest with his own,
But not to pass the Pigeons' Rubicon.

    "Here ends the reign of this pretended Dove,
All prophecies accomplish'd from above,
For Shiloh comes the scepter to remove.
Reduc'd from her imperial high abode,
Like Dionysius to a private rod,   1260
The passive Church that with pretended grace
Did her distinctive mark in duty place,
Now touch'd, reviles her maker to his face.

    "What after happen'd is not hard to guess;
The small beginnings had a large increase,
And arts and wealth succeed (the secret spoils of
    peace).
'Tis said the Doves repented, tho' too late,
Become the smiths of their own foolish fate;
Nor did their owner hasten their ill hour,
But sunk in credit, they decreas'd in pow'r: 1270
Like snows in warmth that mildly pass away,
Dissolving in the silence of decay.

    "The Buzzard, not content with equal place,
Invites the feather'd Nimrods of his race
To hide the thinness of their flock from sight,
And all together make a seeming, goodly flight;
But each have sep'rate int'rests of their own:

[1247-51] Extension of toleration to the most fanatic Sects.
[1256-60] Recalling the defeat of Monmouth, who had crowned himself in
    the west in 1685 and the blessing of Jacob (Genesis 49:8–10). Monmouth
    and Canterbury are Judah, replaced by Shiloh—James and Rome.
[1260] *Dionysius*. The Younger, tyrant of Syracuse (367–343 B.C.), later kept
    school at Corinth. His *rod* was the teacher's *ferula*, not the scepter of
    1258.
[1274] *Nimrods*. See I, 283n.

Two Czars are one too many for a throne.
Nor can th' usurper long abstain from food;
Already he has tasted Pigeons' blood   1280
And may be tempted to his former fare,
When this indulgent Lord shall late to Heav'n repair.
Bare benting times and moulting months may come,
When lagging late, they cannot reach their home,
Or rent in schism (for so their fate decrees)
Like the tumultuous college of the Bees,
They fight their quarrel, by themselves oppress'd;
The tyrant smiles below and waits the falling feast."

 Thus did the gentle Hind her fable end,
Nor would the Panther blame it nor commend,   1290
But with affected yawnings at the close
Seem'd to require her natural repose.
For now the streaky light began to peep,
And setting stars admonish'd both to sleep.
The Dame withdrew and, wishing to her guest
The peace of Heav'n, betook herself to rest.
Ten thousand angels on her slumbers wait
With glorious visions of her future state.

[1278] *Two Czars.* Peter the Great and his brother Ivan were crowned joint rulers of Russia in 1682.

[1279] *usurper.* William of Orange as Buzzard.

[906-1288] The fable of the Pigeons offers an alternative to that of the Swallows in predicting the religious future of England. It is similarly based on John Ogilby's "Of the Doves and Hawks," I, xx, in which the Doves (Pigeons) call in predatory birds to save them from menace, only to have their allies (the Buzzard and his group here) devour them. Dryden again alters the fable, along the lines of Chaucer's Nun's Priest's Tale, with the *plain good man* (James II), not a poor widow, able to control things with a *doom* (Declaration for Liberty of Conscience) granting toleration and peace to all, at which Anglican Pigeons melt away. The threat to Anglicans remains, however, if they invite in Buzzards. Again, there are numerous details from sacred zoography, notably the insistence that the Pigeons are not true Doves (946, 1256), with Doves being the true (Catholic) Church.

[1288] *The tyrant.* The Bear, as during the Interregnum.

[1298] *her future state.* As bride of Christ (II, 517-19).

A SONG FOR
ST. CECILIA'S DAY, 1687

1687. In this year the stewards of a musical society asked Dryden for a lyric in celebration of the feast of St. Cecilia (November 22), patroness of music. The practice of asking writers for lyrics had been followed since 1683 in imitation of continental societies. This *Song* was set by the composer commissioned, Giovanni Baptista Draghi, for a five-part chorus and string orchestra; it was later reset by Handel. Dryden had earlier written creation pieces (for example, *Threnodia Augustalis,* stanza XV; *The Hind and the Panther,* Part I, ll. 251 ff.) and pieces on the end of the world (for example, *Threnodia Augustalis,* ll. 29 ff.; Killigrew Ode, stanza X). In this *Song* he made passages on the creation and end of the world crucial. But between these passages he gave his usual treatment of human history, which here is a progress piece of musical instruments —from Jubal ("the father of all such as handle the harp and organ," Genesis 4:21) to St. Cecilia, traditionally the inventress of the organ, and then beyond her to the last trumpet. Because from antiquity music was thought to have mysterious powers to "raise and quell" the passions, Dryden also uses the progress piece of instruments to arouse a similar, or appropriate, sequence of passions. Ten years later he wrote *Alexander's Feast* for the same occasion. The sources and analogues from Plato to Milton are too numerous to note.

I

From harmony, from heav'nly harmony
   This universal frame began.

When Nature underneath a heap
    Of jarring atoms lay
And cou'd not heave her head,
The tuneful voice was heard from high,
    "Arise, ye more than dead."
Then cold, and hot, and moist, and dry
In order to their stations leap
    And MUSIC's pow'r obey.   10
From harmony, from heav'nly harmony
    This universal frame began;
    From harmony to harmony
Through all the compass of the notes it ran,
The diapason closing full in man.

II

What passion cannot MUSIC raise and quell!
    When Jubal struck the corded shell,
    His list'ning brethren stood around
    And, wond'ring, on their faces fell
To worship that celestial sound.   20
Less than a god they thought there cou'd not dwell
    Within the hollow of that shell
    That spoke so sweetly and so well.
What passion cannot MUSIC raise and quell!

III

The TRUMPET's loud clangor
    Excites us to arms
With shrill notes of anger
    And mortal alarms.
The double double double beat
    Of the thund'ring DRUM   30
Cries, "Hark, the foes come;
Charge, charge, 'tis too late to retreat!"

⁶ *voice*. Of God, Genesis 1.
¹⁴⁻¹⁵ The music runs through all the *notes* of creation, ending in the most
    harmonious creature, *man*.
¹⁶ *passion*. From *man*, 15. *quell*. See 59–63.

IV

The soft complaining FLUTE
In dying notes discovers
The woes of hopeless lovers,
Whose dirge is whisper'd by the warbling LUTE.

V

Sharp VIOLINS proclaim
Their jealous pangs and desperation,
Fury, frantic indignation,
Depth of pains and height of passion   40
For the fair, disdainful dame.

VI

But, oh! what art can teach,
What human voice can reach
The sacred ORGAN's praise?
Notes inspiring holy love,
Notes that wing their heav'nly ways
To mend the choirs above.

VII

Orpheus cou'd lead the savage race,
And trees unrooted left their place,
Sequacious of the lyre;   50
But bright CECILIA rais'd the wonder high'r;
When to her ORGAN vocal breath was giv'n,
An angel heard and straight appear'd,
Mistaking earth for Heaven.

GRAND CHORUS

As from the pow'r of sacred lays
The spheres began to move
And sung the great Creator's praise
To all the bless'd above,

---

[37] *Sharp* VIOLINS. Newly introduced violins seemed *sharp* to ears used to the more liquid viols.
[53-54] Although St. Cecilia is often painted at the organ with an angel beside her, Dryden's myth appears to have been his own.
[55-56] Cf. 1-15.

So when the last and dreadful hour
This crumbling pageant shall devour,   60
The TRUMPET *shall be heard on high,*
The dead shall live, the living die,
And MUSIC *shall untune the sky.*

[60] *pageant.* The world as stage, as illusion; cf. *Absalom and Achitophel*
751–52.

ON THE MARRIAGE OF THE FAIR AND VIRTUOUS LADY, MRS. ANASTASIA STAFFORD,

With That Truly Worthy and Pious Gent.
George Holman, Esq.

A PINDARIC ODE

1687. Anastasia Stafford (or Howard, 1636–1719) came from one of the most prominent of English Catholic families. Her father, William Howard, Viscount Stafford (b. 1614) had been executed in December 1680 after false accusations in the Popish Plot. He was the Plot's most notable victim, and his "martyr's" death is but one of the cluster of December associations in this poem. On or near Christmas (ll. 5, 20–21) the daughter married George Holman (1630–1698) of Warkworth Manor in Northamptonshire. The husband was a Catholic convert, although the son of a Nonconformist moneylender. Dryden refers to the marriage of Anastasia Howard's brother John to Mary Southcote on December 1, 1682 (ll. 53 ff.), and then to the sister's going abroad as the anti-Catholic fever passed (ll. 57–61). Apparently she there met Holman who had gone, at the outset of religious persecution, to "voluntary banishment" (ll. 75–78), in which he aided other Catholic exiles (ll. 79–89). There are numerous appropriate details: the name Anastasia means "resurrection" (l. 17), and the feast of St. Anastasia Martyr is on Christmas Day. The poem combines features of the epithalamium with those of the panegyric, especially two common "places" of praise—noble, pious ancestry (of the bride) and pious acts (of the bridegroom). The elements of marriage hymn and panegyric are brought together by stress upon divine Providence.

Although composed for a wedding in December 1687, the poem was not printed until 1813, when it was published from a manuscript discovered at Tixall Hall, the seat of a Staffordshire Catholic family close to Stafford Castle, the seat of the Howards. The manuscript has now disappeared with the rest of the Tixall collection. By 1813 it was already incomplete, the poem requiring at least one further stanza. Dryden's relations with the Stafford Howards are unknown (his wife was descended from another branch of the Howards, however). Clearly, this ode is his most Catholic work in the sense of consistent emphasis and the contemporary fame or notoriety of Viscount Stafford; and it is his most religious in the sense that, after the opening lines, it employs little imagery of other kinds.

I

When nature in our northern hemisphere
    Had shorten'd daylight and deform'd the
        year,
    When the departing sun
     Was to our adverse tropic run,
And fair St. Lucy with the borrow'd light
Of moon and stars had lengthen'd night,
What more than summer's day slipp'd in by chance
        To beautify the calendar?
What made a spring in midst of winter to advance,
And the cold seasons leap into a youthful dance   10
        To rouse the drooping year?
    Was this by miracle, or did they rise
    By the bright beams of Anastasia's eyes
        To light our frozen clime
    And, happily for us, mistook their time?
    'Twas so, and 'twas imported in her name;

---

5 *St. Lucy.* Her feast day, December 13, was popularly regarded as the shortest day of the year.
12 *they.* The *seasons* (10).

From her their glorious resurrection came,
    And she renewed their perish'd flame.
    The God of nature did the same;
His birth the depth of winter did adorn,   20
And she to marriage then, her second birth,
      was born.
    Her pious family, in every state,
Their great Redeemer well can imitate.
They have a right in Heaven, an early place;
The beauteous bride is of a martyr's race,
    And he above with joy looks down—
I see, I see him blaze with his immortal crown.
    He, on her nuptials, does his beams dispense,
    Blessing the day with better influence;
He looks from Heaven with joy and gives her joy
      from thence.   30

      II
Now, let the reasonable beast call'd man,
    Let those who never truly scan
      The effects of sacred Providence,
But measure all by the gross rules of sense,
    Let those look up and steer their sight
      By the great Stafford's light.
The God that suffer'd him to suffer here
Rewards his race and blesses them below,
Their father's innocence and truth to show,
To show he holds the blood of martyrs dear;   40
He crown'd the father with a deathless diadem,
    And all the days from him he took
He number'd out in his eternal book,
And said, "Let these be safely kept for them,
The long descendants of that hallow'd stem.
    To dry the mournful widow's tears,
    Let all those days be turn'd to years,
      And all those years be whiten'd too;
    Still some new blessing let 'em bring

---

[42] Stafford died at age sixty-six, four short of the biblical three score and ten.

To those who from My martyr spring,   50
    Still let them bloom and still bestow
Some new content upon his race below.
      Let their first revolution
     Bestow a bride upon his darling son
And crown those nuptials with a swift increase,
    Such as the empti'd ark did bless;
    Then, as the storms are more allay'd
       And waves decay'd,
    Send out the beauteous blooming maid;
And let that virgin dove bring to her house
        again,   60
An olive branch of peace in triumph o'er the
        main."
    For whom, ye heavens! have ye reserv'd this
        joy?
     Let us behold the man you chose.
    How well you can your cares employ,
     And to what arms your maid dispose,
Your maid, whom you have chang'd, but cannot
        lose,
     Chang'd as the morn into the day,
     As virgin snow that melts away,
And, by its kindly moisture, makes new flowers
       to grow.
     See then, a bridegroom worthy such a
       bride!   70
    Never was happy pair so fitly ti'd;
    Never were virtues more alli'd;
United in a most auspicious hour—
A martyr's daughter weds a confessor!
When innocence and truth became a crime,
     By voluntary banishment
    He left our sacrilegious clime
    And to a foreign country went,
Or rather there by Providence was sent;
For Providence designed him to reside   80
    Where he from his abundant stock

55–56 Genesis 9.

Might nourish God's afflicted flock
And as His steward for their wants provide.
A troop of exiles on his bounty fed;
They sought and found with him their daily
bread;
As the large troop increas'd, the larger table
spread.
The cruse ne'er empti'd, nor the store
Decreas'd the more,
For God suppli'd him still to give who gave in God's
own stead.
Thus, when the raging dearth   90
Afflicted all the Egyptian earth,
When scanty Nile no more his bounty dealt,
And Jacob, even in Canaan, famine felt,
God sent a Joseph out before,
His father and his brethren to restore;
Their sacks were fill'd with corn, with generous
wine
Their souls refresh'd, their ebbing store,
Still when they came, suppli'd with more,
And doubl'd was their corn;
Joseph himself by giving, greater grew   100
And from his loins a double tribe increas'd the
chosen crew.

79-86 Manna is an emblem of Providence; Exodus 16; Numbers 11; Psalm
78.
87-88 The feeding of Elijah, 1 Kings 18:12–16.
100-101 Genesis 49:22–26. The *chosen crew* (Israel): the Holmans.

ON MILTON

1688. As one of Milton's earliest and staunchest admirers, Dryden wrote these lines anonymously for the first illustrated edition of *Paradise Lost*. They were probably in amplification of two verses by the Italian Selvaggi, written on the young Milton's visit to Rome:

> Graecia Maeonidem, jactet sibi Roma Maronem,
> Anglia Miltonum jactat utrique parem.

In the eighteenth century the English poet William Cowper translated Dryden's lines into Latin. The "Three poets" are Homer, Virgil, and Milton.

Three poets in three distant ages born
Greece, Italy, and England did adorn.
The first in loftiness of thought surpass'd;
The next in majesty; in both the last.
The force of Nature cou'd no farther go:
To make a third she join'd the former two.

BRITANNIA REDIVIVA

A Poem on the Prince

> *Dii patrii indigetes, et Romule,*
>   *Vestaque mater,*
> *Quae Tuscum Tiberim, et Ro-*
>   *mana palatia servas,*
> *Hunc saltem everso puerum*
>   *succurrere saeclo*
> *Ne prohibete: satis iampridem*
>   *sanguine nostro*
> *Laomedonteae luimus perjuria*
>   *Trojae.*
>
>   VIRG. *Georg.* I.

1688. On Trinity Sunday—June 10—1688, a son was born to Mary, queen of James II, arousing wild Catholic hopes and wild Protestant accusations of fraud. The young Prince of Wales was still unnamed (see ll. 192 ff.) when Dryden rushed his poem into print about two weeks after the birth. The baby was subsequently named James Francis Edward Stuart, but came to be known better as the Old Pretender, the forlorn hope of a generation of Jacobites. As usual, Dryden was accurately informed, even to the point of fussing over the fact that doctors had ordered the baby "bred by hand" (ll. 208 ff.), that is, not suckled (later a wet nurse was assigned after all). The poem is also characteristic in its mingling of classical, biblical, scientific, and other imagery or allusions, some of them highly conceited (e.g., ll. 106 ff.). Dryden's transported state is uncharacteristic. He does implicitly warn James at the end of the poem (ll. 339–56), but his immoderate enthusiasm elsewhere is more that of a reprieved Catholic than of the usual clear-sighted judge of his times. In spite of a certain extravagance, the poem has been long admired, perhaps for a style that appears to be "Pindaric" although cast in heroic couplets.

The epigraph is from Virgil, *Georgics* I, 498–502:

> Ye home-born deities of mortal birth!
> Thou father Romulus, and Mother Earth,
> Goddess unmov'd! whose guardian arms extend
> O'er Tuscan Tiber's course, and Roman tow'rs defend;
> With youthful Caesar your joint pow'rs engage,
> Nor hinder him to save the sinking age.
> O let the blood already spilt atone
> For the past crimes of curst Laomedon.
>
> (Trans. Dryden.)

In the Latin epigraph Dryden stresses *puerum* (boy), which he has substituted for *iuvenum* (youth, to make clear the reference to the prince), and *perjuria* (the "past crimes") to evoke the image of infidelity to the throne in the century.

BRITANNIA REDIVIVA

A Poem on the Prince
Born on the 10th of June, 1688

Our vows are heard betimes! and Heaven takes care
To grant before we can conclude the pray'r;
Preventing angels met it half the way
And sent us back to praise who came to pray.
    Just on the day when the high mounted sun
Did farthest in his northern progress run,
He bended forward and ev'n stretch'd the sphere
Beyond the limits of the lengthen'd year
To view a brighter sun in Britain born; ⎫
That was the bus'ness of his longest morn, ⎬   10
The glorious object seen, t'was time to turn. ⎭

---

9 *sun*. Also meaning "son."
5–10 June 10, old calendar, was close to midsummer in the new.

Departing spring cou'd only stay to shed ⎫
Her bloomy beauties on the genial bed,   ⎬
But left the manly summer in her stead   ⎭
With timely fruit the longing land to cheer
And to fulfill the promise of the year.
Betwixt two seasons comes th' auspicious heir,
This age to blossom and the next to bear.

Last solemn sabbath[a] saw the Church attend,
The Paraclete in fiery pomp descend;   20
But when his wondrous octave[b] roll'd again,
He brought a royal infant in his train.
So great a blessing to so good a King
None but th' eternal Comforter cou'd bring.

Or did the mighty Trinity conspire
As once, in council, to create our sire?
It seems as if they sent the new-born guest
To wait on the procession of their feast,
And on their sacred anniverse decreed
To stamp their image on the promis'd seed.   30
Three realms united, and on one bestow'd
An emblem of their mystic union show'd;
The mighty Trine the triple empire shar'd,
As every person wou'd have one to guard.

Hail, Son of pray'rs! by holy violence
Drawn down from Heav'n; but long be banish'd
        thence,
And late to thy paternal skies retire;
To mend our crimes whole ages wou'd require,
To change th' inveterate habit of our sins
And finish what thy godlike sire begins.   40
Kind Heav'n, to make us Englishmen again,
No less can give us than a patriarch's reign.

The sacred cradle to your charge receive,
Ye seraphs, and by turns the guard relieve.

---

[a] *Whit-Sunday*. [The lettered notes are Dryden's; material added to them
in this edition is set off in brackets.]
[b] *Trinity Sunday*.

25–34 Comparing the Prince to Adam (*our sire* 26) and Christ (30).
36–37 See Horace, *Odes* I, ii, 45; the ode provided the basic design of the
poem.
42 See 61–70.

Thy father's angel and thy father join
To keep possession and secure the line,
But long defer the honours of thy fate;
Great may they be like his, like his be late,
That James this running century may view,
And give his son an auspice to the new.   50

  Our wants exact at least that moderate stay; ⎫
For see the dragon[c] winged on his way   ⎬
To watch the travail and devour the prey.[d]   ⎭
Or, if allusions may not rise so high,   ⎫
Thus, when Alcides rais'd his infant cry,   ⎬
The snakes besieg'd his young divinity;   ⎭
But vainly with their forked tongues they threat,
For opposition makes a hero great.
To needful succour all the good will run,
And Jove assert the godhead of his son.   60

  O still repining at your present state,
Grudging yourselves the benefits of fate,
Look up and read in characters of light
A blessing sent you in your own despite.
The manna falls, yet that celestial bread
Like Jews you munch and murmur while you feed.
May not your fortune be like theirs, exil'd,
Yet forty years to wander in the wild;
Or if it be, may Moses live at least
To lead you to the verge of promis'd rest.   70

  Tho' poets are not prophets to foreknow
What plants will take the blight, and what will
        grow,
By tracing Heav'n his footsteps may be found:
Behold! how awfully He walks the round!
God is abroad and wondrous in his ways,

[c] *Alluding only to the Commonwealth party here and in other places of
the poem.*
[d] *Rev. 12. v. 4.*

[48] *like his be late.* James was 51 at accession in 1685.
[49–50] James died in 1701, but with no good *auspice* to his son.
[54] As to compare the infant to Christ.
[55] *Alcides.* Hercules; see *Threnodia Augustalis* 446 ff.
[63] *characters of light.* Exodus 16:7.
[61–70] Numbers 11:4–6.
[73] *his.* Of *Heav'n* in the sense of God; Dryden's pronoun for "heaven"
is sometimes *his*, sometimes *its* (92).

The rise of empires and their fall surveys;
More (might I say) than with an usual eye
He sees his bleeding Church in ruin lie
And hears the souls of saints beneath his altar cry.
Already has he lifted high the sign[e]   80
Which crown'd the conquering arms of Constantine;
The moon[f] grows pale at that presaging sight,
And half her train of stars have lost their light.

   Behold another Sylvester[g] to bless
The sacred standard and secure success,
Large of his treasures, of a soul so great
As fills and crowds his universal seat.

   Now view at home a second Constantine[h]
(The former, too, was of the British line);
Has not his healing balm your breaches clos'd,   90
Whose exile many sought, and few oppos'd?
Or, did not Heav'n by its eternal doom
Permit those evils that this good might come?
So manifest, that ev'n the moon-ey'd Sects
See *whom* and *what* this Providence protects.
Methinks, had we within our minds no more
Than that one shipwreck on the fatal Ore,[i]
That only thought may make us think again
What wonders God reserves for such a reign.
To dream that chance his preservation wrought   100
Were to think Noah was preserv'd for nought,
Or the surviving eight were not design'd
To people earth and to restore their kind.

   When humbly on the Royal Babe we gaze,
The manly lines of a majestic face
Give awful joy; 'tis paradise to look
On the fair frontispiece of nature's book;

---

[e] *The Cross.*
[f] *The crescent, which the Turks bear for their arms.*
[g] *The Pope in the time of Constantine the Great, alluding to the present Pope.*
[h] *K. James the Second.*
[i] *The Lemmon Ore.*

---

95 *whom and what.* "James, and Mary, and the Church" (295).
102 *surviving eight.* Noah, his three sons, and their four wives.
91-103 See Prologue *To the Duchess on Her Return from Scotland,* head-note.

If the first opening page so charms the sight,
Think how th' unfolded volume will delight!
   See how the venerable infant lies   110
In early pomp; how through the mother's eyes
The father's soul with an undaunted view
Looks out and takes our homage as his due.
See on his future subjects how he smiles,
Nor meanly flatters, nor with craft beguiles,
But with an open face, as on his throne,
Assures our birthrights and assumes his own.
   Born in broad daylight that th' ungrateful rout
May find no room for a remaining doubt:
Truth, which itself is light, does darkness shun,   120
And the true eaglet safely dares the sun.
   Fain wou'd the fiends have made a dubious birth,[k]
Loth to confess the godhead cloth'd in earth.
But sicken'd after all their baffled lies,
To find an heir-apparent of the skies,
Abandon'd to despair, still may they grudge,
And owning not the Saviour, prove the judge.
   Not great Aeneas[l] stood in plainer day
When, the dark mantling mist dissolv'd away,
He to the Tyrians show'd his sudden face,   130
Shining with all his goddess mother's grace,
For she herself had made his count'nance bright,
Breath'd honour on his eyes and her own purple
   light.
   If our victorious Edward,[m] as they say,
Gave Wales a prince on that propitious day,
Why may not years revolving with his fate
Produce his like but with a longer date?
One who may carry to a distant shore
The terror that his fam'd forefather bore.
But why shou'd James or his young hero stay   140

---

[k] *Alluding to the temptations in the wilderness.*
[l] *Virg. Aeneid. I.* [Virgil, *Aeneid* I, 588–93.]
[m] *Edw. the Black Prince, born on Trinity-Sunday.*

118-19 Numerous people witnessed the birth.
121 *eaglet*. The royal bird, associated with the royal sun.
122-27 Matthew 4; Milton, *Paradise Regained*.
131 The *goddess mother* is Venus, complimenting Queen Mary's beauty.

For slight presages of a name or day?
We need no Edward's fortune to adorn
That happy moment when our Prince was born;
Our Prince adorns his day, and ages hence
Shall wish his birthday for some future prince.

    Great Michael,[n] prince of all th' ethereal hosts,
And whate'er inborn saints our Britain boasts,
And thou, th' adopted patron of our isle,[o]
With cheerful aspects on this infant smile:
The pledge of Heav'n, which dropping from above,   150
Secures our bliss and reconciles his love.

    Enough of ills our dire rebellion wrought
When, to the dregs, we drank the bitter draught;
Then airy atoms did in plagues conspire,
Nor did th' avenging angel yet retire,
But purg'd our still increasing crimes with fire.
Then perjur'd plots, the still impending Test,
And worse—but charity conceals the rest:
Here stop the current of the sanguine flood;
Require not, gracious God, thy martyrs' blood,   160
But let their dying pangs, their living toil,
Spread a rich harvest through their native soil,
A harvest ripening for another reign,
Of which this royal babe may reap the grain.

    Enough of early saints one womb has giv'n,
Enough increas'd the family of Heav'n;
Let them for his, and our, atonement go,
And reigning blest above leave him to rule below.

    Enough already has the year foreslow'd
His wonted course, the seas have overflow'd,   170
The meads were floated with a weeping spring,
And frighten'd birds in woods forgot to sing;
The strong-limb'd steed beneath his harness faints,
And the same shiv'ring sweat his lord attaints.
When will the minister of wrath give o'er?

[n] *The motto of the poem explain'd.*
[o] *St. George.*

152-58 One of the poem's confessions of guilt; cf. Horace, *Odes* I, ii, 25–44.
160-62 Developing the adage, "Martyrs' blood is the Church's seed."
165 *one womb.* Queen Mary's previous five children had died in infancy.

Behold him at Araunah's[p] threshing-floor:
He stops, and seems to sheath his flaming brand,
Pleas'd with burnt incense from our David's hand.
David has bought the Jebusites' abode
And rais'd an altar to the living God. 180
    Heav'n, to reward him, make his joys sincere; ⎫
No future ills nor accidents appear   ⎬
To sully and pollute the sacred infant's year. ⎭
Five months to discord and debate were giv'n;
He sanctifies the yet remaining sev'n.
Sabbath of months! henceforth in him be blest,
And prelude to the realm's perpetual rest!
    Let his baptismal drops for us atone,
Lustrations for offences not his own.[q]
Let conscience, which is int'rest ill disguis'd, 190
In the same font be cleans'd and all the land
      baptiz'd.
    Unnam'd as yet,[r] at least unknown to fame;
Is there a strife in Heav'n about his name?
Where every famous predecessor vies
And makes a faction for it in the skies?
Or must it be reserv'd to thought alone?
Such was the sacred Tetragrammaton.[s]
Things worthy silence must not be reveal'd;
Thus the true name of Rome[t] was kept conceal'd
To shun the spells and sorceries of those 200
Who durst her infant majesty oppose.
But when his tender strength in time shall rise
To dare ill tongues and fascinating eyes,
This isle, which hides the little thund'rer's fame,

---

[p] *Alluding to the passage in the I. Book of Kings, Ch. 24. v. 20th.* [1 Kings is a misprint for 2 Kings, here alone in the poem presuming the old four books, the first two of which are now called by Protestants 1 Samuel and 2 Samuel.]

[q] *Original Sin.*

[r] *The Prince christen'd but not nam'd.*

[s] *Jehovah, or the name of God, unlawful to be pronounc'd by the Jews.*

[t] *Some authors say that the true name of Rome was kept a secret: Ne hostes incantamentis Deos elicerent.* [The Latin quotation ("Lest enemies should entice away the gods by incantations") is unidentified.]

---

203 *fascinating.* Casting a spell; so also *ill*, Dryden's rendering of *fascinat* in Virgil, *Eclogues* III, 103.

Shall be too narrow to contain his name;
Th' artillery of Heav'n shall make him known;
Crete[u] cou'd not hold the god when Jove was
        grown.
    As Jove's increase,[x] who from his brain was born,
Whom arms and arts did equally adorn,
Free of the breast was bred, whose milky taste   210
Minerva's name to Venus had debas'd,
So this imperial babe rejects the food
That mixes monarchs with Plebeian blood,
Food that his inborn courage might control,
Extinguish all the father in his soul,
And for his Estian race and Saxon strain
Might reproduce some second Richard's reign.
Mildness he shares from both his parents' blood,
But kings too tame are despicably good:
Be this the mixture of this regal child,   220
By nature manly but by virtue mild.
    Thus far the furious transport of the news
Had to prophetic madness fir'd the Muse,
Madness ungovernable, uninspir'd,
Swift to foretell whatever she desir'd;
Was it for me the dark abyss to tread
And read the book which angels cannot read?
How was I punish'd when the sudden blast[y]
The face of Heav'n and our young sun o'ercast!
Fame, the swift ill, increasing as she roll'd,   230
Disease, despair, and death, at three reprises told,
At three insulting strides she stalk'd the town,
And, like contagion, struck the loyal down.
Down fell the winnow'd wheat, but mounted high
The whirlwind bore the chaff and hid the sky.

---

[u] *Candy, where Jupiter was born and bred secretly.*
[x] *Pallas, or Minerva, said by the poets, to have been bred up by hand.* [To
    be bred by hand means, as the following lines show, to be fed by hand
    rather than suckled, especially by a wet nurse; Dryden fusses that an-
    other king weak as Richard II (217) may be reared.]
[y] *The sudden false report of the Prince's death.*

---

[216] *Estian race.* Queen Mary was of Este (and Modena), so her son could
    claim the heroic ancestry of Rinaldo's shield in Tasso, *Gerusalemme
    Liberata* XVII.

Here black rebellion shooting from below
(As earth's gigantic brood by moments grow),[z]
And here the sons of God are petrifi'd with woe:
An apoplex of grief! so low were driv'n
The saints as hardly to defend their Heav'n.   240

    As when pent vapours run their hollow round,
Earthquakes, which are convulsions of the ground,
Break bellowing forth and no confinement brook
Till the third settles what the former shook:
Such heavings had our souls, till slow and late
Our life with his return'd and faith prevail'd on fate.
By prayers the mighty blessing was implor'd,
To pray'rs was granted and by pray'rs restor'd.

    So e'er the Shunamite a son conceiv'd,[a]
The prophet promis'd, and the wife believ'd;   250
A son was sent, the son so much desir'd,
But soon upon the mother's knees expir'd.
The troubled seer approach'd the mournful door,
Ran, pray'd, and sent his past'ral staff before,
Then stretch'd his limbs upon the child and mourn'd,
Till warmth and breath and a new soul return'd.

    Thus mercy stretches out her hand and saves
Desponding Peter sinking in the waves.

    As when a sudden storm of hail and rain
Beats to the ground the yet unbearded grain,   260
Think not the hopes of harvest are destroy'd
On the flat field and on the naked void;
The light, unloaded stem, from tempest freed,
Will raise the youthful honours of his head,
And soon restor'd by native vigour, bear
The timely product of the bounteous year.

    Nor yet conclude all fiery trials past,
For Heav'n will exercise us to the last,

---

[z] *Those giants are feign'd to have grown 15 ells every day.*
[a] *In the second Book of Kings, Chap. 4th.*

---

[237] Dryden's memory exaggerated their growth (*Odyssey* XI, 305–20).
[241–44] Recalling an earthquake leveling Lima, Peru, in 1687, reported in England in May 1688.
[228–48] The Prince fell ill the night of June 11–12.
[249–56] The *prophet* or *seer:* Elisha, 2 Kings 4:8–37.
[264] *honours.* A Virgilianism for hair. See *Aeneid* I, 591; *MacFlecknoe* 134.

Sometimes will check us in our full career,
With doubtful blessings and with mingled fear,   270
That, still depending on his daily grace,
His every mercy for an alms may pass,
With sparing hands will diet us to good,
Preventing surfeits of our pamper'd blood.
So feeds the mother bird her craving young
With little morsels and delays 'em long.
   True, this last blessing was a royal feast,
But where's the wedding garment on the guest?
Our manners, as religion were a dream,
Are such as teach the nations to blaspheme.   280
In lusts we wallow, and with pride we swell,
And injuries with injuries repell;
Prompt to revenge, not daring to forgive,
Our lives unteach the doctrine we believe;
Thus Israel sinn'd, impenitently hard
And vainly thought the present ark[b] their guard,
But when the haughty Philistims appear,
They fled abandon'd to their foes and fear;
Their God was absent, though his ark was there.
Ah! lest our crimes shou'd snatch this pledge away   290
And make our joys the blessing of a day!
For we have sinn'd him hence, and that he lives,
God to His promise, not our practice, gives.
Our crimes wou'd soon weigh down the guilty scale,
But James, and Mary, and the Church prevail.
Nor Amaleck[c] can rout the chosen bands,
While Hur and Aaron hold up Moses' hands.
   By living well let us secure his days,
Mod'rate in hopes, and humble in our ways.
No force the freeborn spirit can constrain,   300
But charity and great examples gain.
Forgiveness is our thanks for such a day;
'Tis godlike, God in His own coin to pay.

[b] *Sam. 4th. v. 10th.* [Should be 2 Samuel 4:10.]
[c] *Exod. 17. v. 8th.*

277–78 Matthew 22:1–14; *this last blessing,* the Prince's recovery.
297 Exodus 17:11–12.

But you, propitious Queen, translated here ⎞
From your mild heav'n to rule our rugged ⎟
    sphere, ⎬
Beyond the sunny walks and circling year; ⎠
You, who your native climate have bereft
Of all the virtues and the vices left;
Whom piety and beauty make their boast,
Though beautiful is well in pious lost,   310
So lost as starlight is dissolv'd away
And melts into the brightness of the day,
Or gold about the regal diadem
Lost to improve the lustre of the gem:
What can we add to your triumphant day?
Let the great gift the beauteous giver pay.
For shou'd our thanks awake the rising sun ⎞
And lengthen as his latest shadows run, ⎟
That, tho' the longest day, wou'd soon, too soon ⎬
    be done. ⎠
Let angels' voices with their harps conspire,   320
But keep th' auspicious infant from the choir;
Late let him sing above, and let us know
No sweeter music than his cries below.
    Nor can I wish to you, great Monarch, more
Than such an annual income to your store;
The day which gave this unit did not shine
For a less omen than to fill the trine.
After a Prince an Admiral beget;
The *Royal Sov'reign* wants an anchor yet.
Our isle has younger titles still in store, ⎞   330
And when th' exhausted land can yield no more, ⎬
Your line can force them from a foreign shore. ⎠
    The name of great your martial mind will suit,
But justice is your darling attribute;
Of all the Greeks, 'twas but one hero's[d] due,
And in him Plutarch prophesi'd of you.
A prince's favours but on few can fall,

[d] *Aristides; see his Life in Plutarch.*

---

[306] From *Aeneid* VI, 797. Cf. *Annus Mirabilis* 639; *Threnodia Augustalis* 353.

But justice is a virtue shar'd by all.
    Some kings the name of conqu'rers have assum'd;
Some to be great, some to be gods presum'd;   340
But boundless pow'r and arbitrary lust
Made tyrants still abhor the name of just;
They shunn'd the praise this godlike virtue gives
And fear'd a title that reproach'd their lives.
    The pow'r from which all kings derive their state,
Whom they pretend, at least, to imitate,
Is equal both to punish and reward;
For few wou'd love their God unless they fear'd.
    Resistless force and immortality
Make but a lame, imperfect deity;   350
Tempests have force unbounded to destroy,
And deathless being ev'n the damn'd enjoy,
And yet Heav'n's attributes, both last and first,
One without life, and one with life accurst;
But justice is Heav'n's self, so strictly He,
That cou'd it fail, the Godhead cou'd not be.
This virtue is your own, but life and state
Are one to fortune subject, one to fate;
Equal to all, you justly frown or smile,
Nor hopes nor fears your steady hand beguile;   } 360
Yourself our balance hold, the world's, our isle. ⎦

349-50 Here and in 339-56 Dryden urges James to justice, not militancy.
359-61 Horace, *Odes* I, ii, 49-52.

Epilogue

AMPHITRYON

1690. Like Plautus and Molière before him, Dryden found a rich comic vein in the subsidiary characters that had entered the story of Jove's visit to Alcmena in the guise of her husband Amphitryon, a union from which Hercules (one of the "godlings" of the Epilogue) was born. Dryden added to the play the story of Mercury's efforts to woo Alcmena's pert and mercenary woman, Phaedra, played by Mrs. Mountfort in 1690. This actress was famous for the variety of her comic moods, as is well revealed by this Epilogue with its incomparable first line.

Spoken by Phaedra. *Mrs. Mountfort.*
I'm thinking (and it almost makes me mad)
How sweet a time those heathen ladies had.
Idolatry was ev'n their gods' own trade;
They worshipp'd the fine creatures they had made.
Cupid was chief of all the deities,
And love was all the fashion in the skies.
When the sweet nymph held up the lily hand,
Jove was her humble servant at command.
The treasury of heav'n was ne'er so bare
But still there was a pension for the fair.   10
In all his reign, adult'ry was no sin,
For Jove the good example did begin.
Mark, too, when he usurp'd the husband's name,
How civilly he sav'd the lady's fame.

The secret joys of love he wisely hid;
But you, sirs, boast of more, than e'er you did.
You tease your cuckolds, to their face torment 'em,
But Jove gave his new honours to content 'em.
And, in the kind remembrance of the fair,
On each exalted son bestow'd a star.   20
For those good deeds, as by the date appears,
His godship flourish'd full two thousand years.
At last, when he and all his priests grew old, ⎫
The ladies grew in their devotion cold,   ⎬
And that false worship wou'd no longer hold,   ⎭
Severity of life did next begin
(And always does, when we no more can sin);
That doctrine, too, so hard in practice lies,
That the next age may see another rise.
Then pagan gods may once again succeed,   ⎫   30
And Jove or Mars be ready at our need   ⎬
To get young godlings and so mend our breed. ⎭

Songs

FROM

KING ARTHUR

1691 (revised from 1684). Styled "A Dramatick Opera" on its title page, *King Arthur* combines ordinary dialogue, numerous masquelike or operatic effects, ten songs set to music "with so great a genius" by Henry Purcell, and dances arranged by Joseph Priest. It proved to be an immediate success upon performance in May or June 1691. Dryden complains in his Dedication of the opera, however, that, having written it seven years earlier for Charles II, he had "to alter the first design" (because of the changed situation under William and Mary) and "take away so many beauties" that little was left of his original conception. He also regretted that writing for music obliged him "to cramp my verses" and make them rugged to the reader. Because the 1684 version has not survived, we cannot judge what violence has been done to his original conception, but the songs selected here show only a few signs of "cramp." Song II celebrates victory by the Britons over the Saxons at the end of Act I. Song IV (from Act II) is a realistic British pastoral sung by "a crew of Kentish lads and lasses." Song VI (Act III) follows the magical acquisition of sight by the blind Emmeline, beloved by King Arthur. Song VIII (Act IV, scene i) shows the temptation of Arthur by two sirens —owing more to Tasso's temptresses in *Gerusalemme Liberata*, XV, than to classical legend. Song X (Act V) is in reality a series of related songs, almost a masque, including the "pudding and dumplin'" song that was the hit of the opera. Although founded, Dryden said, on "that Fairy kind of writing," the songs, and particularly the tenth, possess greater English heartiness.

Song II

A battle supposed to be given behind the scenes, with drums, trumpets, and military shouts and excursions; after which the Britons, expressing their joy for the victory, sing this Song of Triumph.

"Come if you dare," our trumpets sound;
"Come if you dare," the foes rebound:
"We come, we come, we come, we come,"
Says the double, double, double beat of the
    thund'ring drum.

  Now they charge on amain,
  Now they rally again;
The gods from above the mad labour behold
And pity mankind that will perish for gold.

The fainting Saxons quit their ground;
Their trumpets languish in the sound;   10
"They fly, they fly, they fly, they fly;
Victoria! Victoria!" the bold Britons cry.

  Now the victory's won,
  To the plunder we run;
We return to our lasses like fortunate traders,
Triumphant with spoils of the vanquish'd invaders.

Song IV

Enter Shepherds and Shepherdesses.

1 Shepherd ⎱ How blest are shepherds, how happy
    sings. ⎰   their lasses,
        While drums and trumpets are
          sounding alarms!

Over our lowly sheds all the storm
    passes;
And when we die, 'tis in each other's
    arms.
All the day on our herds and flocks
    employing,
All the night on our flutes and in
    enjoying.
Chor.   All the day, etc.

2

Bright nymphs of Britain, with graces
    attended,
Let not your days without pleasure
    expire;
Honour's but empty, and when youth
    is ended,   10
All men will praise you but none will
    desire.
Let not youth fly away without
    contenting;
Age will come time enough for your
    repenting.
Chor.   Let not youth, etc.
*Here the Men offer their flutes to the Women,
    which they refuse.*

2 Shepherdess.   Shepherd, shepherd, leave decoying;
        Pipes are sweet a summer's day,
    But a little after toying
        Women have the shot to pay.

Here are marriage-vows for signing;
    Set their marks that cannot
        write;   20
After that, without repining,
    Play and welcome, day and
        night.
*Here the Women give the Men contracts,
    which they accept.*

Chor. }
of all. } Come, shepherds, lead up a lively
      measure;
The cares of wedlock are cares of
      pleasure;
But whether marriage bring joy or
      sorrow,
Make sure of this day and hang
      tomorrow.

Song VI

Airy Spirits appear in the shapes of Men and Women.

Man sings.   O sight, the mother of desires,
     What charming objects dost thou
        yield!
      'Tis sweet when tedious night
        expires
    To see the rosy morning gild
      The mountain-tops and paint
        the field!
    But when Clorinda comes in sight,
    She makes the summer's day more
        bright,
    And when she goes away, 'tis
        night.
Chor.   When fair Clorinda comes in sight,
      etc.

Woman sings.   'Tis sweet the blushing morn to
      view,   10
    And plains adorn'd with pearly
      dew,
    But such cheap delights to see
      Heaven and nature
      Give each creature;
    They have eyes, as well as we.

> This is the joy all joys above,
> To see, to see
> That only she,
> That only she we love!

Chor. This is the joy all joys above, etc. 20

Man sings. And if we may discover
What charms both nymph and
lover,
'Tis when the fair at mercy lies,
With kind and amorous anguish,
To sigh, to look, to languish,
On each other's eyes!

Chor. of all ⎱ And if we may discover, etc.
Men and Women. ⎰

Song VIII

As he is going to the bridge, two sirens arise from the water; they show themselves to the waist, and sing.

1 Siren. O pass not on, but stay
And waste the joyous day
With us in gentle play;
Unbend to love, unbend thee;
O lay thy sword aside
And other arms provide;
For other wars attend thee
And sweeter to be tri'd.

Chor. For other wars, etc.

Both sing. Two daughters of this aged stream are we, 10
And both our sea-green locks have comb'd
for thee;
Come bathe with us an hour or two;
Come naked in, for we are so.
What danger from a naked foe?
Come bathe with us, come bathe and
share

What pleasures in the floods appear;
We'll beat the waters till they bound,
And circle round, around, around,
And circle round, around.

Song X

Merlin *waves his wand; the scene changes and discovers the British Ocean in a storm;* Aeolus *in a cloud
above;* Four Winds *hanging, etc.*

Aeolus   Ye blust'ring brethren of the skies,
singing.   Whose breath has ruffl'd all the wat'ry
           plain,
     Retire, and let Britannia rise
In triumph o'er the main.
   Serene and calm and void of fear,
   The Queen of Islands must appear:
   Serene and calm, as when the spring
   The new-created world began,
   And birds on boughs did softly sing
   Their peaceful homage paid to man,   10
   While Eurus did his blasts forbear,
   In favour of the tender year.
Retreat, rude winds, retreat
To hollow rocks, your stormy seat;
There swell your lungs and vainly, vainly
      threat.

Aeolus *ascends, and the* Four Winds *fly off. The scene
opens and discovers a calm sea, to the end of the
house. An Island arises to a soft tune;* Britannia *seated
in the island, with Fishermen at her feet, etc. The tune
changes; the Fishermen come ashore and dance
awhile; after which* Pan *and a* Nereid *come on the
stage and sing.*

Pan *and* Nereid *sing.*
Round thy coasts, fair nymph of Britain,
  For thy guard our waters flow;

Proteus all his herd admitting
　On thy greens to graze below.
Foreign lands thy fishes tasting,　　　　20
Learn from thee luxurious fasting.

　　　Song of Three Parts.
For folded flocks on fruitful plains,
The shepherds' and the farmers' gains,
　Fair Britain all the world outvies,
And Pan as in Arcadia reigns,　　．
　Where pleasure mix'd with profit lies.

　2
Though Jason's office was fam'd of old,
The British wool is growing gold;
　No mines can more of wealth supply:
It keeps the peasant from the cold　　　30
　And takes for kings the Tyrian dye.

The last stanza sung over again betwixt Pan *and the*
Nereid. *After which the former dance is varied, and*
goes on.

　Enter Comus *with three Peasants, who sing the*
　　　following Song in parts.

Com.　Your hay it is mow'd, and your corn is
　　　　reap'd;
　　Your barns will be full and your hovels
　　　　　heap'd;
　　　Come, my boys, come;
　　　Come, my boys, come
　　And merrily roar out Harvest Home;
　　　Harvest Home,
　　　Harvest Home,
　　And merrily roar out Harvest Home.
Chorus.　Come, my boys, come, etc.　　　40
1 Man.　We ha' cheated the parson, we'll cheat him
　　　　again,
　　For why shou'd a blockhead ha' one in ten?
　　　One in ten,
　　　One in ten,

    For why shou'd a blockhead ha' one in ten?
Chorus.   One in ten,
     One in ten,
    For why shou'd a blockhead ha' one in ten?
2 [*Man*]. For prating so long like a book-learn'd sot,
    Till pudding and dumplin' burn to pot;   50
     Burn to pot,
     Burn to pot,
    Till pudding and dumplin' burn to pot.
Chorus.   Burn to pot, etc.
3 [*Man*]. We'll toss off our ale till we canno' stand,
    And hoigh for the honour of old England;
     Old England,
     Old England,
    And hoigh for the honour of old England.
Chorus.   Old England, etc.   60
   The dance vari'd into a round country-dance.

      Enter Venus.
Venus. Fairest isle, all isles excelling,
    Seat of pleasures and of loves,
   Venus here will choose her dwelling
    And forsake her Cyprian groves.

    2
  Cupid from his fav'rite nation
    Care and envy will remove,
  Jealousy, that poisons passion,
    And despair that dies for love.

    3
  Gentle murmurs, sweet complaining,
    Sighs that blow the fire of love,   70
  Soft repulses, kind disdaining,
    Shall be all the pains you prove.

    4
  Every swain shall pay his duty,,
    Grateful every nymph shall prove,
  And as these excel in beauty,
    Those shall be renown'd for love.

ELEONORA

A Panegyrical Poem

DEDICATED TO THE MEMORY OF
THE LATE COUNTESS OF ABINGDON

> —*Superas evadere ad auras,*
> *Hoc opus, hic labor est. Pauci,*
> *quos aequus amavit*
> *Juppiter, aut ardens evexit ad*
> *aethera virtus;*
> *Diis geniti potuere.*
>
> VIRGIL *Aeneid. l. 6.*

1692. Eleonora, daughter of Sir Henry Lee of Ditchley in Oxfordshire, was the wife of James Bertie, the first Earl of Abingdon. She had died on May 31, 1691, and, as Dryden says, "some months" before publication in March 1692, Abingdon had commissioned the poem. Dryden's elegies are, in fact, usually panegyrics given to speaking of triumph rather than loss. As his epistle dedicatory makes clear, he had never met either the Earl or the Countess of Abingdon, although he may have known her sister, Mrs. Wharton, one of the bluestockings of the day. He also clearly derived details on Eleonora from the poet Robert Gould, who was patronized by Abingdon. Evidently his lack of personal acquaintance led him to cast his mind back to Donne, who had faced a similar problem when writing his *Anniversaries* on the death of the fourteen-year-old Elizabeth Dury, likewise unmet by him. Dryden returned, with some variation, to his early Metaphysical style and to Donne himself, whose poems he frequently echoes.

It appears that Dryden was attempting to amend the contradictions in Donne's *Anniversaries* that occurred between
alternating passages of eulogy and despairing meditations,
and it is true that *Eleonora* is under far better control. Dryden says himself that his original title was "The Pattern,"
and the finished poem moves from Eleonora as pattern *of*
the divine and good to a pattern *for* lesser mortals. But his
poem suffers less from the "beautiful faults" of the imagery
(that sometimes approaches blasphemy, as does Donne's,
but that, again like Donne's, often proves highly effective)
than from the flawed beauty of a poem in which his lack of
acquaintance with the dead woman prevents full integrity
of feeling (except for that remarkable outburst at the end).
Like Donne, Dryden did not solve the problem of tone.
Although too numerous for full annotation, the main
sources of the imagery are Donne, the Bible, Virgil, and
science—particularly Fontenelle's *Plurality of Worlds*.

The epigraph is from Virgil, *Aeneid* VI, 128–31, concerning the difficulty of reascending from the underworld:

> . . . to return and view the cheerful skies,
> In this the task and mighty labour lies.
> To few great Jupiter imparts this grace,
> And those of shining worth and heav'nly race.
>   (Trans. Dryden.)

To the Right Honourable the Earl of Abingdon etc.

My Lord,

The commands with which you honour'd me some months
ago are now perform'd. They had been sooner, but betwixt
ill health,[1] some business, and many troubles, I was forc'd
to defer them till this time. Ovid, going to his banishment
and writing from on shipboard to his friends, excus'd the
faults of his poetry by his misfortunes and told them that
good verses never flow but from a serene and compos'd
spirit.[2] Wit, which is a kind of Mercury with wings fasten'd

---

[1] *ill health.* Dryden had needed Thomas Southerne's help to finish his
tragedy, *Cleomenes* (1692).
[2] Ovid, *Tristia* I, i.

to his head and heels, can fly but slowly in a damp air. I therefore chose rather to obey you late than ill, if at least I am capable of writing anything at any time which is worthy your perusal and your patronage. I cannot say that I have escap'd from a shipwreck, but have only gain'd a rock by hard swimming, where I may pant awhile and gather breath; for the doctors give me a sad assurance that my disease never took its leave of any man but with a purpose to return. However, my Lord, I have laid hold on the interval, and manag'd the small stock which age has left me to the best advantage in performing this inconsiderable service to my Lady's memory.

We who are priests of Apollo have not the inspiration when we please but must wait till the god comes rushing on us and invades us with a fury which we are not able to resist, which gives us double strength while the fit continues and leaves us languishing and spent at its departure. Let me not seem to boast, my Lord, for I have really felt it on this occasion and prophesi'd beyond my natural power. Let me add, and hope to be believ'd, that the excellency of the subject contributed much to the happiness of the execution, and that the weight of thirty years was taken off me while I was writing. I swam with the tide, and the water under me was buoyant. The reader will easily observe that I was transported by the multitude and variety of my similitudes, which are generally the product of a luxuriant fancy and the wantonness of wit. Had I call'd in my judgment to my assistance, I had certainly retrench'd many of them. But I defend them not; let them pass for beautiful faults amongst the better sort of critics: for the whole poem, though written in that which they call heroic verse, is of the Pindaric nature, as well in the thought as the expression, and as such requires the same grains of allowance for it. It was intended, as your Lordship sees in the title, not for an elegy, but a panegyric, a kind of apotheosis, indeed, if a heathen word may be applied to a Christian use. And on all occasions of praise, if we take the ancients for our patterns, we are bound by prescription to employ the magnificence of words and the force of figures to adorn the sublimity of thoughts. Isocrates amongst the

Grecian orators, and Cicero and the younger Pliny amongst
the Romans, have left us their precedents for our security;
for I think I need not mention the inimitable Pindar, who
stretches on these pinions out of sight and is carried upward, as it were, into another world.

This at least, my Lord, I may justly plead, that if I have
not perform'd so well as I think I have, yet I have us'd my
best endeavours to excel myself. One disadvantage I have
had, which is never to have known or seen my Lady; and
to draw the lineaments of her mind, from the description
which I have receiv'd from others, is for a painter to set
himself at work without the living original before him.
Which, the more beautiful it is, will be so much the more
difficult for him to conceive, when he has only a relation
given him of such and such features by an acquaintance or
a friend, without the nice touches which give the best resemblance and make the graces of the picture. Every artist
is apt enough to flatter himself (and I amongst the rest)
that their own ocular observations would have discover'd
more perfections, at least others than have been deliver'd
to them, though I have receiv'd mine from the best hands,
that is, from persons who neither want a just understanding of my Lady's worth, nor a due veneration for her
memory.

Doctor Donne, the greatest wit though not the best poet
of our nation,[3] acknowledges that he had never seen Mrs.
Drury, whom he has made immortal in his admirable *Anniversaries;* I have had the same fortune, though I have not
succeeded to the same genius. However, I have follow'd his
footsteps in the design of his panegyric, which was to raise
an emulation in the living to copy out the example of the
dead. And therefore it was that I once intended to have
call'd this poem, *The Pattern;* and though on a second consideration I chang'd the title into the name of that illustrious person, yet the design continues, and Eleonora is still
the pattern of charity, devotion, and humility, of the best
wife, the best mother, and the best of friends.

And now, my Lord, though I have endeavour'd to answer your commands, yet I cou'd not answer it to the world

[3] Distinguishing between force of mind (*wit*) and command of art (*poet*).

nor to my conscience, if I gave not your Lordship my testimony of being the best husband now living; I say my testimony only, for the praise of it, is given you by yourself. They who despise the rules of virtue, both in their practice and their morals, will think this a very trivial commendation. But I think it the peculiar happiness of the Countess of Abingdon to have been so truly lov'd by you while she was living, and so gratefully honour'd after she was dead. Few there are who have either had or cou'd have such a loss, and yet fewer who carried their love and constancy beyond the grave. The exteriors of mourning, a decent funeral, and black habits are the usual stints of common husbands; and perhaps their wives deserve no better than to be mourn'd with hypocrisy and forgot with ease. But you have distinguish'd yourself from ordinary lovers by a real and lasting grief for the deceas'd. And by endeavouring to raise for her the most durable monument, which is that of verse. And so it wou'd have prov'd if the workman had been equal to the work and your choice of the artificer as happy as your design. Yet as Phidias, when he had made the statue of Minerva, cou'd not forbear to engrave his own name as author of the piece,[4] so give me leave to hope that by subscribing mine to this poem, I may live by the goddess and transmit my name to posterity by the memory of hers. 'Tis no flattery to assure your Lordship that she is remember'd in the present age by all who have had the honour of her conversation and acquaintance. And that I have never been in any company since the news of her death was first brought me, where they have not extoll'd her virtues and even spoken the same things of her in prose which I have done in verse.

I therefore think myself oblig'd to thank your Lordship for the commission which you have given me; how I have acquitted myself of it must be left to the opinion of the world, in spite of any protestation which I can enter against the present age as incompetent or corrupt judges. For my comfort they are but Englishmen, and as such, if they think ill of me today, they are inconstant enough to think well of me tomorrow. And, after all, I have not much

4 Plutarch, Life of Pericles.

to thank my fortune that I was born amongst them. The good of both sexes are so few in England that they stand like exceptions against general rules; and though one of them has deserv'd a greater commendation than I cou'd give her, they have taken care that I shou'd not tire my pen with frequent exercise on the like subjects, that praises, like taxes,[5] shou'd be appropriated and left almost as individual as the person. They say my talent is satire; if it be so, 'tis a fruitful age, and there is an extraordinary crop to gather. But a single hand is insufficient for such a harvest; they have sown the dragon's teeth themselves, and 'tis but just they shou'd reap each other in lampoons. You, my Lord, who have the character of honour, though 'tis not my happiness to know you, may stand aside with the small remainders of the English nobility, truly such and, unhurt yourselves, behold the mad combat.[6] If I have pleas'd you and some few others, I have obtain'd my end. You see, I have disabled myself, like an elected Speaker[7] of the House; yet like him I have undertaken the charge and find the burden sufficiently recompens'd by the honour. Be pleas'd to accept of these my unworthy labours, this paper monument; and let her pious memory, which I am sure is sacred to you, not only plead the pardon of my many faults, but gain me your protection, which is ambitiously sought by,

My Lord,
Your Lordship's
Most obedient servant,
John Dryden.

---

[5] *taxes.* Highly unpopular levies for the wars of William III.
[6] Cf. poem, 359–70.
[7] *Speaker.* Who has no right to debate.

ELEONORA

A Panegyrical Poem Dedicated to the Memory of the Late Countess of Abingdon

As when some great and gracious monarch dies,   *The*
Soft whispers, first, and mournful murmurs rise   *Introduction.*
Among the sad attendants; then the sound
Soon gathers voice and spreads the news around
Through town and country, till the dreadful blast
Is blown to distant colonies at last,
Who then, perhaps, were off'ring vows in vain
For his long life and for his happy reign:
So slowly, by degrees, unwilling fame
Did matchless Eleonora's fate proclaim,   10
Till public as the loss the news became.
   The nation felt it in th' extremest parts
With eyes o'erflowing and with bleeding hearts;   *Of her*
But most the poor, whom daily she suppli'd,   *charity.*
Beginning to be such but when she di'd.
For while she liv'd they slept in peace by night,
Secure of bread as of returning light,
And with such firm dependence on the day
That need grew pamper'd and forgot to pray:
So sure the dole, so ready at their call,   20
They stood prepar'd to see the manna fall.
   Such multitudes she fed, she cloth'd, she nurs'd,
That she herself might fear her wanting first.
Of her five talents, other five she made;
Heav'n that had largely giv'n was largely paid;
And in few lives, in wondrous few, we find
A fortune better fitted to the mind.
Nor did her alms from ostentation fall
Or proud desire of praise; the soul gave all,
Unbrib'd it gave, or if a bribe appear,   30

1-8 Cf. *Threnodia Augustalis* 19 ff. and 119 ff.
19-21 Numbers 11.
24-25 Matthew 25:14-21.

No less than Heav'n, to heap huge treasures there.
    Want pass'd for merit at her open door;
Heav'n saw he safely might increase his poor
And trust their sustenance with her so well
As not to be at charge of miracle.
None cou'd be needy whom she saw or knew;
All, in the compass of her sphere, she drew;
He who cou'd touch her garment was as sure
As the first Christians of th' Apostles' cure.
The distant heard by fame her pious deeds   40
And laid her up for their extremest needs,
A future cordial for a fainting mind;
For what was ne'er refus'd all hop'd to find,
Each in his turn: the rich might freely come
As to a friend; but to the poor, 'twas home.
As to some holy house th' afflicted came,   ⎫
The hunger-starv'd, the naked, and the lame; ⎬
Want and diseases fled before her name.   ⎭
For zeal like hers, her servants were too slow; ⎫
She was the first, where need requir'd, to go; ⎬   50
Herself the foundress and attendant too.   ⎭
    Sure she had guests sometimes to entertain,
Guests in disguise, of her great Master's train:
Her Lord himself might come, for aught we know,
Since in a servant's form he liv'd below;
Beneath her roof He might be pleas'd to stay,
Or some benighted angel in his way
Might ease his wings, and seeing Heav'n appear
In its best work of mercy, think it there,
Where all the deeds of charity and love   60
Were in as constant method as above;
All carri'd on, all of a piece with theirs,   ⎫
As free her alms, as diligent her cares,   ⎬
As loud her praises and as warm her pray'rs. ⎭
    Yet was she not profuse, but fear'd to waste   *Of her prudent*
And wisely manag'd that the stock might last,   *management.*
That all might be suppli'd and she not grieve,

30-31 1 Timothy 6:17–19.
37-39 Mark 6:56; Acts 9:32–43.
52-55 Matthew 25:35–40.
57-61 Cf. *A Song for St. Cecilia's Day* 51–54.

When crowds appear'd, she had not to relieve.
Which to prevent she still increas'd her store,
Laid up, and spar'd, that she might give the more: 70
So Pharaoh or some greater king than he
Provided for the sev'nth necessity;
Taught from above his magazines to frame,
That famine was prevented e'er it came.
Thus Heav'n, though all-sufficient, shows a thrift
In his economy and bounds his gift,
Creating for our day one single light,
And his reflection too supplies the night;
Perhaps a thousand other worlds that lie
Remote from us and latent in the sky   80
Are lighten'd by his beams, and kindly nurs'd,
Of which our earthly dunghill is the worst.

　　Now, as all virtues keep the middle line,
Yet somewhat more to one extreme incline,
Such was her soul, abhorring avarice,
Bounteous, but almost bounteous to a vice;
Had she giv'n more, it had profusion been
And turn'd th' excess of goodness into sin.

　　These virtues rais'd her fabric to the sky,   *Of her humility.*
For that which is next Heav'n is charity.   90
But as high turrets for their ai'ry steep
Require foundations in proportion deep,
And lofty cedars as far upward shoot
As to the nether heav'ns they drive the root;
So low did her secure foundation lie;
She was not humble, but humility.
Scarcely she knew that she was great, or fair,
Or wise, beyond what other women are,
Or, which is better, knew, but never durst
　　compare.
For to be consc'ious of what all admire   100
And not be vain advances virtue high'r;
But still she found, or rather thought she found,
Her own worth wanting, others' to abound,

71-74 Genesis 41. *some greater king.* God, King of kings.
75-78 With 79-82, 134-53, and 263-69 echoes of Fontenelle.
91-96 Isaiah 2:12-17.

Ascrib'd above their due to ev'ryone,
Unjust and scanty to herself alone.

 Such her devotion was as might give rules *Of her piety.*
Of speculation to disputing schools,
And teach us equally the scales to hold
Betwixt the two extremes of hot and cold;
That pious heat may mod'rately prevail,   110
And we be warm'd but not be scorch'd with zeal.
Business might shorten, not disturb her pray'r;
Heav'n had the best, if not the greater, share.
An active life long oraisons forbids,
Yet still she pray'd, for still she pray'd by deeds.

 Her ev'ry day was sabbath, only free
From hours of pray'r for hours of charity.
Such as the Jews from servile toil releas'd,
Where works of mercy were a part of rest;
Such as blest Angels exercise above,   120
Vari'd with sacred hymns and acts of love;
Such sabbaths as that one she now enjoys,
Ev'n that perpetual one which she employs
(For such vicissitudes in Heav'n there are)
In praise alternate and alternate pray'r.
All this she practic'd here, that when she sprung
Amidst the choirs, at the first sight she sung;
Sung, and was sung herself, in angels' lays,
For praising her, they did her Maker praise.
All offices of Heav'n so well she knew   130
Before she came, that nothing there was new.
And she was so familiarly receiv'd,
As one returning, not as one arriv'd.

 Muse, down again precipitate thy flight, *Of her various virtues.*
For how can mortal eyes sustain immortal light!
But as the sun in water we can bear,
Yet not the sun but his reflection there,
So let us view her here in what she was,
And take her image in this wat'ry glass,

118-19 Deuteronomy 15:1-18.
126-33 Cf. Killigrew Ode 191-95.
134-39 Exodus 33. *this wat'ry glass.* This mirror; this poem.

Yet look not ev'ry lineament to see;   140
Some will be cast in shades, and some will be
So lamely drawn you scarcely know 'tis she.

For where such various virtues we recite,
'Tis like the Milky Way, all over bright
But sown so thick with stars 'tis undistinguish'd
    light.

  Her virtue, not her virtues, let us call,
For one heroic comprehends 'em all:
One as a constellation is but one,
Though 'tis a train of stars that, rolling on,
Rise in their turn and in the zodiac run.   150
Ever in motion, now 'tis faith ascends,
Now hope, now charity that upward tends
And downwards with diffusive good descends.

  As in perfumes compos'd with art and cost
'Tis hard to say what scent is uppermost,
Nor this part musk or civet can we call,
Or amber, but a rich result of all;
So she was all a sweet, whose ev'ry part,
In due proportion mix'd, proclaim'd the Maker's art.
No single virtue we cou'd most commend,   160
Whether the wife, the mother, or the friend;
For she was all in that supreme degree
That, as no one prevail'd, so all was she.
The sev'ral parts lay hidden in the piece;
Th' occasion but exerted that or this.

  A wife as tender and as true withal   *Of her conjugal*
As the first woman was before her fall;   *virtues.*
Made for the man of whom she was a part,
Made to attract his eyes and keep his heart.
A second Eve but by no crime accurst,   170
As beauteous, not as brittle, as the first.
Had she been first, still Paradise had been,
And death had found no entrance by her sin.
So she not only had preserv'd from ill

---

¹⁵⁴⁻⁵⁷ Cf. John Donne, *II Anniversary* 127–30, one of many passages in
   Donne's poetry recalled, if not fully alluded to, in this poem.

Her sex and ours, but liv'd their pattern still.
   Love and obedience to her lord she bore;
She much obey'd him, but she lov'd him more.
Not aw'd to duty by superior sway,
But taught by his indulgence to obey.
Thus we love God as author of our good;   180
So subjects love just kings, or so they shou'd.
Nor was it with ingratitude return'd;
In equal fires the blissful couple burn'd;
One joy possess'd 'em both, and in one grief they
    mourn'd.
His passion still improv'd; he lov'd so fast
As if he fear'd each day wou'd be her last.
Too true a prophet to foresee the fate
That shou'd so soon divide their happy state,
When he to Heav'n entirely must restore
That love, that heart, where he went halves before.   190
Yet as the soul is all in ev'ry part,
So God and he might each have all her heart.

   So had her children, too, for charity   *Of her love*
Was not more fruitful or more kind than she;   *to her children.*
Each under other by degrees they grew,
A goodly perspective of distant view:
Anchises look'd not with so pleas'd a face
In numb'ring o'er his future Roman race
And marshalling the heroes of his name
As, in their order, next to light they came;   200
Nor Cybele with half so kind an eye
Survey'd her sons and daughters of the sky.
Proud, shall I say, of her immortal fruit,
As far as pride with heav'nly minds may suit.

   Her pious love excell'd to all she bore;   *Her care of*
New objects only multiply'd it more.   *their education.*
And as the Chosen found the pearly grain
As much as ev'ry vessel cou'd contain;

176-80 Ephesians 5:22–25.
193-96 Nine children survived Eleonora, who is depicted like Charity, accompanied by, or nursing, numerous children.
197-200 Virgil, *Aeneid* VI, 752–853.
201-2 *Aeneid* IX, 82 ff. and 107 ff.

As in the blissful vision each shall share ⎫
As much of glory as his soul can bear: ⎬   210
So did she love and so dispense her care. ⎭
Her eldest thus, by consequence, was best,
As longer cultivated than the rest;
The babe had all that infant care beguiles
And early knew his mother in her smiles;
But when dilated organs let in day
To the young soul and gave it room to play,
At his first aptness the maternal love
Those rudiments of reason did improve;
The tender age was pliant to command;   220
Like wax it yielded to the forming hand;
True to th' artificer, the labour'd mind
With ease was pious, generous, just and kind,
Soft for impression from the first, prepar'd
Till virtue, with long exercise, grew hard,
With ev'ry act confirm'd, and made at last
So durable as not to be effac'd,
It turn'd to habit and, from vices free,
Goodness resolv'd into necessity.

Thus fix'd she virtue's image, that's her own,   230
Till the whole mother in the children shone;
For that was their perfection; she was such
They never cou'd express her mind too much.
So unexhausted her perfections were
That, for more children, she had more to spare;
For souls unborn, whom her untimely death
Depriv'd of bodies and of mortal breath,
And (cou'd they take th' impressions of her mind)
Enough still left to sanctify her kind.   239

Then wonder not to see this soul extend   *Of her*
The bounds and seek some other self, a friend;   *friendship.*
As swelling seas to gentle rivers glide
To seek repose and empty out the tide:
So this full soul, in narrow limits pent,
Unable to contain her, sought a vent
To issue out and in some friendly breast

Discharge her treasures and securely rest;
T' unbosom all the secrets of her heart,
Take good advice, but better to impart.
For 'tis the bliss of friendship's holy state   250
To mix their minds and to communicate;
Though bodies cannot, souls can penetrate.
Fix'd to her choice, inviolably true,
And wisely choosing, for she chose but few.
Some she must have, but in no one cou'd find
A tally fitted for so large a mind.

   The souls of friends like kings in progress are,
Still in their own, though from the palace far:
Thus her friend's heart her country dwelling was,
A sweet retirement to a coarser place   260
Where pomp and ceremonies enter'd not,
Where greatness was shut out and bus'ness well
     forgot.

   This is th' imperfect draught, but short as far
As the true height and bigness of a star
Exceeds the measures of th' astronomer.
She shines above we know, but in what place,
How near the throne and Heav'n's imperial face,
By our weak optics is but vainly guess'd;
Distance and altitude conceal the rest.   269

   Tho' all these rare endowments of the mind   *Reflections*
Were in a narrow space of life confin'd,   *on the*
The figure was with full perfection crown'd— *shortness of*
Though not so large an orb, as truly round.   *her life.*

   As when in glory through the public place
The spoils of conquer'd nations were to pass
And but one day for triumph was allow'd,
The consul was constrain'd his pomp to crowd,
And so the swift procession hurry'd on,
That all, though not distinctly, might be shown:
So, in the straiten'd bounds of life confin'd,   280
She gave but glimpses of her glorious mind,
And multitudes of virtues pass'd along,
Each pressing foremost in the mighty throng,
Ambitious to be seen, and then make room,

273 *orb.* Emblem of perfection.

For greater multitudes that were to come.
    Yet unemploy'd no minute slipp'd away;
Moments were precious in so short a stay.
The haste of Heav'n to have her was so great ⎫
That some were single acts, though each   ⎬
    complete,   ⎭
But ev'ry act stood ready to repeat.   290
    Her fellow saints with busy care will look
For her blest name in fate's eternal book,
And, pleas'd to be outdone, with joy will see
Numberless virtues, endless charity,
But more will wonder at so short an age,
To find a blank beyond the thirti'th page,
And with a pious fear begin to doubt
The piece imperfect and the rest torn out.   *She di'd in*
                                      her thirty-third year.
But 'twas her Saviour's time and, cou'd there be
A copy near th' original, 'twas she.   300
    As precious gums are not for lasting fire—
They but perfume the temple and expire—
So was she soon exhal'd and vanish'd hence,
A short sweet odour of a vast expense.
She vanish'd, we can scarcely say she di'd,
For but a now did Heav'n and earth divide;
She pass'd serenely with a single breath,
This moment perfect health, the next was death.
One sigh did her eternal bliss assure;   *The manner*
                                        of her death.
So little penance needs, when souls are almost pure.   310
As gentle dreams our waking thoughts pursue,
Or, one dream pass'd, we slide into a new
(So close they follow, such wild order keep,
We think ourselves awake, and are asleep):
So softly death succeeded life in her;
She did but dream of Heav'n, and she was there.
    No pains she suffer'd nor expir'd with noise;
Her soul was whisper'd out with God's still voice:
As an old friend is beckon'd to a feast
And treated like a long familiar guest,   320
He took her as he found, but found her so,
As one in hourly readiness to go.   *Her preparedness*
                                           to die.
Ev'n on that day in all her trim prepar'd,

As early notice she from Heav'n had heard,
And some descending courtier from above
Had giv'n her timely warning to remove,
Or counsell'd her to dress the nuptial room,
For on that night the Bridegroom was to come.
He kept His hour and found her where she lay   329
Cloth'd all in white, the liv'ry of the day;   *She di'd on*
Scarce had she sinn'd in thought, or word, or act,   *Whitsunday*
Unless omissions were to pass for fact,   *night.*
That hardly death a consequence cou'd draw
To make her liable to nature's law.
And that she di'd we only have to show
The mortal part of her she left below;
The rest (so smooth, so suddenly she went) ⎫
Look'd like translation through the firmament, ⎬
Or like the fiery car, on the third errand sent. ⎭   339

   O happy soul! If thou canst view from high,   *Apostrophe*
Where thou art all intelligence, all eye;   *to her soul.*
If looking up to God or down to us,
Thou find'st that any way be pervious;
Survey the ruins of thy house and see
Thy widow'd and thy orphan family;
Look on thy tender pledges left behind,
And if thou canst a vacant minute find
From Heav'nly joys, that interval afford
To thy sad children and thy mourning lord.
See how they grieve, mistaken in their love,   350
And shed a beam of comfort from above;
Give 'em, as much as mortal eyes can bear,
A transient view of thy full glories there,
That they with mod'rate sorrow may sustain
And mollify their losses in thy gain.
Or else divide the grief, for such thou wert   ⎫
That shou'd not all relations bear a part,   ⎬
It were enough to break a single heart.   ⎭

   Let this suffice: nor thou, great saint, refuse   *Epiphonema:*
This humble tribute of no vulgar Muse,   *or close of*
                                                     the poem.

322–28 Matthew 25:1–7.
338–39 The first *errand* was for Enoch (Genesis 5:24), the second for Elijah
   (2 Kings 2:11).
342–43 *Verbatim* from Donne, *Obsequies to the Lord Harrington* 5–6.

Who, not by cares, or wants, or age depress'd, 361
Stems a wild deluge with a dauntless breast
And dares to sing thy praises in a clime
Where vice triumphs and virtue is a crime;
Where ev'n to draw the picture of thy mind
Is satire on the most of human kind;
Take it while yet 'tis praise, before my rage,
Unsafely just, break loose on this bad age;
So bad, that thou thyself had'st no defence
From vice but barely by departing hence. 370
　　Be what and where thou art; to wish thy place
Were, in the best, presumption, more than grace.
Thy relics (such thy works of mercy are)
Have in this poem been my holy care.
As earth thy body keeps, thy soul the sky, ⎫
So shall this verse preserve thy memory, ⎬
For thou shalt make it live, because it sings of thee. ⎭

---

[362] *dauntless breast.* Traditional for sturdy integrity against opposition; cf. *To Sir Godfrey Kneller* 79–80.

TO MY DEAR FRIEND
MR. CONGREVE

ON HIS COMEDY, CALL'D *The Double-Dealer*

1693. *The Double-Dealer*, Congreve's second play, was performed in November 1693, and published in 1694 with this poem before it; but Dryden did send a friend a copy on December 12, 1693. Dryden apparently met Congreve through their mutual friend, the dramatist Thomas Southerne. The two felt deep affection for each other. "I am Mr. Congreve's true lover," Dryden wrote his publisher; and Congreve said, "I loved Mr. Dryden," in his dedication to the Duke of Newcastle of Dryden's *Dramatic Works*. This epistle does not have the blaze of imagery and language of that to the Duchess of Ormond or the breadth of that to John Driden. But its depth of affection, maintained in Dryden's perfect tone, led Edmund Gosse to say of it, "Perhaps since the beginning of literary history there is no other example of such fine and generous praise of a young colleague by a great old poet." Dryden begins the epistle with a progress piece of English drama from the Elizabethan and Restoration dramatists to his young friend (ll. 1–40). He next discusses the irregular "royal" succession among contemporary poets, and includes a prophecy of Congreve's fame (ll. 41–63). He concludes with the charge to Congreve, "Be kind to my remains," as Congreve proved to be in editing Dryden's plays in 1717. The subject and much of the imagery of the poem are uncannily like those of *MacFlecknoe*, with which it may be instructively compared.

Well then, the promis'd hour is come at last;
The present age of wit obscures the past;
Strong were our sires, and as they fought they writ,
Conqu'ring with force of arms and dint of wit;
Theirs was the giant race before the flood;
And thus, when Charles return'd, our empire stood.
Like Janus he the stubborn soil manur'd,
With rules of husbandry the rankness cur'd;
Tam'd us to manners when the stage was rude,
And boistrous English wit with art indu'd.   10

    Our age was cultivated thus at length,
But what we gain'd in skill we lost in strength.
Our builders were with want of genius curs'd;
The second Temple was not like the first,
Till you, the best Vitruvius, come at length;
Our beauties equal but excel our strength.
Firm Doric pillars found your solid base;
The fair Corinthian crowns the higher space:
Thus all below is strength, and all above is grace.

    In easy dialogue is Fletcher's praise;   20
He mov'd the mind but had not power to raise.
Great Jonson did by strength of judgment please,
Yet doubling Fletcher's force, he wants his ease.
In differing talents both adorn'd their age,
One for the study, t'other for the stage.
But both to Congreve justly shall submit,
One match'd in judgment, both o'er-match'd in
    wit.
In him all beauties of this age we see:
Etherege his courtship, Southerne's purity,
The satire, wit, and strength of Manly
    Wycherley.   30
All this in blooming youth you have achiev'd;

7-12 Janus brought agriculture and civilization to Italy by welcoming
Saturn (Ovid, *Fasti* I, 235 ff.). Cf. *To the Earl of Roscommon* 1 ff.
14 *the second Temple*. Built after the Exile and inferior to the first (Ezra
5–6; Haggai 2:1–3).
15 *Vitruvius*. M. Vitruvius Pollio, architect under Augustus and author of
the only extant classical treatise on architecture.
20-25 Cf. *An Essay of Dramatic Poesy*, pp. 80–82.
29 *courtship*. Grace, address. *purity*. Of language, diction.
30 *Manly*. Hero of Wycherley's *Plain Dealer* (1677).

Nor are your foil'd contemporaries griev'd;
So much the sweetness of your manners move,
We cannot envy you because we love.

Fabius might joy in Scipio when he saw
A beardless consul made against the law
And join his suffrage to the votes of Rome,
Though he with Hannibal was overcome.

Thus old Romano bow'd to Raphael's fame
And scholar to the youth he taught became.   40

Oh, that your brows my laurel had sustain'd;
Well had I been depos'd, if you had reign'd!
The father had descended for the son,
For only you are lineal to the throne.

Thus when the state one Edward did depose,
A greater Edward in his room arose.

But now, not I, but poetry is curs'd,
For Tom the Second reigns like Tom the First.

But let 'em not mistake my patron's part,
Nor call his charity their own desert.   50

Yet this I prophesy: thou shalt be seen
(Tho' with some short parenthesis between)
High on the throne of wit, and seated there,
Not mine (that's little), but thy laurel wear.

Thy first attempt an early promise made;
That early promise this has more than paid.

So bold, yet so judiciously you dare,
That your least praise is to be regular.

[35-38] Fabius envied the way Scipio achieved success and a consulship while
yet under age; but he would not envy the agreeable Congreve.

[39-40] Giulio Romano was the *scholar* or pupil of Raphael; perhaps Dryden
confused the former with Pietro Vanucci, Raphael's teacher-collabora-
tor.

[42-48] Royal and literary succession form a complex metaphor. Dryden-
James II should be succeeded by Congreve-James' son, as Edward II
made way for Edward III. Unfortunately, Tom II (Thomas Rymer, now
Historiographer Royal) has replaced Tom I (Thomas Shadwell, Historiographer Royal and Poet Laureate, 1688–1692). There may be a
glance at two purely poetic Toms: "Tom Sternhold's or Tom Shadwell's rhymes" (*Religio Laici* 456).

[48] *my patron.* Charles Sackville (d. 1706), Earl of Dorset, Eugenius in
An Essay of Dramatic Poesy, was said by some to have bestowed an
equivalent of his pension on Dryden when forced to appoint the
Protestant Shadwell in 1688.

[53] *high on the throne,* etc. Cf. *MacFlecknoe* 107.

[55] Southerne reported Dryden as saying that Congreve's *Old Bachelor*
was the best first play he had seen.

Time, place, and action may with pains be wrought,
But genius must be born and never can be taught. 60
This is your portion, this your native store; ⎱
Heav'n that but once was prodigal before ⎰
To Shakespeare gave as much; she cou'd not give ⎰
    him more. ⎰

  Maintain your post: that's all the fame you need,
For 'tis impossible you shou'd proceed.
Already I am worn with cares and age
And just abandoning th' ungrateful stage;
Unprofitably kept at Heav'n's expense,
I live a rent-charge on his Providence;
But you, whom ev'ry Muse and Grace adorn, 70
Whom I foresee to better fortune born,
Be kind to my remains; and, oh, defend
Against your judgment your departed friend!
Let not the insulting foe my fame pursue,
But shade those laurels which descend to you;
And take for tribute what these lines express:
You merit more, nor cou'd my love do less.

[63] *she*. For *Heav'n* (62). Dryden otherwise uses "he" and "it"; because of *native* (61), Dryden must have changed to *Heav'n* from *Nature*, leaving *she*.

Second Song

LOVE TRIUMPHANT

1693. *Love Triumphant*, a tragicomedy and Dryden's last complete play, was performed in January 1694. It met with little success, both because of a Whig claque against it and because of an unconvincing change of character by adamant King Veramond, who relents for the lovers of the play. Much else in the play is of great interest, including this extraordinary song sung by a girl at the age of innocence before cynical comic characters. It became popular, both set to the music of John Eccles and by itself.

Song for a Girl

1

Young I am and yet unskill'd
How to make a lover yield,
How to keep or how to gain,
When to love and when to feign.

2

Take me, take me, some of you,
While I yet am young and true,
E'er I can my soul disguise,
Heave my breasts and roll my eyes.

3

Stay not till I learn the way,
How to lie and to betray;

He that has me first is blest,
For I may deceive the rest.

4

Cou'd I find a blooming youth,
Full of love and full of truth,
Brisk and of a jaunty mien,
I shou'd long to be fifteen.

TO SIR GODFREY KNELLER

1694. Sir Godfrey Kneller (1646–1723), who had succeeded Sir Peter Lely as the leading court painter of England, painted Dryden in 1693. Dryden had long had an
interest in painting as a "sister art" of poetry, and in his
Parallel of Poetry and Painting (1695) there are many of
the same points made in prose about the two arts as are
made in the verse of this poem. The year of publication
(1694, in *The Annual Miscellany*) is therefore the likely
year of composition.

Apart from its comparisons between the sister arts, the
poem includes a progress piece of painting (ll. 28–72).
There are some curiously disgruntled passages (e.g., ll.
81–84, 100–101) and in much of the second half of the
poem a satiric undertone. Dryden may have been getting
at Kneller, who was extraordinarily vain, so much so that
either Kneller's personality or his outright protests led Dryden's publisher, Jacob Tonson, to delete several lines (91–
94, 115–23, and 164–65) when the poem was republished
after Dryden's death. The picture of Shakespeare (ll. 73
ff.) is a copy of the "Chandos portrait." It is 29 inches by
24 inches, and has survived in the collection of the Earl of
Fitzwilliam. As with stanzas VI–VII of the Killigrew Ode,
the epistle to Kneller reveals that Dryden enjoyed most
that kind of painting he felt was closest to poetry and reality—portraiture.

Once I beheld the fairest of her kind
(And still the sweet idea charms my mind);
True, she was dumb, for Nature gaz'd so long,
Pleas'd with her work, that she forgot her tongue,
But smiling said, "She still shall gain the prize;

I only have transferr'd it to her eyes."
Such are thy pictures, Kneller, such thy skill,
That Nature seems obedient to thy will,
Comes out and meets thy pencil in the draught,
Lives there and wants but words to speak her
    thought. 10
At least thy pictures look a voice, and we ⎫
Imagine sounds, deceiv'd to that degree ⎬
We think 'tis somewhat more than just to see. ⎭

  Shadows are but privations of the light,
Yet when we walk they shoot before the sight,
With us approach, retire, arise and fall,
Nothing themselves, and yet expressing all.
Such are thy pieces, imitating life
So near they almost conquer'd in the strife,
And from their animated canvas came, 20
Demanding souls and loosen'd from the frame.

  Prometheus, were he here, wou'd cast away
His Adam and refuse a soul to clay,
And either wou'd thy noble work inspire
Or think it warm enough without his fire.

  But vulgar hands may vulgar likeness raise;
This is the least attendant on thy praise;
From hence the rudiments of art began;
A coal or chalk first imitated man;
Perhaps the shadow taken on a wall 30
Gave outlines to the rude original
E'er canvas yet was strain'd, before the grace ⎫
Of blended colours found their use and place, ⎬
Or cypress tablets first receiv'd a face. ⎭

  By slow degrees the godlike art advanc'd;
As man grew polish'd, picture was enhanc'd;
Greece added posture, shade, and perspective,
And then the mimic piece began to live.
Yet perspective was lame, no distance true,
But all came forward in one common view; 40
No point of light was known, no bounds of art;
When light was there, it knew not to depart,

3-6 Cf. Killigrew Ode 103.
22-25 Ovid, *Metamorphoses* I, 78-86; *To the Earl of Roscommon* 73-74.

But glaring on remoter objects play'd,
Not languish'd, and insensibly decay'd.

    Rome rais'd not art but barely kept alive,
And with old Greece unequally did strive,
Till Goths and Vandals, a rude northern race,
Did all the matchless monuments deface.
Then all the Muses in one ruin lie,
And rhyme began t' enervate poetry.   50
Thus in a stupid military state,
The pen and pencil find an equal fate.
Flat faces, such as wou'd disgrace a screen,
Such as in Bantam's embassy were seen,
Unrais'd, unrounded, were the rude delight
Of brutal nations, only born to fight.

    Long time the sister arts in iron sleep
A heavy sabbath did supinely keep;
At length in Raphael's age at once they rise,
Stretch all their limbs, and open all their eyes.   60

    Thence rose the Roman and the Lombard line,
One colour'd best, and one did best design.
Raphael's, like Homer's, was the nobler part;
But Titian's painting look'd like Virgil's art.

    Thy genius gives thee both, where true design,
Postures unforc'd, and lively colours join.
Likeness is ever there, but still the best,
Like proper thoughts in lofty language dress'd,
Where light, to shades descending, plays not strives,
Dies by degrees and by degrees revives.   70
Of various parts a perfect whole is wrought;
Thy pictures think, and we divine their thought.

    Shakespeare,* thy gift, I place before my sight;
With awe I ask his blessing e'er I write;
With reverence look on his majestic face,

---

* *Shakespeare's picture drawn by Sir Godfrey Kneller and given to the author.* [Dryden's note.]

---

51 *a stupid,* etc. Criticism of the warlike William III.
54 *Bantam's embassy.* Welcomed by Charles II in 1682, their exotic racial features excited great curiosity and long were talked of.
35-72 One of Dryden's longest progress pieces; it includes art with poetry (cf. *To the Earl of Roscommon* 1 ff.) and has some political details (51–54).

Proud to be less but of his godlike race.
His soul inspires me while thy praise I write,
And I like Teucer under Ajax fight,
Bids thee through me be bold, with dauntless breast
Contemn the bad and emulate the best.   80
Like his, thy critics in th' attempt are lost;
When most they rail, know then, they envy most.
In vain they snarl aloof, a noisy crowd,
Like women's anger, impotent and loud.
While they their barren industry deplore,
Pass on secure and mind the goal before;
Old as she is, my Muse shall march behind,
Bear off the blast and intercept the wind.

    Our Arts are sisters, though not twins in birth,
For hymns were sung in Eden's happy earth   90
By the first pair while Eve was yet a saint,
Before she fell with pride and learn'd to paint.
Forgive th' allusion; 'twas not meant to bite,
But satire will have room where'er I write.

    For, oh, the painter Muse, though last in place,
Has seiz'd the blessing first, like Jacob's race.
Apelles' art an Alexander found,
And Raphael did with Leo's gold abound,
But Homer was with barren laurel crown'd.
Thou hadst thy Charles a while, and so had I,   100
But pass we that unpleasing image by.

    Rich in thyself, and of thyself divine,
All pilgrims come and offer at thy shrine.
A graceful truth thy pencil can command;
The fair themselves go mended from thy hand;
Likeness appears in every lineament,
But likeness in thy work is eloquent;
Though Nature there her true resemblance bears,
A nobler beauty in thy piece appears.
So warm thy work, so glows the gen'rous frame,   110
Flesh looks less living in the lovely dame.

---

[75] *Iliad* VIII, 266–72.
[79] *dauntless breast.* See *Eleonora* 362n.
[95–96] Genesis 27.
[100–1] This ungracious couplet is bafflingly out of character.

Thou paint'st as we describe, improving still,
When on wild nature we engraft our skill,
But not creating beauties at our will.

Some other hand perhaps may reach a face,
But none like thee a finish'd figure place;
None of this age, for that's enough for thee,
The first of these inferior times to be,
Not to contend with heroes' memory.

Due honours to those mighty names we grant,   120
But shrubs may live beneath the lofty plant;
Sons may succeed their greater parents gone;
Such is thy lot, and such I wish my own.

But poets are confin'd in narr'wer space
To speak the language of their native place;
The painter widely stretches his command:
Thy pencil speaks the tongue of ev'ry land.
From hence, my friend, all climates are your own,
Nor can you forfeit, for you hold of none.
All nations all immunities will give   130
To make you theirs, where'er you please to live,
And not seven cities but the world wou'd strive.

Sure some propitious planet then did smile,
When first you were conducted to this isle
(Our genius brought you here t' inlarge our fame,
For your good stars are ev'rywhere the same);
Thy matchless hand, of ev'ry region free,
Adopts our climate, not our climate thee.

Great Rome and Venice early did impart*
To thee th' examples of their wondrous art.   140
Those masters then but seen, not understood,
With generous emulation fir'd thy blood;
For what in nature's dawn the child admir'd,
The youth endeavour'd and the man acquir'd.

That yet thou hast not reach'd their high degree
Seems only wanting to this age, not thee:

---

* He travell'd very young into *Italy*.

129 That is, what you have is your own, owed to no one, and so cannot
be taken from you.
132 *seven cities*. That competed for the honor of being Homer's birthplace.
134 *when first*, etc. Kneller arrived in 1676.

Thy genius bounded by the times like mine, ⎫
Drudges on petty draughts, nor dare design ⎬
A more exalted work and more divine. ⎭
For what a song or senseless opera   150
Is to the living labour of a play,
Or what a play to Virgil's work wou'd be,
Such is a single piece to history.

   But we who life bestow ourselves must live;
Kings cannot reign unless their subjects give.
And they who pay the taxes bear the rule:
Thus thou sometimes art forc'd to draw a fool;
But so his follies in thy posture sink,
The senseless idiot seems at least to think.

   Good heav'n! that sots and knaves shou'd be so vain   160
To wish their vile resemblance may remain!
And stand recorded, at their own request,
To future days a libel or a jest.
Meantime, while just encouragement you want,
You only paint to live, not live to paint.

   Else shou'd we see your noble pencil trace
Our unities of action, time, and place,
A whole compos'd of parts, and those the best,
With ev'ry various character express'd,
Heroes at large, and at a nearer view   170
Less, and at distance, an ignobler crew,
While all the figures in one action join,
As tending to complete the main design.

   More cannot be by mortal art express'd,
But venerable age shall add the rest.
For time shall with his ready pencil stand,
Retouch your figures with his ripening hand,
Mellow your colours, and imbrown the taint,
Add every grace which time alone can grant,
To future ages shall your fame convey   180
And give more beauties than he takes away.

174-81 Contrasting *mortal art* with immortal fame in a typical closing
prophecy.

AN ODE ON THE DEATH
OF MR. HENRY PURCELL,

*Late Servant to His Majesty
and Organist of the Chapel Royal
and of St. Peter's, Westminster*

1696. Usually thought to be England's greatest composer, Henry Purcell (1658–1695) was a pupil of John Blow, who set this ode to music. Both before and after his death Purcell was commonly known as England's Orpheus or Orpheus Britannicus (see ll. 16 ff.). The opening simile of birds is in Dryden's more descriptive vein of nature imagery that usually appears in narrative poems rather than in lyrics. The pageant of stanza III seems almost to adapt an effect from one of the "dramatic operas" that Dryden and Purcell did together—and of course this ode was performed as a cantata. The "scale of music" let down by angels is a visual symbol of harmonic intervals that looks rather like a ladder and so is doubly appropriate for Purcell's ascent to heaven.

The Ode

I

Mark how the lark and linnet sing:
    With rival notes
They strain their warbling throats
   To welcome in the spring.
   But in the close of night,
When Philomel begins her heav'nly lay,

They cease their mutual spite,
Drink in her music with delight
And list'ning and silent, and silent and list'ning,
    and list'ning and silent obey.

II

So ceas'd the rival crew when Purcell came;   10
They sung no more or only sung his fame.
Struck dumb, they all admir'd the godlike man,
    The godlike man,
    Alas, too soon retir'd,
    As he too late began.
We beg not Hell our Orpheus to restore;
    Had he been there,
    Their sovereigns' fear
    Had sent him back before.
The pow'r of harmony too well they know;   20
He long e'er this had tun'd their jarring sphere
    And left no Hell below.

III

The heav'nly choir, who heard his notes from
       high,
Let down the scale of music from the sky;
    They handed him along,
And all the way he taught, and all the way they
       sung.
Ye brethren of the lyre and tuneful voice,
Lament his lot, but at your own rejoice.
Now live secure and linger out your days;
The gods are pleas'd alone with Purcell's lays,   30
    Nor know to mend their choice.

ALEXANDER'S FEAST;

Or the Power of Music
An Ode

IN HONOUR OF ST. CECILIA'S DAY

1697. On September 3, 1697, Dryden wrote his sons in Rome that he was "writing a Song for St Cecilia's feast" and his ode, long his most popular lyric, was duly performed on November 22 in the musical setting of Jeremiah Clarke, who is best known today for the "Trumpet Voluntary" that had been long ascribed to Purcell. Although it is less appropriate to the feast of St. Cecilia than was *A Song for St. Cecilia's Day* written a decade before, this poem was at once welcomed with praise by Dryden's contemporaries. In combining the story of Timotheus and Alexander with the amour of Alexander and Thais, Dryden gave renewed life to both by the bounding energy of his style, his virtuoso rhythmical variations, and his humor directed at Alexander. Although St. Cecilia emerges as the unconvincing heroine at the end of the poem, it is Timotheus the artist who controls Alexander, much as Dryden manipulates his effects throughout the poem. The motto might well be the line of the earlier poem: "What passion cannot music raise and quell!" Yet the vain, mad, weeping, drunk, loving "warlike son" of Philip of Macedon is the one who earns our affection.

I

'Twas at the royal feast for Persia won
      By Philip's warlike son;

Aloft in awful state
The godlike hero sat
        On his imperial throne;
His valiant peers were plac'd around,
Their brows with roses and with myrtles bound
    (So shou'd desert in arms be crown'd).
The lovely Thais by his side
Sat like a blooming Eastern bride   10
In flow'r of youth and beauty's pride.
    Happy, happy, happy pair!
    None but the brave,
    None but the brave,
    None but the brave deserves the fair.

                    CHORUS
    Happy, happy, happy pair!
    None but the brave,
    None but the brave,
    None but the brave deserves the fair.

                    II

Timotheus, plac'd on high   20
    Amid the tuneful choir,
    With flying fingers touch'd the lyre;
The trembling notes ascend the sky
And heav'nly joys inspire.
The song began from Jove,
Who left his blissful seats above
(Such is the pow'r of mighty love).
A dragon's fiery form beli'd the god;
Sublime on radiant spires he rode,
    When he to fair Olympia press'd   30
    And while he sought her snowy breast;
Then round her slender waist he curl'd
And stamp'd an image of himself, a sov'reign of the
        world.

---

10 *like.* She was a courtesan.
25-33 Timotheus' song tells the legend of Zeus, in serpent's form, father-
ing Alexander on Olympias. This amused Dryden (34-41), who had
already given Philip of Macedon the honor (2).

The list'ning crowd admire the lofty sound,
"A present deity," they shout around;
"A present deity," the vaulted roofs rebound.
                    With ravish'd ears
                    The monarch hears,
                    Assumes the god,
                    Affects to nod,   40
          And seems to shake the spheres.

                    CHORUS
                    With ravish'd ears
                    The monarch hears,
                    Assumes the god,
                    Affects to nod,
          And seems to shake the spheres.

                         III
The praise of Bacchus, then, the sweet musician sung,
          Of Bacchus ever fair and ever young;
                    The jolly god in triumph comes;
                    Sound the trumpets, beat the drums;   50
                    Flush'd with a purple grace,
                    He shows his honest face;
Now give the hautboys breath; he comes, he comes.
          Bacchus, ever fair and young,
                    Drinking joys did first ordain;
          Bacchus' blessings are a treasure;
          Drinking is the soldier's pleasure;
                    Rich the treasure,
                    Sweet the pleasure,
                    Sweet is pleasure after pain.   60

                    CHORUS
          Bacchus' blessings are a treasure;
          Drinking is the soldier's pleasure,
                    Rich the treasure,
                    Sweet the pleasure,
          Sweet is pleasure after pain.

---

[53] *honest face.* A version of *honestum caput:* handsome, comely.

IV

Sooth'd with the sound, the King grew vain,
   Fought all his battles o'er again,
And thrice he routed all his foes, and thrice he slew
   the slain.
      The master saw the madness rise,
      His glowing cheeks, his ardent eyes;   70
      And while he Heav'n and earth defi'd,
      Chang'd his hand and check'd his pride.
        He chose a mournful Muse
        Soft pity to infuse:
      He sung Darius great and good,
        By too severe a fate
     Fallen, fallen, fallen, fallen,
       Fallen from his high estate
         And welt'ring in his blood;
Deserted at his utmost need   80
By those his former bounty fed,
On the bare earth expos'd he lies,
With not a friend to close his eyes.
With downcast looks the joyless victor sat,
   Revolving in his alter'd soul
    The various turns of chance below;
And now and then a sigh he stole,
   And tears began to flow.

CHORUS

Revolving in his alter'd soul
   The various turns of chance below;   90
And now and then a sigh he stole,
   And tears began to flow.

V

The mighty master smil'd to see
That love was in the next degree;
'Twas but a kindred sound to move,

[66-83] The parallel with *To my Honour'd Kinsman* 150–63 suggests that Dryden may have been shadowing William III in Alexander and James II in *Darius great and good* (75).

For pity melts the mind to love.
  Softly sweet, in Lydian measures,
  Soon he sooth'd his soul to pleasures.
  "War," he sung, "is toil and trouble,
  Honour but an empty bubble;   100
   Never ending, still beginning,
  Fighting still, and still destroying;
   If the world be worth thy winning,
  Think, O think it worth enjoying.
   Lovely Thais sits beside thee;
   Take the good the gods provide thee."
The many rend the skies with loud applause;
So love was crown'd, but music won the cause.
  The Prince, unable to conceal his pain,
    Gaz'd on the fair   110
    Who caus'd his care,
   And sigh'd and look'd, sigh'd and look'd,
  Sigh'd and look'd, and sigh'd again;
At length, with love and wine at once oppress'd,
The vanquish'd victor sunk upon her breast.

    CHORUS
  The Prince, unable to conceal his pain,
    Gaz'd on the fair
    Who caus'd his care,
   And sigh'd and look'd, sigh'd and look'd,
  Sigh'd and look'd, and sigh'd again; 120
At length, with love and wine at once oppress'd,
The vanquish'd victor sunk upon her breast.

    VI
Now strike the golden lyre again,
A louder yet, and yet a louder strain.
Break his bands of sleep asunder
And rouse him, like a rattling peal of thunder.
   Hark, hark, the horrid sound
   Has rais'd up his head,

---

[97] *Lydian measures.* Classical modes (unfortunately lost) like the Lydian
had power to affect men by altering psychic harmony; another theory,
reflected in Dryden's style here and in *A Song for St. Cecilia's Day,* held
that effects stemmed from *rhythmus,* cadence and rhythm.

As awak'd from the dead,
And amaz'd, he stares around. 130
"Revenge! Revenge!" Timotheus cries;
"See the Furies arise!
See the snakes that they rear,
How they hiss in their hair,
And the sparkles that flash from their eyes!
Behold a ghastly band,
Each a torch in his hand!
Those are Grecian ghosts, that in battle were slain,
And unburi'd remain
Inglorious on the plain. 140
Give the vengeance due
To the valiant crew.
Behold how they toss their torches on high,
How they point to the Persian abodes
And glitt'ring temples of their hostile gods!"
The princes applaud with a furious joy,
And the King seiz'd a flambeau with zeal to destroy;
Thais led the way,
To light him to his prey
And like another Helen fir'd another Troy. 150

CHORUS

And the King seiz'd a flambeau with zeal to destroy;
Thais led the way,
To light him to his prey
And like another Helen fir'd another Troy.

VII

Thus, long ago
E'er heaving bellows learn'd to blow,
While organs yet were mute,
Timotheus, to his breathing flute
And sounding lyre,
Cou'd swell the soul to rage or kindle soft desire. 160
At last divine Cecilia came,
Inventress of the vocal frame;
The sweet enthusiast from her sacred store

Enlarg'd the former narrow bounds
And added length to solemn sounds
With nature's mother-wit and arts unknown before.
Let old Timotheus yield the prize
Or both divide the crown;
He rais'd a mortal to the skies;
She drew an angel down.   170

GRAND CHORUS

At last divine Cecilia came,
Inventress of the vocal frame;
The sweet enthusiast from her sacred store
Enlarg'd the former narrow bounds
And added length to solemn sounds
With nature's mother-wit and arts unknown before.
Let old Timotheus yield the prize
Or both divide the crown;
He rais'd a mortal to the skies;
She drew an angel down.   180

[169-70] Cf. *A Song for St. Cecilia's Day* 53–54.

TO MY FRIEND,
THE AUTHOR

Peter Motteux

1698. The tragedy, *Beauty in Distress*, by Peter Motteux (1660–1718) was acted and then published in 1698 with Dryden's poem before it. Dryden took advantage of this opportunity to give his reaction to the accelerating change from the vigorous and sometimes indecent writing of the reigns of Charles and James to the more sentimental and moral tone of the reign of William and Mary. (The title of Motteux' play exemplifies the change.) In particular in this poem, Dryden replies to criticism of the stage, especially the *Short View of the Immorality and Profaneness of the English Stage* (1698) of Jeremy Collier. He confesses to a degree of guilt; but he also reserves the right to satirize bad clergymen, wondering why a divine like Collier should find so attractive the searching of plays for "immorality and profaneness." (There are similar sentiments expressed more strongly in the Preface to *Fables*.) He goes on to praise Motteux, a French Huguenot religious émigré who managed to write so successfully in English. Motteux had already completed Urquhart's translation of Rabelais (1693–1694) and later rendered *Don Quixote* (1700–1703). Although not the most significant of Dryden's verse epistles, the ease with which he discussed a topic of almost professional interest and the well-mannered geniality of the last few lines show how accustomed he had grown to writing in the form.

'Tis hard, my friend, to write in such an age
As damns not only poets but the stage.

That sacred art, by Heav'n itself infus'd,
Which Moses, David, Solomon have us'd,
Is now to be no more; the Muses' foes
Wou'd sink their Maker's praises into prose.
Were they content to prune the lavish vine
Of straggling branches and improve the wine,
Who but a madman wou'd his faults defend?
All wou'd submit, for all but fools will mend.   10
But when to common sense they give the lie
And turn distorted words to blasphemy,
They give the scandal, and the wise discern
Their glosses teach an age too apt to learn.

What I have loosely, or profanely writ,
Let them to fires (their due desert) commit;
Nor, when accus'd by me, let *them* complain:
Their faults and not their function I arraign.
Rebellion, worse than witchcraft, they pursu'd;
The pulpit preach'd the crime; the people ru'd.   20
The stage was silenc'd, for the Saints wou'd see
In fields perform'd their plotted tragedy.
But let us first reform, and then so live
That we may teach our teachers to forgive,
Our desk be plac'd below their lofty chairs,
Ours be the practice, as the precept theirs.
The moral part at least we may divide,
Humility reward, and punish pride,
Ambition, int'rest, avarice accuse:
These are the province of the tragic Muse.   30

These hast thou chosen, and the public voice
Has equall'd thy performance with thy choice.
Time, action, place are so preserv'd by thee ⎫
That ev'n Corneille might with envy see   ⎬
Th' alliance of his tripled unity.   ⎭
Thy incidents, perhaps, too thick are sown,
But too much plenty is thy fault alone;

---

⁴ Moses was thought author of the Pentateuch, David of Psalms, and
    Solomon of Proverbs and Canticles.
¹⁹ 1 Samuel 15:23. (For rebellion is as the sin of witchcraft.) Dryden had
    in mind those bellicose *Saints* (l. 21) who closed the theaters between
    1642 and 1660.
³⁵ The unities of time, place, and action had been more rigorously ob-
    served in French than in English plays.

At least but two can that good crime commit—
Thou in design and Wycherley in wit.
Let thy own Gauls condemn thee if they dare, 40
Contented to be thinly regular.
Born there but not for them, our fruitful soil
With more increase rewards thy happy toil.
Their tongue, enfeebled, is refin'd so much
That, like pure gold, it bends at ev'ry touch;
Our sturdy Teuton yet will art obey,
More fit for manly thought and strengthen'd with
    allay.
But whence art thou inspir'd, and thou alone,
To flourish in an idiom not thine own?
It moves our wonder that a foreign guest 50
Shou'd over-match the most and match the best.
In underpraising, thy deserts I wrong:
Here find the first deficience of our tongue;
Words, once my stock, are wanting to commend
So great a poet and so good a friend.

FABLES ANCIENT
AND MODERN

1699. Dryden's translation of Virgil (1697) had been greeted with such success that soon thereafter he and his publisher entered into an agreement for a more miscellaneous collection of about ten thousand verses. Dryden chose passages or books from the *Metamorphoses* of Ovid, tales by Chaucer or then attributed to him, novels by Boccaccio ("Boccace"), and Book I of the *Iliad*. Dryden made clear that the last was presented to test public interest in a subscription for a translation of Homer. That was left to be done by Pope (and to give Pope a financial security that Dryden had never known), because the illness Dryden speaks of in the Preface was soon to take his life. In addition, *Fables* included poems to the Duchess of Ormond and to Dryden's cousin, John Driden. (There are a number of John Drydens contemporary with the poet and the name is spelled differently, often by the same person.) The two epistles are among the finest of Dryden's poems, and the *Fables* also included *Alexander's Feast*, as well as a minor elegy on "A Fair Maiden Lady." The handsome folio volume also contained a dedication to the second Duke of Ormond (see the headnote to the poem to the Duchess of Ormond), which is omitted here in favor of including the letter to the Duchess printed after the Preface, with her poem.

The Preface is unmistakably Dryden's, at once rambling ("never wholly out of the way nor in it"), personal, profound, and engaging. He begins and ends personally, at

the outset defending himself and at the end reprobating
two who had attacked him. The close shows the hand of a
master satirist, but we would not have thought the worse of
Dryden if he had simply ignored those who had sought to
gain repute on the cheap by attacking the most famous
writer of the time. The main purpose of the Preface is,
however, to elucidate and compare the qualities of certain
celebrated writers, a kind of criticism in which Dryden excelled. Homer appears first, compared favorably with Virgil, followed by a long comparison of Ovid and Chaucer.
Dryden's preference for Chaucer, whose works were still
printed in extremely corrupt texts that spoiled his meter,
must have astonished readers of the *Fables*. The remarks
describing the "most wonderful comprehensive nature" of
Chaucer spring from a love of men and great poetry like
that shown by Neander's preference for Shakespeare over
Jonson in *An Essay of Dramatic Poesy*. And although
scholarship was to clarify the nature of Chaucer's text and
therefore his meter, it was Dryden who became, in his old
age, the father of Chaucerian criticism. After defending his
decision to translate Chaucer, he moves on to consider
"Boccace" in comparison with Chaucer. The relaxed style
of these comparisons has often been compared with the
more studied poise of *An Essay of Dramatic Poesy*. There
is no doubt of the superiority of the earlier work in regard
to critical theory and interior structure. But there are many
who prefer the Preface to *Fables* for what it so attractively
reveals of the humanity of both its author and the great
writers "ancient and modern" whom he so obviously loved.

Preface

'Tis with a poet as with a man who designs to build and is
very exact, as he supposes, in casting up the cost beforehand, but generally speaking, he is mistaken in his account
and reckons short of the expence he first intended. He alters his mind as the work proceeds and will have this or
that convenience more of which he had not thought when
he began. So has it happen'd to me; I have built a house

where I intended but a lodge, yet with better success than a certain nobleman[1] who, beginning with a dogkennel, never liv'd to finish the palace he had contriv'd.

From translating the first of Homer's *Iliads* (which I intended as an essay to the whole work), I proceeded to the translation of the twelfth book of Ovid's *Metamorphoses*, because it contains, among other things, the causes, the beginning, and ending of the Trojan war. Here I ought in reason to have stopp'd, but the speeches of Ajax and Ulysses[2] lying next in my way, I could not balk 'em. When I had compass'd them, I was so taken with the former part of the fifteenth book[3] (which is the masterpiece of the whole *Metamorphoses*) that I enjoin'd myself the pleasing task of rend'ring it into English. And now I found, by the number of my verses, that they began to swell into a little volume, which gave me an occasion of looking backward on some beauties of my author in his former books. There occurr'd to me the Hunting of the Boar, Cinyras and Myrrha, the good-natur'd story of Baucis and Philemon,[4] with the rest, which I hope I have translated closely enough and given them the same turn of verse which they had in the original; and this, I may say without vanity, is not the talent of every poet. He who has arriv'd the nearest to it is the ingenious and learned Sandys,[5] the best versifier of the former age, if I may properly call it by that name, which was the former part of this concluding century. For Spenser and Fairfax both flourish'd in the reign of Queen Elizabeth: great masters in our language, and who saw much farther into the beauties of our numbers than those who immediately followed them. Milton was the poetical son of Spenser, and Mr. Waller of Fairfax; for we have our lineal descents and clans as well as other families. Spenser more than once insinuates that the soul of Chaucer was

---

[1] *a certain nobleman.* Probably Buckingham (see *Absalom and Achitophel* 544n), whose house at Cliveden proceeded very slowly; see *To Sir George Etherege* 74–81.

[2] *speeches,* etc. Ovid, *Metamorphoses* VIII.

[3] *the former part,* etc. Translated as "Of the Pythagorean Philosophy."

[4] *the Hunting,* etc. The three stories are in *Metamorphoses* VIII, X, and VIII.

[5] *Sandys.* George Sandys (d. 1644), who translated the *Metamorphoses* (1626).

transfus'd into his body and that he was begotten by him two hundred years after his decease. Milton has acknowl-edg'd to me that Spenser was his' original, and many be-sides myself have heard our famous Waller own that he deriv'd the harmony of his numbers from the *Godfrey of Bulloigne,* which was turn'd into English by Mr. Fairfax.[6]

But to return: having done with Ovid for this time, it came into my mind that our old English poet Chaucer in many things resembled him, and that with no disadvantage on the side of the modern author, as I shall endeavour to prove when I compare them. And as I am, and always have been, studious to promote the honour of my native country, so I soon resolv'd to put their merits to the trial by turning some of *The Canterbury Tales* into our language, as it is now refin'd. For by this means both the poets being set in the same light, and dress'd in the same English habit, story to be compar'd with story, a certain judgment may be made betwixt them by the reader, without obtruding my opinion on him. Or if I seem partial to my countryman and predecessor in the laurel, the friends of antiquity are not few. And besides many of the learn'd, Ovid has almost all the beaux and the whole fair sex his declar'd patrons. Per-haps I have assum'd somewhat more to myself than they allow me, because I have adventur'd to sum up the evi-dence. But the readers are the jury, and their privilege re-mains entire to decide according to the merits of the cause, or, if they please, to bring it to another hearing before some other court.

In the meantime, to follow the thread of my discourse (as thoughts, according to Mr. Hobbes,[7] have always some connexion), so from Chaucer I was led to think on Boc-cace, who was not only his contemporary, but also pursu'd the same studies, wrote novels in prose and many works in verse, particularly is said to have invented the octave rhyme,[8] or stanza of eight lines, which ever since has been

[6] Dryden was suggesting two lines of English poets: the "genius" line of Chaucer, Spenser, Milton, and (cf. *To the Duchess of Ormond* 1–18) perhaps himself; and the "correct" line of Edward Fairfax (translator of *Gerusalemme Liberata* as *Godfrey of Bulloigne,* 1600), Waller, and, no doubt, Denham.

[7] *Hobbes. Leviathan* I, iii. (Of the Consequence or Train of Imaginations.)

[8] *octave rhyme.* Boccaccio perfected rather than invented *ottava rima.*

maintain'd by the practice of all Italian writers, who are, or
at least assume, the title of heroic poets. He and Chaucer,
among other things, had this in common, that they refin'd
their mother tongues, but with this difference, that Dante
had begun to file their language, at least in verse, before
the time of Boccace, who likewise receiv'd no little help
from his master Petrarch. But the reformation of their prose
was wholly owing to Boccace himself, who is yet the standard of purity in the Italian tongue, though many of his
phrases are become obsolete, as in process of time it must
needs happen. Chaucer (as you have formerly been told by
our learn'd Mr. Rymer[9]) first adorn'd and amplified our
barren tongue from the Provençal,[10] which was then the
most polish'd of all the modern languages. But this subject
has been copiously treated by that great critic, who deserves no little commendation from us his countrymen.

For these reasons of time and resemblance of genius, in
Chaucer and Boccace, I resolv'd to join them in my present
work, to which I have added some original papers of my
own, which whether they are equal or inferior to my other
poems, an author is the most improper judge, and therefore
I leave them wholly to the mercy of the reader. I will hope
the best, that they will not be condemn'd; but if they
should, I have the excuse of an old gentleman, who mounting on horseback before some ladies when I was present,
got up somewhat heavily, but desir'd of the fair spectators
that they would count fourscore and eight before they
judg'd him. By the mercy of God, I am already come
within twenty years of his number, a cripple in my limbs,
but what decays are in my mind the reader must deter-
mine. I think myself as vigorous as ever in the faculties of
my soul, excepting only my memory, which is not impair'd
to any great degree, and if I lose not more of it I have no
great reason to complain. What judgment I had increases
rather than diminishes, and thoughts, such as they are,
come crowding in so fast upon me that my only difficulty is
to choose or to reject, to run them into verse, or to give

---

[9] *Rymer.* In *A Short View of Tragedy* (1963), V.
[10] *Provençal.* Probably meaning Old French.

them the other harmony of prose.[11] I have so long studied and practic'd both that they are grown into a habit and become familiar to me. In short, though I may lawfully plead some part of the old gentleman's excuse, yet I will reserve it till I think I have greater need and ask no grains of allowance for the faults of this my present work but those which are given of course to human frailty. I will not trouble my reader with the shortness of time in which I writ it, or the several intervals of sickness. They who think too well of their own performances are apt to boast in their prefaces how little time their works have cost them and what other business of more importance interfer'd. But the reader will be as apt to ask the question, Why they allow'd not a longer time to make their works more perfect? And why they had so despicable an opinion of their judges as to thrust their indigested stuff upon them, as if they deserv'd no better?

With this account of my present undertaking, I conclude the first part of this discourse; in the second part, as at a second sitting, though I alter not the draught, I must touch the same features over again, and change the dead-colouring of the whole. In general I will only say that I have written nothing which savours of immorality or profaneness; at least I am not conscious to myself of any such intention. If there happen to be found an irreverent expression or a thought too wanton, they are crept into my verses through my inadvertency. If the searchers find any in the cargo, let them be stav'd or forfeited like counter-banded goods; at least, let their authors be answerable for them as being but imported merchandise and not of my own manufacture. On the other side, I have endeavour'd to choose such fables, both ancient and modern, as contain in each of them some instructive moral, which I could prove by induction; but the way is tedious, and they leap foremost into sight without the reader's trouble of looking after them. I wish I could affirm with a safe conscience that I had taken the same care in all my former writings; for it

[11] This famous passage may obliquely allude to his translating Boccaccio's prose into verse.

must be own'd, that supposing verses are never so beautiful
or pleasing, yet if they contain anything which shocks religion or good manners, they are at best, what Horace says
of good numbers without good sense, "*Versus inopes
rerum, nugaeque canorae.*" [12] Thus far, I hope, I am right
in court, without renouncing to my other right of self-
defence, where I have been wrongfully accus'd, and my
sense wire-drawn into blasphemy or baudry, as it has often
been by a religious lawyer[13] in a late pleading against the
stage in which he mixes truth with falsehood and has not
forgotten the old rule of calumniating strongly that something may remain.

I resume the thread of my discourse with the first of my
translations, which was the first *Iliad* of Homer. If it shall
please God to give me longer life and moderate health, my
intentions are to translate the whole *Ilias,* provided still
that I meet with those encouragements from the public
which may enable me to proceed in my undertaking with
some cheerfulness.[14] And this I dare assure the world beforehand, that I have found by trial Homer a more pleasing
task than Virgil (though I say not the translation will be
less laborious). For the Grecian is more according to my
genius than the Latin poet. In the works of the two authors
we may read their manners and natural inclinations, which
are wholly different. Virgil was of a quiet, sedate temper;
Homer was violent, impetuous, and full of fire. The chief
talent of Virgil was propriety of thoughts and ornament of
words. Homer was rapid in his thoughts and took all the
liberties, both of numbers and of expressions, which his
language and the age in which he liv'd allow'd him.
Homer's invention was more copious, Virgil's more confin'd. So that if Homer had not led the way, it was not in
Virgil to have begun heroic poetry. For nothing can be
more evident than that the Roman poem is but the second
part of the *Ilias,* a continuation of the same story, and the

---

[12] *Versus,* etc. Horace, *Ars Poetica* 322. (Verses unendowed with substance, and musical nothings.)

[13] *religious lawyer.* Jeremy Collier (d. 1726) of Gray's Inn, author of
A Short View of the Immorality and Profaneness of the English Stage
(1698).

[14] A main purpose of the Preface was clearly to get support for this enterprise, which later gave Pope financial independence.

persons already form'd. The manners of Aeneas are those of
Hector superadded to those which Homer gave him. The
adventures of Ulysses in the *Odysseis* are imitated in the
first six books of Virgil's *Aeneis*. And though the accidents
are not the same (which would have argu'd him of a servile copying, and total barrenness of invention), yet the
seas were the same in which both the heroes wander'd,
and Dido cannot be deni'd to be the poetical daughter of
Calypso. The six latter Books of Virgil's poem are the four
and twenty *Iliads* contracted: a quarrel occasion'd by a
lady, a single combat, battles fought, and a town besieg'd.
I say not this in derogation to Virgil, neither do I contradict anything which I have formerly said in his just praise.
For his episodes are almost wholly of his own invention,
and the form which he has given to the telling makes the
tale his own, even though the original story had been the
same. But this proves, however, that Homer taught Virgil
to design, and if invention be the first virtue of an epic
poet, then the Latin poem can only be allow'd the second
place.

Mr. Hobbes, in the Preface to his own bald translation of
the *Ilias* (studying poetry as he did mathematics, when it
was too late),[15] Mr. Hobbes, I say, begins the praise of
Homer where he should have ended it. He tells us that the
first beauty of an epic poem consists in diction, that is, in
the choice of words[16] and harmony of numbers. Now, the
words are the colouring of the work, which in the order of
nature is last to be consider'd. The design, the disposition,
the manners, and the thoughts are all before it. Where any
of those are wanting or imperfect, so much wants or is imperfect in the imitation of human life, which is in the very
definition of a poem. Words indeed, like glaring colours,
are the first beauties that arise and strike the sight; but if
the draught be false or lame, the figures ill-dispos'd, the
manners obscure or inconsistent, or the thoughts unnatural,
then the finest colours are but daubing, and the piece is a

---

[15] According to John Aubrey, Hobbes was forty "before he looked on
geometry"; and he was still older when his translation of Homer
(1676) appeared.
[16] In his Preface, "Concerning the Virtues of an Heroic Poem," Hobbes
put "choice of words" first.

beautiful monster at the best. Neither Virgil nor Homer were deficient in any of the former beauties, but in this last, which is expression, the Roman poet is at least equal to the Grecian, as I have said elsewhere,[17] supplying the poverty of his language by his musical ear and by his diligence.

But to return: our two great poets, being so different in their tempers, one choleric and sanguine, the other phlegmatic and melancholic, that which makes them excel in their several ways is that each of them has follow'd his own natural inclination as well in forming the design as in the execution of it. The very heroes show their authors: Achilles is hot, impatient, revengeful, *"Impiger, iracundus, inexorabilis, acer,"* etc.;[18] Aeneas patient, considerate, careful of his people, and merciful to his enemies, ever submissive to the will of Heaven, *"quo fata trahunt retrahuntque, sequamur."* [19] I could please myself with enlarging on this subject but am forc'd to defer it to a fitter time. From all I have said, I will only draw this inference, that the action of Homer being more full of vigour than that of Virgil, according to the temper of the writer, is of consequence more pleasing to the reader. One warms you by degrees; the other sets you on fire all at once and never intermits his heat. 'Tis the same difference which Longinus[20] makes betwixt the effects of eloquence in Demosthenes and Tully. One persuades; the other commands. You never cool while you read Homer, even not in the second book (a graceful flattery to his countrymen), but he hastens from the ships and concludes not that book till he has made you an amends by the violent playing of a new machine.[21] From thence he hurries on his action with variety of events and ends it in less compass than two months. This vehemence of his, I confess, is more suitable to my temper, and therefore I have translated his first book with greater

---

[17] *elsewhere.* In the Epistle Dedicatory for his translation, *Aeneis* (1697).
[18] *Impiger,* etc. Horace, *Ars Poetica* 121. (Restless, furious, obdurate, fierce.)
[19] *quo fata,* etc. Virgil, *Aeneid* V, 709. (Let us follow wherever the Fates may drive or draw.)
[20] *Longinus. On the Sublime* XII.
[21] *machine.* Agamemnon's dream in fact precedes the catalogue of ships in Homer, *Iliad* II.

pleasure than any part of Virgil. But it was not a pleasure without pains: the continual agitations of the spirits must needs be a weak'ning of any constitution, especially in age; and many pauses are required for refreshment betwixt the heats, the *Iliad* of itself being a third part longer than all Virgil's works together.

This is what I thought needful in this place to say of Homer. I proceed to Ovid and Chaucer, considering the former only in relation to the latter. With Ovid ended the Golden Age of the Roman tongue; from Chaucer the purity of the English tongue began. The manners of the poets were not unlike: both of them were well-bred, well-natur'd, amorous, and libertine, at least in their writings—it may be also in their lives. Their studies were the same, philosophy and philology. Both of them were knowing in astronomy, of which Ovid's books of the Roman *Feasts* and Chaucer's treatise of the *Astrolabe* are sufficient witnesses. But Chaucer was likewise an astrologer, as were Virgil, Horace, Persius, and Manilius. Both writ with wonderful facility and clearness; neither were great inventors, for Ovid only copied the Grecian fables, and most of Chaucer's stories were taken from his Italian contemporaries or their predecessors. Boccace his *Decameron* was first publish'd, and from thence our Englishman has borrow'd many of his *Canterbury Tales*. Yet that of *Palamon and Arcite* was written in all probability by some Italian wit in a former age, as I shall prove hereafter. *The Tale of Grizild* was the invention of Petrarch, by him sent to Boccace, from whom it came to Chaucer. *Troilus and Cressida* was also written by a Lombard author but much amplified by our English translator, as well as beautified, the genius of our countrymen in general being rather to improve an invention than to invent themselves, as is evident not only in our poetry but in many of our manufactures. I find I have anticipated already and taken up from Boccace before I come to him. But there is so much less behind, and I am of the temper of most kings, "who love to be in debt," are all for present money, no matter how they pay it afterwards. Besides, the nature of a preface is rambling, never wholly out of the way nor in it. This I have learn'd from the practice of honest Montaigne and return at my pleasure to Ovid and Chaucer, of whom I have little more to say.

Both of them built on the inventions of other men, yet since Chaucer had something of his own, as *The Wife of Bath's Tale, The Cock and the Fox,*[22] which I have translated, and some others, I may justly give our countryman the precedence in that part, since I can remember nothing of Ovid which was wholly his. Both of them understood the manners, under which name I comprehend the passions and, in a larger sense, the descriptions of persons and their very habits. For an example, I see Baucis and Philemon as perfectly before me, as if some ancient painter had drawn them, and all the pilgrims in *The Canterbury Tales,* their humours, their features, and the very dress, as distinctly as if I had supp'd with them at the Tabard in Southwark. Yet even there too the figures of Chaucer are much more lively and set in a better light, which though I have not time to prove, yet I appeal to the reader and am sure he will clear me from partiality. The thoughts and words remain to be consider'd in the comparison of the two poets, and I have sav'd myself one half of that labour by owning that Ovid liv'd when the Roman tongue was in its meridian, Chaucer, in the dawning of our language. Therefore that part of the comparison stands not on an equal foot, any more than the diction of Ennius and Ovid, or of Chaucer and our present English. The words are given up as a post not to be defended in our poet, because he wanted the modern art of fortifying. The thoughts remain to be consider'd, and they are to be measur'd only by their propriety, that is, as they flow more or less naturally from the persons describ'd, on such and such occasions.

The vulgar judges, which are nine parts in ten of all nations, who call conceits and jingles wit, who see Ovid full of them and Chaucer altogether without them, will think me little less than mad for preferring the Englishman to the Roman. Yet, with their leave, I must presume to say that the things they admire are only glittering trifles, and

---

[22] Here and elsewhere in the Preface, one sees how little was then known of Chaucer's sources.

so far from being witty that in a serious poem they are nauseous, because they are unnatural. Wou'd any man who is ready to die for love describe his passion like Narcissus? Wou'd he think of *"inopem me copia fecit,"* [23] and a dozen more of such expressions pour'd on the neck of one another and signifying all the same thing? If this were wit, was this a time to be witty, when the poor wretch was in the agony of death? This is just John Littlewit[24] in *Bartholomew Fair*, who had a conceit (as he tells you) left him in his misery, a miserable conceit. On these occasions the poet shou'd endeavour to raise pity, but instead of this, Ovid is tickling you to laugh. Virgil never made use of such machines when he was moving you to commiserate the death of Dido: he would not destroy what he was building. Chaucer makes Arcite violent in his love and unjust in the pursuit of it. Yet when he came to die, he made him think more reasonably; he repents not of his love, for that had alter'd his character, but acknowledges the injustice of his proceedings and resigns Emilia to Palamon. What would Ovid have done on this occasion? He would certainly have made Arcite witty on his deathbed. He had complain'd he was farther off from possession by being so near, and a thousand such boyisms which Chaucer rejected as below the dignity of the subject. They who think otherwise would by the same reason prefer Lucan and Ovid to Homer and Virgil, and Martial to all four of them.

As for the turn of words, in which Ovid particularly excells all poets, they are sometimes a fault and sometimes a beauty, as they are us'd properly or improperly, but in strong passions always to be shunn'd, because passions are serious and will admit no playing. The French have a high value for them, and I confess they are often what they call delicate when they are introduc'd with judgment; but Chaucer writ with more simplicity and follow'd nature more closely than to use them. I have thus far, to the best of my knowledge, been an upright judge betwixt the parties in competition, not meddling with the design nor the dis-

[23] *inopem*, etc. Ovid, *Metamorphoses* III, 466. (Plenty makes me poor.)
[24] *John Littlewit*. In the first scene of Jonson's play (1631).

position of it, because the design was not their own, and in
the disposing of it they were equal. It remains that I say
somewhat of Chaucer in particular.

In the first place, as he is the father of English poetry, so
I hold him in the same degree of veneration as the Grecians
held Homer, or the Romans Virgil. He is a perpetual fountain of good sense, learn'd in all sciences, and therefore
speaks properly on all subjects. As he knew what to say, so
he knows also when to leave off, a continence which is
practis'd by few writers and scarcely by any of the ancients, excepting Virgil and Horace. One of our late great
poets[25] is sunk in his reputation, because he cou'd never
forgive any conceit which came in his way but swept like a
dragnet, great and small. There was plenty enough, but the
dishes were ill-sorted, whole pyramids of sweetmeats for
boys and women, but little of solid meat for men. All this
proceeded not from any want of knowledge but of judgment; neither did he want that in discerning the beauties
and faults of other poets but only indulg'd himself in the
luxury of writing, and perhaps knew it was a fault but
hop'd the reader would not find it. For this reason, though
he must always be thought a great poet, he is no longer
esteem'd a good writer; and for ten impressions which his
works have had in so many successive years, yet at present
a hundred books are scarcely purchas'd once a twelve-
month; for, as my last Lord Rochester[26] said, though somewhat profanely, "Not being of God, he could not stand."

Chaucer follow'd nature everywhere but was never so
bold to go beyond her. And there is a great difference of
being *poeta* and *nimis poeta*, if we may believe Catullus, as
much as betwixt a modest behaviour and affectation. The
verse of Chaucer, I confess, is not harmonious to us, but 'tis
like the eloquence of one whom Tacitus commends, it was
"*auribus istius temporis accommodata.*" [27] They who liv'd
with him and some time after him thought it musical, and
it continues so even in our judgment, if compar'd with the

---

[25] Apparently Abraham Cowley (d. 1667), although editions of his works
continued to be published at about three-year intervals.
[26] John Wilmot (d. 1680), Earl of Rochester.
[27] *auribus,* etc. *De Oratoribus* XXI. (Accommodated to the ears of another age.)

numbers of Lydgate and Gower, his contemporaries. There
is the rude sweetness of a Scotch tune in it, which is natural and pleasing though not perfect. 'Tis true I cannot go so
far as he who publish'd the last edition of him, for he
would make us believe the fault is in our ears and that
there were really ten syllables in a verse where we find but
nine.[28] But this opinion is not worth confuting; 'tis so gross
and obvious an error that common sense (which is a rule in
everything but matters of faith and revelation) must convince the reader that equality of numbers in every verse
which we call heroic, was either not known or not always
practis'd in Chaucer's age. It were an easy matter to produce some thousands of his verses which are lame for want
of half a foot, and sometimes a whole one, and which no
pronunciation can make otherwise. We can only say that
he liv'd in the infancy of our poetry, and that nothing is
brought to perfection at the first. We must be children before we grow men. There was an Ennius, and in process of
time a Lucilius and a Lucretius, before Virgil and Horace;
even after Chaucer there was a Spenser, a Harrington, a
Fairfax, before Waller and Denham were in being. And our
numbers were in their nonage till these last appear'd.[29]

I need say little of his parentage, life, and fortunes; they
are to be found at large in all the editions of his works. He
was employ'd abroad and favour'd by Edward the Third,
Richard the Second, and Henry the Fourth, and was poet,
as I suppose, to all three of them. In Richard's time, I
doubt he was a little dipp'd in the rebellion of the Commons; and being brother-in-law to John of Gaunt, it was
no wonder if he follow'd the fortunes of that family and
was well with Henry the Fourth when he had depos'd his
predecessor.[30] Neither is it to be admir'd that Henry, who
was a wise as well as a valiant prince, who claim'd by
succession and was sensible that his title was not sound,
but was rightfully in Mortimer, who had married the heir

[28] *he who publish'd*, etc. Thomas Speght, in his second edition (1602),
claimed without demonstration that Chaucer's corrupt text could be
scanned.
[29] Until an accurate text and principles of pronunciation were established
in the next century, Chaucer's verse grew more corrupt and unscannable
with each new edition.
[30] Stories taken from Speght.

of York; it was not to be admir'd, I say, if that great politician should be pleas'd to have the greatest wit of those
times in his interests and to be the trumpet of his praises.
Augustus had given him the example, by the advice of
Maecenas, who recommended Virgil and Horace to him,
whose praises help'd to make him popular while he was
alive and after his death have made him precious to posterity.

As for the religion of our poet, he seems to have some
little bias towards the opinions of Wycliffe, after John of
Gaunt his patron, somewhat of which appears in the tale of
Piers Plowman.[31] Yet I cannot blame him for inveighing so
sharply against the vices of the clergy in his age. Their
pride, their ambition, their pomp, their avarice, their
worldly interest deserv'd the lashes which he gave them
both in that and in most of his *Canterbury Tales*. Neither
has his contemporary Boccace spar'd them.[32] Yet both those
poets liv'd in much esteem with good and holy men in
orders, for the scandal which is given by particular priests
reflects not on the sacred function. Chaucer's Monk, his
Canon, and his Friar took not from the character of his
good Parson. A satirical poet is the check of the laymen on
bad priests. We are only to take care that we involve not
the innocent with the guilty in the same condemnation.
The good cannot be too much honour'd, nor the bad too
coarsely us'd, for the corruption of the best becomes the
worst. When a clergyman is whipp'd, his gown is first
taken off, by which the dignity of his order is secur'd. If he
be wrongfully accus'd, he has his action of slander, and 'tis
at the poet's peril if he transgress the law. But they will tell
us that all kind of satire, though never so well deserv'd by
particular priests, yet brings the whole order into contempt. Is then the peerage of England anything dishon-
our'd, when a peer suffers for his treason? If he be libell'd
or anyway defam'd, he has his *scandalum magnatum*[33] to
punish the offender. They who use this kind of argument

---

[31] The Plowman's Tale (not *The Vision of Piers Plowman*), then considered Chaucer's with many other spurious works.
[32] See *The Hind and the Panther*, To the Reader note 9.
[33] *scandalum magnatum*. Slander of a peer, judge, or other great officer,
punished more heavily than slander of lesser men.

seem to be conscious to themselves of somewhat which has deserv'd the poet's lash and are less concern'd for their public capacity than for their private; at least there is pride at the bottom of their reasoning. If the faults of men in orders are only to be judg'd among themselves, they are all in some sort parties. For since they say the honour of their order is concern'd in every member of it, how can we be sure that they will be impartial judges?

How far I may be allow'd to speak my opinion in this case, I know not. But I am sure a dispute of this nature caus'd mischief in abundance betwixt a king of England and an archbishop of Canterbury,[34] one standing up for the laws of his land, and the other for the honour (as he call'd it) of God's Church, which ended in the murder of the prelate and in the whipping of his Majesty from post to pillar for his penance. The learn'd and ingenious Dr. Drake[35] has sav'd me the labour of inquiring into the esteem and reverence which the priests have had of old, and I would rather extend than diminish any part of it. Yet I must needs say that when a priest provokes me without any occasion given him, I have no reason, unless it be the charity of a Christian, to forgive him. *Prior laesit*[36] is justification sufficient in the civil law. If I answer him in his own language, self-defence, I am sure, must be allow'd me; and if I carry it farther, even to a sharp recrimination, somewhat may be indulg'd to human frailty. Yet my resentment has not wrought so far, but that I have follow'd Chaucer in his character of a holy man,[37] and have enlarg'd on that subject with some pleasure, reserving to myself the right, if I shall think fit hereafter, to describe another sort of priests, such as are more easily to be found than the good Parson, such as have given the last blow to Christianity in this age by a practice so contrary to their doctrine. But this will keep cold till another time.

In the meanwhile, I take up Chaucer where I left him.

---

[34] The *dispute* between Henry II and Thomas à Becket in 1170, but also hinting at the refusal of William III to establish episcopacy in Scotland.

[35] *Dr. Drake*. James (d. 1707), whose *Ancient and Modern Stages Surveyed* (1699) had just come out.

[36] *Prior laesit*. Terence, *Eunuch* 6. (Self-defense.)

[37] *his character of a holy man*. Dryden expanded Chaucer's portrait of the Parson into an "imitation."

He must have been a man of a most wonderful comprehensive nature because, as it has been truly observ'd of him, he
has taken into the compass of his *Canterbury Tales* the
various manners and humours (as we now call them) of
the whole English nation in his age. Not a single character
has escap'd him. All his pilgrims are severally distinguish'd
from each other, and not only in their inclinations, but in
their very physiognomies and persons. Baptista Porta[38]
could not have describ'd their natures better than by the
marks which the poet gives them. The matter and manner
of their tales and of their telling are so suited to their
different educations, humours, and callings that each of
them would be improper in any other mouth. Even the
grave and serious characters are distinguish'd by their
several sorts of gravity; their discourses are such as belong
to their age, their calling, and their breeding, such as are
becoming of them and of them only. Some of his persons
are vicious and some virtuous; some are unlearn'd, or (as
Chaucer calls them) lewd, and some are learn'd. Even the
ribaldry of the low characters is different. The Reeve, the
Miller, and the Cook are several men and distinguish'd
from each other as much as the mincing Lady Prioress and
the broad-speaking gap-tooth'd Wife of Bath. But enough
of this: there is such a variety of game springing up before
me that I am distracted in my choice and know not which
to follow. 'Tis sufficient to say, according to the proverb,
that here is God's plenty. We have our forefathers and
great-granddames all before us as they were in Chaucer's
days; their general characters are still remaining in mankind and even in England, though they are call'd by other
names than those of Monks, and Friars, and Canons, and
Lady Abbesses, and Nuns. For mankind is ever the same,
and nothing lost out of nature, though everything is alter'd.

May I have leave to do myself the justice (since my
enemies will do me none, and are so far from granting me
to be a good poet that they will not allow me so much as to
be a Christian or a moral man), may I have leave, I say, to
inform my reader that I have confin'd my choice to such

---

[38] *Baptista Porta.* Giovanni Battista della Porta (d. 1615), renowned for
his *De Humana Physiognomia Libri IV* (1586).

tales of Chaucer as savour nothing of immodesty. If I had desir'd more to please than to instruct, the Reeve, the Miller, the Shipman, the Merchant, the Summoner, and above all, the Wife of Bath, in the Prologue to her Tale, would have procur'd me as many friends and readers as there are beaux and ladies of pleasure in the town. But I will no more offend against good manners. I am sensible as I ought to be of the scandal I have given by my loose writings and make what reparation I am able by this public acknowledgment. If anything of this nature, or of profaneness, be crept into these poems, I am so far from defending it that I disown it. *Totum hoc indictum volo.*[39] Chaucer makes another manner of apology for his broad-speaking, and Boccace makes the like; but I will follow neither of them. Our countryman, in the end of his characters before *The Canterbury Tales*, thus excuses the ribaldry, which is very gross, in many of his novels.

> *But first, I pray you, of your courtesy,*
> *That ye ne arrete it nought my villany,*
> *Though that I plainly speak in this mattere*
> *To tellen you her words, and eke her chere:*
> *Ne though I speak her words properly,*
> *For this ye knowen as well as I,*
> *Who shall tellen a tale after a man*
> *He mote rehearse as nye, as ever he can:*
> *Everich word of it been in his charge,*
> All speke he, never so rudely, ne large.
> *Or else he mote tellen his tale untrue,*
> *Or feine things, or find words new:*
> *He may not spare, altho he were his brother,*
> *He mote as well say o word as another.*
> *Christ spake himself full broad in Holy Writ,*
> *And well I wote no villany is it.*
> *Eke Plato saith, who so can him rede,*
> *The words mote been cousin to the dede.*[40]

Yet if a man should have enquir'd of Boccace or of Chaucer what need they had of introducing such characters where

---

[39] *Totum*, etc. (I wish it all unsaid.) Dryden's indecencies are much exaggerated in this penitence.
[40] General Prologue, A 725-42.

obscene words were proper in their mouths, but very indecent to be heard, I know not what answer they could have
made. For that reason, such tales shall be left untold by
me. You have here a specimen of Chaucer's language,
which is so obsolete that his sense is scarce to be understood; and you have likewise more than one example of his
unequal numbers, which were mention'd before. Yet many
of his verses consist of ten syllables and the words not
much behind our present English, as for example, these
two lines, in the description of the carpenter's young wife:

> Wincing she was, as is a jolly colt,
> Long as a mast, and upright as a bolt.[41]

I have almost done with Chaucer when I have answer'd
some objections relating to my present work. I find some
people are offended that I have turn'd these tales into
modern English, because they think them unworthy of my
pains and look on Chaucer as a dry, old-fashion'd wit, not
worth receiving. I have often heard the late Earl of Leicester[42] say that Mr. Cowley himself was of that opinion, who
having read him over at my Lord's request, declar'd he had
no taste of him. I dare not advance my opinion against the
judgment of so great an author, but I think it fair, however,
to leave the decision to the public. Mr. Cowley was too
modest to set up for a dictator, and being shock'd perhaps
with his old style, never examin'd into the depth of his
good sense.

Chaucer, I confess, is a rough diamond and must first be
polish'd e'er he shines. I deny not likewise, that living in
our early days of poetry, he writes not always of a piece,
but sometimes mingles trivial things with those of greater
moment. Sometimes also, though not often, he runs riot like
Ovid, and knows not when he has said enough. But there
are more great wits beside Chaucer whose fault is their
excess of conceits, and those ill-sorted. An author is not to
write all he can but only all he ought. Having observ'd this
redundancy in Chaucer (as it is an easy matter for a man

---

[41] The Miller's Tale, A 3263–64.
[42] Philip Sidney (d. 1698), third Earl of Leicester, a Protestant patron to
whom Dryden had dedicated *Don Sebastian* (1690).

of ordinary parts to find a fault in one of greater), I have not ti'd myself to a literal translation but have often omitted what I judg'd unnecessary or not of dignity enough to appear in the company of better thoughts. I have presum'd farther in some places and added somewhat of my own where I thought my author was deficient and had not given his thoughts their true lustre, for want of words in the beginning of our language. And to this I was the more embolden'd, because (if I may be permitted to say it of myself) I found I had a soul congenial to his and that I had been conversant in the same studies. Another poet in another age may take the same liberty with my writings, if at least they live long enough to deserve correction. It was also necessary sometimes to restore the sense of Chaucer, which was lost or mangled in the errors of the press. Let this example suffice at present; in the story of *Palamon and Arcite*, where the Temple of Diana is describ'd, you find these verses in all the editions of our author:

> *There saw I* Danè *turned unto a tree,*
> *I mean not the goddess* Diane,
> *But Venus Daughter, which that hight* Danè.[43]

Which, after a little consideration, I knew was to be reform'd into this sense, that *Daphne* the daughter of Peneus was turn'd into a tree. I durst not make thus bold with Ovid, lest some future Milbourne[44] should arise and say I varied from my author because I understood him not.

But there are other judges who think I ought not to have translated Chaucer into English, out of a quite contrary notion: they suppose there is a certain veneration due to his old language and that it is little less than profanation and sacrilege to alter it. They are farther of opinion, that somewhat of his good sense will suffer in this transfusion, and much of the beauty of his thoughts will infallibly be lost, which appear with more grace in their old habit. Of this opinion was that excellent person whom I mention'd, the late Earl of Leicester, who valu'd Chaucer as much as

---

[43] The Knight's Tale, A 2062–64.
[44] *Milbourne.* Luke Milbourne (d. 1720), who attacked Dryden's *Virgil*, is disposed of subsequently.

Mr. Cowley despis'd him. My Lord dissuaded me from this attempt (for I was thinking of it some years before his death), and his authority prevail'd so far with me as to defer my undertaking while he liv'd in deference to him. Yet my reason was not convinc'd with what he urg'd against it. If the first end of a writer be to be understood, then as his language grows obsolete, his thoughts must grow obscure:

> *Multa renascentur quae nunc cecidere; cadentque*
> *Quae nunc sunt in honora vocabula, si volet usus*
> *Quem penes arbitrium est et jus et norma loquendi.*[45]

When an ancient word for its sound and significancy deserves to be reviv'd, I have that reasonable veneration for antiquity to restore it. All beyond this is superstition. Words are not like landmarks, so sacred as never to be remov'd. Customs are chang'd, and even statutes are silently repeal'd when the reason ceases for which they were enacted. As for the other part of the argument, that his thoughts will lose of their original beauty by the innovation of words, in the first place, not only their beauty but their being is lost, where they are no longer understood, which is the present case. I grant that something must be lost in all transfusion, that is, in all translations, but the sense will remain, which would otherwise be lost or at least be maim'd, when it is scarce intelligible, and that but to a few. How few are there who can read Chaucer so as to understand him perfectly? And if imperfectly, then with less profit and no pleasure. 'Tis not for the use of some old Saxon friends[46] that I have taken these pains with him; let them neglect my version, because they have no need of it. I made it for their sakes who understand sense and poetry as well as they, when that poetry and sense is put into words which they understand.

I will go farther and dare to add that what beauties I lose in some places I give to others which had them not originally. But in this I may be partial to myself; let the reader

---

[45] *Ars Poetica* 70–72; see *An Essay of Dramatic Poesy,* p. 55, note 36, for a translation.
[46] *old Saxon friends.* Old English studies were beginning to flourish, especially at Oxford, although it is unknown who the *friends* were.

judge, and I submit to his decision. Yet I think I have just occasion to complain of them who, because they understand Chaucer, would deprive the greater part of their countrymen of the same advantage and hoard him up, as misers do their grandam gold, only to look on it themselves and hinder others from making use of it. In sum, I seriously protest, that no man ever had, or can have, a greater veneration for Chaucer than myself. I have translated some part of his works only that I might perpetuate his memory, or at least refresh it, amongst my countrymen. If I have alter'd him anywhere for the better, I must at the same time acknowledge that I could have done nothing without him: *"Facile est inventis addere"* [47] is no great commendation, and I am not so vain to think I have deserv'd a greater.

I will conclude what I have to say of him singly with this one remark: a lady of my acquaintance who keeps a kind of correspondence with some authors of the fair sex in France has been inform'd by them that Mademoiselle de Scudéry,[48] who is as old as Sibyl, and inspir'd like her by the same god of poetry, is at this time translating Chaucer into modern French. From which I gather that he has been formerly translated into the Old Provençal (for how she should come to understand Old English, I know not). But the matter of fact being true, it makes me think that there is something in it like fatality, that after certain periods of time the fame and memory of great wits should be renew'd, as Chaucer is both in France and England. If this be wholly chance, 'tis extraordinary; and I dare not call it more for fear of being tax'd with superstition.

Boccace comes last to be consider'd who, living in the same age with Chaucer, had the same genius and follow'd the same studies. Both writ novels, and each of them cultivated his mother tongue. But the greatest resemblance of our two modern authors being in their familiar style and pleasing way of relating comical adventures, I may pass it over, because I have translated nothing from Boccace of that nature. In the serious part of poetry, the advantage is

---

[47] *Facile,* etc. Proverbial. (It is easy to add to what another has created.)
[48] *Mademoiselle de Scudéry.* Madeleine (d. 1701), then over ninety; nothing else seems known of this mystifying story.

wholly on Chaucer's side, for though the Englishman has
borrow'd many tales from the Italian, yet it appears that
those of Boccace were not generally of his own making, but
taken from authors of former ages and by him only
model'd. So that what there was of invention in either of
them may be judg'd equal. But Chaucer has refin'd on
Boccace and has mended the stories which he has borrow'd
in his way of telling, though prose allows more liberty of
thought, and the expression is more easy when unconfin'd
by numbers. Our countryman carries weight and yet wins
the race at disadvantage.

I desire not the reader should take my word and therefore I will set two of their discourses on the same subject in
the same light for every man to judge betwixt them. I
translated Chaucer first, and amongst the rest, pitch'd on
the Wife of Bath's Tale, not daring, as I have said, to ad-
venture on her Prologue, because 'tis too licentious. There
Chaucer introduces an old woman of mean parentage,
whom a youthful knight of noble blood was forc'd to marry
and consequently loath'd her. The crone being in bed with
him on the wedding night and finding his aversion, endeavours to win his affection by reason and speaks a good
word for herself (as who could blame her?) in hope to
mollify the sullen bridegroom. She takes her topics from
the benefits of poverty, the advantages of old age and ugli-
ness, the vanity of youth, and the silly pride of ancestry
and titles without inherent virtue, which is the true nobility.[49] When I had clos'd Chaucer, I return'd to Ovid and
translated some more of his fables, and by this time had so
far forgotten the Wife of Bath's Tale that when I took up
Boccace, unawares I fell on the same argument of preferring virtue to nobility of blood and titles in the Story of
Sigismonda, which I had certainly avoided for the resemblance of the two discourses, if my memory had not fail'd
me. Let the reader weigh them both, and if he thinks me
partial to Chaucer, 'tis in him to right Boccace.

I prefer in our countryman, far above all his other sto-

---

[49] *topics*, etc. Chaucer and Dryden shared a rhetorical training untaught
after the eighteenth century.

ries, the noble poem of *Palamon and Arcite*,[50] which is of the epic kind and perhaps not much inferior to the *Ilias* or the *Aeneis*. The story is more pleasing than either of them, the manners as perfect, the diction as poetical, the learning as deep and various, and the disposition full as artful. Only it includes a greater length of time, as taking up seven years at least; but Aristotle has left undecided the duration of the action, which yet is easily reduc'd into the compass of a year by a narration of what preceded the return of Palamon to Athens. I had thought for the honour of our nation, and more particularly for his whose laurel, tho' unworthy, I have worn after him, that this story was of English growth and Chaucer's own. But I was undeceiv'd by Boccace; for casually looking on the end of his seventh *Giornata*, I found Dioneo (under which name he shadows himself) and Fiametta (who represents his mistress, the natural daughter of Robert King of Naples) of whom these words are spoken: *"Dioneo e Fiametta gran pezza cantarono insieme d'Arcita, e di Palamone."* [51] By which it appears that this story was written before the time of Boccace, but the name of its author being wholly lost, Chaucer is now become an original, and I question not but the poem has receiv'd many beauties by passing through his noble hands. Besides this tale, there is another of his own invention, after the manner of the Provençals, call'd *The Flower and the Leaf*, with which I was so particularly pleas'd, both for the invention and the moral, that I cannot hinder myself from recommending it to the reader.

As a corollary to this Preface, in which I have done justice to others, I owe somewhat to myself, not that I think it worth my time to enter the lists with one M—— or one B——,[52] but barely to take notice that such men there are who have written scurrilously against me without any provocation. M——, who is in orders, pretends amongst the rest this quarrel to me that I have fallen foul on priest-

---

[50] *Palamon and Arcite.* The Knight's Tale.

[51] *Dioneo,* etc. *Decamerone* VII, x, Epilogue. (Dioneo and Fiametta together related a lengthy tale of Arcita and of Palamone.)

[52] *M—— or one B——.* Milbourne (note 44) and Sir Richard Blackmore (d. 1729), physician to William III, author of tedious epics and attacks on Dryden (1695 and 1700).

hood; if I have, I am only to ask pardon of good priests and
am afraid his part of the reparation will come to little. Let
him be satisfied that he shall not be able to force himself
upon me for an adversary. I contemn him too much to
enter into competition with him. His own translations[53] of
Virgil have answer'd his criticisms on mine. If (as they say
he has declar'd in print) he prefers the version of Ogilby[54]
to mine, the world has made him the same compliment; for
'tis agreed on all hands that he writes even below Ogilby.
That, you will say, is not easily to be done, but what cannot M—— bring about? I am satisfi'd, however, that
while he and I live together I shall not be thought the
worst poet of the age. It looks as if I had desir'd him un-
derhand to write so ill against me; but upon my honest
word I have not brib'd him to do me this service and am
wholly guiltless of his pamphlet. 'Tis true, I should be glad,
if I could persuade him to continue his good offices and
write such another critique on anything of mine. For I find
by experience he has a great stroke with the reader, when
he condemns any of my poems, to make the world have a
better opinion of them. He has taken some pains with my
poetry, but nobody will be persuaded to take the same
with his. If I had taken to the Church (as he affirms, but
which was never in my thoughts), I should have had more
sense, if not more grace, than to have turn'd myself out of
my benefice by writing libels on my parishioners. But his
account of my manners and my principles are of a piece
with his cavils and his poetry: and so I have done with him
forever.

As for the City Bard, or Knight Physician, I hear his
quarrel to me is that I was the author of *Absalom and
Achitophel*, which he thinks is a little hard on his fanatic
patrons in London. But I will deal the more civilly with his
two poems, because nothing ill is to be spoken of the dead.
And therefore peace be to the *manes* of his Arthurs. I will

---

[53] *His own translations.* Of *Aeneid* I (1687).
[54] *Ogilby.* John Ogilby (d. 1676), the lively Scot if poor stylist, whom
Dryden sometimes drew upon without proper thanks, had published
translations of Virgil (1649), the *Iliad* (1660), and the *Odyssey* (1665).
The handsome plates for his revised Virgil (1654) were used for Dryden's (1697).

only say that it was not for this noble knight that I drew the plan of an epic poem on King Arthur in my Preface to the translation of Juvenal. The guardian angels of kingdoms were machines too ponderous for him to manage, and therefore he rejected them as Dares[55] did the whirl-bats of Eryx when they were thrown before him by Entellus. Yet from that Preface he plainly took his hint, for he began immediately upon the story, though he had the baseness not to acknowledge his benefactor, but instead of it to traduce me in a libel.[56]

I shall say the less of Mr. Collier, because in many things he has tax'd me justly, and I have pleaded guilty to all thoughts and expressions of mine which can be truly argu'd of obscenity, profaneness, or immorality, and retract them. If he be my enemy, let him triumph; if he be my friend, as I have given him no personal occasion to be otherwise, he will be glad of my repentance. It becomes me not to draw my pen in the defence of a bad cause, when I have so often drawn it for a good one. Yet it were not difficult to prove that in many places he has perverted my meaning by his glosses and interpreted my words into blasphemy and bawdry of which they were not guilty. Besides that, he is too much given to horse-play in his raillery and comes to battle like a dictator from the plough. I will not say, "The zeal of God's house has eaten him up," [57] but I am sure it has devour'd some part of his good manners and civility. It might also be doubted whether it were altogether zeal which prompted him to this rough manner of proceeding; perhaps it became not one of his function to rake into the rubbish of ancient and modern plays; a divine might have employ'd his pains to better purpose than in the nastiness of Plautus and Aristophanes, whose examples, as they excuse not me, so it might be possibly suppos'd that he read them not without some pleasure. They who have written commentaries on those poets, or on Horace, Juvenal, and Martial, have explain'd some vices which without their interpretation had been unknown to modern times. Neither

---

[55] *Dares.* In *Aeneid* V, 400.
[56] In his *Discourse on the Original and Progress of Satire* (1693), Dryden outlined credible use of supernatural agency for his proposed epic.
[57] *the zeal*, etc. Psalms 69:9; John 2:17.

has he judg'd impartially betwixt the former age and us.

There is more bawdry in one play of Fletcher's, call'd
The Custom of the Country, than in all ours together. Yet
this has been often acted on the stage in my remembrance.
Are the times so much more reform'd now than they were
five and twenty years ago? If they are, I congratulate the
amendment of our morals. But I am not to prejudice the
cause of my fellow poets, though I abandon my own defence. They have some of them answer'd for themselves,
and neither they nor I can think Mr. Collier so formidable
an enemy that we should shun him. He has lost ground at
the latter end of the day by pursuing his point too far, like
the Prince of Condé[58] at the battle of Senef: from immoral
plays to no plays, *"ab abusu ad usum, non valet conse-
quentia."* [59] But being a party, I am not to erect myself into
a judge. As for the rest of those who have written against
me, they are such scoundrels, that they deserve not the
least notice to be taken of them. B—— and M—— are only
distinguish'd from the crowd by being remember'd to their
infamy.

> —— *Demetri, teque Tigelli*
> *Discipularum inter jubeo plorare cathedras.*[60]

---

[58] *Prince of Condé.* In Flanders on August 11, 1674, Condé rashly advanced too quickly on the retreating army of William III and suffered
serious losses.

[59] *ab abusu,* etc. Dryden applied an old logical commonplace to mean
that just criticism of abuses should not imply fault in proper uses.

[60] Horace, *Satires* I, x, 90–91. (Demetrius, and you, too, Tigellus, I order
you to go whine among the seats of your female pupils.)

TO HER GRACE THE DUCHESS OF ORMOND,

With the Following Poem of
Palamon and Arcite, *from Chaucer*

1699. Lady Mary Somerset (1655–1733), whose father was descended from Edward III, was a famous beauty of the time and the second wife of James Butler, second Duke of Ormond (1665–1745). In the seventeenth century the Ormond (or Ormonde) family was of all the English nobility among the most wealthy, munificent, and foremost in public esteem and service. The great first Duke (the Barzillai of *Absalom and Achitophel*, ll. 817 ff.) had served Charles I and Charles II, often under impossible conditions, remaining at once loyal to the throne and in personal integrity independent of the court or of any particular royal policy. His son, Thomas, Earl of Ossory, died in 1680 after a distinguished naval career, was mourned by Dryden in *Absalom and Achitophel*, and was mentioned in other writings. The second Duke was now serving the kingdom under William III. The three generations of that noble house covered the century, and Dryden could claim a special relation with them all. For the *Fables* and this poem in particular, however, it is the old poet's gallantry with a noblewoman half his age and the rich association of classical, medieval, biblical, and contemporary detail that is so striking.

The following letter is useful for what it shows of the loose practice of syntax, punctuation, and spelling that flowed from Dryden's pen, but it also provides the best gloss on the gallantry and the constellation of imagery and allusion in the poem itself. The letter (dated "The first day of winter, 1698") and the poem both illustrate his statement in the Preface to *Fables* that "thoughts, such as they are, come crowding in so fast upon me that my only difficulty is to choose or to reject, to run them into verse, or to give them the other harmony of prose."

May it please y^r Grace

What Ireland was before y^r coming thither I cannot tell, but I am sure you have brought over one manufacture wch is not of ye growth of ye country, and that is beauty. But at the same time, you have impoverished y^r Native Land by taking more away y^n you have left behind. We Jacobites have no more reason to thank you than we have our present King who has enriched Holland wth the wealth of England. If this be all the effect of his going over the water for a whole Summer together and of y^r Graces leaving us for a much longer time, we have reason to complain if not of both, yet at least of one of you for the Sun has never Shone on us since you went into Eclipse on Ireland, and if we have another Such a yeare we shall have a famine of Beauty as well as Bread, for if the last be the Staff of life to the rest of the World the first is so to the Nation of Poets; who feed only at the eyes. But you Plantagenets, never think of these mean Concernm^{ts}; the whole race of you have been given to make voyages into ye Holy Land to Conquer Infidells or at least to Subdue France without caring w^t becomes of y^r naturall subjects ye poor English. I think we must remonstrate to you y^t we can no longer live without you: For so our Ancestours have done to some of y^r Family w^n they have been too long abroad. And besides who knows but God who can do all things wch seem impossible to us may raise up another beauty in y^r Absence who may dispute y^r Kingdome with you for thus also has y^r Predecessour Richard Coeur de Leon been servd when his B^r John whose christend name I bear while he was takeing Jerusalem from ye Turks was likely to have Usurpd Eng^d from him And I cannot promise for ye fidelity of a Country which is not over famous for that vertue. The product o[f] Ireland [no doubt a gift of whisky] will onely serve to warm my Body as it does this winter by y^r Graces favour to me but I cannot beare to be cold at heart and the older I am the more I have need of the Sun to comfort me for wch reason I humbly advise you to returne next Spring wth the first Swallow though you falsifie the Proverb for then one Swallow will make a Spring at least to him who is

> Y^r Graces most Obliged and most Obedient Servant
> John Dryden

TO HER GRACE THE DUCHESS OF ORMOND

MADAM,

The bard who first adorn'd our native tongue
Tun'd to his British lyre this ancient song,
Which Homer might without a blush rehearse,
And leaves a doubtful palm in Virgil's verse:
He match'd their beauties where they most excel,
Of love sung better and of arms as well.

Vouchsafe, illustrious Ormond, to behold
What pow'r the charms of beauty had of old,
Nor wonder if such deeds of arms were done,
Inspir'd by two fair eyes that sparkled like your
    own.   10

If Chaucer by the best idea wrought
And poets can divine each other's thought,
The fairest nymph before his eyes he set,
And then the fairest was Plantagenet,
Who three contending princes made her prize
And rul'd the rival nations with her eyes,

---

[1] *bard.* Chaucer.
[2] *song.* The Knight's Tale, Dryden's *Palamon and Arcite.*
[4] Cf. Juvenal, *Satires* XI, 180–81: "Conditor Iliados cantabitur atque Maronis/ Altisoni dubiam facientia carmina palmam." (He who raised up the *Iliad* will be sung, and so too that which disputes the palm, the lofty poem of Virgil.)

Who left immortal trophies of her fame
And to the noblest order gave the name.

    Like her, of equal kindred to the throne,
You keep her conquests and extend your own: 20
As when the stars in their ethereal race
At length have roll'd around the liquid space,
At certain periods they resume their place,
From the same point of Heav'n their course advance
And move in measures of their former dance;
Thus, after length of ages, she returns,
Restor'd in you, and the same place adorns;
Or you perform her office in the sphere,
Born of her blood, and make a new Platonic year.

    O true Plantagenet, O race divine   30
(For beauty still is fatal to the line),
Had Chaucer liv'd that angel face to view,
Sure he had drawn his Emily from you;
Or had you liv'd to judge the doubtful right,
Your noble Palamon had been the knight,
And conqu'ring Theseus from his side had sent
Your gen'rous lord to guide the Theban government.

    Time shall accomplish that, and I shall see
A Palamon in him, in you an Emily.

    Already have the fates your path prepar'd,   40
And sure presage your future sway declar'd;
When westward, like the sun, you took your way

14-18 Referring to Joan, Countess of Kent—"the Fair Maid of Kent"—
who married thrice (15), last to the Black Prince, whom she accompanied to France (16) and by whom she was mother of Richard II.
As Countess of Salisbury, she was thought the woman from whom,
in the usual story of the garter, the Order of the Garter is said to
derive.

19-21 The Duchess' father was created Duke of Beaufort in 1682 for
services to Charles II "and his most noble descent from King Edward
III by John de Beaufort, eldest son of John of Gaunt by Catherine
Swynford" (the patent of nobility).

29 new Platonic year. A celestial cycle; see Plato, Timaeus; some said the
heavenly bodies would return to their original relative positions after
passing through all possible positions, and some that events then would
recur in the same order as before—that is, earlier beauties are reborn
in the Duchess.

33 Emily. Heroine of The Knight's Tale, granted at last to Palamon by
Theseus.

36-37 Referring also to conqu'ring William III, who might send Ormond
from England-Athens to Ireland-Thebes.

42 westward. In the summer of 1697 the Duchess and her daughters vis-
ited, with great applause, the Ormond seat at Kilkenny, Ireland. The

And from benighted Britain bore the day,
Blue Triton gave the signal from the shore,
The ready Nereids heard and swam before
To smooth the seas; a soft Etesian gale
But just inspir'd and gently swell'd the sail;
Portunus took his turn, whose ample hand
Heav'd up the lighten'd keel and sunk the sand,
And steer'd the sacred vessel safe to land.   50
The land, if not restrain'd, had met your way,
Projected out a neck, and jutted to the sea.
Hibernia, prostrate at your feet, ador'd
In you the pledge of her expected lord,
Due to her isle, a venerable name,
His father and his grandsire known to fame;
Aw'd by that house accustom'd to command,
The sturdy kerns in due subjection stand,
Nor hear the reins in any foreign hand.
    At your approach they crowded to the port,   60
And scarcely landed, you create a court;
As Ormond's harbinger, to you they run,
For Venus is the promise of the sun.
    The waste of civil wars, their towns destroy'd,
Pales unhonour'd, Ceres unemploy'd,
Were all forgot, and one triumphant day
Wip'd all the tears of three campaigns away.
Blood, rapines, massacres were cheaply bought,
So mighty recompense your beauty brought.
    As when the dove returning bore the mark   70
Of earth restor'd to the long-lab'ring ark,
The relics of mankind, secure of rest,
Op'd ev'ry window to receive the guest
And the fair bearer of the message bless'd:

Duke joined them briefly in October; the others returned to England
in May 1699.
[46] *Etesian gale*. Soft but steady wind.
[48] *Portunus*. Roman god of shores and harbors.
[59] *hear the reins*. Virgil, *Georgics* I, 514: "neque audit currus habenas."
(Nor does the chariot hearken to the reins.)
[63] *Venus*. The Duchess: as goddess of beauty, as just issued from sea to
land, as the morning star preceding her husband, *the sun*, and as
Venus genetrix (64–85).
[65] *Pales*. God or goddess of sheepherding. *Ceres*. Goddess of agriculture.
[70–74] Genesis 8:8–10. The dove was also Venus' bird.

So, when you came, with loud repeated cries ⎫
The nation took an omen from your eyes,   ⎬
And God advanc'd his rainbow in the skies   ⎭
To sign inviolable peace restor'd;
The saints with solemn shouts proclaim'd the new
    accord.

When at your second coming you appear   80
(For I foretell that millenary year),
The sharpen'd share shall vex the soil no more,
But earth unbidden shall produce her store;
The land shall laugh, the circling ocean smile,
And Heav'n's indulgence bless the holy isle.

Heav'n from all ages has reserv'd for you
That happy clime which venom never knew,
Or if it had been there, your eyes alone
Have pow'r to chase all poison but their own.

Now in this interval which fate has cast   90
Betwixt your future glories and your past,
This pause of pow'r, 'tis Ireland's hour to mourn,
While England celebrates your safe return,
By which you seem the seasons to command
And bring our summers back to their forsaken land.

The vanquish'd isle our leisure must attend ⎫
Till the fair blessing we vouchsafe to send; ⎬
Nor can we spare you long, though often we may ⎭
    lend;
The dove was twice employ'd abroad before
The world was dri'd, and she return'd no more.   100

Nor dare we trust so soft a messenger,
New from her sickness, to that northern air;
Rest here a while, your lustre to restore,
That they may see you as you shone before;
For yet, th' eclipse not wholly past, you wade

75-79 Genesis 9:12–16; 8:21–22. The rainbow signifies the end of general
    death to man and a blessing on the earth; cf. 82–83.
85 *holy isle*. Ireland.
87 *venom*, etc. No poisonous animals exist in Ireland.
80-95 Paralleling *The Prologue To the Duchess* 26–46. The *second coming*
    would be the next visit to Ireland; the inevitable Christian associations
    are modified by details of the classical Golden Age.
102 *sickness*. This poem provides the only known evidence; ultimately her
    angel cures her as she had Ireland.

Thro' some remains and dimness of a shade.
  A subject in his prince may claim a right,
Nor suffer him with strength impair'd to fight;
Till force returns his ardour we restrain,
And curb his warlike wish to cross the main.   110
  Now past the danger, let the learn'd begin
Th' inquiry, where disease could enter in,
How those malignant atoms forc'd their way,
What in the faultless frame they found to make their
    prey?
Where ev'ry element was weigh'd so well
That Heav'n alone, who mix'd the mass, could
    tell
Which of the four ingredients could rebel,
And where, imprison'd in so sweet a cage,
A soul might well be pleas'd to pass an age.
  And yet the fine materials made it weak;   120
Porcelain, by being pure, is apt to break;
Ev'n to your breast the sickness durst aspire,
And forc'd from that fair temple to retire,
Profanely set the holy place on fire.
In vain your Lord like young Vespasian mourn'd,
When the fierce flames the sanctuary burn'd;
And I prepar'd to pay in verses rude
A most detested act of gratitude;
Ev'n this had been your elegy, which now
Is offer'd for your health, the table of my vow.   130
  Your angel sure our Morley's mind inspir'd
To find the remedy your ill requir'd,
As once the Macedon by Jove's decree
Was taught to dream an herb for Ptolemy;
Or Heav'n, which had such over-cost bestow'd,
As scarce it could afford to flesh and blood,
So lik'd the frame he would not work anew
To save the charges of another you;

107-10 A glance at William III and his wars.
117 *ingredients*. The four elements: heat, cold, moisture, dryness.
118-19 Donne, *II Anniversary* 221–23.
125 *Vespasian*. Titus Flavius Sabinus Vespasianus commanded the seige of
   Jerusalem but *mourn'd* the destruction of the Temple.
181 Dr. Christopher Love Morley, physician.
133-34 Alexander dreamed of an herb that cured Ptolemy.

Or by his middle science did he steer
And saw some great contingent good appear, } 140
Well worth a miracle to keep you here;
And for that end preserv'd the precious mould,
Which all the future Ormonds was to hold,
And meditated in his better mind
An heir from you who may redeem the failing kind.

Bless'd be the pow'r which has at once restor'd
The hopes of lost succession to your Lord,
Joy to the first and last of each degree, }
Virtue to courts and, what I long'd to see, }
To you the Graces, and the Muse to me. } 150
O daughter of the rose, whose cheeks unite
The diff'ring titles of the red and white,
Who Heav'n's alternate beauty well display,
The blush of morning and the milky way,
Whose face is paradise, but fenc'd from sin,
For God in either eye has plac'd a cherubin.

All is your Lord's alone; ev'n absent, he
Employs the care of chaste Penelope.
For him you waste in tears your widow'd hours,
For him your curious needle paints the flow'rs: 160
Such works of old imperial dames were taught,
Such for Ascanius fair Elisa wrought.

The soft recesses of your hours improve
The three fair pledges of your happy love;
All other parts of pious duty done,
You owe your Ormond nothing but a son
To fill in future times his father's place
And wear the garter of his mother's race.

---

139 *middle science.* Angelic intuitive reason, midway between man's understanding and God's perfect wisdom.
145 The Christian suggestions become wifely obligations (147, 165–68).
152 *red and white.* Emblems of feminine beauty and colors of the roses of
Lancaster and York, united in the earlier Plantagenet ancestry of the
Duchess.
158 *Penelope.* Faithful wife of Odysseus who, in his absence, delayed suitors
by unweaving at night the work she had woven during the day. She
had promised to choose a new husband when it was finished.
162 *Elisa.* Dido, whose love for Aeneas led her to kindnesses to his son,
Ascanius.

To My Honour'd Kinsman

JOHN DRIDEN

OF CHESTERTON IN THE COUNTY
OF HUNTINGDON, ESQUIRE

1699. Dryden benefited toward the end of his life from the kindness of his cousin, John Driden of Chesterton (1635–1708), whom Dryden and other relatives described as an ideal country gentleman. The poem is a model of the verse epistle in English and is rendered appropriate to praise of country life by its recollections of the Horatian traditions both of the verse epistle itself and of the theme of "the happy man" living a retired country life. But Dryden and Horace combine with this neo-Epicurean strain another to which it was sometimes opposed in the century, the neo-Stoic emphasis upon fulfilling public obligations. Dryden's letters give occasional glimpses of his delight in such country pastimes as fishing, and one can believe that he admired his worthy cousin's settled, retired life. At the same time, his cousin's work as local justice and as Member of Parliament led Dryden to a last statement on politics, "a memorial of my own principles to all posterity," as he wrote Charles Montague (later Earl of Halifax). Dryden remarked in yet another letter that this poem and that to the Duchess of Ormond were so highly admired that some thought "that I never writ better"; he added that, although opinion was divided as to which poem was the better, the majority chose this poem. Both alike share an idealizing of real personalities and of the roles, whether of womanhood and manhood, of the best representatives of the upper levels of society at the close of the century; and both display that love of people and of life that Dryden took to his grave about the time the poems were published.

To My Honour'd Kinsman

How bless'd is he who leads a country life,
Unvex'd with anxious cares and void of strife!
Who studying peace and shunning civil rage,
Enjoy'd his youth and now enjoys his age;
All who deserve his love, he makes his own
And, to be lov'd himself, needs only to be known.
  Just, good, and wise—contending neighbours
      come,
From your award to wait their final doom,
And, foes before, return in friendship home.
Without their cost you terminate the cause   10
And save th' expense of long litigious laws,
Where suits are travers'd and so little won,
That he who conquers is but last undone;
Such are not your decrees, but so design'd,
The sanction leaves a lasting peace behind,
Like your own soul, serene, a pattern of your
      mind.
  Promoting concord and composing strife,
Lord of yourself, uncumber'd with a wife;
Where, for a year, a month, perhaps a night,
Long penitence succeeds a short delight;   20
Minds are so hardly match'd that ev'n the first,
Though pair'd by Heav'n, in paradise, were curs'd.
For man and woman, though in one they grow,
Yet, first or last, return again to two.
He to God's image, she to his was made,
So, farther from the fount, the stream at random
      stray'd.
  How cou'd he stand, when put to double pain,
He must a weaker than himself sustain!

1-6 The Horatian motif, *ille beatus.* Cf. Dryden's *Horace, Ode xxiii, Book
III,* above.
7-13 Added to Driden's epitaph in the church at Chesterton.
17 *concord.* The central concept of the poem, combining various energies
and discords into productive, pacific, and artistic harmony. Marriage was
not Driden's kind of concord; health (including that of the body politic)
was.

Each might have stood perhaps, but each alone;
Two wrestlers help to pull each other down.   30
   Not that my verse wou'd blemish all the fair,
But yet, if *some* be bad, 'tis wisdom to beware,
And better shun the bait than struggle in the
     snare.
Thus have you shunn'd, and shun, the married state,
Trusting as little as you can to fate.
   No porter guards the passage of your door
T' admit the wealthy and exclude the poor;
For God, who gave the riches, gave the heart
To sanctify the whole by giving part;
Heav'n, who foresaw the will, the means has
     wrought   40
And to the second son a blessing brought;
The first-begotten had his father's share,
But you, like Jacob, are Rebecca's heir.
   So may your stores and fruitful fields increase,
And ever be you bless'd, who live to bless.
As Ceres sow'd where'er her chariot flew,
As Heav'n in deserts rain'd the bread of dew,
So free to many, to relations most,
You feed with manna your own Israel host.
   With crowds attended of your ancient race,   50
You seek the champian sports or sylvan chase;
With well-breath'd beagles you surround the wood,
Ev'n then industrious of the common good,
And often have you brought the wily fox
To suffer for the firstlings of the flocks,
Chas'd ev'n amid the folds and made to bleed
Like felons, where they did the murd'rous deed.
This fiery game your active youth maintain'd,
Not yet by years extinguish'd, though restrain'd;
You season still with sports your serious hours,   60
For age but tastes of pleasures youth devours.
The hare in pastures or in plains is found,
Emblem of human life, who runs the round

40-48 Genesis 27:6-29.
47 *bread of dew*. Manna, emblem of Providence; Exodus 16:14.

And, after all his wand'ring ways are done,
His circle fills and ends where he begun,
Just as the setting meets the rising sun.

    Thus princes ease their cares, but happier he
Who seeks not pleasure thro' necessity,
Than such as once on slipp'ry thrones were plac'd,
And chasing, sigh to think themselves are chas'd.   70

    So liv'd our sires e'er doctors learn'd to kill
And multipli'd with theirs the weekly bill;
The first physicians by debauch were made;
Excess began and sloth sustains the trade.
Pity the gen'rous kind their cares bestow
To search forbidden truths (a sin to know),
To which, if human science cou'd attain,
The doom of death, pronounc'd by God, were vain.
In vain the leech wou'd interpose delay;
Fate fastens first and vindicates the prey.   80
What help from art's endeavours can we have!
Gibbons but guesses, nor is sure to save,
But Maurus sweeps whole parishes and peoples
    ev'ry grave,
And no more mercy to mankind will use
Than when he robb'd and murder'd Maro's Muse.
Wou'dst thou be soon dispatch'd and perish whole?
Trust Maurus with thy life and Milbourne with thy
    soul.

    By chase our long-liv'd fathers earn'd their food;
Toil strung the nerves and purifi'd the blood;
But we, their sons, a pamper'd race of men,   90
Are dwindl'd down to threescore years and ten.
Better to hunt in fields for health unbought
Than fee the doctor for a nauseous draught.

50–60 The hunt, peaceable and private emblem of war, ends with an *emblem of human life*, recalling in the hare (and 69–70) Charles I and probably also James II.
76 *forbidden truths.* Those leading to physical immortality.
82 *Gibbons.* William Gibbons (d. 1738), a medical attendant to Dryden.
83 *Maurus.* Blackmore; see Preface to *Fables* notes 44 and 52.
85 Blackmore's failures in epic verse outrage Virgil's (*Maro's*) Muse.
87 *Milbourne.* See Preface to *Fables* note 52.
89 *nerves.* See the Glossary.
90–91 For Dryden a rare employment of the idea of historical decay since the Fall of Man.

The wise for cure on exercise depend;
God never made his work for man to mend.
    The Tree of Knowledge, once in Eden plac'd,
Was easy found but was forbid the taste;
O had our grandsire walk'd without his wife,
He first had sought the better plant of life!
Now, both are lost; yet, wand'ring in the dark,   100
Physicians for the tree have found the bark;
They, lab'ring for relief of human kind,
With sharpen'd sight some remedies may find;   ⎫
Th' apothecary-train is wholly blind;   ⎬
From files a random recipe they take,   ⎭
And many deaths of one prescription make.
Garth, gen'rous as his Muse, prescribes and gives;
The shop-man sells and by destruction lives:
Ungrateful tribe! who, like the viper's brood,
From med'cine issuing, suck their mother's blood!   110
Let these obey, and let the learn'd prescribe,
That men may die without a double bribe;
Let them but under their superiors kill,
When doctors first have sign'd the bloody bill.
He scapes the best, who nature to repair,
Draws physic from the fields in draughts of vital
    air.
    You hoard not health for your own private use,
But on the public spend the rich produce
When, often urg'd, unwilling to be great,
Your country calls you from your lov'd retreat   120
And sends to senates, charg'd with common care,
Which none more shuns and none can better bear.
Where cou'd they find another form'd so fit
To poise, with solid sense, a spritely wit!
Were these both wanting (as they both abound),
Where cou'd so firm integrity be found?
    Well-born and wealthy, wanting no support,

---

101 *bark.* "Jesuits' bark," quinine.
107 *Garth.* Sir Samuel Garth (d. 1719), physician and poet; although a fervent Whig, he and Dryden were friends, and he pronounced a Latin oration at Dryden's funeral. His efforts to provide free medical advice and drugs to the poor were opposed by apothecaries who were satirized later in *The Dispensary*, his major work.
121 Driden was M.P. for Huntingdonshire (1690, 1700–1708).

You steer betwixt the country and the court,
Nor gratify whate'er the great desire,
Nor grudging give what public needs require.   130
Part must be left, a fund when foes invade,
And part employ'd to roll the wat'ry trade:
Ev'n Canaan's happy land, when worn with toil,
Requir'd a sabbath-year to mend the meagre soil.

    Good senators (and such are you) so give
That kings may be suppli'd, the people thrive.
And he, when want requires, is truly wise
Who slights not foreign aids nor over-buys,
But on our native strength in time of need relies.
Münster was bought, we boast not the success;   140
Who fights for gain, for greater makes his peace.

    Our foes, compell'd by need, have peace embrac'd;
The peace both parties want is like to last,
Which, if secure, securely we may trade,
Or, not secure, shou'd never have been made.
Safe in ourselves, while on ourselves we stand,
The sea is ours and that defends the land.
Be then the naval stores the nation's care,
New ships to build and batter'd to repair.

    Observe the war, in ev'ry annual course,   150
What has been done was done with British force:
Namur subdu'd is England's palm alone;
The rest besieg'd, but we constrain'd the town;
We saw th' event that follow'd our success;
France, though pretending arms, pursu'd the peace,
Oblig'd by one sole treaty to restore
What twenty years of war had won before.
Enough for Europe has our Albion fought;
Let us enjoy the peace our blood has bought.
When once the Persian king was put to flight,   160
The weary Macedons refus'd to fight,

---

128 *the country and the court.* The two interests or parties usually dis-
    tinguished at the time.
140 *Münster was bought,* etc. See *Annus Mirabilis* 145n.
142 King William's wars growing unpopular, he concluded them with the
    Peace of Ryswick (1697). Driden was a Williamite and at his request
    certain lines against the Dutch were omitted. As for William's desire for
    a standing army, Dryden praises the defensive navy and hopes for peace.
152 *Namur,* etc. Praise of William's brilliant victory in 1695.

Themselves their own mortality confess'd
And left the son of Jove to quarrel for the rest.
   Ev'n victors are by victories undone;
Thus Hannibal, with foreign laurels won,
To Carthage was recall'd too late to keep his
    own.
While sore of battle, while our wounds are green,
Why shou'd we tempt the doubtful die again?
In wars renew'd, uncertain of success,
Sure of a share as umpires of the peace.   170
   A patriot both the King and country serves;
Prerogative and privilege preserves;
Of each, our laws the certain limit show;
One must not ebb nor t'other overflow;
Betwixt the Prince and Parliament we stand,
The barriers of the state on either hand;
May neither overflow, for then they drown the
    land.
When both are full, they feed our bless'd abode,
Like those that water'd once the paradise of God.
   Some overpoise of sway by turns they share,   180
In peace the people, and the Prince in war;
Consuls of mod'rate pow'r in calms were made;
When the Gauls came, one sole dictator sway'd.
   Patriots in peace assert the people's right,
With noble stubbornness resisting might;
No lawless mandates from the court receive,
Nor lend by force, but in a body give.
Such was your gen'rous grandsire, free to grant
In Parliaments that weigh'd their Prince's want,
But so tenacious of the common cause   190
As not to lend the King against his laws.

160-63 Plutarch's Life of Alexander tells of his difficulties with his troops
after defeating Darius, *the Persian king,* and of the myth that he was *son
of Jove;* cf. *Alexander's Feast.*
165 *Hannibal.* On return from abroad after sixteen years, Hannibal found
trouble with Scipio; the analogy with the frequently absent William
III suggests Jacobitic doubts that he is properly English and hopes that
he will have troubles.
168 *the doubtful die. Dye* in the first edition possibly suggests a pun, especially with *green* (167).
171-79 The requisites for political concord are those of the Clarendon Settlement: throne (*King, Prerogative, Prince*), liberty of subjects (*country,
privilege, Parliament*), and *laws.*

And, in a loathsome dungeon doom'd to lie, ⎫
In bonds retain'd his birthright liberty   ⎬
And sham'd oppression till it set him free. ⎭

   O true descendent of a patriot line,
Who, while thou shar'st their lustre, lend'st 'em
     thine,
Vouchsafe this picture of thy soul to see;
'Tis so far good as it resembles thee;
The beauties to th' original I owe,
Which, when I miss, my own defects I show;   200
Nor think the kindred Muses thy disgrace;
A poet is not born in ev'ry race.
Two of a house few ages can afford,
One to perform, another to record.
Praiseworthy actions are by thee embrac'd,
And 'tis my praise to make thy praises last.
For ev'n when death dissolves our human frame, ⎫
The soul returns to Heav'n from whence it came; ⎬
Earth keeps the body, verse preserves the fame. ⎭

[188-94] Probably Sir Erasmus Driden, grandfather of both Dryden and Driden, sent to prison for not lending money to Charles I. But he was re-
leased just before the parliamentary election of 1628.
[204] Cf. *Absalom and Achitophel* 828.
[209] A traditional closing for elegies and panegyrics; see *Eleonora* 375-77.

THE SECULAR MASQUE

1700. In April 1700 there was a performance for Dryden's benefit of John Fletcher's play, *The Pilgrim*, as revised by Sir John Vanbrugh. Not infrequently a masque of a historical, topical, or political nature was included with a revived old play. To Fletcher's play Dryden contributed, as well as a song, a Prologue, and an Epilogue, this brief masque reviewing his century. The "secular" of the title, like the "age" of the poem, means the century passing, and one legend holds that the play was intended for performance on March 25, when in the old calendar the new year (and century) began; but the date of performance is not certainly known. In his splendid edition of Dryden, Sir Walter Scott wrote of *The Secular Masque:* "By the introduction of the chace, of war, and of love, as governing the various changes of the seventeenth century, the poet alludes to the sylvan sports of James the First, the bloody wars of his son, and the licentious gallantry that reigned in the courts of Charles II and James II." Daniel Purcell and others wrote the music.

Enter Janus.

Janus   Chronos, Chronos, mend thy pace;
        An hundred times the rolling sun
        Around the radiant belt has run
        In his revolving race.
        Behold, behold the goal in sight,
        Spread thy fans and wing thy flight.

Enter Chronos, *with a scythe in his hand and a great globe on his back, which he sets down at his entrance.*

Chronos	Weary, weary of my weight,
	Let me, let me drop my freight
	And leave the world behind.
	I could not bear 10
	Another year
	The load of humankind.

Enter Momus *laughing.*

Momus	Ha! ha! ha! Ha! ha! ha! well hast thou done
	To lay down thy pack
	And lighten thy back;
	The world was a fool e'er since it begun,
	And since neither Janus, nor Chronos, nor I
	Can hinder the crimes
	Or mend the bad times,
	'Tis better to laugh than to cry. 20
Cho. of all 3	*'Tis better to laugh than to cry.*
Janus	Since Momus comes to laugh below,
	Old Time begin the show,
	That he may see in every scene
	What changes in this age have been.
Chronos	Then, goddess of the silver bow, begin.

Horns or hunting-music within.
Enter Diana.

Diana	With horns and with hounds I waken the day
	And hie to my woodland walks away;
	I tuck up my robe and am buskin'd soon,
	And tie to my forehead a waxing moon. 30
	I course the fleet stag, unkennel the fox,
	And chase the wild goats o'er summits of rocks;

With shouting and hooting we pierce
    thro' the sky,
And Echo turns hunter and doubles the
    cry.

Cho. of all   *With shouting and hooting we pierce*
    through the sky,
    And Echo turns hunter and doubles the
    cry.

Janus   Then our age was in its prime,
Chronos   Free from rage————
Diana   ————And free from crime.
Momus   A very merry, dancing, drinking,
    Laughing, quaffing, and unthinking
    time.   40

Cho. of all   *Then our age was in its prime,*
    Free from rage and free from crime,
    A very merry, dancing, drinking,
    Laughing, quaffing, and unthinking
    time.

Dance of Diana's *attendants.*
Enter Mars.

Mars   Inspire the vocal brass, inspire;
    The world is past its infant age:
       Arms and honour,
       Arms and honour
    Set the martial mind on fire
    And kindle manly rage.   50
    Mars has looked the sky to red,
    And Peace, the lazy good, is fled.
    Plenty, peace, and pleasure fly;
       The sprightly green
    In woodland-walks no more is seen;
    The sprightly green has drunk the
       Tyrian dye.

Cho. of all   *Plenty, peace, etc.*
Mars   Sound the trumpet, beat the drum
    Through all the world around;

| | Sound a reveille, sound, sound, | 60 |
| | The warrior god is come. | |

Cho. of all   *Sound the trumpet, etc.*

Momus   Thy sword within the scabbard keep
   And let mankind agree;
Better the world were fast asleep
   Than kept awake by thee.
The fools are only thinner
   With all our cost and care;
But neither side a winner,
   For things are as they were.   70

Cho. of all   *The fools are only, etc.*

     Enter Venus.

Venus   Calms appear when storms are past;
Love will have his hour at last;
Nature is my kindly care;
Mars destroys, and I repair;
Take me, take me while you may;
Venus comes not ev'ry day.

Cho. of all   *Take her, take her, etc.*

Chronos   The world was then so light,
I scarcely felt the weight;   80
Joy rul'd the day and love the night.
But since the Queen of Pleasure left the
     ground,
   I faint, I lag,
   And feebly drag
The pond'rous orb around.

Momus   All, all, of a piece throughout;

*Pointing
to Diana* }   Thy chase had a beast in view;

to Mars   Thy wars brought nothing about;

to Venus   Thy lovers were all untrue.

Janus   'Tis well an old age is out;   90

Chro[nos]   And time to begin a new.

Cho. of all   *All, all, of a piece throughout;*
Thy chase had a beast in view;
Thy wars brought nothing about;

Thy lovers were all untrue.
'Tis well an old age is out;
And time to begin a new.

Dance of Huntsmen, Nymphs, Warriors and Lovers.

GLOSSARY

The words and phrases included are those not in present use or those current but whose meanings have altered since Dryden. Words entered in both *Webster's New World Dictionary of the American Language* and the *Concise Oxford Dictionary* are normally not included, even when not currently used, but a number of such have been entered for convenience. The *Oxford English Dictionary* is the chief source. Dryden sometimes used words that have both an older and a modern meaning (for example, *prevent*, "anticipate" and also "forestall"). Sometimes he coined words (*suffragating*) or phrases (*butt and peace*); sometimes he created new figurative meanings (*gears*) and sometimes gave English words from foreign tongues, chiefly Latin (*biography*) and French (*ballet*). In this Glossary, only the forms (in tense, person, number) actually used by Dryden are given, and when a modern as well as noncurrent meaning exists, only the latter is given.

accomptable.   Accountable.
admiral.   Flagship.
admire.   Wonder at.
allay.   Alloy.
alluded.   Mentioned; suggested; said.
Almain(e).   German.
amaz'd.   Put into a maze; dumbfounded.
apoplex.   Sudden numbness; paralysis; apoplexy.
appears.   Is evident.
art(s).   Medical or similar professional knowledge.
authentic.   A matter of fact; real.
awful.   Inspiring, full of awe.

bait.   *n.* Lure; trick. *v.* Rest for refreshment.
balk.   Check, hinder, thwart.
ballete.   Ballet.
bawdry.   Bawdiness, bawdy.

bent. The twist giving a curve to a bowling ball; hence, a pronounced inclination of some kind.

benting times. Harsh times; when pigeons must feed poorly on bents, a grass.

bilanders. Coastal or canal boats used for trade.

bill. Legal indictment, charge.

bless'd. Made the Catholic sign of the cross, crossed.

blots. Weak or vulnerable points, acts, etc.; literally, to *hit a blot* is to take an exposed piece in backgammon.

blow. Blossom.

bluff. Broad in face or forehead.

breathe. (1) Rest and catch breath; (2) open; let (as a vein).

brew'd. Concocted; contrived.

bubbies. Breasts.

bum. Buttocks.

bumpers. Large toasting glasses.

burnish'd. Fattened, grown plump.

business. Sexual intercourse.

butt and peace. The wine butt and peace; hence, peace and further benefits.

Cambria. Wales.

candour. Freedom from malice; sweetness of temper; fairness; ingenuousness; purity.

cannon. Etymologically related to "canon," on which Dryden sometimes plays.

cant. To talk fanatically of religion or in a religious tone; sometimes with a pun on the root meaning, "to sing."

canting-coat. Geneva-gown; Puritan clerical garb as opposed to Anglican cassock.

careful. Given to, full of, exercising care.

castors. Beavers.

catachresis. (Rhetorical term) abuse of words or terms.

cates. Foods.

champian sports. Sports of the field as opposed to the woods.

Change. The commercial Exchange.

chapel of ease. One built for parishioners' convenience in a large parish; Dryden sometimes plays on *ease*.

character. A description of character; characterization; portrait, as that of Zimri in *Absalom and Achitophel*, but also written in prose.

charity. (1) (In religious contexts) hope for another's salvation; (2) one of the three cardinal virtues; (3) a personification of (2) depicted as a nursing mother.

chemist. Alchemist.

chirurgeon. Surgeon.

choleric. Abounding in the humour of choler; vehement, impetuous, irascible.

circles. Cycles or periods of time.

class. (1) A genus; (2) an ecclesiastical, especially Presbyterian, organization as opposed to Catholic or Anglican episcopacy; a *classis*; hence, "classical" ordination.

clinches (clenches). Puns.

clown. Oaf; rascal.

clubb'd. Crudely came together.

clues. Threads, cords.

colours (of speech). Rhetorical features or ornaments.

common cry. (1) Pack of hounds; (2) pack or noisy group of people; (3) the usual mistaken claims of the vulgar.

commons. Rations, food.

compound. Settle by agreement for partial payment or lump sum.

confessor. One who suffers deeply for religion but not to the death.

conscience sake. See *fashion-sake*.

conversation. Social intercourse.

converses. See *conversation*.

co-ordination. Equality of status and right; opposed to *degree*, hierarchy.

corps. Body, used either as singular or plural.

couchée. Evening reception in a chamber.

cousen. Make a dupe of; cheat.

customs. Customary rents or profits.

dar'd. Frozen with fear.

dead-colouring. The underlayer of color first applied to the canvas.

deceive. Frustrate.

defend. Ward off; oppose.

deform'd. Took away, deprived of beauty or excellence.

depend. Hang down; remain unresolved.

design'd. Described.

detorted. Distorted, wrested.

digits. Temporal units for measuring an eclipse.

discourse. Operation of the mind, reasoning.

discover.   Reveal, uncover, show.

dishonest.   Ugly; disreputable; shameful.

disinteress'd.   Disinterested, involving no selfish interest.

dismission.   A sending away; emission.

disseis'd.   Wrongfully dispossessed another of his property.

doctors.   The learned, especially in divinity.

dominion.   Power, sway, rule.

donors.   Of ecclesiastical benefices.

dorp.   Thorp; village.

doubt.   Suspect.

draughts.   Excrements; the excrement of society.

dreadful.   Causing dread, awe, or fear.

eagles.   The Roman device atop military standards.

eat.   Ate (in the United States, obsolete or vulgar past tense).

element.   The sky.

elocution.   Rhetorical, artistic effectiveness.

empiric.   A quack; impostor, charlatan.

engines.   Plots; contrivances; wiles.

entailed.   Settled on a number of persons in a way that no
one can bequeath at pleasure; limited or set in such fashion.

ephod.   Priestly garment; priestly office.

equals.   *n.* Peers in rank, age, etc. *v.* To render equal in
rank, etc.; to level.

event.   Outcome.

examen.   Examination; analysis.

except.   Unless.

expect.   Await.

fabric.   Product of a workman (Latin, *faber*) and especially a
building or other architectural piece.

factor.   Agent, representative.

faggots.   Throws together; sets down.

fancy.   Imagination; "phant'sy."

fascinating.   Casting under an evil spell.

fashion-sake.   Fashion's sake, a common earlier grammatical
form with -*sake*.

fi'ry.   Sexually hot.

fit.   Get even with somebody; to "show" somebody.

flix.   Fur, down.

fogue.   Passion, ardor.

font.   Baptismal font.

foot.   Infantry.

forgive.   Give up; pass by.

forms.   Customs; ceremonies; mores.

frame.   Physical constitution, as of universe or body.

fraught.   Freight, load.

free.   Possessing stipulated rights or privileges, such as the freedom of the city.

frequent.   Crowded.

front.   Forehead; upper part of head.

frontless.   Impudent.

fuddled.   Drunk.

fulminated.   Condemned ecclesiastically.

fundamental.   As *n.*, fundamental principle.

gears.   Proper employments or situations; harness.

glimps.   Momentary flash.

grace-cup.   A drink before retiring; nightcap.

graff.   Graft, engraft.

grandam (grandame) gold.   Hoarded wealth.

grubble.   Grope; fondle.

gust.   (1) Taste in sensory and artistic senses; (2) gusto.

haggard.   Wild, untamed.

hard-head.   A crude game of butting heads.

hautboys.   Oboes.

heav'n.   A common spelling for "haven," sometimes with wordplay.

heroic.   Epic.

hind.   (1) Adult female deer; (2) peasant.

hoigh for.   Rustic or dialect form of "heigh for," said in applause, enthusiasm, encouragement.

Holland.   Linen fabric.

honest.   Handsome.

horse.   Cavalry.

hovels.   Sheds; granaries.

imps.   Attaches on to, especially as to the wing of a falcon.

indicted.   Written down.

Indies.   The West Indies.

in effect.   In actuality.

infers.   Implies.

inspire.   Breathe; blow into.

intend.   Mean; have in mind.

interess'd.   Interested; having selfish interest.

interfering.   Colliding.

interlope.   Trade without proper license.

invent.   Discover; create; find out.

invention.   Originality; in rhetorical theory, especially, the discovery of a subject.

jolly.   Amorous, wanton.

judgment.   Reason, power of understanding.

keeping.   Keeping a mistress in a separate establishment; concubinage.

kern.   Irish peasant soldier.

kind.   Often meaning sexually indulgent.

ladder.   Gallows.

lampoons.   Low satires.

laveering.   Beating to windward; tacking.

lawn.   The fine, thin breast linen of Anglican clergy.

leave.   Quit, stop.

leeches.   Physicians.

let.   Hinder; also *n.*, hindrance.

levée.   Morning reception in a chamber.

limbecs.   Alchemical processing vessels; retorts.

lin'd.   (Of certain animals) copulated with; "covered."

line.   Equator or other imaginary geographical arc or circle.

link.   A street torch or its bearer.

lubbers.   Fools.

machine.   A literary or theatrical device, especially one involving a supernatural agency; a device, after the stage machines for deities, etc.

mack'rel gale.   A fresh, strong wind.

magazines.   Storage places.

Magi.   Egyptian magicians; sorcerers.

manners.   Character; demeanor; behavior.

manur'd.   Worked with the hands.

marks (of the Church).   Distinguishing, necessary properties.

meagre.   Having little flesh; impotent.

metal.   Frequently with a play on "mettle."

mingle.   Admixture, mingling.

missioner.   Missionary.

missions.   Missionaries.

muck.   "Amok" was earlier considered two words, *a mok* or *a muck*, which might have an adjective between.

mulct.   Punishment by fine.

Muse. (1) One of the nine goddesses of poetry, etc.; (2) a poet; (3) a poetic strain, theme, or subject.

nerve. (1) Bodily nerves and sinews; (2) bowstring; (3) string of an instrument.

news. Considered a plural noun.

nicely. Fastidiously.

nicking. Matching; fitting right in with.

nor . . . nor. Neither . . . nor.

note. Stigma.

nuncius. Messenger (the root meaning of "angel," for which Dryden sometimes uses the word).

obnoxious. Liable; exposed.

octave. An ecclesiastical "week" of eight days, including the feast days at both ends.

offals. Inedible parts of a beast taken in the hunt; parts of slain soldiers.

offices. Duties or obligations in the Stoic concept.

officious. Frequently means obliging, performing good *offices*, q. v.

oleo. Miscellany, mixture.

on liking. On approval.

or . . . or. Either . . . or.

outed. Ousted.

overlook'd. Looked over, watched over.

painful. Painstaking; careful.

palliards. Debauchees; vagabonds.

parts. Human abilities, endowments.

pay the shot. Pay the charge at a tavern, etc.

penetrate. Occupy the same space with another body.

pennyworth. True penny's worth, a bargain.

perspective. (1) Telescope; (2) artistic perspective or a diminishing sight like it.

pervious. Permeable; passable.

Philistims. Philistines.

philology. Love of learning or literature.

philosophic stone. The alchemists' magic stone.

phlegmatic. Abounding in the humour of phlegm; stolid, reserved.

physic. Medicine.

picking-work. Meaning unclear; tedious or fussy work?

piles.   The javelins or pikes of the Roman soldier.

places.   The (common) places are traditional set topics and
  formulas of panegyric, satire, etc.

play.   Games, especially of cards, involving money stakes.

poll'd.   Unclear: either struck with poles, or struck on the
  poll (head).

poppits.   Poppets, dolls; idols, worshipped images.

post.   Posthaste; with all speed.

pounc'd.   Furnished with pounces, claws.

prevent.   Anticipate.

prime.   Spring; beginning of a cycle.

primitive.   First; original.

primum mobile.   The first mover; the outermost, kinetic con-
  centric of the Ptolemaic universe.

prince.   A nobleman; a person of authority, not necessarily son
  of a king.

prizes.   Prize fights.

proceed.   Advance farther.

prole.   Prowl.

protatic.   Relating to *protasis,* the entrance, beginning of the
  play; appearing in a minor role then, hence, unimportant.

provoke.   Call forth.

public.   Published, made generally known.

punks.   Prostitutes.

quality.   Rank, nobility: "person of quality."

remainders.   Remainder.

remarks.   Observations; reflections.

remember.   Remind.

rent-charge.   One not proper owner who benefits from a deed.

reprisal.   Return; compensation.

reprise.   (1) Resumption, renewal; (2) return, compensation.

resort.   A general or habitual going to, visiting, repairing to.

revenge.   Maintain by punishment or threat.

revolution.   Change, not necessarily upheaval.

road.   Channel of the ocean; sheltered water or anchorage.

rummers.   Wineglasses; flagons.

sagacious.   Keen in the sense of smell.

salvo.   Explanation, answer to a question; quibbling evasion.

sanguine.   Abounding in the humour of blood; passionate.

scapes.   (1) Escapes; (2) dubious tricks.

scenes.   Stage scenery; sets.

School. The scholastic world of medieval learning, especially Aristotelianism in philosophy, logic, and science.

science. Knowledge; branch of knowledge.

score. Count.

shards. Dung, in which certain beetles were thought to generate.

shelf. Submerged sandbank or rock ledge.

shores, *especially* common shores. Sewage drains or ditches.

shot. See *pay the shot.*

shrieval. Pertaining to a sheriff or sheriffs.

sincere. Unmixed, unqualified.

slight. A trick.

slubber o'er. Do hurriedly and messily.

smoke along. Pass along at great speed.

span. Mental capacity.

spirituals. Spiritual matters or issues as opposed to *temporals.*

spoomes (or spooms). Runs before the wind; scuds.

sprite. Spirit.

squander. Scatter.

stagers. Veterans; old hands.

standard. A tree left standing when a coppice is cut, or a shoot from it; hence, the original or that directly derived from the original.

stav'd. Broke up; destroyed.

stews. Brothels.

sticklers. Umpires.

still. Always, ever.

stints. (1) Allowances; limits; (2) prescribed amounts.

stoop. (Of a bird) swoop down suddenly.

story. History.

style. Appellation, name.

subsidy. A taxlike fiscal measure; revenue.

success(es). Event(s).

suffragating. Voting; assenting; associated.

table. Votive tablet.

tally. A counterpart; an agreeing or corresponding element.

tax'd. Charged, accused of.

temper. Middle ground; moderate course; compromise; mean.

temporals. Secular, temporal matters or issues as opposed to *spirituals.*

Thrones. An order of angels, like Denominations, Seraphim, etc.

tippled. Drunk, intoxicated.

tire. Volley; broadside; cannonade.

traditive. Referring to ecclesiastical tradition.

traduction. Reception of the soul from one's parent at conception.

traverses. Adversities; obstacles; vexations.

treat. Give an entertainment, party.

trine. (1) The auspicious 120° relation of three stars; (2) the Trinity.

try. Doubt; experiment sceptically, especially in religious matters.

turn. A somewhat obscure literary term, apparently meaning a twist, apposition, or play either upon words or ideas.

tympany. Swelling; tumor.

uncas'd. Unmasked, revealed, undressed.

ungodded. Without a god, atheistic.

unsincere. Mixed, impure, qualified.

vare. Rod, staff, or badge of authority.

vermin. Obnoxious animals as opposed to proper beasts of game.

vindicate. (1) Assert, maintain; justify, uphold; (2) claim for oneself.

virtue. Strength.

volume. Coil, as of snake (Latinism).

vow. Prayer; supplication.

vulgar. _n._ The mere common people.

wain. Wagon; Charles' Wain consists of the seven bright stars of the Big Dipper.

whether. Whither.

whirl-bats. A game or weapon with lead plummets; the Roman _caestus_.

white. Propitious, happy, blest; also _whiten'd,_ made so; also _whiter._

wilder'd. Bewildered; lost.

writ of ease. Literally, certificate of discharge from employment.

Index of Titles and First Lines

MODERN LIBRARY COLLEGE EDITIONS

The Best of the World's Best Books
COMPLETE LIST OF TITLES IN
THE MODERN LIBRARY

A series of handsome, cloth-bound books, formerly
available only in expensive editions.

MISCELLANEOUS

MODERN LIBRARY GIANTS

A series of sturdily bound and handsomely printed, full-sized library editions of books formerly available only in expensive sets. These volumes contain from 600 to 1,400 pages each.

THE MODERN LIBRARY GIANTS REPRESENT A SELECTION OF THE WORLD'S GREATEST BOOKS

G76 ANDERSEN & GRIMM: *Tales*
G74 AUGUSTINE, ST.: *The City of God*
G58 AUSTEN, JANE: *Complete Novels*
G97 BALZAC, HONORÉ DE: *Lost Illusions*
G70 BLAKE, WILLIAM & DONNE, JOHN: *Complete Poetry*
G2 BOSWELL, JAMES: *Life of Samuel Johnson*
G95 BROCKWAY, WALLACE & WEINSTOCK, HERBERT: *The World of Opera*
G17 BROWNING, ROBERT: *Poems and Plays*
G14 BULFINCH: *Mythology* (ILLUSTRATED)
G35 BURY, J. B.: *A History of Greece*
G13 CARLYLE, THOMAS: *The French Revolution*
G28 CARROLL, LEWIS: *Complete Works*
G15 CERVANTES: *Don Quixote*
G33 COLLINS, WILKIE: *The Moonstone* and *The Woman in White*
G94 COOPER, JAMES FENIMORE: *The Leatherstocking Saga*
G27 DARWIN, CHARLES: *Origin of Species* and *The Descent of Man*
G43 DEWEY, JOHN: *Intelligence in the Modern World*
G70 DONNE, JOHN & BLAKE, WILLIAM: *Complete Poetry*
G36 DOSTOYEVSKY, FYODOR: *The Brothers Karamazov*
G60 DOSTOYEVSKY, FYODOR: *The Idiot*
G51 ELIOT, GEORGE: *Best-Known Novels*
G41 FARRELL, JAMES T.: *Studs Lonigan*
G82 FAULKNER, WILLIAM: *The Faulkner Reader*
G39 FREUD, SIGMUND: *The Basic Writings*
G6, G7, G8 GIBBON, EDWARD: *The Decline and Fall of the Roman Empire* (complete in three volumes)
G25 GILBERT & SULLIVAN: *Complete Plays*
G76 GRIMM & ANDERSEN: *Tales*
G37 HAWTHORNE, NATHANIEL: *Compl. Novels & Selected Tales*
G78 HOLMES, OLIVER WENDELL: *The Mind and Faith of Justice*
G19 HOMER: *Complete Works* [Holmes
G3 HUGO, VICTOR: *Les Miserables*
G18 IBSEN, HENRIK: *Eleven Plays*
G11 JAMES, HENRY: *Short Stories*
G52 JOYCE, JAMES: *Ulysses*
G4 KEATS & SHELLEY: *Complete Poems*
G24 LAMB, CHARLES: *The Complete Works and Letters* [Lincoln
G20 LINCOLN, ABRAHAM: *The Life and Writings of Abraham*
G84 MANN, THOMAS: *Stories of Three Decades*
G26 MARX, KARL: *Capital*
G57 MELVILLE, HERMAN: *Selected Writings*
G38 MURASAKA, LADY: *The Tale of Genji*
G30 MYERS, GUSTAVUS: *History of the Great American Fortunes*
G34 NIETZSCHE, FRIEDRICH: *The Philosophy of Nietzsche*
G88 O'HARA, JOHN: *49 Stories*
G55 O'NEILL, EUGENE: *Nine Plays*